MARKETING

PRINCIPLES & STRATEGY

MARKETING
PRINCIPLES & STRATEGY

HENRY ASSAEL

Stern School of Business
New York University

The Dryden Press
Chicago Fort Worth San Francisco Philadelphia
Montreal Toronto London Sydney Toyko

Acquisitions Editor: Rob Zwettler
Developmental Editor: Millicent Treloar
Project Editor: Teresa Chartos
Production Manager: Bob Lange
Director of Editing, Design, and Production: Jane Perkins

Text and Cover Designer: Jeanne Calabrese
Copy Editor and Indexer: Maggie Jarpey
Compositor: York Graphic Services, Inc.
Text Type: 10/12 Sabon

Library of Congress Cataloging-in-Publication Data

Assael, Henry.
    Marketing : principles and strategy / Henry Assael. — 1st ed.
        p.   cm.
    Includes bibliographies and index.
    ISBN 0-03-016622-5
    1. Marketing.   I. Title.
HF5415.A748   1990
658.8'02 — dc20   89-11814
                                                          CIP

Printed in the United States of America
012-032-987654321
Copyright © 1990 by The Dryden Press, a division of Holt,
Rinehart and Winston, Inc.

Address orders:
The Dryden Press
Orlando, FL 32887

Address editorial correspondence:
The Dryden Press
908 N. Elm Street
Hinsdale, IL 60521

The Dryden Press
Holt, Rinehart and Winston
Saunders College Publishing

To Alyce

THE DRYDEN PRESS SERIES IN MARKETING

Two aspects of this book position it differently from competitive offerings. First and foremost is its integration of strategy development with traditional marketing concepts. This approach is based on the author's belief that students in a "Principles of Marketing" course should view the components of the marketing mix in the context of strategy development at both the product and the corporate levels. The stage for this focus is set in the early chapters. Part 1 of the book explores the role of marketing in the firm and the environment, as well as its relationship to other business functions. Part 2 then details how a firm identifies and exploits opportunities in the marketplace.

The second factor that differentiates this book is its *process* approach to explaining how marketing strategy decisions are made. In Parts 3 and 4, the process of marketing planning and the components of the marketing mix are described. Early in each of these chapters, the process of strategy development is outlined, and the chapter is then organized on that basis. Thus, Chapter 8 is organized according to the marketing planning process, Chapter 9 according to the selection of market-segmentation strategies, and so forth.

This process approach emphasizes to students the key requirements in developing strategies in each functional area of marketing. It provides the sequential basis for all major headings in each chapter. It is also the basis for organizing the major parts of the book based on the *process* required to develop marketing strategies, as follows:

PART 2   Identifying Marketing Opportunity
PART 3   Plan and Target the Marketing Effort
PART 4   Implement the Marketing Effort
PART 5   Evaluate and Control the Marketing Effort

An integrative framework for this approach is provided in the opening vignette to each chapter, which focuses on a specific company to illustrate key points. Often the example of that company is carried throughout the chapter. For instance, Campbell's regional marketing strategy is used as the kickoff to the chapter on market segmentation, and Merrill Lynch's strategic moves to become the supreme marketer of financial services provides the initial focus for the chapter on services marketing. This framework is reinforced by up-to-date examples of strategy development and applications throughout each chapter.

The process approach is closely tied to a description of the basic concepts of the marketing discipline. For example, Chapter 4 describes concepts of competitive advantage, Chapter 9 the economic concepts underlying market segmentation, Chapter 11 the concept of the product life cycle, Chapters 18 and 19 demand and cost concepts underlying price determination, and so forth.

OTHER IMPORTANT FEATURES OF THIS BOOK

To complement its process approach, *Marketing: Principles and Strategy* offers other important features:

- In-depth coverage of ethical issues, first considering management's social responsibilities and then focusing on ethics in the context of the marketing mix components. Separate sections deal with product safety, truthfulness in advertising, fair selling practices, pricing issues, and ethics in the international marketplace.

- A unique chapter on competitive advantage (Chapter 4) that shows the importance of competition in evaluating marketing opportunities.

- Integration of services marketing and international marketing into the marketing mix section of the book, reflecting today's greater focus on these areas.
- Integration of industrial marketing throughout the text.
- Emphasis on marketing productivity in the context of control of marketing operations, reflecting the increasing concern of American companies about productivity advantages of foreign competitors.
- Coverage of recent developments in marketing research, including single-source data and People Meters.
- Coverage of recent developments in distribution, including just-in-time distribution systems, scanners, hypermarkets, home shopping, and electronic retailing.
- Focus on the increasingly important strategy of brand leveraging as a means of extending the advantages of existing brands.

PEDAGOGY

The text also includes a number of pedagogical aids, such as

- *Learning objectives* at the beginning of each chapter that also serve as a framework to summarize the chapter at the end.
- *Marketing biographies* in each chapter of successful marketing personalities, including John Sculley of Apple Computers and Sam Walton of Walmart.
- Up-to-date *end-of-chapter cases* on companies such as Hewlett-Packard, American Airlines, and Levi Strauss.
- *End-of-chapter questions* that combine descriptive questions on chapter content with more analytical case-oriented questions.
- *Glossary* of key terms in each chapter.
- *Appendixes* on marketing math and on careers in marketing.

THE PACKAGE

The instructor support material for this text has received special attention. Following is a list of the package materials available. For a more in-depth description of these items, please consult your Dryden representative or the *Package Preview* we have developed for the book, which includes samples as well as descriptions of each package item.

- *Study Guide*
- *Test Bank*
- *Computerized Test Banks* for both IBM and Apple PCs
- *Transparency Acetates* (acetates are also available in slide format)
- Video Support, a total of 23 videos, one for each chapter in the book
- *Media Instructor's Manual*. Includes support material for the videos as well as teaching notes for the transparency acetates and full instructional material for the computer simulation.

- *Computer Simulation*
- *Instructor's Manual*

Finally, a word should be said about the tone and content of the book. This is not a "glitzy" book, although the art is first-rate. There are no extraneous photographs and figures. All the art, diagrams, and tables are fully referenced in the text. This is meant to be a serious book — by no means dry, but serious in content. The book does not talk down to students; its style as well as content are meant to respect them.

ACKNOWLEDGMENTS

This book has been thoroughly researched and tested in an extensive developmental process that included three major focus groups and over twenty reviewers. It has been a team effort in every way. I am indebted to the following group of people whose comments and insights helped shape the manuscript and influenced greatly the many product decisions involved in a project of this nature.

Manuscript Reviewers

Deanna Barnwell
Memphis State University

Craig Kelley
California State University — Sacramento

John Buckley
Orange County Community College

James McAlexander
Iowa State University

Leslie Cole
Baylor University

Bill Moser
Ball State University

Helena Czepiec
California State University — Hayward

Keith Murray
Northeastern University

Hugh Daubek
Central Michigan University

Joe Myslivec
Central Michigan University

Curt Dommeyer
California State University — Northridge

William Panschar
Indiana University

Alan Flaschner
University of Toledo

Clint Tankersley
Syracuse University

Robert Gwinner
Arizona State University

Gerard Tellis
University of Iowa

Mark Johnston
Louisiana State University

Sushila Umashankar
University of Arizona

Peter Kaminski
Northern Illinois University

Van Wood
Texas Tech University

Focus Group Participants

Steve Calvert
University of San Francisco

Joh Hawes
University of Akron

Robert Collins
University of Nevada — Las Vegas

Craig Kelley
California State University — Sacramento

Jerry Conover
Northern Arizona University

Fred Kraft
Wichita State University

Sayeste Daser
Wake Forest University

Fred Langrehr
University of Nebraska — Omaha

Ronald Dornoff
University of Cincinnati

Jim Littlefield
Virginia Polytechnic University

George Lucas
Memphis State University

Barbara McCuen
University of Nebraska

Lee Meadow
Salisbury State University

Dennis Menezes
University of Kentucky — Louisville

Roland Michman
Shippensburg University

Jim Muncy
Texas Tech University

Keith Murray
Northeastern University

Connie Pechman
University of California — Irvine

Dennis Pitta
University of Baltimore

Don Robin
Louisiana Tech University

Kelly Shuptrine
University of South Carolina

Terence Shimp
University of South Carolina

Gerald Stiles
Mankato State University

Joel Whalen
DePaul University

Dale Wilson
Michigan State University

I am also indebted to several people who were involved in developing the ancillaries and peripheral material:

- Deanna Barnwell of Memphis State, who developed the *Study Guide*.

- Thomas Quirk of St. Louis University, who developed the *Test Bank*.

- Craig Kelley of California State University — Sacramento, who prepared answers to the end-of-chapter questions and cases for the *Instructor's Manual*.

- Robert Gwinner of Arizona State University, who prepared the transparency acetates.

- Peter Kaminski of Northern Illinois University, who prepared the Marketing Mathematics appendix.

- Edward Golden of Central Washington University, who developed the Careers Guide appendix.

A number of colleagues at the Stern School of Business at New York University were also very helpful in reviewing portions of the manuscript. These included Bruce Buchanan, who helped on the pricing chapters; Richard Colombo, on marketing research; Sam Craig, on the promotional mix; Arieh Goldman, on distribution and international marketing; Avijit Ghosh, on strategic planning; Eric Greenleaf, on new-product development and sales management; Priscilla La Barbera, on advertising; and Robert Shoaf, on organizational buyer behavior.

Thanks are also due to a top-notch group at The Dryden Press who made this book possible. This project dates back to December 1986 when Dryden's acquisitions editor, Rob Zwettler, and I discussed the philosophy of the proposed book. There was an immediate meeting of the minds, and the project was launched. Rob has been involved in every aspect of the book from the start. His commitment, dedication, and continued support made this project possible and are deeply appreciated.

My first developmental editor at Dryden, Becky Ryan, was equally supportive and helpful. She made the transition from first copy to finished manuscript a smooth one. Millicent Treloar, the current developmental editor, has been instrumental in developing a superb ancillary package and is a further demonstration of Dryden's support. Several other people at Dryden deserve mention. Teresa Chartos, project editor, has organized every detail of the production process, ensuring a finished product. Jeanne Calabrese, art and design director, has developed an art program where design supports content, as it should. Doris Milligan, permissions manager, has been persistent in obtaining the many permissions required in a text long on examples. And thanks are due to Bill Schoof, editor-in-chief of Dryden, for believing in this book from the start and committing the necessary resources to it.

Thanks also go to my research assistants, Suzanne Ochoa, Sherri Jaffe, Robin Comizio, Frann Setzer, Debbi Martin, and Phil Peters. They have brought together much of the research material for the book. Sherri Jaffe and Suzanne Ochoa also wrote a substantial portion of the *Instructor's Manual*. Their commitment and long hours of effort are appreciated. I would also like to thank two stalwarts at the Stern School library, Betty Thompson and Mary Jean Pavelsek, for doing the computerized searches that provided many of the references used in this text.

Final thanks go to my foremost research assistant — my wife, Alyce. Without her, this book could not have been written. She collected by far the major portion of the research materials. Further, her constant review of the manuscript has been invaluable. She has been a companion in this effort and deserves equal recognition for the results.

Henry Assael
January 1990

ABOUT THE AUTHOR

Henry Assael is professor of marketing and chairman of the marketing department at New York University's Stern School of Business. Dr. Assael has led in the application of research and analytical techniques to marketing problems, particularly in the areas of market segmentation, product positioning, survey research methods, and evaluation of advertising. He has served as a consultant to such diverse companies as AT&T, American Can, CBS, Nestlé, the New York Stock Exchange, and GTE.

Dr. Assael has published widely in the *Journal of Marketing, Journal of Marketing Research, Journal of Advertising Research,* and *Administrative Science Quarterly.* He is the author of *Consumer Behavior and Marketing Action* and *Marketing Management: Strategy and Action.* He has edited a 33-volume series on the history of marketing and a 40-volume series on the history of advertising.

Dr. Assael received a B.A. degree from Harvard University in 1957, graduating with honors, an M.B.A. from the Wharton School in 1959, and a Ph.D. from the Columbia Graduate School of Business in 1965.

He is listed in *Who's Who in America.*

CONTENTS IN BRIEF

CONTENTS

PART I
THE MARKETING
PROCESS   1

PART 4
IMPLEMENTING
THE MARKETING
EFFORT *261*

PART 5 STRATEGIC PLANNING, EVALUATION, AND CONTROL   *613*

PART I

• • •

THE MARKETING PROCESS

Marketing is an exciting and increasingly important area in business operations dealing with understanding customers and directing the firm's resources to their needs. No matter what your career path will be, you will probably have to consider issues directly or partially related to marketing.

The two introductory chapters in this section attempt to explain why marketing is central to all business operations. The focus is on the role of marketing in the firm and in the broader business environment, as well as its relation to other business functions such as finance, accounting, and manufacturing.

THINGS ARE GOING BETTER FOR PEPSI

PepsiCo, Inc., is packing more marketing punch these days. Its flagship brand, Pepsi-Cola, has been gaining on Coke. PepsiCo is doing well in its two other business areas, snack foods and fast-food restaurants. Its subsidiary, Frito-Lay, is the leader in the sale of domestic salty snacks, while its acquisition of Kentucky Fried Chicken in 1986 (on top of its ownership of Pizza Hut and Taco Bell) gave it the largest number of restaurants in the world. PepsiCo's management has a close eye on these two food areas since they account for over 60 percent of the company's sales.[1]

What is the reason for PepsiCo's success? One word — *marketing*. The company has demonstrated its marketing capabilities in key areas such as new products, distribution, advertising, and pricing. Consider its distribution system: Pepsi-Cola's strong network of bottlers buy the company's soft drinks in syrup form, prepare and bottle them, and sell them to wholesalers and retailers to ensure the products are at the right place at the right time. In advertising, successful campaigns such as the Pepsi Generation, the Pepsi Challenge, and more recently, use of star personalities such as Michael Jackson and Michael J. Fox have kept the company's flagship brand a hit with teenagers. Finally, the company's use of coupons and in-store promotions ensure that when new products are introduced, they will be tried by a large number of consumers.

Why is PepsiCo so effective in implementing marketing know-how? What makes it, in the words of one writer, a "marketing star"?[2] Its aggressive, risk-

oriented management is quick to act when it sees opportunities in the market-place. PepsiCo managers are given a great deal of independence and are encouraged to move quickly. Moving quickly meant introducing Slice, Pepsi-Cola's entry into the soft-drink market, with one important consumer benefit added, fruit juice. By 1987, two years after its introduction, the brand was generating one billion dollars in sales.

But soft drinks account for less than 40 percent of company sales. Frito-Lay, producing nearly half of the company's earnings, is an important testing ground for new snack food products. PepsiCo's fast-food businesses are significant, too, representing about 12 percent of the fast-food business in the United States and generating $6.7 billion in yearly sales.

All situations are not rosy for PepsiCo, though, despite its marketing savvy. Although Slice started with a bang, sales began sliding by 1988 as consumer interest in juice-added products started to wane and competition in the category began heating up. (However, the brand is still highly profitable.) And, although Coca-Cola's introduction of New Coke was an initial fiasco, it has successfully reestablished Coca-Cola Classic, and made it more difficult for Pepsi-Cola to make dramatic sales increases at Coke's expense.

Despite occasional problems, PepsiCo's record stands as ''a marketer'' that identifies unmet customer needs and develops products and strategies to meet these needs. And that is what marketing is all about. ■

● ● ●

WHAT IS MARKETING?

The most important objective in any business is to identify and satisfy customers. As a result, marketing is central to any business firm, and any business executive must understand its role in his or her organization. Whether you are going into investment banking, financial services, accounting, management, or production, you will never be far from a firm's customers and a firm's competition. Knowing what is marketing and how marketing strategies are developed will help you deal with your customers and competitors.

Marketing can be defined as all activities directed to identifying and satisfying customer needs and wants.[3] It is the focus on the customer that has made PepsiCo a successful company. For example, Pepsi's management realized that the customer benefits introduced into soft drinks in recent years involved taking something *out of* the product — namely calories and caffeine. Satisfying unmet customer needs for nutrition and natural ingredients meant putting something *into* soft drinks, namely fresh juice that might translate into better taste and more nutrition. The result was Slice.

Figure 1.1 illustrates the process of identifying customer needs and satisfying them. It focuses on two elements, the marketing organization and its customers. The marketing organization identifies customer needs. It then develops and implements marketing strategies to meet these needs. Once strategies are implemented, they are evaluated based on customer responses. Customer responses are tracked based on purchases and on surveys of customer attitudes and intentions. These three areas — need definition, marketing strategies, and market feedback — comprise the basic role of marketing within the firm. Let us consider each of these areas below.

IDENTIFYING CUSTOMER NEEDS

Marketing strategies must be based on known customer needs. The first question a marketing manager should ask when considering a new product is, "What customer needs would be better met by this product?" And the first question to ask when developing plans for an existing product is, "How does my product stack up against competition in terms of satisfying customer needs?"

PepsiCo identified a new set of benefits in introducing Slice. Fruit juice was an important taste benefit not provided by its competitors. Diet Slice combined the

Boldface terms and their definitions can be found in the Glossary at the end of the book.

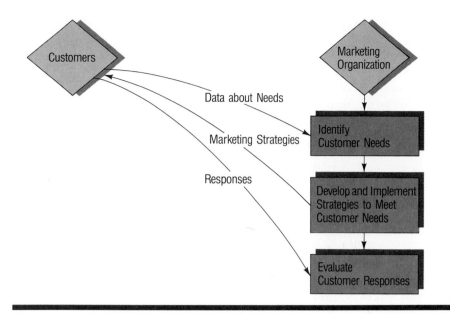

FIGURE 1.1
The Marketing Process

benefits of improved taste with lower calories. Similarly, the substitution of Nutrasweet for saccharin provided the benefit of a more popular sugar substitute.

In identifying a need like a juice-based soft drink, a company must determine what group of consumers have that need. This group is known as the **target segment** — that is, a group of consumers with a similar set of needs that the company can target with its marketing strategies. The target consumers for Slice were young adults.

In the past, Pepsi-Cola has been weaker in the adult market. Adults are more likely to buy lemon-lime drinks and diet sodas. Pepsi-Cola's entry into the lemon-lime category, Teem, never really took off. 7UP and Coke's Sprite dominated that market. In diet colas, Diet Pepsi ran a poor second to Diet Coke. So PepsiCo has always targeted its chief brand to teenagers, as reflected by one of the longest advertising campaigns in history, the 25-year "Pepsi Generation" campaign. With themes like "Catch the Pepsi Spirit" and the use of rock stars such as Michael Jackson, the company has been faithful to maintaining its target as teens (see Exhibit 1.1).

To counter weakness in the lemon-lime category and softer diet soda sales, Pepsi-Cola made two strategic moves: the introduction of Slice and Diet Slice, and the reformulation of Diet Pepsi as the first brand with 100 percent Nutrasweet. Slice became a multimillion dollar brand, and sales of Diet Pepsi soared by 25 percent after the addition of Nutrasweet.[4]

Once customer needs are identified, marketers must respond by (1) developing products to meet these needs, (2) positioning products to target segments, and (3) developing an effective marketing mix.

DEVELOPING STRATEGIES TO MEET CUSTOMER NEEDS

Developing New Products and Offering Existing Ones
A large part of PepsiCo's success has been based on the introduction of new products in all three of the company's business units — Slice in soft drinks; Per-

EXHIBIT 1.1
Using Michael Jackson to Target
Pepsi-Cola to the Teen Market

sonal Pan Pizza, Taco salad, and Chicken Little sandwiches in fast foods; O'Grady's potato chips in snacks. It is also constantly testing new products. In the Frito-Lay division alone it tested Ruffles Cajun Spice potato chips, Doritos Cool Ranch tortilla chips, Lay's brand Crunch Tators and a line of low-oil products.

This kind of new product activity is possible only if management is committed to developing new products as a means of growth, and if an effective new-product development process exists. Such a process requires a mechanism for identifying customer needs, generating new product ideas, developing products, **test marketing** them in selected markets for a period of time to see how well they sell, and finally introducing them nationally. PepsiCo follows such a process, but is not a slave to it. For example, it decided to eliminate the test-marketing phase of new-product development to make sure the new version of Diet Pepsi (with Nutrasweet) was on the shelf before Coca-Cola reformulated Diet Coke.

Marketers do not rely only on new products to satisfy customer needs. They must constantly manage existing products to ensure they continue to meet needs. The addition of Nutrasweet was an important improvement in an existing product. Another strategy for strengthening existing products is to add new flavors or variations, known as **product-line extensions**. For example, Frito-Lay's successful Doritos tortilla chips was extended to include Nacho Cheese, Cool Ranch and Salsa Rio flavors. Similarly, Diet Slice was a product-line extension designed to add a low-calorie benefit to the Slice line of products.

Positioning Products to Target Segments

Once products are developed, their benefits must be communicated to customers. The main product benefits to be communicated define the **product's positioning**. In early tests of Slice, consumers liked the taste but showed no strong preferences for the brand. The research team decided to give consumers all the facts about the new product. When consumers found out about the addition of fruit juice, their attitudes changed significantly. The research team realized they had been focusing on the wrong characteristic — the lemon-lime flavor. As a result, Pepsi-Cola management decided to position the product based on the fruit-juice benefit instead. Once this positioning decision was made, the advertising campaign followed. The basic theme "We Got the Juice" was a logical extension of the positioning.

Similarly, Diet Slice could have been positioned as a new diet lemon-lime product with juice as a secondary benefit or the reverse. Positioning it as a tastier diet product with juice-added as the primary benefit and low-calorie as secondary communicated a *new* benefit to consumers and thus gave Slice a competitive advantage over other diet soft drinks.

Developing the Marketing Mix

Companies must develop a mix of marketing strategies to influence customers to buy their products and services. These strategies have four components, frequently referred to as the **four Ps of marketing**: The *product* component ensures that product characteristics provide benefits to the consumer; the *promotional* component communicates the product's ability to satisfy the customer through advertising, personal selling, and sales promotions; the *place* component distributes the product to the right place at the right time to meet customer needs; and the *price* component ensures the product is priced at a level that reflects consumer value. This combination of strategies is known as the **marketing mix** for a prod-

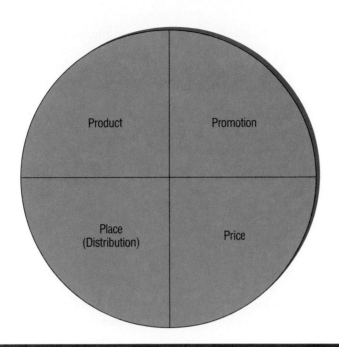

FIGURE 1.2
Components of the Marketing Mix

uct. Together, they work in a single, integrated plan determined by the product's positioning.

The marketing mix is illustrated in Figure 1.2. The basic product advantage for Slice was adding 10 percent juice. This feature gave the brand its basic positioning. A strong promotional campaign identified this point of difference from competitors and effectively communicated it to consumers. Television commercials showed huge pieces of fruit blasting through crystal clear liquid against the consistent refrain, "We Got the Juice." National awareness of the brand was created quickly, and Pepsi-Cola's strong bottler network ensured that once the company produced the syrup for Slice, the product would be quickly prepared, bottled, and distributed.

Price was also an important part of the marketing mix. Pepsi-Cola offered value incentives initially through coupons and in-store promotions to influence consumers to try the brand. In-store displays were coordinated with the national advertising campaign to create immediate brand recognition in the store.

In short, all the elements of the marketing mix were implemented in a well-coordinated plan — a product with an important competitive advantage, strong distribution, an advertising campaign based on the effective positioning of the product, and price incentives to induce initial consumer trial of the brand.

EVALUATING CUSTOMER RESPONSES TO COMPANY STRATEGIES

The test of a successful marketing strategy is customer purchases. PepsiCo tracks customer purchases by determining sales and **market share** for each brand. Market share is the amount consumers spend on a brand as a percent of total expenditures on all brands in the product category. The market share of Slice reached close to 4 percent of the soft drink market by 1987, two years after its introduction, before sliding to 2.7 percent in 1988. Ultimately, though, it is the bottom line — the impact of sales on profits — that counts. PepsiCo closely monitors the profits of each of its offerings. Good profit performance has led business analysts to cite PepsiCo as one of the most effective marketers in business today.

Sales and market share figures do not fully measure the success of marketing strategies. Companies must know what is going on in the customer's mind — that is, attitudes toward the company's and competitive offerings, reactions to proposed new products, awareness of the company's advertising, intention to buy, and so forth. Companies obtain this type of information from product tests and from consumer surveys. Such research has two objectives: first, learn consumer reactions to new product offerings and to marketing strategies before they are introduced; second, determine how consumers react to product offerings once they are introduced.

Pepsi-Cola was given the idea of a fruit-based soft drink when consumer research showed that 75 percent of regular users of lemon-lime soft drinks said they would prefer a carbonated beverage that contained fruit juice.[5] Since lemon-lime beverages accounted for about 13 percent of soft drink sales, a fruit-based drink represented significant potential. Market evaluation identified an important opportunity.

Pepsi-Cola conducts taste tests and in-home tests of new products before introduction. Taste tests of Slice showed that the company had a potential winner. But the taste benefit was relatively weak until it was linked to an awareness of the fruit-juice benefit. These consumer tests led the company to approve product introduction and to establish the brand's positioning. The next step after taste tests was test marketing. In May 1984 Pepsi-Cola entered Slice in four test markets — Tulsa, Milwaukee, Phoenix and Rochester. The results were positive, and national introduction followed in 1985.

The sequence of market evaluation for Slice was thus (1) opportunity identification through a consumer survey, (2) taste tests to determine reaction to the product and to establish product positioning, and (3) introduction into test markets to determine the viability of a national introduction. This process allowed a sound evaluation of market potential before product introduction.

PepsiCo also receives feedback from the market to evaluate existing offerings. Measuring consumer attitudes toward existing brands and advertising campaigns may lead to changes that will make the marketing mix more effective. When PepsiCo bought Taco Bell, a market survey found that Taco Bell needed to modernize its image. First the restaurant's logo — a Mexican dozing under a large sombrero — was replaced by a well-designed logo of a rainbow-striped band and a bell. The survey also showed that customers thought the restaurant's dining rooms were small, dark, and physically unattractive. Taco Bell then committed $200 million to modernization and expansion (see Exhibit 1.2).[6] As a result of these changes, Taco Bell became the fastest-growing restaurant chain in the country. Market feedback provided the basis for revamping and revitalizing an existing offering.

MARKETING IS ALSO A CORPORATE GAME PLAN

So far, our description of marketing has been presented in a product context. Pepsi-Cola had a set of strategies for Slice that made it a successful brand. But marketing also involves looking across brands and asking, "Where is the company heading in the next five years?" For example, given Pepsi-Cola's traditional strength in the teen market, should the company move more aggressively into non-cola drinks to strengthen its position in the adult market? PepsiCo has a strong international presence. Should it put more resources into marketing abroad? Should it acquire additional fast-food chains to expand its position in this market? Since Frito-Lay is such a strong business unit, should it be encouraged to introduce more new snack food products? As these questions suggest, a company needs a *corporate game plan* assessing who its customers and competitors will be five years from now.

PepsiCo's corporate game plan is to challenge Coke at every juncture — in the lemon-lime category, in diet colas, in regular colas, in fountain sales, and in the international market. Where it can, PepsiCo will try to establish a competitive advantage by developing a new market such as the one developed for fruit-based soft drinks.

Part of PepsiCo's corporate game plan is to diversify into areas that can better assure future growth. In fact, it was the merger of Pepsi-Cola Company and Frito-Lay in 1965 that created PepsiCo, Inc., and put it squarely in the food business. Its subsequent acquisitions of fast-food chains provided a basis for profitability in a fast-growing area. In the mid 1980s, PepsiCo decided to define its business solely in soft drinks, snack foods, and fast foods — its areas of expertise. As a result, it divested itself of other acquisitions such as Wilson Sporting Goods and North American Van Lines.

Finance, accounting, and manufacturing managers might have had some input into these decisions, but essentially they were marketing-based, because they relied on an analysis of future customer needs.

EXHIBIT 1.2
Taco Bell's New Logo as a Result of Consumer Feedback

THE ENVIRONMENT: ANOTHER DIMENSION OF MARKETING

Meeting customer needs should be viewed in a broader framework that includes the competition, the economy, technology, government regulations, and demographic and lifestyle trends, because these factors are likely to influence consumer purchases.

Figure 1.3 expands the marketing process shown in Figure 1.1 to include these environmental factors. Generally, the two most important influences on a company are its customers and competitors. Managers identify changes in customer needs, competitive actions, and other environmental factors such as technology, the economy, and legal and regulatory trends. Once changes in the environment are identified, marketing organizations develop strategies to meet customer needs and to establish an advantage over their competitors. Marketing strategies are then evaluated based on customer and competitive responses to these strategies.

Marketers are interested in changes in environmental factors because such changes might help them identify **marketing opportunities** — that is, opportunities to better meet customer needs. For example, a lifestyle trend such as the increasing emphasis on nutrition created the opportunity for Pepsi-Cola to introduce Slice. This opportunity was reinforced by two other environmental factors: first, the absence of any competition in juice-based soft drinks; second, the technology that allowed Pepsi-Cola to develop such a soft drink.

Environmental factors can also constitute **marketing threats** — that is, threats to the success of a product. Once Slice was introduced, competition became a threat. Followers into juice-based soft drinks such as Sunkist soda caused sales of Slice to fall by one-third by 1988.[7]

MARKETING OPPORTUNITIES AND THREATS

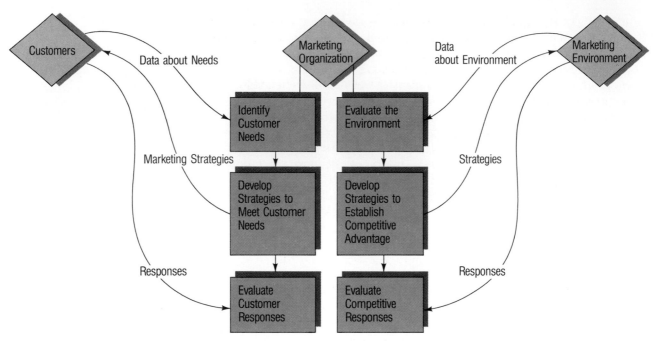

FIGURE 1.3
The Expanded Marketing Process

A more basic threat to PepsiCo over the long term is the decrease in the birth rate and the resultant decline projected for the proportion of cola-drinking teens. This demographic trend means that Pepsi-Cola cannot rely on cola drinks for future growth. But an effective marketing organization will try to turn a threat such as this into an opportunity. For example, PepsiCo saw that a lowering of the birth rate means more women in the workforce and more single-person households. Further, the increase in dual-earning households means more disposable income. What does that add up to? Fast foods! As more women enter the workforce, the need for convenience and carry-out foods increases. Single people generally eat more meals away from home. And more disposable income means that families can afford to eat out more often. As a result, PepsiCo has jumped into fast foods with both feet by buying Pizza Hut, Taco Bell, and Kentucky Fried Chicken. It now has a solid business going with rather than against the demographic tide.

As we saw, part of PepsiCo's strategy to counteract the projected decrease in cola consumption has been to strengthen its position in the adult market by introducing Slice and reformulating Diet Pepsi. In addition, PepsiCo's Wines and Spirits division gives it representation in another adult-oriented beverage market, imported wines.

ESTABLISHING COMPETITIVE ADVANTAGE

One of the most important components in the marketing environment is competition. Marketers identify opportunities based on competitive weaknesses, and they develop strategies with potential competitive responses in mind. They try to develop differences relative to their competitors based on a superior product, better distribution and services, or lower costs and selling price. The development of such differences relative to competitors are known as a **competitive** (or differential) **advantage**.

At times, the drive for competitive advantage takes on battlefield proportions, with all the trappings of military preparations — frontal assaults on competition, attempts to outflank the competitor, wars of attrition to see who can survive in the marketplace, and so forth. Pepsi-Cola has been locked in such battles with Coca-Cola for years and has, until recently, assumed the role of the underdog. Its drive for competitive advantage is constantly centered on Coca-Cola. The introduction of Slice was viewed as a "flanking maneuver" to gain a competitive advantage in a market that Coke had not yet entered.

The result of the introduction was strategy and counterstrategy. After the introduction of lemon-lime Slice, Coke introduced juice-enriched Minute Maid sodas. Pepsi-Cola quickly countered with an expanded line of flavors for Slice such as mandarin orange, apple, and cherry cola.

Pepsi-Cola also attempted to exploit competitive weakness when Coca-Cola introduced New Coke. Roger Enrico, president of Pepsi-Cola USA, made the famous statement, "After 87 years of going at it eyeball to eyeball, the other guy just blinked."[8] The implication was that Coke felt impelled to change its formula to be more like Pepsi-Cola's in order to strengthen its hand in the teenage market. Pepsi-Cola quickly mounted an advertising campaign to take advantage of apparent competitive weakness. In one ad, a young girl, Coke in hand, asks "Why did they do it to me? I liked it (Coke) the way it was." Ultimately, the introduction of New Coke did not create a competitive advantage for Pepsi-Cola. Coke reintroduced the old formula and the net outcome was, if anything, a net increase in Coca-Cola's market share.

Probing for competitive weakness is one aspect of analyzing the competitive environment. Another is assessing competitive strengths and trying to counter them. Pepsi-Cola recognized that Coca-Cola had a distinct advantage in the diet soft drink market. Diet Coke outsells Diet Pepsi two-to-one and sells particularly well among male consumers. Pepsi-Cola introduced diet versions of Slice including lemon-lime, mandarin orange, apple, and cherry cola. These additions were meant to cover all of the company's bases in the diet soft drink market.

D. Wayne Calloway became PepsiCo's chief executive officer in May 1986. A finance man by training, Calloway sees marketing as central to his job. What is his primary marketing objective for Pepsi-Cola? To challenge Coke wherever Pepsi-Cola is lagging behind. For example, Pepsi-Cola trails Coke in fountain sales, and Calloway is pushing to sign up fast-food outlets to sell Pepsi. Pepsi-Cola also lags behind Coke in the international market. Calloway completed an agreement to sell Pepsi in China in the early 1980s to overcome Coca-Cola's exclusive lock on the world's largest market based on an earlier agreement with the Chinese government.[9]

Calloway's marketing vision is not limited to soft drinks. He sees growth in fast foods and snack foods as reflecting the needs of the post World War II baby-

D. Wayne Calloway — Pepsi's Number One Marketing Man

Reprinted by permission of PepsiCo., Inc., Purchase, New York, 1989.

boom generation. His stint as president of Frito-Lay saw a string of new-product successes, most notably, Tostitos Tortilla Chips.[10] Calloway also plans to expand the number of Pizza Hut and Taco Bell restaurants. Part of the plan is the opening of home-delivery Pizza Hut units for the growing number of "couch potato" consumers who want their fast foods at home. Although not looking aggressively for an acquisition, Calloway might consider one. He recognizes that in the long run, the trend to health and nutrition may work against increased consumption of snack items and fast foods. So a good hedge might be to acquire a diversified food company that has a line of low calorie and nutritional foods.

Where did Calloway get his marketing know-how? On the job. His first jobs at Vick Chemical and ITT were as a financial controller. He was then hired by PepsiCo in 1967 to develop a financial reporting system for Frito-Lay. After a stint as controller of the division, he headed Pepsi-Cola Canada and began learning about new-product development, distribution, and advertising. Top management then called him back to Frito-Lay as president. In five and one-half years he tripled profits and saw sales grow by 250 percent.

Not everything at Frito-Lay came up roses for Calloway. After buying Grandma's packaged foods in 1980, the company failed with a soft-cookie entry under the Grandma's label. More established competitors in the cookie market such as Procter & Gamble and Nabisco Brands came in with soft-cookie entries that outsold Grandma's.[11] Also, Frito-Lay could not get Grandma's into stores fast enough to compete effectively. To those who claim that nobody who makes mistakes stays at PepsiCo for long, Calloway says, "Hey, I was one of the guys responsible for Grandma's." Nevertheless, he got the call as number-two man at PepsiCo and now heads the corporation.

Referring to his college days when he was a star guard on Wake Forest's basketball team, Calloway says, "Give me a week, and I'll make 80 percent of my free throws." It may be coincidental, but PepsiCo gave Calloway a few years at Frito-Lay and he got 80 percent of the corn chip market. ■

MARKETING SYSTEMS AND THE PROCESS OF EXCHANGE

Manufacturers rely on **facilitating marketing systems** to provide the means for an exchange process in which there is a transfer of goods from manufacturers to customers, and a reverse transfer of payments from customers to manufacturers. This process of exchange requires three distinct systems: (1) a **marketing information system** that allows management to determine what products to offer to meet customer needs so exchange can take place; (2) a **communications system** that informs customers of products and influences them to buy; and (3) a **distribution system** that delivers what the customer wants, when and where the customer wants it.

Facilitating systems are depicted as part of a total marketing system in Figure 1.4. The customer is at the center. The role of the marketing organization (the

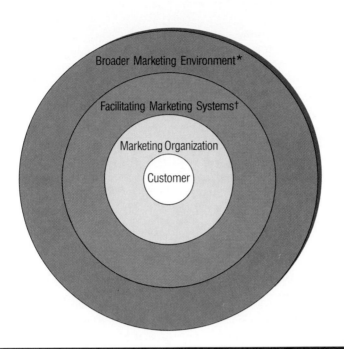

FIGURE 1.4
The Total Marketing System

*Competitive, social, regulatory, and economic forces.

next circle in the figure) is to provide an exchange with the customer, facilitated by information, communications, and distribution systems. These facilitating systems operate in a broader marketing environment composed of competitive, social, technological, legal and regulatory, and economic forces.

THE MARKETING INFORMATION SYSTEM

Management relies on a marketing information system to identify marketing opportunities, test products and strategies, and evaluate customer responses. The system generates information from three sources: the environment, the marketing organization, and marketing research agencies. Environmental information is provided by government agencies, trade associations, the company's management and sales personnel, its distributors, and its competitors. The marketing organization also provides its management important information such as sales data, costs, and cash flow. Also, research firms are called on to evaluate marketing opportunities and strategies by conducting customer surveys and running various experiments to test components of the marketing mix.

THE COMMUNICATIONS SYSTEM

The marketing communications process involves three types of organizations: the marketing organization, advertising agencies, and media. The marketing organization — that is, the manufacturer of the brand being advertised — is responsible for developing the product, positioning it, and paying for the communications process. The company's advertising agency develops a campaign to inform and influence consumers. It also develops an overall communications mix composed not only of advertising, but of direct mail, in-store displays, sales promotions, and public relations. In addition, the agency develops a media plan that might involve TV, radio, magazine, and newspaper ads. The media are responsible for running the ads developed by the agency.

THE DISTRIBUTION SYSTEM

Marketing organizations move their products to their customers through various networks known as **channels of distribution.** The simplest is selling directly to the customer. This form of selling is most common for industrial goods such as generators or automation systems because the cost and complexity of such industrial goods require direct contact between buyer and seller. Most consumer goods are sold through intermediaries. Companies using intermediaries frequently sell to wholesalers, who then sell to retailers. Selling to a few wholesalers is more economical than selling to thousands of small retailers.

Some national marketers sell directly to retailers despite the greater costs. Frito-Lay maintains a competitive advantage by delivering products directly to supermarkets as well as to small retail outlets from 1,800 warehouses through a salesforce of more than 10,000 people. In this way, it can ensure fresh products, shelf space for its brands, and favorable promotions at the point of sale.

MARKETING'S RELATIONSHIP TO OTHER BUSINESS FUNCTIONS

Because of its central role, marketing must be performed in coordination with other business activities. Therefore, it is essential to understand the relationship of marketing to other business functions in the firm; namely, finance, accounting, manufacturing, and research and development (R&D).

Finance is essential to evaluating marketing performance since it determines the profitability of individual products like Slice or Diet Pepsi. If a product is performing poorly, a financial analysis is necessary to determine whether it should be deleted from the line or retained. Wayne Calloway's finance background enabled him to view marketing expenditures with a critical eye, and his control of marketing costs was an important element in the improved profit performance of Frito-Lay. Further, Calloway was in a good position to assess alternative sources of financing for new products and new markets. It was the combination of a finance background and marketing insights that gave Calloway the capability of moving to the top at PepsiCo.

Accounting contributes to the evaluation of marketing performance by allocating costs. Such cost allocations are an essential element in computing profits. In multiproduct companies such as PepsiCo, common activities that cut across products such as research and development, factory overhead, and corporate advertising must be allocated to products to arrive at net profits. Accounting procedures determine such cost allocations. As a result, they directly affect evaluation of a product's profitability. Accounting's cost allocations also help marketers set prices. Prices are often determined on a *cost-plus basis,* that is, by using cost as a base and adding a profit target.

Marketing must also be closely coordinated with *manufacturing*. Production runs are based on marketers' forecasts for new and existing products. Schedules must be developed to ensure distribution of products by a certain date.

Coordination between marketing and *research and development* (R&D) is particularly important in the development of new products. Marketing provides R&D with information on consumers' needs to help scientists and engineers formulate product ingredients and product designs that will meet these needs. R&D then must communicate the product's physical properties and performance capabilities to marketing.

The development of Slice is an example of close coordination between marketing and R&D. Once marketing determined that adding fruit juice to a lemon-

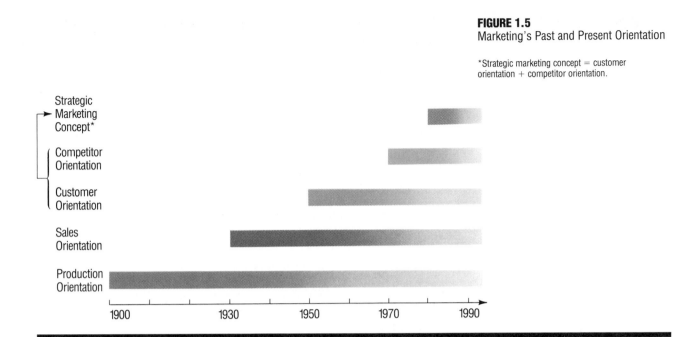

FIGURE 1.5
Marketing's Past and Present Orientation

*Strategic marketing concept = customer orientation + competitor orientation.

lime beverage was an area of opportunity, R&D went to work. The technical problem was that adding juice made a soft drink look cloudy. After over a year of constant testing and a stream of continual failures, R&D finally produced a clear drink with 10 percent juice and a light, crisp, juicy taste. It was then that marketing began testing the new formulation and considering alternative positioning strategies. This R&D/marketing interface would never have occurred without the firm conviction that a juice-based soft drink was a prime area of marketing opportunity.

Smooth integration between marketing and other business functions is not always easy to achieve. For example, manufacturing characteristically strives for efficient production, which requires longer runs and fewer and simpler products. Marketing prefers shorter production runs to facilitate quick distribution, and wants more models to meet varying consumer needs. Similarly, R&D tends to develop products that may have more features and design elements than consumers need. Marketing prefers to eliminate unnecessary design features to keep prices competitive.

MARKETING: PAST, PRESENT, AND FUTURE

In the previous discussion, we have seen that marketing opportunities are defined by analyzing customers and competitors. Interestingly, though, marketing at one time had more of a production and sales orientation, as shown in Figure 1.5. It is only since the 1950s that marketing has been characterized by a *customer orientation*. This customer orientation has come to be known as the **marketing concept**. Its basic premise is that all marketing strategies must be based on known customer needs.

But what about a systematic approach to evaluating competitors' strengths and weaknesses? Surprisingly, this type of evaluation has received attention only since the mid 1970s. We will refer in this book to the newer focus on both customers and competitors as the **strategic marketing concept**. By focusing on both customers and competitors, the strategic marketing concept emphasizes the identification of marketing opportunity as a basis for marketing planning. It also emphasizes marketing's role in developing products and services, as well as its broader and longer-term role in charting a course for corporate growth. Figure 1.5 suggests that this strategic marketing concept will be the primary focus for marketers into the 1990s.

PRODUCTION ORIENTATION

When marketing was first recognized as a business activity at the turn of the century, it was essentially an adjunct of production and agriculture. It was seen as a means of exchanging farm commodities and of bringing manufactured products to market. Management concentrated on increasing output and production efficiencies. Selling was secondary because, in most cases, high-quality products were scarce and could sell themselves.

Firms that focus primarily on production efficiency and product availability with little regard for the needs of consumers have a **production orientation**. This orientation is most likely to succeed in a sellers' market — that is, where demand exceeds supply. In these conditions, the manufacturer does not have to be concerned with selling the product and focuses on increasing production through improvements in manufacturing capabilities.

The former chairman of the Pillsbury company summarized the earlier production orientation at that company as follows:

> We are professional flour millers. Blessed with a supply of the finest North American wheat, plenty of water power, and excellent milling machinery, we produce flour of the highest quality. Our basic function is to mill high quality flour, and of course (and almost incidentally) we must hire salesmen to sell it just as we hire accountants to keep our books.[12]

Production-oriented firms have sometimes become so focused on bringing out the highest quality product that they completely lose sight of the customer. Assuming that "customers will beat a path to the door of the manufacturer that builds a better mousetrap," they have allowed their focus on research and development (R&D) and production to blind them to the fact that customers are not always willing to pay more for higher quality.

Figure 1.5 suggests that a production orientation was prevalent before 1930. But many firms are production-oriented even today. RCA introduced SelectaVision, its entry into the videodisc market, because it was convinced the product would be widely accepted. It failed to understand the importance to consumers of a recording capability. The general acceptance of videocassette recorders forced RCA to withdraw the product in the mid 1980s. Had RCA been more attuned to customer needs, it would have withdrawn from videodiscs and begun marketing VCRs much earlier.

SALES ORIENTATION

Many companies shifted from a production to a **sales orientation** during the Great Depression of the 1930s. Overcapacity spurred management to institute a *hard-sell approach* that sometimes antagonized customers. The philosophy was to sell what the company made rather than to make what it could sell based on customer needs. Most firms had sales departments; few had marketing departments. The predominant factor in the marketing mix was the salesforce.

This sales orientation continued until the 1950s, encouraged by a post–World War II sellers' market caused by shortages. Companies did not have to define customer needs. They could continue to sell what they made. The sales orientation is illustrated by General Electric's approach to marketing before 1950:

> *What we could produce we could sell. Everybody wanted a home and needed a washer, so anyone who could build them could sell them. Mass thinking could prevail since everyone wanted what the neighbors had. Mass production could work because markets were homogeneous . . . forgiving . . . accepting minor differences in products. It was a decade of growth, of suburban tract houses, and the appliances inside . . . of cars and television sets. But it was basically selling, not marketing.[13]*

Even today, many firms use a hard-sell approach characteristic of a sales rather than a marketing orientation. Such an approach is typical of products that consumers do not generally seek out — insurance or magazine subscriptions, for example.

The visibility of a hard-sell approach has created problems for marketing's image. The most effective selling is need-oriented; that is, the salesperson assesses customer needs and directs the sales message accordingly.

CUSTOMER ORIENTATION: THE MARKETING CONCEPT

The philosophy that marketing strategies must be based on known customer needs began to win wide acceptance in the mid 1950s. Pent-up demand for consumer goods after World War II had been met. Consumers had stocked up on durable goods at the onset of the Korean War, and by the mid 1950s demand for these products was decreasing. Consumers now became more selective in their purchases. As a result, supply exceeded demand, yet consumers had plenty of purchasing power. The economy experienced its first true buyers' market — consumers had the money but were not buying.

Some marketers reacted by continuing to be sales oriented — pushing the existing lines, heightening selling efforts, repeating selling themes, unloading excess inventories. These firms continued to sell on a mass-market basis with little thought of targeting products to the needs of particular customer segments. Other firms reacted with more foresight by developing a greater diversity of products directed to segments of customers having similar needs. They became **customer-oriented**.

One of the first companies to recognize the need for a customer orientation was General Electric. A GE executive clearly stated the marketing concept that emerged from this period:

> *The principal task of the marketing function . . . is not so much to be skillful in making the customer do what suits the interests of the business as to be skillful in conceiving and then making the business do what suits the interests of the customer.[14]*

As a result of its new, customer-oriented perspective, GE redefined the meaning of marketing in its 1952 annual report and was the first to use the term *marketing concept*.

> *The marketing concept . . . integrates marketing into each phase of the business. Thus marketing, through its studies and research, will establish for the engineer, the design and manufacturing person, what the customer wants in a given product, what price he or she is willing to pay, and where and when it will be wanted.[15]*

The development of the marketing concept changed the nature of marketing activities by

- *Spurring new product development.* A greater diversity of products was required to meet customer needs.

- *Emphasizing market segmentation.* Customers with similar needs were identified (for example, separate taste, convenience, and decaffeinated segments in the coffee market), and strategies were directed to these segments.

- *Focusing on marketing communications.* Product benefits had to be communicated to customer segments. Advertising became more diverse and informative.

- *Creating greater selectivity in personal selling.* Sales personnel now had to determine customer needs and develop their sales messages accordingly. Standardized sales approaches were no longer as effective.

- *Creating more selective media and distributive outlets.* Specialized magazines began to appear, direct mail was used to reach customer segments, and specialty wholesalers and retailers became more prominent.

- *Encouraging marketing research.* Information on customer needs was required. Consumer surveys were used more frequently to identify opportunity, and new products underwent more rigorous consumer testing.

The shift from a sales to a customer orientation did not occur overnight. Some companies such as General Electric were quick to recognize the changes in marketing strategy required by the acceptance of the marketing concept. Other companies are still operating on the basis of a production or sales orientation.

COMPETITOR ORIENTATION: THE STRATEGIC MARKETING CONCEPT

Although the marketing concept seems perfectly plausible as a basis for developing marketing strategy, some companies began to realize that there was something lacking. A company could be perfectly customer oriented and do all the right things — good marketing research, a strong new-product development capability, products positioned to customer needs and targeted to market segments — yet sustain heavy losses because it was outmaneuvered by competition.

What was lacking was a concept of **sustainable competitive advantage** — that is, meeting the customer's needs while maintaining an advantage over competitors in terms of product uniqueness or lower costs.[16] Before its acquisition by Chrysler, American Motors had decided to produce only Jeeps. It had stopped producing passenger cars, not because it was ineffective in defining customer needs, but because it did not have the resources to compete head-on with Ford, Chrysler, and General Motors. American Motors achieved a sustainable competitive advantage by satisfying the needs of a small segment of the auto market that the Big Three regarded as too small to enter.

A competitor orientation began to be part of the marketing focus of many firms for several reasons. First, rapid inflation in the 1970s, the steep recession in the early 1980s, and the sluggish economic recovery afterward heightened the cost consciousness of many domestic firms. Firms that operated in industries where products were relatively undifferentiated began to realize that they had to gain some advantage over their competitors to make a profit. The only recourses seemed to be to reduce costs by increasing productivity or to find some technological breakthrough to gain product superiority. Competition from lower-cost foreign manufacturers heightened the need to find some sustainable advantage as a basis for long-term profitability.

Second, many firms embarked on a rash of acquisitions of high-growth companies in the late 1960s and early 1970s to increase short-term earnings. In doing so, they strayed from their areas of expertise. These firms then divested their acquisitions so they could go back to core businesses where they had a competitive advantage. As we saw, Pepsi-Cola acquired Wilson Sporting Goods and North American Van Lines, and then divested itself of these companies because of lack of marketing expertise in sporting goods and transportation.

Taking a competitor orientation may not seem new. The concept of competition has been at the center of economic thought for the last two hundred years. Business firms have not ignored competition. In general, though, they did not adequately evaluate it in developing marketing strategies before 1975. Most companies would embark on a certain course of action and then later react to competitors' responses. A competitor orientation requires a more *proactive* stance — evaluating strengths and weaknesses of competitors and anticipating their responses to the company's actions before a particular strategic alternative is selected.

An example of a failure to project competitive responses was Bristol-Myers' introduction of Datril, the nonaspirin pain reliever designed to compete with Tylenol. Bristol-Myers introduced an undifferentiated product at a lower price, not realizing that Tylenol could easily cut its price below Datril's and maintain an acceptable profit margin. It did, and Datril languishes with a tiny share of the market.

A competitor orientation does not displace a customer orientation. It reinforces it. The more competitive the market, the more attuned a company must be to customer needs. In the absence of a competitor orientation, a firm may successfully satisfy customer needs, but at a loss. Figure 1.5 makes the point. The combination of a customer and a competitor orientation produces the new *strategic marketing concept*. This concept states that the firm must satisfy customer needs while sustaining a competitive advantage if it is to ensure long-term profitability.

THE BROADER ROLE OF MARKETING

The description of marketing and the focus on PepsiCo may leave you with the impression that marketing is concerned only with consumer products (products for final consumption). This is not true. Strategies must be developed to market goods sold to businesses (referred to as business-to-business marketing) as well as goods sold to final consumers. Strategies must also be developed to market services as well as products. And these offerings must be marketed in international as well as in domestic markets. Further, these marketing activities can take place in retail and wholesale firms as well as in manufacturing firms.

There is one additional element in the broader concept of marketing: Marketing must extend beyond the business sphere to consider the societal concerns of its customers if marketing organizations are to fulfill their social responsibilities.

Business-to-business marketing involves the sale of products to firms so as to manufacture or process other products (machine tools, generators), or to support such activities (business computers, order forms, copiers; see Exhibit 1.3). The products marketed on a business-to-business basis are called **industrial products** and actually represent a higher sales volume than consumer goods. They are purchased by organizational buyers whereas consumer products are purchased by final consumers. The term *customers* refers to all buyers, industrial and consumer. The term *consumers* refers only to final consumers of the product.

EXHIBIT 1.3
An Example of Business-to-Business Marketing

BUSINESS-TO-BUSINESS MARKETING

The principles in marketing industrial products are usually the same as those that apply to consumer goods. But there are some important differences. Organizational buyers deal with products that are more technically complex than consumer goods. They need to negotiate with a salesperson who can describe product performance and service support. As a result, personal selling plays a more important part in marketing industrial products than consumer goods.

The new-product development process is also likely to differ. Technological development is likely to be more rapid for industrial products. The development process is likely to be longer and capital expenditures on new products greater. Another difference is that postpurchase service is more likely to be important for industrial compared to consumer goods. As a result, service capabilities are a more important factor in influencing the customer to buy.

In general, the business-to-business sector has lagged behind consumer marketers in adopting a strategic marketing concept. The focus in industrial firms tends to be more on internal factors such as company resources and capabilities than on external factors such as customer needs and competitor reactions. But this focus is slowly changing. For example, Dun and Bradstreet, one of the foremost purveyors of information services to corporate America, operated with little regard for customer needs for almost 140 years. Its "take it or leave it" attitude was profitable until the computer and electronic revolution created competition. The company then began to change its focus to develop new services geared to the needs of industrial users. It expanded its staff to include computer experts and marketing researchers, so that it was no longer dominated by salespeople. The new philosophy is summarized by D&B's chairman:

> *Instead of concentrating on new ways to package and sell information we happen to have on hand, we are beginning to look at the changing needs of the marketplace and to devise ways to fill those needs.*[17]

SERVICES MARKETING

EXHIBIT 1.4
An Example of Services Marketing

The American economy is increasingly service-oriented. Services produce about half of the U.S. gross national product. As a result, service marketing is receiving increasing attention. Banks, brokerage houses, insurance companies, airlines, and hotel chains are becoming more marketing-oriented. (See the ad in Exhibit 1.4 as an example of services marketing.) Some of these companies are beginning to hire product managers from such staunch consumer-goods companies as General Foods and Procter & Gamble to apply marketing skills to services.

Any product manager moving from consumer-goods products to services encounters a drastic change in environment. Services are intangible, whereas products are tangible. Services are produced by people, products by machines. As a result, services tend to be more variable in quality, products are more standardized. A consumer buying a box of corn flakes knows what is in the box. A consumer boarding a flight or going into a restaurant is less assured of the consistency of what he or she is buying. Another difference between products and services is that services cannot be stored if they are not used. An airline cannot store empty seats, whereas an auto manufacturer can keep unsold cars in inventory. The perishability of services creates more risks for service compared to product marketers.

Much of the recent attention to services marketing is due to the greater marketing orientation of the financial community. Banks, brokerage houses and insurance companies have become more marketing-oriented because many of the restraints on competition have been lifted. As a result, Merrill Lynch is offering banking services, Citicorp is going into the brokerage and insurance business, and companies like Sears, J. C. Penney, and General Electric have subsidiaries in financial services. These companies are seeking a competitive advantage by better serving customer needs.

Not-for-profit institutions such as hospitals, museums, charities, and educational institutions are also beginning to engage in services marketing. These organizations have the additional task of marketing to the donors of funds as well as to their own customers.

INTERNATIONAL MARKETING

Many American firms such as Coca-Cola and IBM have multinational operations and do over half their business abroad. Some direct products and services to overseas marketers (see Exhibit 1.5). Also, foreign firms such as Nestle and Unilever have substantial operations in the United States. These multinational firms must adjust their marketing operations to differences among countries. Such differences will be much greater than any regional or social differences experienced in marketing at their home base. Therefore, a key strategic question in international marketing is the extent to which operations can be standardized across countries. Such standardization allows for a more uniform global strategy that is much less expensive to implement. But, often, standardization is achieved at the sacrifice of gearing marketing strategies to the particular needs of customers in various countries.

The diversity of needs and customs across countries means that international marketing operations tend to be riskier. Moreover, requirements set by foreign governments to enter their markets and differences in language, customs, media, and distribution make international marketing more complicated than domestic marketing.

EXHIBIT 1.5
An Example of International Marketing

RETAIL AND WHOLESALE MARKETING

The examples in this chapter have described marketing by the producers of goods and services. Intermediaries between manufacturers and customers also engage in marketing. These firms identify opportunities, develop marketing strategies to satisfy customer needs, and seek competitive advantages. The difference is that they are providing a specific set of services to consumers — time, place, and possession *utilities* (or values) in the exchange of goods. They provide **time utility** by ensuring products are distributed so consumers can buy and consume them when they are needed. They provide **place utility** by ensuring consumers can buy these products in convenient locations. And they provide **possession utility** by giving consumers the means to exchange money for product ownership.

Wholesalers and retailers gain competitive advantage by providing superior store facilities and services. For example, 7-Eleven stores established a competitive advantage by offering late-hour and weekend shopping in convenient locations. Retailers and wholesalers also define target segments and position their offerings to these segments. J. C. Penney has tried to appeal to a more affluent segment by upgrading its image and repositioning its line to higher-quality merchandise.

MARKETING MANAGEMENT'S SOCIAL RESPONSIBILITIES

Marketing managers have a responsibility to the consumer to guarantee product safety, provide accurate information to consumers so they can make a reasoned choice, and provide facilities for registering complaints. In recent years firms have become more sensitive to their responsibilities to consumers and to society. One way to demonstrate social responsibility is to ensure that consumer complaints are heard. Whirlpool instituted a "cool line" to provide a 24-hour-a-day facility for consumers to make complaints and inquiries directly to company headquarters. Johnson & Johnson's 22 subsidiaries each have consumer-affairs departments with representatives on call 24 hours a day to hear consumer complaints.[18] Procter & Gamble has an 800 number on each of its packages should consumers want information or have a complaint.

A more important consideration is that products be produced and marketed to avoid these complaints. Marketers must make sure consumers get what they pay for and must, above all, guarantee product safety. In addition, concern for consumer welfare would dictate providing fuller information on product ingredients and company safeguards against polluting the environment. Ultimately, the issue is whether marketing organizations are willing to support a philosophy of social consciousness, one that attempts to resolve the potential conflict between profit maximization and social welfare.

SUMMARY

1.   What is marketing?

Marketing is a dynamic set of activities directed toward identifying and satisfying customer needs. An effective marketing organization defines customer needs; develops new products to meet these needs; positions the product to a defined target segment; develops a mix of advertising, price, and distribution strategies to market the product nationally; and evaluates customer reactions once the product is introduced.

2.   What are the environmental dimensions of marketing?

Managers must evaluate customer needs in a broad marketing environment that includes competition, the economy, technology, government regulations, and demographic and lifestyle trends. Another important component of the environment is the operation of marketing systems that facilitate the exchange of goods and services in the economy. A communications system informs consumers about products and influences them to buy. A distribution system delivers what consumers want, when and where they want it. An information system enables management to develop marketing strategies aimed at introducing products fitted to consumer needs.

3.   What is the relationship of marketing to other business functions?

Marketing plays a central role in the firm in conjunction with other business functions. Finance provides marketing managers the profit criteria for evaluating product performance. Accounting allocates cost to products to permit determination of profits. Manufacturing ensures that the product is ready to be distributed when promised. Research and development formulates and designs new products.

4.   What was marketing's role in the past, and what is its role at present?

In the past, marketing was production- and sales-oriented. A production orientation meant that marketers were more concerned with developing products based on their production and research and development capabilities rather than on customer needs. A sales orientation meant that marketers were willing to sell what the company made rather than to determine what should be made to meet customer needs.

Marketing's current role provides strategic direction to the business firm by ensuring that all marketing strategies are developed based on known customer needs. Marketing also recognizes the importance of developing a sustainable advantage over competitors to prevent the firm from losing ground to competitors. The focus on both customer needs and competitive advantage is called the strategic marketing concept.

5. What is the broader role of marketing?
The broader role of marketing encompasses business-to-business, international, service, and not-for-profit marketing in both the manufacturing and distribution sectors. It also recognizes the social responsibilities of the marketing firm to ensure product safety, product quality, and adequate environmental protection.

KEY TERMS

Marketing (p. 4)
Target segment (p. 5)
Product-line extension (p. 6)
Product positioning (p. 6)
Test marketing (p. 6)
Four Ps of marketing (p. 6)
Marketing mix (p. 6)
Market share (p. 7)
Marketing opportunities (p. 9)
Marketing threats (p. 9)
Competitive advantage (p. 11)
Facilitating marketing systems (p. 12)
Marketing information system (p. 12)
Communications system (p. 12)

Distribution system (p. 12)
Channels of distribution (p. 14)
Marketing concept (p. 15)
Strategic marketing concept (p. 16)
Production orientation (p. 16)
Sales orientation (p. 16)
Customer orientation (p. 17)
Sustainable competitive advantage
  (p. 18)
Business-to-business marketing (p. 19)
Industrial products (p. 19)
Time utility (p. 21)
Place utility (p. 21)
Possession utility (p. 21)

QUESTIONS

1. The owner of a small business producing costume jewelry read the introduction to this chapter. She then made the following comment:

   It is all well and good to talk about Pepsi as having marketing savvy and being successful. They have the resources and the clout. But what about us small firms? We can't spend millions on new product development and advertising. I really wonder how relevant your description of marketing is to our operations.

   a. What is the relevance of the definition of marketing in this chapter to a small producer of costume jewelry?
   b. What is the relevance of the three-step description of the marketing process in Figure 1.1 to this firm?

2. A manager of a medium-sized industrial firm producing electrical cable also read the chapter. His reaction was somewhat different than that of the small business owner in the previous question. He said:

   Yes, Pepsi is a very good marketing-oriented company. We are very different. We rely on our salesforce, not advertising, as the main contact with customers. Occasionally we will develop new products, but our products are pretty much like our competitors'. So we really do not need marketing as you describe it. We need an effective salesforce. We fit into your description of being a sales-oriented company. And that's pretty much where we should be.

   a. Do you agree with this view?

b. What might cause the company to shift from a sales to a customer orientation?

c. What might cause it to shift to a strategic marketing orientation?

3. What do marketers mean by *positioning* a product? What are some examples of positioning products at Pepsi-Cola? What is the link between positioning a product and developing a marketing mix for the product?

4. What is PepsiCo's long-term *corporate game plan?* Why is this game plan based on marketing considerations?

5. One marketer, commenting on PepsiCo's constant attempt to gain competitive advantage at Coke's expense, said

Pepsi has done well in competing with Coke. Such competition keeps management on their toes. But there is a danger of being too focused on your competitors. You wind up developing your strategies based on knee-jerk reactions rather than anticipating what the future environment might hold.

a. Explain the marketing analyst's statement.

b. Is there any evidence that PepsiCo has developed its strategies on a knee-jerk basis? Explain.

6. A pharmaceutical company is considering developing a three-in-one hair care product — a rinse, conditioner, and shampoo all in one. The marketing manager for the project wants to make sure that (1) the right ingredients are developed to make a safe and effective product that will provide rinse, conditioning, and shampoo benefits; (2) financial criteria will be established for product performance; (3) costs will be fairly allocated to the new product; and (4) the product will be available before the advertising campaign is introduced. How can nonmarketing business functions contribute to each of these areas?

7. Consider the statement, "Marketing strategies must be based on known consumer needs." In what ways did acceptance of this statement in the 1950s represent a marked departure from the past? What are the implications of the statement for

a. advertising strategies?

b. product strategies?

c. marketing research?

d. strategies to gain competitive advantage?

8. The chairman of the board of a large oil company states:

The marketing concept is fine for companies providing packaged goods. These are differentiated products in highly competitive industries that need to advertise to stimulate demand. But we are producing standardized products in a situation of scarcity. Our main concern is not satisfying consumer needs, but trying to discover and exploit scarce resources.

a. As executive vice-president for marketing, you take exception to the chairman's statement. On what grounds?

b. Under what environmental conditions might the chairman become more concerned with satisfying customer needs?

9. What is the difference between the marketing concept and the strategic marketing concept? Why does the strategic marketing concept give a firm a sounder basis for developing marketing strategies?

10. What were the reasons companies began to focus more on competition in developing marketing plans and strategies in the 1980s?

11. What is a sustainable competitive advantage? Can you cite examples of companies sustaining a competitive advantage based on

a. product superiority?

b. price?

c. factors other than product or price?

12. A product manager for a deodorant line accepts a job at Citicorp as product manager of its new line of cash management accounts. What differences is the manager likely to find in developing marketing strategies for a financial service such as cash management accounts as opposed to a consumer product such as deodorants?

CASE 1.1

JAKE'S, PEPSI'S GOOD-TASTING DIET COLA

Source: "Jake's, Pepsi's 'Real Good Diet Cola,' to Try to Establish New Market Niche," *Adweek*, December 15, 1986, p. 2. Reprinted with permission of Adweek.

The cola wars' newest David vs. Goliath bout has an unlikely David. His name is Jake.

Pepsi-Cola Co. introduced Jake's Diet Cola to Midwestern test markets in January 1986, confronting Diet Coke's domination of the category with an industry anomaly. For one thing, Jake's has 15 calories per serving — 30 calories in a 12-ounce can. For another, everything about the brand runs counter to the hip, zippy style of most cola marketing from the homespun name to the bracingly straightforward ad theme, "Jake's. A real good diet cola."

Jake's hit the market at a time when the diet segment of the soft-drink industry was growing about 8% a year — more than twice as fast as sugared soft drinks' 3% rate. If they sustain their rapid pace, diet soft drinks could account for 40% of the $30-billion soft-drink market.

That kind of growth has led Pepsi to view diet cola as a market unto itself, "one that could have its own segments within it," says a Pepsi spokesperson.

Currently 41.3% of adults drink diet soft drinks, according to Simmons Market Research Bureau, but while 47% of women are diet soft-drink consumers, only 34.7% of men are diet-beverage drinkers.

That's changing fast, however, and although Pepsi feels Jake's appeal will "cut across all lines," Jake's positioning reflects more than a casual nod to the influx of male drinkers.

Diet Coke not only outsells Diet Pepsi 2-to-1 — a 10% share of the entire soft-drink market to Diet Pepsi's 4.8% share — it also has a greater following among males.

"Diet Pepsi has always been a more female drink than Diet Coke," says a former brand manager at Coke, "and Diet Coke has always been more positioned to males by imagery."

It's not clear, however, whether a mid-calorie cola can shake up the soft-drink market the way Miller Brewing Co.'s mid-calorie Miller Lite beer shook up that industry in the early 1970s, spawning a new category.

"Fifteen calories [per serving] won't work," says the former Coke brand manager, "because it's not a diet cola. It's like selling beer without alcohol."

Pepsi says its research shows that 15 calories per serving is the maximum number of calories consumers will accept in a drink that also promises dietetic benefits. Jake's gets those calories by mixing fructose with NutraSweet, the no-calorie sweetening component in most diet soft drinks.

Roy Burry, a beverage analyst for Kidder Peabody, New York, believes the market is ripe for a mid-calorie cola.

"Part of the problem with diet soft drinks is they just don't taste as good as regular," says Burry. "I think they will sacrifice a little on the diet side for taste. There's a market for the product."

Burry estimates that such mid-calorie soft drinks could account for as much as 5% of the total soft-drink market by the end of the decade.

Jake's sets the stage for the soft-drink industry to follow the beer, fast-food and tobacco industries, which have realized for years that consumers may talk a good game of abstinence, but in effect "they diet, and cheat every third day," says Frank Lane, an Atlanta-based marketing consultant.

"Most of the light beers introduced since Miller Lite have more calories than Miller Lite," the consultant says. "They've done that in an effort to return to taste. And in the cigarette industry the low-tar segment of the market has a bigger share than the ultra-low because there's a perceived taste improvement."

Lane calls such marketing "an awakening to the reality of life."

Says he: "People don't eat all diet or all non-diet food. They monitor the mix."

1. What were Pepsi Cola's marketing objectives in introducing Jake's?
2. Did Jake's have a competitive advantage compared to Diet Coke and other diet colas?
3. What was the target market for Jake's?
4. What alternative ways could Jake's have been positioned?
5. What do you think happened after Jake's was introduced?

NOTES

1. Pepsi-Cola Inc., Annual Report, 1986, p. 4.

2. "Pepsi's Marketing Magic: Why Nobody Does It Better," *Business Week,* February 10, 1986, p. 52.

3. In 1985 the American Marketing Association formulated the following definition of marketing: "Marketing is the process of planning and executing the conception, pricing, promotion, and distribution of ideas, goods, and services to create exchange that will satisfy individual and organizational objectives." This is an equally acceptable definition as the one in the text, and most of its components will be discussed in this chapter.

4. "Pepsi's Magic," p. 53.

5. "Now Soft-Drink Makers Brace for the Juice Wars," *The New York Times,* June 2, 1985, p. F12.

6. *Business Week,* February 10, 1986, p. 56.

7. "Slice: A Cast Study of a Setback," *The New York Times,* July 13, 1988, p. D1.

8. Douglas K. Ramsey, *The Corporate Warriors* (Boston: Houghton Mifflin Co., 1987), p. 89.

9. "Keeping the Party Going at Fast Paced PepsiCo," *The New York Times,* May 25, 1986, p. F25.

10. *Business Week,* February 10, 1986, p. 57.

11. *The New York Times,* May 25, 1986, p. F25.

12. Robert F. Keith, "The Marketing Revolution," *Journal of Marketing,* 24(January 1960): 35–38.

13. John F. Welch, Jr., "Where Is Marketing Now That We Really Need It," General Electric Speech, reprint of address to the Conference Board Marketing Conference, October 28, 1981.

14. J. B. McKitterick, "What Is the Marketing Management Concept?" in *The Frontiers of Marketing Thought and Science,* Frank M. Bass, ed., (Chicago: American Marketing Association, 1957).

15. *General Electric Company,* 1952 Annual Report, New York, p. 21.

16. Michael E. Porter, *Competitive Strategy* (New York: The Free Press, 1980), ch. 2.

17. "How D&B Organizes for a New-Product Blitz," *Business Week,* November 16, 1981, p. 87.

18. John A. Goodman and Larry M. Robinson, "Strategies for Improving the Satisfaction of Business Customers," *Business* (April–June 1982): 40–44.

KODAK: NO LONGER THE COMPLACENT MARKETER

Fifteen years ago, Kodak was virtually unchallenged in its leadership of the U.S. photography market. It held almost 100 percent of the market for amateur film. Its Instamatic cameras were selling well. And it was the darling of Wall Street.

But success spoiled Kodak. Its near monopoly position bred a complacency that led the company to ignore customers and competition. While its technological and engineering skills produced technically superb, easy-to-use products, its management was so averse to taking risks it often strangled new product ideas and marketing initiatives.[1] Thus, Kodak failed to enter the VCR camera market in the late 1970s. It also decided to withdraw from the 35 millimeter camera market in 1970,[2] leaving the Japanese to develop and effectively mass market high-quality, affordable 35 millimeter cameras. And Kodak let Fuji take the lead in introducing higher-speed film into the American market.[3]

Finally, a series of hammer-blows in the early 1980s destroyed Kodak's complacency, forcing the company to become more marketing-oriented. Between 1982 and 1986 Kodak saw the introduction of its disc camera falter as a result of misreading the consumer, its share of the color film market drop from almost 100 percent to 82 percent as Fuji forcefully entered the U.S. market,[4] its 1984 introduction of an 8 millimeter VCR camera achieve disappointing results due to an outdated camera design and the dominance of VHS systems,[5] and its entry into instant photography cost the company $500 million due to the loss of a patent-infringement suit on instant cameras to Polaroid.[6]

Kodak's move to a marketing orientation was quick and vigorous. As early as 1982 the company's chairman quipped, ''It's time to make this elephant dance."[7] How did Kodak start dancing? By reorganizing the company into 17 strategic business units that were focused on specific markets such as photofinishing, electronic photography, and office automation.[8] Each of these business units was given profit responsibility and had to identify new product opportunities as well as revitalize existing products.

Marketing strategy development was now in the hands of managers who were focused on customers and competitors. As a result, Kodak was able to develop products more attuned to customer needs. In 1986 Kodak successfully entered the battery market (90 percent of Kodak's photo retailers sell batteries),[9] first with an alkaline battery, and then with a new lithium battery that lasts twice as long as alkalines. In 1986 Kodak also succeeded with the introduction of the VR-G film line, widely accepted for more accurate and vibrant colors. And the reorganization enabled Kodak to move more quickly in developing and marketing new products.

Kodak made a second important change as it adopted a marketing orientation: It redefined its business. The company was no longer in the photography business; it was in the "imaging" business. It began looking at new marketing opportunities in electronic publishing, factory machine vision systems, digital scanning, color image processing, and microfilm management. Acquisitions in these areas have expanded Kodak's business beyond photography, giving its marketers more responsibility in defining future corporate directions.

Kodak is now poised to enter the environment of the 1990s a very different company, less complacent and more marketing-oriented. ■

2

CHAPTER

MARKETING IN BUSINESS ORGANIZATIONS

● ● ●

THE ROLE OF MARKETING MANAGEMENT IN THE FIRM

The role of marketing management in the business firm is illustrated in Figure 2.1. Marketing managers at Kodak and in other companies are responsible for (1) identifying marketing opportunities, (2) developing plans that will use the firm's resources to effectively exploit these opportunities, (3) targeting these strategies to a defined group of consumers, (4) implementing these strategies, and (5) evaluating and controlling the marketing effort. Figure 2.1 shows that this text is organized based on these steps.

IDENTIFY MARKETING OPPORTUNITIES

The first responsibility of marketing managers is to identify marketing opportunities. As we saw in Chapter 1, this is accomplished by analyzing customer needs and other environmental conditions.

Take lithium batteries. Kodak had clearly identified an opportunity here. With the continuing popularity of the Sony Walkman, electronic toys, portable TVs, and laptop computers, battery sales are at $2 billion a year and sales of alkaline batteries are growing at an annual rate of 14 percent.[10] Kodak also had a competitive advantage because lithium batteries are superior to the longest-lasting alkaline batteries.

The environment the firm faces is the external component in identifying marketing opportunity. The internal component is the firm's ability to exploit these opportunities with its resources. These two dimensions are shown in Figure 2.2. The level of opportunity identified by the firm is on the vertical axis. Opportunity depends on factors such as unmet customer needs, competitors' strengths and weaknesses, new technologies, emerging lifestyle and demographic trends, the regulatory climate, and economic conditions. The firm's ability to exploit such opportunities is on the horizontal axis. A company can better exploit a defined opportunity if it has some previous managerial and marketing experience, distri-

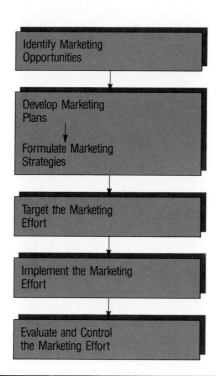

FIGURE 2.1
Role of Marketing Management
in the Business Organization

bution facilities and a salesforce, production capabilities, technological know-how, and financial resources. If one or more of these capabilities is lacking, the question management must answer is whether to acquire it in order to exploit a given opportunity.

The combination of the level of opportunity and the firm's ability to exploit it is titled the *marketing planning matrix* in Figure 2.2, because all marketing plans are formulated based on the two key dimensions in the figure.

Kodak clearly identified an area of opportunity in batteries. But did it have the know-how to exploit this opportunity? Did it have the resources to enter the battery market? Kodak had never sold batteries before; its experience was in films and cameras. Serious questions arose among top management as to Kodak's marketing capabilities, distribution network, and needed production facilities to enter the battery market. While the company had the money to go in, the battery market was only one of several places Kodak could put its money.

The Strategic Window of Opportunity
The combination of an opportunity and the firm's ability to exploit it is called the **strategic window of opportunity** (see the upper left-hand corner of Figure 2.2).[11] If the strategic window is open, this means that the firm has the ability to meet marketing opportunities.

Sometimes, firms mistakenly think the strategic window is open because they do not evaluate their ability to exploit an opportunity carefully enough. A case in point is Levi-Strauss, the jeans maker. Levi thought it saw an opportunity to leverage its name by going into fashion and designer apparel. What the company failed to realize was that designer apparel required a different set of marketing

FIGURE 2.2
The Marketing Planning Matrix

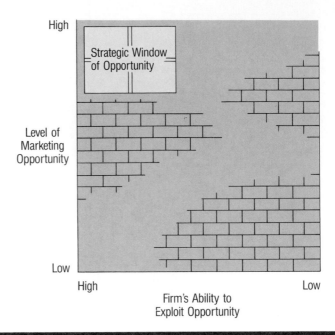

capabilities than that required for jeans. The company had neither the know-how nor the management support to successfully run a string of acquisitions in designer apparel. As a result, it eventually sold most of them off. It is now following a narrower strategy focused once again on jeans.[12]

Kodak was able to compensate for a lack of marketing know-how in batteries by using an interesting strategy. It came out with a line of alkaline batteries over a year before introducing the lithium battery. Its intent was to learn about the battery market while the lithium battery was still being developed. In 1986 it introduced its Supralife alkaline batteries with a $20 million–plus advertising campaign.[13] In the process, it not only developed consumer awareness of the Supralife line, it also established a new distribution network in supermarkets and drugstores. Having gained the ability to exploit the lithium opportunity, Kodak entered the battery market with its Ultralife brand of lithium batteries in the spring of 1987 (see Exhibit 2.1).

Even when the strategic window is open, a firm can get into trouble if it fails to sustain its advantage. Duracell and Eveready have more established brand names in batteries then Kodak. If they quickly follow Kodak's lead into lithium batteries with lower-priced lines, Kodak's advantage could quickly dissipate unless it comes up with some product improvement or cost advantage.

DEVELOP MARKETING PLANS AND STRATEGIES

A second role of marketing management in the firm is to develop marketing plans and strategies, both for new products and existing ones. A set of integrated strategies (the marketing mix) is necessary to exploit opportunities.

Kodak's strategy was to first introduce an alkaline battery in order to pave the way for its lithium battery. The Kodak name featured prominently on each battery made consumers aware of Kodak's new battery line. It also established a marketing mix for the company's battery line. The advertising and distribution

EXHIBIT 2.1
Exploiting Marketing Opportunity: Kodak
Introduces Ultralife Lithium Batteries

facilities developed for the alkaline line made it easier for Kodak to reach its objective — entry with a superior lithium battery.

Marketing strategies must be developed in some organized way. The vehicle for developing marketing strategies is the **marketing plan**; that is, a document that defines

- What a firm wants to accomplish. This must be expressed as specific objectives based on management's assessment of marketing opportunities.
- How the firm plans to accomplish its objectives as defined by the marketing strategies management selects.
- What resources management requires to implement the plan.
- How management should implement the specific strategies.

There are two kinds of marketing plans: a product marketing plan and a strategic marketing plan. The **product marketing plan** charts the marketing strategy for an individual product or service, generally over a one-year period. The product plan is developed by a **product manager** who has responsibility for marketing the product. The product plan for lithium batteries estimated the demand for the product, identified the target market, and established a marketing mix by specifying the price at which it would be sold, the product's positioning, the distribution channels, and the sales promotional incentives designed to influence consumers to try the product.

The **strategic marketing plan** is concerned with all the products that a business unit or company markets (the company's **product mix**). It does not develop plans for each product. Rather, it is concerned with the general makeup of the company's offerings based on its objectives. The plan evaluates longer term (generally five-year) opportunities, such as the projected increase in the need for portable power sources, and judges the firm's product mix based on this evaluation. It then allocates resources to various business units and product lines based on this assessment. For example, the strategic plan would recommend the amount of resources the Consumer Products Business Unit (the unit at Kodak responsible for batteries) should get to market the new battery line.

Companies that develop strategic marketing plans are frequently organized based on **strategic business units** (**SBUs**); that is, units within the company that are organized around markets with similar demand. At Kodak, an SBU would be electronic publishing or office automation, because each of these units markets products to similar buyers. The SBU organization encourages a planning focus directed to meeting customer needs and gaining competitive advantage.

The strategic marketing plan is the responsibility of either a **business manager** at the business-unit level or a **corporate marketing manager** at the headquarters level. For firms operating in many markets such as Kodak, strategic plans are usually developed at each business unit and then coordinated at headquarters. For one-market companies (for instance, Michelin Tires) or medium to small companies, the strategic plan is usually formulated at the corporate level.

Colby Chandler — A Man with a Mission

Source: "Why Kodak Is Starting to Click Again," *Business Week*, February 23, 1987, pp. 134–138; and "Kodak Is Trying to Break Out of Its Shell," *Business Week*, June 10, 1985, pp. 92–95.

Photo Source: *Advertising Age,* © Crain Communications Inc.

When Colby Chandler took over the reins of Kodak in 1984, he was a man with a mission. The company was on the ropes. It let competitors run away with such markets as 35 millimeter cameras, video recorders, and instant photography, markets that were logical extensions of Kodak's photography business.

Chandler knew what he had to do. He commissioned a sweeping review of Kodak's ponderous bureaucracy that resulted in a reshuffling of the company's core photo businesses into 17 strategic business units. The idea was that these individual business units could become more attuned to a dynamic environment that was starting to leave Kodak behind.

Chandler's next step was even more wrenching — drastic cost cuts. Kodak's cost disadvantage compared to Fuji and other Japanese competitors was staggering. Fuji's average sales per employee was four times Kodak's in 1987. Chandler cut the workforce by 15 percent and top management ranks by 25 percent.

Chandler then developed a strategic marketing plan to broaden Kodak's business mission beyond photography and into imaging technology in fields as diverse as biotechnology and graphics.

Chandler's ability to shake up the Kodak bureaucracy can be attributed to his tough-mindedness gained in growing up on a Maine farm and serving as a Marine sergeant in World War II. After the war he earned a degree in engineering and joined Kodak in 1950. In the early 1970s he distinguished himself as project manager for Kodak's first successful diversification effort — into office copiers. From there, he became president and then chairman.

Like Pepsi's Calloway, Chandler does not have a marketing background — he is an engineer. But he has the marketing vision to lead Kodak into the twenty-first century. ▪

TARGET THE MARKETING EFFORT

The third responsibility of marketing managers shown in Figure 2.1 is to target the marketing effort. Both product and business managers must identify segments of the market based on their needs and demographic and lifestyle characteristics. For example, Buick has targeted more performance-oriented cars such as its Skylark to baby boomers. Kellogg targeted its cereals to nutritionally conscious adults to expand demand beyond children.

Kodak identified the target for lithium batteries as battery users who are willing to pay more for a battery with a longer life. This definition may be accurate, but it does not give marketing managers any basis for directing their efforts. More specific information about the demographic characteristics of this segment is necessary for selecting magazines, newspapers, or TV for advertising. More specific information about the lifestyles of this segment is also necessary to gear advertising to their activities and interests.

Such information was provided by marketing research, which tied the future growth of batteries to a few environmental factors, including the electronic explosion, mobility, and the postwar baby boom. More consumers are buying Walkmans, laptop computers, VCRs, and compact discs. Many of them like to carry these products around. These consumers are primarily baby boomers (people born between 1946 and 1960). As they grow older, their disposable income is increasing. They are likely to pay more for a longer-life battery if they see value in the product.

Defining the market as "*upscale* (that is, higher income and better educated) baby boomers" guides marketing managers in media selection and advertising. Television ads should be slotted into shows that this group is most likely to watch. Print ads should be in magazines read by higher-income people age 25 to 40 (the baby-boom age spread when lithium batteries were introduced). Since this group is interested in value, ads should emphasize the performance of Kodak's battery line.

The definition of the target market is typically addressed in the product marketing plan. But the strategic marketing plan must also consider the target market. For instance, before entry into the battery business, the business manager for the Consumer Products Unit had to decide whether the SBU's target should be restricted to film users or whether it could be broadened to include battery users in general. If the unit's strategic plan restricted its new product activities to photography, then the batteries would have been sold as a tie-in to camera needs. Expansion of the target to battery users meant a broader marketing effort.

IMPLEMENT THE MARKETING EFFORT

Implementing the marketing effort is also the responsibility of both product managers and business managers. Marketing strategies in the product-marketing plan are implemented by a marketing mix designed to promote, distribute, and price the product. For instance, Kodak introduced Supralife batteries with a $20 million national advertising campaign that focused on product performance. An additional $22 million effort encouraged people to try the product by offering discounts off battery purchases plus rebates on purchases of Kodak cameras and film.[14] Distribution support was already strong with 200,000 stores selling Kodak film, and Kodak expanded this network to supermarkets and drugstores.

Kodak introduced its lithium battery at a premium price of $5 a battery. The advertising campaign focused on the benefit of twice as much power and twice as much life. The product was also advertised to electronics manufacturers as having a ten-year shelf life, an important benefit for companies whose battery-powered products sometimes sit on retail shelves for months.[15]

Whereas the product manager is responsible for implementing the product plan, the business manager implements the strategic marketing plan. The business manager for the Consumer Products Business Unit is concerned with integrating the marketing efforts of all the products within the SBU — films, cameras, and batteries. The manager's prime responsibility is allocating resources to these products to allow implementation of the various product plans.

EVALUATE AND CONTROL THE MARKETING EFFORT

The final responsibility of marketing managers, as shown in Figure 2.1, is to evaluate and control performance based on the marketing plan. For product managers, this means tracking sales and comparing revenues and costs to those projected in the product marketing plan. If sales are lower than expected, the product may have to be withdrawn or adjustments made in the marketing mix. If advertising, distribution, or sales costs are significantly over budget, the product manager must either bring these costs into line or justify why the budget should be increased. Competitive activity must also be evaluated. The product manager will need to adjust the marketing plan if a competitor comes in with a superior product or a lower price.

A product manager also relies on data from surveys to determine how consumers evaluate the product and competitive offerings as well as their awareness of advertising and their intention to buy. If adjustments have be made in the marketing mix, such surveys indicate what these adjustments should be.

Business managers evaluate marketing performance of each product in the unit's mix. Resources are allocated on this basis. Thus, the business manager for Kodak's Consumer Products Unit may decide to shift resources from film to batteries if sales of batteries exceed expectations and sales of film are relatively flat.

THE ORGANIZATIONAL FRAMEWORK FOR MARKETING

In the previous section, we mentioned two types of managers with marketing responsibility — a product manager, responsible for marketing strategies for a product, and a business manager, responsible for marketing strategies for the business unit.

A third type of executive is also responsible for marketing in the firm — a corporate marketing manager, who is part of the top management of the company and evaluates the marketing performance of all the business units within the firm. At Kodak this means evaluating not only the Consumers Product Unit but the 16 other SBUs such as photofinishing, electronic photography, and office automation. Using this evaluation, a top management group will then decide on the amount of resources the company should allocate to each of its business units. The marketing management and planning responsibilities for these three marketing levels are summarized in Figure 2.3.

THE PRODUCT MARKET UNIT (PMU)

The key planning unit at the product level is the **product market unit** (PMU). A product market unit is a set of products aimed at defined markets. Figure 2.4 shows the organization of the product, business-unit, and corporate levels at

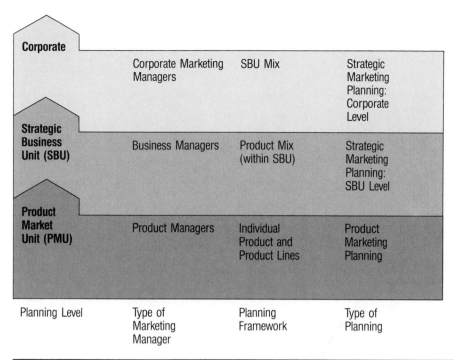

FIGURE 2.3
Three Levels of Marketing
Management and Planning

Kodak. It focuses on the Consumer Products Unit as an example of these levels. Here, there are at least three PMUs: cameras, film, and batteries. Individual products within each PMU are shown. The camera PMU has 35 millimeter, instamatic, disc, and VCR cameras. The film unit has the VR-G line as well as the regular Ektachrome, Kodachrome, and black and white films. The battery PMU has alkaline (Supralife) and lithium (Ultralife) batteries. Each of these products is headed by a product manager.

The next level up in the marketing management hierarchy in Figure 2.3 is the strategic business unit. The concept of the SBU was first developed by McKinsey and Co., a large management consulting firm, for General Electric in the early 1970s in response to GE's need to reorganize its divisions to be more sensitive to customer needs. As a result, McKinsey suggested moving away from a divisional setup that was organized around technologies and production methods in favor of organizing around markets such as small appliances, electronics, and nuclear energy. In this way, managers would be more focused on similar customer needs rather than similar technologies. These organizations were called *strategic business units* rather than divisions because they became the planning focus for business strategies based on customer needs.

Before 1984 Kodak was organized primarily on functional lines. Marketing, manufacturing, and research and development (R&D) were separate divisions that cut across market lines. This meant that one marketing group might be responsible for developing product plans for film, office copiers, and electronic publishing products. It also meant lack of coordination between functional groups, since manufacturing, marketing, and R&D would submit separate plans for the same product. Top management then had to coordinate these plans. The

THE STRATEGIC BUSINESS UNIT (SBU)

FIGURE 2.4
Example of Organizational Structure for
Marketing Planning at Kodak

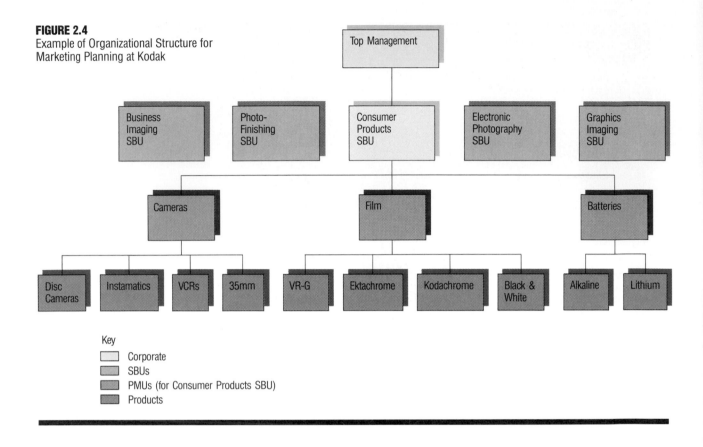

cumbersome planning process stifled initiative and took much too long to introduce new products.

Kodak's reorganization in 1984 resulted in a clearer focus on customer needs and marketing requirements. Each unit was headed by a business manager who had profit responsibility for all products within the unit. Functional areas were represented within each SBU so that marketing, manufacturing, and R&D activities could be integrated. Planning efforts could then be more efficiently directed to specific markets such as business imaging and photo-finishing (see Figure 2.4). The time needed for new-product development and management approval was cut, quickening the pace of new-product introductions. By focusing on markets rather than functions, the SBU structure enabled Kodak to better meet customer needs and gain competitive advantage. It helped make Kodak a marketing-oriented company.

As Figure 2.3 shows, the planning focus of the business manager in an SBU is the unit's product mix. The business manager reviews the plans submitted by the product managers and develops an overall strategy that defines where the SBU is heading for the next five years (the strategic marketing plan). Thus, the business manager for Kodak's Consumer Products Unit might develop a five-year plan that projects substantial growth in batteries, moderate growth in film, and flat sales for cameras. Resource allocations to these product market units would be made based on this assessment. The business manager then submits the strategic marketing plan to top management for approval.

SBUs	Markets			
	Consumer	Commercial/ Industrial	International	Government
Consumer Products	✓	✗	✓	✗
Electronic Photography	✗	✓	✓	?
Business Imaging	✗	✓	✓	?
Photo Finishing	✗	✓	✓	?
Bioproducts	✗	✓	?	?
Health Services	✗	✓	?	?

FIGURE 2.5
An SBU/Market Matrix for Kodak

The SBU framework we have been discussing assumes a multi-unit company such as Kodak. Small to medium-sized companies, and some large companies serving single markets, do not have an SBU organization. In these cases, the company operates essentially like a single strategic business unit.

THE CORPORATE LEVEL

The third and highest level of marketing management within the firm is at the corporate level. Figure 2.3 shows that top management's responsibility is to evaluate the company's mix of strategic business units through a strategic marketing plan at the corporate level. The plan allocates resources to each business unit based on corporate management's evaluation of SBU plans and will chart a five-year course for the company. For example, if top management had felt that Kodak could not develop the know-how in batteries, or if it had felt that potential demand for batteries was overstated in the Consumer Product Unit's strategic plan, it might not have given the green light for entry into the battery market.

In evaluating the SBU mix, top management will consider acquiring new business units or divesting itself of business units that do not meet profit goals. As we saw in the last chapter, Pepsi-Cola's management decided to acquire Kentucky Fried Chicken while divesting Wilson Sporting Goods and North American Van Lines, because the former fit into its corporate game plan whereas the latter did not.

A useful tool for assessing new business areas is an SBU/market matrix. Figure 2.5 lists 6 of Kodak's 24 SBUs down the side of such a matrix and its basic market

Product Marketing Plan
(Product Level)

Formulate Marketing
Objectives

Identify Marketing
Opportunities

Define the
Product-Planning Focus

Develop Marketing
Strategies

Evaluation and
Control

Strategic Marketing Plan
(Corporate and SBU Level)

Formulate Corporate
Objectives

Identify Marketing
Opportunities

Define the Strategic
Planning Focus

Develop SBU/Corporate
Growth Strategies

Evaluation and
Control

areas across the top. Checks indicate areas now served by Kodak products. Crosses indicate areas that are not relevant (for instance, industrial or government markets for the Consumer Products Unit). Question marks indicate areas of potential entry, such as government markets for the imaging and health services SBUs. The SBU/market matrix provides a good summary of top management's evaluation of areas for future growth. This global view of the company also provides an important perspective that is beyond the scope of any single SBU's strategic plan.

MARKETING AT THE PRODUCT LEVEL

Whether it takes place at the product level or at the SBU and corporate level, the steps in the marketing planning process are essentially the same. Figure 2.6 summarizes and compares these steps for both the product marketing plan and the strategic marketing plan.

The plans are far from identical, however. They differ significantly in *scope* (opportunity identification and strategies are more broadly focused in the strategic plan compared to the product plan); in *level of planning* (plans are formulated at a higher level in the strategic plan); and also in *the time horizon* (the strategic plan is generally developed with a five-year horizon and is revised yearly; the product plan is a one-year document).

In this section, we discuss the product marketing plan using the example of planning for the introduction of an acne preparation targeted to the adult market. In the next section, we describe the strategic marketing plan using the example of Toyota's long-term strategy for marketing its cars in the United States.

In 1982 Block Drug Company, a medium-sized producer of such pharmaceuticals as Nytol sleep aid tablets, Tegrin medicated shampoo, and Romilar cough syrup, identified an important area of opportunity, an acne preparation for the adult market.[16] One of Block Drug's guidelines in considering new products was to search for opportunities in which the company could develop a distinct benefit compared to the competition, but in relatively small markets. The company developed this objective because success in mass markets would attract larger and better-funded competitors, and the company did not have the funds to compete with the giants in the industry.

The acne preparation fit into this definition. The company had the competence to develop such a product. At the same time, Block's entry was unlikely to attract bigger companies because the market was relatively small compared to other over-the-counter pharmaceutical products.

The company followed each of the basic steps for a product marketing plan in Figure 2.6.

Formulating Marketing Objectives

Marketing objectives are specific performance criteria set by management. One objective in introducing the acne preparation was that return on investment (profits as a percent of total investment) should reach 15 percent within five years. Another was that the company should recoup its initial investment within three years. Limits were also set on first-year advertising of $5 million. Losses were expected in the first year because of development and startup costs, but an objective was to limit such losses to less than $3 million.

Identifying Marketing Opportunity

The product plan evaluates opportunities in specific markets. Block's marketing research showed that adults, particularly women, had acne problems and found teen acne remedies unsuitable because they left the skin dry and flaky. An area of opportunity was identified based on an unmet need: an acne remedy for adult women that would leave moisture in the skin.

Defining the Product Planning Focus

The focus in a product marketing plan can be directed to developing new products, to revitalizing existing products, or to extending a product line (see Figure 2.7).

New-Product Development The area of opportunity identified by Block Drugs required developing and testing a new product. By 1982, the company had developed an acne preparation with a moisturizer and without the drying agent in teen preparations. It was actively testing the product. These tests indicated that the product would meet the company's marketing objectives.

Revitalizing Existing Products Product plans can also be developed to revitalize existing products. Should competition enter the adult acne market and reduce Block's market share, a product plan would be designed to revitalize the brand. Revitalization strategies might involve introducing a new and improved formulation, reducing the price, or repositioning the product to better appeal to the target segment.

PRODUCT MARKETING PLANNING

FIGURE 2.7
The Product-Planning Focus

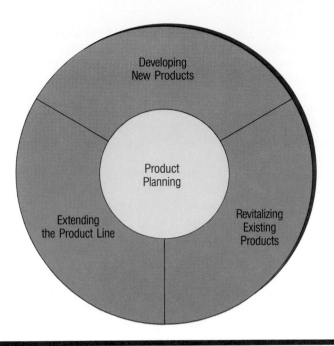

Extending the Product Line The marketing plan can also focus on extending the product line by building on a successful new-product introduction. If Block's adult acne product is successful, the company might expand it into a complete line that would include face and skin moisturizers, cold creams, and hand lotions. In this case, the product plan would be geared to developing strategies for such extensions. A common brand name and common packaging for the line might be developed. Advertising might show the complete line of moisturizing products. And price strategy would have to reflect the appropriate price differentials between products in the line.

Developing Marketing Strategies for the Product
The outcome of product planning is marketing strategies. At the product level, strategies are directed toward three goals: identifying the target segment, positioning the product, and formulating the marketing mix (see Figure 2.8).

Target Market Identification The target market for Block Drug's acne preparation was well defined: working women between ages 18 and 49 who have an acne problem and are dissatisfied with their current acne preparation. Marketing research estimated 10.6 percent of all women in this age group, or 5.5 million women, are in this segment. Market tests of the product projected one-fourth of the targeted segment would try the product.

Positioning Once the target market is identified, the product must be positioned to meet its needs. In Block's case, this meant determining whether the new product should be positioned as an acne preparation with a moisturizer added, or as a moisturizer that helps acne. Since research showed the main problem was the acne condition, Block chose the former positioning. The latter would have diminished its uniqueness and thus its competitive advantage.

Marketing Mix Establishing a positioning for the product sets the stage for developing a marketing mix to deliver the product to the target market. The marketing mix for the acne remedy was a well-integrated plan for advertising, pricing, and distribution. The advertising campaign was designed to create immediate brand awareness among working women between 18 and 49. A $5 million budget was to be split 70/30 between network TV and women's magazines such as *Working Woman, Working Mother,* and *Savvy.*

The product's retail price was set at $3.00 for a one-ounce tube — below the price of most other popular acne preparations. Special introductory discounts through coupons and price specials were planned to encourage consumers to try the product. Block planned to distribute directly to large drug chains, using wholesalers to reach medium-sized and smaller drugstores. Wholesalers and retailers would be offered trade discounts to ensure they stocked the brand. Block's salesforce was instructed to visit retail stores to check whether the new brand had shelf visibility.

Evaluation and Control
Once a product plan is implemented, it continues to serve an important function as the basis for evaluating product performance and controlling costs. The product manager will track sales and market-share (that is, a product's sales as a percent of total sales in a market) on a monthly basis to determine if revenue objectives are being met. Advertising, sales promotion, and distribution costs will also be tracked to make sure marketing-mix allocations do not go over budget.

If performance goals are not being met, the product manager will change components of the marketing plan to more effectively direct the product to the target market. This may involve a change in the product's positioning, a decrease in price, or a change in allocations to TV and print advertising.

Sales and market-share performance for the acne remedy met expectations in the first year, and it looked as if the product would achieve the targeted 15 percent return on investment. Advertising, sales, and distribution costs were also within the budgeted range. On this basis, all systems were go for continuing to market the product.

Block Drug's introduction of an adult acne remedy was one way the company could have directed its efforts at the product level. Figure 2.9 shows that new products are not the only avenue open to the product manager. The product manager could have chosen to spend more money reinforcing existing products. Further, both existing and new products can be directed to a company's existing customers or to new customers. These two dimensions produce the four product strategy alternatives in Figure 2.9: market penetration, market expansion, product line extensions, and new product development.

A company will not follow one strategy to the exclusion of the others. Companies usually support existing products through market penetration or expansion to give them the revenue to pursue new-products for future growth. But the product marketing plan will focus on one of these four strategies for an individual product.

Strategies for Existing Products
Companies use **market-penetration strategies** to try to increase sales of well-established products in existing markets. This is a strategy aimed at maintaining a

FIGURE 2.8
Components of Marketing Strategy

Identify Target Markets

Position Product

Develop the Marketing Mix

PRODUCT STRATEGY ALTERNATIVES

FIGURE 2.9
Product Strategy Alternatives

	Existing Products	New Products
Existing Customers	Market Penetration	Product Line Extension or New Product Development
New Customers	Market Expansion	New Product Development

competitive advantage already gained by strong product performance. Increasing advertising, reducing prices, expanding distribution, or modifying a product may all be implemented in this strategy.

Coca-Cola has tried to increase its share of the cola market by getting users of competitive brands to switch. It has advertised its flagship brand since it became Coca-Cola Classic with themes like "America's Real Choice" in 1985, "Red, White and You" in 1986, and "Can't Beat the Feeling" in 1987. The primary objective in each case has been to get cola drinkers to switch from Pepsi. The persistent battle between Coca-Cola and Pepsi for a larger share of the cola market has come to be called "the cola wars."

Companies like Coca-Cola also use coupons and price reduction to induce consumers of competitive brands to switch, hoping that once they try the company's brand, many will continue to buy it. Another way to try to attract customers of competitive brands is by modifying an existing product to make it more appealing. Changes in color, product ingredients, or packaging are common approaches. An example of this strategy is Heinz's introduction of a squeezable plastic ketchup bottle to make it easier to pour.

A second product strategy used by companies for existing products is **market expansion**; that is, targeting existing products to new markets. This can involve geographic expansion, targeting of new demographic and lifestyle segments, or expanding demand by attracting nonusers to the product.

Converse provides a good example of geographic expansion. Riding the increasing popularity of basketball abroad from Spain to Japan, the company decided to expand its overseas efforts (see Exhibit 2.2). As a result, it sold over $50 million worth of basketball shoes abroad, tripling international sales since 1986.[17]

A company can also seek to expand markets for existing products by appealing to new target segments. Diet Coke was first positioned to male cola drinkers because Coca-Cola's other entry, Tab, appealed primarily to women. Diet Coke's success in the male market led it to successfully broaden its appeal to women so that today it is the third largest selling soft drink.

Market expansion can also be achieved by influencing nonusers of a product category to become users. Arm & Hammer, for instance, developed an effective advertising campaign to get nonusers to use baking soda by emphasizing new uses as a toothpaste, a pot cleaner, and so on.

EXHIBIT 2.2
Example of a Market Expansion Strategy

Strategies for New Products

Strategies for new products require a company to either extend existing product lines or to develop totally new products. As examples of **product line extensions**, Ban capitalized on its strong market position by introducing 17 different versions in its deodorant line, and Procter & Gamble expanded Crest toothpaste to include gels, pump dispensers, and a new tartar-control formula.

Figure 2.9 shows that **new product development** can be targeted to existing or to new customers. Kodak's introduction of its new VR-G film line with improved color quality and richness was intended to keep its existing film users from switching to Fuji film. Its introduction of lithium batteries was directed to a new market — battery users requiring a longer-lasting energy source.

MARKETING AT THE SBU AND CORPORATE LEVEL

While the product marketing plan guides the targeting, positioning, and delivery of a product, the strategic marketing plan guides the overall direction of the company and its business units. The key in guiding the SBUs and the company over a five-year period is to identify strategic windows — that is, opportunities in the environment that can be exploited and sustained for competitive advantage.

We will describe Toyota's successful entry into the U.S. car market as an example of the strategic planning process in Figure 2.6. The difference between the Toyota example and that of Block Drug is that Toyota's entry into the U.S. market determined its future corporate growth, whereas Block Drug's introduction of the acne preparation did not in itself define the company's future.

In 1958 Toyota sold 288 cars in the United States.[18] Its first imported car, the Toyopet, was a flop. Its block shape made it look like a truck, its engine made it sound like a truck, and the rough and uncomfortable interior made it feel like a truck. But by 1980 the company was selling close to 600,000 cars — nearly a 25

THE STRATEGIC PLANNING PROCESS

percent share of foreign car sales in the United States — with star performers like the Toyota Corona and Corolla. What was the cause of this remarkable turnaround? It was a strategic marketing plan to enter the U.S. market by identifying unmet customer needs and exploiting Detroit's weaknesses.

Toyota followed the five planning steps in Figure 2.6 with a single-minded devotion that ensured success.

Define Corporate Objectives

Toyota's failure in the U.S. market in the late 1950s led it to reanalyze its market-entry strategy. Its corporate objectives, supported by the Japanese government, were to look for markets that might provide superior investment returns and international trade benefits over the long term. The U.S. auto market was a prime candidate for fulfilling these objectives — a market that Toyota was not about to give up on.

Toyota also recognized that its long-term survival would depend on establishing a presence abroad. Its forecasters saw tremendous growth in worldwide automobile market demand, and Toyota's foremost corporate goal was to get a share of that demand. With the help of the Japanese government, Toyota was prepared to invest heavily to fulfill this goal.

Identify Marketing Opportunities

Just as identifying marketing opportunities is crucial to marketing at the product level, it is also critically important at the SBU and corporate level. After the failure of the Toyopet, Toyota conducted a complete study of U.S. auto dealers and owners. It identified a substantial gap between what many customers wanted and what Detroit was giving them. By the 1960s, attitudes toward cars were changing. Instead of looking on cars as status symbols, many Americans were looking for fuel economy, durability, easy maintenance, and service reliability. All this added up to a substantial segment of car buyers that wanted a smaller car. At the time, Volkswagen was the only manufacturer that was giving it to them.

Instead of filling this gap, American car manufacturers continued to build larger and more expensive cars in a production oriented mode. The opening was there. Toyota filled it with the introduction of the Corona in 1965, the first viable alternative to the Volkswagen.

Define the Strategic Planning Focus

The strategic focus for Toyota's entry into the American car market was clearly corporate. The company gave virtually total attention, as well as a good portion of its resources, to entry into the American market. By 1965 a series of successful new-car introductions provided Toyota with the means to finance its overseas expansion. But Toyota did not just import its successful domestic cars into the U.S.; it developed cars such as the Corona with the American consumer in mind.

Develop the Corporate (or SBU) Growth Strategy

A company's **growth strategy** is the means by which it plans to exploit marketing opportunities over the next five years. Growth strategies deal with decisions regarding businesses rather than individual products. For example, Toyota's growth strategy was to further its international business by fueling entry into the U.S. car market. It did so with superior products at reasonable prices.

Toyota's success with the Corona paved the way for the next phase in its growth strategy; to consolidate its competitive advantage over American car manufacturers. Toyota introduced the Corolla series as an additional compact alternative. In 1974 it offered an enlarged version of the Corolla to appeal to mid-sized car buyers. In the process, Toyota continuously invested in plant and equipment to maintain product quality.

These efforts paid off. The central element in Toyota's corporate growth strategy — establishing itself in the U.S. car market with a superior line of compacts — was a clear success.

Evaluation and Control

As at the product level, the fifth step in strategic marketing planning is evaluation and control. Toyota constantly evaluated results as it implemented its strategic plan so as to adapt the plan to a changing environment. These efforts began after the Toyopet failure, when Toyota conducted extensive research to identify the move to compact cars. The company continued to monitor consumers' changing tastes toward auto economy and safety: It correctly tracked the growing demand for smaller cars, even before the energy crisis. On this basis, Toyota developed the strategy of first introducing the Corona and then the Corolla.

Toyota has also exerted tight cost controls that enable it to produce many more cars per employee than American manufacturers. These efficiencies result in lower costs, allowing lower prices. Toyota's product superiority and lower costs thus permitted the company to sustain its competitive advantage over domestic car manufacturers.

At the corporate and the business unit level, the company's strategy for growth is the key element in the strategic marketing plan.

Figure 2.10 shows some alternative growth strategies. These alternatives are determined by two key questions: First, does the company seek growth in businesses related to its core markets, or does it seek growth in new business areas. Second, does the company seek growth through internal development of products (as did Toyota), or does it seek growth through external acquisition (a strategy used by Chrysler when it acquired American Motors in 1987). These strategies will be explored in Chapter 22 when we more fully discuss strategic marketing planning and corporate growth strategies.

ALTERNATIVE CORPORATE GROWTH STRATEGIES

THE ROLE OF MARKETING MANAGEMENT: A DESIGN FOR THIS BOOK

We have seen in this chapter that the role of marketing in the firm is essentially defined by the role and planning activities of marketing managers, both product managers and business managers. This role was summarized at the beginning of this chapter in Figure 2.1, and will be used as a basis for organizing the remainder of this book. In Part Two we focus on defining marketing opportunities. Chapters in this section deal with the marketing environment, competition, the customer for both consumer and industrial goods, and the collection and interpretation of marketing data to define opportunity.

Part Three deals with developing marketing plans and strategies, and targeting these strategies to customer segments. We describe the process of product planning. (Strategic planning will be considered later.) In Part Three we also focus on the importance of targeting the marketing effort to customer segments based on their needs by describing strategies for segmenting markets.

FIGURE 2.10
Alternative Corporate Growth Strategies

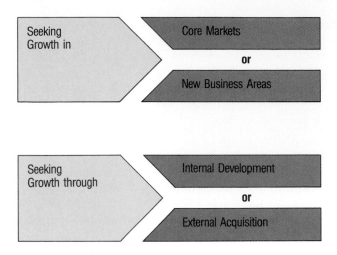

Seeking Growth in → Core Markets or New Business Areas

Seeking Growth through → Internal Development or External Acquisition

Part Four describes how a marketing mix is developed to implement strategies at the product level. This section represents the "guts" of the marketing process since it deals with the basic components of the marketing mix — product, distribution, advertising, sales promotion, and pricing strategies. Although the focus is on product-level planning, chapters in this section tie components of the marketing mix back to the firm's broader directions spelled out in the strategic marketing plan. Because international operations are an increasingly important component of marketing activities, we devote a chapter in this section to developing a marketing mix for international firms.

In Part Five, we consider the broader corporate dimension of marketing by first focusing on strategic planning, and then describing how managers evaluate and control their marketing operations at both the product and corporate levels.

SUMMARY

1.   What is the role of marketing management within the firm?
Marketing managers have the primary responsibility to fulfill the marketing function within the firm. They identify marketing opportunities, develop strategies to use the firm's resources to exploit these opportunities, implement these strategies, and evaluate them. A key factor is the existence of a *strategic window of opportunity,* which is identified not only by the existence of an opportunity, but also by the firm's ability to exploit the opportunity.

2.   What is the dual role of marketing in the firm, from both the product and corporate perspective?
There are two types of marketing managers in most multi-unit firms, a product manager and a business manager. The responsibilities of these individuals reflect their dual role. The product manager for a particular product is responsible for developing, implementing and evaluating strategies for the product. The business manager is in charge of a strategic business unit (SBU) — that is, a division of a company organized to reflect market demand. The business manager evaluates the SBU's product mix, charts a course for the SBU by allocating resources to individual products, and submits a plan for approval to top management.

In a single-market company and in medium-sized and smaller companies, the business manager operates at the corporate level, and the company as a whole operates as a single SBU.

3. *What is the importance of the strategic business unit in the marketing planning process?*

Since the strategic business unit is organized on the basis of market demand, it encourages a more marketing-oriented view of company operations. Before the SBU organization was introduced, most companies were organized on functional lines (i.e. marketing, manufacturing, R&D) or on the basis of similarities in technology. The reorganization at Kodak on SBU lines — as an example — resulted in improving the ability of the company to meet customer needs and gain a competitive advantage because it focused on markets rather than functions. The various functional areas were brought together under one roof and coordinated to better serve market needs.

4. *What is the nature of product marketing planning and strategic marketing planning?*

The product marketing plan charts the marketing strategy for an individual product. It is the responsibility of the product manager. The plan identifies the opportunities for marketing the product, sets performance objectives, identifies a target segment, positions the product to meet customer needs, and develops a mix of pricing, distribution, and advertising elements to market the product. Cost estimates and revenue goals in the plan serve as bases for evaluating the performance of the product.

The strategic marketing plan for a business unit evaluates its product mix and charts a course for the SBU by allocating resources to individual products. SBU plans are submitted to corporate managers, who then evaluate the company's business mix and allocate resources to the business units in the context of a corporate strategic plan.

5. *What strategy alternatives are available to marketing managers at the product level and at the SBU or corporate level?*

Strategic alternatives available to product managers are to strengthen existing products among current customers, to extend existing products to new market segments, or to develop new products to appeal to the company's current customer base. In each case the strategic focus is on individual products.

Strategic alternatives available to business or corporate managers deal with entering new businesses. Management can consider entering new businesses in its core markets, or it can consider acquiring companies outside its areas of core competency. It can move into these new business areas through a process of internal new-product development or external acquisition of companies.

KEY TERMS

Strategic window of opportunity (p. 31)
Marketing plan (p. 33)
Product marketing plan (p. 33)
Strategic marketing plan (p. 33)
Product manager (p. 33)
Product mix (p. 33)
Strategic business unit (SBU) (p. 34)
Business manager (p. 34)

Corporate marketing manager (p. 34)
Product market unit (PMU) (p. 36)
Market expansion strategy (p. 44)
Market penetration strategy (p. 44)
New product development strategy (p. 45)
Product line extension (p. 45)
Corporate growth strategy (p. 47)

QUESTIONS

1. Why is Kodak a more marketing oriented company today than it was before 1984? Specify (a) organizational changes and (b) strategies that suggest a greater marketing orientation.

2. A marketing manager for a large consumer-goods company read the description of Kodak's turnaround in the beginning of this chapter and made the following comment:

    > You don't turn a company around by just reorganizing. An SBU structure is fine, but it doesn't necessarily change the way you think. Kodak still has a lot of old-line managers. Don't forget they rarely brought fresh blood into the company before 1984. What Kodak needs is not just a reorganization, but a change in corporate culture. As far as I'm concerned, the jury is still out as to whether Kodak has really shifted from a production to a marketing orientation.

    a. Do you agree with this statement?
    b. What do you suppose the marketing manager meant by a "corporate culture"?

3. What do we mean by a strategic window of opportunity? Was the strategic window open for Kodak to introduce the lithium battery? What actions did Kodak take to ensure that the strategic window would be open?

4. What is the difference between a product marketing plan and a strategic marketing plan? Specify differences in (a) objectives, (b) opportunity identification, (c) strategies, and (d) the nature of evaluation and control.

5. How does the definition of the target market for lithium batteries as "upscale baby boomers" affect the marketing plan for the product?

6. Why did General Electric shift from a traditional divisional organization to an organization based on strategic business units?

7. What is the purpose of developing an SBU/market matrix such as that in Figure 2.5? What strategic decisions might be made based on this matrix?

8. How do the marketing responsibilities of the product manager for lithium batteries at Kodak differ from those of the business manager for the Consumer Products SBU?

9. What factors made introduction of an adult acne remedy a desirable opportunity to pursue for Block Drug? What risks does the company face in pursuing this opportunity?

10. What are the differences between strategies of new-product development, market penetration, and market expansion? When is a company most likely to follow each of these strategies?

11. How might Kodak apply strategies of (a) market expansion and (b) market penetration to the lithium battery once it is established in the market? What actions would each type of strategy require? Which strategy would Kodak be most likely to use first: market penetration or market expansion? When would it switch from one strategy to another?

12. Why did Toyota's re-entry into the U.S. market after the Toyopet failure represent a strategic window of opportunity for the company?

CASE 2.1

KODAK CONFRONTS DOUBTS ABOUT ITS 35-mm CAMERAS

Source: "Negative Images: Polaroid Faces Tough Sell With Its New Instant, While Kodak Confronts Doubts About Its 35mm," *The Wall Street Journal,* March 25, 1986, p. 33.

Kodak's reentry after 16 years into the crowded $1.4 billion-a-year 35-mm market could be less than a hit among consumers. The Rochester, N.Y.-based photographic giant is arriving late to a market now dominated by Minolta Corp., Canon USA Inc., and other Japanese producers. And Kodak isn't introducing any significant new technology that sets its 35-mm camera apart.

"It's largely a me-too product," asserts Elliott Novak, a photo consultant with Concord Associates Inc. of Concord, Mass.

Thus, marketing — which Kodak has mastered so well in the film business — becomes all the more critical to a company hurt by its forced withdrawal recently from the instant-camera field and battered from intensifying competition in most of its businesses. It introduced two 35-mm models in 1986 and promoted them in a $20 million advertising campaign.

Kodak is aiming its cameras at young buyers who want high-quality photos without the headaches of mastering sophisticated equipment. Its two cameras, being made in Japan by Chinon Industries Inc., don't have the interchangeable lenses that are used with so-called single-lens reflex (SLR) 35-mms. Images are seen through a range finder rather than the lens. That makes Kodak's non-SLR cameras less expensive than SLR models: they'll sell for between $88 and $140 compared with at least $200 for an SLR 35-mm. Since 1975, 13 million non-SLR 35-mms have been sold in the United States.

The new ads are a major departure for Kodak, which has traditionally focused on families, capturing their holidays and other happy memories. Now they feature young professionals, dressed in fashionable sportswear and snapping pictures of each other outdoors. Gone are the children, the grandparents and the Christmas trees.

Kodak's print ads copy that approach. "I think I'm in love," says the headline in full-page ads featuring a handsome, young professional man holding a color picture of an attractive brunette. "With this camera," reads a line below. The ads ran in 12 major magazines, including *National Geographic, Life* and *Esquire.*

Canon, now No. 1 in the market, has targeted the fashion-conscious camera owner with its Snappy line, offered in red, blue and yellow colors.

Minolta, whose non-SLR camera is called the Minolta Talker because a voice tells the user when there's enough light, stresses the technology in its cameras that helps produce sharp snapshots. Fuji Photo Film U.S.A. Inc., Kodak's main competitor in the film and paper industry, stresses the ease and quality of its non-SLR cameras.

So what are Kodak's chances in the 35-mm market? Analysts say the company has two big things going for it. First, its name. "It may be Johnny-come-lately," says Mr. Novak, the consultant, "but it's name is so well-known and accepted."

Second is the huge network of retail outlets that already sell Kodak film and other products; already 10,000 outlets carry Kodak's 35-mm cameras. "If Chinon showed me that 35-mm camera, I wouldn't have bought it," says Chuck Wolf, president of Wolf Camera Inc. of Atlanta, which has 65 photo specialty stores in the Southeast. "I don't need another camera. No dealers need another camera. But when Kodak comes out with a camera, you buy it."

1. Why did Kodak enter the 35 millimeter camera market after an absence of 16 years if, as one photo consultant says, it came out essentially with a "me-too" product?
2. Does the company have any competitive advantage relative to Canon and Minolta in the 35 millimeter camera market?
3. Who is the target segment for its cameras?
4. How is the company trying to appeal to this target?

NOTES

1. "Kodak Pays the Price for Change," *The New York Times*, March 6, 1988, p. F1, F7.

2. "Picture This: Kodak Wants to Be a Biotech Giant, Too," *Business Week*, May 26, 1986, p. 88; and "Has the World Passed Kodak By?" *Forbes*, November 5, 1984, p. 184.

3. *Forbes*, November 5, 1984, p. 185.

4. "Eastman Kodak Co. Has Arduous Struggle to Regain Lost Edge," *The Wall Street Journal*, April 2, 1987, p. 1.

5. "Why Kodak is Starting to Click Again," *Business Week*, February 23, 1987, p. 138.

6. *Business Week*, May 26, 1986, p. 88.

7. *The Wall Street Journal*, April 2, 1987, p. 1.

8. "Kodak is Trying to Break Out of Its Shell," *Business Week*, June 10, 1985, p. 92.

9. "What's Recharging the Battery Business," *Business Week*, June 23, 1986, p. 124.

10. Ibid.

11. Derek F. Abell, "Strategic Windows," *Journal of Marketing* 43(July 1978): 21–26.

12. "Tight Fit," *Forbes*, August 11, 1986, pp. 94–95.

13. "Duracell Adds Acid to Battery Zapfest," *Advertising Age*, November 3, 1986, p. 109.

14. *Advertising Age*, November 3, 1986, p. 109.

15. *Business Week*, June 23, 1986.

16. The example of the adult acne preparation is cited by permission of Block Drug Co. Thanks are due to Mr. James Iseman, product manager at Block Drug, for providing the information reported in this section.

17. "Playing the Global Game," *Forbes*, January 23, 1989, pp. 90–91.

18. This section is based on "How the Japanese Won the West: Toyota's 20-Year Marketing Plan," *Ad Forum*, March 1985, pp. 42–52.

PART 2

• • •

IDENTIFYING MARKETING OPPORTUNITIES

Identifying marketing opportunities is one of the most important tasks of the marketing manager. Marketing opportunities determine the products the company will market and which businesses it will pursue. In Chapter 3, we explore the changes in the marketing environment that might afford an opportunity for profit — changes in the social, technological, regulatory, and economic environment. We then focus on two of the most important sources of marketing opportunity — competitive advantage (Chapter 4) and customer needs (Chapters 5 and 6). In Chapter 7, we describe how firms collect information to identify marketing opportunities and to evaluate their marketing effort.

AVON — CAN IT COPE WITH A CHANGING ENVIRONMENT?

The 1980s have been difficult for Avon. From 1980 to 1985 its sales stagnated, its profits declined an average of 12 percent annually, its credit rating sank, and its value on the New York Stock Exchange was almost halved.[1] Why has the largest fragrance and beauty products company in the world run into trouble? Because of one of the most significant changes in the marketing environment in the twentieth century: the increase in the proportion of working women.

Avon relies on door-to-door selling to market its products, a tactic that has become increasingly ineffective as more women have joined the workforce. With 55 percent of all women now employed outside the home, chances are no one will be home when the Avon saleslady comes calling. Also, fewer women are available to recruit as sales representatives. In 1982, for the first time in its history, Avon's salesforce started to get smaller.[2]

Another factor that hurt Avon was its image. Its low-priced, conservative products had traditionally appealed to downscale, blue-collar consumers. But more women in the workplace means more dual-earning families and greater affluence. As one analyst said, ''In a market that is increasingly upscale, the widespread perception of Avon as a bargain-basement, low-quality producer is a heavy handicap.''[3] Adding to this handicap is a change in the way many women see themselves. A greater equality in male-female roles both in the workplace and in the home has led away from the view of fragrances and beauty items creating a fantasy world of feminine allure. And yet, Avon continued to sell these items the old-fashioned way.

In short, the marketing environment zapped Avon with a triple whammy in the 1980s — fewer women at home to be sold to, fewer women available to do the selling, and a more affluent and aware female consumer at variance with Avon's established product line and image. All these problems arose from basic changes in demography and lifestyles.

How did Avon react? First, it brought in a new management team in 1983 led

MARKETING OPPORTUNITY IN A DYNAMIC ENVIRONMENT

by Hicks Waldron, a dynamic marketing-oriented executive who was former chief executive officer (CEO) at Heublein. Waldron realized that with 100 percent of Avon's products being sold door-to-door, he could not just walk away from that method of distribution. So under his leadership, Avon simply followed the working woman to work. In 1987 it introduced a workplace-selling program where working women sell Avon products in their offices. Today 25 percent of Avon's direct sales are made at work.[4]

But Waldron realized that Avon would have to do more than try to improve direct sales. He developed a three-pronged strategy in which the first prong was the development of new distribution channels. Avon acquired a line of high-priced perfumes targeted to the working woman and sold them through department stores. Then it bought Parfum Stern, a marketer of designer perfumes such as Valentino, followed by Giorgio of Beverly Hills, the nation's largest-selling prestige perfume. In addition, it acquired a 50 percent stake in the high-priced Liz Claiborne line of cosmetics.[5] The company is also relying on catalogs as another distribution channel to reach working women so they can phone in their orders.

Second, Avon is developing its own line of expensive perfumes to appeal to the more affluent woman. For example, it developed Catherine Deneuve perfumes, which sell in department stores for $165 an ounce, using the French actress as a spokesperson for the line. The third prong of Avon's strategy involves upgrading its image with a new advertising campaign that shows a more self-aware and achievement-oriented woman, more in tune with its new product line.

What are the results of Avon's new direction? An increase in sales of close to 20 percent and in operating profits of 25 percent by 1987.[6] Avon appears to be turning an environmental threat into an opportunity for growth that will take it into the 1990s a stronger company. ■

YOUR FOCUS IN CHAPTER 3

(1) *What creates opportunities and threats in the marketing environment?*

(2) *Why does a marketing opportunity always have some threat? How can an environmental threat frequently be turned into an opportunity?*

(3) *How can marketers systematically analyze environmental changes to better shape marketing strategies?*

(4) *What were the basic environmental trends — social, technological, economic, and legal and regulatory — in the 1980s that will shape marketing opportunities in the 1990s?*

● ● ●

THE MARKETING ENVIRONMENT AND THE MARKETING ORGANIZATION

Chapter 1 described the marketing environment as those external forces that are the source of marketing opportunities and profits. But as the Avon example showed, these same forces are also the source of marketing threats.

One of the difficulties facing marketing managers is that environmental forces are generally beyond their control. Marketing organizations try to *adapt* to changing environmental conditions; they rarely can *control* them. Avon could not halt the demographic trend of increasing numbers of working women, but it is adapting to it by changing its distribution and product strategies. Merrill Lynch could not prevent the stock market crash of October 1987, but it is adapting to its aftermath by emphasizing investment alternatives other than stocks. These are examples of adapting to environmental threats. Now consider an environmental opportunity facing Kodak — the rising need for portable power sources stemming from increased use of laptop computers and electronic toys. It is unlikely that Kodak can further stimulate this trend , but it can and did take advantage of it by introducing a line of longer-lasting batteries. In each of these cases, the marketing organization tries to change an environmental threat into an opportunity (e.g. Avon), or tries to exploit an opportunity (e.g. Kodak) through forces they *can* control — their marketing strategies.

The interaction between controllable marketing strategies and uncontrollable environmental forces is illustrated in Figure 3.1. The marketing organization must evaluate key environmental trends: namely, social, competitive, technological, economic, and legal and regulatory influences. The end result of these influences is the creation of environmental opportunities and threats. The marketing organization then responds to these opportunities and threats by developing a mix of product, distribution, promotional, and pricing strategies to satisfy customer needs.

FIGURE 3.1
Marketing Strategies and the
Marketing Environment

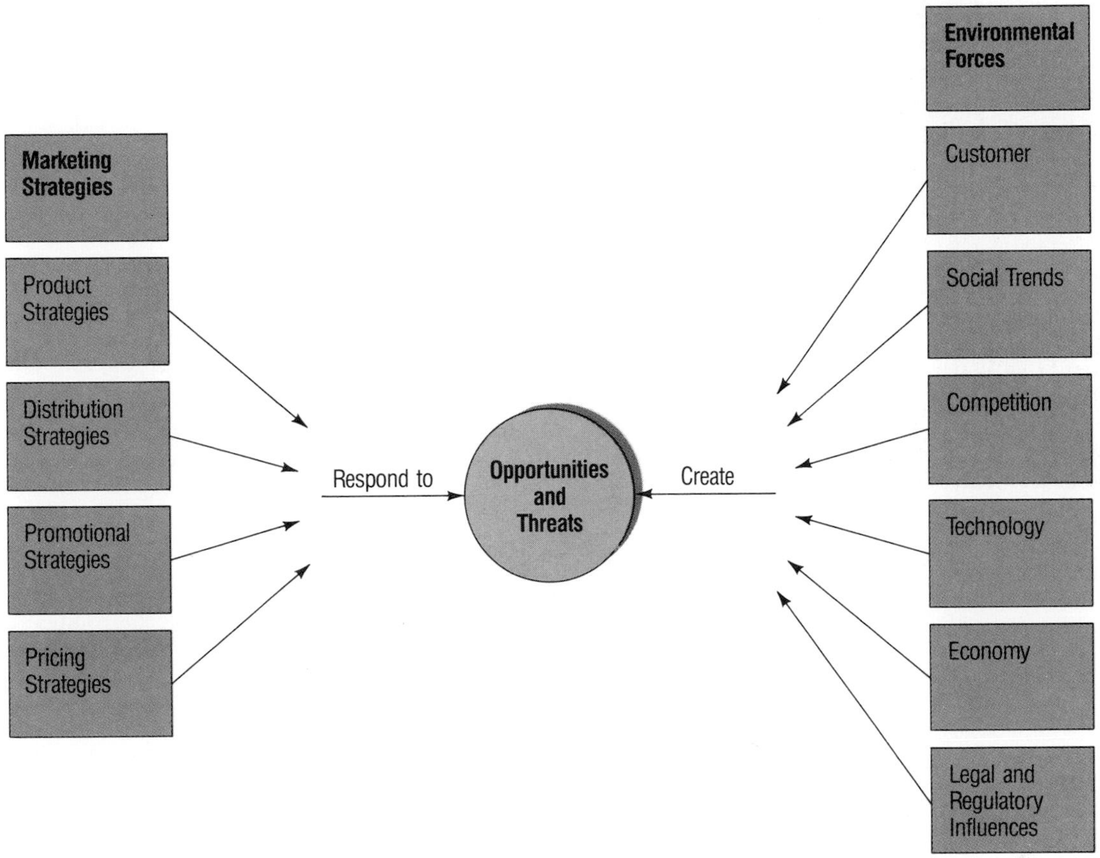

Marketing Strategies
- Product Strategies
- Distribution Strategies
- Promotional Strategies
- Pricing Strategies

Respond to → Opportunities and Threats ← Create

Environmental Forces
- Customer
- Social Trends
- Competition
- Technology
- Economy
- Legal and Regulatory Influences

ENVIRONMENTAL OPPORTUNITIES AND THREATS

There are three general sources of marketing opportunity: unmet customer needs, competitive weakness, and longer-term environmental trends. As we saw in Chapter 2, Kodak filled customer needs by introducing a longer-life battery. Kimberly-Clark's introduction of Huggies Dry Touch disposable diapers succeeded due to the second source of opportunity, competitor's weaknesses. The market leader, Procter & Gamble, became too smug and failed to improve its Pampers brand because it did not recognize a competitive threat. And McDonald's provides a good example of a third source of marketing opportunity, favorable environmental trends. The aging of the baby-boom market, the increasing proportion of singles and working women, and greater affluence have all spelled an increase in demand for fast foods in the last few decades.

Environmental Opportunity Can Become Threat

Opportunity is almost always linked to threat. A company may introduce a new product because it sees a better way to meet customer needs. But in so doing it faces three types of threats: first, misreading customer needs; second, competition coming in with something better; and third, unforeseen changes in the environment (such as a new technology making a product entry obsolete).

RCA's entry into the videodisc market illustrates these threats. Two decades ago, RCA thought it saw an opportunity to create a market for home entertainment through the introduction of videodisc players. The company's objective was to be the leader in electronic technology. It saw videodisc as a way to extend its TV product line so as to use the TV screen in a new way, for customized home entertainment. As early as 1970 it had a prototype ready. Marketing research projected a $1 billion market by 1980.[7] The company was right in predicting a revolution in home entertainment. But by 1984 RCA had withdrawn videodisc players from the market. Why? All three of the environmental threats just cited played a role.

First, RCA misread consumer needs, failing to see the potential of videocassette recorders (VCRs). VCRs had a basic advantage over videodiscs: they could record programs and play prerecorded tapes, whereas videodiscs could play only store-bought discs. Consumers wanted the recording capability. Second, RCA failed to gauge the competitive threat, underestimating the single-minded drive of Japanese manufacturers to penetrate the U.S. market with lower-priced VCRs. When the first VCRs sold for about $1,300 in 1977, RCA did not think Japanese manufacturers could reduce prices to the level of videodisc players. They were wrong. Today, VCRs can be purchased for under $300.

The third threat was unforeseen changes in the environment. RCA simply did not anticipate the superior technology that permitted Japanese manufacturers to cut prices. One RCA executive said, "We did not see the opportunity for mechanization and miniaturization to lower costs."[8] Another environmental factor that it did not anticipate was the role of the rental market. It assumed videodiscs would have a distinct competitive advantage over VCRs because the average price of a disc was $10 to $20 compared to $50 to $80 for prerecorded videotapes. It failed to predict the emergence of a rental market with tapes renting for as little as $2 each.

Faced with declining sales, RCA finally withdrew its videodiscs in April 1984. People simply preferred VCRs. In the end, RCA decided to join rather than fight its competitors. It began marketing Japanese-made VCRs even before it withdrew videodiscs.

Environmental Threat Can Become Opportunity

Not only can environmental opportunity become threat; environmental threat can also become opportunity.[9] Like Avon, the liquor industry faced adverse environmental trends in the 1970s and 1980s. The increasing proportion of baby boomers (those born between 1946 and 1962) entering their adult years represented a threat because these consumers were raised on sugared sodas and developed a sweet tooth that was not conducive to drinking liquor. Added to this, the belief that drinking is a menace to health and safety has been gaining increasing acceptance in American society.

The result was a steady decline in sales of hard liquor until distillers reacted with a simple solution: Schenley, Seagram, National Distillers, and Brown-Forman all came out with lines of sweet-tasting cordials with lower alcohol content to appeal to baby boomers. These products not only helped sales, they also boosted profits, since their return on investment is 20 percent to 30 percent higher than traditional hard liquors.[10] Hiram Walker has taken an even more direct approach, developing nonalcoholic beverages to hedge against further decreases in liquor consumption.[11] Some distillers are diversifying as a further hedge. For example, Seagrams now owns 21 percent of Du Pont Company through stock purchases.[12]

OPPORTUNITY/THREAT ANALYSIS

In order to take advantage of environmental opportunities or to counter environmental threats, management must be able to gauge trends in consumer purchasing, competitive actions, technology, and so forth. Many companies have teams of specialists to collect and assess environmental information from diverse sources and judge where future opportunities and threats might lie. This task is known as **environmental scanning**. Sources of data include the business press, government publications, industry and trade sources, and marketing research studies.

Another source of information is research from companies that specialize in assessing environmental trends. For example, the Value and Life Style Program (VALS) of the Stanford Research Institute surveys American consumers to identify groups with similar values and lifestyles. It has identified three broad groups: outer-directed, inner-directed, and need-driven consumers. Outer-directed consumers, representing about two-thirds of Americans, buy "with an eye to appearances and to what other people think."[13] Inner-directed consumers, representing about one-fifth of Americans, buy to meet their own inner wants rather than in response to social norms. Need-driven consumers are the lowest income group, motivated by need rather than by choice. They represent about 10 percent of Americans.

When Waldron joined Avon, he formed an environmental scanning unit as part of the strategic planning group. The group subscribed to VALS to better determine how to change Avon's image. One consumer segment identified by VALS, the *belongers*, was of particular interest. This group, a subset of the outer-directed consumer group, was described as wanting to "maintain their personal appearance, improve their feelings about themselves, and accept themselves more." They view fragrances and beauty products as a means to this goal. Partly as a result of the VALS research, Avon introduced a campaign directed to this group based on the theme, "We're going to make you feel beautiful."

SELECTING MARKETING STRATEGIES BASED ON ENVIRONMENTAL TRENDS

Ultimately, marketing managers must make strategic decisions based on trends reported by environmental scanning units. One tool for determining the best strategy given certain expected trends is *expected-value analysis*. Let us take the example of Avon in 1983. By 1983, management was aware of the trend toward more working women. Assume it asked the environmental scanning unit to estimate the chances of the trend continuing past 1990, tapering off by 1985, or tapering off immediately. The environmental scanning unit puts a probability of 70 percent, 25 percent, and 5 percent on each of these three possibilities (see Table 3.1)

Avon's management now formulates three alternative strategies, all with the same budget. One is to hire an additional 20,000 sales representatives, the second is to introduce catalog sales, and the third is to develop new lines and introduce them through department stores. Management then estimates the impact of these three strategies on *return on investment (ROI)* for each of the three environmen-

TABLE 3.1
Impact of Environmental Trends
on Marketing Strategies:
Expected Value Analysis

ALTERNATIVE ENVIRONMENTAL POSSIBILITIES	PROBABILITY OF OCCURRENCE	EFFECT OF STRATEGY ON RETURN ON INVESTMENT		
		HIRE 20,000 SALES REPS	INTRODUCE CATALOG SALES	DISTRIBUTE NEW LINES THROUGH DEPARTMENT STORES
1. Proportion of working women will increase past 1990	70%	−3%	+3%	+4%
2. Proportion of working women will increase to 1985	25%	−1%	+1%	+1%
3. No further increases in proportion of working women	5%	+5%	−1%	−4%
Expected value of each strategy		−2.10	+2.30	+2.85

tal possibilities. For example, if the number of working women continues to increase past 1990, management estimates that hiring 20,000 more reps will reduce return on investment by 3 percent because of the greater difficulty in finding women at home. If the number of working women tapers off by 1985, hiring more sales reps would reduce return on investment by 1 percent. If the number of working women tapers off immediately (that is, in 1983), the profit impact of more reps is an increase of 5 percent.

To determine which strategy has the most favorable effect on return on investment, management multiplies the likelihood of each environmental contingency by the profit impact of the particular strategy. This determines the expected value of that strategy. The expected value for hiring 20,000 more reps is $(.70 \times -3) + (.25 \times -1) + (.05 \times +5) = -2.1$ percent, as shown at the bottom of Table 3.1. Thus, given the chances of each of the three environmental contingencies occurring, management's best estimate is that adding 20,000 sales reps is likely to reduce return on investment by 2.1 percent.

The two other strategies, introducing catalog sales and distributing new lines through department stores, are likely to be more profitable since they seek to develop alternative distribution channels to reach working women. The estimated profit outcome for catalog sales is an increase of 2.3 percent; for a new line of products distributed through department stores it is an increase of 2.85 percent. Given the estimates formulated by the environmental scanning unit, the clear choice is to distribute a new line of products through department stores.

The expected-value approach illustrated in Table 3.1 serves as a guide for managers to organize their thinking about the possible impact of environmental trends and the most suitable strategies to exploit these trends.

When Hicks Waldron took on the top job at Avon in 1983, he knew he might be looking for another job in two or three years if he did not turn the company around. Risk and challenge were nothing new to Waldron. As CEO at Heublein, he had engineered the acquisition of Kentucky Fried Chicken as a hedge against declining liquor sales. Soon after, Heublein was in turn acquired by R. J. Reynolds, and sales at Kentucky Fried Chicken began sliding. Waldron now had to answer for Kentucky Fried Chicken's performance to R. J. Reynolds' top management. His plan was to turn Kentucky Fried Chicken around in a year. If he did not, he agreed he would be out of a job.[14]

Waldron succeeded in improving Kentucky Fried Chicken's sales and profits. But he did not stay. He was offered the challenge of turning Avon around and took it. His job at Avon is proving tougher than at Heublein. The turnaround at Kentucky Fried Chicken was easier to engineer because the division was a fast-food operation, and fast foods were going with the environmental tide. When Waldron joined Avon, the company was a door-to-door seller going against the environmental tide and saddled with an old-line management. One marketing analyst equates Waldron's job with trying to "turn around an ocean liner."[15]

Waldron saw his job as transforming Avon from a door-to-door sales company into a consumer-driven brand marketer.[16] His three-pronged marketing strategy was single-mindedly devoted to that goal — expand distribution beyond door-to-door sales to reach the working woman, upgrade the product line to reach the more affluent woman, and improve Avon's stodgy image.

Waldron retired as Avon's CEO in 1989. The jury is still out on whether he turned environmental threat into opportunity for Avon. One thing is certain: He will be remembered for taking a marketing challenge. ■

**Hicks Waldron —
A Risk-Oriented Manager**

Source: © Viviane Moos 1986.

We have reviewed the nature of environmental opportunities and threats and the way managers use information gained from environmental scanning to make strategic decisions. In the remainder of this chapter, we will consider specific trends in the environment that have defined marketing opportunities and threats for managers in many industries. These trends represent changes in four of the five components of the marketing environment shown in Figure 3.1: social, technological, economic, and legal and regulatory. The remaining component, competition, will be considered in the next chapter.

ENVIRONMENTAL TRENDS RESULTING IN OPPORTUNITIES AND THREATS

SOCIAL TRENDS IN THE 1980s

Social trends in American society directly affect marketing strategies since they help determine consumer needs and purchasing decisions. Social trends represent changes in three types of factors: The first, **demographics**, describes the objective

FIGURE 3.2
Women in Labor Force as a
Percentage of All Women

Source: "Employed Persons with Single and Multiple
Jobs by Sex," *Monthly Labor Review,* Department of
Labor, May 1982, p. 48, Table 1; "A Portrait of the
American Worker," *American Demographics,* March
1984, p. 19; *Handbook of Labor Statistics,* June 1985,
Tables 1, 6, and 50; and *Monthly Labor Review,* Feb-
ruary 1986, Table 1, Bureau of Labor Statistics,
Monthly Labor Review, July 1988, Table 5, p. 60. Pro-
jections to 1990 from Bureau of Labor Statistics, De-
partment of Labor. Projections to 1995 from "Societal
Shift," *The Wall Street Journal,* June 29, 1982, p. 1.

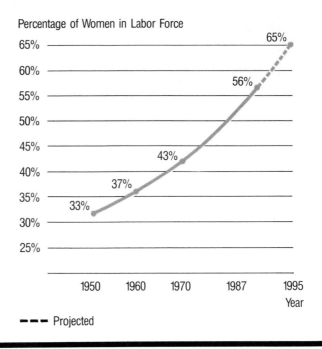

characteristics of an individual — age, education, occupation, income, marital status, location, and so forth. The second, **lifestyles,** is defined by consumers' activities, interests, and opinions. We can talk of an active and outgoing lifestyle, a health-oriented lifestyle, and a conservative lifestyle. The third social factor, **cultural values,** has to do with the beliefs shared by a large number of people in a society. Common values in American culture are materialism, youthfulness, and personal achievement. We will explore trends in each of these social factors in more detail.

CHANGING DEMOGRAPHIC CHARACTERISTICS

Marketers closely track changes in demographic characteristics because they help determine customer needs and purchases. Three demographic trends had the most direct impact on marketing strategies in the 1980s: (1) the increasing pro-portion of working women (2) changes in family composition; and (3) changes in the age composition of the American market.

Increasing Proportion of Working Women
One of the most significant changes in American society in the 1970s and 1980s has been the increasing proportion of women in the workforce. As Figure 3.2 shows, the proportion of working women increased from one-third in 1950 to 56 percent in 1987 and is projected to rise to 65 percent in 1995. Not only are more women working, but they are entering the workforce earlier. Among women in their twenties and thirties, nearly 70 percent are now employed outside the home.[17]

This trend has posed both threat and opportunity for many marketers. At first, food companies such as General Foods and Quaker Oats saw the increasing proportion of working women as a threat in that they would have less time to devote to shopping, food preparation, and homemaking. And, many super-market products directed to the traditional homemaker role suffered. But many

EXHIBIT 3.1
Targeting a Financial Service
to Working Women

food companies have translated this threat into opportunity by emphasizing easy-to-prepare foods. They have also exploited the emphasis on time-saving convenience by buying fast-food outlets. With working wives averaging 7.4 meals out per week, it is not surprising to see General Mills, General Foods, Quaker Oats, and Pepsi-Cola all buying established fast-food companies.[18]

Marketers have also begun directing financial services to working women. For instance, in 1982 American Express began targeting its credit cards to women through an "interesting lives" advertising campaign that portrayed career women in real-life situations (see Exhibit 3.1). Partly as a result, the proportion of American Express cardholders who are women climbed from 16 percent in 1980 to 29 percent in 1985.[19]

Changing Family Composition

The American family is becoming smaller and less cohesive. In 1950, 70 percent of all families were composed of a working father, a nonworking mother, and at least one school-age child. By 1984 only 14 percent of American families had this traditional composition.[20] Why this dramatic change? We already noted one reason — more working women. Two other factors are a decrease in the birthrate after 1960 and a doubling in the divorce rate. (Today 50 percent of marriages end in divorce.) As a result, there are more single-person households, smaller families for married households, and a steady decrease in the proportion of teenagers, a decline that will not end until 1997.

For many food and toiletry companies, these trends seem to represent a threat of lower sales. A decrease in the birth rate and smaller families mean less food consumed. But here again, companies have been turning environmental threat into opportunity. For example, candy bar companies saw consumption steadily decline because of a smaller base of children and teenagers. Nestle and Hershey began to appeal to the adult market by importing high-quality chocolates from

EXHIBIT 3.2
Repositioning a Product to Appeal to a
More Aware Elderly Market

Europe, while M&M/Mars repositioned some of its existing lines to adults.[21]

Similarly, some companies have countered the threat of fewer purchases because of more single-member households by introducing foods in smaller sizes. Campbell introduced Soup-for-One. Even oatmeal cookies are being sold in packs for one.[22]

Changing Age Composition

A third demographic trend has been a change in the age composition of American society. Marketers will be focusing primarily on three age groups in the coming years: baby boomers, the elderly market (65+), and the youth market (primarily teenagers).

Baby Boomers Baby boomers now represent one-fourth of the population and significantly more than one-fourth of the economy's purchasing power. They are better educated and more likely to be dual-income households. As they move into their forties, baby boomers will represent the largest chunk of buying power in the United States.

Several marketers are appealing directly to this group. For example, Levi projected a decrease in sales of its jeans as baby boomers begin to enter middle age. As a result, it introduced a new line of slacks to appeal to the more conservative tastes of the aging baby boomer.[23] Similarly, General Motors, Ford, and Chrysler have all introduced more utilitarian and performance-oriented automobile models styled along European lines to appeal to baby boomers.[24]

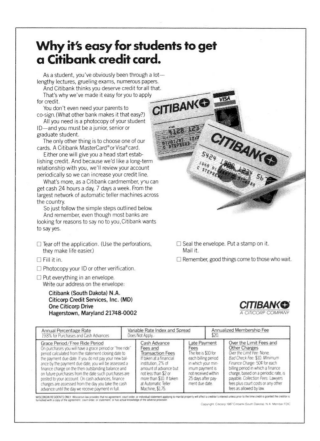

EXHIBIT 3.3
Appeals to the Youth Market by
Credit Card Companies

The Elderly Market The elderly market (65+) is also expanding in both numbers and purchasing power. This group's purchasing power is rising because of better pension and retirement plans and fewer financial burdens in the later years.

Marketers have found it difficult to position products to this market for the simple reason that people do not like to be reminded they are old. Clairol realizes that older consumers prefer to view themselves as active and vital. So when Clairol advertises Instant Beauty hair coloring agent for gray hair, it uses women across various age categories to avoid a connotation of aging (see Exhibit 3.2).

Marriott, the hotel chain, is appealing directly to the housing and care needs of the elderly by committing $1 billion to build 200 retirement communities across the country in the next 10 years. Marriott plans to follow a segmentation strategy by offering several facilities to senior citizens that vary by income level and degree of care required.[25]

The Youth Market Although the youth market (teens and college-age consumers) will comprise a smaller proportion of the total population, it will remain a particularly desirable target for marketers for two reasons. First, its purchasing power is increasing; and second, most of that purchasing power is discretionary. In contrast to the anti-establishment teenagers of the 1960s and 1970s, those of the 1980s became much more conservative, materialistic, and goal-oriented, spending most of their money on clothing, entertainment, personal grooming products, and automobiles.[26] Teenagers are also showing more financial independence by opening up checking and savings accounts, reading business and financial news, and attempting to establish credit.

As a result, credit card companies are making it a point to target their services to the college-age crowd in the hope that they will become the adult subscribers of tomorrow. American Express has directed appeals to college students with the theme "Don't leave school without it," a takeoff on its "Don't leave home without it" theme.[27] And Citibank is targeting its card to the same segment by citing how easy it is for a student to get one. (See Exhibit 3.3.)

CHANGING LIFESTYLE TRENDS

A second social trend that is important to marketers is changing lifestyles. Three recent, broad changes that have had a direct impact on consumer purchases are (1) a change in male and female roles, (2) an interest in a healthier lifestyle, and (3) a more conservative lifestyle, especially in the youth and baby-boom markets.

A Change in Male-Female Roles

The increase in the number of working women and the decrease in family size have significantly changed the male and female purchasing roles. Men are assuming some of the burdens of shopping and child care. As a result, they have become more involved in traditionally female purchases such as cereal, soap, and toothpaste.[28] Marketers of food and household products have begun to pay more attention to men. Campbell Soup Co. now positions its condensed soup to men as well as women, advertising in magazines such as *Field & Stream*, a publication with 82 percent male readership, and in *Sports Illustrated*.[29] Similarly, a commercial for Procter & Gamble's Ivory Liquid soap shows a man helping his wife with the dishes as he exclaims, "Why not? I do the dishes, lots of men do."[30]

Women's purchasing roles have changed as dramatically as men's, and, accordingly, companies selling credit cards, financial services, life insurance, and cars have increasingly appealed to women. Moreover, they have done so in a manner that recognizes women's increasing independence and assertiveness. Gone are the days when a theme like Wisk's "Ring around the collar" could imply that a woman's worth depends on her husband's approval and her homemaking abilities.

A Healthier Lifestyle

Another lifestyle trend with an important impact on marketing strategies is the greater emphasis on health and nutrition. American consumers today are exercising more and are more conscious of food ingredients.[31] They are smoking less, drinking less liquor and coffee, and avoiding red meats. Food marketers have responded with offerings of "light" and "natural" foods, now the fastest-growing category on the store shelf. Carnation even introduced Health and Nutrition Centers to carry diet and natural foods and provide advice on nutritional programs.[32]

A related lifestyle trend is greater emphasis on fitness. More Americans are jogging, doing aerobics, and engaging in sports activities than ever before. One company that has followed this trend is Timex watches. The company used to market plain, low-priced, durable watches. As consumers became more style-conscious, sales fell. Timex then decided to change its image and reposition its watches to younger, sports-oriented consumers. It came out with watches for aerobic fans that can measure pulse rates, for racing fans that can track car speeds, and for skiiers that can measure low temperatures.[33] (See Exhibit 3.4.) As a result of its repositioning to the fitness market, Timex's sales soared.

Companies for whom the health and fitness trend poses a potential environmental threat (for instance, liquor, cigarette, coffee companies) have gone with

EXHIBIT 3.4
Repositioning Timex Watches to
Fitness-Oriented Consumers

the trend by diversifying or adapting their product line. Cigarette companies have diversified into foods and beverages. Philip Morris, for example, has become the second largest food company in the world by acquiring General Foods in 1985 and Kraft in 1988. Coffee companies have responded similarly. Rather than continue to rely on a declining coffee market, Nestle acquired Stouffer's Foods and got on the nutritional bandwagon with the introduction of Lean Cuisine. As we saw, liquor companies have been expanding their product lines into lower-proof products.

A More Conservative Lifestyle

The 1980s has seen the youth market become increasingly conservative. Young people today are more concerned with their careers and are more style- and fashion-conscious than they were in the 1960s and 1970s. As a result, they are spending more money on clothing, personal grooming products, and automobiles.

Teenagers and college students are also more involved with food and household products than were their predecessors. Many, coming from divorced households, are already accustomed to the role of family purchasing agent, and they carry their awareness of food and household products to college.

The anti-establishment youth of the 1960s and 1970s are now heads of households with responsible positions. Ownership of a chunk of the establishment causes them to behave and purchase more conservatively. One indication of this conservatism is that many baby boomers have become "couch potatoes," stay-at-homes who prefer to order in than eat out, and rent a videotape than go to a movie. The result has been a boom in home-delivered foods and is the primary reason that Pepsi-owned Pizza Hut began delivering its pizzas.[34]

We have seen how demographic and lifestyle trends pose both opportunity and threat in the marketing environment. A third significant social trend is cultural change. One cultural trend in the 1970s and 1980s has been a greater "me" orientation, particularly among baby boomers; that is, a more self-indulgent ori-

CHANGING CULTURAL VALUES

entation manifested by a greater willingness to spend money on oneself. The "Me Generation" proclaims the desirability of "doing your own thing." The resultant search for immediate gratification has led to an increase in spending on travel, entertainment, clothing, and personal grooming products. Prudential Insurance's advertisement, "I Need me," and Miss Clairol's "This I do for me," reflects this cultural change.

Some observers predict that the 1990s will see a shift back to a "we" orientation. Traditional values and emphasis on the family are returning. We noted the greater conservatism of teenagers and baby boomers. If this trend continues, we are likely to see more emphasis on savings and more money spent on furniture, appliances, housing, and education in the 1990s.

Another cultural trend of the 1980s has been a greater emphasis placed by consumers on environmental values. The energy crisis of the 1970s and the economic dislocations of the early 1980s caused consumers to be more aware of the limits of natural resources. Such concerns have had a widespread impact on purchasing patterns. There is more interest in buying pollution-free products such as low-phosphate detergents, beverages in returnable bottles, recycled products, and natural foods that do not contain potentially harmful additives. It is likely that ecological concerns will continue through the 1990s.

SUBCULTURAL INFLUENCES

A fourth broad social influence important to marketers involves the values and behavior of **subcultures** in the United States — broad groups that have similar values that distinguish them from society as a whole. American society is so diverse that many subcultures exist defined by region, national origin, religion, or ethnic identification. The two most important are blacks (representing 12 percent of the population) and Hispanics (representing 8 to 10 percent). Together, these two groups comprise over one-fifth of American consumers. The key question for marketers is how blacks and Hispanics differ from whites, and what marketing opportunities these differences might represent.

The Black Consumer Market

Black consumers are as diverse as white consumers, so to refer to them as a homogeneous group is misleading. However, in general, they are more likely to try new products, particularly socially visible products such as clothing, and are more likely to be brand-loyal.[35]

Marketers are paying more attention to this important group. Ford Motor Co. is segmenting the black consumer market by targeting its luxury Lincoln Continental to upscale blacks, and its Ford Escort to an economy segment (see Exhibit 3.5). Brown-Foreman Co., producers of Canadian Mist, is another company that is showing more interest in the black market. The company realized that its campaign featuring scenes of the Canadian wilderness would have little relevance for blacks. So it began portraying an assertive black male in its ads based on research that the black male has remained more dominant than his white counterpart in selecting liquor products.[36]

The Hispanic-American Market

Hispanic Americans are a more distinct subculture than blacks: more than two-thirds of Hispanic Americans prefer to speak Spanish at home.[37] Further, Hispanic Americans tend to be more traditional and conservative than most other

EXHIBIT 3.5
Targeting Luxury and Economy
Segments of Black Consumers

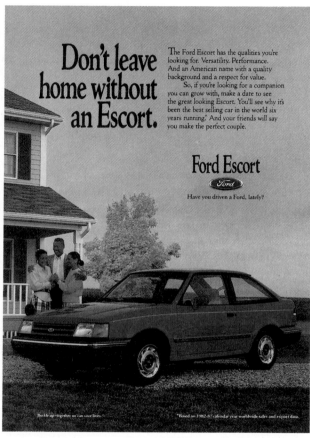

groups. This orientation is reflected in the dominant role of the man, as well as in the view of four-fifths of Hispanic women that having a child is the most important event in their lives.[38]

Like blacks, Hispanics are more likely to be brand-loyal, showing more faith in the quality of nationally advertised products than most other consumers. They are also more likely to be influenced by advertising than are other market segments.

In the mid 1980s, more companies began paying attention to the Hispanic market. For example, Sears Roebuck spent $3 million on advertising to Hispanics in 1987.[39] In a commercial for baby furniture, the company shows Hispanic grandparents surprising an expectant couple with furniture. In the English version, the couple goes shopping alone. Kimberly-Clark also orients its ads differently to reach Hispanic-Americans compared to the general market. The company developed a campaign for its Huggies diapers showing a Hispanic family caring for the baby. In the English version, the baby is the entire focus of the ad.

TECHNOLOGICAL TRENDS

We have been exploring how companies have adapted their marketing strategies to a variety of social trends. But such trends represent only one dimension of the marketing environment. Technological trends are also critically important in identifying marketing opportunities. These trends include new directions in research and development (R&D) that might lead to new products or even to new industries. They also include new technologies that change the way consumers or marketers do things.

RESEARCH AND DEVELOPMENT

The pace of technological change has increased in the 1980s, putting greater pressure on marketers to invest in new-product development and to maintain adequate research and development facilities.[40]

Technology As Opportunity

For many companies, new technology has been the road to marketing opportunity. Polaroid's development of the instant camera, Sony's introduction of the Walkman, RCA's role in developing color TV, and DuPont's development of synthetic fibers all illustrate how technological breakthroughs can give a company a competitive advantage for many years.

The link between R&D and marketing opportunity is shown in one study that found a high correlation between R&D expenditures and corporate profitability.[41] That is why many companies try to maintain research and development facilities that can give them an edge in technology. It is especially important to have an edge in industries such as telecommunications, computers, electronics, chemicals, and pharmaceuticals, where the pace of technological change is rapid. In industries such as paper, furniture, and textiles, the technological pace is slower, and R&D expenditures are low. Here technology is unlikely to be so critical in creating marketing opportunity and competitive advantage.

Technology As Threat

Just as new technologies can present marketing opportunities, they can also present environmental threat to companies whose current technology could be undermined. Railroads were brought close to extinction by the airlines and the automobile, the steel industry was threatened by the development of aluminum, and the wool industry shrunk as a result of the development of synthetic fibers.

But new technologies can also pose a threat to the companies that develop them. A company that pursues new technologies in order to maintain technological leadership may end up developing products the consumer does not need. For example, P&G got involved in the soft-cookie market when it developed a new technology that allowed the outside of cookies to be baked to a crisp while the inside remained soft and chewy. Using this technology, P&G introduced its Duncan Hines line. Even though the company had never made cookies before, it thought that its technological edge and its marketing know-how would allow it to challenge Nabisco, Keebler, and other baking-goods companies. But P&G forgot about the unpredictability of taste: many consumers did not like the taste of soft cookies. Soft cookies wound up representing 13 percent of all cookie sales instead of the 35 percent projected by P&G.[42] In 1987 P&G decided to sharply cut back production and marketing of soft cookies.

P&G remains undaunted, though. It plans to return to the cookie market with a diet cookie made from a new substance it invented — a sucrose polyester that contains no calories. This time, the company promises it will not forget thorough taste tests.

A dramatic change that has had a pronounced influence on the marketing environment has been the development of technologies that provide consumers with new shopping and entertainment options both inside and outside the home. New technologies also give marketers options for dealing with information that have improved the way they implement strategies.

In-Home Shopping and Information Services

Many consumers have changed their shopping habits because of new technologies. One of the most important innovations has been to provide consumers with a greater facility for in-home shopping through cable TV networks. Almost 50 percent of U.S. households have access to cable TV channels, and satellites have permitted cable companies to move from local to national programming. The largest cable channel devoted to shopping, the Home Shopping Network (HSN), operates by offering items on its cable TV network to consumers who then phone in their orders. The fact that 35 percent of all U.S. households regularly watch a home shopping TV show prompted J. C. Penney to introduce its own home shopping service, called Telaction. Subscribers watch Penney's home shopping channel and call a local telephone number to order an item using a pushbutton phone.[43]

Another home shopping technology — **videotex** — is an interactive system that permits subscribers to access product information on their TV screens through a small computer terminal. Consumers can then order items directly through the terminal. There is evidence, however, that many consumers do not perceive this technological breakthrough as an advantage. The success of HSN has proved that many consumers prefer the auction-like atmosphere of seeing various products on the screen. Companies such as Warner Communications, Knight-Ridder, American Express, and AT&T have invested in videotex with poor results.

A more current entry into videotex called Prodigy does not rely on cable TV. It requires using a home computer to call up information on offerings from airline tickets to clothing, and uses telephone lines for the two-way transmission of information through the computer.[44] Jointly backed by IBM and Sears, Prodigy is banking for success on the increasing number of personal computers in people's homes.

Overall, manufacturers see in-home shopping as an area of opportunity since it affords another outlet for their goods. But there are constraints. The main one is the reluctance of consumers to shop at home because they prefer to see the merchandise and interact with salespeople. At the same time, many retailers view home shopping as a threat — an alternative purchasing channel that may lower their sales.

Home Entertainment Technologies

A revolution in technology in the 1980s was the introduction of integrated in-home entertainment systems. VCRs have led the way and are projected to be adopted as widely as TV. Today, over 50 percent of U.S. households have VCRs, a remarkably rapid rate of adoption considering the figure was only 10 percent in the early 1980s.

In-home entertainment is viewed as an opportunity by the electronics and computer industry, but it is viewed as a potential threat by the advertising industry because commercials on programs recorded at home can be "zapped" — that is, bypassed so that only the program is seen. Advertisers have tried to adapt to the threat by placing commercials on VCR tapes. Such advertising would open up a new, if limited, media channel.

New Consumer Technologies Outside the Home

The last decade has seen the emergence of an important shopping technology outside the home, **electronic retailing**, which permits consumers to call up product information through computer terminals in shopping kiosks in various locations and place orders by credit card.

Such electronic retailing affords manufacturers yet another channel for distributing their products. Avon has experimented with it, setting up shopping kiosks in office buildings, shopping malls, and supermarkets.

Although some retailers view electronic retailing as a threat, others have begun placing terminals in their stores to allow shoppers to browse the store electronically by obtaining information on products and prices. For instance, Murjani International, a manufacturer of jeans, introduced electronic kiosks outside many retail stores in 1986, giving shoppers the opportunity to make purchases 24 hours a day and guaranteeing delivery in two days.[45]

New Industrial Information Technologies

New informational and service technologies make marketing more efficient not only for consumers, but also for companies. The widespread proliferation of personal computers and microprocessing capabilities has led to the development of industrial information technologies that give marketers instant access to sales trends, cost data, competitive data, and statistical analysis. Such information is stored in a central computer, but it can be easily accessed through personal computers. As a result, the past decade has seen an increasing reliance by managers on PCs for marketing and financial analysis.

Computer technology has also provided opportunities for improved services to clients. Merrill Lynch introduced one of its most successful products, the Cash Management Account, by using computers to combine information about customer checking, savings, credit card, and securities accounts into one statement and automatically "sweeping" idle money into money market funds. American Hospital Supply Corp. also took advantage of technological opportunity by establishing computer links to its customers and suppliers. Hospitals can now enter orders directly through computer terminals. As a result, American Hospital has seen its market share soar.[46]

ECONOMIC TRENDS

A third environmental influence on marketing opportunity is economic conditions. Economic stagnation inhibits marketers from seeking new opportunities, while a boom in spending may encourage them to increase R&D budgets and accelerate the pace of new-product introductions.

The 1980s started out with a severe recession that had a lasting effect on consumer purchasing habits. The subsequent recovery has been long lasting. Both periods affected assessments of environmental opportunity and threat.

The rampant inflation of the late 1970s and the deep recession that followed in the early 1980s both had the effect of reducing real income for many consumers. In 1980 the median family income was $1,300 less than in 1973 as measured by constant 1980 dollars.[47] The recession led to sharp reductions in **discretionary income** (the amount left after paying for necessities and taxes). And less income lowered consumer confidence in the ability to maintain their current standard of living. As a result, consumers became more price-sensitive. They were more likely to buy low-priced **private brands** (store-owned brands sold at lower prices than national brands) or **generic products** (unbranded products identified by product category only). Consumers were also more likely to hunt for price specials and bargains and to use coupons to save money.[48]

RECESSION IN THE EARLY 1980s

The economic recovery in the mid 1980s increased discretionary income and spending for durable goods. One enduring legacy of the recession, however, was continued price sensitivity. Consumers today are less likely to be loyal to nationally advertised brands than they were 15 years ago. They are more likely to buy private and generic brands, competitive brands that have price promotions, and new brands that are seen as having price or performance advantages. The post-recession period also produced a greater willingness by consumers to spend for services, electronics, and time-saving products.

The American economy grew at an average rate of only 2 percent after 1984, and by 1987 there were signs that consumer spending was leveling off.[49] The stock market crash of October 1987 put a temporary damper on consumer spending by undermining confidence in the economy. But spending quickly rebounded to pre-crash levels with no lasting ill effect on the economy.[50] Fears of a recession in 1989 did not materialize as the economy continued on a slow but steady course.

RECOVERY IN THE MID 1980s

More enduring changes in the economy have also caused some marketers to sound a note of caution in assessing future opportunity. Intensified foreign competition has resulted in a substantial trade gap that has weakened the economy. Finding it difficult to compete with the lower labor costs and higher productivity of foreign competitors, many American manufacturers are scaling back their manufacturing facilities and are buying parts and assembled products from foreign countries, particularly Japan. The net result is a greater emphasis on service than production.[51]

The shift to a service economy and the cutback in America's industrial base may lead to long-term problems that have not yet been played out. If America's manufacturing base continues to shrink, the economy of the 1990s will suffer. Perhaps the best economic assessment for the 1990s is cautious optimism, an upbeat view of marketing opportunity, but not too upbeat.

A LOOK TO THE FUTURE

REGULATORY TRENDS

Regulatory trends are a fourth environmental factor that affect marketing opportunity because they define the constraints that government places on marketing actions. Government has a role in ensuring that products are safe, that advertising is truthful, and that competition is fair.

Two regulatory agencies are particularly important because of controls they can exert on marketing actions. The *Federal Trade Commission* (FTC) was established in 1914 to curb the monopoly powers of big business and unfair trade practices. Since then, it has also taken on a watchdog role to discourage unfair and deceptive advertising. The *Food and Drug Administration* (FDA) was created in 1906 largely as a result of the outcry produced by Upton Sinclair's book *The Jungle,* which exposed unsanitary conditions in Chicago's meat-packing houses. The FDA is empowered to set product standards to ensure consumer safety and to require disclosure of product contents.

The basic issue is the extent to which government regulatory agencies should become involved in ensuring consumer welfare and fair competition. The alternative to government regulation is to let industry regulate itself. The Reagan administration strongly favored industry self-regulation and began to dismantle some of the regulatory apparatus put in place in the 1960s and 1970s.

THE LEGAL CONTEXT OF MARKETING

If we are to understand how regulatory trends affect marketing opportunity, it is necessary to first have some awareness of the laws that affect marketing actions. These laws are grouped in Table 3.2 according to which component of the marketing mix they affect — the company's product, distribution, advertising, or pricing. The product-related laws are designed to protect the consumer by guaranteeing product safety and disclosure of product contents. Laws (namely the Lanham Act) are also designed to protect a company's **trademarks** (that is, the names and symbols used to identify brands and companies by registering them).

Distribution-related regulations are designed to restrict three types of practices: (1) establishing an **exclusive sales territory** wherein a territory is granted by a manufacturer to an intermediary (a wholesaler or retailer), giving it sole rights to sell the company's product in the area; (2) **exclusive-dealing contracts** requiring an intermediary to buy only the company's lines; and (3) **tying contracts** requiring an intermediary to take other products in the company's line in order to obtain the desired product. These restrictions apply only if a court judges the actions by the manufacturer to be in restraint of trade.

Advertising regulations are designed to eliminate deceptive and misleading advertising through the powers of the FTC. For example, the FTC forced Warner Lambert to stop advertising that Listerine mouthwash helps prevent colds, and further required the company to advertise that the former claim was not true.[52] The FTC also monitors and controls advertising to children. As an example, it prohibited advertisements for Spider Man vitamins that could have encouraged children to consume harmful amounts of vitamins.[53]

In the pricing area, government regulations restrict three pricing practices. In **price fixing**, competitors agree to maintain fixed price levels to avoid competition. In **predatory pricing**, a company attempts to establish market dominance by pricing below cost to drive other competitors out of the market, then raises prices once it has established market dominance. In **price discrimination**, a seller charges different prices to intermediaries for the same product. The Robinson-Patman Act prohibits this practice unless there is some cost justification to charge a lower price to one buyer than another (e.g., savings in transportation costs or for large purchase quantities).

REGULATION AND DEREGULATION IN THE 1980s

The regulatory climate for marketing changed considerably during the 1980s as the Reagan administration moved toward deregulating many government controls over business practices. Whereas the 1970s saw an "outpouring of federal rules and standards"[54] and the creation of new regulatory agencies such as the

TABLE 3.2
Selected Laws Affecting
Marketing Actions

PRODUCT RELATED	**PROVISIONS OF LEGISLATION**
Lanham Act (1946)	Provides trademark protection for brand names on goods shipped in interstate or foreign commerce.
Fair Packaging and Labeling Act (1966)	Requires manufacturers to disclose ingredients and volume on the package.
Truth in Lending Act (1968)	Requires full disclosure of all finance charges in consumer credit agreements.
Child Protection Act (1969)	Allows the Food and Drug Administration to remove dangerous children's products from the market.
Consumer Product Safety Commission Act (1972)	Established the Consumer Product Safety Commission to identify, ban, and recall unsafe products.
DISTRIBUTION RELATED	
Sherman Antitrust Act (1980)	Limits right of seller to award an intermediary exclusive rights to a territory if such an exclusive arrangement restricts competition.
Clayton Act (1914)	Prohibits exclusive dealing wherein a seller requires a customer to buy only the company's line. Also prohibits *tying contracts* wherein a seller requires a customer to take other products in the seller's line.
ADVERTISING RELATED	
Federal Trade Commission Act (1914)	Established the Federal Trade Commission to monitor unfair practices, including advertising.
Wheeler-Lea Amendment to FTC Act (1938)	Enlarged the powers of the Federal Trade Commission to prevent deceptive and misleading advertising.
PRICING RELATED	
Sherman Antitrust Act (1890)	Outlaws price fixing and predatory pricing in restraint of trade.
Robinson-Patman Act (1936)	Prohibits price discrimination wherein the same product is sold to intermediaries at different prices without cost justification.

Environmental Protection Agency and the Consumer Product Safety Commission, the 1980s could be labeled "the decade of deregulation." President Reagan's first economic report stated his philosophy clearly: "Unnecessary regulation simply adds to the costs to business and consumers alike without commensurate benefits."[55]

One of the clearest effects of deregulation was the change in the role of the FTC from an active watchdog over industry practices to a passive observer that prosecuted only the more blatant violations. Whereas in the 1970s the FTC would bring action against an advertiser if an advertisement had the potential to deceive, in the 1980s advertising had to be clearly deceptive to most consumers before the FTC took action. In other words, the burden of proof that government action was or was not warranted shifted from industry to the regulatory agencies.

This shift had broad ramifications, as the case of Kraft's Cheese Whiz illustrates. Cheese Whiz was advertised as real cheese even though the product was half processed cheese. A consumer interest group protested that the advertisement was deceptive. Because the FTC had become reluctant to prosecute such cases, the group had to go through the Texas courts to force Kraft to change its advertising.[56]

Not only the FTC, but the Consumer Product Safety Commission and the Food and Drug Administration also scaled back their actions during the Reagan era. The Consumer Product Safety Commission shifted its emphasis from imposed to voluntary standards for product safety, while the FDA softened its regulatory stance on full disclosure of the effects of prescription drugs.[57]

MARKETING ETHICS AND CONSUMER RIGHTS

The laws and regulations just cited are generally designed to protect the consumer from unethical practices by businesses. These laws recognize that consumers have certain basic rights in the marketplace. However, some unethical practices are just one step short of being unlawful and are therefore overlooked by the regulatory agencies. Ultimately, each marketer must rely on his or her own value system to determine what is and is not ethical. That value system should recognize consumer rights to safety, to full information, and to value for the price paid. The American Marketing Association (AMA) has established a code of ethics to provide guidelines for ethical conduct. It says, in part, that

> Marketers shall uphold and advance the integrity, honor and dignity of the marketing profession by being honest in serving consumers, clients, employees, suppliers, distributors, and the public.[58]

The code then outlines responsibilities for each component of the marketing mix. For *products and services*, it says that marketers have the responsibility to ensure product safety, to disclose all product risks, and to identify any factor that might change product performance. Did General Motors fulfill these responsibilities when it was sued to recall 1.1 million X-body cars for faulty brakes?[59] Probably not.

For *advertising*, the code states that marketers must avoid deceptive and misleading communications, must reject high-pressure sales tactics, and must avoid manipulating consumers to buy. Did Warner Lambert fulfill these responsibilities when it advertised Listerine as preventing colds? Probably not.

For *distribution*, the code says that suppliers should not coerce their intermediaries into taking unwanted products, and that they should not create false shortages to drive up prices of their products. Did Chrysler fulfill these responsibilities in the early 1960s when it forced its dealers to take unwanted cars during an economic downturn? Probably not.

For *pricing*, the code stipulates that marketers must not engage in price fixing or predatory pricing, and must fully disclose all prices associated with the purchase including service, installation, and delivery. Did General Electric fulfill these responsibilities in the 1960s when several of its executives were indicted for price fixing? Probably not.

As further insurance of consumer rights, the AMA code states that marketers should provide the means to hear consumer complaints and to adjust them equitably.

Although many of the actions cited by the AMA code as unethical are also illegal, some are not — for example, ignoring a consumer's complaint. But even the AMA code is not sufficient to provide guidelines for ethical action. Should an individual work for a cigarette company if he or she believes that cigarettes cause cancer? Should an international marketer subscribe to the practice of offering bribes if all the company's competitors are doing it? Should a manager approve of the practice of buying a competitor's product, analyzing it, and then duplicating it? Should an advertiser go along with a strategy of promoting a brand as new and improved when there have been only minor changes in the product? These areas are not covered by the law or by the AMA code.

We will be addressing ethical issues from time to time in future chapters, primarily as they relate to product, distribution, advertising, and pricing strategies. As you will see, in every such issue, the question of marketing ethics must bear directly on the level of integrity of the individual marketer.

SUMMARY

1. *What creates opportunities and threats in the marketing environment?*
Opportunities and threats are created by social, technological, economic, and regulatory trends in the environment. Trends such as the increasing proportion of women employed outside the home, a decrease in family size, and more emphasis on health and fitness are opportunities for some companies and threats for other companies.

2. *Why does a marketing opportunity always have some threat? How can an environmental threat frequently be turned into an opportunity?*
A marketing opportunity can pose a threat for several reasons. The three basic sources of opportunity are unmet customer needs, competitive weakness, and longer-term environmental trends. Marketers can misread each of these opportunities, respectively, by underestimating customer demand, misjudging the competition's ability to come in with something better, or misreading an environmental trend such as the potential for a new technology.

Just as opportunity can pose a threat, a threat can also be turned into opportunity when a marketer can adapt to the environment and take advantage of what appears to be an adverse trend.

3. *How can marketers systematically analyze environmental changes to better shape marketing strategies?*
Marketers systematically analyze the environment through a process of environmental scanning. This process requires teams of specialists to collect environmental information and assess its potential impact on the company. Such information is available through a variety of sources, including marketing research surveys, the business press, industry sources, and research companies that specialize in assessing environmental trends. Marketers can also use approaches such as expected-value analysis to assess the impact of environmental trends on particular marketing strategies.

4. *What were the basic environmental trends — social, technological, eco-*

nomic, and legal and regulatory — in the 1980s that will shape marketing opportunities in the 1990s?

Three types of *social trends* directly influence opportunity: changes in consumer demographic characteristics, lifestyles, and cultural values. Demographically, the most significant trends in the 1980s were the increasing proportion of working women, the changing character of the American family as a result of smaller families and more singles, and the greater numbers of baby boomers and elderly consumers in the marketplace.

The 1980s saw significant lifestyle changes, too. Male and female roles have begun to shift as more women have entered the workforce. In addition, consumers are placing greater emphasis on health and nutrition and manifest more concern about the environment. Baby boomers and youth are showing greater conservatism. The American consumer of the 1970s and 1980s displayed different cultural values from consumers of earlier years, emphasizing immediate personal gratification. Some foresee a shift from a "me" to a "we" orientation in the 1990s, though.

Important changes in the *technological environment* have provided consumers with new shopping and entertainment options and have given businesses more powerful data-gathering and analysis capabilities.

Economic trends such as the steep recession in the 1980s had a lasting effect on consumers, making them more price-conscious and less brand-loyal. Slow growth in the late 1980s, more intense foreign competition, and the reduced manufacturing base of many U.S. companies may be some grounds for concern as we move into the 1990s.

The most significant *regulatory trend* of the 1980s was the Reagan administration's dismantling of much of the regulatory apparatus designed to protect consumers. The result has been reduced powers of the FTC to patrol advertising practices and the weakened regulatory roles of the Consumer Product Safety Commission, the Food and Drug Administration, and the Environmental Protection Agency.

KEY TERMS

Environmental scanning (p. 61)
Demographics (p. 63)
Lifestyles (p. 64)
Cultural values (p. 64)
Subcultures (p. 70)
Videotex systems (p. 73)
Electronic retailing (p. 74)
Discretionary income (p. 75)
Private brands (p. 75)

Generic products (p. 75)
Trademarks (p. 76)
Exclusive sales territory (p. 76)
Exclusive dealing (p. 76)
Tying contracts (p. 76)
Price fixing (p. 76)
Predatory pricing (p. 76)
Price discrimination (p. 76)

QUESTIONS

1. One marketing analyst who works for a large consulting firm read the description of Avon in the beginning of this chapter and made this comment:

   You know, a company like Avon that faces an environmental threat is likely to bring in new management. And that's a pretty good idea because you need fresh thinking to turn the com-

pany around. But what is never said is that sometimes a company just can't be turned around, even if these great managers do everything right. Look at Avon. Waldron is stuck with door-to-door selling and can't do much about it. Door-to-door selling is on the decline, even if Avon's sales reps are selling at the office. Environmental threats are just sometimes beyond the control of management to do anything about them.

a. Do you agree with this assessment?
b. If a firm cannot control an environmental threat, does that mean it can do nothing about it?
c. What is Avon trying to do to turn environmental threat into opportunity?

2. The chapter referred to Procter & Gamble's introduction of its Duncan Hines line of soft cookies. P&G thought it saw an opportunity to enter a new market based on a technology that allowed cookies to be crispy on the outside and soft on the inside. But this perceived environmental opportunity became an environmental threat. Why?
3. Social changes in the 1980s created environmental threats for the following companies and industries:

   • Kellogg, faced with a decreasing proportion of children.
   • Pepsi, faced with a decreasing proportion of teenagers.
   • The liquor industry, faced with an increasing proportion of baby boomers.

   In each case, what was the threat? How did each company/industry try to turn threat into opportunity?

4. Why did RCA's videodisc entry fail? How might an effective environmental scanning unit have helped the company in the 1970s?
5. An executive for a large industrial firm producing standardized items was asked about the need for environmental scanning in his company. He made the following comment:

   > You know, we sell a commodity product in a stable environment. Even in the 1981–82 recession, we did not hurt much. I don't see the need for us to be concerned about environmental change. When you're in a stable business without too much product change, you don't have to be that concerned about environmental scanning.

   Do you agree with this assessment? Under what circumstances might environmental changes represent a threat to this company?

6. A manufacturer of home cleaning products introduces a new floor cleaner and wax combination. The advantage of the product is that it gets up dirt more quickly and effectively while protecting the floor. The company decides to advertise with a theme of a wife using the product, then guests coming in and marveling at the floor. The final scene shows the husband extolling the wife's homemaking abilities.

a. In what ways does this advertising approach contradict basic demographic, lifestyle, and cultural changes described in this chapter? (Be specific in citing these trends.)
b. What type of an advertising approach could be used to better conform to the trends you cited above? What are the advantages of your suggested approach?

7. Gerber's, a large producer of baby foods, viewed the decreasing birth rate after 1960 as an environmental threat. What strategic actions could the company take to turn threat into opportunity?
8. What are the marketing implications of changing male-female roles for

a. a financial service company?
b. an automobile manufacturer?
c. a producer of packaged foods?

9. What types of companies might regard the increasing emphasis on health and nutrition as a threat? What types of companies are most likely to regard these trends as an opportunity? How have companies threatened by these trends tried to turn them into opportunities?
10. The chapter suggested that youth and baby boomers were becoming more conservative. What are the marketing implications of such a trend for

a. clothing manufacturers?
b. producers of personal grooming products?

11. One automobile industry executive, commenting on the advisability of designing ads for the black consumer market, said

   > We develop one campaign for the total market based on the performance advantages of our cars. Yes, we could spend money developing a different advertising campaign for blacks. But why should we, when blacks use pretty much the same reasons for buying as whites?

   What are the pros and cons of developing an advertising campaign specifically directed to the black consumer market?
12. Consider the following technological trends in the 1980s: (a) in-home shopping through cable TV,

(b) electronic retailing, (c) widespread adoption of VCRs for in-home entertainment.

What kind of businesses have considered each of the preceding a threat? Why?

13. One marketing executive, commenting on the deregulation during the Reagan administration, said

    Deregulation was overdue. Regulatory agencies were starting to be a real problem for us. Take the FTC. We had to worry about substantiating claims we would ordinarily regard as typical advertising pitches, like "Gets clothes cleaner than most other leading detergents." Now, we don't have that problem. The FTC leaves us alone unless a claim is clearly misleading.

    Do you feel that marketing executives should regard deregulation as favorable and government regulation as unfavorable? Under what circumstances might government regulation help a marketer?

CASE 3.1

TARGETING A NEW DEMOGRAPHIC GROUP: BABY BUSTERS

Source: "Busters May Replace Boomers as the Darlings of Advertisers," *The Wall Street Journal,* November 12, 1987, p. 41.

Enough already about baby boomers. Marketers have analyzed them to death. Now get ready for the baby busters. They're the consumers born after the baby boom subsided — from about 1965 to 1974 — and they're shaping up to be the next hot demographic group.

"They may be fewer in number than baby boomers, but young people today have lots of discretionary income," says Barbara Feigin, an executive vice president at Grey Advertising. "They also make many purchasing decisions on their own because either the parents are divorced or both parents work."

Running the gamut from teens to young adults, baby busters are an amorphous bunch who are harder to pigeonhole than the baby boomers. There isn't even total agreement on what to call them. While busters is most common, consultants also have coined such terms as "afterboomers" and Flyers (Fun-loving youth en route to success).

Experts on consumer behavior do agree, though, on a few distinguishing traits. For example, they note that many baby busters value religion and formal rituals, such as proms and lavish weddings. If this return to tradition takes hold, it will surely affect the look and sound of advertising.

Busters also are characterized as driven people, preoccupied with success in school and in careers. "They're definitely a materialistic group, but unlike yuppies, they're more into being entrepreneurs — starting their own health club or disco," says Larry Graham, a marketing consultant who advises companies on the attitudes and spending habits of consumers 13-to-25 years old.

Among the marketers most interested in baby busters is the sluggish coffee industry. For the coffee industry, Mr. Graham says, the busters are an inviting but difficult market to crack since many of them already have adopted soft drinks as their breakfast beverage.

Some consumer researchers believe marketers may be deluding themselves about the true significance of the busters. Cheryl Russell, editor-in-chief of American Demographics magazine, notes that there are only about 37 million 13-to-22-year-olds, compared with more than 43 million 23-to-32-year-olds, who make up the second half of the baby boom. "It amazes me how interest in baby busters has heated up," she says. "If companies start showing young people jumping around in all their ads, they'll risk turning off people nearing middle age who have much more spending power."

1. Why do "baby busters" represent an opportunity to the coffee industry? How might coffee producers such as Nestle and General Foods appeal to this group?
2. Why might it be risky for a coffee company to target an advertising campaign to baby busters?
3. Is Coca Cola's "Coke for Breakfast" campaign directed primarily to this group? What other demographic groups might it be directed to and why?
4. What other products or services might view baby busters as a prime area of opportunity? Why?

CASE 3.2

CANADA DRY DIRECTS ITS APPEAL TO "COUCH POTATOES"

Source: "Using Pop Psychology." Reprinted with permission from *Advertising Age*, June 6, 1988, p. 70, copyright Crain Communications, Inc. All rights reserved.

Canada Dry Corp. thinks the post-yuppie era is so crucial to the sales growth of its ginger ale that the company hired a social psychologist to better explain its target market of aging baby-boomers.

Joel Brockner, a social psychologist and associate professor of management at Columbia University in New York, interpreted the results of several studies to help Canada Dry fine-tune its ad strategy to the key older-than-30 market.

One of the studies Mr. Brockner analyzed was a survey commissioned by Canada Dry that showed adults are staying home more, are less interested in appearances and no longer follow fads.

Mr. Brockner reaffirmed Canada Dry's ad focus: that promoting wealth as a virtue is as dated as the dress-for-success suit. Homespun values and peace of mind are in vogue as baby-boomers enter middle age.

"People are leading more hectic, fast-paced lives," Mr. Brockner said. ". . . Life is more frenetic and complicated. And in response, people are searching for things that are simple, not unsophisticated but uncomplicated."

The post-yuppie analysis helped Canada Dry evolve its ad strategy into "a change of pace" soft drink, said Edward Moerk, president of Canada Dry Corp.

The studies also convinced Canada Dry to reformulate its diet ginger ale for a less sweet, more gingery flavor.

Canada Dry's ad strategy was developed in 1987 with a commercial showing a woman who says that, though she yearned for excitement as a youth, now she enjoys quiet evenings at home.

The company said the campaign helped turn around declining sales for the No. 1 ginger ale and build brand share in 1987 to 37.2% of the $140 million ginger ale market, up from 36.7% in 1986.

Mr. Moerk said that as the population ages, soft drinks such as ginger ale are likely to experience more growth. He said the drier taste tends to appeal to older drinkers.

In 1988, Canada Dry broke two new TV spots. One shows a bunch of friends in their 30s lounging and reminiscing about the 1960s and 1970s.

The other shows a 30-ish career couple who turn down a night on the town to relax at home with Chinese takeout and Canada Dry.

Mr. Brockner said the campaign tries to articulate the "couch potato" values of the 30-and-older age group.

The Canada Dry survey reveals a new maturity among the so-called yuppie generation.

For instance, the survey revealed that appearance isn't that important in a mate. Survey respondents ranked sensitivity, honesty, intelligence and humor as top qualities in a romantic partner.

Looks ranked fifth of the seven qualities most valued in a mate. And, Mr. Brockner said, when respondents were asked to list things they value, "people weren't giving yuppie answers."

"They weren't listing power and wealth; they were giving answers such as greater sense of wisdom."

1. What lifestyle trend among baby boomers does the Canada Dry campaign reflect?
2. What other products or services might view the "couch potato" trend as an opportunity? Why?
3. What products or services might view the "couch potato" trend as a threat? Why?

NOTES

1. "Direct Selling Is Alive and Well," *Sales & Marketing Management*, August 1988, p. 76; and "A Troubled Avon Knocks at Several New Doors," *Marketing & Media Decisions*, November, 1984, p. 68.

2. "Anyhow, It Was Nice While It Lasted," *Forbes*, January 12, 1987, p. 50.

3. "Fresher Face at Avon," *Management Today*, December, 1984, p. 60.

4. "Get Ready for Shopping at Work," *Fortune*, February 15, 1988, pp. 95–98.

5. "Avon Answers Calling to Higher Scent Lines," *Advertising Age*, March 28, 1988, p. S-4; and *Sales & Marketing Management*, August 1988, p. 78.

6. "Big Names Are Opening Doors for Avon," *Business Week*, June 1, 1987, p. 96.

7. "The Anatomy of RCA's Videodisc Failure," *Business Week*, April 23, 1984, pp. 89–90.

8. Ibid., p. 89.

9. "Eight Ways to Avoid Marketing Shock," *Sales & Marketing Management*, April, 1989, pp. 55–58.

10. "The Spirited Battle for Those Who Want to Drink Light," *Business Week*, June 16, 1986, pp. 84–87.

11. "Hiram Walker Plots Strategy," *Advertising Age*, June 6, 1988, p. 57.

12. "How Seagram Is Scrambling to Survive 'The Sobering of America,'" *Business Week*, September 3, 1984, p. 94.

13. Arnold Mitchell, *Changing Values and Lifestyles* (Menlo Park, Calif.: SRI International, 1981), p. 3.

14. "The Life of a C.E.O.," *The New York Times Magazine*, December 1, 1985, p. 50.

15. *Marketing & Media Decisions*, November, 1984, p. 69.

16. "Avon Crawling," *Forbes*, April 21, 1986, p. 74.

17. *Handbook of Labor Statistics*, June 1986, Tables 1, 6, and 50; and "Baby Boomers Push for Power," *Business Week*, July 2, 1984, p. 52.

18. "Eating Habits Force Changes in Marketing," *Advertising Age*, October 30, 1978, p. 65.

19. "Think Plastic," *New York Magazine*, March 4, 1985, pp. 19–20.

20. "Mass Marketing to Fragmented Markets," *Planning Review*, September 1984, p. 34.

21. "Chocolate Makers Tempt Grown-Ups as Market Matures," *Ad Forum*, February 1984, pp. 37–39.

22. "A Once Tightly Knit Middle Class Finds Itself Divided and Uncertain," *The Wall Street Journal*, March 9, 1987, p. 23.

23. "Levi Line Tailored to Aging Boomers," *Adweek*, September 21, 1987, pp. 1, 4.

24. "Detroit's New Goal: Putting Yuppies in the Driver's Seat," *Business Week*, September 3, 1984, p. 48.

25. "Marriott Corp. Gambles $1 Billion on Communities for Elderly," *Adweek's Marketing Week*, March 6, 1989, pp. 28–30.

26. "Targeting Teens," *American Demographics*, February 1985, p. 25.

27. "Clutter Makes for Marketing Confusion," *Advertising Age*, February 1, 1988, p. S-2.

28. "Real Men Do Wear Aprons," *Across the Board*, November 1983, p. 53.

29. "New Buyers Catch Advertisers' Eyes," *Advertising Age*, March 14, 1985, pp. 15, 26.

30. "Ads Throw Product Pitch in New Direction," *Advertising Age*, October 4, 1984, p. 18.

31. "Whetting Appetites with Healthy Food," *Adweek Special Report*, September 12, 1988, p. F, p. 65.

32. "Heavy Ambitions Feed on a Love of Light," *Advertising Age*, May 9, 1983, p. M-34.

33. *Sales & Marketing Management*, April, 1989, p. 56; and "Sweat Chic," *Forbes*, September 5, 1988, pp. 96, 101.

34. "Pizza Makers Slug It Out for Share of Growing Eat-at-Home Market," *The Wall Street Journal*, January 12, 1988, p. 39.

35. "National Advertisers Rediscover the Black Market," *Ad Forum*, January 1984, p. 36; and "Traditional Brand Loyalty," *Advertising Age*, May 18, 1981, p. S-2.

36. "Trying to Reach Blacks? Beware of Marketing Myopia," *Advertising Age*, May 21, 1979, p. 60.

37. "Spanish Spending Power Growing Dramatically, but Consumers Retain Special Characteristics," *Television/Radio Age*, December 1984, p. A-4.

38. "Reaching the Hispanic Market: A 53 Billion Opportunity," *Listening Post* June 1984, p. 3.

39. "Cosmetic Companies Need to Brush Up," *Advertising Age*, February 8, 1988, p. S-2.

40. "The Innovators," *Fortune*, June 6, 1988, pp. 50–64.

41. "Corporate Growth, R&D, and the Gap Between," *Technology Review*, March–April 1978.

42. "A Shift in Direction at Procter," *The New York Times*, June 23 1987, pp. D1, D5.

43. "Penney's 'TV Mall' To Make Its Late, Humbled Debut," *The Wall Street Journal*, February 16, 1988, p. 6.

44. "Child Prodigy," *Adweek's Marketing Week*, October 3, 1988, pp. 22–25.

45. "Electronic Retailing," *Marketing Communications*, May 1986; and "Murjani to Put Shopping for Coca-Cola Apparel at Customers' Fingertips," *Women's Wear Daily*, June 5, 1986, p. 8.

46. "Information Power," *Business Week*, October 14, 1985, p. 109.

47. "Running Faster to Stay in Place," *American Demographics*, June 1982, pp. 16–19.

48. *Supermarket Shoppers in a Period of Economic Uncertainty* (New York: Yankelovich, Skelly, and White, 1982), p. 15.

49. "A Sense of Limits Grips Consumers," *The New York Times*, March 15, 1987, pp. F1, F14.

50. "Good News: Consumers Bounce Back," *Advertising Age*, November 9, 1987, pp. 1, 91.

51. "The Hollow Corporation," *Business Week*, March 3, 1986, pp. 57–79.

52. William L. Wilkie, Dennis L. McNeill, and Michael B. Mazis, "Marketing's 'Scarlet Letter': The Theory and Practice of Corrective Advertising," *Journal of Marketing* 48(Spring 1984).

53. Dorothy Cohen, "Unfairness in Advertising Revisited," *Journal of Marketing* 46(Winter 1982): 73–80.

54. "A Decade of Deregulation?" *Industry Week,* January 7, 1980, p. 17.

55. "The Consumer Movement: Whatever Happened?" *The New York Times,* January 23, 1983, p. A16.

56. "Firms Fret as States Threaten Taxes and Restrictions on Ads," *The Wall Street Journal,* April 17, 1986, p. 31.

57. "FDA Shows New Taste for Food Health Claims," *Advertising Age,* December 9, 1985, pp. 3, 72.

58. *Code of Ethics,* American Marketing Association, Chicago, Illinois.

59. "Public Interest Groups Achieve Higher Status and Some Permanence," *The Wall Street Journal,* August 27, 1984, p. 1.

How does a company compete with IBM? With a great deal of difficulty. But Apple Computer is committed to doing it. In fact, it is the only personal computer company that is giving customers an alternative to IBM. Other companies have chosen to switch rather than fight by making their machines IBM compatible. Apple has chosen to both fight and switch. While its Apple II PCs and its newer Macintosh use a different operating system than IBM, Apple announced in 1987 that it was also making its Mac compatible with IBM through a plug-in adapter.[1]

Why is IBM such a formidable competitor in personal computers? (After all, Steve Jobs and Stephen Wozniak pioneered the development of PCs when they put together the first Apples in a garage in 1976.) The answer has to do with IBM's competitive strategy. When IBM enters a market, it goes all out to establish competitive advantage. When IBM introduced its first PCs in 1981, it did so with a sales staff and advertising budget that smothered Apple. It successfully undercut one of Apple's prime advantages, ease of use, by using a Charlie Chaplin character in its advertising to convince customers that its machines are user friendly. Most importantly, it established the industry standard for software, pressuring all PC manufacturers to produce IBM- compatible machines. Clearly, IBM threatened Apple's survival.

Apple reacted to IBM's onslaught by attempting to maintain its competitive advantage in the school and home computer markets with its Apple II, a machine that was easy to use and had superior graphics. Most PC profits are in the business market, however, and IBM had an effective lock on that segment. Not surprisingly, Apple's market share for PCs slid from 41 percent in 1981 to 24 percent in 1983.[2] Something had to be done. Steve Jobs, Apple's chairman at the time, did two things. In 1983 he convinced John Sculley, President of Pepsi-Cola USA, to join Apple as its president. And Jobs went back to the drawing boards and developed the Macintosh for the business market.

MARKETING OPPORTUNITY THROUGH COMPETITIVE ADVANTAGE

By all accounts, Sculley saved Apple. His first move was to slash costs in the face of decreasing market share, allowing Apple to show a profit for 1984 and 1985.[3] But his major moves were marketing ones. Rather than competing with IBM head-to-head, Sculley believed that the best way to fight a market leader was to look for emerging markets where a competitive advantage could be established. He saw the Macintosh as the key to implementing this strategy. The Macintosh enabled Apple to develop two markets, desktop publishing and desktop communications as a means of entry into the business market.[4]

Desktop publishing permitted companies to develop their own publishing capabilities based on the Macintosh's superior high-resolution graphics tied to Apple's laser printer. These features coupled with the Macintosh's ease of use made the machine a formidable competitor. Apple is also developing the desktop communications market through its AppleTalk network, which allows PCs at separate workstations to "talk to each other," enabling information sharing and joint development of graphics and reports.[5]

Desktop publishing and communications provided the breakthrough Apple was looking for. Large firms such as DuPont, Motorola, and General Electric began using Macs, paving the way for their acceptance in the business market. Sales of Macs went from 250,000 units in 1985 to 405,000 in 1986.[6] By 1988 Apple could report a 50 percent growth rate and a doubling of its net income in the last two years.[7]

Apple's answer to IBM's competitive threat was to be the David to the IBM Goliath — look for selective areas of competitive advantage and avoid direct confrontation. ■

● ● ●

DEVELOPING COMPETITIVE ADVANTAGE

As we saw in the last chapter, competition is one of the three sources of marketing opportunity. To capitalize on that opportunity is to gain a **competitive advantage** by producing a better product, selling it at a lower price, distributing it more widely, providing better services, or offering a wider variety of product options than competing companies.

IBM AND APPLE: STRENGTHS AND WEAKNESSES ON BOTH SIDES

The combination of a firm's strengths and its competitors' weaknesses is an important source of marketing opportunity. IBM led with its strength when it entered the personal computer market. Its huge production and R&D resources allowed it to develop a good product that could hold its own in the marketplace, and its large sales staff, marketing know-how, and financial resources quickly made it the biggest game in town.

But IBM would not have gone into the market if it had not also seen competitive weakness in Apple. It followed Apple's progress closely, saw it dominate the school and home computer markets, and recognized Apple's strength in graphics technology. However, IBM also saw a gaping hole in the business market. There was no undisputed leader in the PC business market, primarily because the software was lacking. IBM moved in.

IBM saw other weaknesses at Apple. Although Apple at that time dominated the PC market, it had not clearly established itself as the industry standard. Further, Apple did not have strong relationships with its retailers, often delivering shipments late and antagonizing them by selling direct to larger companies. IBM entered the market with the intent of establishing its system as the industry standard and providing superior sales and service facilities.

Just as IBM could not have developed a strategy without analyzing its own and its competitors' strengths and weaknesses, the same held true for Apple. Its strengths gave it reason for hope in the face of IBM's onslaught. It had the best technological capability for developing new products (as it would soon prove with its introduction of the Macintosh). Its Apple II had the best graphics capability and was easier to use than the IBM PC. It had over 70 percent of the educational market. And it had a solid core of loyal users whose first personal computers had been Apples.

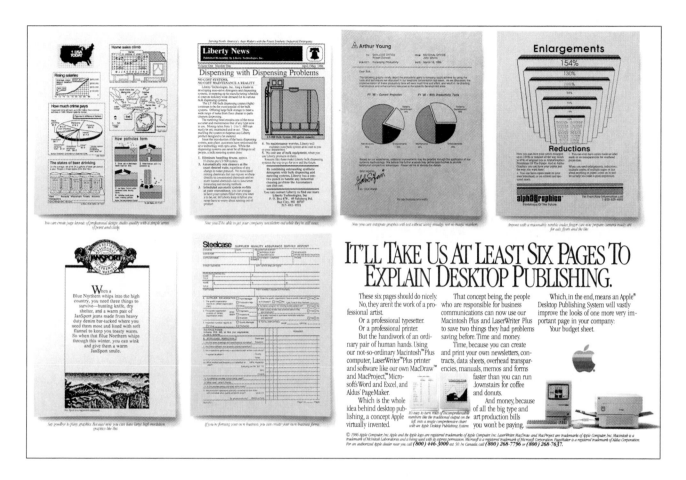

Apple also recognized its weaknesses, and moved quickly to correct them by spending more advertising dollars to promote the Apple II and the Macintosh, improving dealer relations, cutting the fat in production and in staff, and reducing the price of the Apple II to make it more competitive.

But what were IBM's weaknesses? Not many. Yet they were there. Perhaps IBM's biggest weakness was its very size. While IBM had been able to storm the PC market effectively, it did not have the maneuverability to split off small detachments to take advantage of markets of opportunity such as desktop publishing and communications. Sculley saw that the best way to compete with IBM was to take advantage of its lack of maneuverability; to identify emerging markets of opportunity that IBM either had overlooked or was too big to enter.

The net result is that both companies have established competitive advantage in the PC market, but not on each other's turf. IBM has a lock on regular PC usage in the business market, Apple in the educational market. Avoiding head-to-head competition with IBM while pursuing emerging markets means that Apple will survive and coexist with the market leader. But IBM and Apple are not likely to continue to stay off each other's turf. As we saw, Apple has an entree into the business market through desktop publishing. (See the ad in Exhibit 4.1.) And

IBM is increasing its efforts in Apple's strongest segment, the educational market.[8] As a result, the 1990s is likely to see more direct competition between these companies in the PC market.

John Sculley — Bringing Competitive Advantage to Apple

John Sculley is a marketing innovator. When he became president of Pepsi-Cola USA at age 30, one of his first tasks was to develop a bottle to compete with Coke's. He decided that a different-shaped bottle was not the way to gain competitive advantage. Instead, he introduced large-size plastic containers and multiple packs of bottles and cans — innovations aimed at the most profitable segment of the soft drink market, the heavy users.

Sculley applied his innovative bent as president of Apple. He transformed a technology-oriented company into a consumer-products company by using marketing tools to hammer away at the competition. In his first two years, he created a salesforce 350 strong, increased Apple's retail network by one-third, and tripled its advertising budget.[9] He introduced the Macintosh with a $2 million, 60-second spot commercial shown during the 1984 Super Bowl game. The bizarre, attention-getting commercial showed big brother (IBM?) on a movie screen controlling his brainwashed followers. It was unconventional, but it sold Macs.

His strategic approach was straight from Pepsi-Cola: Hit untapped market niches with a superior product before anyone else does. As he now puts it, using his new found "computertalk": "Before Pepsi made strides to segment new markets for its cola, it was really just the 'Coca Cola compatible.'"[10] Pepsi's move to fruit-based drinks, caffeine-free drinks, and diet colas established its independence from Coke.

How did Steve Jobs get Sculley to join Apple? It was partly by offering him the challenge of facing a competitive threat and turning a company around. But an even greater lure was the challenge of changing the face of American technology by offering innovative PCs to offices, homes, and schools. Ironically, two years after joining Apple, Sculley forced Jobs out of the company. Jobs had been focusing the company's efforts entirely on the Macintosh to the detriment of existing products that were proven performers, primarily the Apple II. The split between the Apple and Mac groups was untenable, and Sculley forced a showdown.[11]

Today, Apple is a very different company than in its pre-Sculley days. Sandals and blue jeans are out, suits are in. The talk around the corporate hallways is as much about marketing strategies as about new technologies. And the recognition is that Sculley is taking the company along the road of *niche marketing*, identifying selective markets such as desktop publishing as sources of competitive advantage. Throughout his drive to gain competitive advantage, John Sculley's preoccupation has been both the strengths and the weaknesses of Apple and its main competitor, IBM. ■

Both Apple and IBM required a systematic approach to determining opportunities for competitive advantage and deciding on a strategy for attaining it. Figure 4.1 presents such a framework. The objective of this approach is to develop marketing strategies based on an analysis of competitive strengths and weaknesses.

The first step in the figure is to determine the basis for competitive advantage. For Apple, competitive advantage is based on product superiority through graphics capability, ease of use, and ability to meet the needs of particular market niches (such as desktop publishing). For IBM, it is based on the variety of software options and the weight of the company's name in the business market. As undisputed market leader, IBM is perceived as the low-risk option. As one industrial buyer said, "You can never get fired by buying IBM products."

The next step in Figure 4.1 is to identify existing or emerging opportunities for competitive advantage. This is done through a **competitive analysis** that involves assessing the market's attractiveness, competitors' strengths and weaknesses, and the company's strengths and weaknesses. Based on this analysis, a company then develops marketing strategies (step 3 in Figure 4.1) to exploit the competitive advantages that it identified in the previous steps. Such strategies will depend on whether the firm is a market leader (as IBM is now), a challenger (as IBM was when it first entered the market), or a so-called *nicher*, as Apple was in looking for specific **market niches**; that is, small but profitable segments of the market that are unlikely to attract competitors.

Having determined its strategy, the firm then tries to anticipate what the competitive responses will be. Apple correctly anticipated that IBM would not follow its entry into desktop publishing. Actually, the greatest threat to Apple came from Xerox's introduction of a laser printer that can tie in with an IBM PC to provide desktop publishing capabilities. As is generally the case, pursuit of an opportunity carries with it the threat of competitive entry.

The remainder of this chapter is organized around the steps in Figure 4.1. After discussing the bases for competitive advantage, we will consider how to identify opportunities for competitive advantage. We will then see how marketers develop strategies based on competitive analyses and, finally, how competitive responses can be anticipated.

A FRAMEWORK FOR GAINING COMPETITIVE ADVANTAGE

FIGURE 4.1
A Framework for Gaining Competitive Advantage

Determine the Bases for Competitive Advantage

Identify Opportunities for Competitive Advantage

Develop Competitive Strategies

Anticipate Competitive Responses

DETERMINE THE BASES FOR COMPETITIVE ADVANTAGE

There are two broad bases for developing competitive advantage: a marketing advantage or a cost advantage. **Marketing advantage** can be gained by developing superior products or services that do a better job than competitors in meeting customer needs. It can also be gained by doing a better job in positioning a product, promoting it, or distributing it. **Cost advantage** can be gained by reducing production or marketing costs below those of competitors, enabling the company to reduce prices or to plow excess profits into advertising and distribution.

Generally, a firm seeking a marketing advantage tends to be more consumer-oriented than one seeking a cost advantage, because product or service superiority requires doing a better job than competitors in meeting customer needs. But a

FIGURE 4.2
Three Pathways to Competitive Advantage

Source: Michael E. Porter, *Competitive Strategy*, (New York: The Free Press, 1980).

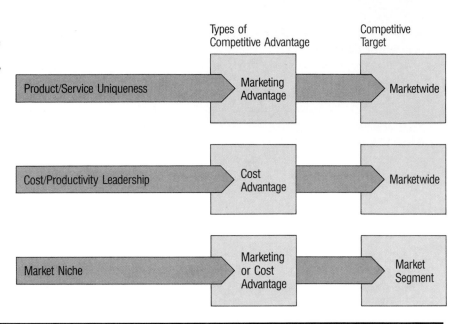

firm seeking a cost advantage cannot ignore customer needs. If a firm is wholly production-oriented and focuses only on cost efficiencies at the expense of customer needs, any competitive advantage gained from lower costs will be short-lived.

A marketing or cost advantage can be sought across all markets or just in particular market segments. IBM sought to establish itself on a market-wide basis when it entered the PC market; Apple chose to aim for targeted market niches, or segments. The combination of marketing or cost advantages on a market-wide or market-segment basis produces the three pathways to competitive advantage shown in Figure 4.2: product/service superiority or uniqueness, cost/productivity leadership, and market niche.

MARKET-WIDE PRODUCT/ SERVICE SUPERIORITY

For a company to enjoy market-wide product or service superiority, some aspect of its product or service must have an edge over the competition. Federal Express gained a competitive advantage by offering a unique service. It first entered the package delivery market by trying to compete with Emery and Airborne as an air-freight forwarder. It then concentrated on the benefit of overnight delivery based on its hub-spoke concept, directing all packages to its Memphis hub and branching out from there. Its focus on overnight delivery established a long-lasting marketing advantage based on superior service.

There are several other ways to obtain competitive advantage through product/service superiority:[12] One is to build a strong brand name that will win shelf space in retail stores and gain customer trial for new products. If Kellogg comes out with a new cereal, Campbell Soup with a new soup line, or Black and Decker with a new line of power tools, both retailers and customers are likely to pay attention because they recognize and respect these companies' products.

Providing superior service support through speed of delivery and responsiveness to customer orders is another way to obtain competitive advantage. Thus, in the construction equipment market Caterpillar Tractor is known for its excellent dealer network that provides reliable service and spare parts availability in situations where downtime is very expensive.

Technological leadership — being consistently among the first to provide innovative product features — can also provide a competitive advantage. One of Apple's advantages over IBM has been its technological leadership in developing computer graphics. However, technological leadership does not always translate into a competitive advantage. As we saw in the last chapter, RCA's leadership in electronics technology did not ensure its success in making videodiscs because it failed to tie technology to customer needs.

A company that offers a full line of products stands a better chance of winning customer loyalty than a company that offers a limited line. Gerber has a competitive advantage in baby foods over Beechnut and Heinz, because "it commands a baby food line so large it creates a billboard effect in supermarkets" by capturing so much shelf space.[13] Carrying a full line is particularly important to industrial buyers because they often need a variety of products to fill technical specifications. For example, corporate computer buyers like to deal with IBM because they can buy mainframe computers, microprocessors, PCs, printers, and software from the same source.

Still another way of gaining a competitive advantage is to develop unique or expanded product distribution. L'Eggs hosiery achieved competitive advantage by distributing its products in a unique way, through supermarkets. One of the reasons Gallo is the leading wine company in the United States is that it handpicked its distributors and demanded their loyalty in return for a strong product line.[14] The result was widespread distribution in liquor outlets.

The strategies just described have a common goal, to create greater customer loyalty that can insulate a company against its competition. This type of competitive advantage allows a company to keep prices at a profitable level. Cuisinart, for example, can sell its food processors for four times as much as competitors because of unique product features. For a long time Clorox was able to maintain a price differential for its bleach, even though it is a standardized product, because of superior name recognition among consumers.

MARKET-WIDE COST LEADERSHIP

Unlike companies such as Cuisinart that rely on product superiority, the primary strategic focus of Heinz is on cost reduction. According to one source, Heinz's management has a "singular devotion to lowering costs."[15] As a result, its profits increased an average of 17 percent in the mid 1980s. Heinz chose to focus on costs because of industry and economic conditions, including slow growth, intense competitive pressures, and low profits. Also, Heinz is in an industry with few product differences among competitors. Product uniqueness or superiority is an unlikely reason for consumers to choose one brand of canned vegetables over another. Thus, cost reduction is the surest way to beat out competitors. Lower costs have produced higher operating margins for Heinz, and the company has chosen to plow these earnings into heavy advertising and sales promotions that in turn help maintain a loyal customer base.

As Figure 4.2 shows, the strategy of attaining a low-cost position on a market-wide basis (as Heinz has done) is a second pathway to competitive advantage. But how can a company reduce costs? One method is to develop **economies of scale** in production and/or marketing; that is, reductions in the per-unit cost of manufacturing or marketing a product as the amount produced increases. Such economies are achieved because certain fixed costs, like the cost of machinery or the cost of trucks to distribute products, are spread out over more units. Such economies are developed in marketing by distributing and advertising a product on a mass-market basis or by advertising and distributing several products jointly. For example, when Folgers expanded its distribution nationwide from its Western base, the increased quantity produced not only reduced per-unit manufacturing costs, it also reduced per-unit costs of distribution.

Experience can also help a company to achieve cost reductions. For example, Texas Instruments was able to establish cost leadership in electronic calculators by achieving lower costs based on its production experience. By lowering prices substantially, Texas Instruments pressured competitors to do the same, driving many of them out of business.

Still another way to reduce costs is by greater productivity resulting either from reduced labor costs or from adopting new technologies that reduce production costs. As we saw in Chapter 2, one of Toyota's biggest competitive advantages in producing cars in this country has been its greater productivity per worker.

MARKET NICHE

A third pathway to competitive advantage is to operate in a protected market niche. The question is how long a market nicher will be able to maintain its niche before the giants come in. Ironically, the better a company does in appealing to a particular market segment, and the more profitable the business, the greater is the likelihood that a large company will step in. The question for Apple is how long its position in desktop publishing will be shielded from competition. As we noted, Xerox is now stepping into this niche in a tie-in with the IBM PC.

Market nichers tread a very fine line between maintaining a protected niche and attracting competition. For example, a small company called Minnetonka established a niche by being the first to introduce liquid hand soap in 1981. The niche quickly attracted the industry giants, including Procter & Gamble. Minnetonka's sales plummeted, and the price of the company's share on the stock market fell from 18 to less than 2. To make matters worse, the company had been advertising its product, Softsoap, based on the slogan "soap without the soapy mess." Because the theme focused on the advantages of liquid soap in general rather than on the particular benefits of Softsoap, it helped pave the way for competition.[16]

As we saw in Figure 4.2, a company can try to dominate a niche based on either product superiority or cost advantage. Most companies, like Minnetonka, rely on product superiority. Martin-Brower relies on cost to achieve a niche strategy. The company, the third largest food distributor in the United States, reduced its customers to eight leading fast-food chains. It met the specialized needs of these customers by stocking only their lines and positioning warehouses based on their locations.[17] As a result, the company was able to reduce the costs of its operations and provide its narrower customer base better service at lower prices.

CONDITIONS FOR SEEKING A PATHWAY TO COMPETITIVE ADVANTAGE

When should a firm seek a marketing advantage, a cost advantage, or a niche? A marketing advantage should be sought if the firm can answer an unmet need in the market place such as the need for more reliable overnight delivery, or the need for reducing companies' in-house publishing costs. Such a marketing advantage is most likely when a product is first introduced and competition has yet to enter.

A cost advantage should be sought in mature markets where sales are stable or declining. In such conditions, few new products have been introduced, so the

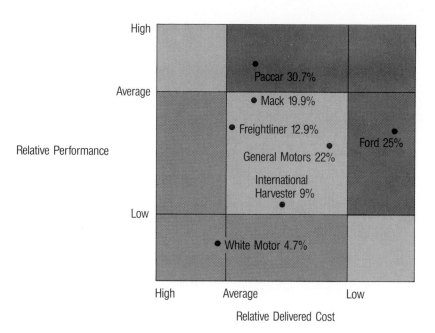

FIGURE 4.3
Relationship of Competitive Advantage to Profitability: The Heavy-Duty Truck Manufacturing Industry

Source: William K. Hall, ''Survival Strategies in a Hostile Environment,'' *Harvard Business Review* 58 (September–October 1980): 81.

most effective pathway to market-wide advantage is to lower costs and use the additional margins to either lower the price to the consumer or increase advertising expenditures. Heinz chose the latter course.

A market-niche strategy is well suited to smaller businesses who are trying to coexist with the giants. Without this strategy, Minnetonka could not have competed for a time as a small company in an industry dominated by giants. A niche strategy can also be used by larger companies who want to stake out a toehold in an industry as a basis for future growth. For example, Procter & Gamble followed a niche strategy in the soft drink market by acquiring Orange Crush and marketing it to a small, loyal segment. It viewed the acquisition as a testing ground to determine whether it should develop additional soft drink brands for a more forceful entry into the industry. It decided against further entry and divested Orange Crush in 1989.

Whether a firm gains a competitive edge through a marketing or a cost advantage, on a market-wide basis or in a particular market niche, the result tends to be greater profitability. However, a company cannot achieve advantage by one route while ignoring the other. A cost advantage is ineffective if customer needs are ignored; and a marketing advantage is worthless if it makes the product prohibitively expensive.

This principle is demonstrated in Figure 4.3, which shows the effects of a marketing and a cost advantage on profitability in the heavy-duty truck manufacturing industry. Marketing advantage is represented on the vertical axis by relative product performance, cost advantage on the horizontal axis by relative delivered cost. Seven companies are positioned on these two dimensions, with their return on investment (ROI) performance listed next to their names.

The firm with the highest return on investment, Paccar, has staked out the quality end of the market. It has almost a 31 percent return on investment. Its Peterbilt and Kenworth trucks are considered the Cadillacs of the industry. The

COMPETITIVE ADVANTAGE AND PROFITABILITY

firm with the lowest-cost position, Ford, has the next highest ROI. Thus, market advantage and cost advantage have produced the best profit performance. It is important to note, however, that neither Paccar nor Ford has ignored the other element of competitive advantage. Paccar is in an intermediate cost position, and Ford gets average ratings on product performance. Thus, competitive advantage requires not only being on top on one criterion (either marketing or cost) but also being at least average on the other.

The firms with the lowest profits, White Motors and International Harvester, have neither a distinct cost nor product quality advantage. (White Motors, the most vulnerable of the two, was subsequently acquired by Volvo.)

IDENTIFY OPPORTUNITIES FOR COMPETITIVE ADVANTAGE

Although firms may take various pathways to gain a competitive edge, these pathways are not always available, nor are they always suitable to a firm's resources. It is necessary for a company to assess a market and identify the opportunities for competitive advantage.

There are three requirements in identifying opportunities for competitive advantage: (1) *determine the attractiveness of a market* that might make it a good target for gaining competitive advantage; (2) *identify competitors' strengths and weaknesses* in the market; and (3) *identify the company's capabilities to gain competitive advantage.*

These three factors are shown as three dimensions in Figure 4.4. You may recognize Figure 4.4 as an offshoot of the marketing planning matrix described in Chapter 2 (see Figure 2.2). In that figure, a strategic window of opportunity is identified by a marketing opportunity that the firm has the resources to exploit. In Figure 4.4 a **window of competitive opportunity** is now defined by a market's attractiveness as a source of competitive advantage, by competitive weakness, and by the firm's ability to exploit such a competitive advantage. Opportunity is thus defined in a competitive context.

MARKET ATTRACTIVENESS

What determines a market's attractiveness as a source of competitive advantage? Two major factors are the intensity of competition in the market and barriers to entry.

Competitive Intensity

When competition in a market is intense, the opportunities for getting an edge over other companies tend to decrease. Minnetonka saw its competitive advantage evaporate as competition intensified; Apple may well see the same happen in desktop publishing.

Competition tends to be most intense when sales industry is stable or decreasing. Competitors are fighting over a shrinking pie. Companies no longer have the opportunity to develop superior products based on technological breakthroughs. Most product advances have been duplicated by competition, and the product is regarded as a virtual commodity.

For example, competition has become more intense in the toothpaste market as toothpaste has become more standardized. Every brand today can claim it fights tooth decay with fluorides. As a result, companies such as Colgate and Procter & Gamble have sought competitive advantage by introducing plaque-fighting toothpastes, tartar-control formulas, and pump dispensers. The net re-

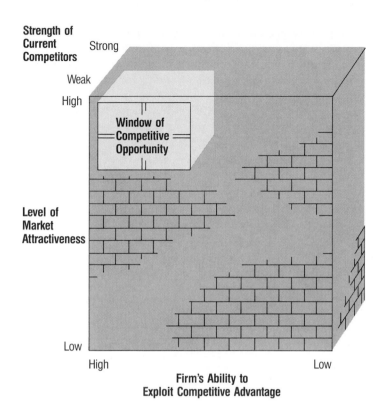

FIGURE 4.4
Identifying the Opportunity for
Competitive Advantage

sult has been to narrow the opportunities for competitive advantage, making it less desirable to introduce new brands.

Competition also becomes more intense when there are fewer opportunities to reduce cost. In mature markets such as toothpaste there is limited potential to reduce marketing or manufacturing costs because cost reductions have already been "wrung out" by long-standing brands. As a result, operating margins are narrower, and there is more intense rivalry for the limited profits available in the industry.

Barriers to Entry

Barriers to entry can be a plus if a company is already established, since they serve to protect the company from further competition, or a minus if the company is considering entry into a market. The greatest barrier to entry is the existence of a competitor with significant competitive advantage — IBM in personal computers, Xerox in copying machines, Kodak in film, Black and Decker in power tools.

At times, companies will consciously develop barriers to prevent the entry of other companies into a market. One of John Sculley's stated intentions when he joined Apple was to spend so much money advertising Apple products that the price of entry into the personal computer business would scare off newcomers.[18]

Entrenched competitors are not the only barriers to entry. In fields such as telecommunications or mineral extraction, capital requirements may be so high that they virtually preclude new companies from entering the market. Legal restrictions such as patent protection may also deter new entries. Polaroid was able to effectively block Kodak's entry into instant photography because of the patents it holds on the process. Lack of distribution facilities are another barrier. Pampers' entrenched position as the leading disposable diaper deterred other companies from entering the market because supermarkets were reluctant to devote shelf space to more than one brand. Only when Kimberly-Clark introduced Huggies with significant product improvements was P&G's stranglehold on distribution broken.

Other Factors Defining Market Attractiveness

Several other factors in addition to competitive intensity and barriers to entry affect a firm's potential for obtaining competitive advantage.[19] One is the threat of substitute products from other industries. For instance, the competitive strength of savings banks has decreased with the availability of other vehicles for saving such as money market accounts and certificates of deposit.

The bargaining power of large customers can also inhibit a firm's ability to gain competitive advantage. At times, companies sell to powerful customers who can force down prices, demand higher quality, or require more service. A large food chain like A&P or merchandiser like Sears can force their smaller suppliers to reduce prices. Such actions by larger buyers increase competitive rivalry among their suppliers and reduce profits, making the market less attractive to enter.

Similarly, the bargaining power of a large supplier might decrease a market's attractiveness for a firm. A large supplier can exert bargaining power by raising prices or dictating the terms on which the product will be sold, making it more difficult for buyers to make a profit. In the past, auto companies have exercised bargaining power over their dealers by forcing them to take additional cars and to offer higher trade-in allowances. When suppliers can exert such power, it lessens the attractiveness of a market for a firm.

COMPETITORS' STRENGTHS AND WEAKNESSES

An analysis of market attractiveness will tell a company the best markets for entry and for winning competitive advantage. But managers must go beyond an overall view of the market to determine the strengths and weaknesses of individual competitors.

There is no formula for analyzing competitors, other than to ensure that information is obtained from as wide a spectrum as possible. Certainly a company will want to evaluate a competitor's *marketing objectives*. (For example, if P&G is thinking of entering the fruit-based soft drink market, it will assess PepsiCo's sales and market-share objectives for Slice.) A firm will also evaluate a competitor's *strategic intentions*. (Will PepsiCo extend Slice's product line by introducing additional flavors?) The competitor's *market assumptions* must also be judged. (Does PepsiCo expect the demand for fruit-based soft drinks to rise?) Finally, a firm must assess the competitor's *resources*. (What are PepsiCo's capabilities for expanding Slice's market share based on its managerial, financial, production, and distribution capabilities?)

Answering these questions is difficult at best. As we saw in the last chapter, many firms have environmental scanning departments that gather competitive information from the business press, salespeople, trade sources, and marketing research. Marketing research includes surveys that evaluate consumer perceptions of competitive products, identify the strengths of those products, and uncover their potential weaknesses. Chesebrough Ponds identified a gap in the hand lotion market through research that revealed significant consumer dissatisfaction with existing brands in that these brands ignored therapeutic needs in favor of cosmetic benefits. As a result, the company came out with its highly successful Vaseline Intensive Care formula.

The most difficult areas to assess are competitors' assumptions and intentions. These can frequently be gleaned from annual reports, articles in the business press, stock reports, and speeches.

Rich as all these sources may be, an assessment of competitors' strengths and weaknesses must also depend on a manager's knowledge of the market, insight into the competitor, and intuition.

COMPANY CAPABILITIES

The third component identifying competitive advantage in Figure 4.4 is the company's capabilities. A company's strengths and weaknesses define its ability to exploit marketing opportunities and competitive weaknesses. In Apple's case, no one was more aware of the company's strengths and weaknesses than John Sculley. His *resource assessment* was that Apple was superior to IBM in technology and product superiority, but that its distribution network and promotional mix were inferior. Thus, one of his first moves was to strengthen Apple's distribution network and advertising campaign.

This type of evaluation cannot be done "off the top of the head." Sculley spent a full year studying the company and the industry, developing an intimate knowledge of computer technology, fully understanding his management, and getting to know IBM almost as well as he knew Apple before making any major moves. Whether he knew it or not, he was doing a **marketing audit** of Apple's capabilities — that is, cataloging the company's resources and needs in key areas such as production, R&D, sales, distribution, product development, and promotion to better assess his future moves.

DEVELOP STRATEGIES FOR COMPETITIVE ADVANTAGE

The next step in a firm's pursuit of competitive advantage as shown in Figure 4.1 is developing strategies to achieve competitive advantage. The need to develop strategies with an eye on competition has led marketers to draw analogies from military science. Let us first consider how these rules of warfare might apply to gaining competitive advantage, and then consider alternative strategies.

RULES OF WARFARE APPLIED TO MARKETING

One of the foremost military strategists, Lidell Hart, said that "the object of war is a better state of peace."[20] Translated into business terms, this means that the object of gaining a competitive advantage is to achieve "peaceful coexistence" with your competitors — but *on your terms*. As a market leader, *peace* means acceptance of the company's leadership position. As a market challenger, it means establishing a secure position in the face of another firm's dominance; or even displacing the firm as the market leader. As a market nicher, "peace" means being left alone to pursue profits in particular market segments.

If peace is not attainable on your terms, then the object of pursuing competitive advantage is *survival*. When Lever Brothers and P&G entered the liquid soap market, Minnetonka was no longer thinking of a niche strategy as a means of peaceful coexistence with the giants. Its goal became survival in the face of market dominance, and its eventual solution was to hook up with a larger firm that had the resources to compete with the market leaders.

A study of the greatest military minds — Clausewitz, Napoleon, von Moltke — has led marketers to borrow four principles for achieving competitive advantage: concentrate resources, take the initiative, maneuver resources, and plan with flexibility.[21]

The first principle is to *concentrate resources* where they will have the greatest effect because a firm's resources are limited. The best way to concentrate resources is not always clear. Should the firm go head-to-head with the market leader? Should it try to probe for weaknesses in the leader's position? Should it try to find select market niches? For Apple, optimal concentration of resources meant following a niche strategy to bypass direct competition with IBM. Head-to-head competition would have dissipated Apple's resources, while probing for weaknesses to attack IBM might have failed, given IBM's resources and marketing prowess.

The second principle is to *take the initiative* by acting rather than reacting to environmental changes. IBM's entry into personal computers caused a basic and unalterable change in Apple's business environment. Apple could have reacted to IBM's entry by forfeiting systems dominance and becoming another IBM compatible, or by ceding dominance of the business market to IBM and concentrating on the home and educational markets. It did neither. Once Sculley was on board, it became an article of corporate faith that Apple would be the "IBM alternative in personal computers."

The third principle is to *maneuver resources* so that overall objectives are accomplished in a coordinated fashion. In other words, "keep your eye on the ball" to ensure that all resources are directed to corporate goals rather than being deflected to secondary areas of competition. Eventually, Apple did focus its resources on its key objective of bypassing IBM in the business market while maintaining leadership in the educational market. It improved its relations with its dealers, increased its advertising budget, decreased prices for the Apple II to maintain price parity in the educational market, and developed a focused niche strategy to exploit desktop publishing and communications in the business market. These were not discrete steps; they were a coordinated plan to attain Apple's overall objectives.

Finally, the fourth military principle is to *plan with enough flexibility* to anticipate both environmental change and competitive actions. Pursuing competitive advantage in a flexible way requires an ability to foresee changes in the environment and to anticipate what competition might do. Apple, for example, must answer some key questions regarding the future market for personal computers. Is the educational market reaching saturation? If so, Apple will have to devote more resources to exploiting the business market. Will Xerox become a major player in desktop publishing? If so, Apple may have to change its strategy by cutting prices on the Macintosh or offering additional features. Will desktop communications take off? If not, what alternative opportunities does Apple foresee for the 1990s? Such questions determine future competitive strategies for Apple.

STRATEGIES FOR ATTAINING COMPETITIVE ADVANTAGE

Firms can develop strategies to attain competitive advantage on a marketing, cost, or niche basis. The application of principles of military strategy suggests two broad approaches to competition: **proactive strategies**, in which a company anticipates competitors' actions and attempts to make the first move, and **reactive strategies**, in which a company lets the competition make the major moves. In

	Proactive Strategies	Reactive Strategies
Market Leaders	Market expansion Market-share protection Preemptive actions	Reaction to competitive challenge
Market Challengers or Followers	Head-to-head competition Flanking strategies Encirclement	Follow the leader
Companies Avoiding Competition	Market niche Bypass the competition	Status quo

FIGURE 4.5
Strategies for Competitive Advantage

military terms, a proactive approach would be identified as an offensive strategy, a reactive approach as a defensive strategy.

Figure 4.5 categorizes various competitive strategies into proactive versus reactive strategies. These strategies are further divided by the firm's market position, since strategies are largely determined by whether a company is a market leader, a challenger or follower, or a company that is trying to avoid competition with the larger firms altogether.

MARKET LEADER STRATEGIES

In a few industries, there is an undisputed leader, such as Campbell Soup, with an 80 percent share of the condensed soup market, and AT&T, with over 90 percent of the long-distance telephone market. A more common situation in consumer-goods industries is what economists call an **oligopoly**, that is, an industry in which two or three firms dominate, and the actions of one firm directly affect those of another. In the soft drink industry, Coca-Cola's introduction of Tab, the original diet soda, prompted Pepsi to introduce Diet Pepsi.

Even though an oligopoly is dominated by more than one company, one firm typically has the highest market share and is acknowledged as the market leader. Thus, Coca-Cola is the market leader in soft drinks, Procter & Gamble in toothpaste, and M&M Mars in candy bars.

The three strategies in Figure 4.5 identified with a market leader are market expansion, market share protection, and preemptive actions.

Market Expansion
In **market expansion,** the market leader tries to expand demand for the product category. With a dominant share of the market for overseas calls, AT&T would clearly benefit from any increase in the demand for such calls. As a result, it has

EXHIBIT 4.2
Market Leader Strategies

Market Expansion: AT&T attempts
to increase the demand for overseas calls.

Market-Share Protection: Kellogg attempts
to retain current users through price incentives.

Preemptive Actions: DHL preempts the
overseas delivery market.

advertised using generic slogans such as "Call Japan" (see Exhibit 4.2). Coca-Cola's "Coke for Breakfast" campaign is also designed to increase demand for a product category — colas. But as we noted in Chapter 2, Pepsi's share of the cola market is almost as large as Coke's, so Coke's campaign could stand to benefit Pepsi.

Another way to expand demand is to develop new uses for a product. S.C. Johnson found a new use for its furniture wax years back when it discovered consumers using it on their cars. It repositioned the product and created the market for car wax.

In each of these cases, the market leader's brands tended to be the beneficiaries because they were the brands adopted by existing users, by new users, or for new uses.

Market-Share Protection
A market leader not only tries to expand the market; it also attempts to protect its current share of the market — **a market-share protection strategy**. Compared with other firms in the industry, a market leader has more to protect. It also should find it easier to protect its share, because the leader operates with higher margins and thus has more resources to devote to capturing customers from competitors.

Kellogg, the cereal industry's profit leader,[22] is attempting to protect its already commanding 42 percent market share not only by expanding cereal consumption, but by trying to hold on to its current customers. It uses its higher margins to support existing brands through heavy advertising and frequent couponing. (See Exhibit 4.2.)

Preemptive Actions

A market leader may take **preemptive actions** by entering a market to anticipate or discourage competitive entry. DHL, the air express company, preempted larger competitors by becoming the leader in overseas package delivery. Its ad in Exhibit 4.2 cites its preemptive strategy aimed at Federal Express and UPS in an attempt to discourage incursions by these competitors into the overseas market.

Reacting to a Competitive Challenge

As Figure 4.5 shows, market leaders might follow reactive as well as proactive strategies by responding to competitive actions. The problem with reactive strategies is that they leave the initiative to the competitor. The principle of flexibility of action calls for contingency plans to anticipate competitive moves so the company will not get caught in a reactive situation.

A good example of a reactive strategy was General Foods' response to Procter & Gamble's challenge when it introduced its Folgers coffee into the Eastern market. The competitive battle between General Foods' leading Maxwell House brand and Folgers was described by *Fortune* as follows:

> As the aggressor, P&G's coffee division is making most of the moves. But [General Foods'] troops countered quickly. When Folgers mailed millions of coupons offering consumers 45 cents off on a one-pound can of coffee, General Foods countered with newspaper coupons of its own. When Folgers gave retailers 15 percent discounts from the list price, General Foods met them head on. [General Foods] let Folgers lead off with a TV blitz that introduced tidy Mrs. Olson to all those Eastern housewives ... Then it saturated the airwaves [with its own TV advertising.][23]

Three major proactive strategies challenge a market leader: head-to-head competition, (that is, a direct frontal attack on the leader), a flanking strategy in which the challenger looks for weak spots or gaps in the leader's offerings, and an encirclement strategy in which several challenges are mounted simultaneously, both directly and on the flanks. These strategies are described as proactive in Figure 4.5 since they take the initiative in challenging the market leader. They are presented visually in Figure 4.6, with examples of each strategy. In the next few paragraphs, we will look more closely at each of these strategies, as well as the reactive strategy of following the leader.

MARKET CHALLENGER/FOLLOWER STRATEGIES

Head-to-Head Competition

Head-to-head competition is characteristic of oligopolies in which the second or third leading company might challenge the leader. For instance, Canon has challenged IBM's dominance in office typewriters by claiming that it can go one better than IBM on features such as memory capacity, type of display, and ease of use. Although the ad in Exhibit 4.3 does not name IBM, Canon's target is clear.

A head-to-head challenge is not viable unless a challenger has some competitive advantage based on product superiority or cost. Canon's advertising campaign implies it has product superiority. Bic challenged Gillette's leadership in the blades and razors market based on cost. Bic's multimillion-dollar ad campaign claimed product parity with Gillette's double-edged Trac II razor, but asked, "Why pay the difference when there's no difference?"[24] Bic's challenge demonstrates the principle illustrated in Figure 4.3: In gaining competitive advantage, a challenge based on one dimension of competitive advantage requires parity in the other. Bic attempted to develop a competitive advantage over Gillette in cost, while claiming equivalent product performance.

FIGURE 4.6
Strategies to Challenge or
Avoid the Market Leader

Source: Philip Kotler and Ravi Singh, "Marketing Warfare in the 1980s," *The Journal of Business Strategy*
(Winter 1982): 34.

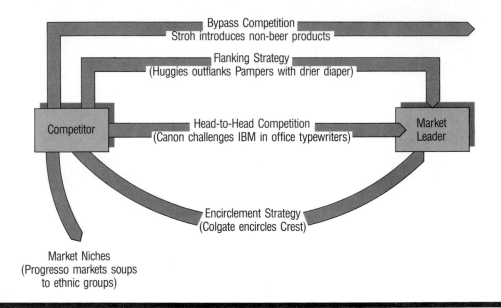

The risk of head-to-head competition with the market leader is that it invites retaliation. When General Mills challenged Quaker's Oatmeal brand in 1987 by coming out with Total Oatmeal, a vitamin-fortified brand, Quaker countered by increasing its advertising budget and extending its oatmeal line to include a vitamin-fortified offering.[25]

A further risk is that the leader's retaliation may occur in other markets. When Campbell Soup introduced its Prego Italian sauces to compete with Chesebrough Pond's Ragu sauces, Chesebrough retaliated by introducing Ragu Pasta Dinners to compete with Campbell's Franco-American line.[26]

Flanking Strategies
Because direct challenges to a market leader are so risky, many firms use the alternative of probing for weaknesses on the leader's flanks. Such **flanking strategies** involve identifying consumer needs the leader may have overlooked and offering product improvements to meet those needs. But unlike head-to-head competition, the challenge in a flanking strategy is in an area not currently contested by the marketing leader.

For example, Kimberly Clark outflanked Procter & Gamble by introducing its Huggies Dry Touch disposable diaper with improved absorbency (see Exhibit 4.3). With this new benefit, Huggies displaced Pampers as the market leader for several years. Flanking strategies have also been used for services. United Jersey, a group of banks in central and northern New Jersey, outflanked the larger banks such as Chase and Chemical by offering a new benefit, speedy loans. Their theme, "the fast-moving bank," hit a responsive chord among customers.[27]

In these cases, the challengers provided consumers a benefit that had been overlooked by the leader. But there are risks in a flanking strategy. If the leader retaliates quickly, it does not give the challenger time to establish an entrenched position. The challenger must have sufficient resources to sustain an attack. Kimberly-Clark had the resources to sustain a counterattack by Procter & Gamble when it came out with a new, improved version of Pampers. But when Seven Up, Inc. began advertising its flagship brand as caffeine-free, Pepsi and Coke introduced their own non-caffeinated brands, undermining 7UP's position. Eventually, the company went back to the "Uncola" theme it was using in the late 1970s, positioning 7UP as a cola alternative.

Encirclement Strategies

The third type of challenge, an **encirclement strategy,** is an aggressive move against the market leader on several fronts. It requires sufficient resources by the challenger to mount several attacks at the same time or in quick succession.

In the early 1980s, Colgate began an encirclement strategy meant to wrest market leadership in toothpaste from Procter & Gamble's Crest. Colgate beat Crest in introducing gels, then pump dispensers. It then opened up a new set of benefits by switching the focus from tooth decay to gum disease and introducing a plaque-fighting toothpaste (see Exhibit 4.3). Colgate's market share then climbed from 18 percent in 1980 to 28 percent in 1985, almost on a par with Crest's.[28]

But Crest counterattacked and went one better than Colgate. It was the first to introduce a tartar-control formula, and Colgate's share began slipping. Crest went back to being the undisputed market leader with a 39 percent market share.[29] Although Colgate's encirclement strategy was successful for a time, it could not maintain a sustainable advantage in the face of Crest's product improvements.

Follow-the-Leader

Figure 4.5 shows that an alternative to challenging the market leader is to take a reactive stance. **Following the leader** is a way to minimize the risks of retaliation due to a direct or indirect challenge. Such a "me too" strategy is unlikely to succeed if it only involves introducing carbon copies of leading brands. A market follower must provide some advantage to consumers, whether in service, location, convenience, or price.

A follower strategy is characteristic of capital-intensive firms that produce standardized items such as steel, aluminum, paper, or fertilizers. Price competition tends to be unprofitable since a price cut will generally be copied, leaving everyone with lower profits. Therefore, the typical strategy is to follow the leader in pricing and attempt to obtain a competitive advantage in service and delivery.

But there are risks in a follower strategy. What if the market leader is pricing at an unprofitable level or offering the wrong services. To quote the vice-president of marketing at Compaq Computer; "To focus too much on the competition means you're relying on them to do their marketing job right. We'd rather make our own decisions."[30]

Many companies seek profits by avoiding competition. They look for targets of opportunity that are unlikely to attract other companies, or that will give them

STRATEGIES FOR AVOIDING COMPETITION

EXHIBIT 4.3
Strategies Challenging the Market Leader

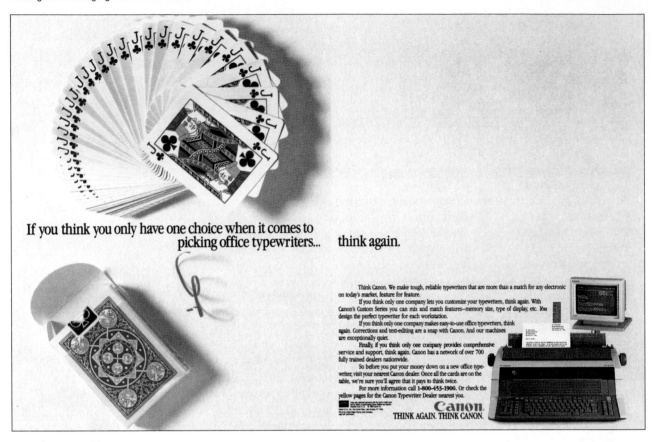

Head-to-Head Competition:
Canon challenges IBM.

enough time in a protected niche to insure profits before competitors come in. Figure 4.5 names two proactive approaches for avoiding competition — a market-niche strategy and a strategy that seeks to bypass competitors. These strategies are depicted visually in Figure 4.6. A reactive approach that avoids competition tries to maintain the status quo.

Market Niche

As we saw in Figure 4.2, one of the primary pathways to competitive advantage is to develop market niches. Such a niche strategy entails pursuing markets that are too specialized or too small to attract the leaders. There are several alternative means of implementing such a strategy. One is to focus on a particular *customer segment*. Although Progresso markets soups, it avoids direct competition with Campbell by directing its appeals to particular ethnic groups. Sun Microsystems and Apollo Computer have established a niche selling high-performance work stations; that is, networks of microcomputers used to generate sophisticated

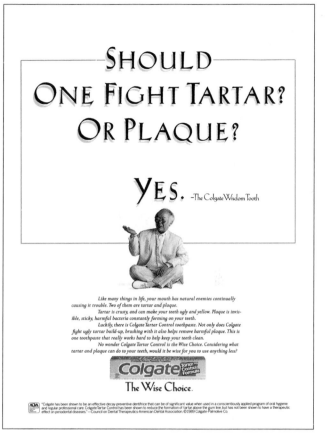

Flanking Strategies: Huggies outflanks Pampers.

Encirclement Strategy: One component of Colgate's attempt to encircle Crest.

graphics and design. By 1988, however, the work station market was profitable enough to attract IBM and DEC.[31]

Another market niche strategy is to focus on a particular *price segment*. Hewlett-Packard, for instance, specializes in high-quality, high-priced hand calculators, thus avoiding direct competition with leaders such as Texas Instruments. A third strategy is to focus on a *geographic area*. Coors beer established a strong regional base in the midwest, building a loyal following. Only when it went national did it lose its niche advantage, opening itself up to direct attack by Budweiser.

On the surface, market-niche strategies may seem similar to a flanking strategy. There is a difference in emphasis, however. While a flanking strategy tries to take advantage of a competitor's weakness on an industry-wide basis, a niche strategy avoids competition by focusing on a market segment. But as we noted earlier, the risk of a niche strategy is that the segment might become profitable enough to attract the industry leaders.

Bypassing the Competition

A second proactive strategy for avoiding competition is to bypass competitors. A company can bypass its competitors by going into unrelated product lines or by entering noncompetitive geographic areas. For instance, Stroh Brewery is finding it increasingly difficult to compete with Anheuser-Busch and Miller, and has had to shut down its biggest plant. Stroh's strategy has been to develop drinks other than beer in small market segments, including a malt-based cooler, a soft drink with 70 percent juice and 30 percent sparkling water, and a nonalcoholic malt beverage while maintaining its current beer line.[32]

Status Quo

A more reactive way to avoid competition is to maintain the **status quo** in an industry. This "don't rock the boat" approach avoids confrontation. Gillette and Schick seemed to be following a status quo strategy in the early 1980s. One industry analyst noted, "It's like, 'Hey, let's both do business and make a good buck and not bother each other.'"[33]

Such a strategy is appealing to these companies because it reduces the costs of competing with each other. But if a status quo strategy is proved to be the result of a direct understanding between companies, it can be regarded as involving collusive practices that are illegal under the antitrust laws.

ANTICIPATE COMPETITIVE RESPONSES

The last step in the process of gaining competitive advantage is anticipating competitive responses. A company must always second-guess a competitor's responses to its strategies. Anticipating what competitors will do defines a proactive approach, since projected competitive responses influence the company's strategy.

An example is Lever Brothers' introduction of Snuggle fabric softener to compete with P&G's Downy in 1985. Snuggle was a parity product offered at a lower price.[34] Lever's strategy had to be conditioned on the response it expected from P&G. If Lever had expected P&G to meet its price immediately, it would not have introduced the brand. If P&G had seemed likely to introduce a lower-priced fabric softener to outflank Snuggle within the first three years after introduction, Lever might have looked at operating margins more closely to see if there was room for a subsequent price cut. If it predicted no specific response from P&G in the first three years, however, Lever would have interpreted this as a clear signal to introduce Snuggle.

A company can use the same approach as that in Chapter 3 (Table 3.1) to estimate the best strategy based on projected competitive responses. The approach would require a company to list (1) its alternative strategies, (2) possible competitive responses, (3) the chance these responses will occur, and (4) the profit impact of company strategy and competitive response. Using the procedure described in Table 3.1, a company can then estimate the expected value of each of its strategies and choose the strategy with the highest profit potential.

SUMMARY

1. How can a firm establish advantages over its competitors?
There are three broad pathways to competitive advantage: market-wide product

or service superiority, market-wide cost leadership, and a market-niche strategy. A company seeking product superiority tries to do a better job than competitors in meeting customer needs in the total market. Product superiority can be obtained by providing a better product, and/or doing a better job in positioning, promoting, and distributing it.

Cost leadership can be gained by reducing production or marketing costs below those of competitors. This gives a company the option of reducing prices or plowing higher operating margins back into advertising and promotions. A firm following a market-niche strategy tries to establish a product or cost advantage in a particular niche as a means of avoiding direct competition with larger companies in the industry.

2. *How can marketing opportunities be identified for establishing competitive advantage?*

Companies identify opportunities for competitive advantage by analyzing a market's attractiveness, competitors' strengths and weaknesses, and their own strengths and weaknesses. A market is attractive to a potential entrant if competitive intensity is low and there are few barriers to entry. A marketer analyzes competitors' strengths and weaknesses by evaluating their objectives, strategies, marketing assumptions, and resources. A company analyzes its own strengths and weaknesses in the same way.

3. *How can principles of military science be applied in developing strategies to win competitive advantage?*

A study of military science has led marketers to borrow four key principles to achieve competitive advantage: (1) concentrate resources where they will have the greatest effect; (2) take the initiative by acting rather than reacting to environmental changes; (3) maneuver resources so that overall objectives are accomplished in a coordinated fashion; (4) plan with flexibility (contingency plans) to anticipate environmental change and competitive actions.

4. *What strategies can be implemented to establish competitive advantage?*

Strategies for competitive advantage can be categorized into proactive (offensive) strategies and reactive (defensive) strategies. The type of strategy to be selected will depend on the position of the firm in the market place — leader, challenger, follower, or nicher.

Market leaders tend to pursue strategies of market expansion, market-share protection, or preemptive actions to prevent competitors from entering new markets. Market leaders may also follow a reactive policy of waiting for a competitive challenge before taking action.

Market challengers pursue offensive strategies involving head-to-head competition with the market leader or flanking attacks that probe for gaps in the leader's offerings. They also pursue strategies of encirclement when they attack simultaneously (or in quick succession) on several fronts. A market follower pursues a reactive strategy of following the leader's initiative.

Companies can also gain competitive advantage by avoiding competition. Companies following a market-niche strategy avoid competition by targeting resources to profitable segments that leaders are unlikely to pursue. Companies can also try to bypass competition by seeking markets that are not closely related to those the leader is in. A company taking a more reactive stance avoids competition by trying to maintain the status quo — a "don't rock the boat" approach.

KEY TERMS

Competitive advantage (p. 88)
Competitive analysis (p. 91)
Market niche (p. 91)
Marketing advantage (p. 91)
Cost advantage (p. 91)
Economies of scale (p. 93)
Window of competitive opportunity
  (p. 96)
Marketing audit (p. 99)
Proactive strategy (p. 100)
Reactive strategy (p. 100)

Oligopoly (p. 101)
Market expansion strategy (p. 101)
Market-share protection strategy
  (p. 102)
Preemptive action (p. 103)
Head-to-head competition (p. 103)
Flanking strategies (p. 104)
Encirclement strategies (p. 105)
Follow the leader strategies (p. 105)
Status quo strategy (p. 108)

QUESTIONS

1. What do we mean by competitive advantage? What are the alternative means of achieving competitive advantage?

2. What were Apple's competitive weaknesses when IBM entered the personal computer market? How did IBM exploit these weaknesses?

3. John Sculley's competitive philosophy regarding IBM was described as looking for emerging markets to avoid a head-to-head confrontation with the industry leader.
   a. How did Sculley implement this philosophy?
   b. Did his actions exploit IBM's weaknesses?

4. One marketing analyst, commenting on John Sculley's strategy of looking for emerging markets that do not directly compete with IBM, said

   > That's smart. They're making good money on desktop publishing. And desktop communications will probably take off. But, and this is a big but, if IBM comes in, they [Apple] could get blown out of the water. The signs are already there, with a possible link up of an IBM PC with a laser printer. What does Apple do then if things really start getting tough in their "emerging markets?"

   a. Do you agree with this assessment of what might happen if IBM enters desktop publishing?
   b. What are Apple's options if IBM does enter this market?

5. A marketing manager for a line of household cleaners commented on the steps described in Figure 4.1 to evaluate the potential for gaining competitive advantage. He said

   > It looks good on paper. But in practice, competition won't give us the time to go through a formal competitive analysis to decide where and how to get competitive advantage. If a competitor comes out with a new ad campaign, increases its couponing, or introduces a special price promotion, you have to look at it and decide how you're going to react. If you go through all the steps suggested in your figure, it may be too late to do anything about a competitor's actions.

   a. Do you agree? Why or why not?

6. Under what circumstances is a company more likely to pursue a strategy of (1) product superiority, (2) cost leadership, or (3) market niche to achieve competitive advantage? What are the relative benefits of pursuing each of these pathways to competitive advantage?

7. What are the risks of pursuing competitive advantage based on cost? Based on a market-niche approach?

8. A company following a low-cost strategy to gain competitive advantage has two options: One is to undercut competition on price (as Texas Instruments did in the hand calculator market). The other is to maintain price at competitive levels and put higher margins into advertising (as Heinz did in packaged foods).

   a. When is each strategy more likely to be used?
   b. What are the risks?

9. P&G's divestment of Orange Crush probably required an assessment of (1) market attractiveness, (2) competitors' strengths and weaknesses, and (3) its own strengths and weaknesses in the soft drink arena. What key questions did P&G probably ask in these three areas in deciding to divest Orange Crush?

10. Did Apple effectively apply the four principles of warfare cited in the text to gain competitive advantage? If so, how?

11. Scripto has decided to challenge Bic's leadership in disposable lighters by introducing a line of lighters from 69 cents to 99 cents. One marketing analyst feels that Scripto is likely to fail because "Bic makes a quality product and its distribution system is far superior to anyone else's."[35]

    a. What must Scripto do to be successful in its attempt at head-to-head competition with Bic?
    b. What are the risks?

12. What are the differences between a (1) preemptive strategy, (2) flanking strategy, and (3) market-niche strategy? What types of companies are most likely to pursue each strategy? Why?

13. Pepsi mounted a successful head-to-head attack against Coca-Cola with its Pepsi Challenge advertising campaign.

    a. What risks did Pepsi run in going head-to-head with Coke?
    b. Did these risks materialize?

14. P&G has found its market dominance challenged by a series of flanker attacks — by Kimberly Clark in introducing an improved disposable diaper, by Colgate in introducing a gel and then a plaque-fighting toothpaste, and by Lever in introducing liquid detergent. Why do you suppose P&G has been a target for these flanking attacks?

CASE 4.1

SODA WAR

Source: Reprinted by permission of *Forbes* magazine from "The Soda War," by Richard L. Stern *Forbes*, May 4, 1987, pp. 82–83. © Forbes Inc.

At just 31, Sophia Collier is co-founder with Connie Best, 33, of American Natural Beverage Co., marketer of the wildly successful Soho Natural Soda, which started at nothing in 1977 and will gross $30 million this year. But Collier noticed something was wrong during a visit last August to her main supplier, a plant in Havre de Grace, Md., then owned by Tetley Tea, which made most of Soho's sodas. Though Soho, which sells 12 flavors in 33 states, was then the biggest customer of the soft drink plant, Collier was startled to discover that the plant was testing a variety of natural soda formulas for St. Louis-based Anheuser-Busch Co. More: Plant officials were anxiously awaiting an official visit from none other than the great Budweiser beer baron, August (Auggie) Busch III himself.

Sniffing a proverbial skunk, Soho Soda a quick month later shifted most of its production from Havre de Grace — just as Auggie Busch bought the entire plant. But Collier claims Soho was not quick enough to keep Busch from grabbing Soho Soda's recipes and customer lists. The plant is now turning out Anheuser-Busch's own "natural soda," which it calls Zeltzer Seltzer.

On top of that, Collier charges, Anheuser-Busch began pressuring independent beverage distributors to stop carrying Soho's sodas. At the same time, the beverage giant was rolling out a national marketing campaign pitching Zeltzer Seltzer as "Something Utterly New."

New? Zeltzer Seltzer, from labels to flavors, is strikingly similar to Soho Natural Soda. Not similar are the ingredients: Soho uses natural fruit juice, Zeltzer a cheaper fruit distillate. But the Zeltzer label carries the same checkerboard pattern on a diamond-shaped background, just like Soho. There is the same shadowed script lettering, with the flavor set out in a bordered oval. "Confusingly similar," Sophia Collier wrote in a letter to Auggie Busch, demanding he change the packaging. Anheuser's big-gun New York law firm, Skadden, Arps, Slate, Meagher & Flom, replied that the "assertions" were "without merit."

The situation has all the trappings of melodrama, with Collier and Best trying to survive against the full weight of a $7.6 billion company. The childhood friends from Brooklyn, N.Y. began concocting a soft drink with no artificial flavoring or coloring in their kitchen a decade ago. They distributed the soda from the back of an old Jeep to stores in Manhattan's artsy and increasingly high-rent Soho district. In the last three years, with a lot of hard work plus $3 million in backing (for 28% of the company) from influential investors that include the Rockefeller family, Soho has improved from $400,000 in sales to $20 million in 1986, with distribution through 10,000 outlets in 33 states.

Soho is firing back at Anheuser-Busch with former Watergate attorney Richard Ben-Veniste, whose law firm is suing the Budweiser brewer in U.S. District Court in Manhattan to get Zeltzer Seltzer pulled from stores. Soho contends, among other things, that Anheuser-Busch is violating New York's unfair-competition statutes, which prohibit a new product from using trademarks or packaging that is similar enough to an existing product to confuse consumers.

Loftily, an Anheuser-Busch spokesman says the company never comments to the press on lawsuits.

With all its problems these days — with payoffs and with product flops — it is little wonder Anheuser is clamming up. Though enormously successful in beer, Anheuser-Busch has so far failed trying to diversify into other beverages. One product, Route 66 Root Beer, never went anywhere. Another, Chelsea, a malt-based nonalcoholic drink, was withdrawn after nuns and nurses, among others, protested that it was an attempt to turn adolescents into beer guzzlers.

More recently, Anheuser misjudged the market with Baybry's, a champagne-based cooler that was too expensive compared with wine coolers. Another, Dewey Stevens, a low-calorie wine cooler, is suffering from a glut of products in that market. LA, the company's elaborately publicized low-alcohol beer, has also not worked. "People either want alcohol or they don't," concludes Manny Goldman, a Montgomery Securities analyst.

All this may explain why Anheuser is pushing Zeltzer Seltzer so hard, to the point of underpricing Soho by about 15 cents a bottle. But Anheuser may again have misunderstood a market. Natural soda is aimed at affluent drinkers who care little about price, says Jessie Meyers, publisher of *Beverage Digest*, the industry bible.

Something seems seriously amiss in St. Louis these days.

1. What are Soho's competitive strengths and weaknesses in the natural soda market? Anheuser-Busch's strengths and weaknesses?
2. Did a competitive window of opportunity exist for Anheuser Busch in natural sodas based on the criteria in Figure 4.4?
3. The chapter talked about the risks to smaller companies of following a niche strategy when larger companies enter the market. Based on this article, what are the risks to larger companies of market entry into niches dominated by smaller companies such as Soho?

NOTES

1. "Apple Finally Invades the Office," *Fortune*, November 9, 1987, pp. 53–64.
2. "Apple Computer's Counterattack Against IBM," *Business Week*, January 16, 1984, p. 78.
3. *Fortune*, November 9, 1987, p. 53.
4. "Apple Cracks the Business Market," *Fortune*, August 17, 1987, p. 10.
5. "Apple Uses New Marketing Strategy to Take a Slice of Competition's Pie," *Marketing News*, September 12, 1988, p. 7; and *Apple Computer, Inc., 1986 Annual Report*, p. 11.
6. "Apple's Comeback," *Business Week*, January 19, 1987, pp. 84–89.
7. "Shedding His Shyness, John Sculley Promotes Apple — And Himself," *The Wall Street Journal*, August 18, 1988, pp. 1, 8; and "Apple's Bite Is Back," *Marketing & Media Decisions*, March 1987, p. 85.
8. "IBM: Still Trying to Go to School," *Business Week*, August 17, 1987, p. 44.
9. "John Sculley: Marketing Methods Bring Apple Back," *Advertising Age*, December 31, 1984, p. 1.
10. Ibid., p. 22.
11. "Sculley's Lessons from Inside Apple," *Fortune*, September 14, 1987, pp. 109–119.
12. George Day, *Strategic Market Planning: The Pursuit of Competitive Advantage* (St. Paul: West Publishing Company, 1984), pp. 27–28.
13. "High Stakes at the High Chair," *Marketing & Media Decisions*, October 1986, p. 67.
14. "How Gallo Crushes the Competition," *Fortune*, September 1, 1986, p. 28.
15. Michael E. Porter, *Competitive Strategy* (New York: The Free Press, 1980), p. 44.
16. "Minnetonka's Revenge," *Forbes*, November 19, 1984, pp. 266, 268.
17. Porter, *Competitive Strategy*, p. 40.
18. *Marketing & Media Decisions*, November 1984, p. 54.
19. See Michael Porter, *Competitive Advantage*, (New York: The Free Press, 1985), Chapter 3.
20. B. Liddell Hart, *Strategy* (New York: Praeger, 1967), p. 351.
21. See William A. Cohen, "War in the Marketplace," *Business Horizons*, March–April 1986.
22. "Kellogg Still the Cereal People," *Business Week*, November 26, 1979, p. 80.
23. "Why Folgers Is Getting Creamed Back East," *Fortune*, July 17, 1978, pp. 68–69.

24. "How Bic Lost the Edge to Gillette," *The New York Times,* April 11, 1982, p. F7.

25. "More Snacking at Quaker," *Adweek,* June 29, 1987, p. 32.

26. "Nestle Prospers by Avoiding Head-On Clashes with Its Competition," *Sales & Marketing Digest,* August 1986, p. 2.

27. "Marketing Warfare," *Marketing Communications,* December 1985, p. 28.

28. "Colgate's Offensive Heats Up Tartar-Control Toothpaste War," *The Wall Street Journal,* August 20, 1987, p. 15; and "Colgate Puts the Squeeze on Crest," *Business Week,* August 19, 1985, p. 40.

29. "P&G Pumps Crest with New Promotion," *Advertising Age,* June 29, 1987, p. 61.

30. "Forget Satisfying the Consumer — Just Outfox the Other Guy," *Business Week,* October 7, 1985, p. 58.

31. "IBM and DEC Take on the Little Guys," *Fortune,* October 10, 1988, p. 108.

32. "New Product Innovators Find Winning Formulas," *Marketing Communications,* February 1988, p. 38; and "And Then There Were Two?" *Forbes,* May 19, 1986, pp. 64, 66.

33. *The New York Times,* April 11, 1982, p. F7.

34. "Lever and P&G Wage a Good, Clean Fight," *Sales & Marketing Management,* June 3, 1985, pp. 47–49.

35. "Sparks Fly in Scripto's Battle to Dump Bic as Lighter King," *The Wall Street Journal,* May 2, 1985, p. 33.

In the early 1980s it looked as if Kellogg lost its snap, crackle, and pop. The leading cereal maker in the country began losing sales to competitors and to lower-priced private brands. New-product introductions were few and far between. It drew heavy criticism from investors for not diversifying like General Mills and Quaker did into more glamorous areas such as fast foods and upscale retailing. Among marketing analysts, the company was cited as being production-oriented — that is, producing cereals first and finding out what consumers wanted later.[1]

Then, in four short years, Kellogg achieved a startling turnaround by zeroing in on health-conscious adults. Its first big step was to reposition an existing product, All-Bran, in 1984 by touting its high fiber content as helping to prevent cancer.

After 1984 Kellogg introduced a barrage of successful new products, and it did so with a surprising amount of savvy in segmenting health-conscious consumers. In 1985 it introduced All-Bran Extra Fiber to extend the appeal of All-Bran to the high-fiber segment, and targeted Special K cereals to a low-cholesterol segment. In 1986 it introduced Nutri Grain cereals, targeted to fitness-oriented young adults, and positioned Product 19 as a dieters' cereal.[2] In 1987 it introduced Nutrific, a combination of barley, bran, almonds, and raisins targeted to consumers wanting a natural cereal.[3]

By 1988 Kellogg had all the health bases covered. In the process, it propelled the growth rate of the cereal industry from an uninspiring 2 percent a year to a respectable 5 percent, a growth rate three times as great as the average grocery product. It increased its share of the cereal market from 38 percent to 43 percent. And its profits were by far the highest in the industry.[4] General Mills, Quaker, and General Foods quickly followed Kellogg's lead with their own lines of cereals aimed at health-oriented adults.

How did Kellogg achieve the turnaround from lackluster to exciting? It started in 1982, when the company faced a basic decision. Should it stick to cereals or diversify? With the help of McKinsey & Co., the management consulting firm, Kellogg took a close look at the potential growth rate for cereals. The long-term outlook was dim. Baby boomers were being weaned away from cereals, regarding them as kid stuff. The decreasing birth rate after the baby-boom generation also meant that fewer kids would be eating cereals. But Kellogg made a simple discovery that had been made by no other cereal manufacturer — baby boomers were becoming increasingly obsessed with finding an alternative to high-fat, high-cholesterol breakfasts.[5]

Kellogg developed a twofold strategy for sticking with cereals: first, to go after the health-oriented baby boomers before anyone else did, and second, to tap the neglected potential for cereals in international markets by trying to change breakfast eating habits. Today, close to one-third of Kellogg's sales come from international markets.[6]

Once Kellogg began to pay more attention to the consumer, it did so wholeheartedly. It doubled its expenditures on new-product development and began to use marketing research more consistently to better understand needs and motives behind cereal consumption. These efforts allowed Kellogg to better meet consumer needs by systematically segmenting the health-oriented market and positioning new products to high-fiber, dieter, fitness, low-cholesterol, and natural-ingredient segments.

Today, Kellogg can look back with satisfaction and realize it made the right decision. It stayed with cereals by recognizing that the American consumer is on a health kick. ■

● ● ●

IMPORTANCE OF CONSUMER BEHAVIOR

In Chapter 1, we defined marketing as all activities directed to identifying and satisfying customer needs. According to this definition, understanding the customer is central to identifying marketing opportunities and to developing strategies for pursuing these opportunities.

UNDERSTANDING CONSUMER NEEDS

Successful marketing strategies hinge on identifying consumer needs. Pepsi-Cola succeeded with Slice because it recognized a need among adults for a nutritious alternative to colas. Kodak was successful with its lithium batteries because it recognized the consumer's need for longer-life batteries to accommodate electronic devices such as laptop computers and portable cassettes. Apple was able to maintain its competitive advantage in the educational market with its Apple II by filling a need for a user-friendly machine that had superior graphics. And Kellogg reversed its decline by recognizing the need among baby boomers for more nutritious breakfast foods.

In contrast, insufficient understanding of the consumer will put a company at a competitive disadvantage, sometimes severe enough to spell disaster. We saw that Avon began a long decline because it did not recognize the negative impact of more working women on door-to-door selling. Similarly, Polaroid and RCA could be cited for a certain corporate arrogance in being driven by their existing technology rather than by consumer needs when they introduced instant movies and videodiscs, products that consumers simply did not need.

CONSUMER BEHAVIOR AND MARKETING STRATEGY

If marketers are to understand their customers, they require marketing research to identify consumers' needs, their perceptions of existing brand offerings, their brand attitudes, and their intention to buy. As we will see in this chapter, terms like *needs, perceptions, attitudes,* and *intentions* have specific meaning that largely determine what the consumer will purchase. Marketers must know these variables if they are to identify opportunities to better meet customer needs. How could Kellogg have defined an opportunity as basic as adult nutritional cereals?

EXHIBIT 5.1
Advertising Based on
Consumer Health Needs

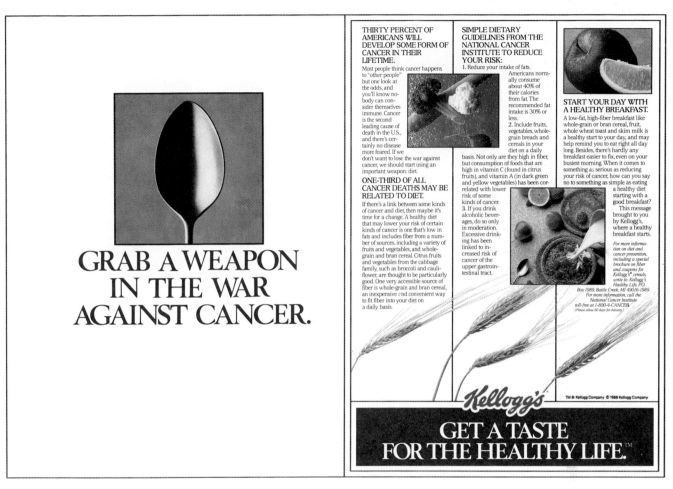

By doing the research that confirmed the baby boomers' desire for more nutritional breakfast foods.

As a result of this type of knowledge, Kellogg developed effective strategies for segmenting the health-conscious market into groupings with somewhat different needs — a diet segment, a fitness segment, a low-cholesterol segment, and so forth. It then developed and positioned separate products to meet the needs of each segment and advertising strategies to convey the benefits of each new product to the target group. For example, it was the first company to establish a link between a food product and cancer prevention in a controversial advertising campaign for All-Bran based on the theme, "At last, some news you can live with."[7] Although the campaign came under attack for implying that eating high-fiber cereals could prevent cancer, it did get the message across that more fiber is better for you. A more general statement by Kellogg of the cancer-prevention benefits of high fiber cereals is shown in the ad in Exhibit 5.1.

Kellogg also developed other components of its strategy to meet the needs of health-conscious consumers. A box of Nutrific comes with a small booklet on nutrition and fitness. Even the colors of the packaging for Kellogg's adult cereals were developed to play up the health positioning — pure white or glowing honey-colored.

Each component of Kellogg's strategy — segmentation, positioning, advertising, and packaging — was developed with the single-minded purpose of appealing to the consumer's health and nutritional needs. Each component of strategy was tested on consumers once it was developed. Product tests determined consumer reactions to new cereals, package tests evaluated their responses to alternative designs, and advertising tests determined the effectiveness of alternative ads in communicating product benefits.

CONSUMERS AND ORGANIZATIONAL BUYERS

In Chapter 1 we cited two types of customers, final consumers and organizational buyers. Final consumers buy for themselves or their family. They are the last link in the chain of creating and distributing a product. Organizational buyers purchase for an organization.

Because there are important differences in the purchasing behavior of these two types of buyers, a chapter will be devoted to each. This chapter deals with consumer behavior and the next, organizational buyer behavior.

A MODEL OF CONSUMER BEHAVIOR

Figure 5.1 presents a simple model of consumer behavior. The marketing organization interacts with the consumer, as shown by the double arrow in Figure 5.1. The organization first seeks information on consumers' needs and their reactions to the company's products and strategies. It then introduces products and supporting strategies (advertising, sales promotions, pricing and distribution strategies) to consumers to influence them to buy.

The consumer will react to the company's offerings and supporting strategies based on three sets of variables. First is the consumer's **psychological set,** or predisposition to react positively or negatively toward a brand, product, or company. For example, a consumer who views cereals as kids' food would probably have a negative psychological set toward the product. The consumer's psychological set is determined by his or her needs, perceptions, and attitudes. The importance of these variables in influencing purchasing behavior will become clear when we define them later in this chapter.

The second set of factors that affect purchasing decisions are the consumer's personal *characteristics:* demographics, lifestyle, and personality. For instance, a consumer's age (a demographic factor) and emphasis on fitness (a lifestyle factor) are likely to influence his or her purchase of cereals.

Third are *environmental factors,* which are as broad as the effects of our culture (cereals are a traditional breakfast food in American culture but not in most other countries) and as specific as family influences on purchasing behavior (a parent forbidding a child to eat sugar-coated cereals.)

Figure 5.1 shows that the consumer's psychological set, characteristics, and environment are the inputs into a decision process that determines what the consumer buys.

In the remainder of this chapter, we will look more closely at the components of consumer behavior shown in Figure 5.1. We will start with the consumer's decision process because it gives us a broader perspective on consumer behavior.

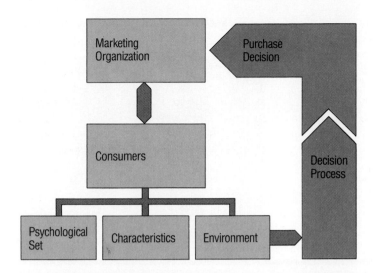

FIGURE 5.1
A Model of Consumer Behavior

THE CONSUMER'S DECISION PROCESS

Consumer decision making is not a singular process. The decision to buy cereals is very different from the decision to buy a car. Figure 5.2 categorizes consumer decisions on two dimensions, the extent of decision making and the consumer's involvement with the purchase. The first dimension distinguishes between decision making and habit. In the process of decision making, a consumer evaluates various brands and searches for information about them. Habit, on the other hand, causes the consumer to buy the same brand repeatedly with little or no brand evaluation and information search.

The second dimension distinguishes between high and low involvement purchases. By involvement, we mean the importance of the product decision to the consumer. The more socially significant the product (clothing) or the greater the risk in its purchase (medicine), the higher the consumer's involvement with the purchase.

Categorizing consumer decisions on these two dimensions produces the four types of decision processes shown in Figure 5.2: complex decision making, brand-loyalty, variety- seeking, and inertia.

HIGH-INVOLVEMENT PURCHASES

Purchases important to the consumer, whether expensive or not, are **high-involvement purchases**. Some require complex decision making whereas others are prompted by brand loyalty.

Complex Decision Making

Complex decision making is associated with a high-involvement purchase that is important to the consumer and requires a great deal of thought and deliberation. A consumer is usually highly involved in a decision to buy a home, a car, or a computer because of the financial outlay and the importance of the product. In making a decision for these types of products, the consumer will search for information and carefully compare a number of alternatives to determine which can best fill his or her needs.

FIGURE 5.2
Types of Consumer Decision Processes

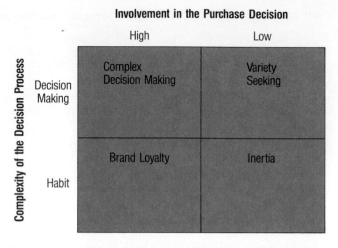

FIGURE 5.3
Complex Decision Making

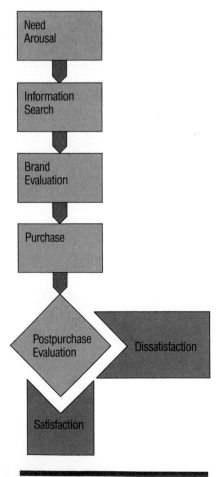

Figure 5.3 shows the process of complex decision making. Consider a business school student who is thinking of purchasing a personal computer. She considers investing in a computer when she realizes she can never finish her work by the time the school's computer lab closes (need arousal in Figure 5.3). Her parents agree to split the cost with her, so one of the first things she does is investigate prices (information search). She quickly realizes she can buy a good computer for between $1,200 and $2,000. With further information search, she realizes she wants to buy a laptop model because of its portability and convenience. But she is concerned about a smaller screen and keyboard compared to the desktop computers she is used to. She is also concerned that the size of the floppy disk for a laptop is smaller than that for the desktop computers she is using at school. A knowledgeable friend, however, assures her that the smaller size will soon become standard for desktop computers as well.

Our student visits several computer stores to check out models (further information search). She is particularly impressed with three brands, Toshiba, Zenith, and NEC, based on the size of the screen and the keyboard. But she also finds that the speed at which commands are executed are slower than the school's desktop computers. After comparing the three makes further, she concludes that the Toshiba's screen is the clearest and that the commands for the machine are executed somewhat faster. It is also the most expensive of the three machines, costing about $300 more than the Zenith or NEC (brand evaluation in Figure 5.3). She decides it is worth the additional cost and buys the Toshiba.

The last step in Figure 5.3 is postpurchase evaluation. A consumer evaluates the brand while consuming it. Continued satisfaction will lead to repurchase and, eventually, to brand loyalty. Dissatisfaction will lead the consumer to switch to another brand. In the process of assessing the level of satisfaction or dissatisfaction, a consumer might experience **dissonance**, that is, doubts whether the right decision was made. After purchasing the Toshiba, our student realizes the screen is not as bright as she thought and the speed of the computer is slower. She begins wondering whether she should have bought the Zenith or NEC for $300 less. Such doubts are particularly likely when the decision is important and there is little difference between brand alternatives. If such dissonance is reduced, the consumer will be satisfied with the purchase; if not, dissatisfaction will occur.

An important objective for marketers is to try to reduce a buyer's dissonance after the purchase. Themes like "Aren't you really glad you bought a Buick" are a direct attempt to assure the buyer that the right decision was made.

Brand Loyalty

Brand loyalty is the result of continued satisfaction with a product that is important to the consumer. It causes repeat purchases made with little thought or deliberation but with high involvement. For example, the consumer might be loyal to a particular make of automobile because of consistent satisfaction with it over the years. Involvement with this type of purchase is high because an auto is an important symbol of achievement, but the complexity of the decision is low. The only decision is when to buy, not what to buy.

Consumer packaged goods may also generate involvement and brand loyalty. The outcry over Coca-Cola's plans to eliminate the original formula for its flagship brand clearly shows that soft drinks are high-involvement purchases for many consumers. Brand loyalty occurs in a high-involvement situation because it requires a positive commitment toward the favored brand. If a store is out of a consumer's usual brand, a measure of involvement and commitment is whether the consumer would buy an alternative or go to another store. Camel cigarettes' old slogan, "I'd walk a mile for a Camel," advertised the involvement of loyal smokers with the brand. To many consumers Coca-Cola was not just another soft drink. It was a symbol of the culture and environment they grew up in, and a brand they would walk a mile for.

In making **low-involvement purchases**, the consumer does not consider the product important or risky enough to give it a great deal of thought and consideration. Most products we buy are not particularly involving — toothpaste, batteries, gasoline, frozen vegetables.

When consumers are not involved with a product, they do not actively search for information about it. They use various strategies to minimize the time and effort in making a decision. One strategy is to buy the most familiar product on the store shelf. Another is to buy the lowest-priced brand or a leading brand that is being sold on a price deal or with coupons.

Figure 5.2 shows two types of low-involvement purchases: variety seeking and inertia.

LOW-INVOLVEMENT PURCHASES

Variety-Seeking Decisions

In **variety seeking**, the consumer tries a diversity of brands to create some interest in the purchase and avoid boredom. A decision process is involved in deciding on the brand to buy, but involvement with the product is low. One study found that consumers who buy products such as salad dressing, potato chips, or cookies switch from one brand to another to try something new and different. These consumers see enough difference between brands of salad dressing or cookies to warrant seeking information about alternatives and to evaluate them.[8]

Inertia

Consumers seeking variety examine alternative brands and make a decision based on a minimal amount of information. In contrast, consumers buying by **inertia** choose the same brand time and again. Items purchased by inertia are unimportant products that are bought frequently. There is no search for novelty or consideration of alternative brands. It simply is not worth the time and trouble to make a decision every time the consumer has to buy. A consumer buying table salt might choose to buy Morton's because it is simpler to buy a recognizable name than to go to the time and trouble to examine alternative brands and make a decision. There would be no novelty in looking for another brand.

HABIT

The level of involvement is one dimension in classifying consumer decisions. Another is the complexity of the decision process. Figure 5.2 makes the distinction between decision making and habit, the basic difference being a process of brand evaluation and information search in decision making, and the absence of such a process in habit. Since we have already discussed decision making in the high-involvement decision section, we will focus on habit here.

By **habit,** we mean an almost automatic response when a need arises, resulting in the purchase of the same brand. For example, a consumer who is out of antacid tablets buys the same brand with little thought or information search. As Figure 5.4 shows, the only elements in buying by habit are need arousal, purchase, and postpurchase evaluation. Thus, habit is the simplest purchasing process.

Both inertia and brand loyalty are classified as habit in Figure 5.2. With brand loyalty, the consumer is committed to a favored brand, and is willing to go elsewhere if a store does not have it. With inertia, there is no commitment or strongly favorable attitude toward a brand. If a store is out of stock, the consumer will just buy an alternative brand. With brand loyalty, the consumer tries to optimize his or her satisfaction; with inertia, the consumer is quick to accept second best.

Whether it reflects brand loyalty or inertia, habit is the result of consumer **learning**, in which past experience influences the consumer's future actions. A consumer satisfied with a particular brand learns that the brand is likely to produce the same level of satisfaction on the next purchase. As a result, the consumer buys that brand again.

Consider a consumer who has bought Coca-Cola since he was a teenager. Every purchase of Coke reinforced his satisfaction with the brand, so today, when he wants a soft drink, he automatically thinks of Coke. He buys the brand almost automatically anytime he is out of stock.

Now assume our consumer buys Coke after the company decided to change the formula. He decides he does not like the new taste. It is too sweet. Figure 5.4 shows that his dissatisfaction leads him to a process of decision making in which he begins to evaluate other brands. Thus, not only can decision making lead to habit when the consumer is satisfied, habit can lead back to decision making when the consumer is dissatisfied.

Habit is on one end of a continuum and complex decision making on the other. In between is **limited decision making,** which does not require extensive information search but is not automatic, either. For example, in choosing a deodorant, a consumer may evaluate several brands but may not search extensively for information or try to find the best brand available.

STRATEGIC IMPLICATIONS OF DECISION PROCESSES

Marketers develop very different strategies based on the type of decision process they think consumers are likely to use in selecting a brand.

Habit versus Decision Making
Different advertising, distribution, and pricing strategies are appropriate for products typically purchased by habit than for those purchased as a result of decision making. In the latter case, advertising is likely to focus on brand attri-

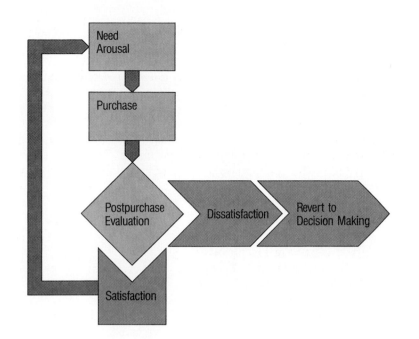

FIGURE 5.4
The Process of Buying by Habit

Source: Henry Assael, *Marketing Management, Strategy, and Action* (Boston, MA: Kent Publishing Co., 1986), p. 133.

butes and features. Auto ads center around gas mileage, four-wheel drive, roominess, and comfort. Ads for over-the-counter pharmaceuticals emphasize quick relief, no side effects, and recommendations by doctors. In contrast, advertising for products purchased by habit aims primarily at reminding the consumer to buy and to reinforce postpurchase satisfaction.

A market leader has a decided advantage if it is in a category purchased by habit, because many of its consumers are likely to be brand loyal. The market leader's objective will therefore be to remind consumers of the brand and reassure them. For example, Coke's former advertising slogan, "It's the real thing," served as a reminder to drink Coke and reassured Coke drinkers by implying that there is no real alternative to Coke. Seven-Up, Inc. tried to break Coke's and Pepsi's hammerlock on the market by advertising a new feature — no caffeine. The strategy was to get loyal Pepsi and Coke users to stop buying those brands by habit and to consider a non-cola alternative.

The purchase process also helps determine distribution strategies. Brands purchased by habit should be readily available because they are frequently purchased. Therefore, widespread distribution is necessary. Hershey is a classic example of a product relying on extensive distribution. Until the 1970s, it did no advertising, relying solely on its availability in almost every food store in the country to maintain its market leadership. Products purchased by complex decision making are bought less frequently. Often, these are technically complex items requiring the help of a salesperson and subsequent service. Consumers are more likely to shop around for such items. As a result, they are more likely to be distributed on a selective basis.

Pricing strategies also differ according to the purchase process. If a brand is purchased by habit, the best way a competitor can get a brand-loyal consumer to try something else is to offer a price deal, special sale, or a free sample. Such promotions are less effective with complex decision making. Consumers are less likely to switch because of a temporary price deal.

EXHIBIT 5.2
Ads for High-Involvement and Low-
Involvement Products

Ad for Low-Involvement Product

Ad for High-Involvement Product Using
Informational Approach

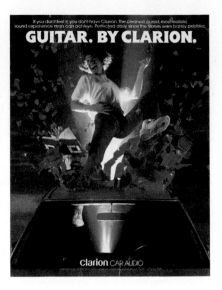

Ad for High-Involvement Product Using
Emotional Approach

High- versus Low-Involvement Decisions

Marketing strategies will also differ depending on the degree to which the consumer is involved with the product. If there is little involvement, consumers are less likely to pay attention to advertising. In this case, ads should focus on a simple message, such as "Bring more shower to your shower" for Irish Spring soap (see Exhibit 5.2), and emphasize one key benefit like freshness. Trying to advertise more product benefits might lose the consumer's attention because of lack of interest.

Ads for high-involvement products should convey more information about product benefits, using an informational or emotional approach. Product benefits can be communicated based on emotions by showing good feelings and sympathetic scenes, or by attempting to enhance the consumer's self-image. Benefits can also be communicated using an informational approach by directly describing product attributes. The ad for the Coustic car stereo in Exhibit 5.2 takes an informational approach. It details the characteristics and performance results of the product. The ad for the Clarion car stereo is clearly emotional.

Product-positioning strategies are also likely to differ based on the consumer's involvement with the product. Uninvolved consumers will not search for the best product; they will look for an acceptable product. Products that minimize problems rather than maximize benefits will catch their attention. Crest achieved its position as the leading toothpaste by advertising that it solves a problem — cavities — rather than maximizes a benefit (like whiter teeth).

Involved consumers will take the time and trouble to look for the best product available to meet their needs. In such cases, a product should be positioned as maximizing a benefit. Kellogg realized that adults would be more involved with cereals if they were positioned as meeting health and nutritional needs. It effectively changed cereals from an uninvolving children's product to an involving adult breakfast food by advertising nutritional benefits.

THE CONSUMER'S PSYCHOLOGICAL SET

One of the three major factors influencing a consumer's purchase decision is his or her psychological set, defined earlier as the consumer's positive or negative predispositions toward a particular brand or company. Most consumers will have some familiarity with a brand or company unless it is totally new. The purchase process does not begin with a clean slate.

The consumer's mind set is formed by his or her needs, perceptions of a brand or company, and attitudes toward that brand or company. These three variables are shown in Figure 5.5. **Needs** are forces that direct consumers toward the achievement of certain goals. For example, a young executive in the market for a car needs one that provides good gas mileage, is stylish, and will be seen as a status symbol among friends and business associates. **Perceptions** are the way consumers organize and interpret information about objects like brands and companies. Based on advertising, friends' and neighbors' comments, and her own driving experiences, our consumer perceives the BMW as a stylish, status-oriented car that provides good gas mileage. In the process of organizing and interpreting information about the BMW, she develops a **brand image** of the car, that is, an overall perception of the brand.

Attitudes are the consumer's tendency to evaluate an object in a favorable or unfavorable way. Our consumer has a positive attitude toward the BMW because she perceives it as meeting her needs. If the BMW outranks other cars on her important need criteria (good gas mileage, stylish, status associated), then she is likely to buy a BMW if it is economically feasible. Our consumer's needs and perceptions thus interact to determine brand attitudes and **purchase intentions**. Since the BMW was *perceived* as meeting our consumer's *needs, attitudes* toward the car were positive and resulted in an *intention to buy.*

Marketers will try to influence the consumer's psychological set by identifying needs, defining need segments, and influencing brand images and attitudes.

Need Identification

A company can gain a competitive advantage by defining unmet consumer needs. Coca-Cola defined the need for a diet cola among male cola drinkers, paving the way for the success of Diet Coke. Pepsi identified a need for a more nutritious non-cola alternative among adults, and successfully established the juice-based soft drink market with Slice.

One approach to identifying unmet needs is through what is known as **need-gap analysis,** in which consumers' needs are identified by using the concept of an *ideal brand.* The ideal represents what the consumer wants. Consumers are then asked to rate various brands on key attributes. If no brand comes close to the ideal, a *gap* in needs exists that could be filled by a new brand.

Assume it is 1982, and Kellogg does a need-gap analysis of the cereal market. It asks consumers to rate cereals on key attributes such as natural ingredients, nutritional value, calories, sweetness, and taste. It also asks consumers how they would rate their ideal cereal based on these attributes. Say that the majority of adult consumers rate their ideal cereal as being highly nutritious and composed of

FIGURE 5.5
The Consumer's Psychological Set

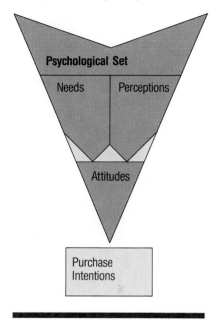

STRATEGIC APPLICATIONS OF THE CONSUMER'S PSYCHOLOGICAL SET

natural ingredients. But they rate the leading cereal brands low on these attributes. These consumers are expressing a need and are saying that there is no brand on the market that currently fills that need. As a result, Kellogg has identified an important opportunity.

Need Segmentation

Consumer needs are the most important basis for identifying target segments. In determining the need for nutritious cereals, Kellogg identified a broad segment of health-conscious consumers. But such a definition of the market was too broad to target specific brands and advertisements. So Kellogg defined more specific market segments such as a low-cholesterol segment, a fitness segment, and a low-calorie segment.

Once Kellogg identified the market by needs, it targeted product development, advertising, and packaging strategies to these need segments. The effectiveness with which it targeted its product line based on need segmentation is shown in Exhibit 5.3.

Brand-Image Formation

Advertisers try to influence a consumer's brand image by positioning a brand so that it communicates desired benefits. Kellogg positioned All-Bran by communicating the benefits of high-fiber content, it positioned Just Right by touting the benefits of natural ingredients. Kellogg was successful in establishing an image for its total line of adult cereals, an image linked to specific nutritional and health needs.

A major issue for a company is when a brand's image should be changed; that is, when the brand should be repositioned. Philip Morris repositioned Miller High Life after acquiring Miller Brewing in the early 1970s. High Life was positioned as "the champagne of bottled beer," conveying a high-quality image to a small segment of occasional beer drinkers willing to pay a premium price. Philip Morris changed the image to a heftier brew for the mass market with a campaign portraying blue-collar workers in positive situations associated with beer drinking. The campaign propelled High Life to the second best-selling brand in the market.

Trying to change a brand's image can sometimes spell trouble for a company. Cadillac began making its cars smaller in the 1970s, after the energy crisis, to improve fuel efficiency. But a smaller Cadillac contradicted the brand image of Cadillac's core market. As Cadillac's director of marketing said, "You develop an image over an 83-year period and it's hard to change."[9] Many loyal Cadillac customers wanted larger, luxurious cars, even if they were gas guzzlers. As a result, sales began to slide, and Cadillac lost about one-fourth of its share of the luxury-car market. In an effort to recoup, the company brought back its king-size cars.

Brand Attitude Formation

Marketers develop strategies to either reinforce brand attitudes (an adaptive strategy) or to change them. Kellogg reinforced positive attitudes toward its cereal line as it introduced additional nutritionally oriented cereals. Philip Morris succeeded in changing attitudes toward Miller High Life when it linked the brand's image to heavy beer drinkers.

Marketers frequently use an adaptive strategy by introducing a line extension of a successful brand. The introduction of Diet Coke was built on the positive

For the High-Fiber Segment

For Dieters

For Nutrition-Oriented Consumers

For the Natural-Ingredients Segment

EXHIBIT 5.3
Targeting Kellogg's Adult
Cereals to Need Segments

associations consumers have with Coca-Cola. The company had avoided using the Coca-Cola name for other brands for fear it would dilute the position of its flagship brand. Its decision to introduce Diet Coke — and later Cherry Coke — reflected a change in management's thinking. The success of both products proved that the positive attitudes toward one product could be effectively leveraged toward others.

Several cosmetics companies, such as Brut, Ralph Lauren, and Lancome, have mounted strategies to change men's reluctance to use skin care products. Their task, in the words of one executive, is to convince men "that there is nothing wrong with taking care of your skin. Your face is your calling card." [10]

CONSUMER CHARACTERISTICS

Another set of factors that influence purchasing behavior in Figure 5.1 are the consumer's characteristics. While the consumer's psychological set describes needs, perceptions, and attitudes toward specific brands, consumers' characteristics such as age or occupation are not brand-specific. Yet the age or occupation of a consumer could be just as important as perceptions and attitudes in influencing brand-purchasing decisions.

Marketers study three types of characteristics to better understand consumers shown in Figure 5.6: demographics, lifestyles, and, to a lesser extent, personality.

DEMOGRAPHICS

We identified demographics as the objective characteristics of the consumer in Chapter 3, and cited broad demographic trends such as the greater proportion of working women, the increasing proportion of singles, and the greater number of older consumers. Marketers also study more specific data on the demographic characteristics of current and prospective purchasers of their brands. In such cases, demographics are used to segment markets, to identify targets for new products, and to buy media to reach these target segments.

Market Segmentation

Companies use demographics to find a particular niche in the market. Kellogg is positioning most of its cereals by age segment — sugared cereals for children, fitness-oriented cereals such as Nutri Grain for young adults, and health-oriented cereals such as All Bran for older consumers. Avon is segmenting the market by income class and occupation, positioning its expensive Giorgio and Deneuve perfume lines to more affluent career women, and its traditional Avon line of cosmetics to middle- to lower-income women.

Identifying Targets for New Products

Demographics are also used to describe targets for new as well as existing products. In the 1970s General Foods tested a new-product concept, a low-calorie breakfast strip designed as a more nutritious substitute for bacon. Research showed that two demographic segments were most likely to buy the product: older, downscale consumers and younger, more affluent consumers. The older consumers were more likely to emphasize cholesterol content and health, the younger consumers, calories and nutrition. Such a split could suggest two ad campaigns for the same product, or two separate products to appeal to each segment.

Media Selection

Demographic characteristics also provide guidelines for media selection. Once the demographic characteristics of a segment are identified, marketers try to select media that are more likely to be read or viewed by that segment. For example, in 1986 Lee introduced a Shawnee line of denim and corduroy jeans targeted to trend-conscious 14- to 19-year olds. The company's mix of media was based on

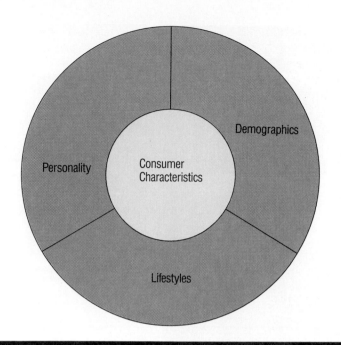

FIGURE 5.6
Types of Consumer Characteristics

this demographic definition of the target. Lee introduced the line with commercials on MTV, the music video station, and ads in magazines such as *Glamour, Seventeen,* and *Young Miss* for the female line, and *Sport* and *Rolling Stone* for the male line.[11]

Lifestyle characteristics are represented by a consumer's activities, interests, and opinions. Activities may be related to work, social events, entertainment, and the community. Interests may focus on the home, recreation, fashion, and food, to name a few areas. Opinions might concern the individual's job and personal achievements.

LIFESTYLES

There is no standard definition of lifestyle variables as there is for demographics. Lifestyle categories are defined based on the nature and potential positioning of a product. A company positioning a detergent might identify segments such as compulsive housekeepers, homebodies, and achievement-oriented consumers because these lifestyles are likely to be related to attitudes toward detergents. A company segmenting a line of perfumes might develop different positionings to self-indulgent, socially active, or inner-directed segments.

As with demographics, lifestyles can identify broad trends, such as the change in male-female roles and increasing emphasis on fitness and nutrition noted in Chapter 3. Lifestyle information has also been used more specifically to develop strategies for brands, particularly in defining market segments, positioning products, and selecting media.

Market Segmentation
The most widely used basis for segmenting consumers by lifestyle is through the VALS (Value and Life Style) program. Chapter 3 cited VALS as identifying three broad lifestyle groupings based on the values and interests of American consumers; outer-directed, inner-directed, and need-driven consumers.

EXHIBIT 5.4
Ads Targeted to Inner-Directed and
Outer-Directed Consumers

One advertising agency that was trying to win Avon's business pointed out that Avon's highbrow ads featuring the theme, "The art and science of beauty," were geared to inner-directed consumers (those who emphasize achievement and self-expression). The ad agency felt that Avon's target segment should be outer-directed consumers (those who emphasize tradition and group influences). For example, an Avon ad showing a high-fashion model gazing at beauty products inside geometric shapes just would not fly with outer-directed consumers.[12]

When Avon shifted its advertising business to the agency that gave it this insight, its new commercials, targeted to outer-directed consumers, featured young women looking like the girl next door eating ice cream bars, sunbathing, or jogging, with the theme, "Look how good you look now."

Product Positioning

The VALS groupings have been used to position products as well as to segment markets. MasterCard International took a look at American Express's "Don't leave home without it" campaign and realized that it was aimed at outer-directed consumers based on the idea of what other people would think about someone who does not have an American Express card. The company decided to distinguish itself from American Express by appealing to inner-directed consumers. Celebrities such as Robert Duvall and Angela Lansbury pitched individualism based on the theme, "Master the possibilities." (See Exhibit 5.4.) "Life's too short to worry about impressing other people," says Angela Lansbury in one commercial. "Don't talk to me about impressions. Give me possibilities."[13]

The fact that more consumers were becoming inner-directed reinforced MasterCard's positioning strategy. The MasterCard executive who conceived of the campaign described its rationale: "The consumer wants to be perceived as being his or her own person, capable of making choices. Substance and freedom have replaced style and status."[14]

Media Selection

Lifestyle characteristics can also be used to select media. For example, the National Turkey Federation tried to increase the consumption of turkey by appealing to all three VALS groups using different media. It appealed to need-driven consumers by advertising bargain cuts in *True Confessions* because readers of that magazine are downscale and older. Traditional cuts of turkey associated with holiday dinners were advertised to outer-directed consumers in *Better Homes and Gardens* because this segment is more likely to read it. And the most expensive gourmet cuts were targeted to the more affluent inner-directed consumers who read *Food and Wine* and *Gourmet* magazines.

Laurel Cutler has been called the most powerful woman in the advertising industry.[15] Why? Because she has the knack to understand consumer lifestyles and where they are heading. The implications of her insights for marketing strategies could be profound. That is why she counts among her clients the top executives of Campbell Soup, Colgate-Palmolive, Chrysler, and Citicorp.

LAUREL CUTLER — LIFESTYLE FUTURIST

Source: © Giorgio Palmisano. New York City.

In the mid 1970s, for example, she correctly predicted the death of mass marketing. She saw consumers becoming more savvy, more value-oriented, smarter shoppers based on greater access to information. She noted that these consumers might buy in the most expensive as well as in the cheapest stores looking for value.[16] Their search would be for distinctive merchandise that would single them out as being independent and different, that would answer the question, "Who am I?"

The shift to a "me" orientation and the greater focus on independence and individuality that followed confirmed her acumen. Consumers were no longer content to buy the most popular, the bland, the undifferentiated. They began looking for the distinctive. And that spelled trouble for many companies. It spelled trouble for Procter & Gamble's reliance on its market leaders like Crest toothpaste and Pampers' disposable diapers. Challengers could come in and steal market share by offering improvements such as gel in toothpaste or greater absorbency in diapers. And the lumbering giants that relied on the mass market were slow to react. As Cutler notes, until the early 1980s a company like General Foods would think only in terms of brands that could make $200 million. Now, with the fragmentation of the market, they would be happy to identify $50 million opportunities.[17]

Cutler began her career as a *Washington Post* reporter and novelist. She entered the field of advertising by writing copy for J. Walter Thompson, then the largest advertising agency in the world. But she quickly tired of copywriting and struck out on her own to better understand what is behind consumer needs.[18]

Rather than rely on formal research to develop her insights into future lifestyles and consumer actions, Cutler goes directly into the marketplace and interacts with consumers one-on-one. What does she see for the future? The Europeanization of the American consumer. The United States is reaching the age of limits — limits on consumption, limits on growth. The European consumer has already learned to live with limited growth and limited resources, and the American consumer will have to learn the same lesson. Cutler also sees the erosion of the purchasing power of the middle class, and a greater emphasis on value and on wise purchasing decisions as a result.

The key to the future, in Cutler's words, is to "help our customers find something to hang onto, to sink roots into. One hundred percent quality, real service, unique design, style."[19] ■

PERSONALITY

Personality variables are those characteristics that reflect consistent, enduring patterns of behavior. Compulsive, aggressive, or compliant behavior, for example, reflects deep-seated predispositions formed in childhood. Personality characteristics have not been used as widely as demographics and lifestyles in developing marketing strategies, possibly because these variables are complex and not well understood. But there have been some applications.

One such application is based on the notion that consumers assign brands and products personality characteristics much as they assign people personalities based on their knowledge of them. Computers are described as friendly, beer as masculine, furniture as intimate. These are all human traits assigned to products. One advertising agency used these types of associations to better understand why McDonald's is more popular than Burger King. It found that people described McDonald's as friendly and nurturing. Gimmicks such as Ronald McDonald and kiddie playgrounds further this nurturing feeling. In contrast, Burger King was described as aggressive, masculine, and distant.[20]

Personality variables have also occasionally been used to define market segments. A study by a large life insurance company identified a target segment of purchasers as "dominant people who like to have control over situations with which they are involved. They tend to be self-reliant and will follow the counsel of experts only if it meets demands for accuracy and reliability."[21]

This personality profile suggests that life insurance advertising to this segment should use an informational approach. An emotional approach such as fear of leaving a family destitute would be unlikely to work because this group prides itself on control over its future and has probably planned ahead for financial security. Consumers in this segment are seeking information on how to better provide for future security; they do not need to be convinced that life insurance is a good idea.

ENVIRONMENTAL INFLUENCES

The final set of factors influencing consumer behavior in Figure 5.1 is the consumer's social and cultural environment. Influences range from broad cultural forces issuing from the society in which the consumer lives to more specific group and family influences. These are categorized into five major groups in Figure 5.7: culture, subculture, social class, reference group, and family.

Culture represents the widely shared norms and values learned from a society and leading to common patterns of behavior. The common patterns of behavior in American society are often reflected in what products consumers buy and the importance they place on those products. The fact that cereal is the traditional breakfast food for children is specific to American culture, possibly the product of an emphasis on a hearty breakfast dating back to pioneer times.

Three American cultural values that have seen particular emphasis in marketing strategies are individualism, materialism, and youth.

The emphasis on *individualism* has manifested itself in the search for distinctive clothing or furniture that reflects one's personality. As mentioned earlier, we often buy important products as extensions of our self-image, and such an extension often demands an expression of the individualism that is emphasized in American society.

Another dominant value in American culture is *materialism*. The traditional emphasis on materialism waned in the 1960s and 1970s as many Americans became increasingly skeptical of business and government because of the Vietnam War and Watergate. But a series of yearly surveys of first-year college students sponsored by the American Council on Education found a rising trend to materialism since the early 1970s. The 1987 survey found that more than three-fourths of the students surveyed feel that being financially well off is an essential goal, the highest proportion ever recorded by the study. Those who gave priority to developing a meaningful philosophy of life were the lowest proportion ever recorded.[22]

Another value emphasized in American society is *youth*. Ads for deodorants and cosmetics typically show young models, even though the products are also directed to middle-aged adults. The ad for Sure deodorant in Exhibit 5.5 is an example.

CULTURE

In Chapter 3 we defined subcultures as groups of people having certain values in common that distinguish them from society as a whole. We also cited the increasing attention marketers are giving to the two largest subcultural groups in the United States — blacks and Hispanics. Diverse companies such as AT&T, McDonald's, Ford, and Procter & Gamble have directed advertising campaigns for their products and services to black consumers. They have advertised most frequently on radio stations targeted to blacks, in black-oriented national magazines such as *Ebony* and *Essence*, and in specialty magazines such as *Black Enterprise*.

Marketers have taken two approaches in appealing to blacks. One is to develop specific campaigns that foster black identity. The other is to use the same advertising campaign for blacks and whites, but to place some ads in black media. The ad for Delta Airlines in Exhibit 5.6 is directed specifically to the black male. The ad for American Airlines does not use an ethnic appeal, but has been run in black media.

Marketers have taken the same two approaches in appealing to Hispanic-Americans. One is to use the same ads for the general market in Hispanic media such as the 112 Spanish-speaking local TV stations in the United States and Spanish-language magazines like *Vanidades*, using Spanish copy in these ads. For example, Philip Morris runs the same ad depicting the Marlboro cowboy in general-circulation magazines and in Spanish-language magazines. The other

SUBCULTURE

FIGURE 5.7
The Consumer's Environment

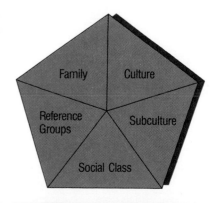

EXHIBIT 5.5
Emphasis on Youth in American Culture

approach is to target specific appeals to Hispanics. For instance, Anheuser-Busch develops different advertising for different segments of Hispanic consumers. Commercials for Budweiser targeted to the Puerto Rican community are set in a disco and feature salsa rhythms; commercials to consumers of Mexican origin are set in a rodeo to mariachi music; commercials to the Cuban segment take place on a private boat because Cubans are the most affluent Hispanic group.[23]

SOCIAL CLASS

Social classes define broad consumer groupings according to their degree of prestige and power in society. In our society, prestige and power are defined by income, occupation, and education. In general terms, these criteria define the "haves" and "have nots." The most common way to categorize social classes are as upper, upper-middle, lower-middle, and lower.

The social class we belong to influences what we buy. The upper class, composed of the social elite and top managers tend to buy conservative clothing and avoid showy purchases. The upper-middle class, composed of professionals, managers, and some small businesspeople are career-oriented and emphasize educational attainment. They stress quality and value in their purchases and are more likely to be comparison shoppers. Lower-middle class consumers, composed of white-collar employees and well-paid blue-collar workers, are more home- and family-oriented and buy with an eye to conformity and respectability. The lower class is composed of lower-paid blue-collar and unskilled workers.

Marketers have used social-class differences to define their advertising campaigns. Power and dominance have been used in advertising across different social classes. For example, working-class consumers (lower-middle and lower

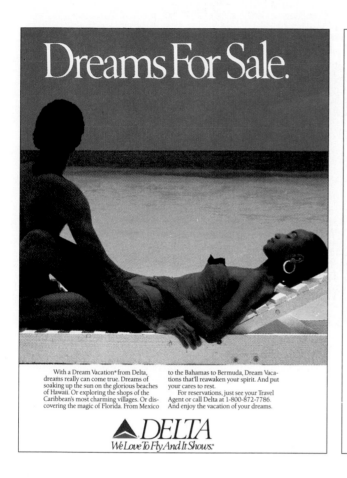

class) seek an escape from everyday drudgery. They express a need for power by buying more powerful cars.[24] The "power and passion" of the Cherokee Jeep ad in Exhibit 5.7 is an expression of freedom and independence targeted to this group.

In contrast, members of the professional and managerial group (upper and upper-middle class) express the need for power in terms of getting ahead in their occupations. The ad for the Macintosh in Exhibit 5.7 also advertises power. But in this case, it is "the power to be your best" in terms of getting ahead. Whereas the power appeal for the Cherokee is the independence of getting away from work, the power appeal for the Macintosh is one of getting ahead in work.

REFERENCE GROUPS

Consumers are also influenced by **reference groups,** that is, groups that serve as a reference point for individuals in defining their needs and developing opinions. In deciding what to buy, a consumer usually relies more on the opinions of reference groups than on information from ads or salespeople. Advertisers have a vested interest in providing only positive information about a brand; reference groups do not.

The most important reference groups are an individual's peer group (friends, neighbors, business associates) and family. Marketers frequently portray these

EXHIBIT 5.7
Power Themes in Advertising Directed to
Different Social Classes

Power Theme Directed to Professional and
Managerial Class

Power Theme Directed to Working-Class
Consumers

groups in advertising. Ads for beverages as diverse as Hawaiian Punch, Lowenbrau beer, and Dry Sack sherry all show friends drinking the brand in a congenial setting. Fast-food chains such as McDonald's and Burger King usually advertise in a family-related context.

Reference groups exert three types of influence on consumers: informational, comparative, and normative. **Informational influence** means the group is the source of believable information about brands and companies. **Comparative influence** means the group gives consumers something to compare their beliefs, attitudes, and behavior against. The greater the similarity between a consumer's opinions and those of his or her reference group, the greater the comparative influence is of that group. **Normative influence** means the group persuades members to conform to its norms. Sometimes groups use rewards and punishments to gain compliance. The family can reward children with praise and punish them with a scolding; social groups can reward members with compliments on their clothing or behavior and punish them by ignoring their words and actions.

To take advantage of the importance of reference groups, marketers try to duplicate these three forms of influence in advertising (see Exhibit 5.8). Marketers attempt to exert informational influence by using expert spokespersons who tell consumers about product features and performance. Such testimonials are accepted only to the degree that consumers view the spokesperson as being an expert on the product. Thus, information from Julius (Dr. J) Erving, the basketball star, about Dr. Scholl's foot powder is likely to be viewed as credible.

Marketers attempt to exert comparative influence by using a "typical consumer" approach to persuade consumers that people similar to themselves have chosen the advertised product to fill their needs. The ad for Hartz Blockade flea repelent in Exhibit 5.8 is an example of this approach.

Normative influence is wielded by depicting social approval from reference-group members. Praise from friends for good sherry or a comfortable auto ride are examples. The American Airlines ad in Exhibit 5.8, links on-time reliability with the reward of business people coming home to their families more quickly. Normative influence can also be used more as a threat than as a reward. For example, the Hart Schaffner & Marx ad for men's suits says that even though the right suit might not ensure success in the job, the wrong suit could lead to failure.

Reference groups influence consumers through **word-of-mouth communication,** that is, face-to-face communications between group members. Such personal communication is the single most powerful influence on consumer behavior. One researcher summarized 6,000 consumer case studies and found that nearly 80 percent of all purchases can be traced to word-of-mouth influence.[25]

The importance of such communication is illustrated by the quick success of Corona beer in the United States. The brand, a little-known Mexican import until the mid 1980s, did no advertising. It was sold on a limited basis and became the "in" beer among the young, affluent, urban set based on word-of-mouth communication. The beer's popularity spread like wildfire and caught the company by surprise. It had to quickly increase capacity and its distribution network to allow for expanded distribution into other areas. By 1987 Corona was the second largest imported beer in the United States next to Heineken.[26]

A central element in word-of-mouth influences is the role of **opinion leaders,** that is, individuals regarded by the reference group as having expertise and knowledge on a particular subject. Marketers are interested in identifying opinion leaders because if they can be convinced to buy a product, it will most likely be accepted by others in their reference group.

THE FAMILY

The most important reference group is the family. Spouses influence each other's choice in clothing. Parents influence the college choice of their children. Children influence parents' choice of computers or stereo equipment because they often know more about these products.

The family often makes group decisions for certain purchases, such as a new home or a summer vacation spot. In these group decisions, family members will play one or more roles as follows: The **information gatherer** collects product information and is likely to be the most knowledgeable about what sources of information to consult. The **influencer** establishes the criteria by which brands are compared and is instrumental in influencing others in the family. The **decision maker** is responsible for the final selection. The **purchasing agent** may also be the decision maker or may just be an "order taker." The **consumer** could be the whole family or one or more members of it. It is the consumer who determines the level of satisfaction with the decision and influences future decisions regarding the brand or activity.

Family influences occur between husbands and wives and between parents and children. Marketers are interested in who is likely to have the most influence on purchasing decisions so they can develop advertising and select media targeted to that person.

EXHIBIT 5.8
Showing Reference Group
Influences in Advertising

Informational Influence

Comparative Influence

Normative Influence Using Implied Reward

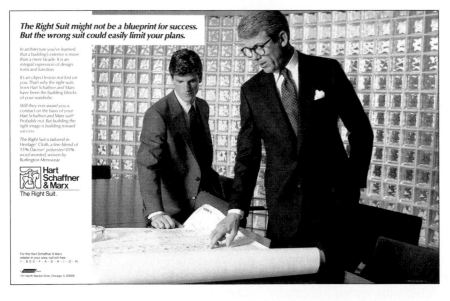

Normative Influence Using Implied Threat

Husband-Wife Influences

Traditionally, wives have had the most influence in buying foods, toiletries, and small appliances, while husbands have dominated decisions for automobiles, insurance, and financial services. But as we saw in Chapter 3, these traditional patterns have changed. The increasing power of working wives have given them a greater say in decisions for financial services, insurance, and automobiles.

Car makers are beginning to recognize these changing family roles by targeting more of their effort to women. In the mid 1980s, Chevrolet began targeting 30 percent of its ad budget to women. But even then, much of this advertising was geared to fashion and style rather than to performance. One study found that 65 percent of women felt misrepresented in auto advertising that implied they were more interested in appearance than in technical data.[27]

On the other side of the coin, greater involvement by husbands in home and child care have given them more influence over purchases of foods and household items.

Parent-Child Influences

Most consumers learn how to be consumers as children. This process of **consumer socialization** is perhaps the most important legacy of the family in marketing terms. Parents can try to teach children to be more effective consumers by helping them to distinguish fact from fantasy in advertising, by trying to show them the relationship between price and product quality, and by teaching them how to be effective comparison shoppers.

In recent years, children have acquired more purchasing influence than ever before. Since many children come from dual-earning and one-parent families, they often have to do the shopping and take care of the house when they come home from school. As a result, the process of consumer socialization is occurring much faster than it used to. Children have to learn to be consumers because they are often the purchasing agents for the family. This recognition led Kraft Inc. to tailor more of its food advertising to girls 12 to 19. It places ads for convenience dinners in magazines such as *Seventeen*.

Many marketers try to influence the consumer socialization of children by getting them to recognize company and brand names early, even if these companies do not sell children's products. Black & Decker has licensed its name to a line of toys that are miniature versions of its small appliances. One company executive reasoned, "Youngsters don't buy Black & Decker drills. But they might someday, if they start out on toy Dustbusters."[28]

Such strategies might be effective in capturing a child's loyalties at an early age. But they must be closely monitored by parents to avoid exploiting children, especially since children are more easily influenced by a marketer's appeal than adults.

The Family Life Cycle

Another dimension of family influence is the **family's life cycle**, which is the progression of a family from formation to child-rearing, to middle age, and finally to retirement. The stage of the life cycle influences purchasing behavior. For example, newly married couples are more affluent because both frequently work and do not have the expenses of child care. They are good markets for travel, entertainment, autos, and durable goods. As children arrive, discretionary income decreases as expenditures on appliances, furniture, and infant products increase.

As children grow, financial pressures continue, especially if they enter college. Discretionary income then increases sharply as children leave home. At this point, husband and wife are probably at the peak of their earning potential, yet expenses have decreased. Such middle-aged "empty nesters" are excellent markets for travel, sporting goods, apparel, and home-improvement items.

In the later stages of the life cycle — older married couples and widows and widowers — discretionary income starts decreasing, as these individuals begin to live off fixed income pensions and annuities. Expenditures increase for drugs, medical services, hobby-related items, and leisure products.

As an example of targeting products by stage of the life cycle, banks and brokerage houses have targeted financial services according to the desire for growth in equity in the early phases of the life cycle, for short-term appreciation (and willingness to take risks) in the middle years when discretionary income is greatest, and for protection of equity in the later years when husband and wife may be living on a fixed income.

SUMMARY

1.   How do consumers go about making purchasing decisions?
Consumers first determine their needs, then search for information on brands that might fill their needs, next evaluate alternative brand choices, and finally choose the brand that they feel will most likely fill their needs.

Decisions will vary depending on the extent to which such information search and brand evaluation takes place. They will also vary depending on the degree of involvement of the consumer with the brand. Complex decision making involves extensive information search and brand evaluation. Where brand loyalty exists, information search is minimal. In low-involvement decision making, the consumer wants to minimize the time and effort spent in selecting a brand.

2.   What factors influence a consumer's purchase decisions?
Three sets of factors influence a consumer's purchase decisions: the consumer's psychological set, characteristics, and environment. The psychological set is the prior notions and predispositions the consumer carries into a purchase situation. Consumer characteristics are the consumer's demographic, lifestyle, and personality variables that are likely to influence brand choice. The consumer's environment is the society in which brand choice takes place and the groups the consumer associates with, particularly the peer group and the family.

3.   How do a consumer's needs, perceptions, and attitudes influence his or her purchase decisions?
Needs are forces that direct consumers toward the achievement of certain goals. Perceptions are the way consumers organize and interpret information about brands and companies. Consumers develop brand images that represent their overall perceptions of a brand. Attitudes are the tendency to evaluate a brand or company in a favorable or unfavorable way. Needs, perceptions, and attitudes constitute a consumer's psychological set toward a brand. When a brand is perceived as filling a consumer's needs, a positive attitude is likely to result, leading to a greater likelihood the brand will be purchased.

4.   How do the consumer's characteristics and environment influence purchases?
Whereas a consumer's perceptions and attitudes are specific to a brand, consumer characteristics are more general. Three types of characteristics affect brand choice: demographics, lifestyles, and personality. Demographics are the objective characteristics of the consumer, such as age, income, and education. Lifestyles represent the consumer's activities, interests, and social attitudes. Personality variables are characteristics that reflect consistent and enduring patterns of behavior, such as compulsiveness, compliance, and dominance.

Environmental factors also influence consumer behavior. These factors range from broad cultural influences to more specific group and family influences. Cultural values such as the emphasis in American society on youth and materialism influence our choice of brands. Social class — that is, the status grouping in which a consumer belongs based on income, education, and occupation — influences preferences for a range of products from beer to cars. Groups have the most direct influence on brand choice through face-to-face influence.

Family influences occur between husbands and wives and parents and children. A key element in family influence is the consumer socialization of children, that is, the process by which children learn how to evaluate marketing information and select brands.

5. *How do marketers use knowledge about consumers and their environment to develop marketing strategies?*

Marketers use the three basic influences on consumer behavior — the consumer's psychological set, characteristics, and environment — to develop a range of marketing strategies. These variables are most commonly used to define market segments. Once the target segments are defined, brands are positioned to the needs of these segments. Definition of the target segments also helps identify the proper media to reach these groups. In particular, demographic and lifestyle characteristics are used to identify magazines or newspapers most likely to be read and TV or radio shows most likely to be seen or heard by the target group.

KEY TERMS

Psychological set (p. 118)
High-involvement purchases (p. 119)
Complex decision making (p. 119)
Dissonance (p. 120)
Brand loyalty (p. 121)
Low-involvement decision making (p. 121)
Variety seeking (p. 121)
Inertia (p. 121)
Habit (p. 122)
Learning (p. 122)
Limited decision making (p. 122)
Needs (p. 125)
Perceptions (p. 125)
Brand image (p. 125)
Attitudes (p. 125)

Purchase intentions (p. 125)
Need-gap analysis (p. 125)
Personality (p. 132)
Culture (p. 133)
Social class (p. 134)
Reference groups (p. 135)
Informational influence (p. 136)
Comparative influence (p. 136)
Normative influence (p. 136)
Word-of-mouth communication (p. 137)
Opinion leaders (p. 137)
Information gatherer (p. 137)
Influencer (p. 137)
Purchasing agent (p. 137)
Consumer socialization (p. 139)
Family life cycle (p. 139)

QUESTIONS

1. What strategy did Kellogg use to revitalize its cereal business?

2. Consider the four types of decisions in Figure 5.2. Which decision process is most likely to apply to each of the following product categories:

   a. cigarettes   d. cookies
   b. adult cereals   e. automobiles
   c. canned vegetables

   Describe your rationale for associating a particular decision process with each product category.

3. Use the model of complex decision making in Figure 5.3 to describe the decision-making process you went through in selecting a business school. What are the implications of the decision process you described for the school's

   a. positioning strategy (features to meet student needs)?
   b. product strategy (course offerings)?
   c. pricing strategy (tuition level and financial assistance programs)?

4. (a) Under what circumstances might a consumer switch from complex decision making to habit in buying a car? What might cause the consumer to stop buying by habit and to revert to complex decision making?

   (b) What might cause a consumer to switch from being uninvolved to being highly involved with a product like cereals?

5. A product manager for a well-known brand of bar soap commented on the distinction between low- and high-involvement purchasing decisions as follows:

   > Your emphasis on low-involvement decisions is overblown. I just don't agree that consumers aren't involved with most decisions. Consumers get their egos tied up with a lot of packaged goods — soaps, toothpaste, deodorants, hair spray. Anything that has to do with how we come across socially has to be involving. Even items like detergents and floor cleaners are going to be involving for many consumers that take pride in the way they and their homes look. So I just don't buy your focus on low involvement.

   Do you agree with the product manager's statement? Why or why not? Are marketing executives likely to think consumers are more involved with their products than they actually are?

6. An electronics company decides to diversify and buys a company that produces canned vegetables. Company executives have been used to marketing electronics as items purchased based on information search and brand evaluation. They must now get used to marketing products likely to be purchased by habit. What are the different strategic implications the company's executives are likely to face in marketing a product purchased by habit rather than complex decision making?

7. Kellogg effectively changed cereals from an uninvolving to an involving product for many consumers. What are the different strategic implications in advertising cereals as an uninvolving product versus advertising them as involving?

8. How did Kellogg effectively apply principles of (a) need segmentation and (b) brand-image formation in marketing its line of adult cereals?

9. How have marketers used demographic and life-style characteristics to (a) segment their markets and (b) select media? Cite specific examples.

10. How have companies used the emphasis on youth in American culture in developing their marketing strategies? Cite examples.

11. An auto manufacturer is targeting a new high-priced model to professionals and managers. Its main line of cars is targeted primarily to blue-collar workers based on themes of escaping from everyday drudgery. What differences in positioning strategies might be developed in appealing to professionals/managers versus blue-collar workers.

12. How do the ads in Exhibit 5.8 demonstrate the three types of reference group influences?

13. Why have children gained more purchasing influence in the family? How have some marketers targeted more of their effort to children?

CASE 5.1

SMALL-SIZE FOODS ARE A BIG DEAL

Source: Laurie Freeman and Julie Liesse Erickson, "Small-Size Foods Are a Big Deal." Reprinted with permission from *Advertising Age,* May 16, 1988, p. 12, Copyright Crain Communications, Inc. All rights reserved.

When comedian Steve Martin decreed, "Let's get small," he wasn't referring to the American diet.

Only 10 years ago, package-goods marketers were of the "bigger is better" mentality, bringing out giant and king-size packages of popular foods and snacks.

Today, many of the same companies are introducing downsized versions of those same products.

Nabisco Brands' Ritz Bitz, the offspring of long-famous Ritz crackers, are showing up at cocktail parties with or without toppings. A Cheese Ritz Bitz line extension is rolling out.

"People are eating less at one time, and they are eating on the run or in front of the TV," said Herbert Meyers, principal of Gerstman & Meyers, a package-design company.

Instead of pushing huge buckets of chicken, Kentucky Fried Chicken Corp. is into Chicken Littles. And Burger King Corp. may add the leprechaun-size Burger Bundles to its permanent menu. Could the two-handed Whopper be bound for fast-food heaven?

For those who don't want to go out for fast food, Oscar Mayer Foods Corp. is testing Zappetites, an eight-item line of minimeals designed specifically for the home microwave oven.

The Zappetites line includes snack-size cheeseburgers, pizza slices, hot dogs, ham and cheese sandwiches and a Mexican-style stuffed pastry.

A TV and radio ad campaign, positions Zappetites as food easy enough for children to make on their own.

If the shoppers have children, that is.

Marketers are facing the cold reality that more than half of all U.S. households now consist of one or two people. Minifoods are made mostly for the convenience of smaller families and more active lifestyles.

In the 1950s and 60s, food companies promoted multiple-serving packages to handle the appetites of larger families. Now these same companies have found that smaller portions and single-serve sizes better meet the needs of today's "grazing" society.

"People are doing things on a grazing, or single, basis. Not many people indulge in a sit-down meal. Food is picked up and eaten on the basis of an individual's schedule," said Alan Miller, a consultant.

He pointed out that an old Hunt-Wesson product — Hunt's Snack-Packs, individual servings of puddings and fruits — is enjoying a resurgence in sales not because they're packed in more school lunches but because "they can be eaten between meals as a minisnack."

Yet convenience isn't the only goal of minifoods.

Kitchens of Sara Lee last fall completed national distribution of Sara Lee Snacks, a four-item line of single-serving desserts.

Although most Sara Lee frozen pastries are designed to be heated or thawed before eating, the company is recommending consumers try the Snacks right out of the freezer.

But Sara Lee Snacks are individually packaged partly to help health and diet-conscious consumers avoid overeating.

The product's tagline? "Just a *little bit* dangerous."

1. Does the introduction of smaller-sized foods fill a gap in consumer needs? What needs are these products satisfying?

2. Would a company trying to influence consumers to buy small-size foods be following a strategy of attitude change or attitude reinforcement?

3. What demographic groups should these foods be targeted to?

4. Zappetite's basic theme — "Kids can make it on their own" — advertises that children can easily cook the product in microwave ovens. Do you think the product should be positioned to children?

CASE 5.2

TARGETING THE "TWEEN" MARKET

In the latest effort to reach the newly targeted "tween" market, the National Dairy Promotion & Research Board today launches a $9.3 million TV campaign aimed at 9-to-15-year-olds.

A recent study indicates the age group has at least $4 billion and possibly as much as $30 billion in pocket money and influences the spending of another $40 billion annually.

The first companies to target the group were fashion marketers and entertainment equipment manufacturers such as Sony Corp. of America.

Lately, however, youngsters too young to be treated as freedom-loving teen-agers but too old for babyish appeals also have been targeted by food product marketers such as Borden Inc., which designed its Spirals snack with tweens in mind. General Mills is reported to be considering recasting a product for tweens.

The age group is of special interest to the Arlington, Va.-based dairy board because it represents the time when children's milk-drinking begins a dramatic downward spiral.

In 1986, children ages 6 to 12 drank milk for up to 40% of their liquid consumption. That number dropped to 25% for 13-to-19-year-olds and to 15% for people in their 20s.

For that reason, the board for the first time is targeting a large chunk of its $63 million budget at tweens.

Children in the age group "go from having choices made for them in home to being on their own," said Bill McEwen, senior VP-strategic planning and research, McCann-Erickson, San Francisco, which handles the campaign. At the same time, he added, "these children are doing shopping for their families. Our goal is to get them to continue to make milk a choice."

The campaign consists of two 30-second commercials.

In "Late Bloomer," a girl tells a preteen "hunk" who does not notice her that she will grow up to be an attractive woman because she drinks milk. As the camera transforms her into an adult, she tells the boy that when she is older, "you'll be history."

A second spot, called "Bullies," shows a boy talking to two threatening-looking youths. As the camera transforms him into an adult, he tells the other youths that he probably will forgive them for the way they treat him by the time he grows up. But he becomes a curly-haired boy again in the closing seconds and adds, "but you never can tell."

Both commercials conclude with the theme "Milk: It does a body good."

1. Do you think the National Dairy Board will be successful in influencing "tweens" to continue drinking milk?

2. Would you classify their campaign as an attitude-reinforcement or an attitude-change strategy? Why?

NOTES

1. "How King Kellogg Beat the Blahs," *Fortune,* August 29, 1988, pp. 55–64; and "Crunching the Competition," *Marketing & Media Decisions,* March, 1988, p. 72.

2. "Brantastic," *Marketing & Media Decisions,* April, 1987, pp. 98, 100.

3. *Marketing & Media Decisions,* March 1988, p. 70.

4. *Fortune,* August 29, 1988, p. 58; and "The Health Craze Has Kellogg Feeling G-R-R-Reat," *Business Week,* March 30, 1987, p. 52; and *Marketing & Media Decisions,* March 1988, p. 71.

5. *Marketing & Media Decisions,* March 1988, p. 82.

6. "Kellogg: Snap, Crackle, Profits," *Dun's Business Month,* December 1985, pp. 32–33.

7. "Tell Us It's New and Improved — But Keep Health Out of It," *Business Week,* August 10, 1987, p. 47.

8. "Former Customers Are Good Prospects," *The Wall Street Journal,* April 22, 1982, p. 31.

9. "Cadillac Wants to Attract Younger Buyers, but Its 'Old Man' Image Gets in the Way," *The Wall Street Journal,* November 18, 1985, p. 33.

10. "Marketing Skin Care to Men," *Marketing Communications,* November 1985, pp. 32, 33, and 36.

11. "Lee Maps New Line of Jeans," *Advertising Age,* March 10, 1986, p. 28.

12. "Agencies Zero in on Segments of the Baby-Boom Generation," *The Wall Street Journal,* June 26, 1986, p. 33.

13. " 'Inner-Directed' Is Where It's at in New Strategies," *Adweek,* May 26, 1986, p. 17.

14. "MasterCard Shuns Status," *Advertising Age,* February 24, 1986, p. 3.

15. "Futurist Laurel Cutler," *Inc.*, November 1987, p. 45.

16. "Laurel Cutler: Consumers are Tougher Customers," *Fortune,* July 3, 1989, p. 76.

17. *Inc.*, November 1987, p. 45.

18. Laurel Cutler: Two Hats and Velvet Gloves," *Adweek,* December 12, 1988, p. 36.

19. *Inc.*, November 1987, p. 54.

20. "Advertisers Put Consumers on the Couch," *The Wall Street Journal,* May 13, 1988, p. 21.

21. Shirley Young, "The Dynamics of Measuring Unchange," in Russell I. Haley, ed., *Attitude Research in Transition* (Chicago: American Marketing Association, 1972), p. 72.

22. "Freshman Found Stressing Wealth," *The New York Times,* January 14, 1988, p. A14.

23. "Hispanic Market Profile: Resisting the Winds of Change," *Marketing Communications,* July 1983, p. 37.

24. "The Masculine Dreamscape," *Marketing Communications,* April 1987, pp. 17–18.

25. "The Shifting Power of Influentials in Purchase Decisions," *Ad Forum,* July 1983, p. 55.

26. "Corona's Unlikely Conquest," *The New York Times,* July 11, 1987, pp. 39, 41; and "Anheuser Beer Arrives without Ads," *Advertising Age,* July 6, 1987, p. 2.

27. "Auto Makers Set New Ad Strategy to Reach Women," *Advertising Age,* September 23, 1985, p. 80.

28. "As Kids Gain Power of Purse, Marketing Takes Aim at Them," *The Wall Street Journal,* January 19, 1988, p. 15.

ntil 1985 IBM might as easily have stood for *I*nvincible *B*usiness *M*arketer as for International Business Machines. The company had experienced 40 years of sustained growth, establishing the industry standard for computer hardware and commanding a market share of over 70 percent for mainframes and over 40 percent for microcomputers.[1] Moreover, it had just successfully established the business market for personal computers, leaving its competitors in such a trail of dust that its greatest fear was renewed government interest in breaking up the company on antitrust grounds.

Then its performance started to unravel. In 1985 and 1986 IBM experienced seven straight quarters of decreased earnings. It saw earnings drop by 55 percent in 1986 alone and revenue fall by 12 percent, its worst performance in over 40 years.[2] Instead of Big Blue (the company's nickname), analysts started calling IBM "black and blue." What happened? In the words of IBM's chairman, John F. Akers, the company simply lost touch with its business customers. It kept trying to sell them products, when what they were looking for was *systems solutions.*

Somehow, in the early 1980s the company stopped being marketing oriented and became sales oriented. Business was booming; selling products to organizational buyers used to dealing only with IBM became a breeze; and the company's salespeople became complacent. IBM failed to notice that the needs of organizational buyers were becoming more systems-oriented; that is, they wanted to buy total packages rather than single components. What is more, greater customer savvy was diminishing the "FUD factor" — fear, uncertainty, and doubt — that once caused buyers to shy away from anything but IBM equipment.[3] IBM's customers wanted more for their dollar, and were consider-

ORGANIZATIONAL BUYING BEHAVIOR

ing competitors' offerings. Unless IBM did something, it was facing the prospect of a continued loss in sales to companies such as Digital Equipment Corp. that were more attuned to customer needs.[4]

Big Blue reacted quickly with a two-pronged strategy. First, to better meet customer needs, IBM initiated a Value-Added Program that meant it had to break down some long-standing taboos. Perhaps the most radical change was its decision to produce its products on a customized basis. In the past, its engineers were awarded bonuses for finding ways to use the same products across many applications. Now their charge was to fit products to customer needs. By the end of 1986 a new laboratory was turning out customized workstations and data-processing systems for specific companies in the insurance, banking, oil, and automotive industries.[5]

Breaking down another of its taboos, IBM began working with other companies to provide the installation, consulting, and training needs for its customers' information systems.[6]

The second prong of its strategy was to reeducate its sales staff to think in terms of systems rather than products and to focus on specific customer needs. This process was facilitated by reorganizing the sales staff on industry lines rather than a geographic basis. Salespeople could thus focus on the information needs of specific industries and even act as consultants in fulfilling their customers' systems requirements. Twenty-four new sales offices and 5,000 salespeople were added to accomplish this goal.

Big Blue's downward slide was reversed by its new-found marketing orientation. Net earnings were up 10 percent in 1987 and 14 percent in 1988.[7] Catering to the needs of its organizational customers paid off. ■

● ● ●

THE NATURE OF ORGANIZATIONAL BUYING BEHAVIOR

Most of the buying and selling in the American economy is not from an organization to a final consumer, but from one organization to another. In fact, organizational buying represents more dollar volume than the purchase of goods by final consumers.

Organizational buyers purchase for manufacturing firms, for institutions such as hospitals and schools, for government agencies, and for intermediaries such as wholesalers and retailers, which then resell the goods. As we saw in Chapter 1, marketers to business organizations are known as **business-to-business marketers**. And just as marketers of consumer goods must base marketing strategies on an understanding of the needs of final consumers, business-to-business marketers must base their strategies on an understanding of the needs of organizational buyers.

IMPORTANCE OF A CUSTOMER ORIENTATION

A business-to-business marketer can become product-oriented more easily than a consumer-goods marketer for one reason: Business-to-business marketers are more likely to sell high-technology, finely engineered products. As a result, they are more likely to become wed to their technologies rather than to the customer. This was true for IBM. It had become more focused on its product lines than on customer needs.

In some cases, business-to-business marketers that become technology-oriented are too late in recognizing the need for a customer orientation and go out of business as a result. On occasion, these are the same companies that were the technological innovators in the industry. For example, an English company called Electric and Musical Industries (EMI) developed the CT-scanner, the device that takes hundreds of X-ray slices from different angles and then uses a computer to reconstruct the total picture. EMI rested on its laurels as the innovator without ever developing a marketing capability to keep a pulse on customer

TABLE 6.1
Examples of Purchases by
Organizational Buyers

TYPE OF BUYER	PRODUCTS	SERVICES
INDUSTRIAL BUYERS	Pollution control company buys industrial generator	Auto producer buys maintenance and repair contract for machinery
	Metal processor buys forklift trucks to transport fabricated parts	Industrial cable company buys inventory control system
		Computer manufacturer buys marketing research study
INSTITUTIONAL BUYERS	Hospital buys drugs	Hotel buys janitorial and cleaning services
	Hotel buys food	Airline buys consulting services
GOVERNMENT AGENCY	Census Bureau buys computers	State Department of Tourism hires an advertising agency
	Department of Defense buys military equipment	City drug-rehabilitation program hires professional counseling services
	School system buys educational supplies	
RESELLERS	Distributor buys electrical cable for resale to utility company	Retailer buys store location study
	Wholesaler buys drugs for resale to drug stores	Distributor buys accounting services
	Retail druggist buys pharmaceuticals for resale to final consumer	

needs. EMI's first device was a head scanner, but customers (hospitals) wanted a body scanner capable of faster resolution time in taking the X-rays.[8]

EMI was slow to respond, and its take-it-or-leave-it attitude turned off many customers. By the time it produced the desired machines, General Electric had already developed a third generation of CT-scanners, a superior salesforce, and an ability to adapt to market needs. Six years after EMI had introduced the device, it was out of the CT-scanner market, and losses incurred as the result of declining sales made it an acquisition target.[9]

If business-to-business marketers are to develop strategies based on the needs of their customers, they must be aware of the different types of organizational buyers — industrial buyers, institutional buyers, resellers, or government agencies. Table 6.1 lists some examples of products and services purchased by these buyers.

Industrial buyers buy products and services that they use to further process other products. They buy products used in manufacturing, mining, or construction. For example, a manufacturer might buy generators to create power or forklift trucks to transport fabricated parts from one part of the plant to another. The

**TYPES OF
ORGANIZATIONAL
BUYERS**

manufacturer might also buy services such as a contract to service generators or trucks, an inventory control system to ensure adequate inventory levels, or a marketing research study to identify prospective buyers.

Whereas industrial buyers buy for organizations that process goods, **institutional buyers** buy for organizations that provide services, such as hospitals and schools, hotels and restaurants, airlines and railroads. In each case, products (such as drugs for a hospital) and services (such as consulting expertise for an airline) are purchased to provide other services rather than to process products. (Table 6.1 lists specific examples.)

Government agencies represent a significant proportion of organizational buying. There are over 80,000 federal, state, and local government units in the United States that account for over $1 trillion in purchases. Federal agencies like the Census Bureau or Department of Defense will buy products ranging from computers to military equipment. A local school system might buy educational materials. Government agencies also buy services. For example, a state agency might hire an advertising firm to promote tourism. Or a city drug rehabilitation program might hire psychologists for professional counseling services.

Resellers are wholesalers and retailers that buy products to resell. They do not process goods. Rather, they act as purchasing agents for other organizational buyers or for the final consumer. A distributor such as W. W. Grainger buys electrical cable from a manufacturer and sells it to a public utility. A drug wholesaler such as McKesson buys from pharmaceutical companies to resell to drugstores. A retailer such as Sears buys a wide range of products to resell to the final consumer. Here also, resellers buy services to support their activities, such as studies to determine the best location for new store outlets or accounting services for bookkeeping and tax returns.

We will consider reseller activities in a later chapter. For now we will focus on industrial and institutional buying behavior.

COMPARISON WITH CONSUMER BEHAVIOR

Organizational buyer behavior is similar to consumer behavior in many respects. Each of the steps in complex decision making cited in the previous chapter—need arousal, information search, brand evaluation, purchase, and postpurchase evaluation — apply to organizational buying. Further, the types of factors influencing organizational buyers are similar to those influencing consumers — the buyer's psychological set, characteristics, and group influences through word-of-mouth communications.

Traditionally, organizational buyers have been thought of as more rational and scientific in their purchase decisions. Since they often rely on a set of technical product specifications, their purchasing is more likely to be based on measurable product attributes and seller capabilities. Yet studies have shown that organizational buyers are also governed by emotion, inertia, and interpersonal relations in making purchasing decisions. For example, one study of purchasers of computer terminals found that word-of-mouth influence was as important in making the decision as objective sources such as technical specifications.[10]

The differences between organizational and consumer behavior tend to outweigh the similarities, primarily because of the greater complexity of products purchased by organizational buyers. Greater complexity means a lot more can go wrong with the product, so more risk is involved in the purchase. Organizational buyers have more at stake — sometimes including their jobs — if they make the wrong decision. Because of this risk, organizational buying decisions are more

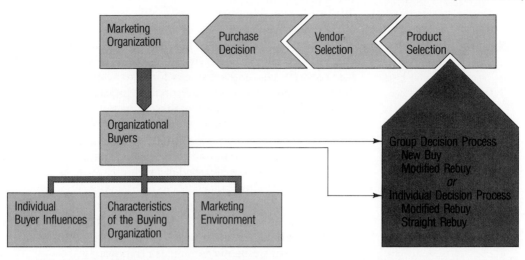

FIGURE 6.1
A Model of Organizational Buyer Behavior

likely than consumer buying decisions to be made on a group basis. Also, organizations frequently form **buying centers**, in which a group of executives — most often, a purchasing agent, an engineer, and a production manager — provide the different skills necessary to make important, risky buying decisions.

Technical complexity also means that buyers are likely to purchase based on a set of formal **product specifications**, that is, the performance requirements set by prospective users of the product (such as lifting capacity for forklift trucks). As a result, a purchase decision is based on the degree to which product or service attributes meet these specifications. The purchase decision will also be based on vendor (i.e., supplier) attributes such as reliability, on-time delivery, and service. In consumer buying, the consumer usually decides on a product first, then on the store to buy it from. In organizational buying, the product and vendor decision are closely intertwined.

Business-to-business marketing and consumer-goods marketing also differ from the seller's standpoint, primarily as regards the greater role of personal selling in business-to-business marketing. The salesperson's technical knowledge of the product is essential and postpurchase follow-up and service are necessary. In business-to-business marketing, buyers negotiate with sellers on price, delivery dates, and product specifications. In consumer buying, such negotiations are rare.

Advertising is likely to play only a supportive role to personal selling in organizational buying, and serves to provide information to lay the groundwork for a subsequent sales call.

A MODEL OF ORGANIZATIONAL BUYER BEHAVIOR

Figure 6.1 presents a basic model of organizational buyer behavior. The components of the model are the same as those for consumer behavior (see Figure 5.1) — a marketing organization, a buyer, the buyer's decision process, and a purchase.

The differences involve the specific influences on the buyer and the nature of the decision process.

THE ORGANIZATIONAL BUYER

As with consumer buying, the marketing organization (in this case the business-to-business marketer) interacts with the buyer. Assume that Citicorp wants to buy a customized computer system for its retail banking divisions so that managers can have instant access to information for each branch. A buying team made up of the information systems manager, the purchasing manager, and the data-processing manager solicits information from several computer firms. These companies provide information on a customized system, including specifications on software and hardware. They also provide information on price, prospective installation dates, training schedules for users of the system, and maintenance service.

Individuals in the buying center will evaluate information from sellers and decide on the system to select. The decision will be influenced by each individual in the buying center, by the nature of the organization, and by the environment in which the buying center is making its decisions.

The *individual buyer* will be influenced by his or her psychological set and characteristics. For example, assume that the purchasing manager has purchased mostly IBM equipment in the past and has a favorable attitude toward that company (the buyer's psychological set). He is older and more risk-averse than the other members of the group (the buyer's characteristics), and does not want to make any waves by trying a totally new supplier. Based on these individual buyer influences, the purchasing manager is initially in favor of the IBM system, whereas the information systems and data-processing managers have no strong preferences.

The second major influence on the organizational buyer, the *characteristics of the buying organization* in which he or she works, includes factors such as purchasing roles, the nature of personal influence, and the degree to which decision making is centralized. In the Citicorp example, the information systems manager has the most influence over software specifications because she is familiar with the data and analytical needs of managers in a branch office information system (purchasing role). As a result, she wants to consider a wider range of software alternatives, and tries to prevail on the purchasing manager not to be so committed to past vendor relationships (personal influences). Since Citicorp is relatively decentralized, the lines of authority between the data processing, information systems, and purchasing managers are not clear-cut (degree of centralization). This means the information systems manager has to rely on persuasion rather than on direct power and authority in trying to get the purchasing manager to consider other vendors.

Influences of the *marketing environment* such as the level of competition, technology, and regulatory constraints will also affect the decision of the buying group. For example, several of Citicorp's competitors are considering establishing similar systems to provide their managers with quick information on the status of branch deposits and transactions. Advances in information-processing technology make it essential that Citicorp maintain a state-of-the-arts system. The economic uncertainty after the 1987 stock market crash has also made banks more cost-conscious, and an effective system to track deposit and transaction activity might help reduce costs. Finally, the trend toward deregulation means that new competitors are coming in to challenge the traditional banking system, putting more pressure on the banks to improve efficiency through better information.

Figure 6.1 shows that individual buyer influences, the characteristics of the buying organization, and the marketing environment determine the organizational decision process. Organizational buying decisions can be made by groups or by individuals. These decisions can be of three types: a straight rebuy, a modified rebuy, and a new buy.[11] The **straight rebuy** is a recurring purchase that can be handled on a routine basis, such as an institution buying office supplies or a manufacturer buying metal fasteners. These purchases involve standardized products with routine usages. Little information search is required. Vendors are often selected from an approved list, so there is little vendor evaluation. Usually, a straight rebuy will be triggered by a low inventory level. It is similar to habitual purchasing in consumer behavior.

ORGANIZATIONAL DECISION PROCESS

A **modified rebuy** is a recurring purchase that is less routine. Some information search is required on product specifications and vendor capabilities. A modified rebuy might involve reevaluating a straight rebuy because of a new product or a change in technology — for example, the introduction of a bonded adhesive in place of a metal screw.

The **new buy** is a decision that has not occurred before, as in the example of Citicorp establishing a microcomputer network for a branch-banking information system. Since there is little experience to go on, the buyer must conduct an extensive information search on product specifications and vendor capabilities.

As Figure 6.1 shows, new-buy decisions are usually made by groups, straight-rebuy decisions by individuals, and modified-rebuy decisions by either groups or individuals depending on their relative complexity. Organizational decisions also require selection of a product and a vendor. Selection of the product should determine selection of the vendor. In the Citicorp example, each of the companies being considered provided different sets of specifications for the microcomputer network. Therefore, selection of the system determines selection of the vendor.

But frequently, it is the other way around — the vendor is selected based on past loyalties or plain inertia, and the product is selected as a result of vendor selection. One study found that many organizational buyers are reluctant to change to new sources because of an inability to cope with any complications resulting from such a change.[12] The purchasing manager in the Citicorp example would have selected the IBM system, regardless of systems specifications. He felt comfortable with IBM based on past associations and was trying to minimize risk by avoiding selection of a new vendor.

ORGANIZATIONAL BUYING DECISIONS

In the rest of this chapter, we consider the basic components of organizational buyer behavior in Figure 6.1. We will start by considering the organizational buyer's decision process, because it gives us a perspective on different types of organizational buying. We will then discuss each of the three main influences on organizational buyers — individual, organizational, and environmental influences.

TYPES OF BUYING DECISIONS

The three types of organizational buying decisions — new buys, modified rebuys, and straight rebuys — parallel the processes of complex decision making, limited decision making, and habit cited in the last chapter (see top of Table 6.2). Habit is further broken out into vendor loyalty versus inertia. In vendor loyalty, the same vendor is chosen because of prior satisfaction with the vendor's performance. In inertia the same vendor is chosen to minimize risk and avoid change, even though that vendor may be performing poorly.

Complex Decision Making

Complex buying decisions (new buys) are usually made by a group because of the financial and performance risks involved in buying a new product. There is extensive information search in evaluating vendor capabilities. Once the decision is made, postpurchase evaluation is also extensive, since product performance is monitored carefully. In a new-buy situation, the person with the most influence is usually an engineer because they have the best capability to set and evaluate specifications for complex products.

Complex decision making processes in organizational buying have the same five steps as in the consumer behavior model — need arousal, information search, product and vendor evaluation, purchase, and postpurchase evaluation (see Figure 6.2). Initially, an organization determines a product need.The company then forms a buying center that develops the product specifications for a product to meet this need. In the Citicorp example, the company first determined it needed an on-line branch information system to provide deposit and transaction information to its managers. A buying center was then formed, and it devel-

TABLE 6.2
Types of Organizational Buying Decisions

DECISION-MAKING PROCESS	COMPLEX DECISION MAKING	→	LIMITED DECISION MAKING		→	HABIT		
						Vendor Loyalty		Inertia
TYPE OF ORGANIZATIONAL BUYING BEHAVIOR	NEW BUY ————→		MODIFIED REBUY ————————————→			STRAIGHT REBUY		
TYPE OF DECISION MAKING	Group ———→		Group or Individual ————————→			Individual		
FINANCIAL AND PERFORMANCE RISK	High ————→		Moderate ————————————→			Low		
INFORMATION SEARCH	Extensive ——→		Limited ——————————————→			None		
EVALUATION OF ALTERNATIVE VENDORS	Extensive ——→		Moderate ————————————→			Minimal		
USE OF APPROVED VENDOR LIST	Rarely ———→		Sometimes ————————————→			Usually		
POSTPURCHASE EVALUATION	Extensive ——→		Moderate ————————————→			Minimal		
POSITION WITH GREATEST PURCHASE INFLUENCE	Engineering ——→		Production or Purchasing ————→			Purchasing		

oped specifications for the type of information required, linkages between micros and mainframe computers, and core capacity requirements.

Information search involves soliciting information from vendors regarding their capabilities. Based on this information, the buying center determines a list of vendors from which it will solicit proposals. These may be totally new vendors or vendors with which the company has dealt in the past.

Product and vendor evaluation involves submitting the product specifications to the approved vendors and requesting a proposal detailing how each vendor plans to fill the specifications. Proposals are then evaluated by the buying center based on its original specifications.

In the final stages, the buying center selects a vendor and then evaluates the vendor's performance on delivery, product installation, product performance, and service to determine if the company should buy from that vendor again. Assume that based on its overall assessment, the buying group at Citicorp concluded that Digital Equipment would do the best job in developing, installing, and maintaining an on-line branch information system. The other members prevailed on the purchasing manager (who favored IBM) to go along with their decision for Digital Equipment. All were satisfied with Digital's installation, personnel training, and service performance, and decided to consider the company in future systems purchases.

Limited Decision Making

Limited decision making is analogous to a modified rebuy. If a company decides to buy an existing product with some modifications, a buying group may not be required. The decision might instead be made by one or two individuals with a more limited search for information and fewer vendors under consideration.

The characteristics of limited decision making in Table 6.2 are limited information search and vendor evaluation, occasional use of an approved vendor list, and limited postpurchase evaluation. Production and purchasing are the most influential parties — production initiating a request, and the purchasing department filling it. The expertise of an engineer is less important since the product or service is not new.

An example of a modified-rebuy process is the purchase of steel plate by James Hampden Ltd. The Glasgow-based company is a producer of customized and standardized units of air- and gas-handling equipment such as large fans and blowers, circulators for gas-cooled nuclear reactors, and rotary heat exchangers.[13] When producing customized units, it buys steel plate on a special-order basis. This is not a new buy, but a modified rebuy, since these steel products have been purchased before.

An order for steel plate is usually initiated by a production manager or engineer. The order states the product specification, quantity required, and when it is required. The purchasing agent then initiates a request for quotes from an approved vendor list. (Companies get on the approved vendor list if they meet Hampden's requirements for product quality, financial soundness, and condition of plant and equipment.)

The purchasing agent selects a supplier to fill the order from the approved list. Sometimes the purchasing agent negotiates price and delivery with the vendor, but usually the vendor with the lowest price and best delivery date is selected. Postpurchase evaluation of product quality and on-time delivery determines whether the vendor stays on the approved list.

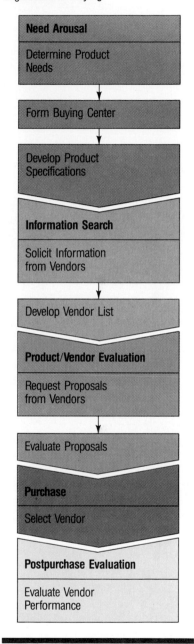

FIGURE 6.2
Complex Decision Making in Organizational Buying

Need Arousal

Determine Product Needs

Form Buying Center

Develop Product Specifications

Information Search

Solicit Information from Vendors

Develop Vendor List

Product/Vendor Evaluation

Request Proposals from Vendors

Evaluate Proposals

Purchase

Select Vendor

Postpurchase Evaluation

Evaluate Vendor Performance

FIGURE 6.3
Habit in Organizational Buyer Behavior

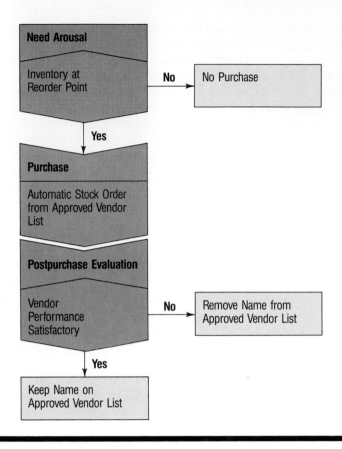

Habit

Straight rebuys are similar to habitual purchasing behavior. As Figure 6.3 shows, straight rebuys are usually initiated when a product's inventory level reaches a reorder point. Purchasing is then automatic. A purchase order is issued to an approved vendor, who fills it based on prearranged terms for price and delivery. A vendor is on the approved list because past performance has been satisfactory. If its prices become higher than those of competitors, or product quality deteriorates, or delivery slows down, the vendor will probably be taken off the approved list.

The process in Figure 6.3 can be better described as ordering rather than purchasing. The vendor is only filling an order rather than meeting a set of specifications. As Table 6.2 shows, ordering is the responsibility of the purchasing department. There is no information search or vendor evaluation, and postpurchase evaluation is minimal. Hampden buys steel for standardized products based on a straight rebuy process. Steel plate for standardized products is maintained at specified stock levels. When inventory falls below these levels, the stock control department issues a purchase order that is sent to an approved vendor and quickly filled.

Vendor Loyalty Straight rebuys can reflect vendor loyalty or inertia. Vendor loyalty is the result of past satisfaction, causing the buyer to use the same vendor any time an automatic reorder point is reached. One study found that vendor loyalty is most likely for small orders and when significant cost savings can be had by dealing with the same vendor.[14]

Dealing with the same vendor has the advantage of providing a constant and assured source of supply. Xerox has cut its approved vendor list from 2,000 to less than 350 highly reliable suppliers. As a result, it has been able to substantially reduce the need to inspect incoming parts.[15]

But when the price of a product is high and the product is technologically complex, vendor loyalty can be risky. As technology advances, other vendors may offer superior products or the same product at lower costs. A company that buys complex products should be wary of consistently buying from the same vendor.

Inertia Sometimes buyers rely on the same vendors in the belief that it is better to avoid the risk of trying someone new, even if another supplier might offer better prices, quality, or delivery dates. Also, the organizational buyer may wish to avoid starting a new process of information search and vendor evaluation. In addition to the advantage of a long-term relationship, dealing with the same vendor offers the benefits of *reciprocity*. For example, an auto manufacturer might buy materials from a steel company, which then buys its fleet of cars from the auto manufacturer. Such reciprocity encourages inbreeding and a failure to look for more efficient sources of supply.

A new-buy or modified-rebuy situation involves two interrelated decisions: which product to purchase and which vendor to supply the product. Figure 6.1 suggests that the product decision should be made first and then vendors selected to fill predetermined product specifications. The decision process for product and vendor selection will differ in several respects: First, buyers will use different criteria in selecting products and vendors; second, they will use different sources of information in evaluating each; third, the influence of members of a buying center will differ when product and vendor decisions are made.

PRODUCT AND VENDOR SELECTION

Selection Criteria

Quality and performance are likely to be the most important criteria in choosing a product, with technical specifications dominating. Suppliers are most likely to be chosen based on price, service, delivery, and dependability.[16] (See Table 6.3.)

An important factor in vendor selection is potential risk. Selecting the wrong vendor could mean product failure, missed delivery dates, or poor service, and organizational buyers naturally want to reduce these risks. Buying from the same vendors on an approved vendor list helps. So does the strategy of **multiple sourcing**, that is, buying from several vendors so that the risk is spread among them.[17] A third strategy to reduce risk is simply to select the vendor that offers the lowest price so as to minimize the potential for financial loss.

None of these strategies completely eliminates the risk of poor vendor selection. Using the same vendor from an approved list can mean missed opportunities to get better prices or performance elsewhere. A few bad performers in the selected group will cause multiple sourcing to fail. And buying based on price leaves one open to possible product or service failure.

Sources of Information

Buyers turn to different sources of information, depending on whether they are selecting a product or a vendor. As mentioned, technical information is likely to

TABLE 6.3
Criteria Used for Product
and Vendor Selection

Sources: Donald R. Lehmann and John
O'Shaughessy, "Difference in Attribute Importance for
Different Industrial Products," *Journal of Marketing* 38
(April 1974):38; and John I. Coppett and William A.
Staples, "Product Profile Analysis: A Tool for Indus-
trial Selling," *Industrial Marketing Management*
9 (1980):208.

PRODUCT CRITERIA	VENDOR CRITERIA
Overall quality	Overall reputation
Quality of parts	Financing terms
Features conform to buyer's specifications	Flexibility in adjusting to buyer's needs
Durability	Technical services
Compatibility with present equipment	Confidence in salespeople
Speed of obsolescence	Convenience in placing order
Economy	Price
Value	Training offered by vendor
Flexibility to accommodate future growth	Reliability of delivery
Product reliability	Ease of maintenance
Ease of use	Post-purchase service
Training time required	

be most important in product selection. Such information is obtained from technical journals, trade magazines, customer catalogs, trade shows, and government publications.

For information on vendor capabilities, the most important sources are the vendor's salespeople and past performance. The salesperson can describe the vendor's product offerings, pricing structure, and service and delivery capabilities. If the vendor has been used over time, then the buyer's purchasing agent can track vendor performance on product reliability, delivery, and service.

The vendor's advertising and sales literature can provide additional information. So can more objective sources such as trade and government publications. A key source of information that is sometimes overlooked in both product and vendor selection is word-of-mouth communication from colleagues both inside and outside the company. Studies of both product and vendor choice have found that such personal sources are particularly important in the later stages of complex decision making, when the buyer is close to making a decision,[18] and also when the purchase involves a high degree of risk.[19]

Relative Influence in the Organization

Some areas in the organization exert more influence on product selection, others on vendor selection. Generally, engineers have more influence on product selection, particularly for new buys and modified rebuys. They have the technical expertise and are more likely to influence setting product specifications.

There is a danger, however, that engineers may set product specifications that are too technology-oriented. They tend to want better designs and more features than their organization may need. For example, if the engineering group at Hampden Ltd. develops specifications for a large fan blower for an automobile assembly line, it may decide to buy finely tempered steel for quieter operation, whereas the plant manager may be willing to pay less for a noisier fan system, since noise is not a critical factor on the assembly line.

When it comes to vendor selection, the purchasing agent generally has the most say. Purchasing agents are responsible for maintaining relations with vendors on an ongoing basis and know more about delivery and service capabilities. In a straight-rebuy situation where product choice is predetermined, the purchasing agent usually acts alone. In a new-buy situation, the product specifications set by engineering may narrow the choice down to a few vendors, at which point purchasing steps in for the final decision.

Group decision making is particularly important for new buys. It is organized around a buying center.

GROUP DECISION MAKING: THE BUYING CENTER

Roles in the Buying Center

Members of the buying center assume various roles in the decision process, termed gatekeeper, influencer, buyer, and user. These roles are similar to those described as part of the family decision-making process in the last chapter. The **gatekeeper** controls the flow of information into the buying center by introducing materials from salespeople, ads, or technical journals. Gatekeepers identify alternative products and vendors in the process of gathering information. The *influencer* sways other members of the buying group based on his or her expertise.

The *buyer* has formal authority to select the supplier and to arrange terms of purchase and also has a role in identifying and evaluating alternative vendors. At times the buyer's authority may be restricted, as when engineering establishes product specifications that only certain vendors can fill. The ultimate *user* of the product identifies product needs, helps establish product specifications, and evaluates the product once it is used.

These roles are not always firmly defined by the buying group and may vary depending on whether a product or a vendor is being selected. For example, the engineer is likely to be the gatekeeper for product information, whereas the purchasing agent usually serves as gatekeeper in controlling the flow of information regarding vendors. Engineers exert influence regarding technical specifications, purchasing agents regarding cost and delivery criteria.

Conflict in the Buying Center

In the process of group decision making, conflicts are likely to arise between members of a buying center. For example, engineers are interested in product specifications and are more likely to sacrifice quick delivery or a cheaper price to get the materials they want. Production managers are most interested in keeping the factory running smoothly and avoiding delays. Like engineers, they will emphasize quality products, but they also emphasize on-time delivery. Purchasing agents are most interested in getting good products at the lowest cost, with adequate delivery and service. They are more focused on good vendor relations, whereas engineers and production managers are more concerned with product specifications. Frequently, engineers and production managers view the purchasing department as a service function operating to fill their needs, while purchasing agents see themselves as having independent authority to select vendors and negotiate terms of sale.

Usually, these differences in opinion are resolved when the buying center collects information about a product or vendor and reaches a joint decision. In the hypothetical example cited above, the information systems manager at Citicorp felt that Digital Equipment had the capability to provide the services necessary to install and maintain an on-line branch information system, but the purchasing manager felt that IBM was better able to perform these functions. As additional information was collected, members of the buying center decided on Digital Equipment, and the purchasing manager was persuaded to go along.

At times, however, conflict among members of a buying center can be intense, particularly if there is mistrust among groups in the organization. Consider the following statements by a purchasing agent and a production manager:[20]

> *Purchasing Agent: The company doesn't realize that we are an important contributor to profits and not merely a service-providing mechanism for other departments.*

> *Production Manager: Those people in purchasing are trying to build their own little empire without regard for our needs. It's about time they were put in their place.*

In such cases, the only option might be to ask top management to step in and resolve the conflict.

INFLUENCES ON ORGANIZATIONAL BUYERS

Throughout the decision-making process, organizational buyers respond to three types of influences: individual buyer influences, the characteristics of the buyer's organization, and the marketing environment (see Figure 6.1).

INDIVIDUAL BUYER INFLUENCES

Like consumers, organizational buyers are influenced by their psychological set and characteristics in deciding on vendors and products. The only major difference is that consumers purchase according to individual needs and preferences, whereas organizational buyers attempt to purchase to maximize organizational profits.

Organizational buyers go into purchasing situations with prior notions and predispositions about products and suppliers. The importance of this psychological set was apparent in the Citicorp example where the purchasing agent preferred IBM. Since he placed the most emphasis on service, delivery, and installation, and since he had a positive perception of IBM's capabilities in that regard, he naturally had a positive attitude toward the company.

The characteristics of organizational buyers also affect their approaches to decision making and their choice of products and suppliers. One early study of the decision to buy computers found that less educated buyers who were more closed-minded were less likely to purchase computers for their company.[21] Another study found that younger and better educated buyers were more likely to use a variety of information sources in evaluating products and suppliers.[22]

The purchasing agent in the Citicorp example was older and more risk-averse than the other members of the buying center. As a result, he did not seek new vendors. His past relationship with IBM led him to favor it.

ORGANIZATIONAL CHARACTERISTICS

The organizational characteristics of the buyer's firm will influence his or her actions. Studies have shown that the firms most likely to adopt new products are larger and are in industries with rapid technological change.[23] Organizational buyers in such firms are more likely to experience new-buy situations and to make group decisions in a buying center.

The structure of the organization is important, too. Highly centralized, bureaucratic organizations are more likely to adopt routine purchasing procedures and are less likely to consider new products or vendors. Firms with a freer and more open decision style are more likely to encourage risk taking. One study found that such firms are more open to information and facilitate the flow of information into the firm.[24] Such a flow is likely to encourage consideration of new products and vendors.

ENVIRONMENTAL INFLUENCES

The environmental factors that most influence organizational buyers are (1) competitive intensity, (2) technological advances in the buyer's industry, (3) the state of the economy, and (4) legal and regulatory factors. Another important component of the environment is the availability of the materials being purchased. In the 1970s companies became increasingly aware of their vulnerability to shortages in fuel, precious metals, and other raw materials. As a result, many are signing longer-term contracts with their suppliers.

Another characteristic of the environment facing the organizational buyer is that the demand for industrial products is **derived demand**; that is, it is dependent on the demand for the final product. Hampden Ltd. buys steel plate according to the demand for blowers and other air- and gas-handling systems. The demand for these systems, which are used in factories that make autos, appliances, and other products, is in turn ultimately dependent on the demand for those final products.

When demand for a product is derived, it fluctuates more. Any cutback on purchases of the final product has a ripple effect throughout related industries. As a result, organizational buyers must be careful not to overbuy, or they may find themselves with excess inventory when a decrease in demand for consumer goods decreases the demand for industrial goods.

STRATEGIC APPLICATIONS OF ORGANIZATIONAL BUYER BEHAVIOR

Business-to-business marketers must develop effective strategies to meet the needs of organizational buyers. As we saw, the most important component of the marketing mix in business-to-business marketing is personal selling. The salesperson is the main channel for communicating information about product offerings and vendor capabilities. Advertising, though important, plays a supportive role by paving the way for the salesperson rather than a dominant role by influencing purchases.

Before marketing strategies can be developed, prospects for sales must be identified. Today the average cost of a sales call on a prospective customer is over $300. In some high-technology industries, requiring careful preparation and a more detailed presentation, the cost rises to more than $1,000. With costs like these, it is essential to screen companies and carefully identify prospective customers.

In this section, we deal with these three major components of business-to-business marketing strategies — customer prospect identification, personal selling, and supportive advertising strategies.

PROSPECT IDENTIFICATION

Traditionally, business marketers have pinpointed customers for sales calls by relying on industry classifications. The government has established a detailed system of identifying organizations called the *Standard Industrial Classification (SIC)*. Each class of business in the United States is given an SIC code. For example, the code for companies producing blowers and exhaust fans, like Hampden, is 3564. A company specializing in selling steel plate to manufacturers of air blowers can consult the SIC codes and find that there are 337 such plants in the

United States. This information may be sufficient for the seller to identify its prospects.

But the steel plate company may also want to sell to other industry groups such as companies making machine tools and accessories. Now its prospect list is several thousand prospects. To concentrate its sales effort, it therefore decides to sell its products only in one region of the country, the western states. Further, it might decide it is uneconomical to call on firms with net sales of less than $20 million. So it now wants to identify prospects by size and location.

The government does not have data on the organizational characteristics of individual businesses. Dun & Bradstreet (D&B), the information conglomerate, has such data on most companies in the United States based on its file of companies' credit ratings. The steel plate company decides to use the D&B database to identify air blower and machine tool companies in the West with sales of over $20 million. As a result, it pares its prospect list from 2,000 companies to 280. The company's 20-person salesforce can directly contact this prospect group.

Identifying Purchase Influencers

The procedures for prospecting just described identify an organization. But they do not identify those with purchasing influence within the organization. Usually the first person to contact is the purchasing agent, who then directs the seller to those with purchase influence, such as a design engineer or production manager.

But some organizations are a labyrinth of divisions, customer groups, and business units. If a certain individual is more likely to have purchase influence for particular types of products, then the job of prospecting is greatly facilitated. Advertising can be used to introduce a company's product line, and salespeople can follow up by contacting a specified individual within a company. Exhibit 6.1 shows an ad for *Computer Graphics Review*, a magazine for high-level managers and engineers who use computer graphics systems and products. The ad is targeted to sellers of computer graphics systems, and points out that the magazine reaches most of its prospective customers.

Need Segmentation

Business marketers identify customers with unmet needs and then direct marketing strategies to them. For example, a study of over 300 organizational buyers responsible for buying computers identified four need segments based on the computer needs of each company.[25] Segment 1 emphasized price and delivery in buying computers, segment 2 the supplier's visibility among the company's top management, segment 3 performance factors such as ease of operation and amount of training required, and segment 4, which was more systems-oriented, the software support and broad line of products that would facilitate establishing systems networks.

This information allowed computer marketers to pinpoint prospects. For example, before IBM's slide, segment 2 would have been its strongest prospect because of the company's leadership in the industry and visibility among top management. But the increasing emphasis on systems solutions makes segment 4 more important.

SALES STRATEGIES

The overriding importance of personal selling means that a business marketer's sales strategy is the central component of its marketing mix. The single most important factor in IBM's turnaround was its shift in strategy from selling indi-

EXHIBIT 6.1
Advertising the Importance of Reaching
the Right Organizational Buyer

vidual products to selling systems solutions. Salespeople had to become intimately familiar with their customers' needs and organization to sell systems solutions. A central part of this strategy is the **National Account Marketing (NAM)** concept in which a team of salespeople is responsible for satisfying the needs of a single organization.

The NAM concept is becoming more widely accepted among business-to-business marketers selling to large accounts. A NAM team coordinating a seller's marketing effort is better able to determine customers' needs and also to overcome any obstacles or misunderstandings between buyer and seller. One study confirmed that organizational buyers prefer to deal with a team from a supplier rather than separate salespeople offering different lines from the same company.[26]

Measurex, a California-based seller of computerized manufacturing control systems, has implemented the NAM concept very successfully, making the same transition as IBM, from being product-oriented to being customer-solutions-oriented. The heart of Measurex's strategy was to make salespeople more aware of customer needs and operations. Its focus on personal selling is reflected in an average field cost for each of its salespeople of over $250,000 a year. The average cost of a sales call is $1,000.[27]

Business marketers are beginning to use **telemarketing**, that is, contacting prospects by phone, on a widespread basis to supplement the efforts of their salespeople. Telephone selling is becoming a cost-efficient means of reaching smaller accounts or those hard to reach by salespeople. Trained company representatives can provide smaller customers with product information, answer questions, and send them more detailed information by mail.

**For John Akers —
A New Sales Strategy to Get
IBM off the Boards**

Source: Courtesy of International Business Machines
Corporation.

When John Akers, IBM's current CEO, was playing varsity hockey for Yale in the 1950s, he was checked into the boards quite a few times, but he also did some checking himself. One teammate described Akers' first goal: "He had to make a superhuman effort to get the puck on the pass and put it in the net. We were amazed. He was the toughest guy on the team."[28]

Akers is going to need all that toughness these days. He had the bad luck of picking up the reins at IBM in 1985, just when sales started slumping. His single-minded determination to stage a turnaround led him to immediately attack an IBM sacred cow — secure employment — by slashing 12,000 positions from the payroll and cutting expenses by $700 million in 1986.[29] He then tackled another sacred cow — avoiding making IBM systems compatible with those of other manufacturers — by announcing a new framework for integrating all software applications for IBM computers.[30] He saw the latter move as necessary for IBM to develop custom-made systems solutions for its customers.

But the most important change Akers engineered was a shift in IBM's sales strategy toward a greater customer orientation. Akers knew that IBM had lost touch with many of its customers, and he realized becoming customer-oriented was not just a matter of integrating IBM software, but of understanding the customers' information needs so that custom-made systems could be developed. Based on this understanding, Akers developed a sales strategy known as *Information Systems Investment Strategies (ISIS)*. An extension of the National Account Marketing (NAM) concept, ISIS sends an IBM team into a company to study its finances, business goals, and information needs for an average period of two months.[31] In tandem with data collection, the team compiles a profile of the company and the industry. The final output is a comprehensive plan for the company to make investments in information systems over time.

Akers has the reputation of being a team player at IBM. He has been described as "decisive yet not stubborn, demanding but not tyrannical," but also as hiding "a steel hand in a velvet glove."[32] Maybe he got that steel hand playing hockey at Yale. It seems to be coming in handy these days in implementing IBM's turnaround. ■

ADVERTISING STRATEGIES

Advertising's main function in business-to-business marketing is to pave the way for a subsequent contact, whether directly or by phone. As such, it must (1) communicate product features, (2) address the specific needs and concerns of organizational buyers, and (3) communicate the vendor's capabilities.

Advertising Product Features

Business marketers choose specialized business publications directed to a particular target group for each product's advertising. *Computer Decisions* is a good magazine for advertising microcomputers and software for business information

EXHIBIT 6.2
Advertising Product Features to
Organizational Buyers

systems. *Engineering and Mining Journal* is a good magazine for advertising air blowers used in mines.

Traditionally, business ads communicating product features tend to be descriptive and unimaginative. But recently business marketers have tried to take more creative approaches. The ad for Scotch Polyurethane Protective Tape in Exhibit 6.2 is an example. The use of a rhinoceros gets the point across that the product is tough, durable, and protects exposed surfaces.

Addressing the Needs of Organizational Buyers

Business marketers also use advertising to address specific needs and concerns of organizational buyers. The ad for Mobil's synthetic lubricants (syn for short) in Exhibit 6.3 focuses on a concern of many organizational buyers — overheated machinery. The ad cites Syn as a solution that is better than conventional oils for reducing friction and increasing the life of gears and bearings.

Advertising Company Capabilities

A third role of advertising in business-to-business marketing is to communicate the overall capabilities of the company (including its technological competence) rather than specific product features or problem solutions. Also, a company might want to advertise a change in its policies or in its corporate name.

The ad for 3M's Health Care Specialties Department in Exhibit 6.4 is directed to buyers for hospitals and health maintenance organizations. It accomplishes three objectives. First, it creates awareness of 3M's capabilities in this area. Second, it indicates the types of drug delivery services and supplies that 3M offers. And, third, it shows how interested prospects can get more information.

EXHIBIT 6.3
Addressing the Needs and Concerns
of Organizational Buyers

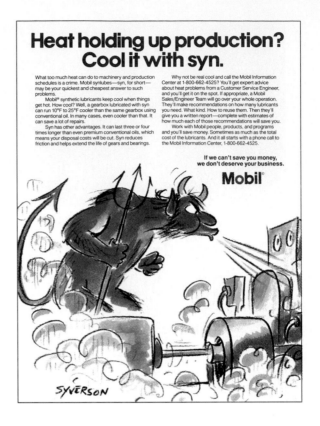

SUMMARY

1. *What are the similarities and differences between organizational buyer behavior and consumer behavior?*

The same types of factors that influence consumers influence organizational buyers, namely, the buyer's mind set, characteristics, and environment. Like consumers, organizational buyers are governed by their needs, attitudes, and perceptions of product offerings. The main differences between organizational buyers and consumers are a function of the technical complexity of business products, which leads to more decisions being made on a group basis through buying centers. Organizational buyers are also more likely to develop product specifications to fill their needs and to negotiate the fulfillment of these specifications at particular prices with sellers.

2. *What types of decisions do organizational buyers make?*

Organizational buyers make new-buy, modified-rebuy, and straight-rebuy decisions. A new buy can be characterized as complex decision making. It requires extensive information search on product specifications and vendor capabilities, careful consideration of a number of alternative vendors, and a process of group decision making. Generally, new-buy decisions are made by a buying center.

A modified rebuy is a recurring decision that is not routine. It can be characterized as limited decision making. It might involve reevaluating a straight rebuy or repurchasing a new product. Some information search is required, but it is not extensive, and brand evaluation is limited to a few vendors.

A straight rebuy is a recurring decision that can be handled on a routine basis. It parallels habit in consumer decision making. Little or no information search is required, and a vendor is chosen from an approved list.

3. *What is the role of group decision making in organizational buyer behavior?*

Group decisions are likely in organizational buying because products are complex and decisions risky, requiring the collective expertise of several individuals organized into a buying center. Members of a buying center serve a number of roles. The gatekeeper controls the flow of information into the group; the influencer sways other members; the user evaluates product needs and assesses the product's performance; and the buyer has formal authority to select a supplier and arrange terms of purchase.

4. *What are the individual and environmental influences on organizational buyers?*

Organizational buyers are influenced by their psychological set — their needs, perceptions of vendors, and attitudes toward these vendors — and their demographic characteristics. The nature of the buyer's organization also influences organizational buyers. For example, highly centralized, bureaucratic organizations are likely to encourage routine purchasing procedures and to discourage the flow of new information or consideration of product alternatives. The broader business environment also influences buyers through factors such as technological change, the degree of competitive intensity in the buyer's industry, the state of the economy, and government laws and regulations.

5. *What strategies do business-to-business marketers use to influence organizational buyers?*

Business-to-business marketers must first identify prospects based on factors such as industry grouping, size, and location. Then they must develop sales and advertising strategies to meet the needs of these prospects. Personal selling is the most important component of the business-to-business marketing plan. Advertising strategy is used to pave the way for the salesperson and has three objectives: to advertise product features, to advertise solutions to buyers' problems, and to advertise vendor capabilities.

KEY TERMS

Business-to-business marketing (p. 148)
Industrial buyers (p. 149)
Institutional buyers (p. 150)
Government agencies (p. 150)
Resellers (p. 150)
Buying center (p. 151)
Product specifications (p. 151)
Straight rebuy (p. 153)

Modified rebuy (p. 153)
New buy (p. 153)
Multiple sourcing (p. 157)
Gatekeeper (p. 159)
Derived demand (p. 161)
National account marketing (NAM) (p. 163)
Telemarketing (p. 163)

QUESTIONS

1. What was the cause of IBM's downturn in the mid 1980s according to its CEO, John Akers? What is the company doing to reverse the slide? What do these strategies have to do with organizational buyer behavior?

2. What are the differences among industrial buyers, institutional buyers, and resellers?

3. What are the differences between organizational buying behavior and consumer behavior? What are the strategic implications of these differences for business-to-business marketers?

4. Consider the three types of decisions in Table 6.2 — new buy, modified rebuy, and straight rebuy. Which decision process is most likely to apply to each of the following categories and why?

   a. Purchase of a pollution control system for a chemical company's processing plants.
   b. Purchase of office supplies for a bank's branch offices.
   c. Purchase of various grades of aluminum by a manufacturer of kitchen utensils.
   d. Purchase by an airline company of a computerized scheduling and booking system.

5. Under what circumstances might a company switch from a new buy to a modified rebuy in making a decision to purchase industrial generators? Under what circumstances might the company switch from a straight rebuy to a modified rebuy in making a decision to buy metal fasteners?

6. A purchasing agent for a large industrial company tends to buy products from the same vendors because of long-established relationships with the salespeople from these companies. The purchasing agent is confident about the vendor's products and service reliability.

   a. How is this vendor loyalty an advantage to the buyer?
   b. What are the potential risks?

7. An organizational buyer responsible for purchasing petrochemicals used to manufacture plastics considered the difference between vendor loyalty and inertia, and made the following comments:

   > Any organizational buyer that buys from the same vendor based on inertia should be fired. When we buy petrochemicals, even on a straight rebuy to replenish stocks, we are always evaluating a supplier's performance. We would take a supplier off the approved list in a minute if we saw a decrease in quality or a failure to meet delivery dates. Just because a buyer feels comfortable with the same vendor is no reason to continue to deal with the company. We are supposed to maximize our company's profits, not to lie low and avoid making waves.

   a. Do you agree with the buyer's views on dealing with the same vendor based on inertia?
   b. Would you fire an organizational buyer who is motivated to buy based on inertia?

8. What strategies do organizational buyers use to reduce the risk of vendor selection? What are the problems with each of these strategies?

9. A pharmaceutical company is considering converting its plants to reduce industrial emissions and limit pollution. What are likely to be the differences in criteria used to evaluate alternative vendors' proposals by the (a) purchasing, (b) engineering, and (c) production departments?

10. How do the characteristics of the buyer's organization and the buyer's environment influence product and vendor choice?

11. Why is personal selling the most important component of the business-to-business marketing mix?

12. What roles does advertising play in the business-to-business marketing mix? Cite examples.

CASE 6.1

HEWLETT-PACKARD TARGETS ITS CUSTOMERS

Source: Based on "Mild-Mannered Hewlett-Packard Is Making Like Superman," *Business Week,* March 7, 1988.

In the early 1980s, Hewlett-Packard (HP) had the reputation of being an engineering-oriented company with an inadequate understanding of customer needs. It built high-quality mainframe computers. The failure of its 1983 plunge into personal computers did not surprise most industry analysts. The company did not have the marketing savvy to compete with Apple and IBM in the PC market. Its lack of customer orientation was reflected in one buyer's comments: "I feel HP's raining features on me, rather than understanding the problems I have and finding a solution."

Even when it became apparent that a solution to many customers' problems lay in a systems orientation that would establish information networks by tying together mainframes, microcomputers, and PCs, HP's salesforce still tended to sell one product at a time. Its decentralized structure created barriers against selling systems.

By 1984 HP's management realized it had to get rid of its product orientation and decentralized structure if it was to meet customer needs. First, it eliminated its product-oriented organization by reorganizing its 54 product divisions into market groupings that sold to particular sectors of the economy such as financial services or local governments. Its second step was to retrain its salesforce to become more systems-oriented and sell on a team basis. For example, in the past, one salesperson might sell AT&T's signal network division a computer to control microwave instruments, while another salesperson from a different HP division might sell the same group a signal processor. Now an HP team sells an overall signal network system composed of computers, processors, and microwave instruments.

HP's systems capability rests on the concept of a National Account Marketing (NAM) group, described earlier in this chapter. HP demands that its NAM groups be intimately familiar with the systems needs of its customers, even if it requires them to work for a customer for months.

Analysts are still somewhat skeptical of HP's marketing abilities. But they feel the company's reorganization and more customer-oriented perspective is moving it in the right direction.

1. What are the similarities between HP and IBM in

(1) the requirement to more effectively adjust to customer needs and (2) the steps they took to do so?

2. Why did HP establish National Account Marketing groups to sell its customers systems solutions?

3. Does this case support the statement that personal selling is the most important component of the marketing mix for the business-to-business marketer? Why or why not?

NOTES

1. "IBM's Big Blues: A Legend Tries to Remake Itself," *Fortune*, January 19, 1987, p. 34; and "Vaunted IBM Culture Yields to New Values: Openness, Efficiency," *The Wall Street Journal*, November 11, 1988, pp. A1, A9.

2. "The Moment of Truth for Big Blue," *The New York Times*, January 3, 1988, pp. F1, F6; "IBM's Travails Test Its Sales Force," *Sales & Marketing Management*, June 1987, p. 60; and "How IBM Is Fighting Back," *Business Week*, November 17, 1986, p. 152.

3. *Fortune*, January 19, 1987, p. 35.

4. *The New York Times*, January 3, 1988, p. F6.

5. "The Great Value-Added Push Revolutionizes IBM," *Business Marketing*, November 1987, p. 70.

6. *IBM 1987 Annual Report*, p. 8.

7. *The Wall Street Journal*, November 11, 1988, p. A1; and *Sales & Marketing Management*, June 1987, p. 60.

8. *EMI and the CT Scanner (B)* (Boston: Harvard Business School, HBS Case Services, 1983).

9. "The Rise and Fall of EMI," *International Management*, June 1980, pp. 21–25.

10. Rowland T. Moriarty, Jr., and Robert E. Spekman, "An Empirical Investigation of the Information Sources Used During the Industrial Buying Process," *Journal of Marketing Research* 21 (May 1984): 137–147.

11. See P. J. Robinson, C. W. Faris, and Y. Wind, *Industrial Buying and Creative Marketing* (Boston: Allyn and Bacon, 1968).

12. Peter Lawrence Bubb and David John van Rest, "Loyalty as a Component of the Industrial Buying Decision," *Industrial Marketing Management* 3 (1973): 25–32.

13. Anita M. Kennedy, "The Complex Decision to Select a Supplier: A Case Study," *Industrial Marketing Management* 12 (1983): 45–56.

14. Yoram Wind, "Industrial Source Loyalty," *Journal of Marketing Research* 7 (November 1970): 450–457.

15. "Crafting 'Win-Win Situations' In Buyer-Supplier Relationships," *Business Marketing*, June 1986, p. 43.

16. Donald R. Lehmann and John O'Shaughnessy, "Difference in Attribute Importance for Different Industrial Products," *Journal of Marketing* 38 (April 1974): 36–42.

17. Christopher P. Puto, Wesley E. Patton III, and Ronald H. King, "Risk Handling Strategies in Industrial Vendor Selection Decisions," *Journal of Marketing* 49 (Winter 1985): 89–98.

18. See M. Baker and S. Parkinson, "Information Source Preference in Industrial Adoption Decisions," in Barnett A. Greenberg and Danny N. Bellinger, eds. *Proceedings of the American Marketing Association Educators' Conference*, Series No. 41 (1977), pp. 258–261; and Urban B. Ozanne and Gilbert A. Churchill, Jr., "Five Dimensions of the Industrial Adoption Process," *Journal of Marketing Research* 8 (August 1971): 322–328.

19. Moriarty and Spekman, "An Empirical Investigation."

20. Ronald H. Gorman, "Role Conception and Purchasing Behavior," *Journal of Purchasing* 7 (February 1971): 57.

21. Michael P. Peters and M. Venkatesan, "Exploration of Variables Inherent in Adopting an Industrial Product," *Journal of Marketing Research* 10 (August 1973): 312–315.

22. Ozanne and Churchill, "Five Dimensions of the Industrial Adoption Process."

23. Charles R. O'Neal, Hans B. Thorelli, and James M. Utterback, "Adoption of Innovation by Industrial Organizations," *Industrial Marketing Management* 2 (1973): 235–250.

24. John A. Czepiel, "Decision Group and Firm Characteristics in an Industrial Adoption Decision," in Kenneth L. Bernhardt, ed., *Proceedings of the American Marketing Association Educators' Conference*, Series No. 39 (1976), pp. 340–343.

25. Rowland T. Moriarty and David J. Reibstein, "Benefit Segmentation in Industrial Markets," *Journal of Business Research* 14 (1986): 463–486.

26. John A. Barrett, "Why Major Account Selling Works," *Industrial Marketing Management* 15 (1986): 63–73.

27. "Measurex: The Results Company," *Business Marketing*, November 1985, pp. 64, 66.

28. "Be Nice to Everybody," *Forbes*, November 5, 1984, p. 245.

29. "John Akers," *Business Week*, April 17, 1987, p. 210; and "Letting the Sun Shine in," *Fortune*, August 3, 1987, p. 29.

30. "IBM's Very Tough Guy," *Business Month*, February 1988, pp. 22–28.

31. *Fortune*, August 3, 1987, p. 29.

32. "IBM: More Worlds to Conquer," *Business Week*, February 18, 1985, p. 86.

SONY — RESEARCHING THE MARKET FOR ELECTRONIC PHOTOGRAPHY

In 1981 Sony's chairman demonstrated a prototype of the company's ProMavica electronic photography system on the Tonight Show. The system allows the user to take a picture on a two-inch disk that fits into a special camera, requires no developing, and can be shown immediately by inserting the disk in a recorder connected to a video monitor. In December 1987 the company started to market the camera.[1]

What happened in the intervening six years? Exhaustive marketing research and information collection to identify the market, define customer needs, and redesign the product based on these needs.

Initially, Sony identified 20 to 25 business markets with imaging needs that the ProMavica might fill. To pare the number of targets down, it conducted informal interviews with managers in each of these markets to determine their specific imaging needs. On this basis, the primary target was identified as the newspaper industry with its need for electronic news gathering. A secondary target was the *Fortune 500* (the largest corporations in the United States), to fill presentations and corporate communications needs.

Sony next developed a detailed questionnaire based on the information it had gained from the informal interviews and sent it to a large sample of newspaper publishers. The survey asked about respondents' current photographic procedures, including their volume of photo processing and film use and the number of staff photographers. The results revealed a need for higher-resolution pictures than the ProMavica could provide, so the company went back to the drawing boards.

The next step, in 1987, was to conduct 150 tests of prototypes of an improved ProMavica among both newspaper publishers and companies in the *Fortune 500*.[2] The company actually installed the camera system on site in companies in the United States, Japan, and Europe and, after two to four weeks, interviewed users. The ProMavica was further modified based on these product tests. For example, many users asked for lighter-weight recorders so that pictures could be shown outside the office. As a result, Sony introduced a portable viewer in 1988.

The last step in Sony's research was to determine how to position the ProMavica so as to best communicate user benefits in its advertising. Should advertising focus on the camera or the total system, including camera, recorder, and video monitor? Interviews with about 200 prospective users found a clear preference for a systems approach. The survey concluded that the market was not defined as photography but as "imaging," which required advertising the total system.[3]

Sony's systematic approach to researching the ProMavica market included informal interviews to define the market on a preliminary basis, more detailed surveys to define customer needs, product tests to determine customer reactions to the product, and additional surveys to determine how to best position the product when it was introduced. Sony has yet to determine whether the ProMavica is a success, but sales figures in 1988 were encouraging. Sony appears to have established the informational base for a successful product. ■

YOUR FOCUS IN CHAPTER 7

(1) *What is the role of a marketing information system in developing marketing plans?*

(2) *What is the role of marketing research in marketing planning?*

(3) *How is marketing research conducted?*

(4) *What are the sources of marketing data?*

(5) *What is the nature of the "information revolution" that has occurred in marketing in the 1980s?*

● ● ●

DEVELOPING A MARKETING INFORMATION SYSTEM

In the last four chapters, we have seen how marketers use knowledge of customers, competition, and the environment to identify opportunities as a basis for developing marketing strategies. The foundation of opportunity identification is *information* — on consumer needs, competitive activities, consumer reactions to the company's products, advertising strategies, salespeople, and changes in the marketing environment.

Marketers must also collect information on product and company performance in the form of sales and cost data. Environmental and company information must be integrated into a **marketing information system** (MIS), so it can be used effectively by managers in developing marketing plans and strategies. A MIS is a company facility that collects and analyzes information from diverse sources, then disseminates it in usable form. This definition implies that a marketing information system must have two capabilities: (1) to integrate information and (2) to disseminate it to decision makers.

The first capability, integration, allows management to look at the relationship between environmental factors, competition, customers, and company sales. A prototype of a MIS is presented in Figure 7.1. It shows three broad sources of information — internal company information on performance, environmental information, and customer information. These three sources are organized into three subsystems: an internal reporting system that obtains information on company sales and marketing expenditures; an environmental scanning system that obtains information on competition, technology, the economy, and legal and regulatory changes; and a marketing research system that obtains information on customer attitudes, perceptions, and behavior.

Integration means tying this information together through data analysis to determine what factors affect sales results. For example, the MIS must be able to link changes in technology, competitive actions, or company advertising expenditures to a product's performance.

Dissemination of information means sending the right data at the right time to those managers who require it to develop marketing plans and strategies. The MIS must be able to identify the type of information needed by various decision centers in the organization. For example, a business manager responsible for Sony's photography business unit will need information on broad environmental trends such as technological changes, changes in foreign import quotas, or capabilities of U.S. competitors such as Kodak or Polaroid. The product manager for Sony's ProMavica would need more specific information on results of product tests, customers' intention to buy, and their reaction to alternative product positionings. Whereas the business manager would rely primarily on the environmental scanning component of a MIS, the product manager would rely on the marketing research component.

We will consider each of the three MIS reporting systems in Figure 7.1. We will then focus on the marketing research system for the rest of the chapter, because marketing research is the primary source of information on customer needs — and customer needs must be central to the development of all marketing plans and strategies.

INTERNAL REPORTING SYSTEM

The internal reporting system provides management with data on retail sales, factory shipments, and marketing expenditures. **Factory shipments** are the amount of goods the firm sells to retailers and wholesalers. Retail sales data are provided to companies by independent firms that specialize in such measurements. Without such data, firms do not know how much of their products are sold by retailers at any given time.

Information from the internal reporting system provides marketing managers with revenue and cost data that are the basis for evaluating the profit performance of each product. Some firms have a system that provides immediate access to such data. For example, sales managers at General Mills receive daily reports on shipments in their area, which they can compare with sales targets and the previous year's performance.

ENVIRONMENTAL SCANNING SYSTEM

The environmental scanning system tracks changes in the marketing environment that might create future opportunities or threats. Information compiled from diverse sources reveals potential changes in consumer demand, competition, technology, the economy, or government regulation. Compared to the internal reporting and marketing research systems, environmental scanning is relatively unstructured. It does not rely on existing databases or formal studies, but rather on a loose network of information that is channeled to a manager or department to review for insights and trends.

At Levi Strauss a small environmental scanning group watches closely for environmental changes that might affect the demand for clothing, particularly demographic and lifestyle trends, changes in family roles, and government regulations. The group also tracks economic factors, such as clothing imports, and technological trends, such as improvements in synthetic fibers and in stretch fabrics.[4]

A firm that makes a business of environmental scanning, Inferential Focus, reviews more than 200 publications to find early warnings of political, economic, or social change that could affect the businesses of its subscribers. More than 50 clients pay $25,000 a year for this service. Recently, it detected a shift by baby boomers to a more sedentary, at-home lifestyle. One projected result of that trend is increased sales of microwaves and frozen foods and decreased restaurant sales.[5]

FIGURE 7.1
The Marketing Information System

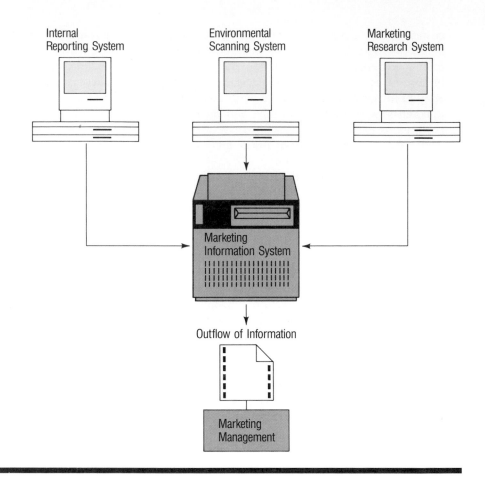

MARKETING RESEARCH SYSTEM

The marketing research system reports on consumer needs, attitudes toward the firm's product offerings, and reactions to advertising, price, and promotional strategies. Of particular importance are data on consumer purchase intentions.

The primary sources of information are consumer studies conducted by the marketing organization, marketing research firms, and advertising agencies. We will be discussing these activities in the rest of this chapter.

THE NATURE OF MARKETING RESEARCH

We will discuss the nature of marketing research by considering its importance and its role in the planning process.

**IMPORTANCE OF
MARKETING RESEARCH**

The importance of marketing research is evident by its impact on marketing strategies. It was marketing research that gave Ford a competitive edge in its introduction of its Taurus and Sable models in 1985. Inroads by Japanese car makers spurred Ford to launch the largest series of market studies it had ever conducted on consumer preferences. Four years of these studies led to a "want" list of 1,401 features that car buyers were looking for.[6]

Marketing research also led to the introduction of American Express's successful Buyer Assurance Plan, giving purchasers warranty protection on certain items bought with their American Express card. In looking for a way to expand the use of its card beyond travel and entertainment, the company discovered, through marketing research, that consumers were concerned about paying hard-earned dollars for appliances that might break down, furniture that might crack, or electronics that might fail. Its novel concept of extending the manufacturer's warranties increased use of the card on warranty items by 40 percent, and card applications soared.[7]

A measure of the importance of marketing research is its scope. Procter & Gamble interviews well over 1 million people each year on literally thousands of projects to evaluate current brands and identify new opportunities. More money is also being invested in refining the accuracy of information on which decisions are made. For example, for the first time, marketers can determine which commercials specific households have watched and what their purchases were before and after seeing those commercials.

In each of the cases discussed thus far, marketing research identified an unmet need and management successfully developed a product or service to meet it. But marketing research does not guarantee success. Companies sometimes conduct the wrong kind of research, or they conduct the right research but ignore it. Consider the decision by one of the most savvy marketing companies, Coca-Cola, to change the formula of its flagship brand. The rationale was logical — the brand was losing market share to Pepsi primarily among teenagers. So why not change the formula to make it sweeter and more appealing to that major segment.

In extensive taste tests, the new Coke was a consistent winner over the old Coke, and it won over Pepsi more than 50 percent of the time.[8] Yet the uproar was heard around the world when Coca-Cola withdrew old Coke from the market and replaced it with new Coke. Disaffected Coke drinkers wanted their brand back. In two short months Coca-Cola's management was forced to reintroduce old Coke as "Coca-Cola Classic."

What happened? The tests Coca-Cola conducted were "blind" taste tests; that is, there was no label on the can. As a result, consumers were reacting solely to taste, not to image. What would have happened if tests had been conducted with labels intact? Old Coke might very well have been a winner, because it represented more than just a soft drink to many people. Coca-Cola's competitive position could not be determined based on taste alone. How consumers *felt* about the product was the key element Coca-Cola overlooked.

Coca-Cola's "mistake" did not turn out too badly. Both classic and new Coke are now in supermarkets, classic to make the loyal Coke drinkers happy and new Coke positioned to compete with Pepsi. But lack of adequate research could seriously hurt a company, as when Procter & Gamble failed to recognize the taste deficiency of Pringle's potato chips when they were first introduced because management was so focused on the cylindrical container that keeps the chips fresh.

As we saw, the role of marketing research is to provide marketing managers information to identify marketing opportunities and to develop strategies to exploit these opportunities. Figure 7.2 shows a flow of information from the marketing environment to the marketing organization through the marketing re-

RISKS OF MARKETING RESEARCH

ROLE OF MARKETING RESEARCH

FIGURE 7.2
The Relationship of Marketing Research
and Marketing Management

Source: Adapted from Henry Assael, *Marketing Management* (Boston, Mass: Kent Publishing, 1985),
p. 191.

search process, and a flow of marketing strategies from the organization to the environment through the marketing management function.

In the first step, a marketing opportunity or problem is identified. For instance, Stouffer's management felt that an opportunity to introduce a tastier line of diet foods might exist, based on the increasing weight and health consciousness of the American public and the lack of enthusiasm for diet foods. Marketing research confirmed this opportunity: A survey of dieters identified four objections to existing diet foods; they were bland, lacked variety, were not filling, and did not look particularly appetizing. This dissatisfaction gave Stouffer's management the opening to introduce Lean Cuisine, which became the leading brand of frozen diet foods.

In Step 2, management develops alternative strategies to exploit opportunity. Stouffer's strategy was to try to develop a tasty line of low-calorie entrees, a task that had eluded other marketers. The company spent five years in this effort.[9] Its development kitchens ground their own meat to control fat content and made heavy use of vegetables and herbs to develop tastier diet dishes. Simultaneously, management was considering how to position the prospective line. Three positionings were considered — a good-tasting food with a low-calorie appeal as secondary, a low-calorie food with good taste as secondary, or an emphasis on the line as a light food.

In the third step in Figure 7.2, marketing research tests alternative strategies formulated by management. Stouffer's tested the entrees developed by its kitchens on a panel of consumers to determine whether they regarded them as tasty, filling, and appetizing. In addition, mock-ups of sample ads were developed representing alternative positionings for the product line. One ad focused on the low-calorie appeal of the product based on the fact it had only 300 calories. Another emphasized good taste with the calorie appeal as secondary. These ads were tested on consumers to determine which had the greatest appeal for dieters.

In Step 4, management selects a set of marketing strategies based on this research and implements them. In the case of Stouffer's, ten entrees were selected for market introduction based on consumer evaluations. Stouffer's also decided that the product should not be identified as a diet food, since dieters dislike being reminded they are on a diet. As a result, the name Lean Cuisine was selected. Consumer responses to alternative positionings also led management to decide to emphasize good taste, with low calories and weight watching as secondary themes. The rationale was that any diet food could emphasize low calories. Lean Cuisine's distinctive advantage was its good taste and appetizing appearance.

Once the marketing strategy is implemented, marketing research evaluates consumer reactions (step 5). Sales results will be tracked. In addition, consumers will be surveyed to determine their awareness of the brand and the advertising, and whether they are likely to buy the product. Consumer surveys after introduction of Lean Cuisine showed high awareness of the name. A high percentage of consumers also recalled the advertising. Based on sales results, it was apparent that Lean Cuisine was a huge success. Two months after introduction, it was the leading frozen diet food. Its market share continued to climb, and it became the second-largest-selling frozen food line, second only to Stouffer's regular frozen entree line. In two short years, it became a $500 million brand.[10]

In step 6 of Figure 7.2, management adjusts the marketing strategy based on feedback from marketing research. Any adjustments that were made in Stouffer's strategies for Lean Cuisine involved increasing expenditures for the brand. The number of entrees was quickly expanded from 10 to 13 based on consumer responses, the advertising budget was increased, and production capacity was expanded by 47 percent.[11] In addition, advertising emphasis began to shift. The initial ads were informationally oriented, explaining that Lean Cuisine was tastier and more appetizing because it had beef with less than 10 percent fat content and used naturally flavored foods. Marketing research showed that the target market was aware of these features. But consumers still had to be sold on what the product would do for them. So advertising shifted to a more image-oriented appeal based on the theme, "I love the way it looks on me."[12] (See Exhibit 7.1.)

MARKETING RESEARCH PROCESS

Marketing research must be conducted rigorously and systematically to fulfill its intended role.

RIGOROUS MARKETING RESEARCH

Research is conducted rigorously when the data collected are valid, reliable, and representative.

Validity is the collection of the *right* information to meet the purposes of the research. One might question the validity of Coca-Cola's blind taste tests to measure preference for what is now Coke Classic versus new Coke and Pepsi. The assumption was that taste is the primary component of preferences for soft drinks. As we saw, brand image also has a lot to do with preferences. A labeled test might have been more valid.

By **reliability**, we mean the accuracy with which the data was collected. Researchers should attempt to collect data without any inherent measurement biases. A reliable study should yield similar results if repeated.

A case in which reliability was missing occurred in the late 1970s when Pepsi tested its flagship brand against Coke. It conducted blind taste tests, giving consumers two identical bottles, one labeled with the letter M that always contained

EXHIBIT 7.1
Shift in Lean Cuisine's Advertising Based
on Marketing Research

From: Information Advertising　　　　　　　　　　　　To: Image Advertising

Pepsi, and the other with the letter Q that always contained Coke. Pepsi was the clear favorite and the company advertised this fact. Coca-Cola then did some research and found that consumers preferred an item labeled M rather than Q, regardless of its contents. In other words, many respondents preferred Pepsi not because of its taste but because it was labeled M and Coke was labeled Q. Coca-Cola concluded that on this basis, Pepsi's test was clearly unreliable. It advertised this fact, showing that when consumers were given two identical glasses of Coke marked M and Q, M was the clear favorite.

Representativeness is the degree to which a sample of consumers represents the characteristics of a population. Researchers can rarely interview every consumer in the market, so a *sample* is usually selected to represent the **population,** that is, the total market under study. For example, in testing new Coke, the population was defined as all cola drinkers. A sample can never be a perfect representation of the population, but researchers can try to make it as representative as possible. Generally, the larger the sample size, the greater its representativeness.

In testing new Coke, assume that 60 percent of the sample was teenagers, but that data shows that only 40 percent of all cola consumption is accounted for by teenagers. Teenagers would thus be overrepresented in the sample. Since teenag-

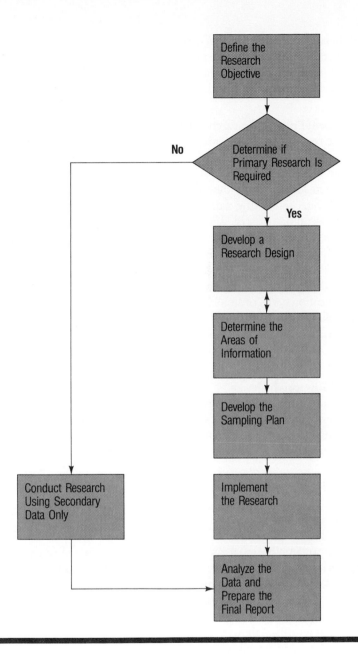

FIGURE 7.3
Steps in the Marketing Research Process

ers prefer a sweeter cola, overrepresenting them in the sample would create an unfair advantage for new Coke, given its sweeter taste. Actually, it appears that Coca-Cola did select a representative sample of cola drinkers.

Besides being rigorous, marketing research should be systematic, meaning it should follow a logical series of steps to achieve the research objectives. These steps are outlined in Figure 7.3.

SYSTEMATIC RESEARCH: STEPS IN THE MARKETING RESEARCH PROCESS

Define Research Objectives

The first step in the research process is defining the research objectives. For example, AT&T determined that it had little information on the telephone needs of its small-business customers. Its research objective was to obtain information on how to adapt its services and equipment to small businesses. This objective dictated all subsequent steps in the research process — the type of research to be conducted, the questions asked, the sample, and the data analysis.

Determine If Primary Research Is Required

Once the research objectives are defined, the next step is to consider whether a research study is required, and if so, what type. Frequently, a company's questions can be answered by past studies, by information collected by industry or government sources, or by the company's own data on shipments and expenditures. We refer to existing data from such sources as **secondary data**. Data collected by a company for the specific purpose of answering its research questions are known as **primary data**.

A logical first step in the research process is for a researcher to determine whether existing (secondary) data can answer the research questions. AT&T conducted a computerized search for secondary data, turning up 40 articles on communication needs of small businesses. But these articles did not refer directly to attitudes of small businesses toward AT&T or its equipment.

Because of the lack of sufficient information from secondary data, it was apparent to AT&T's management that it would have to conduct primary research.

Develop a Research Design

If the researcher decides that primary information must be collected, the next step is to determine how. Figure 7.4 shows that researchers can use qualitative research, survey research, experimentation, observation, and case studies to implement a research plan.

Qualitative Research **Qualitative research** is research that asks consumers to respond to questions in an unstructured manner. As a result, analysis of the results rely totally on the interpretation of the researcher. Qualitative research is often used to collect primary data when the required information is too complex, vague, or potentially embarrassing to ask the respondent directly. It is also used to better identify a research area, so that researchers will know what kinds of questions to ask in more structured surveys or experiments.

Marketing researchers use two types of qualitative approaches: focus-group or depth interviews, and projective techniques. **Focus-group interviews** are informal interviews with eight to twelve respondents. The group is asked to focus on a particular topic in an open-ended discussion guided by a trained moderator. Focus groups are a good vehicle for obtaining information, because respondents can talk freely and often encourage each other to talk more openly. When such interviews are conducted on an individual rather than a group basis, they are called **depth interviews**.

One study, conducted before flying was so commonplace, used focus groups to try to determine why men resisted flying for business purposes. The discussions found it was not so much fear of flying as guilt that if they died they would leave behind their loved ones. As a result, the airline sponsoring the study developed a campaign that focused on the joy of coming back to the family from a business trip rather than the more rational appeals of on-time arrival and direct flights. It is unlikely that this information could have been obtained by directly asking these businessmen why they chose not to fly.

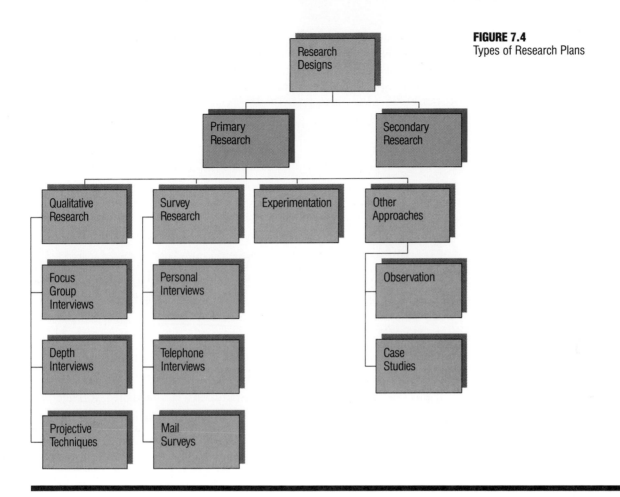

FIGURE 7.4
Types of Research Plans

Another approach is to collect qualitative data through **projective techniques**. If information is very personal or potentially embarrassing, then respondents can be given a situation, a cartoon, or a set of words and asked to react to these stimuli. They are more likely to project their true feelings because the questions are not asked directly.

A classic example of the application of projective techniques was an attempt by a coffee producer to determine why women resisted using instant coffee when it was first marketed in the late 1940s. The researcher constructed two identical shopping lists, except that one included regular coffee and the other instant coffee. Housewives were then asked to project the type of woman most likely to have developed each shopping list.

The woman who included instant coffee was characterized as being lazy and not concerned with her family. Women in the study apparently had a deep-seated fear that if they used instant coffee, they would be seen by their husbands as avoiding their traditional homemaker roles. As a result, the company advertised instant coffee in a family setting portraying the husband's approval.[13] Today, such a study would produce very different results since women's acceptance of a traditional homemaker role is not as widespread.

Qualitative research studies can also be used to develop hypotheses that are then tested in subsequent research that is more quantitative. AT&T conducted focus-group interviews with small-business owners and found that those who were unwilling to consider competitive equipment gave AT&T's service reliability as their reason. As a result, a primary objective of a subsequent survey was to determine perceptions of AT&T's telecommunications services, and the interaction between these perceptions and the willingness to consider competitive equipment.

Ernest Dichter — Father of Qualitative Research

Source: UPI/Bettmann Newsphotos.

What happens to some consumers when they get behind the wheel of a car? They get a sense of freedom and power. They look for the surge of acceleration to free themselves from the mundane aspects of everyday life. So if you want to advertise gasoline, go along with this feeling and advertise, "There is a tiger in your tank."[14] Why do some men resist giving blood? Because they equate it with a loss of potency. So have the Red Cross advertise to potential donors that they are lending rather than giving their blood, because blood gets regenerated in a short period of time.[15]

Although such reasoning is well-accepted today, the idea of exploring the "why" of consumer behavior was not always widely accepted. It began to gain favor as the result of one man's efforts, Ernest Dichter. Now in his eighties, Dichter can look back to his early training in Freudian psychoanalysis in Vienna as the springboard for his future attitude to marketing research. When he came to this country in 1938 to escape the Nazi takeover of Austria, Dichter found work in a marketing research firm. What he found was a superficial research process. For example, when Chrysler tried to find out why 64 percent of consumers bought the same make of car, the answer was that they were satisfied with their previous car. Today we know that deeper motives are often involved in such choices.

In applying his training in psychology to investigate consumer motives, Dichter borrowed the techniques of depth and focus-group interviewing and projective techniques. One of his first applications of qualitative research was for Procter & Gamble around 1940. Asked to investigate soap usage to determine if there was a way to revitalize Ivory Soap, he did some depth interviews with teenagers and found that bathing was almost a ritual, especially before a date. It was a means of "getting rid of all your bad feelings, your sins, your immorality, and cleansing yourself."[16] On this basis, Dichter developed the slogan, "Be smart, get a fresh start with Ivory soap . . . wash all your troubles away." That classic study was the beginning of Dichter's success and cost P&G all of $400.[17]

Today, over 5,000 studies and 17 books later, Dichter continues to head the company he founded, the Institute for Motivational Research, and is internationally acclaimed as the father of qualitative research. ■

	PERSONAL INTERVIEWS	TELEPHONE INTERVIEWS	MAIL SURVEYS
Amount of data that can be collected	Large	Moderate	Moderate
Feasibility of complicated questions	Yes	Sometimes	No
Ability to present visual stimuli	Yes	No	Sometimes
Likelihood of cooperation (response rates)	Moderate	Moderate	Low
Time required to get data	Moderate	Quick	Slow
Potential response bias	High	Moderate	Low
Cost	Very high	Moderate	Low

TABLE 7.1
Characteristics of Three Methods of Survey Research

Survey Research The most important and commonly used method of collecting primary data is through a consumer survey. Surveys involve selecting a representative sample of respondents from a population, developing a questionnaire, asking the respondents questions, and analyzing the results.

A researcher must determine whether the survey will be conducted in person, by telephone, or by mail. Each method has its advantages and disadvantages, as summarized in Table 7.1. For example, a *personal interview* is usually necessary when a large amount of information is required, when more complicated questions must be asked, or when visual stimuli such as an advertisement or a new-product concept must be shown to consumers. But the potential for *response bias* due to the interaction between interviewer and respondent is high (many respondents like to give the answers they think the interviewer wants), and personal interviews are the most expensive method of data collection.

Telephone interviews are best used for shorter interviews that require no visual stimuli, and when data is needed quickly. *Mail surveys* are frequently used as an inexpensive means of collecting data. There is less chance of response bias on the respondent's part, since there is no interaction with an interviewer. But returns from mail surveys are low, and a longer period of time is required to get data.

In the AT&T survey, the company could have used any of the three methods in Table 7.1. It decided to test all three to see which was best. It found that mail surveys were the best approach since small-business owners did not have the time to give to a phone call or personal interview. They could take a mail questionnaire home and send it back. Although response rates to mail questionnaires are generally much lower than for personal or telephone interviews, in this case response rates were high to the mail questionnaire because of the respondents' interest in the survey.

Experimentation Marketing researchers often want to test how marketing variables such as advertising, sales promotions, or price level are related to sales results. This requires establishing a cause-and-effect relationship between these variables and sales. The researcher must try to control all outside factors so that sales results can be attributed to the particular marketing strategy being tested.

Experimentation is this type of research that attempts to test for cause and effect under controlled conditions.

For example, if a marketer wants to test the effects of in-store displays on sales, two groups of stores might be selected and in-store displays introduced into one and not the other. But suppose the stores having displays are larger or in higher-income neighborhoods than the stores not carrying displays. Then if sales are higher for the stores with displays, the researcher does not know to what extent this is due to the displays and to what extent it is due to the other factors. One solution is to *match* the stores so that each group has the same number of larger and smaller stores and the same number of stores in high- and low-income areas.

Now assume sales go up 10 percent in the stores with displays and 4 percent in the stores without displays over the test period. Then management can safely attribute higher sales in the stores with displays to the effects of the displays, since the stores are equal in other respects.

Observation Observation can be direct or indirect. As an example of *direct observation,* Q-tips were created when their inventor observed midwives wrapping cotton around wooden sticks.[18] Similarly, Curad Battle Ribbon adhesive bandages were developed as a result of direct observation of children decorating bandages with crayons and felt-tip pens.[19] Researchers used *indirect observation* when, having determined that they could not get reliable estimates of alcohol consumption through direct questioning, they then measured the number of empty bottles in the garbage.[20]

Case Studies Case studies are comprehensive analyses of a particular situation. They are used mainly by industrial marketers to study the purchasing process of their customers. For example, if an industrial firm wants to determine how buying groups operate in its industry, it might select four or five companies for intensive study to determine the composition of their buying groups, the criteria used by members for selecting vendors, and potential conflicts within the groups.

Determine the Areas of Information

Concurrent with establishing a research approach, the marketing researcher determines the areas of information to be collected (thus the double arrow between these two steps in Figure 7.3). In most cases, information is collected using a questionnaire administered by an interviewer. In the AT&T study, the questionnaire asked small-business people for information on their telephone usage and equipment, their view of the importance of telephone service, the role of the telephone in conducting their business, and the likelihood of their buying competitive equipment.

The questions in a questionnaire should be carefully crafted, since the same question asked two different ways can produce very different results. For example, when one researcher showed a picture of Ronald Reagan to respondents and asked, "You know who this man is, don't you?", most people correctly identified the picture. But when the researcher asked, "Do you have any idea at all who this man is?", only one out of fifteen people identified Reagan.[21] Similarly, consumers are more likely to answer that they purchased a particular brand when asked, "Did you buy brand X in your last purchase?" than if they are asked, "Which of the following brands did you buy the last time you purchased this product?"

Researchers should be aware of several principles of questionnaire construction. One is to avoid putting the respondent on the defensive by asking questions such as, "Why didn't you buy brand X the last time you purchased?" A second principle is to avoid identifying the sponsor of the survey. For example, questions on attitudes or perceptions of a company's brand should be asked along with those for competitive brands. A third principle is to ask more sensitive questions, such as those pertaining to income, at the end of the questionnaire, after a willingness to answer questions has already been established.

Develop the Sampling Plan

As we saw, a sample of consumers is selected to represent a population, which is the market of interest to the researcher. In the AT&T study, the population was small businesses, defined in telecommunications terms as a business establishment with three lines (telephone numbers) or less. The sample size in the study was about 1,600 small businesses, selected to be representative of all small businesses in the United States.

There are two approaches to selecting a sample: probability and nonprobability sampling. In **probability sampling**, researchers use scientific rules to ensure that the sample is representative of the population. Each individual in the population has an equal or known chance of selection. The AT&T study used this method by choosing respondents randomly from its list of small-business customers. Though probability sampling is more accurate in assuring representativeness, it is also much more costly than nonprobability sampling.

In **nonprobability sampling**, selection is based primarily on the researcher's judgment. This method is often used when the sample's representativeness is less important. For example, if a researcher is testing ten alternative package designs for a product, the purpose might be to weed out the clear losers so that two or three potential winners can be further investigated. Nonprobability sampling is adequate for such screening purposes.

Implement the Research

Once the areas of information and sampling plan are defined, the research is implemented. Most companies do not do their own research. In the small-business study, AT&T commissioned an outside research company to implement the research. Research companies may have their own interviewers or may contract out for them. They try to ensure reliability by training interviewers to ask questions without bias and to carry out the instructions for collecting information.

Analyze the Data and Prepare the Final Report

Once interviews are complete, marketing research companies will then collect and analyze the data to be presented to management. *Data analysis* summarizes the data and shows the relationship between key variables. For example, the AT&T study found that only 13.5 percent of small-business owners were considering buying competitive equipment, but among those who felt present AT&T telephone service was inadequate, the figure was 44 percent. Thus, a negative attitude toward AT&T telephone service meant that there was more than three times as much chance that a small-business owner would consider buying equipment from an AT&T competitor.

Once the data is analyzed and the report submitted, management develops action recommendations. In the AT&T study, management decided to target small businesses dissatisfied with service with ads for better service delivery, since these were the customers most likely to buy competitive equipment. Based on the

FIGURE 7.5
Sources of Marketing Data

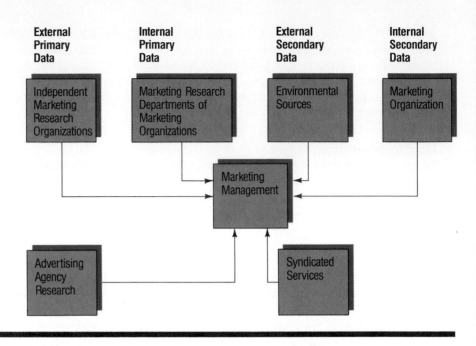

findings, management also decided to offer small businesses new products such as pagers and automatic dialers to better meet their telecommunication needs.

SOURCES OF MARKETING INFORMATION

In our discussion of the marketing research process, we focused primarily on collecting primary data — that is, data collected by a marketing organization for a specific research purpose. But, as mentioned, an important source of marketing information is secondary data — that is, past data that has been collected by other organizations such as trade associations, the government, or syndicated research firms that run continuous studies for subscribing organizations.

Figure 7.5 shows the sources of primary and secondary marketing data. These are further divided into data collected by the marketing organization *(internal data)*, and data collected by outside agencies such as marketing research firms, advertising agencies, government organizations, and other environmental sources *(external data)*. All data are directed to marketing managers to allow them to identify opportunities, and to plan for product and corporate strategies.

SOURCES OF PRIMARY DATA

Figure 7.5 shows that primary data can be collected externally or internally.

External Primary Data
Most companies use outside marketing research firms to conduct consumer surveys and product tests and to test alternative advertisements. When Coca-Cola ran its taste tests for New Coke it first used Schrader Research, a New Jersey–based company specializing in taste tests, which had specially equipped trailers located in major markets nationwide to conduct the tests. It then turned to Cambridge Survey Research, a Washington D.C. company owned by political pollster

Patrick Caddell, to do surveys to determine public reaction to a formula change.[22]

Another important source of external primary data is a firm's advertising agency, which conducts research to determine the best advertising approaches and to select the most effective media to reach the target group. Buick used its advertising agency, McCann-Erickson, to help it develop both the concept and the advertising for its Regal coupe, introduced in 1987. The effort began in 1982 with 20 focus groups across the country being asked what they wanted in a new car. Results showed they wanted a stylish but conservative car, one with lots of room, good acceleration, and gas mileage of over 20 miles a gallon. The agency then developed 20 ad concepts that were screened by consumers and narrowed down to 4, which were developed into TV commercials and print ads. These four alternative advertising approaches were again shown to consumers to help the agency select the best approach.[23]

Internal Primary Data

Marketing organizations sometimes conduct their own studies. Procter & Gamble has a staff of 250 people in its marketing research department, with specific groups responsible for qualitative research, advertising tests, product and package testing, and data analysis.[24] It also has a bank of WATS (Wide Area Telephone Service) lines it uses to do consumer surveys. At one time, the company ran 80 percent of all its studies internally, but now it uses outside services more frequently.

Most marketing firms cannot afford the in-house marketing research facilities of Procter & Gamble, but on occasion they might initiate their own small-scale studies. For example, Sony initially conducted informal interviews with prospective customers to determine the target market for the ProMavica.

Figure 7.5 shows that secondary data are available from external sources or from internal company records. Most firms will evaluate such data before incurring the costs of collecting primary data, since secondary data alone may satisfy the firm's research needs.

SOURCES OF SECONDARY DATA

External Secondary Data: Environmental Sources

There are two major sources of secondary data: (1) environmental sources such as government agencies, trade associations, or competition, and (2) syndicated research services.

The U.S. government is the largest environmental source, providing a rich storehouse of data useful to marketers in every field. The most important government source is the demographic information provided by the Bureau of the Census. We saw in Chapter 3 that key demographic trends such as the increasing proportion of working women, more singles, and the decrease in the birth rate have affected the longer-term strategies of companies like Avon, Kellogg, and Gerber. Census information is essential if these companies are to project future purchasing trends for their products. Marketers also use census data for planning. *Time* magazine uses census data to identify zip code areas that have the highest income so that it can concentrate subscription mailings in these areas.[25]

Competition is another environmental source for secondary data. Firms can obtain valuable information from a competitor's annual report and financial reports required by the Securities and Exchange Commission, in addition to competitors' salespeople and distributors.

Trade and industry publications are a valuable source of information on demand trends, competitive activities, and government regulations. *Sales & Marketing Management* provides a yearly survey of buying power that contains data on population, retail sales, and household income by county and city. The magazine develops an index of buying power based on this information for each area. An automobile manufacturer could use this buying-power index to determine purchase potential for its cars by region and thus identify areas warranting new dealerships. *Fortune* publishes a directory of the 1,000 largest U.S. companies, with information on sales, assets, profits, and number of employees.

External Secondary Data: Syndicated Research

Marketing organizations often rely on **syndicated research** firms, which collect data periodically and sell their research results to subscribing companies. The most important use of syndicated research services is to obtain retail sales data and data on advertising and media exposure.

Sales Data In the past, retail sales have been measured by **store audits**. The A. C. Nielsen Company, the largest marketing research company in the world, periodically audits the sales of a representative sample of food and drug stores nationwide. Its employees measure sales by subtracting end-of-period inventory for a particular brand from beginning inventory plus shipments. But Nielsen store audits were subject to the inaccuracies of the store auditors and were available to management only three months after an audit.

In the 1970s, **Universal Product Codes** (**UPC**) began appearing on products. These are the small vertical lines that are an identifying mark on most food and drug items. Shortly after, in-store checkout **scanner systems** appeared allowing a clerk to move a product over a laser scanner to record its UPC code both on the cash register and in a central computer file.

By 1987 over 50 percent of all supermarkets had scanner facilities.[26] Since the scanner recorded the price of the item, its size, and whether it was purchased on sale, services providing scanner data supplied manufacturers with a wealth of data that previously could be obtained only from less reliable store audits. Scanners also provided sales data much more quickly than store audits. Since scanners are not in all stores, however, store audits are still necessary to fill in the gaps.

Advertising and Media Exposure Several research firms offer services designed to determine exposure to print and TV advertising. For example, the Starch service conducts 240,000 interviews yearly, evaluating 30,000 ads, to measure awareness and readership of advertisements in magazines and newspapers.[27] It asks respondents whether they have seen the ad, remembered reading about a particular product or company, and whether they read the copy. Firms also offer services to measure exposure to TV advertising. Burke Marketing Research uses a day-after recall method in which a sample of consumers is asked whether they recall seeing a TV commercial the day after it appears.

Simmons Market Research Bureau provides the most comprehensive data on exposure to print media. The company interviews 15,000 respondents yearly and obtains data on readership of 136 magazines and purchases of 500 product categories.[28] It can then determine whether purchasers of a particular product category are more likely to read certain magazines or newspapers. For example, if Simmons finds that purchasers of camping equipment are twice as likely to read *Popular Mechanics* as the average respondent, then a company knows that advertisements in that magazine would be very effective in reaching the camping market.

The A. C. Nielsen company is the largest service that measures TV exposure. It attaches an **audimeter** to a sample of 1700 TV sets nationwide that records what each household is viewing. Households in the sample also keep a diary of what each individual member watches. In this way Nielsen can estimate not only if the set was on at a given time, but who was watching it. On the basis of this sample, the company projects TV exposure to the country as a whole, and supplies the number of viewers watching a program, as well as a demographic profile of viewers by time of exposure. This information enables companies to determine what programs they should advertise on to best reach a particular demographic target. For example, assume purchasers of camping equipment tend to be non-urban, middle-income, blue-collar individuals between 25 and 40, and that this group is more likely to watch late-night movies. Then TV commercials for camping equipment should be shown on late-night movies.

Nielsen's data on TV exposure are also important to companies because TV networks use the program ratings to sell advertising time. The higher the rating, the more costly it is to advertise on a show. One of the costliest time slots on TV is the Super Bowl because of the millions of consumers watching the broadcast.

Internal Secondary Data

Internal secondary data includes data on factory shipments, showing the amount of revenue generated by each of the company's products, and cost data such as expenditures for research, advertising, personal selling, and distribution. The combination of revenue and cost data permits a company to evaluate a product's profit performance.

An industrial firm that analyzed its profits by product category based on internal company data found that 10 percent of its products accounted for 80 percent of its profits. Further, the most profitable products were generally targeted to a small, well-defined group of customers. By eliminating many of its products and concentrating sales effort on the remaining product line and a smaller number of customers, the firm substantially increased its profits.

THE INFORMATION REVOLUTION

A description of marketing research does not capture the remarkable changes that have taken place in the late 1980s in information technology. The quantity, quality, and accessibility of information have increased significantly. Today, marketers are capable of obtaining more reliable sales information through scanner data, of accessing this information quickly through microcomputers, and of relating sales information to marketing expenditures, allowing managers to better measure the effectiveness of their advertising and sales promotions.

Three developments have made this information revolution possible: electronic measures of TV exposure, scanner data, and the microcomputer. These three components are depicted in Figure 7.6 in a series of steps that illustrate the information revolution.

COMPONENTS OF THE INFORMATION REVOLUTION

FIGURE 7.6
Components of the
Information
Revolution

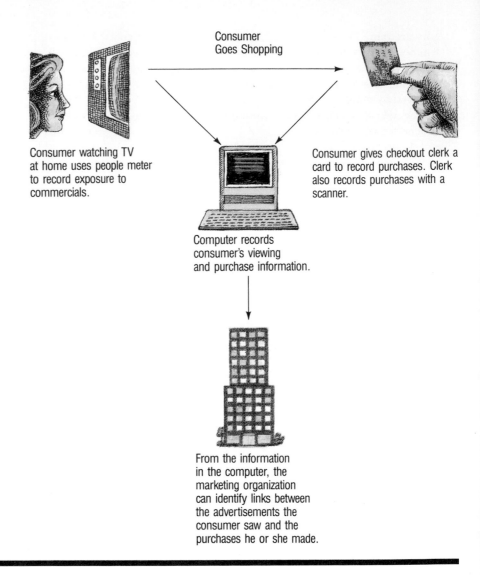

Consumer
Goes Shopping

Consumer watching TV
at home uses people meter
to record exposure to
commercials.

Consumer gives checkout clerk a
card to record purchases. Clerk
also records purchases with a
scanner.

Computer records
consumer's viewing
and purchase information.

From the information
in the computer, the
marketing organization
can identify links between
the advertisements the
consumer saw and the
purchases he or she made.

Electronic Measures of TV Exposure

The first component of the information revolution in Figure 7.6 is the electronic measurement of TV exposure (step 1). As we saw, Nielsen attaches an audimeter to sets to record what channel they are tuned in to. Consumers used to record who was watching the set through a diary questionnaire. But diaries were sometimes unreliable since they required consumers to recall what they were viewing. In 1987 Nielsen replaced audimeters and consumer diaries with **People Meters,** hand-held devices that are supposed to be pressed when a member of the household starts and stops watching TV.

Whereas audimeters could only determine whether the set was on or not, People Meters could record who was watching TV and what commercials were seen. Exposure to TV commercials could now be measured without asking consumers direct questions and having to rely on the accuracy of their recall. People Meters still lack perfect reliability, since there is no assurance that viewers will in fact "punch in" and "punch out" when viewing TV programs.

Scanner Data

The second component in the information revolution, scanner data, allows an instant record to be made of a consumer's purchases through UPC codes (steps 2 and 3 in Figure 7.6). The information is stored in a central computer and can be accessed by managers from microcomputers in other locations. A manager can thereby determine sales of a particular product by size, type, price paid, and store in which it was purchased.

Several research firms have established *consumer scanner panels,* groups of consumers who are asked to shop in stores with scanner equipment and are given computer-coded cards to be presented to the checkout clerk when they make a purchase. The researcher knows the demographic characteristics and past purchases of each consumer in the panel. When a consumer buys merchandise, the checkout clerk records the purchases by a laser scanner and punches in the consumer's card. This way, purchases can be associated with the demographic and purchase characteristics of a particular consumer based on the card identification.

The Microcomputer

As Figure 7.6 shows, marketers have immediate access through microcomputers to purchase data from scanner stores and to TV exposure data from People Meters. For example, sales data can be broken out by whether it was purchased through a coupon in each sales region. Similarly, TV exposure data could be broken out by demographic characteristics of households in the sample.

SINGLE-SOURCE DATA

Research firms that run scanner panels make sure that consumers in the panel also have TV sets equipped with People Meters. This way, they know what a particular consumer watches on TV and what purchases were made by that consumer (steps 1 and 2 in Figure 7.6). This capability is known as **single-source data**, because purchases and media exposure are both determined from the same source — the individual consumer.

Single-source data allow the researcher to determine whether exposure to TV commercials for a brand is related to subsequent purchase of the brand. Such data can answer the question, "Did a consumer buy Coca-Cola after seeing a Coke ad on TV?" Before single source data, this question could not be answered directly because there was no way to link what a consumer purchased to what the consumer saw on TV. At best, a consumer could be asked what he or she remembered seeing on TV and when. By directly linking advertising exposure to sales, single-source data provide a more reliable measure of advertising effectiveness.

The information revolution shown in Figure 7.6 was an improvement in research quality in another respect. Consumers are never directly asked any questions. Rather, questions are answered by electronic measurement of their behavior and media exposure. This eliminates inaccuracies due to the potential bias in asking questions and relying on imperfect consumer recall.

Campbell effectively used single-source data in a test of two TV commercials for its line of Swanson frozen dinners. Campbell ran the test through Information Resources Inc. (IRI), a research firm that established a single-source system like that shown in Figure 7.6. One commercial showed a young man impressing his girlfriend with a fine meal she thought he had cooked but that turned out to be a Swanson frozen dinner. The other showed Swanson as an alternative to hot dogs or hamburgers. Campbell found that Swanson purchases were 20 percent higher among viewers of the first commercial.[29]

As the Campbell example demonstrates, the information revolution is providing managers with a powerful tool: the ability to relate marketing mix variables directly to product performance. For the first time, managers can evaluate how consumers respond in a store after they have been exposed to TV commercials. Scanner systems can also tell managers how consumers respond after having been exposed to various price levels and in-store sales promotions. Never before has it been possible to evaluate so accurately the impact of alternative marketing strategies on a product's sales performance.

SUMMARY

1. *What is the role of a marketing information system in developing marketing plans?*

A marketing information system provides the capability to collect and analyze information from diverse sources and then disseminate it to decision makers. It should provide management with three capabilities: (1) to gauge a product's profit performance from information on sales revenues and costs, (2) to evaluate changes in the environment that might affect product performance, and (3) to evaluate customer perceptions, attitudes, and behavior that might affect product sales. These three requirements are filled by three subsystems of a marketing information system: an internal reporting system to provide company data, an environmental tracking system to identify environmental changes, and a marketing research system to provide customer data.

2. *What is the role of marketing research in marketing planning?*

The role of marketing research is to provide management with information to (1) identify marketing opportunities or problems, (2) develop alternative strategies to exploit these opportunities, and (3) evaluate consumer reactions to these strategies.

3. *How is marketing research conducted?*

Marketing research involves systematic steps to achieve a set of research objectives. Investigators first define the research objectives. They then review existing (secondary) data to determine if it might be sufficient to fulfill the research objectives. If not, they develop a plan to collect primary data, whether through qualitative research, a survey, or experimentation. If a survey is required, the researchers must determine if it is to be conducted in person, by telephone, or through the mail. Once the research approach is established, the researcher develops a questionnaire to collect the information and selects a sample of respondents for the study. Data is then collected and analyzed, and a final report is submitted to management.

4. *What are the sources of marketing data?*

Marketing data can be categorized as primary (data collected for the specific area being investigated) and secondary (data collected previously). Primary and secondary data can also be categorized as external (collected by outside agencies) or internal (collected by the firm).

Most companies use outside marketing research firms to collect primary data. Some large firms such as Procter & Gamble have internal facilities for implementing surveys, product tests, and other types of research. Outside sources for secondary data include government agencies, competitors, publications, trade associations, and syndicated services.

5. What is the nature of the "information revolution" that has occurred in marketing in the 1980s?

Three developments have created an information revolution in marketing: scanner data, electronic measures of TV exposure, and the microcomputer. Scanner data allows an instant record to be made of a consumer's purchases from the universal product code. Electronic measures of TV exposure determine what channel the TV set is tuned to and who is watching. Microcomputers make both sets of data quickly available to managers. Using these developments, researchers can collect single-source data, which link TV exposure to purchases and allow more accurate measurement of the effectiveness of advertising.

KEY TERMS

Marketing information system (MIS) (p. 174)
Factory shipments (p. 175)
Validity (p. 179)
Reliability (p. 179)
Representativeness (p. 180)
Population (p. 180)
Secondary data (p. 182)
Primary data (p. 182)
Qualitative research (p. 182)
Focus-group interviews (p. 182)
Depth interviews (p. 182)

Projective techniques (p. 183)
Experimentation (p. 186)
Probability sampling (p. 187)
Nonprobability sampling (p. 187)
Syndicated research (p. 190)
Store audits (p. 190)
Universal product code (p. 190)
Scanner systems (p. 190)
Audimeter (p. 191)
People meters (p. 192)
Single-source data (p. 193)

QUESTIONS

1. What were Sony's research objectives in testing the ProMavica electronic photography system?

2. What are valid, reliable, and representative marketing data? In testing new Coke versus old Coke and Pepsi, how well did Coca-Cola meet the requirements of validity, reliability, and representativeness?

3. Assume Pepsi-Cola conducted a study before it introduced Slice to determine the potential for a new fruit-based soft drink. Its research objectives were to (a) determine if a fruit-based soft drink might better meet the nutritional needs of adults than existing colas and (b) identify the market for such a product. Describe the research process the company might have implemented based on the steps in Figure 7.3.

4. What type of research approach — qualitative, survey, or experimental — would a company be most likely to use in the following cases, and why?

   a. Identifying the demographic and lifestyle characteristics of potential buyers of a new fruit-and-nut snack.

   b. Testing two or three formulations of the product on consumers to determine which is most effective.

   c. Determining if consumers might have any deep-seated resistance to accepting fruit as a snack.

5. Because sales of men's hats have been slowly decreasing, a hat manufacturer is considering whether to get out of the business. Before it does, it would like to determine why sales have been decreasing to see if it can do something to reverse the trend.

   a. How can the company use focus-group interviews and projective techniques to evaluate why sales of men's hats are decreasing?

   b. What are the purposes of each of these techniques?

6. One marketing executive, commenting on Ernest Dichter's qualitative approach to marketing research, said:

   I always take Dichter's findings with a grain of salt. It's fine to say, for example, that men did not like to fly because of guilt in leaving their families behind, or that bathing is a ritual. But these findings are based on the comments of just a few consumers and rely on Dichter's insights. Even Dichter will admit that he might develop a hypothesis based on the comment of one respondent. What happens if he is just plain wrong?

   a. Is this marketing executive's concern with qualitative research justified?
   b. What might be a possible solution to the concern about (a) small samples and (b) relying on the interpretations of the researcher?

7. What are the advantages and disadvantages of personal interviews, telephone interviews, and mail surveys?
8. What is an example of an experiment in a marketing research study? Why would you classify the study you cited as an experiment?
9. The investigation of the small-business market by

AT&T warranted the collection of primary data through survey research. Why was it necessary to collect primary data? Under what circumstances might secondary data be sufficient to investigate a marketing research area? What are the dangers of relying only on secondary data?
10. An industrial producer of auto parts finds its sales slipping. Management feels the cause could be inefficient allocation of sales effort. How can the company use internal secondary data to investigate the cause of this decline?
11. What is the significance of scanner data for marketing managers?
12. What are single-source data? What is the significance of single-source data in evaluating advertising effectiveness?

CASE 7.1

DETERMINING THE MARKET POTENTIAL FOR THE FROOKIE

Source: "Luscious Low-Cal," *The East Hampton Star*," October 20, 1988, p. 22. Reprinted with permission. *The East Hampton Star*/ Robert Marchant.

The sweet smell of success means no cholesterol and no fat for Richard Worth, an entrepreneur whose line of naturally sweetened cookies will go on sale throughout the nation. Worth said his new cookie is called R. W. Frookie.

While the main ingredient is flour, and it looks like a cookie, the Frookie shares little in common with its gustatory brethren, Mr. Worth said. The Frookie has no cholesterol, is low in fat, has no added sugar, and, Mr. Worth said, tastes good, too.

Mr. Worth, who concedes he could probably stand to lose a few pounds himself, said his cookie and the premise behind it was not a fad, but a lasting change in the American diet.

"For the first time, the consumer knows he's under attack," said the cookie-maker. "The consumers are reading the ingredients, and they're starting not to like it.

"People are being threatened by their environment, and realizing that what they put into their body is what they are," said Mr. Worth. "The consumer's looking for an excuse to be healthy," he added. "The Surgeon Gen-

eral has laid it [the connection between high cholesterol and heart disease] on the line."

Despite the fierce competition of a market saturated with almost every possible brand and marketing technique conceivable, Mr. Worth said he expected the Frookie to be in a category by itself. It will follow in the tradition of such other mass-market products that appeal to the head as well as the stomach, like Celestial Seasonings teas.

"There's nothing in the cookie category that's low-fat, no cholesterol, and tastes good," said the entrepreneur. The cookies available on the market now, he said, are baked with heavy oils and animal starch, not to mention sugar. "It really makes them an unhealthy experience," he said.

His brand would "put the fun back into cookies by taking the guilt out," said Mr. Worth. In addition to the cookies, available in four varieties, carrot and banana cakes sweetened with fruit juices are also in the works.

Assume Richard Worth hires you to do marketing research to evaluate the potential for Frookie.
1. What might be the role of qualitative research in evaluating the potential for Frookie?
2. How might experimentation be used in evaluating the product?
3. How might a survey be used?

4. What type of a survey would you propose — personal, telephone, or mail? Justify your choice.
5. How would you define the population for the study?

6. What areas of information would you want to collect?

CASE 7.2

THE INFORMATION REVOLUTION REACHES WILLIAMSPORT

Source: Michael Days, "Wired Consumers: Market Researchers Go High-Tech to Hone Ads, Weed Out Flops," *The Wall Street Journal*, January 23, 1986, p. 33.

Joann Alter shops at the Weis Market near her home at least four times a week. But even if she's just dashing in for a quart of milk or a dozen eggs, she always remembers to give the cashier her Shopper's Hotline card.

By showing the card, Mrs. Alter gets a chance at a variety of enticing prizes, including vacations in Mexico and Hawaii, small electrical appliances and gift certificates–such as the one she and her husband used for dinner at a fancy local restaurant. "How could I ever forget to show my card, when with so little effort you can gain so much?" she asks.

That's the sort of thing the people at Information Resources Inc. like to hear. The card is a vital link in the Chicago-based company's BehaviorScan test-marketing program. It makes it possible to monitor purchases by consumers like Mrs. Alter and correlate them with information collected by gadgets on their TV sets about what commercials they watch and with other data about what coupons they use.

Weeding Out Flops

Marketers have for years depended on willing consumers in relatively isolated communities to weed out products that are likely to flop and to identify the best ways to promote those that are likely to succeed. But electronic testing techniques — such as those being used here, as well as in several other markets by Information Resources and two major competitors, A. C. Nielsen Co. and Burke Marketing Services Inc. — have made it possible to evaluate consumer tastes with much greater precision.

Traditionally, research on buying habits has depended heavily on diaries kept by test participants. But diaries are only as reliable as the people who keep them, and human recall has its frailties.

As an example, Information Resources points to the discrepancies it found when it asked some of the consumers in its BehaviorScan research about what products they had bought in a recent three-month period and compared their answers with their actual purchases. Among the findings: Only about a third of those who reported buying Kellogg's Frosted Flakes had done so; only about one in 10 of those claiming to have purchased Pledge furniture polish had bought the product.

Anthony Adams, director of marketing and research at Campbell Soup Co., says that electronic testing also allows researchers to observe consumers' reactions without tipping them off about what is being studied. That's not possible with questionnaires and focus groups, two other common market-research techniques.

Campbell Soup, which has been a BehaviorScan client since 1980, is one of several companies that use the electronic-testing service to evaluate new products and to determine what marketing strategies will help sell them most effectively. Others include Procter & Gamble Co., Dart & Kraft Inc., and General Foods Corp.

The Williamsport area, with a population of about 93,000 and an average annual discretionary household income of $24,000, provides an unusual opportunity for electronic market testing. Because the community sits in an Appalachian valley at the foot of Bald Eagle Mountain, TV reception is poor, and most residents depend on cable. The extensive network of cable hookups is ideal for Information Resources' purposes.

Inside an electronic control room at the local cable-TV franchise, the market-research firm's employees work from 6:30 a.m. until after midnight "cutting" into commercials on the three network affiliates. Clients buy local time to test new ads, or Information Resources can "overlay" a test ad or two in place of the client's national commercial, which the rest of the country is seeing.

Late each night, a computer calls the 3,000 Williamsport households participating in BehaviorScan to link up with the microprocessor inside each of their cable converters. Information Resources knows exactly what they watch each day and whether family members view an entire show or flip the channel several times.

Information Resources spent about $2 million in start-up costs to establish its electronic network here, equipping nine of the 10 local supermarkets with barcode scanning equipment that generates a computer file of each participating consumer's purchases. (One store already had such equipment.)

The company also works hard to keep participants happy. For instance, whenever cable reception at a participant's home goes bad, the company's own repair people investigate without charge.

1. What are the advantages to marketers of using the BehaviorScan system to evaluate marketing strategies?
2. What are the advantages of using BehaviorScan to study influences on consumer behavior compared to using questionnaires or focus groups?

NOTES

1. "Sony: Sorting Out the Sales Suspects," *Business Marketing,* August 1988, p. 44.
2. Ibid., p. 46.
3. Ibid., pp. 46, 48.
4. David W. Cravens, Gerald W. Hills, and Robert B. Woodruff, *Marketing Decision Making* (Homewood, Ill.: Richard D. Irwin, 1980), pp. 75–77.
5. "Straws in the Wind," *Financial World,* November 3, 1987, pp. 126–128.
6. "Listening to the Consumer Again," *The New York Times,* April 6, 1988, p. D6.
7. "New Product Excellence at American Express," *Marketing Review,* January–February 1988, p. 20.
8. Betsy D. Gelb and Gabriel M. Gelb, "New Coke's Fizzle — Lessons for the Rest of Us," *Sloan Management Review* (Fall 1986): 71.
9. "Stouffer's Lean Cuisine Fattens Up Frozen Food Market," *Madison Avenue,* March 1983, p. 94.
10. "Reading the Consumer's Mind," *Advertising Age,* May 3, 1984, p. M-16.
11. "Meticulous Planning Pays Dividends at Stouffer's," *Marketing News,* October 28, 1983, p. 26.
12. *Madison Avenue,* March 1983, p. 96.
13. Mason Haire, "Projective Techniques in Marketing Research," *Journal of Marketing,* 14(April 1950): 649–656.
14. "Work Motivates Psychoanalyst," *Advertising Age,* November 1, 1984, p. 45.
15. Rena Bartos, "Ernest Dichter: Motive Interpreter," *Journal of Advertising Research* 26(February–March 1986): 20.
16. Ibid., p. 16.
17. *Advertising Age,* November 1, 1984, p. 44.
18. "Using Marketing Research to Explore for Exciting New Product Ideas," *Sales & Marketing Management,* April 4, 1983, pp. 126–130.
19. Ibid., p. 128.
20. David A. Aaker and George S. Day, *Marketing Research* (New York: John Wiley & Sons, 1980), p. 102.
21. "Excuse Me, What's the Pollster's Big Problem?" *Business Week,* February 16, 1987, p. 108.
22. *Advertising Age,* July 22, 1985, p. 58.
23. "Listening, the Old-Fashioned Way," *Forbes,* October 5, 1987, pp. 202, 204.
24. "Dawn of the Computer Age," *Advertising Age,* August 20, 1987, pp. 120, and 209.
25. "Businesses Capitalize on Data from Census," *The New York Times,* March 31, 1980, pp. D1–D2.
26. *Supermarket Business,* Research Department, May 1988.
27. *Starch: Scope, Method, and Use* (Mamaroneck, N.Y.: Starch/INRA/Hooper, 1973), p. 2.
28. *The 1980 Study of Media and Markets* (New York: Simmons Market Research Bureau, 1980).
29. "Big Brother Gets a Job in Market Research," *Business Week,* April 8, 1985, p. 96.

PART 3

• • •

PLANNING AND TARGETING THE MARKETING EFFORT

The marketing plan is the vehicle by which firms identify and pursue opportunities. Marketing strategies are defined in the marketing plan to give management a blueprint for pursuing opportunities. These strategies must be targeted to meet the needs of defined groups of consumers if they are to be successful. The process of marketing planning is illustrated in Chapter 8. In Chapter 9 we describe how firms segment their markets into consumer groups for purposes of targeting marketing strategies.

MOTOROLA'S INTRODUCTION OF CELLULAR TELEPHONES — A NEED FOR A MARKETING PLAN

When Motorola introduced cellular telephones in 1984, it thought it had a sure thing. Because the company was the acknowledged market leader in mobile communications, with over 60 percent of the total market, cellular telephones were a natural extension of its line of car telephones, two-way radios, pagers, and beepers.[1]

Cellular telephones are portable phones that use radio waves rather than telephone lines, making wires unnecessary. Calls made while traveling are based on a series of area-to-area hookups known as cells (hence the term *cellular*); each cell has an antenna over which telephone messages are passed when a caller enters a new region. Motorola produces both the cellular networks that transmit the calls and the telephone itself. It markets two types of cellular telephones, stationary phones for cars and walk-around phones that can fit into a briefcase.

Although AT&T pioneered the basic technology for cellular phones, Motorola spent $100 million to develop and test the phones.[2] Their potential seemed unlimited, particularly in the business market, when Motorola began marketing the new product line in early 1984. Doctors, salespeople, and business people all had the need for portable communications. Estimates were that Motorola would help create a $12 billion industry by the mid 1990s.[3]

It now seems that Motorola may have been overly optimistic.[4] It failed to anticipate several events in its marketing planning. First, there were problems with the product: sound quality was poor, and callers frequently lost connections as they drove between cells. Second, Motorola did not anticipate the inten-

8
CHAPTER

MARKETING PLANNING

sity of the competition. As in some other industries, lower-cost Japanese manufacturers drove the price of cellular phones substantially below the original price of $3,000 per unit, cutting into Motorola's anticipated operating margins for the product. Third, the resources required to sustain the market were much higher than anticipated. One research firm estimated that it costs $2,000 to sell a unit to one cellular subscriber.[5] If that figure is accurate, Motorola must be operating at close to break-even on the product line.

Fourth, Motorola could have done a better job planning its entry and countering competitive inroads. *Fortune* reports that "Motorola alienated its distributors with a clumsy marketing strategy" that involved competing with them by selling directly to larger customers. Further, many customers complained about the quality of Motorola's phones, (which was perceived as poorer than that of Japanese phones).[6] Such complaints from dealers and customers hurt the company's ability to counter competitive inroads.

Will Motorola make it in the cellular market? Overall, the answer seems to be yes. The company has regained lost ground with product improvements, a more competitive pricing strategy, and closer relations with its distributors. But with the benefit of some Monday morning quarterbacking, Motorola's shaky start suggests that the company might have done a better job in key aspects of marketing planning, including estimating marketing opportunity, forecasting sales, determining the resources necessary for marketing entry, cementing distributor relations, and ensuring product superiority. ■

YOUR FOCUS IN CHAPTER 8

① *How does a firm develop a marketing plan for a new or existing product?*

② *How should the market for the product be evaluated?*

③ *What are the strategic issues in identifying a target market and positioning the product?*

④ *What mix of marketing elements — advertising, distribution, and price — should be used to implement the strategy for the product?*

⑤ *How can a firm estimate future sales?*

● ● ●

THE MARKETING PLANNING PROCESS

A company needs a plan for each product it markets, specifying strategies to be used and resources required. The process of developing such plans is called **marketing planning**, and is conducted by the product manager responsible for that product. In a later chapter, we will describe a broader planning focus, the **strategic marketing plan,** which is designed to coordinate the company's marketing activities for all its products across its business units.

The steps involved in marketing planning are shown in Figure 8.1. The product manager first conducts a **situation analysis,** which is a preliminary evaluation of the market for the product. The situation analysis will define the market (what products are likely to compete with the company's brand); determine the market's key characteristics, such as competitive intensity, required capital investment, means of distributing the product, and stability of demand; and estimate its size to determine its potential.

Next, the product manager evaluates marketing opportunity for the company's product based on an assessment of customer needs, competitive strengths and weaknesses, and other factors. Since we have described these determinants of opportunity in the last few chapters, we will touch on them here only as they bear on the marketing planning process. An *opportunity/threat analysis* requires information on the competition, customers, and the environment. (These are factors *external* to the company that are generally beyond its control.) An evaluation of the company's strengths and weaknesses (a *strength/weakness analysis*) requires information on its resources and capabilities to market a product. These are factors *internal* to the company that are generally within its control.

The product manager uses the situation analysis and evaluation of marketing opportunity to develop product objectives in the form of sales and profit goals. In Motorola's case, a reasonable goal for the cellular line in the first year after introduction might have been sales of 150,000 units representing revenue of about $270 million.

The next step in the marketing planning process is to formulate marketing strategies to fulfill product objectives. Two key elements are to determine the target market and position the product accordingly. For Motorola, the target for cellular telephones was clearly the business or industrial market; but Motorola would also have to identify specific components of this market, such as salespeople, doctors, manufacturers, and so forth, and differences in their needs for mobile communication.

Product positioning refers to the way in which a product's features and benefits are presented to the customer. This requires an integrated advertising and sales strategy that focuses on a few key customer benefits. Cellular telephones cannot be positioned as just another mobile communications device. Their unique advantages must be demonstrated. Motorola's original positioning was based more on technology and product features. As competition intensified, its positioning shifted to specific benefits such as the capability of creating a "portable office" through mobile communications. The ad in Exhibit 8.1 positions Motorola's "Tough Talker" as a transportable cellular phone that is rugged enough for a construction site yet attractive enough for the Board Room.[7]

Once the target market has been identified and the positioning decided upon, the next step is to develop a marketing mix. As we saw in Chapter 1, the marketing mix is composed of advertising, pricing, and distribution elements that work together to implement the product's positioning. One of the product manager's important responsibilities is to develop a budget for the various elements of the marketing mix. From this budget profits can be projected for the product.

Motorola's initial marketing mix for cellular phones was composed of a product that was supposed to represent superior technology, a high price ($3,000), distribution through its own salesforce and independent distributors, and advertising that focused on the phone's high-tech elements. As we saw, the marketing mix contained some basic flaws: a lack of product superiority, poor distributor relations, advertising that emphasized product technology at the expense of customer benefits, and a price that was not competitive with low-cost Japanese cellular phones.

The product manager next develops a final *sales forecast* based on the proposed marketing strategy. While sales forecasts are developed at various times in the process of marketing planning, they are more reliable at later stages. Next, expected profits from the product are estimated based on revenue projections from sales forecasts and cost projections from marketing and other expenditures.

The final step in marketing planning is evaluation and control. Product managers track product performance and make adjustments in positioning strategies and the marketing mix to ensure that product objectives are met. Feedback to management on product performance may lead to changes in product objectives.

In the rest of this chapter, we will explore each of the steps in Figure 8.1 in more detail, using the example of Motorola developing a marketing plan for entry into the cellular telephone market.

Larry Goldstein was the premiere marketing planner for Motorola's Land Mobile Group (the division responsible for marketing cellular telephones) when he was working there. He was on a crusade to make the division marketing-oriented by focusing more on customer needs and less on number crunching.

LARRY GOLDSTEIN — LAWYER TURNED MARKETING PLANNER

FIGURE 8.1
The Marketing Planning Process

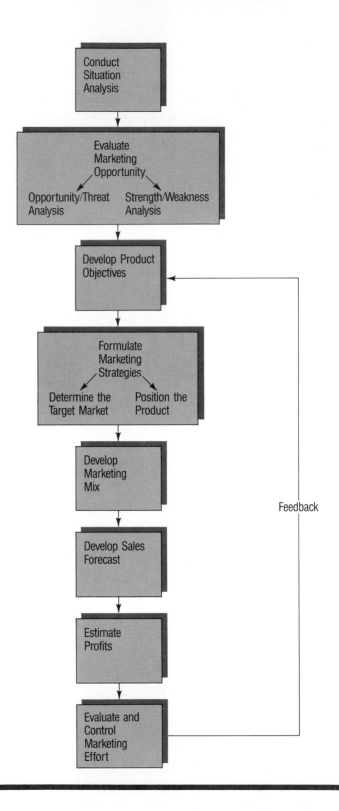

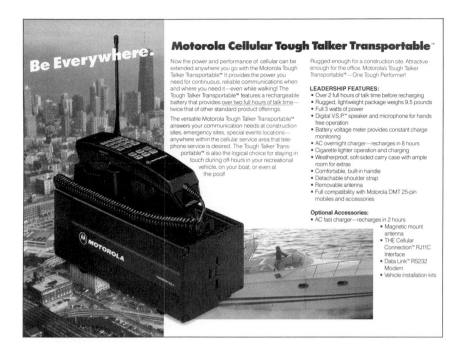

Goldstein, a 1979 graduate of the University of Chicago law school, found that "law was a little too slow for me."[8] After two years with a law firm, he decided to get an MBA degree from Northwestern University. The excitement of the business world attracted him to marketing, and he had his heart set on working for an industrial marketing firm. After a year at Motorola, his new assignment was to find business opportunities for the Land Mobile Group.

When Goldstein joined the Land Mobile Group's planning staff in 1984, it was already apparent that Motorola would have a tougher time than anticipated marketing its cellular telephones. Japanese competitors were reducing prices, and Motorola was struggling to maintain its distributors' loyalty while trying to deal with customer complaints about quality.

One of the first things Goldstein did was to revamp the marketing planning process. He developed teams of marketing, sales, and production managers, and gave these teams the assignment of studying each of the customer markets of the Land Mobile Group.[9] Under Goldstein's direction, the teams became the marketing planners for each market, identifying customer segments, Motorola's opportunities in each segment, and consequent product applications. The teams then developed two strategies for each segment, one aggressive and the other more gradual. Their last step before presenting their plan to top management was to perform a cost-benefit analysis to evaluate revenue expectations of their proposed strategies against their costs.

Goldstein's marketing planning process was similar to that in Figure 8.1. It gave the Land Mobile Group a better capability to identify specific market segments for cellular telephones as well as to estimate potential in the consumer market. It also gave the group the ability to determine the dollar potential for cellular products into the 1990s, to anticipate the impact of competition on the market, and to develop alternative strategies to meet the needs of market segments with a variety of cellular telephone products. ■

CONDUCTING THE SITUATION ANALYSIS

The first step in marketing planning is to conduct a *situation analysis*, which consists of three steps: defining the market for a certain product, determining the market's characteristics, and estimating its size.

DEFINING THE MARKET

A **market** is a group of customers who seek similar product benefits. Thus, we can refer to a market for mobile communications, in-home entertainment, or nutritional breakfast foods. Note that in each case, the market is defined by customer benefits (mobile communications, entertainment, or good nutrition), rather than products (cellular telephones, compact discs, or high-fiber cereals).

Customers can satisfy their needs for mobile communications through cellular telephones or car radios. But they can also satisfy this need through beepers, pagers, and cordless telephones. All of these might be regarded as product offerings directed to the mobile communications market. Therefore, a key question for the product manager is how broadly or narrowly to define the market.

One way to answer this question is to let the customers define the market by describing their communications needs. Then the products that most closely meet these needs can be identified. Assume Motorola identifies five key communications needs of business people as shown by the arrows in Figure 8.2. The company then determines which telecommunications devices are perceived as meeting these needs. A visual representation of customer needs associated with products (like Figure 8.2) is known as a **perceptual map**. Such a map also shows those products that are seen as competitive in meeting the same needs.

For example, beepers and pagers are seen as similar in meeting the need for walk-around communications devices. Car telephones are seen as providing mobile communications in fixed facilities. Stationary telephones are associated with interference-free communications and, possibly as a result, greater control over the communications process. Picturephones and Centers provide a visual capability; and fax, telex, and electronic mail are seen as providing documentation. Cellular telephones satisfy the need for mobility both in terms of walk-around transportability (as in the ad in Exhibit 8.1), and in fixed hookups. Respondents also see cellular phones as being free of interference (thus, there is an arrow linking this need to cellular in Figure 8.2). Documentation and video capabilities are two needs not seen as being met by this product.

The circles represent three ways to define the market. One would be to focus on customers who need walk-around transportability (area #1 in the map), meaning that cellular phones would be competing primarily with beepers and pagers. A second definition would identify the market as those who need fixed hookups (area #2), meaning that cellular phones would be competing primarily with car telephones. A third definition would combine these two and include those who need either transportable or fixed mobile communications (area #3).

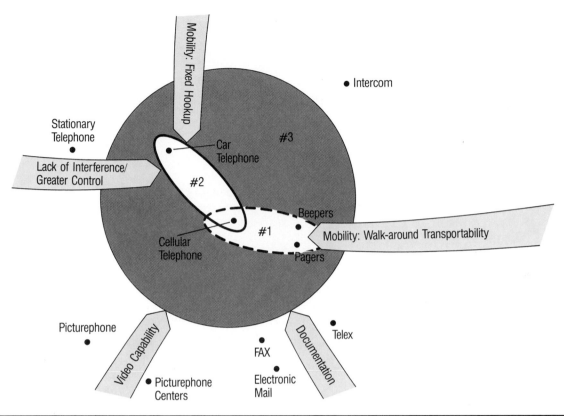

FIGURE 8.2
A Perceptual Map of the Mobile Communications Market

A fourth definition would identify the market as telecommunications in general, rather than mobile communications, meaning that the cellular phone is competing with all the products in Figure 8.2.

Seven desirable characteristics of a market targeted for entry by a new product, or for intensified effort by an existing product are:[10]

IDENTIFYING MARKET CHARACTERISTICS

1. Good potential for market growth.
2. Few barriers to entry (for new product only).
3. Opportunity for competitive advantage.
4. Stability in customer demand.
5. No large capital investment required.
6. Good prospects for increased market share.
7. A high return on investment relative to other markets.

   To see how these criteria operate, consider the situation analysis conducted by General Telephone & Electronics (GTE) in the early 1980s when it was considering entering the consumer appliance market. Market segments and products are listed at the top of Table 8.1, showing the boundaries of the consumer appliance market as defined by GTE.

TABLE 8.1
GTE's Situation Analysis of the
Consumer Appliance Market

Source: Private communication from General Telephone & Electronics

---

MARKET DEFINITION
  MARKET SEGMENTS
      Dealers
      Housing contractors
      Commercial laundries and laundromats
      Final consumers

  PRODUCTS
      Laundry appliances
      Dishwashers
      Disposal units
      Ranges
      Refrigerators

  MARKET CHARACTERISTICS
      Barriers to entry: High, because of large capital investment required to achieve
      economies of scale.
      Competition: Intense, with an increase in private-label brands creating more
      competition.
      Industry leaders: Large, with integrated operations.
      Products: Mature, with little difference among products.
      Price: Increasing, to keep pace with inflation of labor and raw material costs.
      Industry growth: Slow; e.g., laundry products at 2 percent growth per year.
      Demand: Cyclical. Tied to housing starts.

The bottom of the table paints a rather discouraging picture of the market's characteristics. Barriers to entry are high due to strong competition and a necessarily large capital investment. Also, the market is becoming less differentiated, providing little basis for competitive advantage based on product or service uniqueness. Had it entered this market, GTE would have faced entrenched market leaders such as General Electric and Whirlpool with no prospect for competitive advantage except as a low-cost producer — and, given the high cost of entry, it was not likely to gain even that advantage.

Other discouraging characteristics were that customer demand was cyclical, tied primarily to housing starts; both costs and prices were rising; and potential for market growth was poor, since many products were stagnating. Not surprisingly, GTE decided against market entry.

Just as GTE's situation analysis discouraged it from entering the appliance market, Motorola's encouraged entry into the mobile communications market with the cellular telephone. That market represented good potential for growth; there was little competition; demand was not expected to be cyclical or seasonal, and Motorola expected to be the market leader, with a high return on investment based on a price of $3,000 per unit. The only negative seemed to be the need for significant investment in plant and equipment. As we have seen, however, many of these market characteristics changed in unanticipated ways.

ESTIMATING MARKET POTENTIAL

Market potential, the third element in a situation analysis, represents the total demand for the product category in the market. Demand in units can be defined as the number of potential new purchasers plus existing owners who must replace an item.

Assume that as part of its investigation of the consumer appliance market, GTE estimates the market potential for washing machines as follows: There will be 4 million housing starts in the coming year, each of which will require a washing machine; 2 million existing households do not own a washing machine and will buy one; and an additional 8 million households will replace a washing machine. This represents 14 million units a year. If the average price of a washing machine is $400, then total market potential for washing machines is $5.6 billion (14 million times $400).

As we noted earlier, market potential for the total cellular market was estimated at $12 billion by the mid 1990s. This estimate was broken down into $4 billion in sales of cellular telephones, $4 billion in monthly call charges for cellular subscribers, and $4 billion in sales of switching equipment and peripherals.[11]

Once market potential is determined, the product manager can use an estimate of a product's expected market share to calculate a preliminary sales forecast. Assume Motorola projects its share of cellular telephones at 30 percent and its market share for switching equipment at 60 percent by the mid 1990s. Then, accepting the market potential figures cited for cellular phones, its yearly sales estimate would be $3.6 billion at retail (30 percent times $4 billion plus 60 percent times $4 billion = $3.6 billion). Assuming that Motorola's revenue represents about 60 percent of the retail price, the estimated sales revenue to the company by the mid 1990s would be $2.16 billion.

EVALUATING MARKETING OPPORTUNITY

With the situation analysis completed, the next step in the marketing planning process is to evaluate marketing opportunities. As Figure 8.1 shows, there are two components to evaluating marketing opportunities: an opportunity/threat analysis and an analysis of company strengths and weaknesses.

OPPORTUNITY/THREAT ANALYSIS

The product manager uses opportunity/threat analysis to evaluate how changes in customer demand, competitors' actions, and other environmental forces will affect projected profits for an individual product. To begin, a manager must make certain assumptions about the environment, both positive and negative, and assess how these assumptions will affect the profitability of the product. Motorola's decision to enter the cellular market, for instance, was probably influenced by a number of positive environmental assumptions, as follows:

> That demand for cellular phones in the business market would grow at a steady rate into the 1990s.
> That cellular phones would begin to be accepted on a widespread basis by the consumer market during the 1990s.
> That the Federal Communications Commission would regulate market entry into cellular phones.
> That competitive entry would be slow.

The "threat" part of the opportunity/threat analysis is just as important as the "opportunity" part, since product managers must take into account potential risks. In Motorola's case, potential threats prior to entry included the following:

> A lower than expected demand in the business market.
> A lack of acceptance by the consumer market.

Quick entry by lower-cost producers, driving prices down faster than expected.

Higher than anticipated costs of entry (investment in plant and/or selling costs).

The possibility that new technologies might replace the cellular phone, in which case a significant amount of capital investment would be lost.

The product manager for the cellular line must take such positives and negatives into account in developing a preliminary sales forecast for the first year of operations. Assume that three forecasts are developed. The first projects sales of 200,000 units or more, based on most of the positives and few of the negatives operating. If this forecast proves true, the company estimates a profit of about $20 million in the first year. There is a probability of 25 percent, according to the product manager, that this will happen.

At the other end of the continuum, sales of 100,000 or less would mean that many of the negatives were operating and would produce an estimated loss of $10 million. The product manager also assigns this forecast a probability of 25 percent.

The third forecast is for sales between 100,000 and 200,000, with about 150,000 units as the best estimate. This is the most realistic forecast, representing a mix of positive and negative factors operating, but with the positive outweighing the negative. If this forecast proves true — a 50 percent probability — the company estimates about $10 million in profits in the first year, with profit growth expected in succeeding years.

A summary of expectations based on the opportunity/threat analysis follows:

SALES LEVEL	PROBABILITY OF ACHIEVING THIS SALES LEVEL	×	AVERAGE NET PROFIT OR LOSS (IN MILLIONS)	=	EXPECTED VALUE (IN MILLIONS)
200,000 and over	25%	×	+20	=	+5.0
100,000– 200,000	50%	×	+10	=	+5.0
Under 100,000	25%	×	−10	=	−2.5
		Total expected value of market entry		=	+7.5

The *expected value* of entry in the first year is calculated by multiplying the profit or loss by the probability of reaching each sales figure. In this case, expected value of entry equals 25 percent times $20 million, plus 50 percent times $10 million, minus 25 percent times $10 million, or a total of $7.5 million. The product manager should use this expected-value estimate in determining whether market entry is warranted, since it takes account of both opportunities and threats. It is, in a sense, the current value of entering the market based on the anticipated future environment.

STRENGTH/WEAKNESS ANALYSIS

The second essential element in evaluating market opportunity is a strength/weakness analysis to evaluate the company's ability to exploit opportunities in the product's market. Such an analysis is most important when a company (1) en-

	IMPORTANCE OF FACTOR (10 = MOST IMPORTANT, 1 = LEAST IMPORTANT)		MATCH WITH COMPANY RESOURCES (10 = PERFECT MATCH, 1 = WORST MATCH)		RESOURCE UTILITY SCORE
1. Managerial know-how	10	×	9	=	90
2. Knowledge of business market	9	×	9	=	81
3. Knowledge of consumer market	5	×	4	=	20
4. Financial resources	8	×	5	=	40
5. Distribution system	5	×	9	=	45
6. Sales force	5	×	9	=	45
7. Technology	10	×	9	=	90
8. Product service	7	×	9	=	63
9. Raw materials	2	×	10	=	20
10. Manufacturing facilities	4	×	10	=	40
	Overall resource utility score			=	534
	Corporate norms for new products based on past experience			=	350

TABLE 8.2
Hypothetical Example of Strength/ Weakness Analysis for Motorola's Entry into the Cellular Telephone Market

ters the market for the first time, (2) is facing rapid environmental changes that may require reevaluating its resource needs for an existing product, or (3) faces the threat of competitive entry.

Such an analysis for Motorola's entry into cellular phones might have included the ten criteria in Table 8.2. Each of these represent the resources and skills necessary to succeed in the cellular market. Managers first rate the relative importance of each factor. On a ten-point scale, the average rating given by Motorola managers to managerial know-how is a 10, indicating that this is an extremely important factor compared to the availability of raw materials, which is rated a 2.

The next step (column 2 of the table) is to rate Motorola's capabilities for meeting each criterion. Because of its leadership in mobile communications and its market share of over 60 percent, the company is rated strongly on most factors. Knowledge of the consumer market, however, is rated lower. Motorola is much more familiar with marketing to industrial buyers. Financial resources is also rated lower in recognition of the significant financial commitment required for entry into the cellular phone market, which may draw resources away from other opportunities.

The overall *resource utility score* for each criterion is computed by multiplying Motorola's capability score in column 2 by the importance rating in column 1. These scores are then summed to arrive at the total resource utility score of 534. This score does not mean much unless it is compared to strength/weakness analyses for other markets. In Motorola's case, the average resource utility score for its other markets which include semiconductors, computers, and industrial electronics, is 350. Opportunity in the cellular market therefore appears stronger than other opportunities Motorola has investigated. Motorola concluded that it had the resources to establish cost leadership and maintain product quality to give it a sustainable competitive advantage, permitting it to maintain market leadership.

In hindsight, of course, we can see that Motorola did not adequately gauge potential weaknesses in its capabilities and resources. This tells us that just as a company should be alert to potential threat when evaluating opportunity, it should also look for potential weaknesses when evaluating its strengths.

DEVELOPING PRODUCT OBJECTIVES

The situation analysis and identification of marketing opportunities gives the product manager a basis for the next step in marketing planning: developing realistic objectives for the product. A marketing plan can state three types of marketing objectives for product performance — sales-volume, market-share, and profitability. Additional marketing objectives might be stated in terms of the marketing mix (advertising, distribution, and pricing goals) required to achieve sales, market-share, and profit objectives.

SALES VOLUME

Sales-volume objectives will depend on a company's opportunity assessment. For example, PepsiCo has stated it will consider only markets representing potential sales of $250 million or more for new-product entries. Its sales goal for Slice, based on its assessment of the opportunity for introducing a fruit-based soft drink, was $500 million.

Sales-volume objectives are also frequently stated in units. In our hypothetical example, Motorola's best forecast was 150,000 cellular units to be sold in the first year. Assuming its price to distributors is an average of $1,800 per unit (60 percent of an average $3,000 retail price), its sales objective would then be $270 million in revenue in the first year (150,000 units times $1,800).

MARKET SHARE

Market-share goals are closely tied to sales objectives. In PepsiCo's case, a minimum market-share objective for any entry into the soft drink market is 1 percent, since each share point represents $250 million in sales.

Some firms might first establish a sales goal and determine if the resultant market share places it in a viable competitive position. A sales objective of $500 million for Slice produced a market-share goal of 2 percent, meeting PepsiCo's criterion for entering the soft drink market. Other firms might establish market-share objectives first, and then estimate sales. For example, Motorola might have established a goal of capturing 75 percent of the cellular phone market in the first year as a means of discouraging competitive entry. If the total market was estimated to buy 200,000 units in the first year, the objective would thus be 150,000 units.

PROFITS

The third category of product goals, profitability objectives, are most frequently stated in terms of **return on investment** (**ROI**), which equals net profits divided by total investment. A reasonable basis for establishing an ROI objective might be to compare ROI for a product to an alternative investment.

Assume that PepsiCo determines it could take the money it plans to use to introduce Slice, invest it in high-yield bonds and gain a 9 percent return. Then a reasonable ROI objective for Slice might be 10 percent. Can the company's sales goal of $500 million and market share goal of 2 percent produce this ROI level? If not, sales and profit goals are out of line. PepsiCo would then have to determine whether it should settle for the lower ROI produced by $500 million in sales, or whether it can realistically increase its sales goal to achieve the required ROI.

MARKETING MIX

The marketing plan should also set goals for the components of the marketing mix, including distribution, advertising, and price. These goals establish the requirements for meeting sales, market-share, and profit objectives. For example, PepsiCo might establish a goal of making 80 percent of all households aware of Slice six months after introduction. It establishes this goal as a minimum requirement if it is to reach $500 million in sales in the first year. Further, it might establish a distribution goal of 95 percent of all supermarkets and 80 percent of all food stores.

Since the price of Slice will have to be higher than the average soft drink because of its fruit base, a reasonable pricing goal might be to keep Slice no more than 10 percent above Pepsi-Cola's price, since too high a price might discourage customer trial of the new product.

FORMULATING MARKETING STRATEGIES

Once product objectives have been developed, the next step in the marketing planning process is to formulate a **marketing strategy**, which is the basic approach a company will take in trying to influence customers to buy the product. Formulating marketing strategy requires identifying a target market and positioning the product to the target. The target market and positioning strategy will determine the marketing mix elements designed to implement this strategy.

IDENTIFYING THE TARGET MARKET

A **target market** is a group of consumers with similar needs that can be identified and appealed to by a specific product or product line. Targets for cellular telephones and their needs for mobile communications are presented in Figure 8.3 in the form of a needs/market matrix. There are three broad market classifications: business, consumer, and international. Since Motorola plans to target the business market in the first few years, this market is broken out into more specific segments. Three mobility-specific needs are shown: walk-around transportability, fixed hookup, and lack of interference. Documentation is included because Motorola has developed the technology to permit receiving written messages over cellular phone hookups.

Several strategic questions must be answered in identifying the appropriate target in the marketing plan. First, should effort be directed to the total market or to specific segments. Although Motorola targeted its effort to the total business market, some pinpointing might have been desirable. For example, it might have been reasonable to initially target cellular phones to sales firms to meet the needs of salespeople for clear communications in autos. Another group that might have been targeted is doctors and medical personnel, since beepers and pagers do not provide for voice communications.

FIGURE 8.3
Market Segments for Cellular Telephones

| | Business Market | | | | | |
	Corporate Executives	Salespeople	Services	Doctors and Medical Personnel	**Consumer Market**	**International**
Mobility: Walk-around Transportability						
Mobility: Fixed Hookup						
Lack of Interference						
Documentation						

A second strategic issue is whether and when the company should expand its market coverage beyond the target market. As Motorola meets its marketing objectives in the business market, it would be reasonable to begin paying more attention to the consumer and international markets. The company is becoming heavily involved in international markets, selling its cellular network system to countries in Europe, South America, and Asia.

A third strategic issue is whether the company should market one basic product to the total market or develop a line of products, each targeted to specific segments. Motorola chose to develop a full product line with features such as call memory, hookups to answering machines, and even printout capabilities to provide written messages over cellular networks in a car or other location. These features can be targeted to specific segments — call memory to salespeople, written documentation to doctors or ambulances requiring immediate medical reports, and hookups to answering machines for professionals who need to get messages from home offices.

PRODUCT POSITIONING

Once the target market has been identified, the product manager must develop a strategy to communicate product benefits to the target. Managers can use three broad approaches in positioning a product: an informational approach, an imagery approach, and an approach based on comparisons with competitive brands.

An informational approach to positioning requires communicating product characteristics to the target segment. For example, Allstate advertises the items included in renter's insurance and the fact that liability coverage is part of the policy (see Exhibit 8.2). An informational approach can also communicate particular problems a product can solve. Crest tartar control formula is positioned to emphasize its ability to help the consumer avoid tartar buildup and prevent gum disease. A third informational approach is to position a product for use in a particular situation. Campbell's "Soup for Lunch" is an example.

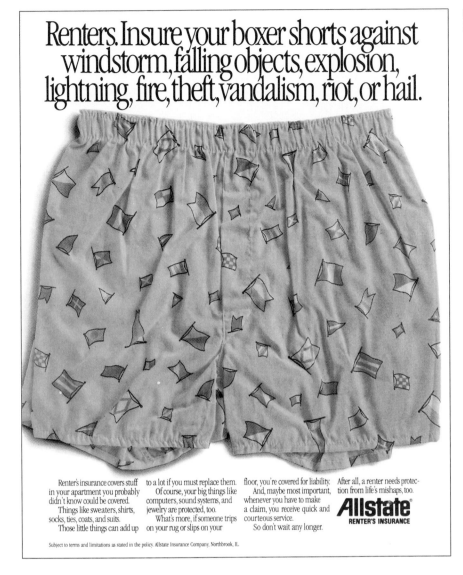

Renters. Insure your boxer shorts against windstorm, falling objects, explosion, lightning, fire, theft, vandalism, riot, or hail.

Renter's insurance covers stuff in your apartment you probably didn't know could be covered.

Things like sweaters, shirts, socks, ties, coats, and suits.

Those little things can add up to a lot if you must replace them.

Of course, your big things like computers, sound systems, and jewelry are protected, too.

What's more, if someone trips on your rug or slips on your floor, you're covered for liability.

And, maybe most important, whenever you have to make a claim, you receive quick and courteous service.

So don't wait any longer.

After all, a renter needs protection from life's mishaps, too.

Allstate
RENTER'S INSURANCE

Subject to terms and limitations as stated in the policy. Allstate Insurance Company, Northbrook, IL.

EXHIBIT 8.2
Informational Positioning

EXHIBIT 8.3
Positioning by Symbolism

An alternative approach is to position a product based on imagery and symbolism. For example, Lenox positions its china based on the theme, "Because Art Is Never an Extravagance." (See Exhibit 8.3.) The implication is that a consumer who buys Lenox is expressing a lifestyle of luxury and distinctiveness. Positioning by imagery is most applicable to products related to a consumer's self-concept, such as clothing, furniture, and china. Automobile companies have taken both approaches: Subaru takes an informational approach by advertising Turbo Traction and four-wheel drive, whereas Lincoln-Mercury takes a more symbolic approach by positioning its Continental line to communicate luxury.

As a product is established and competition intensifies, many companies shift to a more competitive positioning approach by advertising product superiority compared to competitors, or by using **comparative advertising**, that is, naming a competitor in their advertising. MCI names AT&T in its ads for long-distance calls, citing the advantages of MCI's service compared with the market leader (see

EXHIBIT 8.4
Competitive Positioning

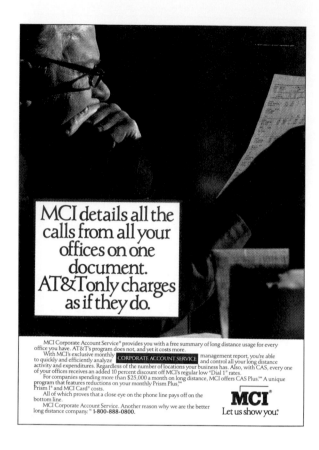

Exhibit 8.4). Avis does not name Hertz in its advertising, but it comes close, with the theme, "We're number 2, but we try harder."

Occasionally, the market position originally developed for a product becomes weakened due to competition, technological developments, or some other factor, and the product must be repositioned. People Express, once the fifth largest domestic air carrier, showed a $58 million loss in the first quarter of 1986 as a result of the maturing of the no-frills air travel market and matching price reductions by the leading airlines.[12] The company's response was to abandon its no-frills policy and begin emphasizing first-class service, a frequent-flier program, and additional ground and on-board services. But People's repositioning was not accepted by fliers, because the airline was too strongly identified with no-frills flying. After more losses, it was eventually taken over by Texas Air.

DEVELOPING THE MARKETING MIX

Once the marketing strategy has been formulated, the next step is to develop a marketing mix, including product, advertising, distribution, and pricing strategies that can effectively position the product to the target market.

Three steps are required. The first is to determine the components of the marketing mix. The second step is to determine how consumers respond to these components — that is, assess how they respond to proposed price levels, sales promotions, personal-selling strategies, and advertising executions. The third step is to determine the appropriate level of expenditures for marketing mix components; that is, the amount of money to spend on advertising, sales promotion, personal selling, and distribution. We will explore all three steps.

DETERMINING THE COMPONENTS OF THE MARKETING MIX

We saw in Chapter 1 that the marketing mix components are often referred to as the *four Ps:* product, place, price, and promotion. *Product* is the most basic component of the mix. It represents the product features, the package, the brand name, and post-sales service support. In the case of cellular telephones, critical product decisions dealt with the technical features of the product required to develop a relatively small unit that would ensure static-free reception, and service guarantees on such a unit.

Place represents the actions the company takes to make sure the product gets to the right target group at the right location and at the right time. Motorola used its own salesforce as well as independent distributors to market cellular telephones. An important component of distribution strategy is the trade support and allowances the company gives its distributors to induce them to stock and actively sell the product. Many food companies give large chains cash payments known as *slotting allowances* to induce them to put a new product on the shelf. Manufacturers will also give retailers advertising allowances to support local advertising of their products. For example, an auto manufacturer like Ford will agree to pay a percentage of its dealers' local advertising costs.

The third component of the marketing mix is *price*. Should cellular telephones be introduced at a high price to try to attract the business segments that place the highest value on the product? This pricing tactic is known as a *skimming strategy*. It produces high operating margins, but it also encourages competitive entry. Alternatively, a low-price strategy known as a *penetration strategy* might be instituted to try to get the greatest share of market possible. Although this tactic might preempt competition and establish a strong market position for the company, it might not bring in enough revenue to recoup the high developmental costs during a product's introduction. Motorola chose a skimming strategy, but in so doing it encouraged lower-cost competitors to enter the market and undercut its prices.

The tactics the company uses to communicate the product's positioning are collectively called *promotion*. Three key elements are involved: advertising, sales promotions (such as coupons, on-package deals, and in-store displays), and personal selling. Since these elements are so varied, they are often referred to as a **promotional mix** within the broader context of the marketing mix.

While each of these components must be individually developed, it is also important that they be integrated within the marketing plan. For instance, the plan must ensure that the product is available to customers before the advertising campaign begins. Advertising a product before it is distributed will result in consumer ill-will. It is also critical that the advertising be in tune with the price level. A number of years ago, an attempt was made to create a quality image for a low-priced beer by using status symbols such as a fox hunt. The imagery was lost on the blue-collar target market for the beer. Similarly, the price level must be consistent with product quality. Generally, higher prices connote higher quality. But if consumers pay a higher price and then quality expectations are not met, sales are likely to suffer.

DETERMINING CONSUMER RESPONSES TO THE MARKETING MIX

The marketing plan must provide for testing alternative marketing mix strategies to determine which will be most effective. Motorola, for example, might want to determine whether cellular telephones should be advertised on a benefit claim (e.g., "Just put the phone in your briefcase and carry communication around with you all day") or on a problem-solution claim (e.g., "If you want distortion-free mobile communication at long distances, buy a cellular telephone.")

Prices should also be tested to determine sales results at various price levels. Similarly, sales promotion devices should be tested in various markets to determine how consumers respond.

Products can also be tested to determine the final form of the product offering. Managers can first test the product idea before incurring production costs by asking consumers to react to a description of the product. The company can then produce prototypes and test customer reactions to them. For packaged goods, in-home use tests or controlled tests in company facilities can be conducted. When product features are close to being finalized, product alternatives can be evaluated in test markets.

DETERMINING THE BUDGET FOR THE MARKETING MIX

The third step in developing the marketing mix is to determine a budget, specifying both the total marketing expenditures and the expenditures for each component of the marketing mix. For example, a firm that plans multimedia advertising must establish an advertising budget as part of the marketing budget and allocate expenditures to various media such as television, newspapers, and magazines. It must also determine a sales promotion budget, allocating money for coupons, in-store displays, and trade promotions. And budgets must be established for personal selling, distribution, and product development.

In general, two types of approaches are used: a top-down and a bottom-up approach. In the *top-down approach,* the product manager first establishes an overall budget by determining the amount of marketing expenditures necessary to meet sales goals. This amount is then allocated among the various marketing mix components. In the cellular phone example, the product manager might have determined that a $20 million marketing budget would be required to introduce the product and achieve the sales goal of 150,000 units in the first year. This $20 million would then be divided among product, promotion, and distribution efforts. The $20 million figure is determined by estimating the expenditure levels necessary to achieve sales and profitability objectives.

In contrast to the top-down approach, the *bottom-up approach* first determines what marketing mix elements are required to implement product strategy, then estimates the marketing budget as the sum of expenditures required for product development, advertising, sales promotion, and distribution. The required marketing expenditures are then subtracted from estimated sales revenues to determine whether profit goals will be met. If not, management must either scale down the marketing mix, or consider withdrawing the product.

The bottom-up approach is more widely used because it is easier to estimate a marketing budget. However, it could result in an excessively high estimate of marketing expenditures, since each component of the marketing mix is estimated separately. Advertising, distribution, and sales managers might have a vested interest in setting a high estimate for their respective functions. Further, integration between components of the marketing mix might be more difficult. The advantage of a top-down approach is that it starts with an overall budget figure derived from estimated sales and is thus more likely to avoid overestimation of marketing requirements.

FORECASTING SALES

The next step in the marketing planning process, forecasting sales, provides the revenue base for estimating profits from marketing strategies. Sales forecasts will be based on an estimate of marketing opportunity and the marketing strategies management develops to exploit opportunity. Sales can be forecast based on past trends, on managerial judgment, on consumer responses, or on quantitative models designed to predict sales. Each of these approaches will be considered.

FORECASTS BASED ON HISTORICAL DATA

When products have been on the market long enough to establish a sales trend, one of the most practical approaches to forecasting sales is to extrapolate a sales trend into the future. This assumes, however, that changes in the environment will not alter these trends.

That assumption may be warranted in a stable industry, but environmental changes could occur to alter these trends. Until the health craze, demand for corn oil was fairly static. Then the American public discovered the value of using unsaturated oils, and suddenly the sales of a lackluster product took off way beyond its projected trend line.

Another approach is the use of **historical analogy**, in which past sales results of one product are used to forecast sales of a similar new product. For example, past sales of car telephones might be used to estimate the sales growth for cellular telephones. This technique is most reliable when the new product is very similar to past products. But there may be differences between the new and the old product. For instance, relying entirely on data about car phones to project sales of cellular phones could be misleading because of differences in ease of use, clarity of reception, and price.

Despite the weakness of historical methods of forecasting, a survey found that 60 percent of the companies reported using them.[13]

JUDGMENTAL FORECASTS

Sales forecasts often rely on managerial judgment. One study found that 96 percent of the companies interviewed used some form of judgmental method in forecasting sales.[14] Yet few of these companies relied only on managerial judgment. Most used historical analysis or customer surveys as well.

A panel of experts is sometimes used to develop judgmental forecasts by trying to reach a consensus on expected sales. An example of this kind of approach is the **Delphi method**, in which a number of experts are asked to make individual forecasts, stating their reasoning in writing. Forecasts are pooled and sent back to the panel of experts, who are then asked to make a second forecast. Generally, a consensus emerges after three or four rounds based on a free exchange of information.

Another judgmental technique is the **expected-value approach**. Here, managers are asked to estimate the probability of various scenarios occurring — for example, the introduction of new technology, entry into the market by the company's chief rival within one year, or shortages in raw materials — and to predict the sales results as a consequence. Managers then weight the estimated sales by the probability of occurrence to arrive at a forecast for the product. The sales forecast for cellular telephones on page 212 is an offshoot of this approach.

FORECASTS BASED ON CONSUMER RESPONSES

Tests of potential customers' responses to products are also commonly used in developing sales forecasts. A company might test product prototypes before market introduction by asking consumers their intention to buy. Although consumer intentions are used to forecast sales, they are not always reliable by themselves, so most companies take the additional step of introducing a product into test markets prior to national introduction. Test areas are selected to reflect national market conditions.

If test-market areas could be guaranteed to be representative of the national market, an accurate sales projection could be obtained simply by multiplying the sales results in the test market by a factor equal to the national population. Thus, if the market size in the test areas is one-twentieth of the national market, sales results multiplied by 20 would yield the sales forecast. However, absolute representativeness in test areas is hardly ever achieved; therefore, some adjustments must be made in sales results in test areas before projecting to the national market.

Assume for example, that PepsiCo selected four markets to test Slice — San Diego, Minneapolis, Dallas, and Boston. Yet soft drink consumption in these areas is somewhat below the national average. PepsiCo would then adjust the sales estimates for Slice in these four markets upward to better reflect national soft drink consumption.

SALES FORECASTING MODELS

The weakness of historical forecasts and managerial judgment has led some companies to develop statistical models to forecast sales. Two types of models are probabilistic and deterministic. **Probabilistic models** rely on past consumer purchasing behavior to estimate the probability that consumers will purchase. For example, if a consumer bought the same brand four times in a row, the model might estimate a 95 percent chance the consumer will buy the same brand again. While probabilistic models are useful, they do not take into account environmental factors such as new technology or aggressive pricing by competitors, which may change even long-standing consumer purchase behavior.

Deterministic models use marketing variables such as advertising expenditures, price level, couponing, and so forth, as their basis for predicting sales or market share. A deterministic model might forecast that a product will attain a certain market share or sales level if a specified amount is spent on advertising and sales promotions, if a certain price level is established, and if the company attains a certain level of distribution. As these marketing mix components change, the model will forecast different market-share and sales levels.

Deterministic models are important because they are the only sales forecasting technique to provide diagnostic as well as predictive information to management. For example, a deterministic model might predict an increase in sales with a certain increase in advertising expenditures, and conclude that the increase in sales is not sufficient to warrant the increase in advertising expenditures. It is not only predicting sales, but also telling management not to increase the advertising budget.

PROFIT ESTIMATES

Sales forecasts provide the revenue base for the next step in marketing planning, estimating a product's profits. Profit estimates must also take into account the costs of marketing a product.

TABLE 8.3

Hypothetical Profit Estimate for Cellular Telephones in the First Year after Introduction (In Millions)

Revenue			$270.0
Marketing costs		$20.0	
Advertising	$10.0		
Sales promotions	4.0		
Distribution	6.0		
Indirect costs		60.0	
Research and development	50.0		
Marketing research	3.0		
Administration	7.0		
Manufacturing costs		180.0	
Total costs		260.0	
Net profits before taxes		10.0	

Investment in cellular telephones = $100 million.
Return on investment = $10 million/$100 million = 10%

Cost estimates are derived from the estimated research and development effort necessary to develop the product, the strategy planned to market the product, and the facilities required to produce the product. Table 8.3 shows hypothetical profit estimates for Motorola's cellular telephones in the first year after introduction. Revenues are estimated at $270 million based on projected sales of 150,000 units at an average of $1,800 per unit. Marketing costs are broken down into advertising, sales promotion, and distribution costs. Indirect costs are those costs that can not be directly assigned to cellular telephones and are shared across several product categories. These include such costs as research and development facilities, marketing research, and administration. Manufacturing is the third major cost item.

Net profits before taxes are total costs less revenues, or $10 million. If investment in the introduction of cellular telephones is $100 million, then return on investment (ROI) would be 10 percent, which is Motorola's target.

VALUATION AND CONTROL

The final steps in marketing planning are ongoing evaluation and control. Once a marketing plan is implemented, the product manager will evaluate actual product performance, particularly the effectiveness of the marketing mix, during the first year, and these data then serve as input into the planning cycle for the following year. This is represented by a feedback loop in Figure 8.1 from evaluation and control back to product objectives.

If sales are below estimate, the product manager must determine what steps are necessary to remedy the situation. Often, changes in advertising, promotion, price, or distribution are required. Before being implemented, though, such changes must be supported by data indicating how they would improve sales performance.

Sometimes a failure to meet sales or profitability objectives requires more basic changes than an adjustment in the marketing mix. For instance, management might have miscalculated consumer needs or competitive reaction. In such cases, it may be necessary to make basic changes in the positioning of the brand or in the definition of the target market. Management must also be prepared to consider withdrawing the product, painful as this action might be.

Control is maintained by the product manager monitoring marketing costs to ensure they are within budget. There must be enough flexibility to allow advertising and promotional costs to be increased if necessary — for instance, if competitive activity requires an increase in coupons or if greater trade promotion expenditures are needed to convince the trade to accept the new product — without bringing the total amount significantly above budget.

Motorola's experience in introducing cellular phones shows the importance of evaluation and control. It was quickly apparent that the marketing plan would need adjustment, since sales were not close to expectations. Two problems were immediately pinpointed — product quality and dealer relations — and corrective action was taken to improve both.

SUMMARY

1. How does a firm develop a marketing plan for a new or existing product?
A process must be established under the direction of the product manager that involves the following:

> Conducting a situation analysis to evaluate the market for the product.
> Evaluating the opportunities and threats in marketing the product and assessing the company's strengths and weaknesses in the market.
> Developing product objectives on the basis of the opportunity/threat and strength/weakness analyses.
> Identifying the target market for the product and establishing a strategy to position the product to meet the needs of the target.
> Developing a marketing mix to implement product strategy.
> Forecasting sales and establishing initial profit projections.
> Evaluating and controlling the marketing effort.

2. How should the market for the product be evaluated?
The product manager should first identify the market for the product, which would entail identifying customer needs and the products customers perceive as filling these needs. Next, the characteristics of the market should be evaluated on criteria such as growth in demand, capital investment, and potential profitability in order to determine market attractiveness. The total potential for the market should be estimated on this basis.

3. What are the strategic issues in identifying a target market and positioning the product?
The plan should indicate whether the target for the product is the total market or specific segments. Further, it should indicate if an expansion of the target market is feasible and, if so, what segments should be targets for future effort. The plan should also indicate the strategy for positioning — that is, whether the product should be positioned based on its attributes and features, on imagery and symbolism, or on comparisons with competitive products.

4. What mix of marketing elements — advertising, distribution, and price — should be used to implement the strategy for the product?
The marketing plan must specify the components of the marketing mix: namely, product features; a promotional mix that includes advertising, promotion, and

sales plans; a distribution plan to identify distribution channels and trade support; and strategies for setting and changing prices. The product manager must specify a budget for the marketing effort and the amount allocated to each component of the marketing mix.

5. *How can a firm estimate future sales?*

Future sales will be based on market potential and the firm's planned marketing strategy. Methods for sales forecasting include (1) relying on past sales data, (2) managerial judgment, (3) basing forecasts on consumer responses, and (4) marketing models.

KEY TERMS

Marketing plan (p. 204)
Strategic marketing plan (p. 204)
Situation analysis (p. 204)
Product positioning (p. 206)
Perceptual mapping (p. 208)
Market potential (p. 211)
Return on investment (ROI) (p. 214)
Marketing strategy (p. 215)
Target market (p. 215)
Comparative advertising (p. 217)
Promotional mix (p. 219)
Historical analogy (p. 221)
Delphi method (p. 221)
Expected-value method (p. 221)
Probabilistic models (p. 222)
Deterministic models (p. 222)

QUESTIONS

1. What are the key steps in the marketing planning process for a product? Why do you suppose

   a. the situation analysis is the first step in the process?

   b. the situation analysis and identification of opportunity precede establishing product objectives?

2. What environmental factors encouraged Motorola to enter the cellular telephone market? What were some of the problems Motorola encountered when it entered the market? Should it have anticipated these problems in the marketing planning process?

3. An executive for a small electronics firm was asked for a general reaction to this chapter. In part, he said:

   > You know, we do most of what you say here — situation analysis, opportunity/threat analysis, strength/weakness analysis, identifying target markets, etc. But a couple of things you should know: First, we don't call it that. A "situation analysis" is our baseline review to assess the market potential for a new product. The "opportunity/threat analysis" is looking at the pros and cons for introducing the product. The "strength/weakness analysis" is our way of asking "What do we need to go into the market?"
   >
   > Second, and as you probably gather, we are

   not nearly as formalized as you indicate in your chapter. Sometimes I'm a one-man planning operation, walking around with the opportunity/threat analysis in my head.

   a. Do the executive's comments suggest that the marketing planning process in Figure 8.1 is not useful for small businesses?

   b. Is there a problem with the executive "walking around with the opportunity/threat analysis in his head"?

4. The executive cited in question 3 made another point:

   > I take issue with your statement that Motorola should have done a better job in anticipating the threats in the cellular telephone market. That really does sound like Monday morning quarterbacking. Any company going into a major venture like cellular telephones is going to face unanticipated risks. It's inevitable. If they're always going to worry about environmental threats, their management might start getting cold feet about everything and wind up doing nothing. You know, if you take this formalized planning process too far, it can shackle the more entrepreneurial and innovative part of your business. And that's the part that's going to ensure a company's survival for the next 50 years!

    a.   Do you agree with the statement?

    b.   Is there a danger of making the marketing planning process too structured and formalized?

5. Apply the marketing planning model in Figure 8.1 to one of the following:

    a.   Kodak's decision to develop lithium batteries (see Chapter 2).

    b.   Apple's introduction of the Macintosh (see Chapter 4).

    c.   Pepsi's introduction of Slice (see Chapters 1 and 10).

In each case, what were (a) the environmental opportunities and threats, (b) the company's capabilities to enter the market, (c) the target market for the product, (d) the general positioning strategy, and (e) key components of the marketing mix?

6. Two companies producing cellular telephones define the market differently. One defines it as "mobile communications," whereas the other defines it as "cellular telephones."

    a.   What is the difference in these market definitions?

    b.   What are the implications of each definition for identifying marketing opportunity, competition, and a target market?

    c.   Which definition do you find more useful for marketing planning? Why?

7. Where would you establish the market boundaries for mobile communications based on Figure 8.2? Why?

8. Use the seven criteria on page 209 to rate the market attractiveness of one of the following:

    a.   Kodak's entry into lithium batteries.

    b.   Apple's entry into desktop publishing.

    c.   Motorola's entry into cellular telephones.

9. What are some of the strategic issues regarding target-market identification cited in the text? How do these issues apply to Motorola's entry into cellular telephones?

10. How might Motorola position its cellular telephones by

    a.   attributes and features?

    b.   problems the product can solve?

    c.   a particular situation?

    d.   symbols and imagery?

    e.   focusing on a competitive product?

11. What are the pros and cons of the four approaches to sales forecasting based on (a) historical data, (b) managerial judgment, (c) consumer responses, and (d) models?

12. In each of the following instances, a company wants to forecast sales for one or more of its products. Which of the sales forecasting methods cited in the chapter would you recommend in each case? Why?

    a.   A firm that has experienced a steady rate of sales growth in the last ten years.

    b.   A company in a highly volatile industrial market that is controlled by a few large producers.

    c.   A consumer-goods company that frequently tests new hair-care and toiletry items.

    d.   An industrial products company that finds a predictable relationship between its price and promotional activities and its sales results.

    e.   A company that is introducing a new diet drink similar to one it introduced several years ago.

CASE 8.1

MARKETING PLANNING: LUNCH BUCKET FOR THE OFFICE

Source: John Birmingham, "Dial's Hearty Office Meal," *Adweek*, June 27, 1988, pp. 20–23. Reprinted with permission of AdWeek.

One Friday in September 1987, as part of its regular run of in-store demonstrations, Jewel Food Stores set up microwave ovens on small tables at its 135 outlets in the Midwest. Employees spent the next two days zapping a new product called Lunch Bucket and doling out 1-ounce samples to customers. The result was staggering. Within 48 hours, the grocery chain sold some 420,000 containers of the microwaveable meals.

Executives at The Dial Corp., the $870-million Phoenix company behind the Lunch Bucket launch, were naturally pleased — but not entirely surprised. After seven arduous years of product development, market research and test marketing, they knew their product was a winner.

Microwave foods constitute the hottest area of the food business. And since Lunch Bucket was shelf stable, it wouldn't have to fight for space in overcrowded freezer sections found in most grocery stores.

Most important, consumers could easily bring Lunch Bucket to the workplace, an unexplored market where Dial saw prospects for dramatic growth.

Lunch Bucket was something altogether rare in the food industry, a truly new product. Although food companies last year introduced well over 3,000 products, the vast majority were unabashed knockoffs and line extensions, merely adding to the clutter on grocers' shelves. Lunch Bucket, by contrast, forged the way for a completely new category — shelf-stable, microwaveable meals — Lunch Bucket has given Dial a considerable lead in the untapped market for lunches cooked up in the office microwave. That alone has excited the envy of large competitors and given Dial a head start in what could develop into a large new market.

Dial needed that edge. As a food marketer, Dial suffered a number of disadvantages, starting with a name that connoted soap. The company had evolved from Greyhound Corp.'s 1968 purchase of Armour Foods, which came with Dial's soap division. Renamed Armour-Dial, the company fared well with household products but fell short in the food business.

In 1983, Armour-Dial sold the bulk of its Armour lines to ConAgra but hung on to Armour Star shelf-stable meat products. The line had sales of $250 million, was turning a profit and boasted a 28% market share. The products also lent themselves to preparation in microwave ovens, a field that clearly would occupy much of the food industry's attention in years to come.

But Dial Corp. — it renamed itself again in 1986 — had other plans in the food business. In 1985 it tested a five-item version of the Lunch Bucket line, but the test ran through the Southland Corp.'s 7-Eleven retail stores. When it entered the market, distribution through 7-Eleven stores had skewed the product toward blue-collar men. In grocery stores, the product attracted a more upscale following, mainly women between the ages of 25 and 54. And that audience demanded more sophisticated fare.

"One thing we learned early on is that you can't take a basic canned-meat item, put it into a plastic container and hope that will be enough to sell it," says one Dial executive. "We've had to look at lower salt levels, better qualities of beef and better vegetables."

Hash soon disappeared from the line. Dial also decided against some items that would have been natural for another company — in other words, items that would play to the competition's strengths and would run the risk of being knocked off.

When Lunch Bucket began to roll out in March 1987, the line included the current 15 varieties. Each contains 8 ounces of what the Lunch Bucket label calls "a hearty half-pound meal." That pits it directly against fast-food fare. The nine entrees range from beef stew and lasagna to scalloped potatoes flavored with ham chunks. There also are six soups, among them vegetable beef and chicken noodle. They range in price from $1.09 for the soups to $1.29 for the entrees.

Even Dial's competitors concede that, so far, Dial has done just about everything right and could be pulling away from the pack. "That's what makes us cringe," says Bill Piszek, marketing research manager for the Microwave Institute at Campbell Soup Co. "Their product is in a container that's absolutely right for the times."

Campbell's research has already confirmed many of the consumer trends that bolster Lunch Bucket sales. According to one of its recent studies, microwave ovens are in 70% of American homes. With some 60 million in use, America currently has more microwave ovens than either dishwashers or VCRs.

Tests of consumer attitudes also consistently underscore the popularity of food products that can be zapped.

In the same Campbell study, roughly 90% of consumers said they liked the taste of food heated in a microwave as much as they like food prepared in a conventional oven. Most mothers reported no qualms about letting their kids use the microwave, either.

Even more important, from Dial's point of view, is the rise of microwave ovens in the workplace. According to Campbell, 68% of workers now have access to a microwave oven. And 79% of these workers who can use a microwave at work do — a third of them at least every other day. "There's no question that this market has big potential," says Piszek. "We estimate that Lunch Bucket could be worth anywhere from $90 million to $110 million if it stays in the market alone."

Dial gets credit for identifying the workplace market, but it wasn't until it test marketed the product that the company discovered the true value of the market. As it turns out, 6 out of every 10 Lunch Buckets are being eaten at work. That's not surprising, given the declining number of people at home for lunch. But it took Dial to make prepared-food marketers contenders in the segment.

Currently, 54% of American women hold jobs, and that figure is expected to climb to 60% by 1995. Furthermore, career-conscious men and women alike are working longer hours, often eating lunch at their desks. By focusing on the workplace, Dial put its finger on a market that is both untapped and growing.

Oddly, Lunch Bucket advertising does little to promote dining in the workplace. Although one TV spot depicts the product being eaten in a firehouse, the central message simply stresses convenience. "We've found that people don't need to be told where to use it," says Paul Vernon, group account director at FCB/Chicago, the ad agency responsible for the Lunch Bucket account. "Even in the first group-studies back in 1985, we saw that once consumers understood the product, they figured out how it would fit into their lives."

Dial doesn't have the luxury to rest on its microwaveable laurels, however. Hormel and American Home Food Products, under its Chef Boy-Ar-Dee label, recently unveiled shelf-stable, microwaveable lines aimed at the lunch-at-the-desk crowd. These are packaged versions of existing products. But with Dial paving the way, that may be enough. And both of the new lines undercut Lunch Bucket on price.

Within a few months Campbell and others will join the fray. But Dial is counting on its competitors to help draw attention to the category as a whole. At the same time, the company is building its own franchise with a first-year marketing program worth $22 million, $15 million of which is slated for advertising. Dial also is using extensive promotions.

Dial's early start also remains an advantage, since it enabled the company to learn precisely how to market its products at retail. Expect considerably more growth ahead. Predictions are that Lunch Bucket's sales will exceed $100 million by the early 1990s. They will level off as national competitors begin to chip away at its market share.

Still, Dial faces a struggle. Food industry leaders like Hormel, General Foods and Campbell have a distinct advantage. "Dial doesn't have a lot of shelf space in the food section of the supermarket," says Wall Street analyst L. Craig Carver. "Hormel, on the other hand, has a fair amount of shelf space in the canned area. Even if they're coming in late, that may give them more leverage."

But Dial is working on new lines that will join Lunch Bucket. As one executive sees it, "We'll certainly be hit with lots of competition from other companies in the food industry. But I think Lunch Bucket will eventually put us in the big leagues."

1. What are the opportunities and risks in marketing Lunch Bucket?
2. What are Dial's strengths and weaknesses in marketing the product?
3. What are the key target segments for Lunch Bucket?
4. How is Dial positioning the product?

NOTES

1. "Lawyer Turned Marketing Crusader," *Business Marketing,* July 1987, p. 12.

2. "A Phone War That Jolted Motorola," *Fortune,* January 20, 1986, p. 43; and "The Race to Put a Phone in Every Car," *Business Week,* October 25, 1982, p. 87.

3. "Mobile Phones: Hot New Industry," *Fortune,* August 6, 1984, p. 108.

4. "Churning the Cellular Phone Channels," *Business Marketing,* June 1988, pp. 49–58.

5. "Cellular Phone Companies Call Business a Tough One, with Profits Years Away," *The Wall Street Journal,* June 25, 1985, p. 12.

6. *Business Marketing,* June 1988, pp. 49–58; and *Fortune,* January 20, 1986, p. 43.

7. "Say Hello to Car Phones," *Sales & Marketing Management,* October 1986, p. 102.

8. *Business Marketing,* July 1987, p. 12.

9. Ibid., pp. 12–16.

10. Glen L. Urban and John R. Hauser, *Design and Marketing of New Products* (Englewood Cliffs, N.J.: Prentice-Hall, 1980), pp. 80–84.

11. *Fortune,* August 6, 1984, p. 108.

12. "New People Express Strategy Expected to be a Hard Sell," *Adweek,* May 12, 1986, p. 6; and "A Hybrid Strategy for People Express," *The New York Times,* May 1, 1986, p. D4.

13. James T. Rothe, "Effectiveness of Sales Forecasting Methods," *Industrial Marketing Management* 7(1978): 116.

14. Ibid.

CAMPBELL SOUP — FROM MASS MARKETING TO SEGMENTED MARKETING

For years, Campbell Soup Co. was one of the supreme mass marketers in America. Its red-and-white soup cans neatly stacked on supermarket shelves were the symbol of standardized marketing on a national basis — one product line, one advertising campaign, one price.

The company did a 180-degree turn in the 1980s, becoming one of the most astute followers of a market-segmentation strategy. It began introducing new products directed to the needs of singles, baby boomers, working women, yuppies, weight watchers, and nutritionally oriented consumers. As these new product lines were added, the proportion of revenues accounted for by soups fell from 50 percent to 30 percent.[1]

Why did Campbell shift from mass marketing to segmented marketing? Because a new CEO, R. Gordon McGovern, believed that the company had to start adapting to changing customer needs and stop acting as if it were the only act in town. When McGovern took over in 1980, soup sales were stagnant. Campbell's share of the soup market fell from more than 80 percent in the early 1970s to about 60 percent in 1988.[2] The company had little in the hopper in the way of new products. Management was conservative, risk-averse, and production-oriented, lacking the capability to identify new food opportunities from the changing demographic and lifestyle characteristics of the American consumer.

In the next few years, Campbell introduced an average of 100 new products a year, including Le Menu low-calorie frozen dinners, Great Start breakfast sandwiches, Fresh Chef salads and sauces, and Prego spaghetti sauce. The Le Menu and Prego lines accounted for $400 million in sales by 1986, representing over 10 percent of revenues.[3]

By 1986 McGovern was able to translate his market-segmentation philosophy into one of the most effective strategies developed by a large company —

regional segmentation. The strategy was simple: Because tastes and food preferences frequently vary by region, Campbell developed variations in products to meet those regional needs. Thus, a spicier version of Campbell's nacho cheese soup was introduced in Texas and California, Creole soups were introduced to Southern markets, a red-bean soup to Hispanic markets, and "Today's Taste," a line of low-fat, low-salt prepared foods, was designed for upscale, health-conscious, northeastern urbanites.[4]

This regional segmentation strategy was innovative — and complex to implement. Not only product runs, but advertising and promotions had to be differentiated by region. Accordingly, McGovern formed 21 regional marketing centers, each with responsibility for promoting and distributing certain products.[5] It was almost as if Campbell were selling its products to 21 countries with different needs.

McGovern saw regional segmentation as the only means of effectively competing in mature markets that were producing lower and lower profits. Otherwise, competitors would flank Campbell through product improvements region by region. Clearly, the days of mass marketing were over.

The jury is still out whether regional segmentation will turn Campbell around. By 1987 sales were growing at about 10 percent a year and earnings at about 11 percent, just under the average for the food processing industry.[6] But without the strategic shift to segmentation, performance would probably have been worse. Since Campbell was one of the first mass marketers, there is some poetic justice in its systematic move from mass marketing to segmented marketing — a response to the demographic and lifestyle changes of a dynamic environment. ■

IDENTIFYING AND TARGETING MARKET SEGMENTS

● ● ●

PURPOSE OF MARKET SEGMENTATION

Market segmentation is a strategy of identifying customers with similar needs and meeting those needs with product offerings. It is the opposite of **mass marketing**, in which a company offers one basic product without distinguishing among different customer needs and characteristics. Today almost all companies follow a strategy of market segmentation to some degree.

Market segmentation sometimes requires developing a new product or targeting an existing product more accurately. Campbell's Le Menu, for instance, was a new product directed to a weight-watcher segment that wanted quick foods it could pop into a microwave. Campbell also targeted its existing condensed soup lines to various regions of the country by introducing new flavors such as Creole and red bean, and by developing regional promotions such as free hot soup for skiers at resort areas. In each case, a segment of consumers with similar needs was identified, and the company's marketing effort was directed to that segment.

WHY SEGMENT MARKETS?

A strategy of market segmentation is a reasonable, marketing-oriented approach to satisfying consumer needs. But does it lead to greater profitability? Someone could reasonably argue just the opposite — that mass marketing is more profitable since a company can enjoy economies of scale in both production and marketing. One advertising campaign is bound to be cheaper than fragmented campaigns geared to various market segments.

Despite its higher costs, segmentation may nevertheless be the more profitable strategy. First, it allows marketers to better identify marketing opportunities. For example, identifying soft drink consumers based on needs or lifestyles might lead a soft drink company to recognize an opportunity to introduce a calcium-based soft drink for health-conscious women, or a soft drink that can be mixed with the increasingly popular low-alcohol products.

Second, segmentation promotes new-product entries. The introduction of Slice was largely the result of Pepsi's focus on the adult market, and more particularly on nutrition-conscious adults. Campbell's focus on convenience-oriented working women led to the introduction of Le Menu as a tasty, microwaveable line of frozen foods.

A third advantage of segmentation over mass marketing is that it helps marketers develop an effective marketing mix. Understanding a segment's needs helps in developing an advertising strategy. Slice's theme, "We've got the juice," was based on the importance customers attached to juice content in soft drinks. Knowing the demographic characteristics of the juice-oriented segment also helped in selecting the right advertising media. Further, the target segment's emphasis on nutrition meant that Pepsi could charge a higher price based on the fruit content of the drink.

A fourth benefit of a segmentation strategy is that it helps guide the allocation of marketing resources to various products. Thus, an evaluation of the potential of various segments such as business or vacation travelers might give airlines an indication of how much money to spend to promote frequent-flyer programs to each segment. Or the growth in health concerns might prompt a large urban hospital to devote more resources to promoting preventive care in clinics rather than in-hospital care.

In all, market segmentation takes into account the diversity of demand within a market — and this can, and usually does, translate into greater profitability.

When Gordon McGovern became CEO at Campbell in 1980, he had just finished a successful 12-year stint as head of its Pepperidge Farm subsidiary. He had introduced a slew of successful new products targeted to specific market segments and increased sales five-fold during his tenure. He knew changes would have to be made at Campbell. The company was stagnant, having made few new-product introductions directed to the changing demographics and lifestyles of the American consumer.

McGovern's plan was a simple one: Apply the same new-product philosophy that had been successful at Pepperidge Farm. But he knew implementation of that plan would be difficult, and he was right. Facing a conservative, engineering-oriented corporate culture, McGovern started to change things rapidly. He brought in some new managers that were less risk-averse and started emphasizing new-product development, but not haphazardly. "What I'm preaching around here," he said, "is adapting the product attack to demographics and the way people eat."[7] To support this new product push, McGovern doubled the advertising budget and increased marketing expenditures by 72 percent.

McGovern's new-product push seemed to be a success at first. Sales and earnings were up, and the company could cite some real winners — Prego spaghetti sauce and Le Menu frozen foods. But Campbell was coming out with new products faster than the company could market them or consumers could absorb them. Failures started popping up — The Juice Works, introduced in single serving cans when competition was offering asceptic packaging; Fresh Chef, a line of

Gordon McGovern — The Trials and Tribulations of a Market Segmenter

Source: © Rob Kinmonth.

refrigerated soups and sauces with limited shelf life; and Star Wars, a cookie line that never made it among kids. Worst of all, the emphasis on new products led managers to ignore existing money-making brands, leading to a loss in market share in soups and frozen foods.

McGovern realized that new products alone were not the answer. The company was not adequately implementing a segmentation strategy. As a result, he began shifting the focus from developing new products to a less risky strategy of extending existing product lines by introducing regional variations in brands. One consequence of this shift was a 40 percent drop in new-product introductions in 1988.[8]

To implement a regional segmentation strategy, McGovern established 21 regional divisions responsible for marketing the company's total product line. But there were problems in implementation here, too. Regional divisions began to focus only on marketing in their local area, forgetting that Campbell was a national company. One local manager decided to give up TV advertising in favor of local radio; another put the bulk of the local promotional budget into sponsoring sports events, with little impact.[9] With experience, however, these regional managers began to better coordinate their marketing plans with corporate management.

McGovern takes these ups and downs in stride. He still drives his run-down Volkswagen Beetle to work, mixes easily with employees in the company cafeteria, and roams supermarket aisles to see Campbell displays. But he has steadfastly held to a segmentation philosophy, and his regional approach seems to be paying off. ■

CUSTOMIZED, SEGMENTED, AND MASS MARKETING

Figure 9.1 shows various levels of marketing effort on a continuum from the individual consumer to the total market. At the most micro level is **customized marketing**, involving the development of tailor-made products to meet the needs of individual buyers. Firms producing pollution-control systems, for instance, must design them to the specifications of individual companies. Clothing can be made to the specifications of individual consumers. Even "mass-produced" cars have come close to being produced on a customized basis. The number of options on a Ford Thunderbird resulted in 69,120 combinations, meaning that consumers came close to designing their own cars if they specified all the available features. At the other extreme is the total market level. Here, the strategy of mass marketing is directed uniformly to the aggregate market.

Our interest in this chapter is neither customized marketing nor mass marketing; it is what lies between the two, segmented marketing. As we saw, segmented marketing requires targeting products to the specific needs of well-defined customer groups. Figure 9.1 suggests that market segmentation is on a continuum, meaning that a marketer can target a very small segment and approach customized marketing, or target a larger segment and approach mass marketing.

For example, L&M is targeting smaller segments because, according to its CEO, it "couldn't compete head-to-head with Philip Morris or R. J. Reynolds in advertising spending."[10] The company introduced Eve 120mm to appeal to fe-

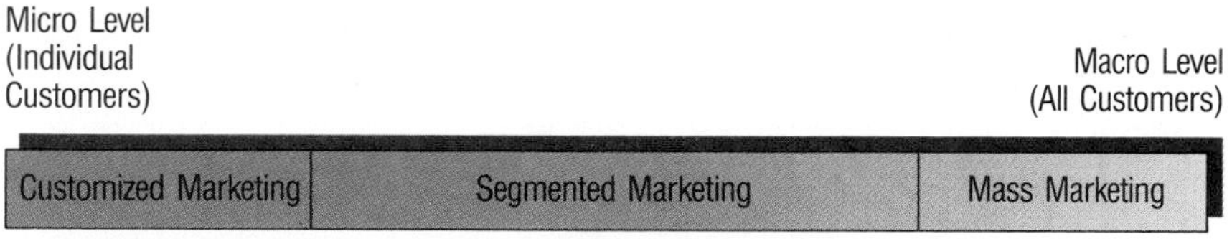

FIGURE 9.1
Levels of Market Segmentation

Micro Level
(Individual
Customers)

Macro Level
(All Customers)

Customized Marketing	Segmented Marketing	Mass Marketing

male smokers who buy 120mm cigarettes, even though this segment accounts for only 2 percent of all smokers. Eve sales totaled over $50 million, a small but profitable sales level for the brand.

In contrast, Philip Morris targets larger segments that generate more sales revenues. Its Benson & Hedges brand is positioned to an upscale segment of both male and female smokers. Marlboro is positioned to a more downscale male macho segment, Virginia Slims is positioned to independent, modern women, and Merit is positioned to concerned smokers who want a low tar and nicotine cigarette. Each of these segments is larger than the niche targeted by Liggett & Myers' Eve, and pursuing them all allows Philip Morris to cover most of the cigarette market.

Like Campbell, many venerable names in corporate America have shifted from a mass-marketing to a segmented-marketing strategy. Companies such as Ford, Chevrolet, Coca-Cola, Pepsi-Cola, Hershey, and Kodak used to sell one or two product lines to a national market. By the 1960s these companies began to recognize the benefits of a more segmented approach. If anything, Campbell is a latecomer to the shift from mass marketing to segmented marketing. Its strategy of one product line to a mass market was a part of the American landscape since the turn of the century. (See Exhibit 9.1 for an example of Campbell's mass marketing approach.)

THE TREND TO MARKET SEGMENTATION

Why the changeover from mass to segmented marketing? There were two major reasons, economic change and demographic or lifestyle change. Economic change came first. As we saw in Chapter 1, until the 1960s marketers did not have to pay that much attention to customers. During the Depression, customers could not afford to buy; during World War II and the Korean War, customers could afford to buy, but the goods were frequently unavailable. Only by the 1960s were customers becoming more selective, because they finally had the buying power at the same time that the goods were available.

Many marketers reacted by trying to offer customers what they wanted. The best way to do that was to recognize the diversity of customer needs. In the automobile industry, for instance, car makers began to divide the market into middle-aged and younger segments, luxury and economy segments, performance and style segments, and rural, suburban and urban segments. A similar pattern emerged in the soft drink industry, where manufacturers divided up the market first into cola and noncola segments, and then into taste, diet, and health oriented segments. In each case, new products or extensions of existing products were directed to these segments.

A second change that contributed to the emergence of market-segmentation strategies was the shift in demographics and lifestyles that became apparent in the 1970s. As we saw in Chapter 3, the increase in working women (a demographic change) led to a shift away from the traditional assumption that car purchases

EXHIBIT 9.1
An Example of Campbell's Former
Mass-Marketing Approach

were a male preserve. Car features and advertising began to be targeted more specifically to women. Similarly, the increasing proportion of singles (another demographic change) led to the introduction of more sporty car models, and, as another example, smaller-sized versions of existing products such as soft drinks. The greater focus on health and nutrition (a lifestyle change) prompted the introduction of adult cereals, caffeine-free versions of soft drinks, and a host of low-calorie foods. In each case, companies began to identify different demographic and lifestyle segments because of changing needs, targeting their marketing effort to these segments.

COCA-COLA — A SEGMENTED PRODUCT LINE

Coca-Cola's product line illustrates the extent of the shift from mass marketing to segmented marketing. Figure 9.2 is a **product-market matrix** of Coca-Cola's products. It is produced by the intersection of six market segments defined by common needs and five product types directed to these needs. Coca-Cola was one of the first to recognize the importance of diet products when it introduced Tab in 1963 as a diet cola positioned to women. Twenty years later, it used the magic name Coke on a product other than its flagship brand, introducing Diet Coke positioned to men. The year 1983 also saw Coke introduce caffeine-free versions of Coca-Cola, Diet Coke, and Tab, positioned to the health-oriented consumers.

In 1985 Coca-Cola introduced Cherry Coke to meet the needs of teenagers who wanted a sweet cola drink and to break Pepsi's lock on the teenage market. The most famous move of all, the introduction of New Coke, was made for the same reason — to better appeal to teenagers who favored Pepsi.

When Coca-Cola brought back the original brand due to the consumer outcry, it inadvertently followed a sound segmentation strategy: positioning one brand (New Coke) to the segment that wants a sweeter drink and another brand (its flagship brand) to the segment that does not.

FIGURE 9.2
Market Segmentation of Coca-Cola's Product Line

Market Segments	Products				
	Cola	Diet Cola	Caffeine Free	Fruit Based	Lemon–Lime
Taste Oriented: Like sweet-tasting colas	New Coke Cherry Coke				
Taste Oriented: Like unsweetened colas	Coca Cola Classic				
Taste Oriented: Like fruit juice				Minute Maid	
Taste Oriented: Like lemon–lime					Sprite
Health/Nutrition Conscious			Caffeine-Free Tab, Coke, and Diet Coke	Minute Maid	
Weight Watchers		Diet Coke, Tab, and Diet Cherry Coke			

Coca-Cola also introduced Minute Maid soda as a fruit-based drink in reaction to Pepsi's introduction of Slice. The brand is positioned to appeal to a segment that likes the taste of fruit juice, as well as to health- and nutrition-conscious consumers. Filling out the product line is Sprite, the company's lemon-lime entry positioned to consumers who like a lemon-lime flavor.

Coca-Cola's actions in segmenting its markets were primarily a series of responses to its competitors in an attempt to maintain its market leadership. RC Cola was the first to introduce a diet cola. Coke and Pepsi followed. RC Cola was also the first to introduce a caffeine-free cola; but Seven Up popularized the notion and opened up the health-oriented segment. Coke and Pepsi followed. Because Pepsi's sweeter taste was popular with teenagers, Coca-Cola followed with New Coke. And Pepsi's introduction of fruit-based Slice prompted Coke to follow suit with Minute Maid. In each case, Coca-Cola moved in relatively quickly to ensure representation in each of the segments in Figure 9.2.

Although segmented marketing has become the norm in our economy, mass marketing is still a strategic option. Indeed, until recently, some savvy marketers like Procter & Gamble successfully used a mass marketing approach despite the overall trend to segmented marketing.

CAN MASS MARKETING BE EFFECTIVE?

Mass marketing was a successful strategy for P&G because its products — toothpaste, soap, and detergents — had a relatively homogeneous market; they could be sold to consumers across age, income, and regional lines. Also, brands such as Crest, Ivory soap, and Tide detergent were the market leaders. Consumers were convinced they were among the best offerings in the market. If a brand has established itself as a leader over the years through mass marketing, it can continue to be marketed uniformly until it faces a competitive challenge. And as we saw in Chapter 4, challenging a market leader is difficult.

But P&G's environment was changing because the assumption of homogeneous demand no longer held true. As one marketer put it,

> [P&G and other mass marketers] soon discovered that demographic and lifestyle changes had delivered a death blow to mass marketing and brand loyalty. A nation that once shared homogeneous buying tastes had splintered into many different consumer groups — each with special needs and interests.[11]

As competitors recognized this diversity in demand, they began to chip away at P&G's dominance — Kimberly Clark in disposable diapers, Colgate in toothpaste, Lever in detergents. P&G's response was to offer more product options to try to accommodate the diversity in demand. Where Tide had once been a single product sold uniformly across the country, today consumers can choose from regular Tide, liquid Tide, Tide in 10-box Redi-Paks, and Tide in multi-action sheets.[12] The largest mass marketer finally had to adopt market segmentation in order to survive.

THE MARKET-SEGMENTATION PROCESS

Although Procter & Gamble's shift to a segmentation strategy was prompted by the flanking strategies of its competitors, the process of identifying segments is far more complicated than simply looking over one's shoulder to see what the competition is doing. Figure 9.3 illustrates this process. It shows market segmentation as part of the marketing plan that we discussed in the previous chapter. Before selecting segments for a marketing effort, the company conducts a situation analysis of the market and identifies marketing opportunities. After these steps, it can start identifying market segments.

There are three approaches to identifying market segments: The first, **benefit segmentation**, identifies segments by what consumers want. An example would be a weight-watcher segment among soft drink consumers. A second approach, **behavioral segmentation**, focuses on what consumers do. An example would be heavy cola drinkers. A third approach is **segmenting by consumer characteristics**. An example would be a male versus a female segment of diet cola drinkers, or a teenage versus an adult segment of fruit-based soft drink consumers.

Having identified the market segments, the next step is to determine which ones to target for new-product introductions or for positioning existing products. Criteria for selecting a segment might be its size, its growth potential, the presence or absence of competitive offerings that are directed to the segment, and the ease with which products can be advertised and distributed to the segment.

The third step in the market-segmentation process is to develop an integrated segmentation strategy based on company objectives. A company could follow a strategy of pursuing one segment with one product (just as Seven-Up Company has targeted the health-oriented segment with its no-caffeine claim), several seg-

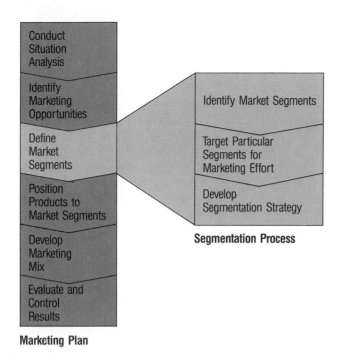

FIGURE 9.3
The Process of Identifying and
Targeting Market Segments

ments with several products (Coca-Cola's strategy as reflected in Figure 9.2), or some strategy in between.

Once the target segment has been selected and a segmentation strategy established, the firm then takes the next steps in the marketing planing process: to position its product to the target segment and to develop a marketing mix. Positioning and marketing mix strategies follow segment identification, since these strategies are determined by the needs of the target segment. For example, Iveco, a manufacturer of medium-sized trucks, found that truck owners who deliver food are particularly concerned with maneuverability in food distribution centers.[13] Having defined this segment, Iveco then developed an integrated strategy to meet its needs. The company improved the maneuverability of its trucks and positioned them to food delivery companies on this basis. Its advertising and personal-selling programs were coordinated to emphasize this feature.

In the remainder of this chapter, we will discuss each of the three steps in identifying and targeting market segments.

IDENTIFY MARKET SEGMENTS

As we saw, market segments can be identified in one of three ways: by the benefits consumers desire, by their behavior, or by their characteristics. Table 9.1 summarizes the types of variables marketers use to identify segments by these three approaches. As we will see, the approach marketers use will depend on their strategic purpose.

Marketers use benefit segmentation to determine the potential for new products. For example, a soft drink company that wants to determine the potential for a soft drink with high fiber content will segment the market by what consumers

BENEFIT SEGMENTATION

TABLE 9.1
Variables Used to Identify Consumer
Market Segments

BENEFIT SEGMENTATION	Nutrition	Prestige/luxury
	Health	Performance
	Economy	Style
	Good taste	Service

BEHAVIORAL SEGMENTATION	Brands purchased (e.g., users of Tide)
	Product category purchased (e.g. users of liquid detergents)
	Frequency of purchase (e.g, heavy, medium, or light purchasers of liquid detergents)

SEGMENTING BY CONSUMER CHARACTERISTICS

Demographics	Income	Race	Family size
	Age	Occupation	Stage in family life cycle
	Sex	Region	

Lifestyles	Achievement-oriented	Isolate
	Societally conscious	Venturesome
	Health-conscious	Innovative
	Sociable	Outdoor type
	Family-oriented	

Personality	Aggressive	Compulsive
	Compliant	Authoritarian
	Dominant	Ambitious

want, probably focusing on those who seek health and nutritional benefits from soft drinks. The new product will then be targeted to this benefit segment.

The second row of Table 9.2 shows how the snack food market can be segmented according to benefits. This figure is based on data compiled by a large food manufacturer that was investigating new product opportunities for nut and chip-type snacks. The company interviewed 1,500 snack food users and identified six segments according to the similar benefits perceived by consumers in each group. For example, nutritional snackers want a nutritious, natural snack with no artificial ingredients, whereas weight watchers want a low-calorie snack that provides quick energy. The study also identified the demographic, lifestyle, and personality characteristics of each benefit segment and the types of snacks they usually eat.

The company already was doing well in the "party" and "indiscriminate snacker" segments with its existing chip and nut snacks, but it also wanted to reach the nutritional and weight-watcher segments. It developed a nut-and-dried-fruit snack positioned to these two segments. Preliminary product tests showed that consumers in the nutritional and weight-watcher segments liked the product, and it was then introduced in test markets.

Data on the demographic, lifestyle, and personality characteristics of these two segments suggested that many of these consumers might be in the "yuppie" (young, urban professionals) category. As a result, the company developed an

TABLE 9.2
Benefit Segmentation of the Snack Food Market

	NUTRITIONAL SNACKERS	WEIGHT WATCHERS	GUILTY SNACKERS	PARTY SNACKERS	INDISCRIMINATE SNACKERS	ECONOMICAL SNACKERS
Percentage of Snackers	22	14	9	15	15	18
Benefits Sought	Nutritious No artificial ingredients Natural snack	Low-calorie Quick-energy	Low-calorie Good-tasting	Good to serve guests Proud to serve Goes well with beverage	Good-tasting Satisfies hunger	Low price Best value
Demographics	Better educated Have younger children	Younger Single	Younger or older Females Lower socioeconomic group	Middle-aged Nonurban	Teens	Larger families Better educated
Lifestyle and Personality Characteristics	Self-assured Controlled	Outdoor types Influential Venturesome	High anxiety Isolate	Sociable	Hedonistic	Self-assured Price-oriented
Consumption Level of Snacks	Light	Light	Heavy	Average	Heavy	Average
Type of Snacks Usually Eaten	Fruits Vegetables Cheese	Yogurt Vegetables	Yogurt Cookies Crackers Candy	Nuts Potato chips Crackers Pretzels	Candy Ice cream Cookies Potato chips Pretzels Popcorn	No specific products

advertising campaign featuring young, upwardly mobile consumers on the go, having a tasty and nutritional snack. Demographics also helped the company select magazines for its print advertising and time slots for its TV advertising targeted to yuppies.

BEHAVIORAL SEGMENTATION

While benefit segmentation is most effective in guiding new-product development, marketers who want to develop strategies for existing brands and product categories are guided by what people do. In behavioral segmentation, consumers are grouped by their purchases. For example, the adult cereal market might be segmented by those consumers who buy bran cereals, vitamin-fortified cereals, low-calorie cereals, and sugared cereals. Marketers would then determine the demographic and lifestyle characteristics of each behavioral segment. If, for example, the group buying bran cereals has more consumers who are over 50, in a higher income group, and express health concerns, then this information would be used to position the product (use health-oriented claims in the advertising), and to select media (buy TV time on programs most likely to be watched by upscale consumers over 50, or select magazines most likely to be read by this group).

Segmenting Consumers by Brands Purchased
In behavioral segmentation, markets are usually segmented by what brands or product categories people buy. As an example of brand segmentation, when VF,

the producer of Lee jeans, bought Wrangler dungarees in 1986 it found itself dealing with two very different segments. Lee purchasers tended to be stylish suburbanite women who bought their jeans in specialty stores; Wrangler purchasers were rural consumers, frequently cowboys, who bought dungarees at mass-merchandise outlets such as K Mart.

VF made sure to market differently to each segment so as to maintain the loyalty of both. In the words of its president, "These are separate companies that will operate separate businesses, and what one does will have no bearing on the other."[14] Segmenting by brand-purchasing behavior led VF to a strategy of ensuring brand distinctiveness and separation. The brands continued to be sold in separate stores with separate advertising campaigns, rather than being linked under a single corporate umbrella.

Another reason to segment by brands purchased is to identify prospective users. For example, if purchasers of air pollution control systems are usually companies with over $100 million in sales in the chemical or oil industries, then any company with these characteristics that does not have an air pollution control system would be a good prospect. Yamaha uses this principle in choosing the cities in which to open new motorcycle dealerships. It identifies the demographic characteristics of owners of its motorcycles, and assumes that prospective purchasers will have similar characteristics to existing Yamaha owners. It then uses census data to determine the demographic characteristics of prospective dealership areas. Yamaha locates dealerships in those areas whose demographic profile most closely matches the demographic profile of Yamaha owners.[15]

Segmenting Consumers by Product Categories Purchased

Another basis for segmenting markets behaviorally is by identifying users of a product category rather than a brand. For example, Yamaha could have determined the characteristics of motorcycle owners in general rather than owners of Yamaha motorcycles and selected dealer locations based on this broader market definition.

Companies often segment a market by frequency of product use, identifying heavy, medium and light users of a product category. A company then has two strategic options: to position products to the heavy users, since they generate more product volume and revenues; or to position a product to light users since they may represent an ignored niche in the marketplace. Nestle segmented the iced-tea market by level of usage to determine how to better position its iced-tea brand to heavy users. It found that the heaviest-user segment (17% of iced-tea users) drank twice as much (47.5 glasses a month) as the average drinker (about 24 glasses a month). By questioning the heavy users, it learned that this group emphasized two things in drinking iced tea — that it restores energy and that it is a good year-around drink. Nestle then developed its advertising around these two benefits to appeal to the heavy-user segment.

SEGMENTING BY CONSUMER CHARACTERISTICS

The third approach to market segmentation involves grouping consumers by their demographic, lifestyle, and personality characteristics. Such groupings can provide guidelines in developing a marketing mix for a product.

Demographic Segmentation

In **demographic segmentation**, consumers are grouped according to variables such as income, education, occupation, age, sex, or race. (See Table 9.1.) This type of segmentation is used most frequently for two reasons: First, demographics are often linked to consumer needs and behavior. As we saw, age largely determines brand preferences in the soft drink market, with teenagers preferring sweeter drinks and adults noncola fruit based drinks. Second, demographics are easier to determine than benefits or behavior and thus are more easily applied in segmenting markets.

The usual categories for demographic segmentation are income, age, sex, and race. Each will be discussed.

Segmenting by Income Holiday Inns uses income as the basis for demographic segmentation of its markets, dividing hotel users into three categories — affluent, middle-income, and budget-conscious. Its Holiday Inns chain has an established position in the middle-income group. To appeal to the upper and lower end of the market, it developed two other chains, Crowne Plaza hotels for the affluent segment and Hampton Inns for the budget-conscious. Holiday's strategy for each of its chains is a function of the income segment it is targeted to. Hampton Inns, for example, has low rates, minimal service, and is advertised as a no-frills chain, using media that reach a downscale segment. Segmenting by income thus provides Holiday Inns with a basis for differentiating marketing strategies for its three chains.

Segmenting by Age Companies often position their products to different age groups. GM, Ford, and Chrysler have all introduced more performance-oriented cars styled on European models to appeal to baby boomers. Buick's TV ads for its Skylark are targeting baby boomers by showing a young family exercising to stay in shape, rushing to work, putting the baby in the car, and then stopping in the playground. Richardson Vicks also targets its Life Stage vitamin line based on age segmentation, with Children's Formula in chewable form designed for 4- to 12-year-olds, Teens Formula for teenagers, and Men's and Women's formula for adults. (See Exhibit 9.2 for another example of age segmentation.)

Segmenting by Sex American Express segments its market on the basis of another demographic characteristic, sex. In attempting to increase the number of women who are American Express cardholders, it waged an "interesting lives" campaign (see Exhibit 3.1 in Chapter 3) that provided a realistic portrayal of women's roles in a series of short vignettes. Toiletry companies that have long segmented their cosmetic and hair-care lines for women are now beginning to segment male consumers. Lancome, for example, advertises its line of skin-care products for men with, "Take what you have and make it better."

Segmenting by Race As we saw in Chapter 3, the vast purchasing power of the black and Hispanic markets has led marketers to segment by race. Products, advertising appeals, and distribution channels are targeted this way. Liggett & Myers developed a new more full-flavored cigarette blend for the Hispanic market. Similarly, Fabergé introduced a shampoo and conditioner designed to accommodate Hispanic women's tendency to shampoo their typically long, thick hair frequently.[16] In developing advertising strategies, Procter & Gamble appointed a black-owned advertising agency in 1984 to run a campaign for Crest directed to blacks. In developing distribution strategies, Zayre Discount Stores located branches in black urban areas and tailored its product line to the needs and tastes of black consumers.[17]

Lifestyle Segmentation

Lifestyle segmentation groups consumers according to their attitudes, interests, and opinions. Achievement orientation, societal consciousness, health consciousness, and family orientation would be examples of the characteristics associated with consumer needs and brand preferences.

Merrill Lynch used lifestyle segmentation to change its corporate image. In the early 1980s, the company found that its advertisements portraying a herd of bulls with the theme, "We're Bullish on America," appealed to conventional and risk-averse consumers. To attract those more upscale and willing to experiment, the company identified a more achievement-oriented group as its target. It then changed its advertising theme to "A Breed Apart." (See Exhibit 9.3.)

Segmenting by Personality Characteristics

Personality characteristics are another important basis for segmenting markets. Traits such as aggressiveness, compliance, and compulsiveness are more deep-seated than lifestyles since they reflect more enduring patterns of behavior. As a result, they are particularly relevant to consumer purchase behavior.

Anheuser-Busch developed personality profiles of beer drinkers in an effort to determine which market segments the company's major brands were reaching. It

EXHIBIT 9.2
An Example of Segmenting by Age

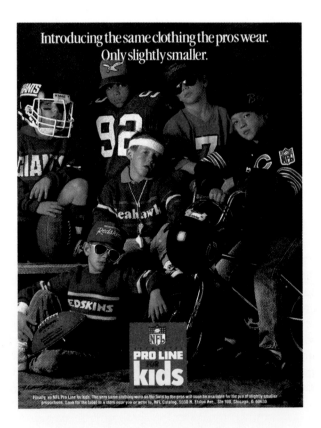

Example of ''We're Bullish on America'' Campaign.

Example of ''A Breed Apart'' Campaign.

linked four drinking types to personality factors (see Table 9.3). Reparative drinkers are light drinkers who are attuned to the needs of others; social drinkers tend to be ambitious and manipulative; indulgent drinkers drink heavily when alone and blame others for their shortcomings; and oceanic drinkers drink heavily with others to escape awareness of their shortcomings.

The study found that Michelob and Budweiser appealed to different personality segments and allowed the company to specify target segments to be reached by each brand based on personality types. For instance, advertising aimed at reparative drinkers might show men and women drinking beer together in a relaxed, congenial setting. Michelob would be well-positioned to this group. An appeal to oceanic drinkers might use a male-oriented setting geared to the heavier drinker by linking beer-drinking to some occupational or social success to overcome a sense of failure. Budweiser would be well-positioned to this group.

The study was also helpful in pinpointing the best advertising media for each beer. For example, reparative drinkers were more likely to watch TV, while oceanic drinkers were more likely to read *Playboy*. Personality segmentation thus enabled more effective advertising directed to particular market segments.[18]

TABLE 9.3
Segmenting by Personality Factors

Source: Russell L. Ackoff and James R. Emshoff,
"Advertising Research at Anheuser-Busch (1968-
1974)," *Sloan Management Review* 14 (Spring 1975);
1-15; as adapted from Leon G. Schiffman and Leslie
L. Kanuk, *Consumer Behavior* (Englewood Cliffs, N.J.:
Prentice-Hall, 1983), p. 98.

TYPE OF DRINKER	PERSONALITY TYPE	DRINKING PATTERNS
Reparative drinker	Sensitive and responsive to needs of others; adapts to these needs by sacrificing own aspirations; well adjusted to this situation.	Drinks at end of day, usually with a few close friends; controlled drinker, seldom drunk; drinking is self-reward for sacrifices made to others.
Social drinker	Driven by own ambitions; attempts to manipulate others to get what he/she wants; not yet attained level of aspirations, but expects to.	Drinks heaviest on weekends; in larger groups in social settings; drinks as means of acceptance of and by others; controlled drinker.
Indulgent drinker	Considers self a failure; blames environment and others.	Heavy drinker; drinks in isolation as a form of escape.
Oceanic drinker	Considers self a failure but blames own shortcomings.	Also heavy drinker and drinks to escape recognition of shortcomings; does not drink alone.

TARGET SEGMENTS FOR MARKETING EFFORT

Two criteria are especially important in targeting segments for a marketing effort. They are the same criteria as those used to identify marketing opportunities in general: (1) opportunities for profit in the segment, and threats that affect the segment's market potential; and (2) the firm's ability, in terms of internal strengths and weaknesses, to exploit these opportunities. The opportunity/threat criteria generally deal with the segment's potential for generating revenue, while a company's strengths and weaknesses generally relate to the costs required to market to the segment. We will explore both of these criteria in more detail.

OPPORTUNITY/THREAT CRITERIA FOR TARGET SELECTION

Nestle used five criteria in a study that segmented the instant coffee market and eventually led to the introduction of Taster's Choice:

1. Similarity in customer needs within the segment.
2. Degree to which customer needs are being met by competitive products (competitive intensity).
3. The segment's growth potential.
4. The size of the segment.
5. The accessibility of the segment.

Similarity in Customer Needs
The basis of segmenting markets is similar needs. In the early 1970s Nestle did a study of instant coffee drinkers and identified four benefit segments: convenience, taste, lift and pickup, and lack of interference with sleep (that is, the decaffeinated segment). (See Figure 9.4.) Each of the segments could be identified by consumers who emphasize one of these four primary needs, although secondary needs were frequently almost as important as the primary need. For example, a large group of the decaffeinated segment was dissatisfied with current brands and wanted a better-tasting decaffeinated coffee.

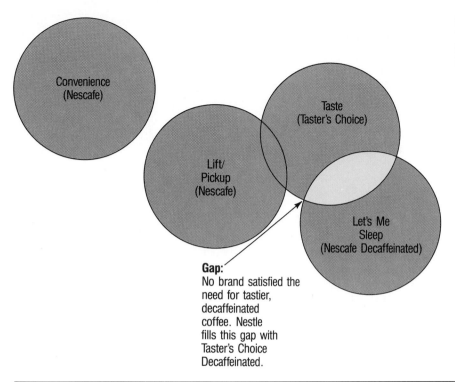

FIGURE 9.4
Targeting a Segment with Unmet
Needs: Nestle's Taster's Choice
Decaffeinated Coffee

The similarity in needs within a segment permitted Nestle to direct specific instant coffee brands to specific targets. Thus, Nescafe is positioned to two segments, the convenience and lift/pickup segments, Nescafe decaffeinated is positioned to the "Lets Me Sleep" segment, and Taster's Choice freeze-dried coffee was introduced for the taste segment. The study prompted Nestle to come out with a decaffeinated version of Taster's Choice because it revealed a gap in the "Lets Me Sleep" segment. Taster's Choice freeze-dried decaffeinated coffee was developed for those decaffeinated coffee drinkers who are dissatisfied with the taste of their current brands.

If a group's needs are not similar, there is little basis for directing marketing strategies to a segment, since no single product will offer the benefits that the segment wants, and no supporting marketing mix will appeal to a majority of consumers in the segment. Even when firms use an approach other than benefit segmentation, the assumption is that needs within the segment are similar. Hence, when Holiday Inn segments its market by consumer characteristics (income), it is assuming that low-, and middle- and higher-income consumers will have different traveling needs in terms of the service and amenities they are willing to pay for.

Competitive Intensity

A second basic criterion in targeting a particular segment is whether its needs are already being met by competitors. If they are, a firm entering the segment runs the risk of being a "me-too" brand with little competitive advantage. If the segment's needs are not being met, then a strategic window exists, assuming the firm has the competency to target the segment.

Nestle defined a strategic window when it identified a significant group of decaffeinated users who were dissatisfied with the taste of existing brands. The breakthrough was not so much in identifying this group, for it was long known that many decaffeinated users thought existing brands such as Sanka tasted medicinal. Rather, the breakthrough came with the technology that developed the freeze-drying process allowing a decaffeinated coffee to be developed that retained more of the flavor of the original beans. Having already developed Taster's Choice, Nestle obviously had the know-how to introduce a freeze-dried decaffeinated version.

Size of the Segment

Another important criterion in selecting segments for targeting is the size of a segment, because size is linked to profitability. A firm would prefer to go after a segment with more consumers and, therefore, higher revenue potential as long as the segment is identified by similar needs and the company can establish some competitive advantage. The segment of coffee drinkers who wanted a better-tasting decaffeinated coffee was large enough to pursue, and so Nestle targeted this segment for its Taster's Choice decaffeinated brand.

The size of a segment is not always related to profitability, however. Relatively small segments may be highly profitable as long as the company can establish a unique and sustainable competitive advantage. For example, Le Peep International is a breakfast-only restaurant chain that targets young professionals who are attracted to the idea of a "power breakfast."[19] The company is providing a unique offering — reasonably priced breakfasts in a quiet setting with tablecloths, flower vases, and skylights — to a small but profitable segment.

Potential for Growth

Still another criterion in targeting segments for marketing efforts is potential for growth. A segment that is likely to attract more consumers in the future is preferable to one that is in a stagnant position in a mature market.

Although coffee consumption is decreasing due to greater health awareness, the decaffeinated market segment is increasing for the same reason. Thus, Taster's Choice decaffeinated is well-positioned to address these concerns in a growing segment of the coffee market. Similarly, Le Peep is likely to find a growing segment of young professionals attracted to the idea of breakfast in a nice environment. The danger of a growth segment is that growth is likely to attract competitors. Le Peep may soon find it will not be the only elegant breakfast chain in town.

Accessibility of Segments

The last opportunity-related factor in evaluating a segment is its accessibility. A firm must be able to reach a segment with media to deliver its advertising messages and with store outlets to deliver its products.

Demographics provide the basis for selecting media and for targeting distribution efforts to reach the segment. Le Peep, for instance, can select media to reach young urban professionals by advertising in magazines such as *Time* or *Fortune*. The chain can also locate its restaurants in urban downtown office areas where young professionals are most likely to work. Similarly, Nestle can use the fact that most decaffeinated drinkers tend to be over 50 to help target its advertising for Taster's Choice decaffeinated coffee.

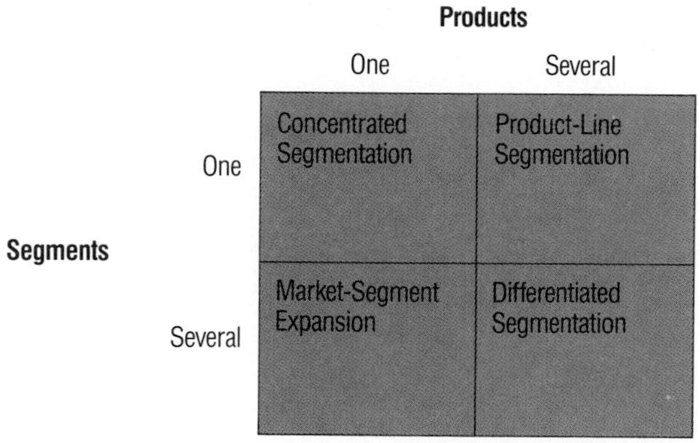

Products

One   Several

	One	Concentrated Segmentation	Product-Line Segmentation

Segments

	Several	Market-Segment Expansion	Differentiated Segmentation

FIGURE 9.5
Alternative Segmentation Strategies

If a segment does not have certain distinctive demographic characteristics, then accessibility may be difficult. The only way to appeal to such a segment is to advertise to everyone through the mass media. This is inefficient, however, for the vast proportion of advertising dollars will be wasted on consumers outside the target group. Demographics that identify a segment permit the marketer to pin-point advertising to the specific target.

The second set of criteria in selecting segments for targeting deal with the firm's competence in exploiting opportunity. Most firms prefer to target segments within their core area of expertise, where the know-how and most of the necessary resources already exist.

A FIRM'S COMPETENCE IN TARGETING SEGMENTS

Nestle was highly competent to exploit opportunity in the decaffeinated segment. It had the marketing know-how, the salesforce, the distribution network, and the production facilities. Because it had already established the technology for freeze-drying, product-development costs were limited. Campbell ran a somewhat higher risk when it introduced Prego spaghetti sauce. Although the product was generally within Campbell's area of competence, the company did not have prior experience in marketing ethnically oriented foods. It was also unsure whether its distribution strength in soups would carry over to the Prego line. Yet Campbell succeeded in competing with more established brands by hiring managers who had experience in the market, and by using its distribution clout to get the product on the shelf.

DEVELOP A SEGMENTATION STRATEGY

Once a firm has evaluated marketing opportunities and selected one or more segments for targeting, it must decide what type of segmentation strategy will be most effective. As Figure 9.5 shows, firms can target one or several products to one or more segments, producing the four alternative strategies of concentrated segmentation, market-segment expansion, product-line segmentation, and differentiated segmentation.

Concentrated segmentation involves targeting one product to one segment. For example, Le Peep targets one product, power breakfasts, to a single segment,

CONCENTRATED SEGMENTATION: ONE PRODUCT TO ONE SEGMENT

EXHIBIT 9.4
One Product Directed to Several
Segments: DuPont's Kevlar

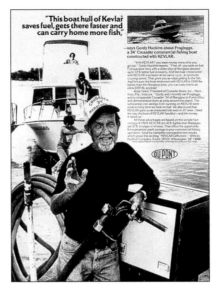

young professionals. Similarly, Subaru's advertising targets one product, its four-wheel drive cars, to a particular segment, rural consumers.

Concentrated segmentation tends to appeal to smaller firms with limited resources. These firms become profitable by gaining a strong market position in one segment. But putting all your eggs in one basket can be risky. As we have noted, a large firm can enter a segment and undercut a smaller firm.

MARKET-SEGMENT EXPANSION: ONE PRODUCT TO SEVERAL SEGMENTS

A firm that uses **market-segment expansion** targets one product to several segments. Thus, the market base for one product is expanded. DuPont used a strategy of segment expansion in marketing Kevlar, a synthetic material that is lighter yet stronger than steel. The product was targeted to three very different market segments, commercial fishermen, aircraft designers, and plant engineers. Commercial fishermen found that a boat hull made from Kevlar saves fuel, increases speed, and permits more fish to be carried in the boat because of its light weight. Aircraft designers like Kevlar because of its high strength-to-weight ratio and the additional lift it provides. And plant engineers like Kevlar because it eliminates the need for asbestos in pumps and other devices.[20] DuPont developed three different advertising campaigns to communicate these benefits to each target group (see Exhibit 9.4).

Market-segment expansion offers the advantage of being able to increase a product's potential profitability. The strategy is viable, however, only if specific segments have well-defined needs for the same product, and if appeals directed to one segment will not alienate another segment. For example, Coors is the first beer company to direct its advertising specifically to women, even though women buy only 17 percent of the beer sold in the United States. Other companies have not targeted women for fear that their ads may alienate male users. As one industry analyst said, "If you gear ads to men, women will buy the product. But if you gear ads to women, men won't buy the product. You're dealing with the fragile male ego here."[21] Coors is willing to take the risk since women's 17 percent share of the beer market still amounts to $6.5 billion a year. That means almost $400 million to Coors for each additional share point it can gain by appealing to women.

A third segmentation strategy is to direct several products to one segment. This is called **product-line segmentation** because the several products being directed to the one segment are usually part of a single product line. Deere, a large farm equipment manufacturer, focuses on one major segment, larger farms that require large-horsepower equipment, and targets it full line of farm machinery to this segment. The segment is sufficiently large and profitable so that Deere does not have to appeal to other segments.

PRODUCT-LINE SEGMENTATION: SEVERAL PRODUCTS TO ONE SEGMENT

Many firms, particularly larger ones, operate in several segments by targeting several specific products to each. This fourth strategy is referred to as **differentiated segmentation** because the firm is differentiating its product offerings to meet the needs of particular segments. Nestle, for example, has different offerings targeted to the taste, decaffeinated, and convenience segments of the coffee market, and in recent years has further differentiated its offerings into milder versus stronger blends. Nescafe Silka is a smooth, light coffee aimed at 18- to 35-year-olds, whereas Maragor Bold is a heartier coffee positioned for older coffee drinkers.[22]

DIFFERENTIATED SEGMENTATION: SEVERAL PRODUCTS TO SEVERAL SEGMENTS

Differentiated segmentation is a powerful strategy, but it carries risks. As a firm appeals to more segments, it must fragment its efforts and increase its costs. Production costs go up as production runs become smaller. Advertising costs also increase, since different campaigns must be used to reach different segments. And product-development costs go up as products are modified to meet the needs of each segment.

The higher costs of differentiated segmentation have led some firms to conclude that their markets are oversegmented. Figure 9.6 is a tongue-in-cheek representation of the dangers of oversegmentation, but this danger is real enough to have caused some firms to try to broaden the markets for some products by seeking additional segments (that is, shifting from a differentiated-segmentation strategy to a market-segment-expansion strategy.)

MARKET SEGMENTATION AND PRODUCT POSITIONING

Once a company has decided which market segments to enter, it must position products to meet the needs of these segments. Chapter 8 defined positioning as communicating product benefits to customers. Nestle positions Taster's Choice decaffeinated as the better-tasting decaffeinated coffee; DuPont positions Kevlar as the synthetic material as strong as steel; Pepsi positions Slice as the fruit-based soft drink. In each case, specific segments were targeted for these appeals. And in each case, other competitors were going after these same segments, meaning that an effective positioning strategy is a means of gaining an advantage over these competitors in a segment.

We also saw in Chapter 8 that there are various ways to position products to communicate benefits — by focusing on product features, solutions to problems, symbols, or comparisons with competition. All these approaches to positioning

FIGURE 9.6
A Hypothetical Example of
Oversegmentation

Source: "Ultimate in Product Segmentation,"
Advertising Age, September 23, 1985, p. 18.
© Terry Sharbach.

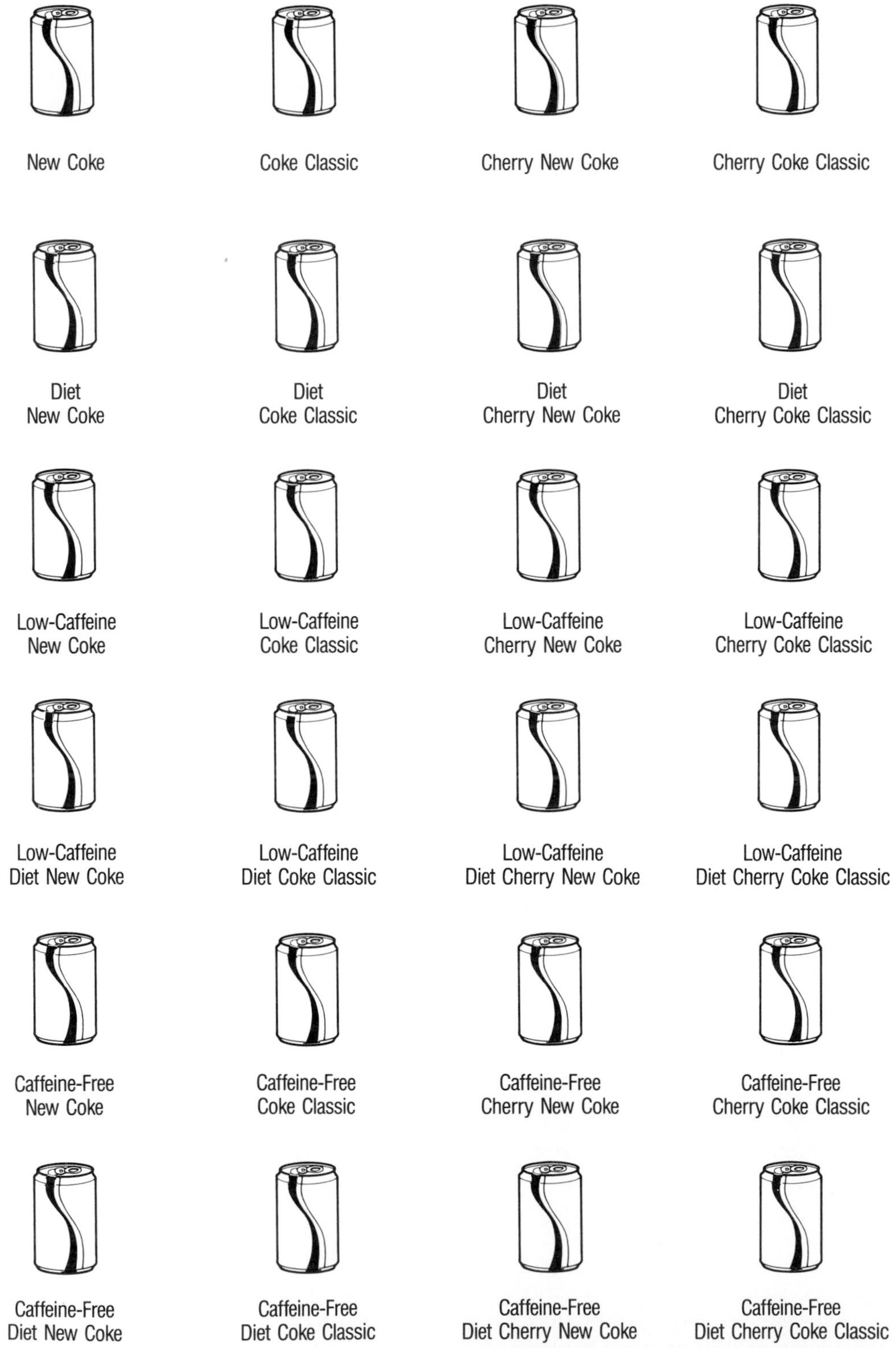

New Coke

Coke Classic

Cherry New Coke

Cherry Coke Classic

Diet
New Coke

Diet
Coke Classic

Diet
Cherry New Coke

Diet
Cherry Coke Classic

Low-Caffeine
New Coke

Low-Caffeine
Coke Classic

Low-Caffeine
Cherry New Coke

Low-Caffeine
Cherry Coke Classic

Low-Caffeine
Diet New Coke

Low-Caffeine
Diet Coke Classic

Low-Caffeine
Diet Cherry New Coke

Low-Caffeine
Diet Cherry Coke Classic

Caffeine-Free
New Coke

Caffeine-Free
Coke Classic

Caffeine-Free
Cherry New Coke

Caffeine-Free
Cherry Coke Classic

Caffeine-Free
Diet New Coke

Caffeine-Free
Diet Coke Classic

Caffeine-Free
Diet Cherry New Coke

Caffeine-Free
Diet Cherry Coke Classic

have one common element: the need to first define a target segment before developing the positioning strategy. Therefore, market segmentation and product positioning go hand-in-hand in the marketing plan: Market segments are defined, and products are positioned to meet the needs of these segments.

INDUSTRIAL MARKET SEGMENTATION

The same reasons apply for segmenting markets in the industrial as in the consumer sector — developing products to meet the needs of customer groups. However, industrial firms have lagged behind in applying segmentation strategies for several reasons. For one, industrial firms tend to be more engineering-oriented, focusing on product specifications. As a result, they frequently let product design rather than consumer needs drive marketing strategy.

Another factor is that industrial marketers are more likely to be in one of the two extremes on the marketing continuum in Figure 9.1, customized marketing or mass marketing. Buyers often require customized products; for example, tailor-made telecommunications or information systems. As a result, many industrial marketers do not have to segment markets into groups of buyers. They are producing for individual customers.

When customized marketing is not required, a mass market mentality seems to prevail. As one industrial marketing expert said:

> *Industrial firms frequently have a product emphasis and little or no real market segmentation identification . . . Many industrial companies tend to think of a market as one large unit that buys and uses similar products.*[23]

Despite these limitations, we have seen the application of effective segmentation strategies in some of the examples cited in this chapter. DuPont developed a market-segment-expansion strategy that positioned Kevlar to three different industrial buyer groups, and Deere effectively applied product-line segmentation in marketing high-horsepower machinery to larger farms.

Industrial firms that implement segmentation strategies use the same three bases for segmentation as consumer firms, segmenting by benefits, by behavior, or by customer characteristics. But as Table 9.4 shows, the variables used to segment the market differ from those in consumer marketing. For example, industrial marketers are likely to identify benefit segments by the need for performance, durability, or economy because industrial buyers tend to emphasize these factors in selecting products. Industrial marketers also identify benefit segments by the buyer's emphasis on delivery, reputation, or convenience because industrial buyers emphasize these factors in selecting vendors.

Industrial buyers can be segmented behaviorally by the products they buy or the frequency with which they buy them. We also saw in Chapter 6 that industrial buyers can be classified by the type of purchase (new buy, modified rebuy, straight rebuy), and buyer segments can be defined on this basis.

As for the third approach to segmentation — by customer characteristics — consumer-goods firms use demographic characteristics to segment consumers, whereas industrial firms use organizational characteristics. Industrial marketers might segment buyers by size of the firm, total number of employees, industry grouping, and number of years in business.

We saw a good example of benefit segmentation in the industrial sector in DuPont's segmentation of potential Kevlar users into three segments, customers

TABLE 9.4
Variables Used to Identify Industrial
Market Segments

BENEFIT SEGMENTATION	
Product Criteria	Product performance
	Durability
	Economy
	Ease of use
Vendor Criteria	Delivery
	Reputation
	Economy
	Convenience
BEHAVIORAL SEGMENTATION	Products purchased
	Frequency of purchase
	Type of purchase (new buy, modified rebuy, straight rebuy)
SEGMENTING BY ORGANIZATION CHARACTERISTICS	Location
	Number of employees
	Annual sales volume
	Net worth
	Number of years in business
	Number of establishments
	Industry grouping

who need a stronger synthetic material, a lighter material, and a material that can be an asbestos substitute. An AT&T study is an example of behavioral segmentation in industrial marketing. AT&T separated the telecommunications market into large, medium, and small businesses based on the number of telephone lines owned. It then determined the telephone needs and characteristics of each segment. The AT&T study cited in Chapter 7 described the steps taken to further research the needs of the small business segment. Both Hewlett-Packard and IBM provide an example of segmenting by organizational characteristics. They group computer buyers by industry type and then develop systems for these industry groupings — for example, systems for aircraft designers, branch bank managers, or retail inventory managers.

SUMMARY

1.   What are the advantages of a strategy of market segmentation?
Market segmentation generally leads to greater profitability because it better satisfies the diverse demands of the market place. In general, firms can generate more revenue by appealing to the needs of specific consumer segments. Market segmentation also helps a firm identify opportunities, develop new products, and allocate marketing resources to areas of opportunity.

2. Why has there been a recent trend toward market segmentation?

Many companies have recently shifted from a mass-marketing to a market-segmentation approach for two reasons. First, economic conditions since the 1950s have prompted firms to focus on consumer needs in order to remain competitive. The best way to focus on consumer needs is by developing products to meet the needs of particular consumer segments. Second, demographic and lifestyle changes in the 1970s and 1980s have fragmented the market into more discrete groupings, furthering the need for a market-segmentation approach.

3. How can companies identify market segments?

Companies can identify segments by the benefits they seek, by their behavior, and by their characteristics. Benefit segmentation identifies segments by their needs; it is an effective tool for developing new products because it pinpoints segments with unmet needs. Behavioral segmentation focuses on the brands consumers buy or the extent to which a product category is used. This approach assists marketers in developing strategies for brands or product categories. Segmenting by consumer characteristics such as age, income, race, lifestyle, and personality traits is useful in providing guidelines for positioning products in advertisements and also for selecting media to reach target segments.

4. What criteria can marketers use to decide which segments to target for marketing effort?

Marketers use two sets of criteria in selecting segments for targeting: (1) opportunities for revenue in marketing to the segment and (2) a firm's competency to pursue these opportunities. Factors related to revenue potential are the extent of similarity in the needs of customers within a segment; the existence of unmet needs within the segment; the size and growth potential of the segment; and the segment's accessibility through marketing efforts such as advertising or distribution. The firm's competence is a function of its marketing and manufacturing know-how in targeting a particular segment, as well as its resources.

5. What alternative strategies can companies use to segment markets?

A company can follow a strategy of pursuing one or several segments with one or several products. Directing one product to one segment, concentrated segmentation, is most often chosen by smaller firms seeking to gain competitive advantage. Market-segment expansion, which targets one product to several segments, allows a firm to expand the market base for a product. Targeting several products to one segment, product-line segmentation, usually involves the products of a single product line being directed to one segment. Differentiated segmentation involves targeting several specific products to several segments.

KEY TERMS

Market segmentation (p. 232)

Mass marketing (p. 232)

Customized marketing (p. 234)

Product-market matrix (p. 236)

Benefit segmentation (p. 238)

Behavioral segmentation (p. 238)

Segmenting by consumer
  characteristics (p. 238)

Demographic segmentation (p. 242)

Lifestyle segmentation (p. 244)

Personality segmentation (p. 244)

Concentrated segmentation (p. 249)

Market-segment expansion (p. 250)

Product-line segmentation (p. 251)

Differentiated segmentation (p. 251)

QUESTIONS

1. What are the advantages of Campbell's regional segmentation strategy?
2. Why was Procter & Gamble successful in following a mass-marketing approach in the face of the trend to segmented marketing?
3. Why have many companies such as P&G shifted from a mass-marketing to a segmented-marketing approach?
4. A marketing executive for a producer of household cleaning products takes a cautious view when it comes to market segmentation strategies. He says:

   Market segmentation works for companies who can offer consumers something different, something they need that competitors are not giving them. But many of our products are standardized items in mature, low-growth industries. We can't segment markets and offer something different to each segment. We advertise across the board and try to attract consumers with couponing and low prices. On this basis, we pretty much fall on the right-hand side of your continuum [Figure 9.1]. We are likely to remain mass marketers for the foreseeable future.

   a. Do you agree that market segmentation is not applicable for relatively standardized products such as detergents and bleach?
   b. What is the danger of this company following a mass-marketing approach for the foreseeable future?
5. Consider the following situations:

   a. A company wants to target its marketing efforts to heavy snackers.
   b. A company wants to determine the potential for a new nut-and-dried-fruit snack.
   c. A company wants to determine the lifestyle characteristics of its customers to obtain insights for developing its advertising strategy.

   What kind of segmentation approach should be used to identify segments in each of these cases? What is the strategic purpose of each approach?
6. What are the implications of the benefit-segmentation study of the snack market (Table 9.2) for

   a. new-product development?
   b. developing advertising themes?
   c. media selection?
7. Why is it important to identify a segment whose consumers have similar needs? What problems arise if a company targets a segment whose consumers have different needs?
8. Why is it difficult to market to a segment whose consumers have no distinctive demographic characteristics?
9. What are the risks of a

   a. concentrated-segmentation strategy?
   b. market-segment-expansion strategy?
   c. differentiated-segmentation strategy?
10. Why do product-positioning decisions necessarily follow market-segmentation decisions? Cite examples from the chapter of the link between market segmentation and product positioning.
11. Why have industrial firms lagged behind consumer-goods firms in applying market-segmentation approaches?
12. What is the main difference in segmenting markets for industrial versus consumer-goods firms?

CASE 9.1

AMERICAN AIRLINES REGIONAL SEGMENTATION STRATEGY

Source: Jennifer Lawrence, "American Air Books New Regionalized Ad Strategy." Reprinted with permission from *Advertising Age,* September 12, 1988, pp. 1, 114, Copyright Crain Communications, Inc. All rights reserved.

American Airlines is taking the wraps off a new regional marketing strategy, making it the first national carrier to develop distinctly separate campaigns in various areas of the country.

While a number of major package-goods marketers have turned to regionalized marketing, until now the big national airlines have relied on national ad campaigns and themes, sometimes tailored to local markets.

Those secondary drives typically are used to push price and destination.

But American is the first to address specific regional goals with full-fledged campaigns using separate creative executions.

The first, which began Sept. 8 in Los Angeles and San Francisco and will expand to other West Coast markets, shows laid-back California scenes of beaches, sand and seagulls.

"They aren't like airline commercials . . . they are almost environmental — there are no airplanes," said Jim Simon, American managing director-advertising.

Each spot addresses a separate concern: number of airports served, number of hourly non-stops and number of West Coast non-stops.

"American's regional move makes some sense to me, because usually travelers have wildly different expectations in different markets like the East and West coasts," said David Sylvester, analyst at Kidder, Peabody & Co.

Airlines now are concentrating on refining their service image, he said.

But others are skeptical about the wisdom of not linking the regional spots to the airline's national theme.

A veteran airline executive downplayed American's strategy, saying, "It sounds like they are cashing in on the current fad toward regional marketing — like maybe they've reinvented the wheel."

James O'Donnell, Continental Airlines senior VP-marketing services, said: "In anyone's case, it's better to take into account local market realities than to spread advertising around the country like mayonnaise on white bread."

1. Why is American Airlines following a regional-segmentation strategy?
2. Do you think the skeptics of American Airlines' strategy are right in saying regional segmentation is a fad? Why or why not?

CASE 9.2

STROH MOVES INTO SOFT DRINKS

Source: "Stroh Leverages Strengths with Sundance Sparklers,"
Marketing Communications, February 1988, p. 44.

What do you do when your industry is flat or declining, with no upturn in sight? You look outside your individual product niche or category. That was Stroh Brewery's strategy when developing Sundance Natural Juice Sparkler — a sparkling beverage with a 70 percent juice content. "Stroh took the position that it was a beverage company, not (just) a brewery," notes Scott Rozek, brand manager, Sundance.

Stroh looked at the demographic and lifestyle influences that were affecting the entire beverage category before launching this product. It saw a population that was increasingly health-conscious and active. So, it created a product that taps into the age of moderation and health.

Sundance's target audience is upscale adults, 25 to 45, in urban areas, who are health- and fitness-conscious. Advertising ties in with these active consumers' lifestyles by focusing in on vignettes. It also harkens back to these adults' youths by setting the theme, "It's a natural time for a Sundance" to Van Morrison's "It's a marvelous night for a Moondance."

Stroh went through the "acid test" when introducing Sundance in California and Nevada in the Spring of 86, according to Rozek. "We knew that if the product sold in California, we had a success." That's because fully 50 percent of the sparkling water business is in that state. Sundance is currently in seven or eight additional markets around the country with plans to expand nationally.

1. What were Stroh's reasons for introducing Sundance?
2. On what basis has the company segmented the soft drink markets — by benefits, by behavior, or by consumer characteristics?
3. What type of segmentation strategy is Stroh following in introducing Sundance — concentrated, product-line, or differentiated segmentation?

NOTES

1. "The Fly in Campbell's Soup," *Fortune,* May 19, 1988, p. 67; and "Campbell's Soup Stirs Up a New Marketing Strategy," *Sales & Marketing Digest,* January 1988, p. 1.

2. *Fortune,* May 19, 1988, p. 67.

3. "Marketing's New Look," *Business Week,* January 26, 1987, p. 67.

4. Ibid., "The Eye of the Stranger," *Marketing Communications,* March 1987, p. 65.

5. "M'm! M'm! Okay," *Adweek,* October 10, 1988, p. 22; and "Hungry Man, NFL Team Up: Campbell Suits Up Regional Effort," *Advertising Age,* April 24, 1989, p. 3.

6. Ibid., p. 23.

7. "There's More on the Stove Than Soup At Campbell's," *Marketing & Media Decisions,* Spring 1984, p. 26.

8. "Firms Grow More Cautious about New-Product Plans," *The Wall Street Journal,* March 9, 1989, p. B1; and "We're Not Running the Company for the Stock Price," *Forbes,* September 19, 1988, p. 48.

9. *Adweek,* October 10, 1988, p. 24.

10. "Revamped Tobacco Firm Targets New Consumer Segments," *Marketing News,* July 6, 1984, p. 8.

11. "Marketing: The New Priority," *Business Week,* November 21, 1983, p. 95.

12. "Upheaval in Middle-Class Market Forces Changes in Selling Strategies," *The Wall Street Journal,* March 13, 1987, p. 27.

13. "Niche Marketing: What Industrial Marketers Can Learn from Consumer Package Goods," *Business Marketing,* November 1984, p. 58.

14. "Jean Makers' Task is to Find the Best Fit," *The Wall Street Journal,* July 31, 1986, p. 6.

15. "Computer Mapping of Demographic Lifestyle Data Locates 'Pockets' of Potential Customers at Microgeographic Level," *Marketing News,* November 27, 1981, Section 2, p. 16.

16. "Competition Heats Up for Hispanic Consumer's Dollar," *Ad Forum,* July 1983, p. 30.

17. "Zayre's Strategy of Ethnic Merchandising Proves to be Successful," *The Wall Street Journal,* September 25, 1984, p. 31.

18. Russell L. Ackoff and James R. Emshoff, "Advertising Research at Anheuser-Busch, Inc. (1968–1974)," *Sloan Management Review* 16 (Spring 1975): 1–15.

19. "Big, Small Chains Sling Hash for Morning Glory," *Adweek,* March 31, 1986, p. 20.

20. "Not All Prospects Are Created Equal," *Business Marketing,* May 1986, p. 54.

21. "New Print Ads for Coors Beer Target Women," *The Wall Street Journal,* June 2, 1987, p. 33.

22. "While Coffee Makers Fight Loss of Younger Drinkers," *The Wall Street Journal,* March 1, 1986, p. 33.

23. James D. Hlavacek and B. S. Ames, "Segmenting Industrial and High-Tech Markets," *The Journal of Business Strategy,* p. 41.

PART 4

• • •

IMPLEMENTING THE MARKETING EFFORT

The central component of the marketing process is implementing the marketing plan. An appropriate mix of product, distribution, promotional, and pricing strategies is necessary to ensure that the product will meet the needs of the targeted consumer. This section considers each of these four components of the marketing mix. Included in this section is a chapter on international marketing which considers marketing strategies for firms operating in the world marketplace.

SLICE'S GOT THE JUICE, BUT DOES PEPSI HAVE THE PROFITS?

I n 1983 PepsiCo was all but out of the lemon-lime soft drink competition. Its entry, Teem, was languishing almost unnoticed in the market while Coca-Cola's spruced-up Sprite brand was biting big chunks out of top-selling 7Up's market share.

Roger Enrico, president of Pepsi USA, dreamt of a new brand that would have $500 million in first-year sales and grow to capture a significant share of the market. Such a product would need to be distinct from other soft drinks in some way that could easily translate into a competitive advantage. Juice-added soft drinks were already popular in Japan and South America. In the fall of 1982, Enrico began wondering if this type of product might be equally appealing to the American palate.

By February 1983, PepsiCo's labs had produced the first lemon-lime test batches. Enrico dubbed the project "Overlord," the code name for the allied invasion of Europe in World War II. He wanted 7Up and Sprite to "feel as if they were on the receiving end of the Normandy invasion."[1]

PepsiCo began testing the new product on groups of regular lemon-lime drinkers with samples of 5 and 10 percent fruit juice. The results were encouraging, and the company plunged ahead. PepsiCo and J. Walter Thompson (its ad agency for the product), created a task force that pushed the research on an expanded scale. During the early summer, tests confirmed Enrico's initial hopes: the juice-added soft drink scored well against 7Up.

These tests indicated that the product could be favorably positioned as a

DEVELOPING NEW PRODUCTS

mainstream adult beverage. They also indicated, however, that the product had two major problems: cloudy coloring and lack of long-term stability. PepsiCo's research and development team went back to work and quickly solved both problems.

In the next four months, PepsiCo developed plans for distribution, store promotions, and pricing. At the same time, the ad agency developed a campaign that focused on what consumers saw as Slice's biggest plus with the theme "We've got the juice."[2] The name Slice was also selected from a group of names tested on consumers because it conveyed an image of a slice of fruit.

In May 1984 test marketing began in Tulsa, Milwaukee, Phoenix, and Rochester. Results persuaded PepsiCo to expand Slice into the West Coast. In March 1985 PepsiCo released the product nationally. At about this time, it successfully introduced a mandarin orange flavor, followed shortly by apple and cherry cola flavors.

By the end of 1986, Slice had a 4 percent share of the soft drink market, a market where each point of market share represents $250 million. It was a billion-dollar brand.[3] PepsiCo's success led to competitive entries. By 1988, Slice's market share slipped to under 3 percent as competitors such as Coca-Coca-Cola's Minute Maid and Procter & Gamble's Orange Crush introduced juice-enriched entries.[4] But Slice remained a profitable market leader. PepsiCo's new-product development process had succeeded in establishing a successful new category to meet consumer needs. ■

● ● ●

WHAT IS A PRODUCT?

When we think of a product, we visualize a tangible object with physical properties. But often we also ascribe intangible attributes to a product. When you think of your car as "powerful," a soft drink as "refreshing," or a computer as "user friendly," you are citing performance characteristics that describe the product's ability to satisfy consumer needs.

The success of many products is due more to such intangible attributes than to tangible characteristics. Reebok sneakers are a prime example. When Reebok introduced its first aerobic shoes in 1982, they were an overnight hit, but not only because they were comfortable and well-made. Their soft leather and range of colors made them a fashion item that women were willing to spend $40 on. Cybil Shepherd clinched that image for Reebok when she wore her red ones in evening dress to the Emmy awards.

PRODUCT COMPONENTS

The Reebok example implies that a product is defined as much by how the consumer sees it as by its physical characteristics. There are three components to a product: the benefits it conveys, its attributes, and its support services. These components are shown in Figure 10.1.

The benefits of the product are those characteristics consumers see as potentially meeting their needs. They are identified as the **core product** in Figure 10.1 because they determine whether the consumer buys it. For many Reebok purchasers, the shoe's key benefit is fashion. For purchasers of Slice, the drink's key benefits are nutrition and natural ingredients.

Marketers must turn desired benefits into product attributes. These attributes are identified as the **tangible product** in Figure 10.1. Reebok turned the desire for fashion in sneakers into a tangible product by introducing bright colors and soft leather. Pepsi-Cola turned the desire for a nutritious soft drink with natural ingredients into a tangible product by introducing fruit-based Slice.

Figure 10.1 shows that product attributes not only include physical characteristics like fruit in soft drinks or soft leather in shoes but are also represented by the package, the brand name, and the product's design. What is on the outside of a product can sometimes be more important than what is on the inside. For example, the ingredients in a product like baby shampoo are fairly standardized across

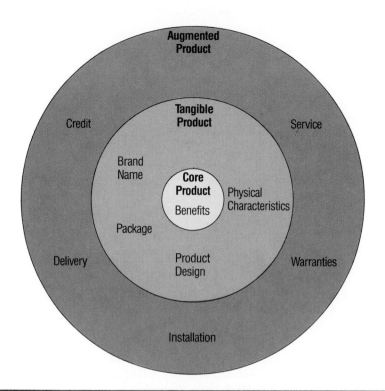

FIGURE 10.1
The Components of a Product

Source: Philip Kotler and Gail Armstrong, *Principles of Marketing,* (Englewood Cliffs, N.J.: Prentice-Hall, 4 ed., 1989), p. 244.

brands. But many parents prefer Johnson & Johnson because they regard it as a known and dependable brand, and they do not want to risk using anything else on their baby. In this case, brand name is more important than ingredients. The packaging can also be critical. As we saw in the last chapter, one of the reasons Campbell's Juice Works failed was because competitive brands were in asceptic packages and Juice Works was not.

Product design is another important product attribute. Products such as automobiles, electronic items, and many industrial goods require good design of the visible components of the product. These may be as important to purchasers as their mechanical characteristics. A Chrysler LeBaron is designed to look luxurious. Its design is as much a part of the tangible product as what is under the hood.

The third element of a product is post-sale support. Many products are purchased on credit. Purchases also sometimes include delivery, installation, warranties and service. A product that includes these features is referred to as an **augmented product** because terms of sale include elements other than the tangible product. The augmented product is particularly important in industrial marketing, since many industrial products require post-sale support. In recent years, Digital Equipment Corp. established a competitive advantage over IBM by providing stronger post-sales support for computer systems in the way of instruction, servicing, and software.

Recognizing that a product is composed of benefits, tangible characteristics, and at times, post-sales support leads us to the following definition: A **product** is a bundle of attributes and benefits designed to satisfy customer needs. The fact that consumers seek different benefits means that they will see products differently. Therefore, a product is not a uniform, well-defined entity. One consumer may view Slice as having the benefit of nutrition; another may see adding fruit as a gimmick to increase prices. One consumer may see the LeBaron as a car that provides luxury and prestige; another may see it as crass and tasteless. These consumers will define each brand very differently.

BRANDS AND PRODUCT CATEGORIES

So far, we have used the term *product* as a single classification. Actually, a product can represent a brand or a product category. A **brand** is a name or symbol that represents a product. A **product category** is the generic class to which the brand belongs. Slice is a brand name; the product category is soft drinks. MacIntosh is a brand name; the product category is personal computers.

The distinction between brand and product category is important for several reasons. First, the product category defines the brand's competition. Defining the product category broadly or narrowly will therefore affect a brand's strategy. Slice's product category could be defined as soft drinks or as fruit-based drinks. If it is defined as soft drinks, then Slice is competing with a wide range of brands including cola drinks. As a result, it might decide to advertise a broader set of benefits than its fruit base and set a price at parity with most other cola drinks. If the product category is defined as fruit-based drinks, then nutrition and natural ingredients are likely to be the main benefits advertised, and the brand can be priced at a higher level than other soft drinks.

A second reason why the distinction between brand and product category is important is that a company may wish to develop a **product line**, that is, a line of offerings within a certain product category. PepsiCo developed a line of different flavored drinks under the Slice label, all in the fruit-based category. Ban has a complete product line in the deodorant category composed of roll-ons, dry sprays, and sticks. The definition of the product category determines what is in the product line.

A third reason for distinguishing between brand and product category is that, at times, a company may be as interested in stimulating demand for the product category as for its brand. Campbell's share of the condensed soup market is over 60 percent. When it advertises "Soup for Lunch," or "Soup for One," its objective is to stimulate demand for the condensed soup category as well as for its brand.

PRODUCT CLASSIFICATIONS

The large number of different products in the marketplace makes classifying them difficult. Yet, marketers need to classify products so that similar strategies can be developed for those in the same class. Two important types of product classifications bear on marketing strategies: degree of product tangibility and type of product user.

DEGREE OF PRODUCT TANGIBILITY

Products can be classified by the degree to which they represent tangible physical characteristics. Figure 10.2 shows three categories on this dimension, durable goods, nondurable goods, and services.

The most tangible product offerings are **durable goods**, products that are used over time. Cars, appliances, and electronics are durable goods. **Nondurable goods** are items consumed in one or a few uses. These products are divided in Figure 10.2 into packaged goods, such as toothpaste, detergents, or candy bars, and nonpackaged goods, such as gasoline.

Most Tangible   Least Tangible   **FIGURE 10.2**
Classifying Products by
Degree of Tangibility

Durable Goods	Nondurable Goods—Packaged	Nondurable Goods—Nonpackaged	Services

Services are defined as intangible benefits purchased by consumers that do not involve ownership. When we buy an airline ticket, we are buying the services offered by riding in someone else's plane. We will be considering the classification and marketing of services in Chapter 12.

As we will see, there are major differences in marketing strategies for durables, nondurables, and services. For example, customers are likely to deliberate more in buying durables and consult a wider range of information sources. As a result, personal selling is a more important part of the marketing mix. Advertising is more likely to provide consumers with information. Durables are also distributed selectively rather than on a widespread basis. Nondurables involve less consumer deliberation. Advertising is more likely to be used to convey images and symbols than to provide information. Distribution is fairly extensive, and sales promotions such as couponing and price deals are used frequently to encourage consumers to switch to a company's brand.

Since services are intangible, advertising is used to try to make their benefits more tangible. Most services are delivered on a person-to-person basis and are often variable, so an important element in the marketing mix is to ensure that services are offered at a standard level of quality.

The other important product classification is by type of buyer. The most important distinction is between products directed to consumers versus organizational buyers. As we saw in Chapter 1, consumer goods are sold directly to individuals for final consumption. Industrial goods are designed to be used in producing other goods (raw materials such as steel or lumber), or in support of such production (generators to produce electricity, typewriters to prepare reports, post-sales service to maintain products). The distinction between a consumer and industrial good is not based on the characteristics of the product, but on the purpose for which it is used. A typewriter or computer used at home is a consumer good; the identical product used in a business organization is an industrial good.

TYPE OF BUYER

Consumer Goods

Consumer goods can be classified as convenience, shopping, and specialty goods (see Table 10.1). **Convenience goods** are goods that consumers purchase frequently with little deliberation or effort. They are generally packaged goods such as toothpaste, detergents, cereals, and coffee. We saw in Chapter 5 that such low-involvement products are characterized by little information search and by repeat buying based on inertia rather than on brand loyalty.

The product classifications in Table 10.1 are of interest because they suggest different marketing strategies. Because consumers purchase convenience goods frequently, they must be distributed widely. Since product involvement and brand loyalty are low, coupons and price promotions are frequently used to try to get consumers to switch brands. High advertising expenditures are necessary

TABLE 10.1
Classification of Consumer Goods

	CONVENIENCE GOODS	SHOPPING GOODS	SPECIALTY GOODS
CONSUMER PURCHASING CHARACTERISTICS	Frequent purchases Low involvement Purchase by inertia or limited decision making	Less frequent purchases Higher involvement Purchases by extensive decision making	Infrequent purchases Highest involvement Purchases by brand loyalty
TYPES OF PRODUCTS	Toothpaste Detergents Cereals Coffee	Appliances Clothing Cars Medical services: general practitioner	Rolex watch Nikon camera Gucci handbags Medical services: specialist
STRATEGIC CHARACTERISTICS	Low price Widespread distribution Fewer product differences Frequent use of sales promotions High level of advertising expenditures Frequent use of symbols and imagery in advertising	Higher price Selective distribution Many product differences Emphasis on product features in advertising Importance of personal selling	Highest price Exclusive distribution Unique brand Emphasis on status in advertising Importance of personal selling

because of intense competition in many convenience goods categories. Low involvement also means that advertising strategies are more likely to use symbols and imagery rather than information to increase brand awareness and to influence purchases. For example, ads for colas might show teens on the beach to capture the spirit of youth and vigor the marketer is trying to associate with the brand. Rarely will a cola ad focus on product attributes such as sweetness or carbonation.

Shopping goods are those products that consumers are likely to spend more time shopping for and comparing on specific characteristics because they are involved with the product. As a result, a process of extensive decision making is likely, requiring greater information search. Examples of shopping goods are clothing, furniture, major appliances, cosmetics, and medical services.

The marketing mix for a shopping good is very different from that for a convenience good. Prices are higher. Coupons and other price incentives are unlikely to be used, since it is difficult to get buyers in a high-involvement category to switch brands based on price. Distribution is likely to be selective, since products are not purchased as frequently. Product characteristics are likely to be more distinct. Whereas the ingredients in toothpaste or detergents brands are similar, the characteristics of clothing, cars, or medical services can differ markedly. As a result, advertising is likely to focus on these differences. Personal selling is likely to be important, since consumers seek information about alternative brands.

Specialty goods are goods with unique characteristics that consumers make a special effort to search for and buy. These products have the highest level of consumer involvement. Their purchase is often the result of brand loyalty. These are products of high status, prestige items such as Rolex watches, Gucci handbags, or a Mercedes car, and brands having a reputation for high performance such as a Nikon camera. Medical services could also be a specialty good if a consumer seeks treatment from a specialist rather than a general practitioner.

Strategies for specialty goods are characterized by high prices, since consumers in this case are insensitive to low-price appeals. Distribution is on an exclusive basis to ensure a status image. Products must have an element of uniqueness for consumers to view them as specialty items, and this uniqueness will be advertised. Personal selling is particularly important in guaranteeing continued loyalty and good service.

It is important to recognize that the same item could be a convenience, shopping, or specialty good. This is because products are classified based on how consumers view them rather than on any inherent physical characteristics. Thus, a skin moisturizer is a convenience good for the consumer who thinks all moisturizers are alike and buys the cheapest one. It is a shopping good for the consumer who sees distinct differences between brands and goes through a process of extensive decision making in comparing them. It is a specialty good for the consumer who seeks out one particular moisturizer that can only be purchased from exclusive cosmetics retailers. Consequently, marketers might position their brand either as (1) a convenience good, as the lowest-priced moisturizer on the market; (2) a shopping good, as the product that has the best and safest ingredients to moisturize the skin; or (3) a specialty good, as the most distinctive and highest-quality product on the market, available only from certain exclusive sources.

Another point is that many consumers view certain product categories differently as they lose their distinctiveness. When compact disc players were first introduced, they were a specialty item, a new way to play music with little distortion. As they are becoming more widespread, they are viewed as shopping goods with consumers comparing many alternative brands more closely.

Industrial Goods

Industrial goods can be classified in three ways: production goods, installations and accessories, and supplies and services (see Table 10.2).

Production goods are products used to manufacture a final product. Examples are steel, aluminum, and lumber products. Component parts required by manufacturers are also included in this category — for example, a producer of computer chips selling this component to a manufacturer of computers. Since production goods are fairly standardized, they are usually bought on a straight-buy or modified-rebuy basis. A purchasing agent or materials-ordering manager is responsible for buying, and often purchases are made from the same vendor. In some cases, however, production goods are specialized and purchased on a new-buy basis. An example would be highly tempered steel plate used in the construction of submarines. Since most production goods are standardized, companies selling them are likely to gain a competitive advantage by offering superior ser-

TABLE 10.2
Classification of Industrial Goods

	PRODUCTION GOODS	INSTALLATIONS AND ACCESSORIES	SUPPLIES AND SERVICES
CUSTOMER PURCHASING CHARACTERISTICS	Straight rebuy or modified rebuy Vendor loyalty Purchased by purchasing agent or materials-ordering manager	New buy Purchased by buying center	Straight rebuy or modified rebuy Vendor loyalty Purchased by purchasing agent
TYPES OF PRODUCTS	Steel Aluminum Lumber Component parts	Generators Trucks Factory automation systems Pollution-control systems	Typewriters Maintenance and repair services Business stationery
STRATEGIC CHARACTERISTICS	Marketed based on delivery and vendor reliability Price competition Salesforce acts as order takers	Marketed based on product performance Salesforce requires technical expertise Price not a determining factor	Marketed based on vendor reliability Price competition Salesforce acts as order takers

vice and delivery. Buyers tend to be price-sensitive, so lower prices can create a competitive advantage.

Industrial goods categorized as **installations and accessories** are used in support of the manufacturing process. Examples are generators, truck fleets, factory automation systems, or pollution-control systems. These are differentiated products often produced to specification. Purchases are made on a new-buy basis by a buying center, with little loyalty to any single vendor. Sold primarily based on their features rather than on price or delivery, these products are likely to be developed to meet buyers' specification. Consequently, salespeople must have the technical expertise necessary to describe product performance. Buyers tend to be more price-insensitive and buy based on product performance.

Supplies and services are products that support the manufacturing process but are not part of it. Examples are typewriters, maintenance and repair services, or business stationery. Like production goods, these products are likely to be purchased on a straight-rebuy or modified-rebuy basis by a purchasing agent, often from the same vendor. Reputation and reliability of the vendor and price are particularly important selection criteria.

WHAT IS A NEW PRODUCT?

An understanding of the nature of a product and types of consumer and industrial products allows us to consider the specifics of product strategy. Perhaps the most important strategic concern of marketers is developing and introducing new products to the marketplace. As we will see, the ability to effectively develop and market new products largely determines a company's profitability and competitive position.

Before we consider the nature of new-product development, we should address the question, "What is a new product?" This question has some strategic relevance because a product viewed as new is likely to go through a more rigorous development and testing process than one viewed as a simple extension of an existing product. For example, when Coca-Cola considered introducing Diet Coke, it could have viewed it as a new product or a line extension of its flagship brand. It chose to view it as a new product because it was positioned to appeal to a different segment of the market, and it was the first time that an offering other than the flagship brand was to be marketed under the Coke name.

NEW TO THE CONSUMER OR NEW TO THE COMPANY?

Booz Allen & Hamilton, a leading consulting firm, studied 13,000 new products introduced by 700 companies in the early 1980s.[5] It classified them based on whether they were new to a company, new to consumers, or new to both. A product is new to a company when the company goes through a process of development, testing, and market introduction. (Pepsi's Slice is an example.) A product is new to consumers when they have no prior awareness of the product category when it is introduced; for example, cellular telephones or fruit-based soft drinks.

This classification produces three types of new products, as shown in Figure 10.3. A product that is new to both consumers and to a company is an **innovation**. The Sony Walkman, when it was first introduced, was this kind of product. About 10 percent of the products in the Booz Allen & Hamilton (BAH) study were classified as innovations. A product that is known to the market but is new to the company is classified as a **new-product duplication**. Kodak's introduction of instant cameras in the mid 1970s to challenge Polaroid was such a product. Consumers were aware of instant cameras, but Kodak was introducing the line for the first time. About 20 percent of the products in the BAH study were in this category.

Products known to the company but that have some new dimension for consumers are generally **product extensions**. There are three types of product extensions: revisions, additions, and repositionings. Product revisions are improvements in existing products — for example, adding fruit to yogurt or vitamins to cereals. The BAH study classified 26 percent of new products as revisions. Product additions represent extensions of an existing product line, as when Prince introduced graphite tennis rackets or when Colgate introduced a tartar-control toothpaste. The BAH study classified another 26 percent of new products as additions.

Product repositionings represent communicating a new feature of a brand without changing its physical characteristics. For instance, when 7Up was repositioned as a new caffeine-free soft drink, most consumers were unaware that soft drinks contained caffeine. Similarly, when Tums was repositioned as a product that would fight calcium deficiencies in women, most consumers were unaware of its high calcium content. The BAH study classified 7 percent of new products

FIGURE 10.3
New-Product Classifications

[a]Percentages cited are new products classified in the Booz Allen & Hamilton study. See *New Product Management for the 1980s,* (New York: Booz Allen & Hamilton, 1982), pp. 8-10.
[b]Percentage of new products adds up to 89% of those studied in the Booz Allen & Hamilton study. The remaining 11% were classified in ambiguous categories.

New to the Consumer

	Yes	No
Yes	Product Innovations (10% of new products)[a]	New-Product Duplications (20% of new products)
No	Product Extensions Revisions (26% of new products) Additions (26%) Repositionings (7%)[b]	Not a New Product

New to the Company

as such repositionings. Each of these product extensions represented a new offering to the consumer that did not require an extensive product-development process by the firm.

INNOVATIONS OR NEW-PRODUCT REFORMULATIONS?

This classification of new products shows that the vast majority are either reformulations of existing products or additions to existing product lines. Only one out of ten new products in the Booz Allen & Hamilton study are classified as *innovations* — that is, new to the world. Such innovations usually result in some change in consumer behavior and consumption patterns. Videocassette recorders are a clear example of an innovation because they changed consumer behavior in the area of entertainment. Consumers now watch less network TV, and can "zap" commercials on taped programs by bypassing them.

Companies that emphasize innovations put more of their resources into research and development and technical expertise. Such firms are willing to take the risk of introducing new and untried products, and to spend advertising dollars on educating consumers on their use. In contrast, firms that introduce non-innovative products put more focus on existing markets, spending marketing dollars to attract customers from competitors rather than to create new customers. Their rationale for being a follower is that new-product development is expensive, and it is less risky to leave it to others to develop and introduce new products. Further, in high-technology areas, frequent changes in technology increase the risk of new-product development. Polaroid was the innovator in instant photography, establishing the category and educating customers in product use. Kodak was the follower in this category, attempting to convince customers its cameras were as good as Polaroid's.

FIGURE 10.4
Profits and New-Product Introductions

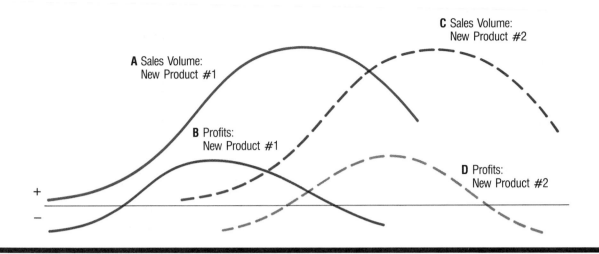

C Sales Volume:
New Product #2

A Sales Volume:
New Product #1

B Profits:
New Product #1

D Profits:
New Product #2

+

−

NEW PRODUCTS AND PROFITABILITY

Even though some firms do not emphasize new-product development, most leading companies try to ensure a continuous flow of new products because new product development is closely tied to profitability. Although Kodak was the follower in instant photography, we saw in Chapter 2 that it was the innovator in other categories, including lithium batteries. Firms active in new-product development expect to see a substantial part of their sales represented by new products. At 3M Co. and at Johnson & Johnson, about one-fourth of company sales are targeted to come from products introduced during the previous five years.[6]

New products have especially strong profit potential because they are designed to satisfy unmet customer needs. The link between new-product development and profitability is illustrated in Figure 10.4. The first curve (curve A) is the sales volume for a typical product over time. When the product is first introduced, brand awareness and distribution must be established. As a result, expenditures usually exceed revenues, and the brand shows a loss. As the brand begins to be accepted, sales accelerate, and it shows a profit (curve B). (The horizontal line in Figure 10.4 is the dividing line between profits and losses.)

Higher profits tend to attract competition. As this happens, sales continue to increase, but not as rapidly, and profits begin to level off. As competition intensifies, the firm loses its competitive advantage, since many brands now have the same basic features and advertise the same benefits. As sales begin decreasing, the brand starts showing a loss.

The sales history of the new product in Figure 10.4 is known as the product's life cycle. We will be discussing the concept of the product life cycle in the next chapter. Here, the life cycle shows that a firm can not rely on any one new product for profitability. Profits can be maintained only by a constant flow of new products. This is demonstrated by the introduction of a second new product just as the profits of the first begin to decline. Sales from the second product (curve C) begin to increase, and profits (curve D) take up the slack just as losses begin to appear for the first product. As a result, overall profitability is maintained. Over time, a third and a fourth new product will be introduced to maintain profits. This scenario assumes that many of the firm's new products will be successful. Any firm recognizes that some of its new products must fail. But if the firm has an effective new-product development process, its overall success rate should assure profitability over the long term.

The introduction of the Apple computer is a good illustration of the link between new-product introductions and profitability in Figure 10.4. When the Apple was first introduced, it showed a loss because of the need to spend for advertising and distribution before the product was established. As consumers accepted the Apple, sales increased, and it became profitable. IBM's entry into the personal computer market slowed Apple's growth. Profits began to decrease. If Apple was to survive, it would have to begin developing new products. Apple recognized the need to revitalize its product line. It first introduced a series of variations of the original model and then introduced the MacIntosh, targeted for the business market. These successful new-product introductions enabled it to maintain profitability over time.

FACTORS IN THE SUCCESS AND FAILURE OF NEW PRODUCTS

The failure rate for new products is high. The Booz, Allen & Hamilton study cited earlier found that about one in every three new products fails.[7] Other studies have found a much higher failure rate, depending on how a new product is defined. Since new product failures are expensive, marketers must be aware of the factors associated with successful product introductions to avoid the risks of such failures.

WHY NEW PRODUCTS SUCCEED

Factors generally recognized as keys to new-product success are as follows:

1. *The degree to which the product matches customer needs.* Miller successfully introduced light beer to meet the need for a less filling beer that did not sacrifice taste. Yet the first low-calorie beer, Rheingold's Gablingers, was a failure. Why? Because it was positioned as a diet beer. Beer drinkers did not want to link the enjoyment of beer to the pain of dieting. Miller succeeded in meeting consumer needs by introducing a "light" beer; Gablingers failed by introducing a "diet" beer.

2. *Use of existing company know-how.* A new product is most likely to succeed if it is developed within the company's core markets, so that the company can use its expertise in marketing it. Gillette was successful in introducing a line of women's products such as facial scrubs and shampoos because it had already developed expertise in marketing men's toiletries.

3. *A superior product.* A new product is more likely to succeed if it is superior to those already on the market. Kimberly-Clark's Huggies was able to displace Pampers as the leading disposable diaper in the mid 1980s because it was a superior product that improved fit and absorbency. It took a major effort by Procter & Gamble to regain its market leadership by reformulating Pampers and mounting an advertising campaign to counter Huggies' threat.

4. *An organizational environment that fosters entrepreneurship.* Successful new products are often developed within an entrepreneurial business envi-

ronment. This environment is found when top management encourages its middle managers to take risks in the process of new-product development. Top management at Johnson & Johnson encourages such risk-taking by "creating a corporate culture where even mistakes can be a badge of honor," because they recognize that such mistakes are an inevitable by-product of effective new-product development.[8] As a result, the company has successfully developed new products in biotechnology and pharmaceuticals.

5. *An established new-product development process.* Finally, successful new products are often the result of a well-defined new-product development process. Companies like General Foods, P&G, Johnson & Johnson and 3M have such a process. General Foods was well-positioned to meet the need for new food products in the early 1980s because it had a sound new-product development process in place. It successfully introduced a string of new products including Crystal Light powdered soft drinks packaged in individual serving sizes for active singles; Pudding Pops, the first of a line of frozen desserts brought out under the Jell-O name; and Soft Swirl, the first soft ice cream that can be stored in the freezer.[9] As a result of this new-product push, General Foods increased its earnings and reduced its dependence on its coffee line, resulting in a more balanced product mix that put more emphasis on deserts and beverages.

WHY NEW PRODUCTS FAIL

There is no easy formula to predict product failures. But marketing managers can use past failures to develop the following general prescriptions as to why new products fail:

1. *Misreading customer needs.* One of the main reasons why new products fail is that management misreads customer needs. In some cases, companies misread the market because of inadequate market analysis as when P&G did not match improvements in diaper absorbency introduced by Huggies. In other cases, the failure is due to management's commitment to the wrong technology — for example, RCA's commitment to videodisc technology when superior product alternatives were available.

2. *Poor product positioning.* The annals of marketing are full of cases of poor product positioning resulting in new-product failures. For example, R. J. Reynolds lost $200 million when it introduced Real cigarettes as the first "natural" cigarette. The problem was that a positioning based on natural ingredients worked against rather than for Reynolds since it reminded consumers of health concerns about smoking.[10]

3. *Poor product performance.* A product can always be repositioned if it provides consumer benefits. But an inferior product is doomed to failure, regardless of its positioning, unless the company goes back to the drawing boards and reformulates it. This is what Procter & Gamble did with Pringles potato chips once it determined that the taste was unacceptable to many consumers. Technical products such as consumer electronics or industrial goods are most likely to be compared on specific performance criteria; they are therefore more likely to fail based on poor performance rather than poor positioning. Coleco's attempt to enter the home computer market with its entry, called Adam, failed because the product's performance did not live up to its promises.[11]

4. *Inadequate marketing research.* Companies sometimes fail to adequately

project product performance before they incur the costs of market entry. For example, General Mills introduced a salted snack food called Bugles and Whistles, based on positive results in product tests. The company had projected high sales based on the number of consumers who had tried the product. But it had not tested adequately to determine how many consumers would buy again. This was a major shortcoming in a category such as snacks, where success must be measured by repurchasing through four or five purchase cycles.[12]

5. *Inadequate competitive analysis.* Another reason why new products fail is that companies often seem to have blinders on when it comes to estimating competitive reactions. A case in point is Lever's introduction of Signal mouth wash. The product was positioned to combat bad breath, particularly from eating garlic and onions. To determine whether the new product should be introduced nationally, Lever first tested Signal in several test markets. However, Signal was in test markets for so long that it gave Scope a chance to preempt Signal's positioning by emphasizing the same benefits in a national advertising campaign. Signal lost potential competitive advantage by failing to anticipate Scope's intentions.[13]

THE PROCESS OF NEW-PRODUCT DEVELOPMENT

FIGURE 10.5
The New-Product Development Process

Identify New-Product Opportunities

Formulate New-Product Objectives

Establish Product Idea

Test Product

Develop Product

Develop Marketing Plan

Test Market the Product

Introduce Product

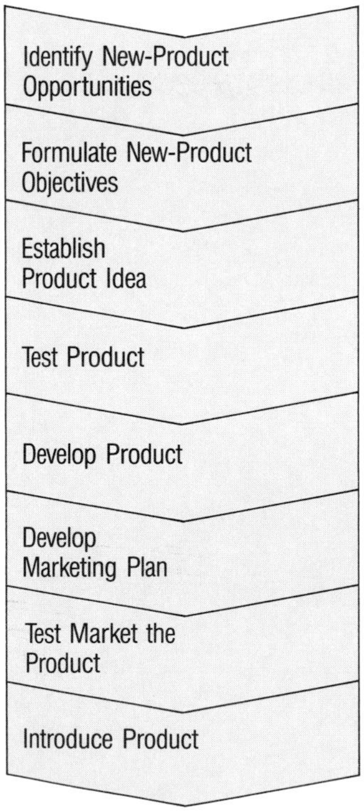

Whatever the explanation for new-product failure, its high costs have caused marketing management to put more emphasis on an effective process of new-product development. Figure 10.5 presents an outline of this process.

The first step in the new-product development process is to identify new-product opportunities. The last chapter cited a large food company that identified a segment of consumers who wanted a nutritional snack, but found current snack food brands inadequate. This segment tended to snack on fruits, vegetables, and yogurt rather than on snack food brands. Once the opportunity was identified, new-product objectives were established. The main objective was to extend the company's snack food line to appeal to nutritional snackers, with a target *return on investment* for such products of 15 percent. In the third step in Figure 10.5, new-product ideas are generated and screened. Based on these steps, the company decided to test a dried-fruit-and-nut snack.

The fourth step in the new-product development process involves testing both the product idea and the actual product. The dried-fruit-and-nut snack idea was translated into several alternative concept statements that positioned the product differently (for instance, nutritious, tasty, or healthy). These alternative concepts were then tested on consumers. A number of preliminary samples were then produced to conduct product tests. These tests uncovered some problems with the product — the fruit was too dry, and consumers found the selection of different types of fruits and nuts too limited. As a result, the product was reformulated (step 5 in Figure 10.5) and tested again until enough consumers expressed buying interest to warrant evaluating the product in test market.

At this point, a marketing plan was developed for the product (step 6) to set the strategy to be used in test marketing and possibly in national introduction. The product was then test marketed in four cities for a six-month period (step 7). Sales projections and budget estimates based on test-market results warranted a national introduction (step 8).

In the following pages, we will review each of these steps.

As we saw in Part II, unmet customer needs are one of the main sources of marketing opportunity. There are other bases for new product opportunities, including competitive weakness, new technologies, and changes in laws and regulations. But the most systematic approach to identifying opportunities has been in the analysis of customer needs. Gaps in the marketplace — determined by identifying target segments dissatisfied with current offerings — represent potential new-product opportunities. Consider the following examples:

- Several companies are testing new products to fill the needs of working couples who want to be able to eat traditional meals at home, but do not have time to cook them from scratch. For instance, Kroger supermarkets is introducing Table Ready Meats that are boned and precooked; Armour is introducing a line of fully prepared breakfast items including crepes and omelets; and General Foods has come out with Jell-O pudding in ready-to-eat form.[14]

- Food companies are viewing with interest research to develop products that make food tastier for a growing market of elderly consumers. As people grow older, they often lose their ability to discriminate tastes. Flavor-enhanced foods would meet an important need for many senior citizens.[15]

- There is a growing awareness of problems of calcium deficiencies in women past the age of 50.[16] As a result, Borden is testing calcium-fortified milk. Many other companies are either developing calcium-fortified products or repositioning calcium-rich products as good sources of this mineral. As we saw, Tums, an antacid, was repositioned to advertise the high calcium content of its product.

IDENTIFY NEW-PRODUCT OPPORTUNITIES

Each new product should have specific profit and sales goals as a basis for evaluating performance. We saw in Chapter 8 that the three performance goals most frequently cited are sales volume, market share, and return on investment. *Dollar sales volume* is the most frequently stated new-product objective. Sales goals are also stated in units, because *unit sales* objectives can be more easily translated into production requirements.

Market-share goals indicate expected product performance relative to the competition. Usually, market-share goals for products entering established markets are relatively modest. For example, PepsiCo's goal for Slice was to attain a 2 percent share in the first year. In relatively new markets, goals might be much higher. Procter & Gamble anticipated obtaining a substantial share of the relatively new liquid soap market when it introduced Ivory Liquid.

Return on investment provides a key performance measure in terms of a product's contribution to company resources. The basic assumption in most strategic plans is that existing products provide the resource base to support new products until they are profitable, and that successful new products will provide the resource base for the next generation of new products.

Another frequently used performance measure for new products is its **payback period,** the period of time it takes for the cash flow generated by the product to become positive (that is, to be on the plus side after accounting for all past expenditures and investments). The payback period is important in showing how long it takes the product to be a cash generator with the ability to support other new-product ventures.

FORMULATE NEW-PRODUCT OBJECTIVES

FIGURE 10.6
Mortality of New-Product Ideas During
Product Development: 1969 versus 1981

Source: Adapted from "New Product Strategy: How
the Pros Do It," *Industrial Marketing,* May 1982,
p. 50.

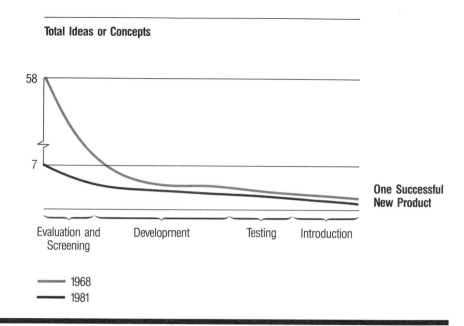

ESTABLISH THE PRODUCT IDEA

The third phase of new-product development is establishing the product idea. This is a two-step process. First, many new ideas are generated. Next, these ideas are screened to narrow the field down to a few alternatives. The Booz Allen & Hamilton study found that organizations are putting more emphasis on these steps and increasing their efficiency. As a result, companies have had to test fewer ideas per successful new product. In a 1968 study, Booz Allen & Hamilton found that companies screened an average of 58 new-product ideas to get one new-product success (see Figure 10.6). By 1981 it took an average of only seven new ideas to get a success.

Idea Generation

If new products are expected to be an ongoing source of profits to the firm, product ideas must be generated. The most important sources are

- *Research and development:* Basic breakthroughs often come from an R&D group. Examples are Kodak's development of lithium batteries and GE's development of factory automation systems.

- *Focus groups:* We saw in Chapter 7 that focus groups are often used to identify unmet customer needs. One set of focus groups uncovered the need for a cold remedy that was free of antihistamine ingredients. The result was the introduction of Sine-Aid by McNeil Labs.[17]

- *Customer suggestions:* Some companies encourage customers to suggest new products. For instance, IBM is looking for software packages developed by users through an Installed User Program.[18]

- *Competitors:* Products introduced by competitors are often acquired and tested in company labs. Companies might develop a competitive edge in their labs and introduce an improved version of the product.

- *Salespeople and distributors:* Suggestions often come from the company's own salesforce and its distributors, both of whom have direct contact with customers. Industrial firms are much more likely to rely on the salesforce for new-product ideas and opportunities. A good salesforce has the technical proficiency to identify and interpret customer needs.

Idea Screening

As Figure 10.6 shows, a firm cannot afford to develop and market all the ideas it generates. Thus, screening is an essential part of establishing the product idea. Companies use two general approaches to weed out ideas that do not warrant further consideration: managerial judgment and customer evaluations.

Managerial judgment refers to a process in which managers rate new-product ideas on key criteria related to a product's profit potential, such as market size, projected growth rate, and required resources. Since managerial judgment is usually not sufficient, *customer evaluations* are also used to screen new-product ideas. Mobil Chemical asked consumers to rate 20 new ideas for products such as storage bags, trash bags, and bug killers against competitive offerings. They were also asked whether they would buy the new product if it was introduced. Ideas that scored highest on "intention to buy" were then subjected to the next step in the new-product development process, testing the product.

The next step in new-product development often involves two phases: testing the product concept and then testing the actual product. In a **concept test** consumers evaluate the product idea, providing a final check before the company incurs the expense of developing prototypes for a product test. For example, when Nestle was considering introducing a line of casserole dishes that required only the addition of boiling water, it asked consumers what they liked and did not like about the product idea. Because consumers rated the concept positively, Nestle decided to develop limited samples for product testing.

The second step, the *product test,* is the first actual exposure consumers have to the product. Consumers might be given the product to use over a period of time at home and compare it to their regular brand, or they might be invited to company facilities to try the product and then rate it. Based on their response, the company decides whether to evaluate the product further in test markets.

Product testing for industrial firms is sometimes limited by the expense of prototype production. For example, a firm developing nuclear imaging machines that cost close to $1 million might be able to develop, at most, one or two prototypes to test their effectiveness. Some industrial firms use their salesforce to conduct informal concept tests on customers before committing to expensive prototype production.

Whether testing is for consumer or industrial goods, an important indication that the product-development process is on-track is a good "fit" between results in the concept and product tests. The benefits that appeal to consumers in the concept must be actually delivered when the product is used.

At one time, a large food company tested an artificial bacon product. Figure 10.7 illustrates the concept-product fit for this product by four benefits — low-calorie, nutritious, appetizing, and convenient. In both panels of the figure, point X shows how consumers rated the concept, and point Y shows how they rated the product after they tried it. As the left panel shows, consumers rated the

TEST THE PRODUCT

FIGURE 10.7
The Product-Concept Fit for an
Artificial Bacon Product

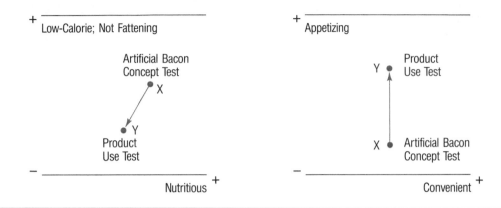

concept of an artificial bacon product positively on the key benefits of nutritious value and low in calories. The right panel shows that they also rated the concept positively on convenience, but did not think it sounded particularly appetizing.

The arrows show how the ratings moved after consumers tried the new product. As the left panel indicates, consumers were disappointed in the nutrition and low-calorie benefits that the product actually delivered. The right panel shows, however, that ratings on appetizing actually improved after use. Consumers had expected the product to be nutritious and not particularly appetizing, but during the product test they found it to be fattier yet much tastier than expected. Since the bacon substitute was meant to be positioned as leaner and more nutritious than the real thing, it was sent back to R&D for reformulation. The reformulated product showed higher ratings on nutrition, leading to its eventual introduction.

DEVELOP THE PRODUCT

If the concept and product tests are positive, the company has a green light to go on to the next step, developing the new product. We tend to think of a product in terms of its physical attributes and what it can do, but another product quality is also important to a company: its design. We will examine how companies formulate both physical attributes and design as they develop new products.

Formulating the Product's Physical Attributes

Formulating the product requires translating consumer preferences into physical product attributes. For example, the idea of an artificial bacon product had to be translated into a product that looked and tasted like bacon but was less fatty and more nutritious.

This process of developing physical product attributes to satisfy intangible consumer benefits is one of the most difficult tasks in marketing. R. J. Reynolds failed in its attempt to introduce Premier, a smokeless substitute for regular cigarettes, because the company could not create the combination of physical attributes to duplicate the taste sensation of a regular cigarette in a cigarette that did not burn tobacco.[19]

Part of the problem in developing products to meet consumer needs is that research and development (R&D) and marketing have very different objectives and perspectives in the new-product development process. R&D personnel tend to emphasize high-quality, well-engineered products, and such products require sufficient time for development. Although marketing personnel also appreciate quality, they argue that perfectly engineered products may not be what consumers want, and that the long development period necessary to develop such products may give competitors an edge.

Coordination between R&D and marketing is particularly important for industrial firms because of the high development costs of many industrial products. Frequent advances in technology result in more product changes, and these changes have to be attuned to customer needs. Industrial marketers must work closely with their R&D counterparts to ensure that products meet customer specifications. Industrial buyers will often work directly with marketers and R&D personnel in setting specifications, making coordination with R&D even more important and potentially more difficult.

Production as well as R&D must be coordinated with marketing in formulating new-product attributes. New production facilities may have to be established, and the nature of these facilities will determine the quantity that can be produced and the speed with which products can get to the marketplace. These are critical factors for the marketing manager. Marketers are more likely to emphasize speed and product quality in the production process, whereas production managers are more likely to emphasize cost-effectiveness.

Developing an Effective Product Design

For many products exterior design is almost as important as development of the product itself — although product design cannot save a product that fails to deliver consumer benefits. Consumers buying cars, typewriters, or kitchen appliances are often first drawn to the product by its design.

For example, Philips Industries, the giant Dutch electronics firm, designed its Roller radio with huge circular speakers to convey a sense of sound and an outsize handle "that blares 'pick me up and carry me.' "[20] The company had forecast sales of 70,000 units for 1986; the product sold 500,000 in that year, largely due to the new design. But designs can fail, just as products do. Philips also introduced a microwave oven that could be used on the dining-room table and was supposed to remind people of an old-fashioned cooking vessel. Instead, the product reminded consumers of a nuclear power plant, something few people wanted on their tables while they ate! (See Figure 10.8.)

At five-foot-two and 98 pounds, Georgena Terry does not exactly look as if she could handle a blowtorch. But that is exactly what she did to build a bicycle specially designed for women. The result was a successful new product and a successful company.[21]

What prompted Terry to head down to her basement one day in 1985 with blowtorch in hand to build a bicycle? After working as a financial analyst, she decided she was bored, got a degree in engineering, and went to work for Xerox. While there, she befriended a lot of bike-riders. Biking was just right for Terry, because as a childhood polio victim, her physical activities were restricted, but she could bike all she wanted.

FIGURE 10.8
Product Designs from Philips that Succeeded and Failed

Source: "Foresaking the Black Box: Designers Wrap Products in Visual Metaphors," *The Wall Street Journal,* March 26, 1987, p. 39. Reprinted by permission of *The Wall Street Journal,* © Dow Jones & Company, Inc. 1987. All Rights Reserved Worldwide.

Philips' Roller Radio: A Success

Philips' Microwave Oven: A Failure

Georgena Terry — Developing a New Product Single-Handedly

Source: © 1985 Phil Matt.

The problem was that she was very uncomfortable on most of the bikes she was riding, and the women she knew felt the same way. Women's bikes were simply not built for women. Terry decided to experiment in building a better bike. She learned how to use a blowtorch and constructed a bike with a smaller frame. Friends borrowed it and liked it. Terry then decided to go into business for herself, making the whole bike, not just the frame. She decided on a line with four different sizes, made eight prototypes, and hauled them to several bike rallies. She made her first sale August 1985, selling one of her models for $775. She sold a total of 20 bikes that year.[22]

She began selling more bikes the following year and established a marketing plan. Terry convinced local bike dealers to stock her bikes through sheer perseverance. She could not afford any advertising, so she hired a public relations firm that positioned her as the David against the Goliaths of the industry. That got her favorable reviews for her product in several bicycle magazines. She also established a line of bikes priced from $319 to $1,560. The combination of a superior product and a good marketing plan began to produce results. By the end of 1986 she had sold 1,300 units. In 1987 she was projecting sales of 5,000 units.[23] Terry Bikes was an established company.

Terry has no illusions about the difficulty of remaining profitable. As the first to develop a superior design for a women's bicycle, she has a competitive advantage. But she recognizes that larger companies could easily duplicate her design. At some point she realizes that she may have to think about selling out or joining forces with a bigger company. But for now, she is having fun reaping the benefits of a successful new product. ◼

DEVELOP THE MARKETING PLAN

Once the product is developed and tested, management must formulate a marketing plan that will be effective for introducing and sustaining it in the market. Because the marketing planning process was already described in Chapter 8, we will not repeat the points made there.

It is important to note, however, that there are generally two marketing plans, a plan for introducing the product into test market, and a plan for a subsequent regional or national introduction. The test-market plan sets out the product's positioning, defines target segments, establishes a marketing mix, and identifies media schedules and distribution requirements for the markets in which the product will be tested. The second plan, the marketing plan, is then modified on the basis of test-market results. The target segment might be redefined, advertising themes changed, budgets for specific marketing mix components increased or decreased, and price levels adjusted based on demand in test markets. The revised marketing plan provides the blueprint for introducing the product.

TEST-MARKET THE PRODUCT

The last step in new-product development before introduction is **test marketing**, which requires introducing the product in several markets with a complete marketing plan to simulate a national introduction. Results of the test market are then projected nationally to determine if it is likely to be successful. This stage differs from earlier concept and product tests, which ask the consumer, "If this product were in the market, would you buy?" Test marketing gives consumers an actual opportunity to buy, and is the "dress rehearsal" for introduction. If results do not meet sales and profit goals, there is still time for management to withdraw the product to avoid market failure. In addition to determining consumer reactions in a realistic environment, test marketing also allows management to evaluate marketing strategy before introducing the brand nationally, and to project sales and revenues from test areas to the national market.

In selecting test markets, management tries to ensure that they are representative of the product's target segment and reflect competitive conditions nationally. Introducing a product into test markets where competition is weak would bias sales results upward. Management must also ensure that the product is in test markets long enough to determine the repurchase rate — an important factor in national projections of sales.

In addition to providing data on purchase and repurchase rates, test markets provide information that the company can use to fine-tune the marketing mix. For example, in 1984 Campbell test marketed its Home Cookin' Soups, a thicker soup that looked more homemade with chunks of meat and vegetables. These tests provided the company with a clear idea of what worked and what did not. What worked was that consumers thought the soup tasted good; what did not work was everything else, from the packaging to the variety of flavors available.

As a result of these findings, Campbell reformulated the marketing plan for the product. It broadened the line of flavors, introduced a larger 19-ounce can that would appeal to family users, and at the same time captured more shelf space. And the original "Tastes like I made it myself" advertising message changed to focus more on the nutritional benefits of the food. Management attributes the success of the brand to the lessons learned in test market.[24]

Alternatives to Test Marketing

Despite successes such as Campbell's, test marketing is both costly and time-consuming. Also, having a product in test market for months allows competitors to duplicate the product. As a result, many firms are using alternatives to test marketing that are of shorter duration and are less expensive. One type of test, known as a **simulated store test**, asks consumers to shop in experimental supermarket facilities in which new products are introduced, and then tracks their purchases. Another, known as a **sales wave experiment**, places new products in consumer homes, determines reactions to the product, and then gives consumers a chance to purchase them over time to track repurchase rates. Companies are increasing their use of these techniques to avoid the risks of competitive duplication and the high costs associated with test marketing.

Most test marketing and less costly market tests are conducted by consumer rather than industrial firms. It would be prohibitively expensive to test-market complex, high-technology products — and such tests would invite competitors to acquire and possibly duplicate the new technology. Further, many industrial markets have a limited number of customers, often located in a few regions. Test marketing prior to introduction is not necessary since these firms can go directly to individual customers to do a concept test or to test product prototypes.

NATIONAL INTRODUCTION

A company's most crucial decision is whether to introduce the product nationally. The substantial investment in production and marketing makes this a risky decision. If a company decides to introduce the product, it must choose between a region-by-region *rollout* or an immediate national introduction. To minimize risk, most companies choose a rollout, releasing the product first in regions where competition is weakest. Procter & Gamble rolled out Folgers coffee from its strong regional base in the West across the center of the country, introducing the brand last on the East Coast where General Foods' Maxwell House brands were strongest.

In contrast, Gillette went national immediately in 1981 when it introduced Aapri, a facial scrub meant to compete with Noxzema, Ponds, and Oil of Olay. The company introduced a well-integrated marketing plan in June 1981 with network TV advertising.[25] In August, full-color two-page ads appeared in national magazines, and in September 15 million samples were distributed by mail. Retail trade support in the form of cooperative advertising was provided during this period to ensure adequate stocks.

The decision to use a regional rollout or a national introduction depends on the company's competitive position and risk orientation. Folgers' weaker position relative to Maxwell House prompted P&G to tackle one region at a time. Gillette, on the other hand, was in a strong competitive position, since Aapri was the first facial scrub. The company was willing to take the risk of going national immediately because it felt Aapri would fill an important customer need, and Gillette did not want to risk competitive duplication by taking a more cautious region-by-region approach.

INCREASING COSTS OF NEW-PRODUCT DEVELOPMENT

The description of the new-product development process in the preceding pages left out one important subject: the increasing costs of development as a company progresses through the process. In the initial phases of idea generation and screening, costs are relatively low. If a company decides to test a product, prototypes must be made, and the company incurs its first substantial costs. Research and development must be brought into the process to work on the development and design of the product. In many cases, new production facilities must be built. When the company begins test marketing, it incurs costs of advertising, sales promotions, and distribution. Finally, when the product is introduced, costs escalate because of the expenses of national advertising and distribution.

These costs have increased in recent years, so that by 1988 it cost an estimated $20 million to introduce the average new brand.[26] Costs of market entry have increased correspondingly. Transportation costs and the costs of TV advertising have outpaced inflation. As a result, the risks of new-product introductions have escalated.

These risks are particularly high for small firms that cannot afford potential multimillion-dollar losses resulting from new product introductions. As one marketing analyst noted, "Skyrocketing expenses of new entries means that smaller firms are literally betting the company on each rollout."[27]

ETHICAL AND REGULATORY ISSUES IN NEW-PRODUCT DEVELOPMENT

Consumers have a right to safe products, to products that perform well, and to full information regarding product ingredients. These three rights constitute the major ethical responsibilities of marketers in developing new products.

Most companies try to ensure product safety and reliability in the course of new-product development. But abuses exist, and the consumer's welfare dictates that government have a role in ensuring product safety. The primary government agency responsible for product safety is the Consumer Product Safety Commission (CPSC), established in 1972.

The CPSC can ban the sale of products, require manufacturers to perform safety tests, and require repair or recall of unsafe products. It operates a hot line, allowing consumers to report hazardous products, and runs a National Electronic Injury Surveillance System, a computer-based system that monitors 119 hospital emergency rooms across the country. On the basis of this system, the commission computes a *Product Hazard Index*. Among products with the highest hazard index are cleaning agents, swings and slides, liquid fuels, snowmobiles, and all terrain vehicles (ATVs).

The CPSC's action against manufacturers of ATVs illustrates how it tries to ensure product safety. ATVs have been associated with over 900 deaths since 1982, and in December 1987 the commission filed suit against ATV manufacturers. In April 1988 all ATV manufacturers signed a consent decree agreeing not to sell any three-wheel ATVs and to restrict sale of four-wheel models to certain age groups.[28] A preferable solution might have been for ATV manufacturers not to have developed or sold three-wheel models in the first place, or to have provided adequate instruction for those already in use, but such self-regulation was not forthcoming.

The CPSC has also been active in recalling products. It recalls an average of 200 products a year.[29] Another agency with recall powers is the National Highway Traffic Safety Administration, which sued General Motors to force a recall of 1.1 million X-body cars because of faulty brakes.

The Food and Drug Administration (FDA) also has an important role in ensuring product safety. It has the authority to ban or seize food and drug products it regards as a menace to public health. It can also require extensive testing for food and drug products before they are marketed. Recently, the agency required NutraSweet Co. to test a new, low-calorie fat substitute. It has also challenged R. J. Reynold's new smokeless cigarette, claiming that it should be treated as a drug because of its ingredients and should be tested as such before being marketed.

In addition to government regulation, consumers have recourse to sue manufacturers for damages. Unfortunately, such product-liability claims come into play only after consumers have incurred some harm as a result of product use. Over 10,000 former users of Dalkon Shield, an intrauterine device, brought suit against A.H. Robbins, its manufacturer, only after experiencing illness and infertility.

Although there is a need for government to regulate product safety, some companies recognize their responsibilities in this area. A good example is Gillette. The company has a 29-member quality-inspection group whose head is empowered to stop the development of a new product or to recommend a change in its ingredients if there is a potential danger. On the group head's say, Gillette pulled a product off the market just as it was being introduced: an aerosol antiperspirant containing zirconium salt, an ingredient that was later found to inflame lungs.[30] An inspection team also convinced Gillette's R&D group to reduce the amount of apricot aroma in Earth Born shampoo so the apricot scent on freshly shampooed hair would not attract bees. Gillette's quality-inspection group is a good example of self-regulation to ensure product safety.

PRODUCT SAFETY

PRODUCT PERFORMANCE

Manufacturers should be concerned with more than product safety. They also have a responsibility to ensure that products perform in an acceptable manner. If a fabric shreds, a kitchen appliance fails, or a battery goes dead soon after it is purchased, performance, not safety, is the issue.

Most companies try to ensure that a product will meet consumer expectations for the simple reason that otherwise consumers will not buy again. Also, negative word-of-mouth communications about the product will discourage new buyers.

Since good product performance is generally in their interest, most manufacturers use quality controls to achieve it. They also reduce the financial risk to consumers of purchasing expensive products such as cars or appliances by offering warranties that assure repairs or replacement in a certain period of time. Industry associations have also established performance standards such as energy usage for major appliances.

The government can do little to legislate adequate product performance if consumer safety or environmental concerns such as pollution are not at issue. Consumers can bring a manufacturer to court when it has not adequately remedied a product failure; but few do unless product safety is involved. Fortunately, the link between good performance and profitability is a compelling motivator for most companies to regulate themselves.

PRODUCT INFORMATION

Another consumer right that bears on new-product development is information on product ingredients provided on the package. Consumers have a right to know these ingredients so as to make a safe and informed choice. In 1975 rules assuring this right were formulated by the Food and Drug Administration for certain food labels and cosmetics. Additional laws seeking to protect consumers through full information have resulted in health-warning labels on cigarettes and sugar substitutes.

§UMMARY

1. What is the definition of a product? A new product?
A product is an offering by an organization represented by a bundle of product attributes and benefits designed to satisfy customer needs. Products are classified as consumer goods (products sold directly to individuals for final consumption) and industrial goods (products to be used in producing other goods or in support of the production process). New products are products new to consumers, to a company, or to both. A product is new to consumers when they have no prior awareness of the brand or product category. A product is new to a company when it has to go through a process of development, testing, and market introduction. Many products that are new to both companies and consumers are classified as innovations — that is, products that result in changes in consumer behavior and consumption patterns.

2. Why are new products essential to a firm's profitability?
Because existing products eventually mature and begin to decline, firms need a series of successful new-product entries to maintain profits over time.

3. What are the reasons behind new-product successes and failures?
New products tend to be successful when the company has matched product characteristics to customer needs well, when it has been able to use its know-how

in marketing the new product, when the product has a distinct competitive advantage, and when the company's environment fosters risk-taking.

New-product failure results from misreading customer needs, poor positioning of the product, a product that does not perform up to par, and inadequate marketing research and competitive analysis.

4. What steps are involved in new-product development?

- Identifying new-product opportunities based primarily on unmet customer needs.
- Developing new-product objectives.
- Generating and screening new-product ideas to fill customer needs.
- Testing the product concept and then the product itself.
- Developing the product.
- Developing a marketing plan for product introduction.
- Testing the product in several market areas.
- Introducing the product.

5. What are some of the ethical issues in new-product development?
The major ethical issue in new-product development is the marketer's responsibility to ensure safety. Most marketers try to do so during the development process. But abuses have occurred, making action by government agencies necessary. The most important of these is the Consumer Product Safety Commission (CPSC). Another key issue is full disclosure of information about product ingredients on packages. Again, most marketers do so, but laws had to be passed to guarantee full information on packages of all appropriate products.

KEY TERMS

Core product (p. 264)
Tangible product (p. 264)
Augmented product (p. 265)
Products (p. 265)
Brand (p. 266)
Product category (p. 266)
Product line (p. 266)
Durable goods (p. 266)
Nondurable goods (p. 266)
Convenience goods (p. 267)
Services (p. 267)
Shopping goods (p. 268)
Specialty goods (p. 269)
Production goods (p. 269)
Installations and accessories (p. 270)
Supplies and services (p. 270)
Innovations (p. 271)
New-product duplication (p. 271)
Product extensions (p. 271)
Payback period (p. 277)
Concept test (p. 279)
Test marketing (p. 282)
Simulated store test (p. 283)
Sales wave experiments (p. 283)

QUESTIONS

1. An industrial engineer commented on the definition of a product as follows:

   As far as I'm concerned, the product is the various parts that make it work. It's fine to say that the brand name and package may influence sales when we are dealing with consumers goods. But for industrial goods, it is the physical product entity that counts. Everything else is window dressing.

   a. Do you agree with this statement?
   b. Could product components other than the physical product be decisive in influencing sales for industrial goods?

2. Why is the distinction between a brand and a product category important?

3. A manufacturer of major appliances is considering acquiring a company that produces cleaning products such as oven and floor cleaners to offer a broader range of products for the kitchen and home. It staffs some product management positions with managers from its appliance business. Based on Table 10.1, what changes in the marketing mix will these managers most likely have to consider in shifting from appliances to cleaning products? Would you consider the transition from one type of business to the other an easy one to make?

4. The chapter cited five reasons why new products succeed. Were each of these factors important in PepsiCo's successful introduction of Slice? Explain.

5. A company that has tended to rely on product reformulations and extensions of its existing line is considering putting more emphasis on innovations. What risks might the company face as a result?

6. The president of a firm that manufactures small appliances says:

> New products are one road to profitability, but not the only road. The problems with investing heavily in new product development are that (a) it is expensive, (b) it is risky because competition can follow you in very easily, and (c) it opens you up to losses due to changes in technology. I would prefer to let the other fellow take the lead and then follow when I think the market is ripe.

What are the pros and cons of this position?

7. A company introduced a new hand-cream preparation targeted to older women and positioned to "get the wrinkles out of aging hands." Consumers liked the product in concept and product tests. Trial rate for the product in test markets was so high that the company decided to shorten the test-marketing period and introduce the product nationally. It flopped badly. What hypotheses could you develop as to why the product was successful in tests but failed after national introduction?

8. The chapter mentioned a company considering the idea of a nut-and-dried-fruit snack concept to fill the need for a nutritious snack.

   a. What information would you need in order to decide whether to develop samples of the product for testing?

   b. What information would you need in order to decide whether to introduce the product nationally?

9. What is meant by a product-concept fit? How does the idea of a product-concept fit apply to Figure 10.7? What alternatives does a company have if the product-concept fit is poor?

10. Consider the following statement made by a marketing manager at a large electronics firm:

> We have some of the best engineers and scientists in our R&D labs. But those people waste most of their time on esoteric ideas with no market applications. And when they do hit on an idea that is marketable, they're interested in making the perfect product. Well consumers aren't usually willing to pay for the perfect product. If it was up to me, I would have R&D report to marketing to ensure product development is geared to what the market wants.

   a. Do you agree with this statement?

   b. What problems might arise if R&D were under the control of marketing?

   c. What problems might arise if R&D were divorced from marketing?

11. Many companies are avoiding test marketing. Why? What are the risks of not test marketing a product? What are the alternatives to test marketing?

12. How have federal agencies operated to ensure product safety? What can companies do to ensure that they market safe products?

CASE 10.1

A NEW PRODUCT: CARBONATED MILK?

Source: "The New Style is Fizzy," *The New York Times*, February 18, 1987, p. C6. Copyright © 1987 by The New York Times Company. Reprinted by permission.

Their penchant for sweet carbonated beverages gave rise to scores of soft drinks and to fruit-flavored, low-alcohol wine coolers. In the next year or so, baby boomers may have a new drink designed with their taste preferences and health concerns in mind: carbonated milk in an array of flavors — strawberry, orange, coconut, piña colada, mint, cola, even rum.

Milk for the Pepsi generation?

"It's a fun kind of casual, sporty drink," said Marilyn Wilkinson, speaking for the United Dairy Industry Association in Rosemont, Ill., which represents 95 percent of American dairy farmers. "It's the dairy industry's entry into the casual snack market, as well as into the restaurant and fast-food industry."

An affiliate of the association, Dairy Research Inc., is developing the milk-soda hybrid by carbonating skim milk, then adding flavorings and sweeteners. It is perhaps the culinary kin to the colorization of old movies.

Industry analysts say that carbonated milk is designed to tap the upscale, young-adult market, particularly calcium-conscious women. It will be marketed, they say, as a tasty drink with milk's calcium, vitamins and minerals and carbonation's light, fizzy taste.

Carbonated milk is part of the dairy industry's effort to create a successful range of products, much as the soft drink industry has done. Consumers who buy soft drinks constitute the beverage industry's fastest growing market.

Just as soft drinks come in many flavors and containers targeted for different groups of consumers, the dairy industry is now offering or developing milk with greater amounts of calcium for women and older people; milk with the low-calorie sweetener aspartame, marketed as NutraSweet, for dieters; milk more easily digestible for people who are lactose intolerant; "long life" milk kept in aseptic cartons that needs no refrigeration and can travel in lunchboxes, and milk marketed in six-color packaging to create brand identification.

Why all these changes? "The dairy industry has not kept pace with soft drinks because milk has been out-marketed, out-distributed and out-packaged," said Michael Bellas, president of the Beverage Marketing Corporation, an independent research group in New York.

Americans are now drinking twice as many gallons of soda a year as they were 15 years ago. Soft drinks sailed past milk in popularity in the early 1970's. By the 1980's, soft drinks had become the country's leading beverage, with 25 percent of the market.

Meanwhile, the consumption of coffee, milk, liquor and wine has dropped or stagnated. "Baby boomers like sweet, slightly carbonated, chilled drinks," Mr. Bellas said.

If milk and carbonation appear to be unlikely bedfellows, it is a marriage of necessity. Milk consumption has been flat for more than a decade. "The reality is that if dairy farmers are going to survive, and if they're going to be competitive, they must come out with new products," Mrs. Wilkinson said.

She conceded that some people may not accept changing a product that is an American mealtime tradition, one whose taste and color are often associated with physical growth and wholesomeness.

"There will always be people who resist change," she said, "but we're after people who don't drink milk."

Carbonated milk, she said, does not taste like milk. The prototype being developed is thinner, with only a slight dairy flavor; moreover, it won't leave a mustache.

Adding flavors will give the drink some punch and add color. The basic product will have the same caloric and nutritional value as skim milk, although the sweeteners and flavors being tested are likely to add calories.

In addition, researchers are trying to develop a carbonated milk that will not require refrigeration so that it can sit on the supermarket shelf side-by-side with soft drinks.

That strategy has succeeded with Yoo-Hoo, a chocolate-flavored, dairy-based, noncarbonated drink. Yoo-Hoo, developed in the 1920's, is now offered in bottles and boxes and competes on the same shelves with soft drinks and juices. According to Patrick Ferro, president of Yoo-Hoo in Carlstadt, N.J., the product's placement, packaging and marketing as a sweet drink fortified with vitamins and minerals has helped the refreshment beverage carve out a 1 percent market share in the soft-drink industry.

1. How should the United Dairy Industry Association identify the opportunities for a carbonated milk product?
2. What are the alternative ways of positioning carbonated milk?
3. How should these positionings be tested?
4. Who do you think is the target for the new product?
5. Who would United Dairy be competing against?

CASE 10.2

PROCTER & GAMBLE EXTENDS ITS SNACK LINE

Source: Laurie Freeman, "P&G May Try Corn Chips Next." Reprinted with permission from *Advertising Age,* June 15, 1987, p. 12, Copyright Crain Communications, Inc. All rights reserved.

Procter & Gamble Co. continues to chip away at the nearly $7 billion salty-snack market dominated by Frito-Lay.

Sources indicate P&G plans to introduce a corn chip by yearend. It is not known if the chip will come under the Pringle's umbrella.

The Cincinnati-based marketer's 16-year-old Pringle's brand holds a 7.5% share of the $1.75 billion potato chip segment. In moving into the $350 million corn chip segment, it would go up against F-L's popular Fritos brand as well as Bordon's recently introduced Spirals.

P&G refused to comment on the possible corn chip.

Some sources said the corn chip has been in development since the mid-1970s. Others suggested any new salty snack by P&G would be placed in a "holding pattern" until P&G receives Food & Drug Administration approval for its olestra fat-substitute compound.

P&G has filed a petition to substitute olestra, formerly called sucrose polyester, for up to 35% of the fats in home cooking oils and up to 75% of the fats in commercial cooking oils and salt snacks. P&G "would not want to introduce a corn chip unless they had a major point of difference" between it and rival brands.

They can't compete with Frito-Lay's store-door delivery system for freshness quality, so they'll get the corn chip ready, get production lines going, then wait for olestra's approval.

1. How should P&G test its new corn chip?
2. Should the product be test marketed? Why or why not?
3. What is the corn chip's competitive advantage?

NOTES

1. "The Anatomy of an Ad Campaign," *New York Newsday,* October 27, 1986, Part III, City Business, pp. 1, 6.

2. Ibid.

3. PepsiCo Annual Report, 1986, p. 10.

4. "Can A New Ad Blitz Put the Fizz Back in Slice," *Business Week,* February 8, 1988, p. 95.

5. *New Product Management for the 1980s* (New York: Booz Allen & Hamilton, 1982), pp. 8–10.

6. "Masters of Innovation," *Business Week,* April 10, 1989, p. 58; and "At Johnson & Johnson, a Mistake Can Be a Badge of Honor," *Business Week,* September 26, 1988, p. 126.

7. *New Product Management for the 1980s,* pp. 8–10.

8. *Business Week,* September 26, 1988, p. 126.

9. "General Foods' Strategy for Tomorrow," *Dun's Business Month,* May 1985, pp. 49–53.

10. "Rx for New Product Survival," *Marketing Communications,* February 1986, p. 29.

11. Ibid., p. 30.

12. Ibid., p. 28.

13. Ibid., p. 32.

14. "Working Couples Get More Than Just Desserts," *Advertising Age,* December 2, 1985, p. 96.

15. "Scientists Working to Develop Products That Make Food Tastier for the Elderly," *The Wall Street Journal,* November 4, 1985, p. 33.

16. "Borden Bones Up on Calcium," *Advertising Age,* March 24, 1986, p. 28.

17. "Creating Products for the Marketplace," *The New York Times,* December 10, 1981, p. D22.

18. Eric Von Hippel, "Get New Products from Customers," *Harvard Business Review* 60(March/April 1982): 117–122.

19. "'Smokeless' Cigarette A Failure for Reynolds," *The New York Times,* March 1, 1989, p. D1.

20. "Foresaking the Black Box: Designers Wrap Products in Visual Metaphors," *The Wall Street Journal,* March 26, 1987, p. 39.

21. "Spokeswoman," *INC.,* June, 1987, pp. 31–32.

22. Ibid., p. 31.

23. Ibid.

24. "Test Marketing Put to the Test," *S&MM,* March 1987, pp. 67–68.

25. "Gillette Spends $17.4 Million to Introduce Aapri, Gain Foothold in Skin Care Market," *Marketing News,* May 29, 1981, p. 6.

26. "Giving Fading Brands a Second Chance," *The Wall Street Journal,* January 24, 1989, p. 31.

27. "How Smaller Companies Meet the Test," *S&MM,* March 10, 1986, p. 89.

28. "For Want of a Wheel," *Regulation* 12(1988):7.

29. Ibid., pp. 7–8.

30. "Gillette's Dr. No Guards Company Against Liability," *Business Insurance,* April 18, 1988, p. 157.

REEBOK — CAN IT STAY AHEAD OF THE PACK?

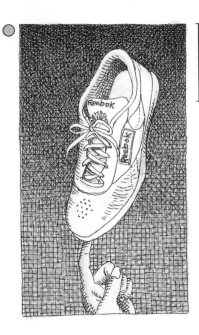

How does a company like Reebok grow from almost nothing to become the largest athletic footwear supplier in the United States in five short years? Simple. Create a high-style aerobic shoe to catch the growing aerobic exercise trend among women at exactly the right time. Then promote the shoe at the grass roots level by enlisting the support of aerobic instructors and by starting aerobic services and clinics. Finally, when aerobic shoe sales are growing at a phenomenal rate, cash in on the increasingly popular REEBOK® name by expanding the customer base to include basketball shoes for teenagers, casual and walking shoes for the older set, and even athletic shoes for children and infants. (You guessed it, they are called WEEBOK® brand shoes.) This product strategy propelled Reebok from $3 million in sales in 1982 to an industry leading $1.8 billion in 1988.[1] By then, Reebok represented more than one-fourth of total sales of athletic footwear.[2]

Although the British-based company had been producing custom racing shoes since 1895 (it made the shoes used by Britain's 1924 Olympic racing team, immortalized in the movie *Chariots of Fire),*[3] the story really starts in 1979 when a camping goods distributor, Paul Fireman, saw REEBOK shoes at a Chicago trade fair. Impressed by the shoe's construction and styling, he bought North American rights to Reebok the following year.

Fireman was well aware of the fitness trend and the growth of running shoes in the United States. He also recognized that other forms of exercise besides running, particularly aerobics, were beginning to be popular among women. His genius was to link fashion and exercise in a garment leather aerobic shoe targeted to women. In his words, ''There was enormous pent-up demand for a shoe that not only performs but fills a burning need for more style, more comfort, more fit, and more fashion, particularly for women.''[4]

Reebok's aerobic shoe was that product. The first athletic shoe designed for women, it came in different colors to match different exercise outfits. Shortly

after its 1982 introduction, the company moved from a low-budget strategy of building word-of-mouth advertising by getting the support of aerobic instructors, to more expensive advertising in general circulation magazines.

By 1984 sales of Reebok's aerobic shoes reached $36 million, and Fireman could finance other lines.[5] Reebok's primary asset was its brand name, and the question was whether this name could help the company sell shoes outside the aerobics market. Tennis shoes were introduced in 1984; they were an immediate success. In 1985 Reebok created another category, fitness shoes, designed to be used in health clubs as the man's counterpart to aerobic shoes. Then came basketball, casual, walking, and children's shoe lines in quick succession. The transition from a one-line, one-segment company to a broad-based athletic footwear leader was complete.

By 1988 the company could boast of sales over $1 billion, a $60 million advertising budget that included a national TV campaign to introduce its basketball sneaker line, and the acquisition of two other shoe companies: ROCKPORT for its casual shoe line, and AVIA for its sturdy, well-built running shoes. But 1988 also saw Reebok's first earnings decline as it faced more intense competition from companies such as Nike because of its attempt to move into high-performance footwear.[6]

Reebok made it to the top by following sound product strategy principles: Find a gap in the market, fill it by introducing a product to meet the needs of a particular segment, then build on success by using the now established brand name to introduce other lines targeted to new segments within the company's core area of competence.

Will Reebok stay on top, or are its shoes a fad that consumers will tire of? Only time will tell — but if Reebok passes into oblivion, it will not be because of a lack of a sound product strategy. ■

YOUR FOCUS IN CHAPTER 11

(1) *What is the role of the product manager in marketing a brand?*

(2) *What are the responsibilities of product managers for brands, product lines, and the company's overall product mix?*

(3) *What important decisions must product managers make for brands and product lines?*

(4) *What do we mean by a product life cycle? How does this concept help managers develop brand and product line strategies?*

● ● ●

THE NATURE OF PRODUCT MANAGEMENT

Marketers must not only develop new products, they must also manage existing products. Reebok went through a process of new-product development in introducing aerobic and other types of shoes. It then had to establish a system to maintain growth of existing products. It did so by placing each of its product lines under the direction of a manager responsible for the profit performance of the line and for establishing marketing strategy. Most firms refer to these individuals as *brand* or *product managers*.

THE PRODUCT MANAGEMENT SYSTEM

The system within which brand or product managers work is known as the **product management system.** It ensures that a product manager has profit responsibility for a brand or product line by placing all marketing strategies under that manager's control. The product management system was first developed by Procter & Gamble in the late 1920s, when the company assigned responsibility for marketing Camay Soap to one person. Before then, one person had been responsible for product development, another for advertising, another for sales, and another for manufacturing. P&G then realized that as it introduced more brands, it would need a manager to oversee each one.

As the number of brands in the marketplace proliferated after World War II, the product management system became the norm for large packaged-goods firms such as General Mills, Lever Brothers, and General Foods. By the 1970s banks and other financial institutions began adopting the system, too, as they strove to become more marketing-oriented. Citicorp, Chase, Chemical, and other banks began hiring product managers from consumer packaged-goods firms such as Procter & Gamble and Lever Brothers to integrate marketing strategies for various services such as bank cards, student loans, and integrated checking services.

THREE LEVELS OF PRODUCT MANAGEMENT

Product managers operate at three levels: the brand, the product line, and the product mix. As we saw in the last chapter, a brand is a name or symbol that has come to represent the product. Pampers is a brand of disposable diapers made by

Procter & Gamble; Pepsi-Cola is a brand of cola made by PepsiCo. In Reebok's case, the name of the company has become the brand name associated with all the company's products. (Actually, a *reebok* is a speedy African gazelle.) The Reebok Phase 1, Reebok ACT 600 and Reebok Newport Classic are all individual brands of Reebok tennis shoes.

A **product line** is a group of products in the same category, frequently with the same name to facilitate identification. Reebok tennis shoes (including Reebok Phase 1, Reebok ACT 600, etc.) and Ban deodorants (including Ban Solid, Ban Roll-On, etc.) are product lines under one name. A product line can also be a collection of brands with different names in the same product category. For instance, General Mills' line of children's cereals includes Cheerios, Cocoa Puffs, Circus Fun, and Rocky Road.

A **product mix** is a company's or strategic business unit's (SBU's) mix of products offered to the public. (We defined SBUs in Chapter 2.) Reebok has three business units: footwear, apparel, and an international unit. The footwear SBU's product mix includes all the athletic shoe products it offers in the United States. The apparel SBU's product mix includes exercise suits, tennis clothes, and accessories such as hats, socks, and bags. The international unit's product mix combines footwear and apparel, and offers this mix outside the United States.

Table 11.1 shows the three types of product managers associated with each of these three levels, and the strategic decisions they are responsible for. Brand managers are responsible for particular brands in companies that emphasize the brand as the focal point for marketing strategy. For instance, Procter & Gamble has always followed a marketing strategy of focusing on individual brand names rather than on a corporate umbrella, because it feels brand identification is more important than corporate identification. As a result, P&G's brand managers operate as business managers for individual brands. They are responsible for positioning a product, identifying the target segment, and establishing price, promotional, and distribution strategies.

Although P&G uses brand managers to develop strategies, it has recently begun to use **product-line managers** (also known as **category managers**) to coordinate marketing strategies between brands in a line, rather than let each brand manager act independently. For example, assume that brand managers for P&G's Tide and Cheer detergents both want to position their brands as "removing tough dirt." A product-line manager would determine how to position each brand to avoid such conflicts. As a result of this change, brand managers at P&G now report to product-line managers.[7]

The product line can also be the focal point in setting marketing strategies rather than the brand. This is the case at Reebok, where strategies are developed for each line of athletic shoes under the direction of a product-line manager. For example, the word-of-mouth strategy used to help introduce aerobic shoes was not used for basketball shoes because there was no need to educate existing and prospective users on the nature of the sport. Since basketball shoes was a highly competitive market, Reebok used national TV for the first time to get teenagers to notice the basketball shoe line.

In addition to developing marketing strategies, product-line managers are also responsible for additions to or deletions from the line. For example, the product manager for the tennis line would have been instrumental in adding the Phase 1 and Act 600 models as product-line extensions.

Product-mix decisions involve evaluating a firm's or business unit's product offerings and allocating resources to the firm's product lines. As we saw in Chap-

TABLE 11.1
Three Levels of Product Management

	THE BRAND ⟶	THE PRODUCT LINE ⟶	THE PRODUCT MIX
MANAGEMENT	Product or brand management	Product-line management	Business unit or corporate management
STRATEGIC CONCERNS	Product positioning	Product-line positioning	Resource allocation to existing lines
	Identify target segments	Identify target segments	
	Develop price, distribution, and promotional strategies	Develop price, distribution, and promotional strategies	Evaluate product portfolio
		Additions of brands to existing lines; deletions of brands from existing lines.	Additions of new lines; deletions of existing lines
PLANNING	Marketing plan	Marketing plan	Strategic marketing plan

ter 2, such decisions are made by business-unit or corporate managers in the context of a strategic plan. Product-mix decisions shape a company's future growth and affect its profitability. Arm & Hammer was a one-product company in the early 1970s, relying on its baking soda for sales. It then embarked on a program of product expansion by extending its trusted name to toothpastes, carpet deodorizers, and laundry detergents.[8]

In the remainder of this chapter, we focus on the three levels of product management just described.

Mara Michele (Mitch) Myers — Brand Manager Supreme

Source: Reprinted with permission of ADWEEK, July 1987.

Mitch Myers thought her days at Anheuser-Busch were numbered when she first introduced Spuds MacKenzie, the black-eyed English bull terrier that has become the symbol of Bud Light, to August Busch III, the tough CEO of the company that bears his name.

It was 1985, and sales of Bud Light were slumping as Miller Lite strengthened its hold on the light-beer market. Myers, associate brand manager for Bud Light, figured that the usual appeal to blue-collar workers paying tribute to the American work ethic was overused. It is true these are the heaviest beer drinkers, but using the same approach as Miller Lite would mean going head-to-head with the market leader, and that was unlikely to get Bud Light out of the doldrums. The problem was that Busch himself "applauded advertising that exalted the American can-do spirit."[9]

Myers' solution was a $20 million advertising campaign to make a party animal, Spuds MacKenzie, the symbol for Bud Light just as Max Headroom had become the symbol for New Coke. The difference was that Max was a human that teens could relate to. It was not at all obvious that Spuds was a symbol that Bud Light's target group was likely to accept.

Myers went into the meeting to present the proposed Spuds campaign to Busch, prepared with a simple warning from her boss, the brand manager for Bud Light: "You're going to be fired." Myers passed around stuffed versions of Spuds, gave her presentation, and waited for a reaction. She recounts, "August didn't say anything. He just sat there holding the stuffed dog. I thought, that's it. After the meeting, August walked over to me shaking the dog . . . 'This is terrific,' he said."[10]

The rest is history. The Spuds campaign was accepted by Bud's target group and has become one of the most successful campaigns in the industry. Myers' gamble paid off. As a brand manager for the product, she knew it needed a distinctive position compared to the market leader, and she had the foresight to realize that a "far-out" symbol like a stuffed dog might do it.

Myers went from associate brand manager to product manager for bottled waters and then to manager of all nonalcoholic beverages. In December 1986, only in her mid-thirties, she was named director of brand management, overseeing the brand managers of all the company's beverages. She was responsible for reviewing the marketing plans of all the brand managers and integrating strategies across brands. Her successful rise made her the highest ranking marketing person in the beverage group.

Success has not been easy for Myers. She was passed over for promotion at a previous job at Seven-Up Co. and had to face an "old boy network" when dealing with Anheuser-Busch's brewery personnel. But she earned their respect by her hard work, competence, and a good dose of self-confidence. Success as a brand manager was the stepping stone to a top corporate position for Myers in a tough, male-dominated company. ■

THE BRAND

A brand name associated with a quality product is one of the most valuable assets a company can have. The name Hershey is worth more than all of the company's candy-making facilities. The name Reebok, although unknown before 1981, had in four years become synonymous with stylish athletic footwear.

Most products in the marketplace are **branded**; that is, they have a name and/or symbol that is identified with the product. If we accept the broad definition of a product in the last chapter, then a brand means more than a name, such as

COMPONENTS OF A BRAND

EXHIBIT 11.1
Importance of a Brand Name

Coca-Cola, or a symbol, such as the McDonald's arch. It is also represented by the benefits it conveys (the *core product*), the package it is in (the *tangible product*), and any warranties and services associated with it (the *augmented product*). We will consider each of these.

Brand Names

Companies spend millions of dollars establishing brand names and keeping them before the public eye. The value of a brand name is illustrated by Sunkist's entry into soft drinks. Until 1978 Sunkist was the brand name for oranges and lemons grown by a cooperative group, Sunkist Growers. One of the best-known brand names, Sunkist accounted for 50 percent of the oranges and 70 percent of the lemons sold in the United States.

In 1978 the company capitalized on its strong association with orange flavor and nutrition by introducing an orange soda — an undeveloped flavor category that at the time had no brand leadership. The brand quickly gained leadership of the orange-flavor category, capturing a 2 percent share of the soft drink industry that was worth $500 million in revenue.[11] The main ingredient in Sunkist's success was its well-known name (see Exhibit 11.1).

The term **brand equity** refers to the tremendous value of names such as Hershey, Coke, and Sunkist to manufacturers.[12] Brand equity, not the value of the company's facilities, was the reason for the record buyout price of $25 billion for RJR Nabisco in 1988. RJR's Del Monte line of fruits and vegetables was alone valued at $4 billion.[13]

Attributes of a Good Brand Name If possible, a brand name should suggest product benefits. Sunkist suggests a well-ripened, good-tasting orange. Easy Off oven cleaner, Beautyrest mattresses, and Pampers disposable diapers are other examples of names that suggest product benefits.

Also, a brand name should fit the brand image. Apple is a good name for a personal computer because it gives the impression of being friendly, familiar, and easy to use. Comanche is a good name for a jeep because it brings to mind the ruggedness, and durability of an Indian scout.

The name should be easy to pronounce and recognize as well. When Reebok was first introduced, it conveyed neither benefits nor a particular brand image, but because the name was simple and recognizable, a strong positive link was established between name and product.

For international marketers, the name should be able to be translated into other languages without altering its meaning. For example, General Motors discovered it could not use the name Nova on a universal basis because in Spanish the name translates into "won't move."[14]

Finally, as we saw in Chapter 3, the Lanham Act forbids use of a brand name previously registered by another company.

How Are Brand Names Selected? Given these objectives, companies use both managerial judgment and consumer tests to select a brand name. A management team at Sony selected the name Walkman. Names such as "Hot Line" and "Sound-About" were considered and rejected as not reflecting product benefits. Managers liked another name, "Stereo-Walky," but Toshiba had already registered the name. The team liked Walky, and Sony's ad agency even developed a logo with two legs sticking out from the bottom of the A in "walk." That gave someone the idea of combining walk and man, and the name was born.[15]

EXHIBIT 11.2
Symbols that Play Key Roles
in Brand Identification

Instead of relying entirely on managerial judgment, most companies use some kind of consumer testing as well. Typically, the company generates a large number of names, which are then weeded down by management to 10 or 20 finalists. These are then tested on consumers. This was the process used by Coors beer, in a joint venture with Molson of Canada, when it introduced a super-premium beer to compete with imported beers. It started out with a list of 500 candidates which was reduced to 13 by using a computerized program that matched the 500 names to company brand-name objectives. The finalists were tested on heavy beer drinkers by labeling the identical beer with different names, then asking consumers to taste and rate each beer. Even though the beers were identical, the different names made consumers think they were tasting different beers. Consumers gave the beer labeled Masters by far the highest ratings because, apparently, it conveyed an image of old-world skill and tradition.[16]

Brand Symbols

Brand symbols, such as McDonald's golden arch or the Pillsbury doughboy, can be as important as a brand name in establishing product associations and a brand image (see Exhibit 11.2).

When brand identification is weak, symbols may be even more important than names. Because consumers regard all glass-fiber products similarly, Owens-Corning decided to exploit the one visual factor that distinguished it from competitors — its pink coloring. It adopted the Pink Panther as its symbol. This cartoon character became the centerpiece for the advertising campaign with the theme "Put Your House in the Pink." For the first time, buyers began to specify Owens-Corning Fiberglass insulation.[17]

The Package

A third important component of a brand is packaging. Its importance is reflected in the fact that 10 cents of every dollar spent by consumers goes to package development.[18]

Role of the Package The package plays a number of important roles. First, it identifies and promotes the brand. Hershey's distinctive brown package was so successful in this regard that the company found advertising unnecessary until the early 1970s. Second, distinctive package design can attract consumers' attention and increase sales. When General Foods bought Ronzoni, it redesigned the dull and unappetizing package for Ronzoni's frozen entrees to make it look like a line of premium foods. The result was increased sales.

Third, a package can identify a line of products. Miller-Morton, producers of Chapstick, successfully introduced Lip Quencher based on moisturizing benefits. It then extended the line to moisturized facial makeup and powders by introducing Face Quencher and Skin Quencher. Central to its strategy was a common silver-and-black carded package for the Quencher line. The package was meant to establish a link to Chapstick's black-and-white container and to convey the key moisturizing benefits of the products.[19]

Fourth, packaging communicates information on ingredients, quantity, and product use. Government regulation requires disclosure of ingredients for many food and drug products and dating of perishable packaged products. Packaging also communicates product benefits or changes in product characteristics that might appeal to consumers.

Packaging has a functional as well as a promotional and informational role. It can provide convenience, preservation, storage, and safety benefits. Pumps make it easier to dispense toothpaste, plastics make ketchup more squeezable, cylindrical cans make potato chips crush-proof, zip-lock bags make foods fresher, and seal-tight openings make over-the-counter drugs tamper-proof. All are examples of improvements in packaging functions. In the interest of functional benefits, even the Campbell's Soup can will be making room for other packaging for the first time since 1897, as Campbell introduces asceptic containers, bowls for microwave ovens, and plastic cups for its soup products.

Package Design Companies either design packages internally or employ special package design firms for this purpose. Package design was central in Coca-Cola's decision to bring back the original brand after introducing the new formula. A new can had to be developed that would distinguish what is now Coca-Cola Classic from New Coke. The challenge for the package designers was to fit the product into the Coke family while giving it a distinctive identity that would appeal to traditionalists.[20] The name Coca-Cola would be used instead of Coke, and Classic would be attached to appeal to the brand's loyal followers. The name appeared in a script style reminiscent of old ads, and the words "original formula" encased in a circle resembling an official seal were added to the can. The redesign of the package was a central component of the strategy to bring the old formula back.

The Warranty

Another component of brands is the **warranty** that is sometimes provided by manufacturers, a written statement of the manufacturer's commitment if the product is defective or performs poorly. Companies may provide limited warranties that state the extent of coverage and stipulate areas that are not covered or full warranties that have no such restrictions. Peugeot, for example, provides a full warranty of three years or 36,000 miles and a limited warranty on the engine, driveshaft, and transmission of five years or 50,000 miles.

The Magnuson-Moss Warranty Improvement Act of 1975 requires manufacturers to state the limits of any warranty including its length, specific areas of performance, and whether it includes labor and routine maintenance. The act also requires full warranties to meet certain minimum standards, including reasonable repairs and replacement.

Manufacturers sometimes use warranties to gain a competitive advantage. For instance, Chrysler was the first to come out with a five-year, 50,000 mile warranty to get the edge on Ford and General Motors. The warranty was an important factor in Chrysler's recovery in the auto industry. Similarly, General Electric was the first appliance company to offer to replace appliances within 90 days if buyers were not satisfied or fully refund the purchase price. Whirlpool countered by offering replacement up to a full year after purchase. Both companies developed their warranty strategy based on research showing that consumers preferred replacement to a service call.[21]

Brand Image

A brand's physical characteristics, name, symbols, package, and reputation for service combine to create an overall impression, or **brand image**, in the consumer's mind. That image may be the most important factor in a purchase decision, especially for brands such as cars, clothing, liquor, and cigarettes, which are often purchased for visibility or social effect.

One of the most effective brand images ever created, the Marlboro Cowboy, is also the basis for the longest-lasting advertising campaign to date. Marlboro was first introduced in 1924 with an ivory red tip targeted to women. After languishing for 30 years, the brand was repackaged and repositioned by Philip Morris, using the symbol of a cowboy on horseback. The image that was created — strong, quiet, confident, and masculine — was an immediate success in this country and abroad.

It became clear to Philip Morris executives that smokers were buying Marlboro not so much for the taste as the image. This was demonstrated when the company offered Marlboro smokers the brand at half-price, but in generic brown boxes. Only one out of five smokers took the offer.[22] The other four out of five were more interested in the image produced by pulling out a pack of Marlboros. It was this image that produced $2 billion in operating profit for Philip Morris in 1986 and that allowed the brand to increase at 3 percent per year while the rest of the industry was declining by 2 percent. Philip Morris's management estimates that the Marlboro Cowboy is worth $10 billion, one-third of the company's total market value.

If the marketing strategy for a brand is successful, all of its components — name, symbol, packaging, and service reputation — act to form a strong positive association in consumers' minds. As a result, branding can be valuable to both the company and the consumer.

THE VALUE OF BRANDING

Advantages of Branding for Manufacturers

When a brand name is associated with a successful product, it will continue to attract customers. Apple Computer was able to maintain its position in the educational market because it became identified as the best personal computer for students. Even after intense competition from IBM, Apple continues to maintain a loyal base in this market.

A brand that has built a loyal consumer base has staying power. One study found that of 30 leading brands in 1930, 27 are still leaders in their category today, including brands such as Ivory Soap, Campbell Soup, Gold Medal flour, and Crisco shortening.[23]

Another reason why branding is important to manufacturers is that a brand with strong consumer loyalties also tends to win distribution support more easily. Reebok had to scrounge for support from shoe distributors in its early years. Now that it is an established brand, it has no problem getting distribution.

Finally, a strong brand can be leveraged by using it in other product categories to gain more profits for the firm. We saw that Sunkist successfully leveraged its name from fruits to soft drinks.

Advantages of Branding for Consumers

Branding also gives consumers some important advantages. A brand name identifies a product so that consumers know what they are getting. Consumers do not have to worry about variations in content and quality from one purchase to the next. As a result, branding facilitates shopping. Recognizable brand names allow consumers to buy with little need for comparisons and information search.

Brand names also give consumers information. Consumers remember the taste, ingredients, price, and performance of brands; they remember which brands satisfied them and which did not. This is why branding creates the opportunity for consumers to become brand-loyal. Crest toothpaste has many loyal users because the brand has become equated in consumers' minds with cavity protection: It was the first fluoridated toothpaste and received the endorsement of the American Dental Association. That association is still invaluable, almost 30 years later.

Protecting Brands

Because brand recognition is so important in guiding consumer purchases, a brand is valuable property to the company that has established it. Companies protect their brand names and symbols by registering them as **trademarks** with the U.S. patent office. As we saw in Chapter 3, the Lanham Act (1946) protects such trademarks from duplication. For instance, the large toy retailer, Toys "Я" Us, successfully sued a retailer of children's clothes for trademark infringement for using the name Kids "Я" Us, and then proceeded to use the name itself in establishing a line of children's apparel. One of the keys to the case was that Kids "Я" Us used the symbol of a backwards R, which was considered a unique mark of Toys "Я" Us.

Such vigilance is necessary to protect the millions of dollars companies spend on advertising and promotion to build a positive brand image. But ironically, companies can be too successful in establishing a strong brand image. Some brands have become such strong leaders in their field that they have become associated with the product category. When this happens, a company is in danger of losing its distinctive brand association. For instance, how many of us have said we wanted a "xerox" rather than a photocopy, or asked for a "kleenex" instead of a tissue? Xerox and Kleenex are trademarked products that have been marketed so successfully that their names are frequently used in a generic rather than a brand sense. Formica, Jell-O, Scotch Tape, and Fiberglas are other examples.[24]

Why does generic use of a brand name pose a threat to the brand's manufacturer? Because if a brand is too successful, its name may pass into the vocabulary, and as a result, companies may lose the right to use them. Thermos, cellophane, and shredded wheat were once brand names until the companies that produced them lost the right to their names in court cases because they were so commonly associated with the product category. For this reason, Xerox is currently trying to protect its name with an advertising campaign to educate the public to avoid

EXHIBIT 11.3
Protecting a Valuable Brand Name

using the word xeroxing as synonymous with copying. (See the ad in Exhibit 11.3.)

MARKETING DECISIONS CONCERNING BRANDS

We have been looking at the advantages of branding and the stake that companies have in the brands they own. Because brands are so important, the way in which they are marketed is of great strategic relevance. Let us look at two important marketing decisions concerning brands: first, the extent to which the manufacturer controls the marketing of its brand; and second, the way in which a company identifies its brands.

Brand Control

Although we have seen that many companies go to great lengths to develop and protect their brands, not all manufacturers choose to control the marketing of their products. Some even permit their products to be sold without brand names. Companies must make two decisions regarding brand control. First, will they control the marketing of their brand, or will they produce for retailers and wholesalers and let these intermediaries control the product? Second, regardless of who controls the brand, will it be supported by advertising and promotional efforts?

Yes-or-no decisions on these two issues produce the four alternatives to brand control shown in Figure 11.1 — manufacturer's brands, private brands, generic products, and price brands.

Manufacturer's Brands Brands that are both produced and marketed by the manufacturer are called **manufacturer's brands**. These are also known as **national** or **regional brands**, depending on the geographic area in which they are marketed. Most of the brands cited in this chapter, including Reebok shoes, Sunkist oranges, and Budweiser beer, are manufacturer's brands sold nationally. Coors beer was a regional brand centered in the midwest until it began to expand nationally to challenge Budweiser.

FIGURE 11.1
Types of Brands Based on
Who Controls Them

Control over Brands

Manufacturer   Retailer/Wholesaler

	Manufacturer	Retailer/Wholesaler
Yes	Manufacturer's Brands	Private Brands
No	Price Brands	Generic Products

Marketing Support

Private Brands **Private brands** are manufactured for retailers or wholesalers and sold under their label rather than the manufacturer's label. Large retailers such as Sears and A&P often buy products from leading manufacturers such as Michelin, Heinz, or Ralston Purina, then sell them to consumers under their own brand name. Advertising expenditures on private brands such as Sears' DieHard battery or A&P's Ann Page coffee may be equal to expenditures on leading manufacturer's brands.

Why do retailers and wholesalers market private brands when they have to support them with advertising and promotional expenditures? Because they can buy these products at lower cost from manufacturers who want to use up excess capacity. As a result, prices for private brands average 15 percent to 30 percent below those of national brands.[25] Even after spending money on advertising, retailers and wholesalers can offer goods that are often comparable in quality to manufacturer's brands at substantially lower prices. Thus, Safeway can claim that its Truly Fine deodorant soap is comparable to Dial, and its Nu-Made mayonnaise is comparable to Hellmann's.

The next question is why manufacturers sell products for private branding when they know that they may undercut the price of their own brands? There are several reasons. First, excess capacity may cost a manufacturer heavily if production facilities go unused. Second, manufacturers can eliminate marketing costs by selling products for private branding. This is one reason why companies such as Ralston Purina, Scott Paper, and Heinz regularly sell products for private branding, in some cases using up to 40 percent of their production capacity for this purpose. However, other manufacturers, such as Procter & Gamble and Kellogg, refuse to produce for private brands, citing their product superiority and market leadership as evidence that their efforts are best directed to their own brands.

The competition between retailer's brands and manufacturer's brands has been called the **battle of the brands.** The battle is over shelf space and the consumer's dollar, and in this battle, retailers have the advantage. Consumers have become more educated regarding brand alternatives and recognize the value of private brands. Also, retailers control shelf space and can give their own brands preferred positions. On the other hand, many manufacturer's brands have the ability to build strong loyalties to protect themselves from the price competition of private brands. Procter & Gamble was able to fend off private brands in the liquid dishwasher market through a $12 million advertising campaign that emphasized the superior quality and value of its leading brand, Ivory.

Generic Products A third brand category, **generics**, are unbranded products sold with no promotional support. They are produced by manufacturers and controlled by resellers, generally supermarkets. They often appear in plain white boxes with black letters identifying the product category — detergent, paper towel, and so forth. Generic products sell at an average of 40 percent below national brands and 15 percent to 20 percent below private brands.[26]

Generics first appeared in the United States in 1978; by 1982 they were selling in 80 percent of American supermarkets. Consumers accepted generics in the early 1980s because of greater price sensitivity during a steep recession. Their popularity peaked in 1982 with a 12 percent share of unit sales in supermarkets; since then this share has been declining. However, sales of generics continue strong in certain categories that consumers view as undifferentiated, such as granulated sugar, apple juice, baking soda, and canned vegetables.[27]

Manufacturers are even less willing to produce generic items than private brands. Yet some manufacturers who are losing market share and looking to utilize capacity will probably opt to produce generics. L&M's sharp decline in cigarettes, for instance, prompted it to begin producing generics in 1981. By 1984 L&M's generics had captured a substantial 4 percent of the cigarette market. Its success prompted other cigarette companies to introduce generics and lower-priced brands.

Price Brands **Price brands** are low-priced brands under the manufacturer's control that are sold with minimal advertising and promotional expenditures. A manufacturer introduces price brands to compete with private brands and generics. This strategic purpose has also led price brands to be called **fighting brands**.

Procter & Gamble has adopted this strategy because it avoids producing private brands and generics. It introduced a line of low-priced paper towels called Summit without advertising support in an attempt to counteract the inroads being made by generics and private brands. Similarly, Ralston Purina eliminated advertising and reduced the price of its Mainstay brand of dog food to compete with generics. And, L&M introduced Pyramid, a cigarette priced 25 percent below regular brands to further support its dominant position in lower-priced cigarettes.

As the number of low-priced brands in the market increases, however, greater pressure is placed on higher-priced manufacturer's brands to maintain both advertising and product quality in order to insure the loyalty of current users. Many of these brands are experiencing a decline in their market shares as consumers switch to price brands, private brands, and generics. As a result, there may be fewer manufacturer's brands in the future.

Brand-Identification Decisions
Companies have several options in trying to establish brand identity, depending first on whether the brand is an individual brand or part of a product line, and second on whether its name is specific to the brand or part of a corporate umbrella. These decisions produce the four alternatives for brand identification shown in Figure 11.2.

FIGURE 11.2
Brand-Identification Alternatives

		Type of Name Identification	
		Brand Name	Corporate Name
Single Brand or Product Line	Single Brand	Individual Brand Name	Corporate Brand Name
	Product Line	Product-Line Name	Corporate Family Name

Individual Brand Names Each brand a company offers can be sold individually and stand or fall on its own. Procter & Gamble follows this strategy of **individual brand names**. New brands are identified with the P&G name only for the first few months after introduction; from that time on, all reference to P&G is discontinued. Even when P&G offers several products in the same category, there is no strong product-line identification. Thus, P&G's detergents — Tide, Bold, Dash, Cheer and Duz — are all regarded as separate profit centers with separate brand managers; with the one proviso that a product-line manager integrates strategy between these brands to avoid conflicts.

An individual-brand strategy such as that used by P&G offers some advantages but also some risks. The company can target separate brands in a category to separate market segments and thus capture more consumers. But the possibility of **cannibalization** exists, in which a new brand that the company introduces draws consumers from the company's existing brands. For example, when P&G introduced Cheer, some of its users had previously been Tide purchasers. Cannibalization should not deter a company from introducing a new brand, especially if it is an improvement over the existing brand that is being cannibalized. An improved brand will probably draw more customers from the competition than from the company's own brands. But if most of the new brand's business represents consumers switching from one of the company's existing brands, cannibalization could lead to a net loss.

Corporate Brand Name Instead of identifying products by individual brand names, many companies choose a strategy of using **corporate brand names** that link the brand name to the company's name. Kellogg follows this strategy for its cereal products — for example, Kellogg's Rice Krispies and Kellogg's Raisin Bran — because the diversity of these products might otherwise lead to confusion and lack of consumer loyalty. In contrast, P&G does not feel the need for corporate brand name identification because it establishes such strong individual brand names, such as Pampers, Crest, and Folgers, with intensive advertising.

Product-Line Name A **product-line brand name** may be applied to several products within a product line, as in Sears' Kenmore appliance line, its Kerrybrook women's clothing line, and Homart its home-installations line. Sears' product lines require separate identification because of their diversity. The alternative — naming all products under the Sears corporate umbrella — would create too much confusion in consumers' minds.

Corporate Family Name The alternative to Sears' strategy is to have all of a company's products identified under the corporate umbrella — that is, a **corporate family name**. This strategy requires all of a company's products to be advertised under the company's name as a family of brands. It is feasible under three conditions: (1) if the company's product mix is not too diverse and can be easily identified by consumers with the company name, (2) if the company has a strong corporate identity, and (3) if individual brand identification is difficult. Heinz follows a corporate-family-name strategy because it has a relatively homogeneous mix of food products, it has a strong corporate identity, and it would be difficult to establish separate brand identities for each of its 57 varieties of food products. An important advantage of this strategy to Heinz is the economies of scale available in promoting many products in the same advertisement.

THE PRODUCT LINE

Whereas branding decisions are concerned with the marketing strategy for a particular brand, product-line decisions are concerned with the makeup of the brands offered in a given product line. As we saw earlier in this chapter, a product-line manager is responsible for determining how many brands will be included in the line, whether brands should be added to or deleted from the line, and the overall positioning of the line.

The key questions determining the makeup of the product line concern its depth and its breadth.

PRODUCT-LINE DECISIONS

Depth of the Line

The **depth of the line** refers to the number of different types of brands, sizes, and models within a particular product line, such as the number of adult cereals offered by Kellogg or the number of detergents offered by P&G. Some companies provide a wide range of offerings for a product, while others offer just a few items.

Line managers may add additional items to the line to give consumers a full range of options. Bristol-Myers has traded on the strength of its Ban deodorant by introducing 17 variations of Ban including four pump sprays, two "'dry" roll-ons, three solid sticks, and six Ultra Ban versions. A full line is particularly important for industrial sellers since buyers often want a full range of products. A company may carry hundreds of variations of industrial valves or fasteners, even if some of them are losing money. It is worth losing money on a few items to avoid losing customers because the particular product they need is not produced by the company.

There is such a thing as too much depth, however. Brand additions that offer nothing new are likely to get sales from existing products in the line, resulting in cannibalization. As a result, the company has incurred the costs of introducing a line extension without increasing sales.

FIGURE 11.3
Product-Line Strategies

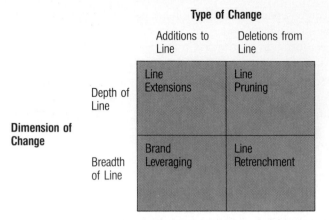

Breadth of the Line

Whereas deepening a product line means adding items within its current range, broadening a line means stretching it beyond its current range. Thus, the **breadth of the line** refers to its diversity.

General Foods has a broad line of coffee products. It offers four brands of regular coffee that also come in decaffeinated form; a wide line of instant coffees including regular instant, freeze-dried, and regular and freeze-dried decaffeinated versions; and also a line of imported premium coffees. This broad coffee line is designed to satisfy various segments of the market. Its breadth is strategically important to GF, which regards coffee as a mainstay of its business. In contrast, Procter & Gamble has a narrow coffee line, offering only a single brand, Folgers. P&G has not yet identified an opportunity to introduce another brand to challenge the market leaders, General Foods and Nestle.

Although broadening a product line can be strategically important, it is not without risk. As with increasing the depth of a line, the primary danger is cannibalization. When General Foods introduced Maxim, its freeze-dried extension of Maxwell House coffee, it realized that a large part of the brand's sales would come from Maxwell House users. It accepted this probability, however, because if it had not introduced a freeze-dried coffee, it would have been at an important competitive disadvantage. Nestle was developing Taster's Choice freeze-dried coffee, and GF concluded it was preferable to cannibalize Maxwell House than to risk losing Maxwell House users to Nestle. As it turned out, Maxim attracted many users other than Maxwell House drinkers, resulting in a substantial net increase in sales.

PRODUCT-LINE STRATEGIES

Product-line managers may try to modify existing lines by adding or deleting brands to change the depth or the breadth of a line. These possibilities create the matrix of four strategies shown in Figure 11.3: line extensions, brand leveraging, line pruning and line retrenchment. We will examine each of these.

Line Extensions

Line extensions are additions to the line in the same product category, and they serve to deepen the line. Line managers introduce line extensions to give customers a full range of alternatives in the product category, and to avoid being flanked

EXHIBIT 11.4
A Line Extension Strategy
for Arrow Shirts

by a competitor's introduction of a similar modification. Arrow Shirt's strategy of extending its line beyond the traditional, conservative, white shirt it was known for is shown in Exhibit 11.4.

Brand Leveraging

Line managers may use another strategy besides line extensions for adding to a line. Instead of deepening a product line, a company may broaden it by leveraging a successful brand through the introduction of additional forms or types of products under the same brand name. The introduction by Gillette of Silkience shampoo leveraged the Silkience name from conditioners to shampoos, whereas the introduction of Silkience deep conditioner merely extended the conditioner line.

Brand leveraging has become a popular strategy because companies find it is about 40 to 80 percent less expensive to introduce a new product under an existing brand name than to launch it under a new name.[28] Brand leveraging works

EXHIBIT 11.5
Three Examples of Brand Leveraging

best when the brand name has value, is well-known and has the consumer's trust. (See Exhibit 11.5 for three examples.) Castle & Cooke found through research that its Dole brand connotes more than pineapples; consumers associated the name with juices and fruit bars. As a result, the company extended its line into these categories. Similarly, Eastman Kodak found that the Kodak name easily transferred into batteries. In fact, its research showed that a significant segment of consumers thought the company sold batteries, even before it actually introduced them.[29]

There are limits to brand leveraging, however. The Disney name has always had a certain amount of magic. But when the company tried to get into movies for adults, the Disney name failed because that magic applied only to child-oriented products. As a result, Disney developed adult films under a different name, Touchstone.

Line Pruning

Both line extensions and brand leveraging strategies add to the number of products in a line. But these strategies may lead to overextending a line. When this happens, products must be deleted either through line pruning or line retrenchment.

Line pruning refers to reducing the depth of a product line by cutting back on the number of offerings in a particular product category. Pressure often comes from salespeople to offer additional variations in flavors, sizes, packages, or composition to satisfy buyers, and many line managers have a tendency to favor such line extensions. But as items are added, the costs of design, inventory, order processing, and transportation all rise, and the line may become unprofitable.

The effective line manager realizes that line pruning can be just as important as line extensions. But when should a line be pruned? Three conditions serve as a signal: (1) a number of items in the line are not making an adequate contribution to profits, either because of low sales or because they are cannibalizing other items in the line; (2) manufacturing and distribution resources are being disproportionately allocated to slow moving items; and (3) many items in the line may be outdated because of product improvements.

Line Retrenchment

Whereas line pruning reduces the depth of the line by cutting back on offerings in a given product category, **line retrenchment** reduces the breadth of the line by cutting back on the diversity of items offered across product categories. Such retrenchment is usually caused by a failure to leverage a brand into a related category.

Successful brand leveraging requires the right conditions: a strong brand name; a logical association of the new product with the brand umbrella; and successful introduction of the leveraged product without alienating users of other products in the line. When these conditions are not met, companies are likely to fail in leveraging their brand. Pillsbury's Green Giant line failed in its entry into frozen dinners because consumers associated Green Giant with vegetables, not contemporary foods. The result was discontinuation of the product, or line retrenchment.

THE PRODUCT MIX

While product-line decisions are concerned with the individual items in a line, product-mix decisions are concerned with the combination of product lines offered by the firm and the possible addition of new lines or deletion of existing lines. As we saw in Table 11.1, product-mix decisions are made by business-unit or corporate mangers, usually in a strategic marketing plan that specifies how much money will be allocated to each line.

Like a product line, a company's product mix can be described as having breadth and depth. The breadth of a product mix refers to the number of product lines offered by the firm. General Electric has a very broad mix because it offers a wide number of lines in diverse business units such as lighting, major appliances, medical imaging, aerospace, and factory automation. Michelin has a narrow product mix, offering just a few tire lines.

The breadth of the product mix raises the question of brand leveraging. Brands can be leveraged across a diversity of product lines, as Bic showed when it leveraged its name from pens, shavers, and lighters to perfumes with a $22 million advertising campaign in 1989 for Parfum Bic.[30]

The depth of the product mix is the average number of product variations in each line — different brands, models, and colors. Michelin has a narrow but deep product mix because of the large number of different tires it carries within its lines. In contrast, L&M's product mix is both narrow and shallow. It offers only a few lines of cigarettes and a small number of variations within each line.

A product mix may also be described as having **consistency**, which refers to the relation of the product lines to each other. Kellogg has a very consistent product mix, for virtually all of its products are cereals. In contrast, General

Electric has a very diverse product mix. Its lines vary by industry, and they include consumer goods, industrial goods, and services.

The breadth, depth, and consistency of a company's product mix pose some important strategic issues that we will consider in Chapter 22 when we discuss strategic planning.

THE PRODUCT LIFE CYCLE

The marketing strategy for a brand or product line cannot stay constant over a **product's life cycle**, that is, the phases through which a product goes from introduction to growth to maturity and decline. Variations in positioning, advertising, pricing, and distribution strategies occur in each of these stages.

LIFE CYCLES FOR PRODUCT CATEGORIES AND BRANDS

The concept of a life cycle can apply to product categories as well as to brands. Consider the automobile. As a product category, the automobile's life cycle extends over decades and is now in its mature phase since automobile sales have been fairly level in recent years.

Defining a product category as "the automobile" is probably too broad for strategic purposes, though. More specific categories could be defined such as compact cars, luxury cars, or station wagons. The life cycle of these categories would have more strategic relevance. The compact car, for instance, is now about 30 years into its life cycle; it is currently moving from a growth to a mature phase, since sales have leveled off after a rapid spurt due to the energy crisis. Brands of cars such as Honda's Acura have their own life cycles. The Acura is in its introductory phase.

Our interest is primarily in the life cycles of brands, since they are the focal point for strategy development. But brand managers must also be aware of the life cycle for the product category, because brand sales are often tied to product-category sales. The decrease in the demand for cigarettes has hurt most brands, with some exceptions such as Marlboro. The failure of RCA's Selectavision was due more to the shortcomings of the product category, videodiscs, than to problems with RCA's brand.

Figure 11.4 shows the sales curves for movie cameras and for VCRs, with movie cameras in the declining stage and VCRs in the growth stage of their respective life cycles. The reason movie camera sales are declining is the increase in sales of video cameras whose pictures can be played on VCR equipment. The movie-camera life cycle proved disastrous for Polaroid. The company introduced its Polavision system that instantly develops movie film in 1976, just at the tail end of the increase in movie camera sales. The company failed to see the effect of the advent of the VCR market on movie cameras. Similarly, Kodak was late in switching out of the eight-millimeter camera market into video camera products and lost any competitive advantage to Japanese manufacturers such as Sony and Panasonic.

STAGES OF THE PRODUCT LIFE CYCLE

Figure 11.5 shows the traditional, bell-shaped sales curve for a product or a brand as it passes through the life cycle stages of introduction, growth, maturity, and decline. These stages tend to be associated with certain types of brand strategies shown at the top of the figure: brand development, reinforcement, revitalization, harvesting, and possibly revival. The figure also shows the strategic objec-

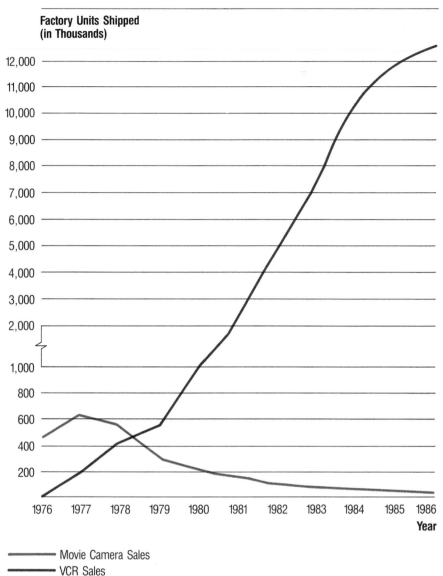

**Factory Units Shipped
(in Thousands)**

FIGURE 11.4
Product Life Cycle for Movie
Cameras and VCRs

Sources: Movie Camera Sales from *Predicasts'
Basebook,* 1987, p. 663. VCR Sales for 1976-1980
from "Sales of Home Movie Equipment Falling as
Firms Abandon Market, Video Grows," *The Wall Street
Journal,* March 17, 1982, p. 29; VCR Sales for 1981–
1986 from *Statistical Abstract of the U.S.,* 1987, Table
1356, p. 751.

tives as well as the four Ps — product, place (distribution), promotion, and price strategies — associated with each stage. In the following paragraphs, we will look more closely at each stage in the life cycle.

The Introductory Stage

When a brand is first introduced, the main purpose of marketing strategy is to establish it, not only with consumers, but with wholesalers and retailers as well. **Brand establishment** thus entails building a distribution network to make the product available to consumers and convincing consumers to try the product.

The product must have some competitive advantage in terms of quality or cost in order to attract consumers. The goal of advertising is to inform them of these benefits. To influence wholesalers and retailers to stock a brand, firms may

FIGURE 11.5
Marketing Strategies over
a Brand's Life Cycle

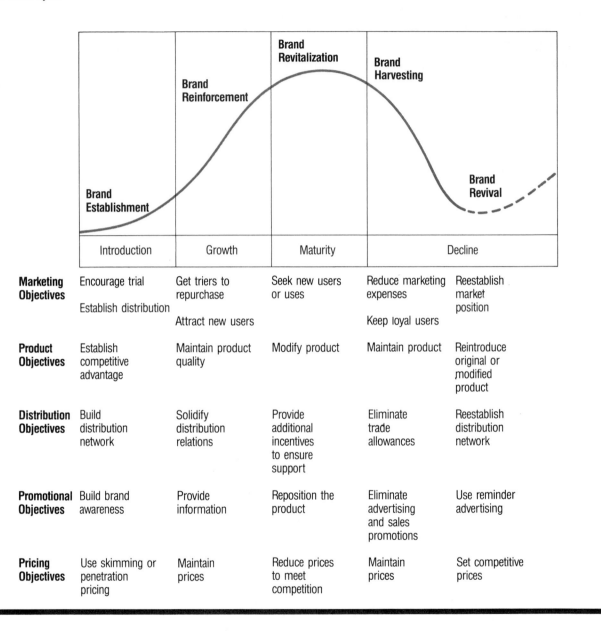

	Introduction	Growth	Maturity	Decline	
Marketing Objectives	Encourage trial Establish distribution	Get triers to repurchase Attract new users	Seek new users or uses	Reduce marketing expenses Keep loyal users	Reestablish market position
Product Objectives	Establish competitive advantage	Maintain product quality	Modify product	Maintain product	Reintroduce original or modified product
Distribution Objectives	Build distribution network	Solidify distribution relations	Provide additional incentives to ensure support	Eliminate trade allowances	Reestablish distribution network
Promotional Objectives	Build brand awareness	Provide information	Reposition the product	Eliminate advertising and sales promotions	Use reminder advertising
Pricing Objectives	Use skimming or penetration pricing	Maintain prices	Reduce prices to meet competition	Maintain prices	Set competitive prices

offer favorable trade discounts and allowances for advertising and in-store promotions.

Brand managers can follow two types of pricing strategies in the introductory stage. As we noted in Chapter 8, with a **penetration strategy,** the brand is introduced at a low price to induce as many consumers as possible to try it. A penetration strategy is usually coupled with the use of price deals and coupons, particularly for food products and toiletries. With a **skimming strategy,** the brand is introduced at a high price so as to maintain a select image and appeal to a smaller target segment. As competition intensifies, prices are slowly lowered.

Coca-Cola's successful introduction of Minute Maid Fruit Juice bars in 1986 illustrates the basic principles of brand establishment. The booming frozen fruit bar market was dominated at the time by Dole's Fruit 'N Juice bars and General Foods' JELL-O Pudding Pops. Coca-Cola began by purchasing a small company that produced fruit juice bars with a unique wrapper that avoided a drippy bar on a stick, then leveraged the Minute Maid name by putting it on the product. To establish a competitive advantage, the company decided to target the children's market, leaving the nutritionally oriented adult market to the leader, Dole. To build brand awareness and encourage consumers to try the new product, it launched a multimillion-dollar marketing campaign that included TV spots, 120 million coupons, and a special in-store freezer compartment promotion. Coca-Cola already had a 300-person Minute Maid salesforce, so distribution was no problem. A penetration strategy was chosen for the price: Its bar sold at an average price of 27 cents per portion compared to Dole's 43 cents.

The Growth Stage

A brand enters the growth stage when sales increases are sustained and the brand begins to become profitable. If it is an innovation, by this time it will have attracted competitors. When Minnetonka introduced the first liquid soap, 42 competitors appeared on the market after only one year.[31]

The main objective of the growth phase is **brand reinforcement**, that is, to reinforce the brand's position by getting consumers who have tried the brand to repurchase it, and by continuing to attract new users. If a substantial number of first-time purchasers do not rebuy, the brand will fail.

Marketing mix strategies during the growth stage are all aimed at maintaining and building upon the competitive advantages won during the introductory stage. The primary product objective is to maintain product quality, although if competition is intense, a company may have to add new features, improve packaging, or add services. The objective of distribution strategies is to solidify relations with distributors by continuing to offer trade discounts and allowances. At the same time, the company will seek additional outlets in areas where brand sales are weak. During this stage an attempt is made to maintain prices; occasionally, however, prices must be reduced due to competitive pressure, as in Minnetonka's case when it lowered its price as competitors entered the liquid soap market.

Whereas the promotional goal of the introductory stage was to create brand awareness and encourage users to try the product, the goal of the growth stage is to inform consumers about brand performance. Gallo reinforced its successful 1985 entry of Bartles and Jaymes wine cooler by allocating over $20 million to its advertising campaign, which featured two crafty old sidekicks named Frank Bartles and Ed Jaymes touting the product in a folksy manner. To further strengthen distribution for the brand, Gallo salespeople have been carrying video machines to show prospective retailers upcoming commercials of Bartles and Jaymes. Gallo's strategy has made Bartles and Jaymes the leading wine cooler, overtaking the original entrant, California Coolers.[32]

The Maturity Stage

During the maturity stage, sales begin to level off because of increasing competition. The brand attracts few new buyers; instead, it relies on repeat purchases to maintain its market position. Greater competitive intensity leads to more price competition, lower prices, and reduced operating margins. As a result, profits begin to decrease.

Few firms are content to remain in the mature phase of the life cycle and face decreasing profits. Most follow a strategy of **brand revitalization**, which can be approached three ways: (1) market expansion, (2) product modification, and (3) brand repositioning. A firm may follow one or all of these strategies.

Market expansion can mean finding new users for the brand, new uses of the brand, or getting existing users to use more of the brand. Thus, cereal companies attempt to attract new users for mature brands like Cheerios and Wheaties by advertising them to adults. And market leaders like Campbell Soup employ packaging innovations such as soup in single-serving pouches in an effort to get existing users to use more of their product.

Industrial products go through the same life cycle stages as do consumer products, and marketers may apply similar strategies. For instance, aluminum is in the mature phase of its life cycle, and some aluminum-producing companies are trying to find new uses for it. One such company, Alcan, has developed aluminum-powered batteries and is pushing for new uses such as aluminum rail coal cars, aluminum containers for microwave cooking, and aluminum-coated hard disk drives for computers.[33]

A strategy of *product modification* attempts to revitalize a product by changing it in some substantial way in order to increase demand. Miller beer is trying to stem the decrease in sales for Miller High Life by coming out with a *flanker brand*, High Life Genuine Draft, in the hope that draft beer will attract more beer drinkers to High Life. Although the original brand has not changed, the addition of draft beer is an important product modification in an attempt to revitalize High Life.

Brand repositioning requires changing the brand's appeal to attract new market segments. Repositioning a brand may or may not require modifying it. Campbell's V-8 juice has been stagnant for a number of years. The company is trying to revitalize it by appealing to a new segment, health-conscious consumers such as joggers, with the theme, "Things don't have to be hard on you to be good for you." It is also appealing to exercise-minded consumers with a tongue-in-cheek ad called the "Supermarket Shelf Stretch" showing consumers using a V-8 six-pack to exercise.[34]

Product Decline

The fourth product life cycle stage, decline, is characterized by decreasing sales and profits, and eventually by losses. Decline may be due to a variety of causes: technology making the brand obsolete, lower-cost competitors undercutting the brand, changes in consumer preferences, or ineffective revitalization attempts. A company cannot sustain a brand in a declining phase for long. It must choose either of the two strategies outlined in Figure 11.5: brand harvesting, with a likelihood of eventual elimination, or brand revival.

Brand Harvesting As we have seen, one of the product-line manager's most important responsibilities is to prune the line to eliminate unprofitable brands. Most companies do not give enough attention to brand-elimination decisions, and few brand managers get rewarded for eliminating brands. Companies prefer to add new products than eliminate unprofitable ones. Unprofitable brands are often carried for too long, creating a drag on profits and decreasing the cash available for pursuing new market opportunities.

Although some products are dropped abruptly, a company will often **harvest** a brand before eliminating it; that is, it will decrease marketing expenditures to almost zero and allow the brand to continue on its own steam by relying on the purchases of loyal customers. This strategy might make the brand profitable on a much smaller sales base, and some brands have been harvested for years. For example, Lever Brothers has been harvesting its Lux Beauty Bar since it stopped advertising the brand in 1970, yet Lux is generally available because it is distributed with other Lever toiletry products. Without advertising, Lux's profit margin is 5 percent greater than most other soaps. This situation will not continue indefinitely, however, for Lux's loyal consumer base is literally dying out. Once the brand begins to lose money, it will then be eliminated.

Brand Revival In some cases, brands that are being harvested or have been eliminated are brought back to life on the strength of their names (**brand revival**). Managers realize it is much cheaper to resurrect a brand name than to create a new one. Although a resurrected brand usually has no competitive advantage other than its name, that one advantage may be significant in a mature market where few brands are in a unique position.

For instance, Beecham is reviving Geritol, the iron and vitamin supplement for older consumers, by advertising it as "the brand for amorous middle-aged people, not the Lawrence Welk generation."[35]

Old names can also be leveraged and used on new products. For example, Barbasol, originally a shaving cream in a jar, was brought back as an aerosol foam shave cream. It soon achieved the number-one spot in the category.

The product life cycle is a useful tool in suggesting strategies over the life of a brand and in indicating when changes in strategies should take place. But brand sales do not necessarily follow the symmetrical curve in Figure 11.5. As a result, it is not always easy for a brand manager to determine a brand's position in the life cycle. Sales may rise during the introductory stage, for instance, and then suddenly drop off. In this case, reliance on the life cycle concept would have led the brand manager to mistakenly predict a growth phase, perhaps allocating more money to advertising and distribution in the coming period.

LIMITATIONS OF THE PRODUCT LIFE CYCLE

Another complication is that the length of the life cycle may vary. It is very hard to predict how long it may take a brand to move from introduction to growth to maturity. New technologies may shorten a product's life cycle, much as the advent of the VCR shortened the life cycle of the videodisc. A successful strategy of revitalization may lengthen the maturity phase beyond what might have been predicted, and may even cause a product to go from growth to maturity back to growth.

Figure 11.6 illustrates some of the more common variations from the normal life cycle curve. The first curve shows a product that has a long introduction stage because it is adopted slowly by consumers. Home computers are an example of this type of product. The second curve illustrates products such as VCRs, which are rapidly adopted and have a shorter than expected introductory stage. The third curve is yet another deviation, a fad product with a rapid rise and a rapid decline. Coleco's Cabbage Patch dolls followed such a curve. Finally, the fourth

FIGURE 11.6
Variations from the Normal
Product Life Cycle Curve

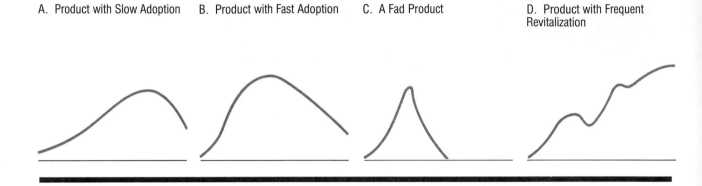

A. Product with Slow Adoption   B. Product with Fast Adoption   C. A Fad Product   D. Product with Frequent
                                                                                                    Revitalization

curve shows a product that has been frequently revitalized, going through periods of decline and subsequent growth. High-technology products such as semiconductors might follow such a life cycle.

In each of these cases, it is difficult for a brand manager to determine what stage the product is in and the appropriate strategic course based on its position in the life cycle. Thus, while principles derived from the life cycle provide useful guides for strategy, their application must be tempered by the particular nature and history of each brand.

SUMMARY

1. What is the role of the product manager in marketing a brand?
The product (or brand) manager is responsible for developing marketing strategies for a brand and for the brand's profit performance. Product managers collect all information that might affect brand performance, set goals for the brand, and plot marketing strategies to achieve these goals.

*2. What are the responsibilities of product managers for brands, product
     lines, and the company's overall product mix?*
Product managers develop strategies at three levels: for brands, product lines, and the firm's product mix. Brand managers are responsible for positioning the brand, identifying its target segments, and establishing it in the marketplace. Product-line managers are responsible for a group of brands in the same category. They coordinate the marketing strategies for the brands in the line, and decide on additions to and deletions from the line.

SBU or corporate managers are responsible for product-mix decisions that involve evaluating a firm's or business unit's overall product offerings. These managers evaluate the portfolio of product offerings and allocate resources to the firm's product lines.

*3. What important decisions must product managers make for brands and
     product lines?*

A brand represents the name and symbols associated with the product as well as the package in which it is purchased. In some cases, a warranty is given with the brand.

A firm must decide whether it will control its brands or produce for private branding to allow retailers to put their own name on the company's products and to market them. Managers must also decide on whether a brand will stand alone or will be part of a family of brands, and if it will bear a corporate name.

Managers also make product-line decisions. They must decide on the depth and breadth of the product line. In addition, they must determine brands to add to the line to provide more depth or breadth. They must be wary of cannibalization when making additions to the line, that is, taking sales away from existing products when adding a new brand with little net addition in sales. It is as important to delete unprofitable products as to add potentially profitable ones.

4. *What do we mean by a product's life cycle? How does this concept help managers develop brand and product line strategies?*

Most products pass through stages of introduction, growth, maturity, and decline. The product life cycle concept proposes that a manager can develop marketing strategies depending on where a brand or product is in its life cycle. Taking advertising strategy as an example, the introductory phase is marked by an objective of creating brand awareness, the growth phase by informing consumers of product benefits to gain a competitive advantage, the maturity phase by trying to differentiate the brand from competitors, and the decline phase by a cutback in advertising. Integrated strategies can be associated with each phase in the life cycle — brand establishment in the introductory phase, reinforcement in the growth phase, revitalization in the maturity phase, and either harvesting or revival in the decline phase.

KEY TERMS

Product management system (p. 294)
Product line (p. 295)
Product mix (p. 295)
Product-line manager (p. 295)
Category manager (p. 295)
Branded (p. 297)
Brand equity (p. 298)
Warranty (p. 300)
Brand image (p. 301)
Trademark (p. 302)
Manufacturer's brand (p. 303)
National/regional brands (p. 303)
Private brands (p. 304)
Battle of the brands (p. 304)
Generics (p. 305)
Price brands (p. 305)
Fighting brands (p. 305)
Individual brand name (p. 306)

Cannibalization (p. 306)
Corporate brand name (p. 306)
Product-line brand name (p. 306)
Corporate family name (p. 307)
Product-line depth (p. 307)
Product-line breadth (p. 308)
Line extensions (p. 308)
Brand leveraging (p. 309)
Line pruning (p. 310)
Line retrenchment (p. 311)
Product-mix consistency (p. 311)
Product life cycle (p. 312)
Brand establishment strategy (p. 313)
Penetration pricing strategy (p. 314)
Skimming pricing strategy (p. 314)
Brand reinforcement strategy (p. 315)
Brand revival strategy (p. 316)
Harvesting strategy (p. 317)

QUESTIONS

1. What is the product management system? Why was it developed?

2. The president of a large financial services company offering insurance, brokerage, and financial plan-

ning services does not believe in the product management system. He says:

> Brand managers are fine for firms producing
> packaged goods that spend millions advertising
> their brand name. But we do not build brand
> identification for our services; we build corporate
> identification. Without brands, what is the point
> of having brand managers?

   a. Is the brand or product management system ir-
       relevant if a firm advertises its corporate name
       rather than advertising individual brand
       names?
   b. Should a financial service firm use a product
       management system, even though it is selling
       services rather than products?

3. Why is creating a strong brand name such an essential ingredient of marketing strategy? Cite an example of a company that created a strong brand name.
   What were the key strategic elements in doing so?
4. Is there a danger that a company can be too successful in establishing a strong brand name? Explain.
5. When Coca-Cola brought back the original formula
   as Coca-Cola Classic, it was essentially admitting
   that brand image can be more important than taste
   in influencing consumer purchases of soft drinks.
   Explain why.
6. Most consumer-goods manufacturers produce national brands and frequently spend millions of dollars to establish a positive brand image. In view of

this, why would a firm manufacture products to be
sold by retailers or wholesalers as private brands or
generic products?

7. Why does Procter & Gamble follow an individual
   brand strategy, whereas Heinz and Reebok follow
   family brand strategies? What are the advantages
   and disadvantages of each approach?
8. What do we mean by cannibalizing a product? Why
   did General Foods introduce Maxim freeze-dried
   coffee when it knew the brand was likely to cannibalize its Maxwell House brand? When should a
   company forego introducing a new product because
   of projected cannibalization?
9. What do we mean by brand leveraging? Cite examples of successful and unsuccessful leveraging strategies. Why were these companies successful or unsuccessful in leveraging their brands?
10. Minute Maid juice bars were recently introduced by
    Coca-Cola. What changes in marketing objectives
    are likely to occur if the brand follows the life cycle
    curve in Figure 11.5? What changes are likely to
    occur in advertising strategy over the brand's life
    cycle?
11. What are the alternatives in revitalizing a brand in
    the mature stage of its life cycle? Are these alterna-
    tives mutually exclusive, or could a firm use all of
    them for the same brand?
12. What are the limitations of using the product life
    cycle concept to develop strategies for a brand? How
    should the product life cycle concept be used by a
    brand manager?

CASE 11.1

THE MATURING OF THE COOLER MARKET

Source: Alison Leigh Cowan, "A Weaker Market for Coolers," *The New York Times*, October 19, 1987, pp. D1, D10. Copyright 1987 by The New York Times Company. Reprinted by permission. Last paragraph from "Cooler Makers Retrench in Face of Sobering Future," *Adweek*, April 4, 1988, p. 6.

Wine and malt coolers, the fruit and alcohol concoctions that just a few years ago were hailed as the savior of the alcoholic beverage industry, have hit a plateau. It seems that everyone has seen their advertising and tried them, but far fewer people are drinking them than the industry had predicted.

Ever since the 1981 introduction and subsequent success of California Cooler, the first such product packaged and marketed like soft drinks, many industry experts have predicted that coolers would help the entire alcoholic beverage industry, which was plagued by declining consumption and stiffer regulation. These experts figured that the coolers would appeal to people who had shunned alcoholic beverages, and that from coolers they would graduate to more expensive wines and hard liquor.

As many in the business have discovered, "that's proven to be a myth," said Carl Martignetti, co-owner of Martignetti Liquors, a large retail chain in Massachusetts.

John Bissell, the executive in charge of the Stroh Brewery Company's White Mountain malt cooler, is equally concerned. "I think we're seeing the first signs of the category's maturing," he said.

The signs of trouble became painfully clear this summer, the peak season for coolers. Sales were lower than expected, causing many consultants to reduce their projections for the year. Consumption is slowing at a time when cooler makers are pouring vast sums into promotion — suggesting that profit margins are slim to nonexistent. More dollars are spent per case on advertising coolers than on any other alcoholic drink.

Last year the industry spent $150 million on advertising, or an average of $2.16 per case. By comparison, $1.55 was spent on advertising each case of distilled spirits, 58 cents on wine and 36 cents on beer.

With sales so disappointing, cooler makers are finding it increasingly difficult to persuade distributors, liquor stores and restaurant proprietors — who have already been dissatisfied with profit margins on coolers — to carry their products.

One big problem amid all the competition is to distinguish one's product. "They're all about the same proof, the same price, and they all look alike," Mr. Martignetti, the liquor store chain owner, said.

When one competitor adds a frill, the others copy it. For instance, word in the industry has it that Gallo is working on a berry flavor to compete with Seagram's and that California Cooler, which has made a pulpy drink until now, is coming out with a clear product more in line with Seagram's.

As if the competitive scene were not grim enough, another big company recently joined the fray: the Miller Brewing Company, which just introduced a malt cooler, which uses beer instead of wine, called Matilda Bay.

That expensive move has some people scratching their heads because it's an unusual time to introduce a new cooler.

The fate of the cooler market is likely to be played out by the end of this summer (1988). Price discounting and a retrenchment in advertising and promotion budgets will force the industry into a classic profit squeeze, and it seems inevitable that at least one or more of the major brands eventually will drop out of the market.

1. What evidence is there, other than stagnant sales, that wine coolers are in the mature phase of their life cycle?
2. What can manufacturers do to revitalize sales?
3. What types of product-line strategies might you suggest for wine coolers based on the alternatives in Figure 11.3?

CASE 11.2

LEVERAGING ARM & HAMMER'S NAME

Source: Ronald Alsop, "Arm & Hammer Baking Soda Going in Toothpaste as Well as Refrigerator," *The Wall Street Journal,* June 24, 1988, p. 24.

People have brushed their teeth with Arm & Hammer baking soda for more than 100 years, but it has never mattered much to toothpaste marketers Colgate-Palmolive Co. and Procter & Gamble Co. Now Arm & Hammer hopes to become more of a threat.

This summer, Church & Dwight Co. will take on the two toothpaste powers when it rolls out nationally its Arm & Hammer Dental Care toothpaste and tooth powder with baking soda. To introduce the products, Church & Dwight plans an $8 million television advertising campaign.

Arm & Hammer toothpaste and powder have an edge over most new products because they start with a small, built-in market of loyal baking soda brushers. Even so, they won't find the going easy against Colgate and P&G, which control more than 70% of the $1.3 billion toothpaste market and fight bitterly to maintain it.

Perhaps the toughest struggle of all will be in getting prominent display in stores. "Colgate and Procter's Crest own so much shelf space that it's extremely difficult for a new brand to penetrate the toothpaste category," says Richard Winger, a partner at Boston Consulting Group.

It won't be easy to motivate consumers to try Arm & Hammer either. "Toothpaste is a low-involvement category that people don't think much about," Mr. Winger says. "It's hard to come up with a convincing reason for them to switch brands."

The company really faces a challenge in clearing up people's perceptions of how bad a baking soda toothpaste might taste," says Jack Trout, president of Trout & Ries Inc., a marketing strategy firm. "I'm not sure you want to freshen your breath with the same stuff you use to freshen your refrigerator."

Church & Dwight believes line extensions like toothpaste are critical to Arm & Hammer's growth. It's the rare consumer today who uses baking soda for its original purpose, as a leavening agent. Recent TV commercials for plain baking soda tout its effectiveness, not for cooking, but for deodorizing refrigerators and freezers.

In addition to the toothpaste, the Arm & Hammer name has been tacked on a deodorizing spray and carpet freshener in recent years. While both of those are baking soda-based products, Church & Dwight also is marketing Arm & Hammer bleach and fabric-softener sheets, which don't contain baking soda.

Marketing experts warn that Arm & Hammer may be falling into the perilous line-extension trap. Sometimes companies put a well-known brand name on such a variety of products that its image becomes blurred and loses its marketing clout. "Arm & Hammer toothpaste isn't as much of a stretch as Adidas cologne, which calls to mind eau de sweat sock," Mr. Trout says. "But the more products (Church & Dwight) hangs the Arm & Hammer logo on, the more it destroys the original meaning of the brand."

Church & Dwight executives disagree with Mr. Trout's assessment. In fact, the company plans more personal-care products that, like the dental-care line, will carry the Arm & Hammer name.

1. What is the rationale for leveraging Arm & Hammer's name by extending the product line to include toothpaste?
2. In following its strategy, is Church & Dwight adding depth or breadth to the Arm & Hammer line? Why?
3. What are the risks of Church & Dwight's strategy for Arm & Hammer?

NOTES

1. "Reebok Responds to Nike," *Advertising Age,* February 20, 1989, p. 2.
2. "Reebok's New Models, Fully Loaded," *New York Times,* February 14, 1989, p. D1.
3. "Reeboks: How Far Can a Fad Run," *Business Week,* February 24, 1986, pp. 89–90.
4. "Setting the Pace," *Marketing & Media Decisions,* Winter 1986, p. 35.
5. *Reebok Annual Report,* 1986, p. 15.
6. *Advertising Age,* February 20, 1989, p. 2; and, "Nike is Bounding Past Reebok," *New York Times,* July 11, 1989, p. D1.
7. "The Marketing Revolution at Procter & Gamble," *Business Week,* July 25, 1988, pp. 72–76.
8. "Growing Pains–and Gains," *New York Magazine,* March 13, 1989, p. 22.

9. "Mitch Myers: Woman of the Year," *Adweek*, July 6, 1987, pp. W. R. 16–W. R. 17.

10. Ibid.

11. "What's in a Name," *Marketing & Media Decisions*, Spring 1982, pp. 149–155.

12. "What Is Your Brand Really Worth," *Adweek*, August 8, 1988, pp. 18–24.

13. "The Brands with the Billion-Dollar Names," *The New York Times*, October 28, 1988, pp. A1, D21.

14. "Maintaining a Balance of Planning," *Advertising Age*, May 17, 1982, p. M–21.

15. "The Selling of the Walkman," *Advertising Age*, March 12, 1982, p. M–37.

16. "Brewing Up a Name for Masters," *Sales & Marketing Management*, March 10, 1986, pp. 107–110.

17. "How Owens-Corning Turned a Commodity Into a Brand," *Management Review*, December 1986, pp. 11–12.

18. "Packages Bear Up Under a Bundle of Regulations," *Fortune*, May 7, 1979, p. 179.

19. "Chapstick 'Quenches' More Consumer Thirst," *Product Management*, July/August 1977, pp. 8–10, 12.

20. "New Coke Packaging Designed in Secret Marathon," *Marketing News*, October 11, 1985, pp. 1, 24.

21. "Appliance Companies Bolster Warranties to Tempt Shoppers," *The Wall Street Journal*, June 25, 1987, p. 27.

22. "Here's One Tough Cowboy," *Forbes*, February 9, 1987, p. 109.

23. *The New York Times*, October 28, 1988, p. A1.

24. "It's Slim Pickings in Product Name Game," *The Wall Street Journal*, November 29, 1988, p. B1.

25. "What's in a Name Brand?" *Money*, February 1974, p. 41; and "Fragmented Markets Complicate Setting New HBA Product Positions," *Product Marketing*, March 1981, p. 8.

26. "Paper Towel Battle: Generic Savings vs. Brand Quality," *The New York Times*, September 1, 1981, p. D4.

27. Brian F. Harris and Roger A. Strang, "Marketing Strategies in the Age of Generics," *Journal of Marketing*, Fall 1985, p. 74.

28. *New York Magazine*, March 13, 1989, p. 24.

29. "The Elephant Dances," *Forbes*, April 7, 1986, pp. 104–105.

30. "$22M Campaign Urges: Spritz Your Bic," *Advertising Age*, February 20, 1989, p. 3.

31. "Some Big Ideas from P&G . . . Is Liquid Soap Field Saturated?" *The Wall Street Journal*, June 18, 1981, p. 25.

32. "Another Coup for the Fighting Gallos," *The New York Times*, July 6, 1986, pp. 1, 22.

33. "Alcan Search: New Products," *The New York Times*, May 7, 1986, pp. D1, D6.

34. "Back to the Future," *Sales & Marketing Management*, November 1986, pp. 61–62.

35. "Giving Fading Brands a Second Chance," *The Wall Street Journal*, January 24, 1989, p. 21.

MERRILL LYNCH — IT'S BULLISH ON MARKETING FINANCIAL SERVICES

The year 1975 was a watershed for Merrill Lynch. For the first time, the company had to start thinking of marketing its financial services. Deregulation removed the Securities and Exchange Commission's gentlemanly restraints on competition among financial service businesses. Fixed commissions on stock sales were eliminated, ushering in discount brokers, who offered to sell stocks at substantially lower commission rates.

Suddenly Merrill Lynch was in a whole new ballgame, competing with discount brokers on one side and, eventually, with new giants in the brokerage business such as American Express, Sears Roebuck, and Prudential-Bache on the other. It was no longer enough to take orders for stocks and to offer financial advice, for in the new competitive environment, consumers were becoming increasingly sophisticated in selecting alternative investments, and competitors were offering more of these alternatives.

How did Merrill Lynch react? The only way it could — by beginning to market its financial services. First, in 1977 it developed one of the most creative financial services to date, the Cash Management Account (CMA), which permits consumers to invest in a wide array of financial instruments while providing checking, loan, and credit card privileges, all in one account. By 1986 Merrill Lynch had 1.2 million CMA customers with an average balance of $65,000.[1] CMAs gave the company $78 billion in assets to manage and entered it into the banking and credit card business in one stroke.

Merrill Lynch also reacted to deregulation by being the first brokerage house to mount a national advertising campaign with its now famous "We're Bullish on

MARKETING SERVICES BY PROFIT AND NONPROFIT FIRMS

America'' theme. The company's $45 million advertising campaign effectively tied together all its financial services under one symbol, the Merrill Lynch bull.[2]

With the CMA program in place and a highly successful advertising campaign, Merrill Lynch did not rest on its laurels. In the mid 1980s, realizing the need to develop services targeted to more specific market segments, such as the ''emerging investor'' segment of baby boomers, the company introduced the Capital Builder (a CMA with a lower cash requirement) and Sharebuilder (a plan allowing employees of a company to buy stocks by monthly dollar investments rather than by shares). These plans allowed younger consumers to begin investing with Merrill Lynch and to move from emerging to established investors.

Merrill Lynch also followed Sears' lead in offering one-stop financial shopping, widening its services to include insurance, real estate sales, and mortgages under one roof.

If anything holds Merrill Lynch back in its quest to become the supreme marketer of financial services, it will be the necessity to reorient its over 10,000 sales representatives to being financial consultants rather than stockbrokers.[3] The stock market crash of 1987 hurt Merrill Lynch because its sales reps had continued to focus on stocks instead of broadly diversified portfolios: They had been selling a product instead of marketing financial services. And they still have a broker mentality that will be hard to change. Unless Merrill Lynch's sales reps develop a facility to identify investors' needs and to effectively manage their assets, it could be tough going for Merrill Lynch in the future. ■

● ● ●

THE IMPORTANCE OF SERVICES

Services are big business in today's economy — bigger business than products. By 1988, over two-thirds of our gross national product (GNP) was generated by services, with over 75 percent of American workers employed in service industries. Today, consumers spend more on services than on products.

THE EMERGENCE OF A SERVICE ECONOMY

After World War II, services accounted for about one-third of our GNP and products two-thirds. It is startling to realize that in about 40 years, these proportions have been reversed.

Why have we become a service economy? The main reason has to do with demographic changes such as those mentioned in Chapter 3 — increasing proportions of working women, single-person households, and senior citizens, and greater affluence because of more dual-income households.

Of these trends, the increase in working women has been the most significant. The massive time crunch suffered by most dual-income families, with less time at home to cook, to clean house, and to take care of children — has compelled many families to pay to have someone else take care of their needs, with the result that fast-food establishments, laundries, child-care centers, and catalog shopping services are booming.

Smaller families, more singles, and more dual-income households have also created the affluence that allows consumers to purchase more services. Just as the demand for personal services from lawn care to beauty care to car care to child care has increased, so have expenditures for services such as travel and entertainment.[4] More Americans are in hotels, in restaurants, on the road, and in the air than ever before.

There has also been an explosion in health care and fitness services fueled by the increasing longevity and greater health-consciousness of Americans. Exercise and fitness centers are now a part of the American landscape; and health maintenance organizations (HMOs) have been established on a nationwide basis to provide more comprehensive medical services at reasonable costs.

American consumers are also spending more on financial services than ever before. Increased affluence has spawned a giant industry offering a host of investment alternatives and another industry of financial advisors to help investors select the right alternatives.

In addition to these trends, still another factor operating to make America a service economy is foreign competition, which has flooded American markets with goods that are cheaper and often of higher quality than homemade products. For example, intense Japanese competition has driven General Electric out of manufacturing televisions and small appliances and into service and technology businesses such as insurance and factory automation. Our trade deficits are a stark reminder of how effective foreign competitors have been in reducing America's manufacturing base. They are also a big reason why companies such as GE are finding it more profitable to sell services than products.

With the emergence of a service economy, it has become increasingly important for service firms to develop a marketing orientation. We saw this is true for Merrill Lynch; it is equally true for many other service companies. Hotel chains such as Holiday Inns, Hyatt, and Marriott, for instance, are targeting specific income segments by expanding their offerings to include luxury, medium-priced, and budget-oriented facilities. Hospitals are beginning to advertise to consumers for the first time; and they are also redesigning drab facilities to meet consumer needs. Professionals such as lawyers, accountants, dentists, and doctors are also beginning to advertise their services. And nonprofit organizations such as universities, charitable organizations, and museums are beginning to recognize that they must gear their services to customer needs to survive.

DEVELOPING A MARKETING ORIENTATION FOR SERVICES

The Slow Emergence of a Marketing Orientation

This attention to marketing is relatively recent for the service sector of the economy. Before deregulation, it was less important. Banks and brokerage houses, for example, were protected from competition by firms outside the "exclusive club." The idea of competing with discount brokers or paying interest rates on checking accounts was unthinkable. As a result, financial institutions could offer their services to customers on a take-it-or-leave-it basis. This was demonstrated as recently as 1983, when Citicorp (one of the more astute marketers in the banking industry) forced customers with average balances of less than $5,000 to use automatic teller machines (ATMs). The hue and cry from disgruntled customers forced Citicorp to rescind the requirement.

Another reason why service firms have traditionally been less marketing-oriented is that services are more differentiated than products. Manufacturing firms produce similar products that compete directly and must therefore be marketed more aggressively. Services such as financial counseling, hospital care, lodging, or education to some extent sell themselves.

Also, services are produced and delivered for the most part by people — bank tellers, hotel clerks, waiters, baggage handlers — who may not be highly motivated to provide quality service. The quality of a product can be controlled more easily than the quality of services provided.

EXHIBIT 12.1
Advertising a Medical Service

The Current Emergence of Service Marketing

Usually it is some change in the environment that makes service managers more aware of the importance of marketing. We noted that changes in demographics revealed to marketers consumers' need for time-saving services. The result was a boom in personal services.

Legal and regulatory changes have created more competition for services and resulted in a greater marketing orientation. It took deregulation to get Merrill Lynch to accept the idea of price competition. It took restraints on Medicare and Medicaid payments, as well as many empty beds, to make hospitals realize that they had to attract potential patients. It took the removal of restraints on advertising by lawyers to make staid and conservative law firms begin advertising their services to attract clients.

Humana Inc. is a good example of a service firm that moved quickly to become customer-driven. In the mid 1980s, the Louisville-based multi-hospital company (with more than 80 hospitals in over 50 cities) realized that it could not continue to absorb the costs of having one-third of its beds unoccupied.[5] The clampdown on health-care spending by both government and employers was starting to hurt, and Humana's management realized that it needed to begin relying on customer as well as physician preferences to define many of its facility and service offerings. As a result, it reorganized its marketing resources and hired an executive with over 12 years of experience in marketing at Ralston Purina and Nabisco to head it.

Its marketing perspective led Humana to develop medical services such as freestanding primary care clinics, Humana Health Care Plans healthcare insurance packages, and individual hospital programs such as Humana DaySurgery, which provides quick outpatient surgical care.[6] Humana then embarked on a $20 million TV, print, and direct-mail advertising campaign in 1986 to make it a household word in medical care.[7] The company also began aggressively creating new products such as its Humana Seniors Association, Humana Gold Plus Plans, Medicare HMO, and Humana On Call. (See Humana's newest theme line, introduced in 1989, in Exhibit 12.1.)

Richard Braddock is the embodiment of the greater marketing orientation of financial service firms. A Dartmouth Phi Beta Kappa, he got his start as a product manager at General Foods handling products such as Shake 'n Bake, Good Seasons salad dressing, and Tang drinks. He joined Citicorp in the mid 1970s as part of the initial wave of marketing talent that the firm was hiring out of consumer packaged-goods firms.

Braddock rapidly moved up the Citicorp ladder from director of marketing for consumer products to director of all consumer banking services as a result of his marketing savvy. Under his direction, the number of Citibank Visa and Master Charge accounts jumped 3 million in one year (1984), and the credit card business became a profit center. As a result, net revenue for consumer services jumped by 30 percent.[8] Credit cards became the workhorse of the consumer products division, providing the means for advertising Citicorp's other financial services such as savings instruments, lines of credit, catalog shopping, and product discounts through the credit card mailer.

Braddock has also been pushing for a greater service orientation after he committed a classic blunder — forgetting about the consumer. He was the executive behind the policy of forcing customers with balances under $5,000 to use ATM machines. He admits "We shot ourselves in the foot."[9] Since then, Braddock has helped introduce a series of services more to the customer's liking, including no-frills, low-cost bank accounts, faster funds availability, simplified consumer accounts, and easier to read bank disclosure statements.[10]

Except for his one blunder, Braddock has been quick to recognize the importance of service delivery in bank marketing. Yet he also recognizes that Citicorp still has a long way to go in ensuring service reliability.[11] Among the future opportunities he sees, is the possibility of offering insurance and brokerage services if restraints on banks marketing such services are removed.

As Braddock sees it, consumers will be the final judge of which financial institutions do the best job in meeting their needs, and he is determined that Citicorp will be out in front of the pack. Marketing financial instruments to consumers may be more demanding than marketing Shake 'n Bake, but that is the reason Braddock made the switch from products to services. ■

THE NATURE OF SERVICES

We have just seen a few reasons why services have traditionally been less marketing-oriented than products. But even when a service firm is marketing-oriented, its strategies will differ from those of a consumer-goods firm. In order to understand these differences in marketing strategies, we must first understand the characteristics that distinguish services from products, and the different types of services that are offered.

CHARACTERISTICS OF SERVICES

Four elements distinguish services from products. They are more intangible, more variable, more perishable, and their production is often simultaneous with their consumption. As we will see, each of these characteristics creates more risks for the marketer, but also creates more opportunities.

Intangibility

A consumer can squeeze Charmin paper towels, pour a Diet Coke, and smell Aramis cologne. Products can be examined before purchase and compared to competitive offerings; and after purchase, consumers have something to show for the money they spent. But consumers cannot feel, see, or smell services before they are purchased; and although some services produce tangible results, such as a haircut or clean laundry, most do not.

This intangibility does not mean that consumers get less for their money when they buy a service compared to a product. Travel, entertainment, or financial services probably provide more important benefits than toothpaste, detergents, or packaged foods. However, intangibility makes it more difficult to communicate the benefits of what is being sold. Consider selling the security of life insurance (an intangible service) as opposed to the comfort of a car (a tangible product). There is also opportunity, however, for marketers to gain a competitive advantage by making their service more tangible to consumers than competitors' services. One way to do this is to link the service to a tangible symbol such as the Merill Lynch bull, or Prudential's rock (see Exhibit 12.2) so as to convey consumer benefits. (The bull is associated with financial success; the rock with stability.)

Another way to make a service more tangible is to focus on the people who provide it — because the service provider is more tangible than the service. Airline ads thus show competent pilots and courteous flight attendants, ads for health maintenance organizations show caring doctors, and bank advertising emphasizes the personal attention of its executives (e.g., "Your Anchor Banker," or "You've Got a Friend at Chase").

Variability

Because services rely primarily on people to provide them, they are much more variable than products. A shopper may find salespeople helpful and courteous on one trip and rude on another; a traveler may have a flawless flight on one occasion, but may lose her baggage the next time she flies the same airline. Such variability makes it a risky business to market services, because customers experiencing poor service delivery may not come back, and may tell others of their experiences.

Like intangibility, variability also provides an opportunity to gain a competitive edge. Consumers will try to minimize the risk of variable services by choosing the most reliable service providers. More standardization in service offerings helps create such reliability. Federal Express has become the leader in air package delivery in this way, launching its own airplane fleet and ensuring on-time delivery through its innovative hub-spoke concept in which all packages are routed to one location (Memphis) and then forwarded to their destination.

EXHIBIT 12.2
Creating Tangibility for
an Intangible Service

Another way to reduce variability is to switch service delivery from people to machines. Banks have reduced the variability of teller services by giving customers the option of using ATMs. Again, risk is involved, for consumers who like to ask questions and obtain advice tend to resist machine-delivered services. As we saw, Citicorp ran into trouble when it tried to force smaller depositors to use ATMs.

Perishability

A third distinction between services and products is perishability. If services are not consumed when offered, they immediately go to waste. An airline seat cannot be stored in inventory: if it is not filled, it is lost. The lawyer whose services are not being used cannot store them for use at some future time. Whereas shifts in demand for products can be accommodated through inventory control, services do not have the same flexibility to regulate supply to meet demand.

Perishability provides service marketers with a basis for competitive advantage if they can regulate supply or demand. On the supply side, marketers can try to cut back on facilities during slack periods. Thus, a restaurant might close off one of its rooms and hire fewer waiters when demand is low. In peak periods, marketers can try to increase capacity by using part-time employees or by letting customers perform certain services at a discount, such as pumping their own gas.

Service marketers can also use several strategies to regulate demand to avoid unsold capacity. Airlines, telephone companies, and utilities provide lower rates in off-peak periods to encourage greater use by consumers and higher rates during peak periods when demand might exceed available supply. Service companies also like to pre-sell services so they can more easily determine the facilities that will be used at a given time. That is why airlines stipulate that customers taking advantage of lower fares must buy their tickets in advance.

A failure to adequately manage supply and demand can cause a service firm to go out of business. This is what happened to the airline, People Express. The company overestimated demand and bought fifty Boeing 727 jets in 1985, then was unable to book enough passengers during the winter months, when only 50 percent of its seats were filled.[12] Because of People Express's low-fare policy, it had to fill a higher percentage of seats than its competitors to break even. As a result, the company reported a net loss of $27.5 million in 1985 and was eventually acquired.[13]

Simultaneous Production and Consumption

Unlike products, which are produced, sold, and then consumed, services are often sold first, then produced and consumed at the same time. A consumer paying school tuition, buying an airline or theater ticket, or giving a lawyer a retainer for services to be delivered will consume these services at some future time as they are being produced.

Like the other characteristics of services, simultaneous production and consumption creates both risk and opportunity. The risk is that the service being consumed might be provided by an unmotivated representative of the company, and the customer will be turned off and unlikely to repeat the purchase.

As we saw, one solution is to avoid human contact by using machines in service delivery. But most services must rely on people, so other ways to improve service delivery must be employed. When American Express found its performance in processing new charge cards and replacing old ones was poor, it responded by developing specific performance criteria for processing cards, ranging from simple courtesy requirements to more complex criteria for financial approval. As a result, it reduced the time to replace lost cards from an average of two weeks to two days. Speeding up replacements resulted in consumer good will — and $2.4 million in added revenue.[14]

CLASSIFYING SERVICES

The risks and opportunities we have been discussing vary according to the type of service being offered. Therefore, it is important to categorize services to understand strategy development. Figure 12.1 presents a classification of services and

FIGURE 12.1
A Classification of Services

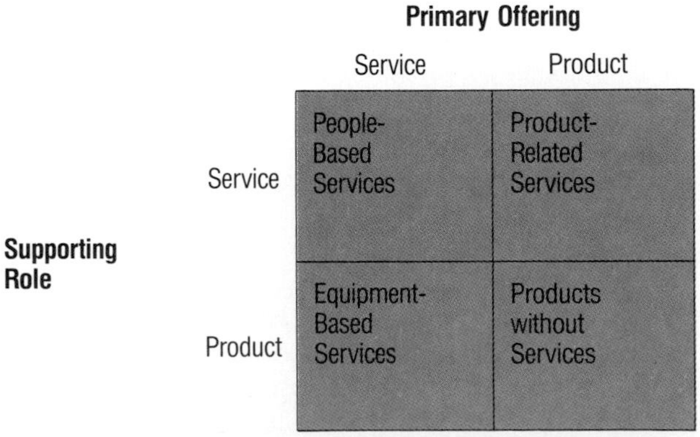

Primary Offering / Service / Product / Supporting Role / Service / Product / People-Based Services / Product-Related Services / Equipment-Based Services / Products without Services

products. Note that the classification in the figure depends on whether the product or service is the primary offering or is in a supportive role.

Although we have discussed services as primary offerings, services can also play a supporting role to products (as is indicated in the **product-related services** category in the upper right-hand box in Figure 12.1). For instance, warranties provide post-sale service support to purchasers of automobiles or appliances. Such service support is sometimes the determining factor in a product's success. Domino has become the leading pizza chain in the country because it provides home delivery within 30 minutes (and a free pizza if delivery takes more than 45 minutes). In contrast, Olivetti failed to crack the U.S. office equipment market, despite a superior product, because of poor service reliability.[15]

In the case where the service is the primary offering, products play a supportive role if they are needed to deliver a service (as in the lower left portion of the figure). Thus, planes provide travel service; telephone switching equipment provides telecommunications services; and ATMs provide bank services. These services are **equipment-based** in contrast to **people-based** services, which do not require products for their delivery, such as child care or legal counseling (upper left portion of the figure).

Services, as well as products, require an organizational framework to market them. In the last chapter, we saw that the organizational framework for products was the product or brand management system. The organizational framework for service firms is a **service management system**. It is similar to the product management system in that it is run by a **service manager** who develops marketing strategies and has profit responsibility for service performance.

The service manager's responsibility is to identify target segments for services and develop advertising, personal selling, and pricing strategies to deliver these services. As we saw, many services require both physical installations and personnel. For instance, when we fly on an airplane, we use the airline's physical facilities (airplanes, airport lounges, and baggage conveyors); but we also interact with the flight attendants and ticketers, as well as relying on the skill of the pilots, flight engineers, and baggage handlers. The service manager is responsible for ensuring the quality and reliability of the physical facilities and service personnel. This dual responsibility is critical since consumers evaluate both the facilities and the personnel in selecting services.

Of equal importance to ensuring service delivery, the service manager must also obtain feedback from customers regarding the adequacy of these services. Many service firms have established a customer service division within the marketing department for this purpose. As we saw, American Express established such a division to speed replacement of lost credit cards.

THE SERVICE MANAGEMENT SYSTEM

FIGURE 12.2
Marketing Planning for Services

Identify Service Opportunities

Define Target Market

Position Service

Develop Service Marketing Mix

Evaluate and Control Service Performance

DEVELOPING SERVICE MARKETING STRATEGIES

Service managers must develop strategies for their services based on a marketing plan. The marketing planning process is essentially the same as that described in Chapter 8 for products. (See Figure 12.2.) As with products, the service manager must first identify opportunities for a service, define the market segment the service will be targeted to, position the service to meet the needs of the target segment, develop a marketing mix for the service, and evaluate and control service performance. This section considers each of these steps.

IDENTIFYING MARKETING OPPORTUNITIES

The first step in developing service marketing strategies is to identify opportunities, which requires monitoring customers, competition, and the broader marketing environment. When Merrill Lynch developed the cash management account (CMA), it identified an important need for one-stop servicing of financial accounts. Seeing that no one else was offering consolidated financial management, Merrill Lynch successfully stepped into the strategic window of opportunity.

The company obtained an important competitive advantage as the innovator of the CMA because it recognized several converging environmental trends. More baby boomers meant more sophisticated investors seeking multiple financial options; more dual-earning households meant greater affluence; and more working women meant less time to devote to juggling several financial accounts. These demographic trends spelled the need for more flexibility and simplicity in financial management, and the CMA was the answer.

In this case, identifying a service opportunity led to developing a new service. Sometimes it leads instead to revitalizing an existing one. An example is Republic Health Corp., which manages 90 hospitals and medical facilities. Like Humana Inc., Republic was threatened by a clampdown on health-care spending by government and business institutions that resulted in unfilled beds. It responded by becoming the Procter & Gamble of hospital companies: It developed a series of promotional packages for the various services offered by its hospitals. For example, "Gift of Sight" advertised its cataract surgery and "Miracle Moments" its childbirth facilities. Republic Health did not develop any new services; instead, it repackaged existing services by giving them brand names and advertising them with a $20 million campaign featuring print ads in magazines such as *Cosmopolitan* and *Playboy*.[16] The campaign was successful in increasing utilization of its facilities.

DEFINING MARKET SEGMENTS

A plan to develop new services or revitalize existing ones must define the target segments for these services. Although service firms have lagged behind product firms in recognizing the importance of market segmentation, some are beginning to catch up. For instance, when Holiday Corporation found that its mid-priced Holiday Inn hotels were caught in a squeeze between budget hotels and luxury chains, the company responded by expanding into the high- and low-priced ends of the market. On the high end, it developed Embassy Suites, a luxury hotel chain of multiple-room suites targeted mainly to upscale business travelers; and at the low end, it developed Hampton Inn hotels, a limited-service chain targeted to the value-conscious business or pleasure traveler, offering prices 25 percent to 30 percent below typical Holiday Inns.[17] For good measure, Holiday Corporation has also introduced Homewood Suites, a chain of hotels designed for guests usually staying five nights or more. (See Exhibit 12.3.)

POSITIONING SERVICES

Positioning a service is more difficult than positioning a product because of the need to communicate intangible benefits. Merrill Lynch adopted the symbol of the bull and the slogan "We're Bullish on America" to convey its optimism about the economy and to encourage consumers to invest through the company. But research showed that the theme was attracting the wrong kind of customer. It appealed to people who "flow with the crowd and prefer the conventional," whereas Merrill Lynch wanted to appeal to more affluent and innovative consumers who were willing to experiment with new investment services.[18] As a result, the company kept the symbol of the bull but changed its slogan to "A

Holiday Inn

Embassy Suites

Hampton Inn

breed apart." This repositioning effectively attracted the more entrepreneurial
investor the company was targeting.

The service manager must develop a marketing mix designed to deliver a service
to the target segment based on the same mix of elements as for a product —
namely, establishing brand identity, advertising the service to the target segment,
ensuring delivery (i.e., distribution), and setting a price.

DEVELOPING THE SERVICE MARKETING MIX

Brand Identity

Services have brand names just as products do. Frequently, services are identified
by the corporate name — for example, McDonald's and Pan Am. But separate
brand names are often developed for individual services, as when Merrill Lynch
established CMA as a trademarked logo for its cash management account, and
Holiday Corp. established three hotel chains with a brand identity distinct from
the corporate name.

Unlike products, however, brand identity for services cannot be associated
with a physical entity such as Pepsi-Cola's red, white, and blue circular logo on its
bottle and can. It is consequently all the more important for a company to establish brand names and symbols for its services, since such identification makes the
intangible service more tangible in the consumer's mind.

Advertising

The intangibility of services makes it more difficult to communicate their benefits
in advertising. One approach to solving this problem is to try to spell out the
service as clearly as possible through informative advertising. American Express
has used such an informational approach in advertising to baby boomers. Its
direct-mail campaign helps educate prospective investors about financial facts,
even sending consumers a wallet-sized card with practical information such as
tips on how to purchase insurance. The company is also running seminars for
working women on managing their finances.

Metropolitan Life initially took an informational approach in advertising its
health-care plans. This informational approach was beginning to encourage a
negative image of Metropolitan as a faceless entity, however, and company management decided it had carried the educational campaign far enough.[19] It decided
instead to use symbols as tangible manifestations of the service, selecting Snoopy

EXHIBIT 12.4
Symbol-Oriented Approach
to Service Advertising

and the Peanuts comic strip gang as its official representatives (see Exhibit 12.4). The Peanuts characters gave Metropolitan a friendly face. The campaign was effective in conveying an image of personal and reliable medical care.

Distribution

Since the delivery and consumption of services usually occur together, the channel of distribution for services is generally limited to a buyer and seller. Occasionally, however, intermediaries are needed. For example, a travel agent serves as an intermediary between the customer and the hotel or airline personnel that deliver the service.

Service firms can establish a competitive advantage through distribution strategies by providing more convenient access. Home delivery of pizza is one example. Another strategy is to provide more outlets. Thus, banks may increase their number of branches, and further extend the distribution of services by means of ATMs.

Providing many outlets to consumers is costly, however. To make this strategy more cost-effective, many service firms have developed one-stop service shopping. By concentrating several services in one location, service firms can decrease the cost and give the customer the convenience of broader facilities. The tradeoff is that often customers must travel a longer distance to reach the facility. Health maintenance organizations have followed this strategy. They provide a broad range of health services in one facility, thereby decreasing medical costs and providing the customer with more medical services, but at more remote locations.

Personal Selling

Since most services are produced and consumed simultaneously, the service provider is often both manufacturer and salesperson. This link between personal selling and service delivery means that the salesperson plays a more important role in service firms than in those producing products.

The point of contact between the service provider and the customer is, potentially, the weakest element in the service marketing mix. We have seen the variability in service quality caused by lack of motivation on the part of service providers. One of the service manager's most difficult tasks is to try to motivate salespeople to deliver better and more consistent service, to be sensitive to customers, to gain their trust, to determine how satisfied they were with service delivery, and in so doing to convey an impression of professional competence. Establishment of customer service departments with responsibility for motivating service salespeople and tracking customer satisfaction is a step in the right direction.

Pricing

The cost of a product to a consumer is its price. Consider, however, the diversity of terms used in referring to the price of services — college tuition, finance charges, insurance premiums, lawyer's fees.

Services can be priced on a *cost-plus* basis by determining service costs and adding a fixed margin, or they can be priced by a *target return* method that determines the price that will yield a targeted return on investment. Both methods may be difficult to apply for people-based services, since it is harder to establish the cost of a service delivered by a person than by a machine. As a result, many firms offering personal services use a **value basis** in setting prices by determining what the consumer is willing to pay. For example, an accountant may set the fees for preparing tax returns based on what individual customers are willing to pay for the service, rather than on actual costs of preparation.

Services are much more difficult to evaluate and control than products because of the variability in service performance. Although no simple prescriptions exist for improving a service manager's ability to evaluate and control services, two essential requirements are (1) to minimize performance variability by motivating service providers and (2) to obtain feedback from customers as to their satisfaction with the services provided.

A few strategies are useful in motivating service providers. One approach is to "sell" them on the importance to the firm of the services they provide. Management is essentially marketing the firm to its employees. American Express paved the way for improving its card-replacement services by educating service personnel on the importance of their function to customers and their strategic role in the company's overall efforts. Another strategy is to establish customer service divisions in which managers try to establish clear standards for performance, defining goals for service personnel and specifying the means to attain these goals.

Equally important is the need for systematic feedback from customers. Hotels, airlines, and other service establishments encourage customers to fill out questionnaires rating facilities and personnel. Larger firms also rely on national surveys to obtain more reliable and systematic information on the customer's image of the firm and reactions to its services.

MARKETING NONPROFIT SERVICES

Although this chapter has focused primarily on marketing services for a profit, services provided by nonprofit institutions also represent big business in our economy. Institutions such as colleges, museums, charitable organizations, cultural centers, and religious institutions are not necessarily motivated by profit-maximizing goals in providing services to the public. Few people realize that the nonprofit sector accounts for over 20 percent of economic activity in the United States. Charitable organizations alone account for over $30 billion in revenues.[20]

Nonprofit services are similar to services in the profit sector in that they are intangible, variable, immediately perishable, and are produced as they are consumed. As most students know, a class taught by an instructor (a service in the nonprofit sector) is difficult to evaluate objectively; can be highly variable from one week to the next; is perishable (that is, it is lost to students who do not show up); and is "consumed" by student as it is "produced" by the instructor.

Marketing nonprofit services is more difficult than marketing services in the profit sector. Before considering why, let us briefly consider the types of organizations offering nonprofit services, and the slow emergence of a marketing orientation in the nonprofit sector.

Types of Nonprofit Organizations

Different types of nonprofit organizations can be classified as follows:

- Cultural (for instance, museums, operas, and symphonies).

- Knowledge-oriented (colleges, schools, research organizations).

- Philanthropic (foundations, charities, welfare organizations).

- Social causes (environmental, consumerist, feminist groups).
- Religious (churches and religious associations).
- Public (city, state, federal services; quasi-governmental services such as the U.S. Post Office and Amtrak).

Slow Emergence of a Marketing Orientation

Like firms delivering services for profit, nonprofit organizations have recently begun to realize that marketing can help them to influence their constituents. Nonprofit services at one time had an almost total lack of awareness of the benefits of marketing. Many were relatively unresponsive to client needs because their revenues were derived from contributions, endowments, and subsidies and were therefore not dependent on satisfying customers. This seeming independence from the consumer led many nonprofit organizations to place considerations such as adequacy of facilities or service delivery lower on their scale of priorities than they should have been. Museum managers, for example, would typically ignore lack of parking and long lines, assuming that art should be able to sell itself despite all obstacles.

This view has had to change in recent years. Rampant inflation in the late 1970s, the deep recession of the early 1980s, and cutbacks in grants by the Reagan administration intensified competition for funds and made the nonprofit sector aware of the need to use marketing techniques both to attract funds and sell their services. Colleges now use marketing to influence alumni to give donations, as well as to recruit students. Charitable organizations such as the Heart Fund and the American Cancer Society use national advertising campaigns to influence people to stop smoking. Government institutions such as the Department of Agriculture use marketing techniques to sell ideas such as improving children's eating habits.

Difficulties in Marketing Nonprofit Services

Developing marketing strategies for nonprofit services is particularly difficult because of several characteristics of such services. First, nonprofits market to **multiple publics** since they must attract resources from donors as well as allocate resources to clients. Marketing to donors is likely to be very different from marketing to clients. For example, the American Cancer Society uses direct mail to solicit contributions from donors, and then uses these funds to prepare antismoking commercials for the general public.

A second characteristic of nonprofits is the use of **multiple exchanges** of resources in dealing with donors and clients. A charitable organization such as Save the Children Foundation must deal with individuals, corporate contributors, and government agencies in trying to attract funds. It then allocates funds to projects ranging from basketball courts on Indian reservations to nutrition-training centers in the Dominican Republic. Similarly, a nonprofit hospital must be concerned with exchanges among financial contributors, physicians, nurses, drug and equipment suppliers, and patients. Exchanges for services tend to be simpler in the profit sector, usually occurring directly between consumer and service provider, occasionally with the help of an intermediary.

A third characteristic of nonprofit companies is that they are more likely to be influenced by government agencies, lobbyists, and other public agencies than are organizations with a profit goal. Such nonmarket pressures require many nonprofit firms to offer services to uneconomical segments: for example, the post office maintains rural services, and Amtrak provides services to thinly populated areas. Many rates charged by nonprofits are also subject to review by government agencies. Examples of this are postal rates, as well as fees for health services under Medicaid and Medicare.

Another reason why it is more difficult to market services in the nonprofit than in the profit sector is that many nonprofit firms are trying to change people's behavior by selling them ideas. Examples are influencing consumers to drive more slowly, to use mass transit, or to buy nonpolluting products. Such actions are beneficial to society, but represent either inconvenience or added cost to individual consumers. Trying to convince people of the dangers of smoking, drinking, or drugs is difficult because these actions are often habitual, and, as we saw in Chapter 5, a marketing strategy is more likely to be effective when it reinforces current behavior than when it attempts to change it.

Still another difficulty in marketing nonprofit services is that what they have to offer is often vaguer and less tangible than services for profit. The benefits of air travel, telecommunications, or bank services, are easier to convey than the benefits of religion, culture, or knowledge.

And finally, marketers of nonprofit services find it harder to control their resources than do marketers of services for profit. In many cases, nonprofit organizations must use the commercial air time that is contributed by media and thus have no say as to when their ads will be shown or heard.

Despite these difficulties, managers in nonprofit institutions have become increasingly adept at developing and implementing marketing strategies. The process of developing strategies in the nonprofit sector are the same as those for services in the profit sector — identifying opportunities, defining target segments, positioning the service, developing a marketing mix, and evaluating and controlling service delivery. We will briefly explore each of these.

DEVELOPING MARKETING STRATEGIES FOR NONPROFIT SERVICES

Identifying Opportunities for Nonprofit Services

A study conducted for the Kennedy Center, a cultural facility for music and drama in Washington, D.C., serves as a good example of identifying new opportunities to attract clients for nonprofit services. In trying to attract people who did not ordinarily attend its performances, the center interviewed a sample of residents of the greater Washington area. The survey found that non-attendees placed a higher priority on parking facilities and convenience than those who attended Kennedy Center events, and rated the center low on both criteria. The clear implication was that the Kennedy Center should advertise the adequacy of its parking facilities and the convenience of its location to public transportation.

The survey also found that those who did not attend the Kennedy Center enjoy dinner theater, country and western music, and pop music more than attendees. If the Kennedy Center changes its mix of entertainment to provide more of these types of shows, it might attract more customers.

Segmenting Markets for Nonprofit Services

Nonprofit firms must identify targets for their efforts, from the standpoint of identifying both donors and clients. Thus, colleges identify donor targets from their alumni list based on income, age, and past history of donations. The Department of the Army identifies its "clients" as potential recruits, specifically young people who want independence, the chance to mature, and the opportunity to

EXHIBIT 12.5
Positioning a Nonprofit
Service: The U.S. Army

travel.[21] Demographically, these individuals are most likely to be lower-middle-class males aged 17 to 21 who live at home. The army targeted a $30 million-plus advertising drive to this segment.

Positioning Nonprofit Services

The importance of positioning services in the nonprofit sector can be seen in the case of the Kennedy Center, which discovered, through research, that non-attendees were more likely to view it as overdone and stuffy. To dispel these notions, the center was repositioned as friendly and unimposing. Similarly, the U.S. Army positioned its advertising campaign to attract recruits with a basic appeal to self-enhancement in the theme, "Be All You Can Be." (See Exhibit 12.5.)

Marketing Mix for Nonprofit Services

Like other service firms, marketers of nonprofit services must develop a mix of brand, advertising, distribution, and pricing strategies to attract funds and deliver services to clients.

Brand Identity The U.S. Postal Service established Express Mail services after research showed that customers would be willing to pay a significant amount to guarantee overnight delivery. It established a brand identity for Express Mail through advertising to compete with air express services in the profit sector such as Federal Express and Purolator Courier. It succeeded in establishing an association between Express Mail and next-day service. (See Exhibit 12.6.)

EXHIBIT 12.6
Establishing Brand Identity

Advertising Advertising is used by nonprofit firms to influence both donors and clients. Direct-mail advertising is most frequently used to solicit contributions, and it is often effective. For instance, when the Light Opera Works of Evanston Illinois hired a direct-mail professional in an effort to raise crucial funds, the group raised enough money to continue its performances. The direct-mail campaign succeeded by expanding solicitations beyond the Opera Works' current subscription list, using appeals showing young singers in training.[22]

Advertising is also an effective means of encouraging people to use nonprofit services. Colleges, museums, opera companies, charities, and public institutions frequently advertise their services in newspapers, and on radio and TV. The creative use of advertising by nonprofit firms with limited budgets sometimes rivals that of larger profit-making firms. Consider the relatively low-budget campaign for the San Diego Zoo on its seventieth birthday in 1986. (See Exhibit 12.7.) The campaign helped increase attendance to over 3 million people a year.[23]

Even religious institutions are beginning to advertise. One ad shows Bubba Smith sitting under a tree, reading as Dick Butkus approaches. TV viewers might expect a Miller Lite ad coming up when they see these two burly former football players. But Butkus snatches the book from Bubba Smith and begins pouring through it with interest. It is the Bible.[24]

Distribution Unlike services for profit, distribution strategies for nonprofit services are usually directed to both donors and clients. Increasing the number of locations where donations can be made can stimulate contributions. That is why Salvation Army collectors solicit funds at so many locations between Thanksgiving and Christmas.

EXHIBIT 12.7
Advertising a Nonprofit Service:
The San Diego Zoo

Celebrate the San Diego Zoo's 70th birthday.

Increasing the number of service locations can also expand the use of nonprofit facilities. Thus, many health maintenance organizations (HMOs) are allowing people to use an expanded network of doctors. Similarly, colleges in cities have added branches in suburban areas to increase enrollment. Adelphi College in New York conducted courses on a commuter train at one time to try to gain a competitive advantage.

Personal Selling Since direct mail is effective in soliciting funds primarily from smaller contributors, nonprofit agencies use personal selling to attract funds from larger donors. The United Fund found that 1 percent of its contributors donated 10 percent of its funds.[25] When giving is so concentrated, direct contact is an effective means of fund raising. Stanford University, like many other educational institutions, uses personal solicitations to appeal to donors who have the potential to contribute large amounts.

Nonprofit organizations may also use personal selling to deliver their services. Outreach workers in social programs, family planners, and community organizers try to get individuals in need of social services to use them.

Pricing A major difference between profit and nonprofit services is that the former are priced to maximize profits, whereas the latter are priced at a "fair" level based on clients' needs and ability to pay. Most nonprofit firms do not expect to recoup costs. College tuition payments rarely cover costs, and social agencies often provide their services for free.

Nonprofit firms must also take account of the nonmonetary costs incurred by their clients. Health-care facilities should be aware of the costs of waiting time, inconvenience, discomfort, and insecurity involved in medical care. Minimizing such costs helps to attract more customers. Alcoholics Anonymous charges a very high nonmonetary cost for membership — public admission of being an alcoholic and commitment to refrain from drinking.

Evaluating and Controlling Nonprofit Services

Evaluating the performance of nonprofit institutions is both simpler and more complex than for profit-making organizations. It is simpler because it is relatively easy to track the effectiveness of a nonprofit organization's fund-raising efforts. Institutions such as the United Way can easily measure the number of new donors attracted yearly and the average amount of giving per donor. But the amount of resources a nonprofit organization attracts is only one dimension of performance. The difficult part is evaluating how these resources are used. The American Cancer Society might be effective in obtaining funds. But how effective is it in allocating these funds to activities such as research, patient care, and education?

Similarly, consider a college. Administrators might attempt to obtain feedback from students concerning many aspects of college service, from the quality of teachers to the adequacy of library, dorm, and computer facilities. But ultimately, such feedback provides only short-term answers. The real criterion of effectiveness for a college is how well it has performed in equipping its students to be successful in society, whatever path they choose. But this kind of measure is highly difficult to obtain, given the diverse factors that affect individual success.

Nonprofit organizations also face the same problems as the profit sector in controlling performance: Management must motivate personnel to provide services in a customer-oriented fashion. Presumably, employees in nonprofit firms are motivated by the altruism of working for worthy causes such as fighting cancer, protecting the environment, or improving minority education, not by the pay, which is much lower than in the profit sector. But judging by the low level of performance in many public and private agencies, such altruism does not always result in effective service delivery. Nonprofit firms need to institute the same types of educational programs as in the profit sector to motivate employees to provide services effectively.

SUMMARY

1. Why have services become a major part of our economy?

Basic demographic changes have propelled services to the forefront of our economy. First, the increase in the proportion of working women made time more valuable, then the greater affluence of dual-earning households made it possible to buy more personal services to alleviate the time crunch. More health-conscious and fitness-oriented lifestyles have also resulted in increased expenditures on services.

Foreign competitors have added to the emergence of a service economy by winning out over domestic manufacturers with superior goods at lower prices. As a result, many manufacturers have been forced to shift to service businesses to ensure growth.

2. *What are the differences between services and products? What are the strategic implications of these differences?*

Services are less tangible and more variable in quality than products. They are also more perishable because they cannot be stored. If they are not used when offered, they go to waste. Another difference between services and products is that services are usually consumed as they are produced.

These differences make the marketing of services more difficult than products. Managers try to overcome these difficulties by employing various strategies. They try to make their services (1) more tangible by associating them in the consumer's mind with physical objects or people; (2) less variable by using machines, where they can, to create standardization and by training their salespeople to provide better and more reliable service; and (3) less perishable by varying price to encourage use during off-peak periods.

3. *How do service firms develop marketing strategies for their offerings?*

Service firms develop marketing strategies in the same way firms producing products do. Service managers first identify an opportunity in the marketplace leading to the development of a new service or the revitalization of an existing service. Services are then targeted to defined segments and positioned to meet their needs. Service managers must then establish a marketing mix to deliver services to the target segment.

A service marketing mix will involve a plan to (1) establish brand identity for the service, (2) distribute it by ensuring that it can be obtained conveniently, (3) communicate its benefits through advertising, and (4) price the service to provide an adequate return on investment. The final step in strategy development is to provide for evaluation and control. Such evaluation is more difficult for services than products given their variability and intangibility.

4. *What are the distinctions between marketing nonprofit services and marketing services at a profit?*

Nonprofit services are distinct from services in the profit sector in that they must attract resources from donors as well as allocate these resources to clients. The service manager must develop marketing strategies for these multiple publics. As a result, nonprofit agencies must establish multiple exchanges when they market to donors and clients. Resources must be donated to service organizations and then passed on to their clients, often through an intermediary. A third difference is that nonprofit firms are more likely to be influenced by nonmarket forces such as government agencies, lobbyists, and other public agencies.

5. *Why is it more difficult to market nonprofit services than services in the profit sector?*

There are a number of reasons why nonprofit service marketing is more difficult. First, many nonprofit agencies are trying to sell ideas and to change behavior. Second, nonprofit services are vaguer and less tangible than services in the profit sector. Third, nonprofit firms have less control over their resources and marketing strategies.

KEY TERMS

Product-related services (p. 332)
Equipment-based services (p. 333)
People-based services (p. 333)
Service management system (p. 333)
Service manager (p. 333)

Value-based pricing (p. 336)
Nonprofit services (p. 337)
Multiple publics (p. 338)
Multiple exchanges (p. 338)

QUESTIONS

1. If service marketing is different from product marketing, why have financial service firms such as Citicorp hired product managers from consumer packaged-goods firms such as Procter & Gamble and General Foods?

2. One service industry manager said, "In service industries, people just aren't oriented to marketing." Why have most service firms lagged behind manufacturers of products in developing a marketing orientation?

3. Assume a life insurance company has developed a new life insurance plan targeted to working women to make benefits more comparable to those for men. It is concerned about the difficulties of communicating intangible benefits such as security, protection, and peace of mind. What strategies can the company develop to communicate these intangible benefits?

4. One airline executive in the business since right after World War II reflected on the variability in airline services as follows:

   I'm tired of hearing how variable services are compared to products. Yes, we have had delays, bumped passengers, lost baggage, and even had discourteous flight attendants at times. But these things are the exception, not the rule. Airline service is a lot better than when I got started in this business. And, I think it is less variable than some products. Personally, I think there is more variability in the cars I buy than in the service we provide. Overall, I think our customers understand some degree of variability in service is inevitable, and are willing to accept it.

   a. Do you agree with this executive's position? Why or why not?
   b. Are there any risks in a service company assuming that "customers understand some degree of variability in service is inevitable and are willing to accept it?"

5. A fast-food chain finds significant variability in service, particularly in several locations where customer complaints are frequent. The company fears if it does not decrease the variability of its service, it will begin to lose customers to competition. What strategies can it develop to reduce service variability?

6. A regional airline finds it is overbooked during peak periods and has significant excess capacity during slack periods. It is trying to compete with larger airlines on its routes by offering better service and price. It recognizes the inherent problems of service perishability in transportation.

   a. What strategies can it develop to try to manage supply and demand?
   b. How would these strategies put the company in a better competitive position?

7. What are the marketing responsibilities of the service manager in the service management system?

8. In what way did Merrill Lynch's introduction of the cash management account fill an important gap in customer needs for financial services? What demographic trends identified an opportunity for introducing this service?

9. Some marketers feel that establishing brand identity for services is more important than for products.

   a. Do you agree? Why or why not?
   b. What are some examples of services that have established brand identity? Has the brand name or symbol helped market the service?

10. What service distribution strategies can be developed to give a firm a competitive advantage?

11. The director of marketing at a large cultural institution has felt frustrated in trying to influence top management to use more constructive pricing and promotional strategies to market musical and theatrical events. She says, "I am beginning to think that top management feels there is no reason to be marketing-oriented because they are used to being in a sellers' market. But that may change, forcing them to take a closer look at marketing techniques."

    a. What factors are likely to cause nonprofit organizations to be more marketing-oriented?
    b. What factors have caused management in nonprofit firms to resist the use of marketing techniques?

12. A marketing manager who moved from a large consumer packaged-goods company to head the marketing effort for a large philanthropic agency said, "My former job was a piece of cake compared to this one. Not only is marketing more complicated here; it's less controllable." Explain what characteristics of nonprofit services make it more difficult to formulate strategies and make these strategies less controllable.

13. How do distribution and advertising strategies differ in attracting donors versus attracting clients for non-profit services?
14. Evaluate your college as a provider of a nonprofit service.

a. Is it effective in communicating its programs and facilities to prospective students?
b. Overall, is your college marketing-oriented? Why or why not?

CASE 12.1

BANK ONE BANKS ON SOME RETAILING EXPERTISE

Source: Steve Weiner. "Banks Hire Retailing Consultants for Help in Becoming Financial Products 'Stores'", *The Wall Street Journal*, May 20, 1986, p. 31.

The Bank One branch here is trying to look more like a small shopping mall than a bank these days.

Gone are most of the tellers' windows and the rows of lending officers. In their place are several small boutiques: an insurance agency in one corner with a real estate office next to it, a travel agency and a discount stock brokerage in another. Across the room is the bank itself — three tellers, an automated-teller machine and a new-accounts desk, all clumped by the vault. Bright informational banners stand out against the decidedly high-tech decor.

Searching for new ways to attract customers, Bank One and a few other big financial institutions are trying to turn themselves into "money stores." They are hiring retailing consultants — people who usually work with department and specialty stores — to teach them how to package products, build exciting displays and induce people to buy their services.

"What we're doing now with financial-service centers is merchandising banks to the level of the Neiman-Marcuses, the Bonwit Tellers and the Bergdorf Goodmans," says George R. Frerichs, a Chicago consultant who is working with half dozen banks.

Ripe for Change

Most bankers agree the industry is ripe for change. Despite deregulation and years of talk about marketing tactics, most banks haven't changed much since the Depression. They still have tellers lined up on one side of the lobby, officers lined up on the other and little salesmanship in between. Meanwhile, Juggernauts like Sears, Roebuck & Co., with its Dean Witter Financial Group unit, and Merrill Lynch & Co. are grabbing deposits by the billions through aggressive selling.

"This is a survival issue," says John F. Fisher, senior vice president of Banc One Corp., Bank One's parent company. "Our old branches don't work for what we need them for today. We must learn to compete with Sears and K mart (which offers banking at some stores) in all the things they do."

Bank One, despite its "store" approach, hasn't fully adopted retailing techniques (the travel agent isn't permitted to hang colorful posters, and city rules blocked plans to outline the automated-teller machines in neon). But it has gone further than most. The doorway to the Upper Arlington branch is a dramatic, arched canopy that makes it look like a retail shop. Bank One plans to equip yet another branch with additional "stores" for tax preparers, financial consultants and lawyers.

Leslie Wexner, a director of Bank One and the chairman of the clothing chain Limited Inc., has even proposed turning the bank's main branch in Columbus into a glittering, two-story showcase. To create visual excitement, he wants to install the whirring machines that count coins and sort checks in the front window. John B. McCoy, the parent's president, says the Wexner plan may be adopted.

Are the changes doing any good? At Bank One, deposits are up 15%, to about $70 million, since the renovation was completed in November. The travel agent says she hasn't done badly, with as many as 50 customers a week. And because the branch now offers brokerage services, Banc One's Mr. Fisher believes the bank has retained "dozens" of customers it might otherwise have lost. "I'd like to think there's some rub-off, some impulse business, just from having those extra things there," he says.

'Still a Bank'

However, few people have used the other services, which aren't affiliated with the bank. The insurance agent says that he's been busy on the phone, but that only five bank customers walked into his office and bought policies. The real estate agent has averaged only 10 walk-up customers a week. "It's not a store where I would go shopping," says Jenny McDaniel, a Bank One customer. "It's still a bank to me."

The retail consultants say banks aren't going far enough. They would make banks into marketing organizations that de-emphasize human tellers in favor of electronic transactions, then devote most of the floor space to selling real estate, travel packages and such financial products as loans, insurance and stocks.

The biggest stumbling block may be that such overhauls rub many bankers the wrong way. Some say retail techniques aren't suited to banks because their business requires long, private talks with customers. Others believe that people just won't make an impulse purchase of a financial product the way they might buy something in a department store.

Some bankers cite an even more fundamental problem. Most people, they say, don't like places that sell financial products, because thinking about their financial condition makes them uneasy.

Among bankers, the resistance is sometimes fierce. Robert J. Dorsey, a retailing consultant in Columbus, says one bank ordered him to stop halfway through a presentation on retailing ideas. Says Mr. Dorsey, "They couldn't cope."

1. What is the objective of Bank One's attempt to make its branches "look more like a small shopping mall"?
2. Will this strategy overcome some of the problems in marketing services? Why or why not?
3. Do you think attempting to create one-stop shopping for a variety of services is a sound strategy? Is it likely to help Bank One to deliver its services?

CASE 12.2

MARKETING HARVEY MUDD COLLEGE

Source: "College Recruiting Gets Fresh, Man." Reprinted with permission from *Advertising Age*, February 2, 1987. Copyright Crain Communications, Inc. All rights reserved.

Every college and university in America annually sends out promotional brochures, hoping the best and brightest and wealthiest high school seniors will give their campuses the once-over and perhaps enroll for the fall.

At best, most of that literature is interchangeable; at its worst it is horribly dull.

Students get something completely different from Harvey Mudd College, a small science and engineering school here.

For one thing, it's funny. The first piece to arrive is called the "Harvey Mudd College Junk Mail Premium Kit," an eight-page overview of the school that displays a sense of humor as well as the usual litany of campus advantages.

As soon as the prospective student opens the brochure, it's clear this is not your average college pitch: "What self-respecting institution of higher learning would pull a stunt like this? Probably one that's hurtin' for students, right?

"Wrong! We're Harvey Mudd College and we're not hurting for students, and our self-respect is in great shape. But because of the demanding, rigorous, difficult, intensive and highly charged* place we are, we try not to take ourselves too seriously . . . at least not all the time. [*We borrowed these adjectives from other college brochures]."

Harvey Mudd dean of admissions Duncan Murdoch, who developed the mailing four years ago, says he has simply borrowed techniques from consumer advertising and direct marketing and used them in an industry — college recruitment — that doesn't like to see itself as an industry.

His job, like Procter & Gamble's, is to cut through the clutter with his message.

Best of all, Mr. Murdoch says, the approach works (which has kept some of the faculty from demanding his head).

"With a name like Harvey Mudd College, you have to take some risks, and it helps if you have a little fun," Mr. Murdoch says.

Nearly a third of the 14,000 high school students receiving the mailer return the card, requesting more information. The percentage of Mudd students from outside California has risen to 55 percent from 40 percent before the humorous approach was tried.

This year, Mr. Murdoch has added a new wrinkle. If the "Junk Mail Premium Kit" doesn't get a response, the student gets a mailing announcing "You may already be an Instant Winner in the College and University Sweepstakes!"

Inside are six scratch-off dots and the promise of an instant prize and two bonuses if any three match.

Surprise! Three of the dots cover the name Harvey Mudd. Lurking under the others are competitors M.I.T., Caltech and Stanford (or Harvard in the East). The instant prize is a free Harvey Mudd catalog and application form. The bonuses are an admission interview and an overnight stay. With free meals!

"High school kids get deluged with entreaties from schools that come in nice, plain envelopes," Mr. Murdoch says. "Those sit on their desks. Ours get opened. And nobody, *nobody*, can resist scratching off those dots.

"We're saying, 'If you can't laugh, maybe you don't belong here.' It's a very tough school academically, and a sense of humor helps you get through."

And what if scratch cards don't get their attention?

The dean of admissions says: "I'm thinking of sending out campus photos during the coldest part of the winter. Maybe put some sand in the envelope."

1. Do you think Harvey Mudd College's promotional campaign is effective in overcoming some of the problems of marketing nonprofit services?
2. What other actions are required to effectively market an educational institution?
3. Would you respond to Harvey Mudd College's direct-mail brochure? Why or why not?

NOTES

1. *Merrill Lynch Annual Report,* 1986, p. 38.
2. "Shopping the Financial Supermarket," *Advertising Age,* September 26, 1987, p. M–32.
3. "The New Order at Merrill," *Institutional Investor,* January 1986, pp. 1–4.
4. "Presto! The Convenience Industry: Making Life a Little Simpler," *Business Week,* April 27, 1987, pp. 86–94.
5. "A High-Powered Pitch to Cure Hospitals' Ills," *Business Week,* September 2, 1985, p. 60.
6. "Healthy Competition: The Human Touch," *Marketing & Media Decisions,* April 1986, pp. 96–101.
7. "New Ad Campaign Prescribes Humana's Brand of Medicine," *The Wall Street Journal,* May 15, 1986, p. 31.
8. "Citibank's Braddock: 'Service' Now Key Tool," *Bank Marketing,* July 1985, pp. 42–43.
9. "Can the Performance Match the Promise?" *Forbes,* January 27, 1986, p. 87.
10. "Banks are Making a Vigorous Play to Satisfy Customers," *American Banker,* November 8, 1985, pp. 1, 39.
11. *Bank Marketing,* July 1985, p. 42.
12. "People Express Wants All the Frills It Can Get," *Business Week,* May 12, 1986, p. 31.
13. "People Express, in Major Strategy Shift, Will Seek to Attract Business Travelers," *The Wall Street Journal,* April 29, 1986.
14. "Boosting Productivity at American Express," *Business Week,* October 5, 1981, pp. 62, 66.
15. Melind M. Lele, "How Service Needs Influence Product Strategy," *Sloan Management Review,* Fall 1986, p. 63.
16. *Business Week,* September 2, 1985, p. 61.
17. "Holiday Inns Thinks Sinatra's a Winner," *Advertising Age,* June 1, 1987, p. 84.
18. "How Business Tunes into Living Trends to Sell Products," *The Christian Science Monitor,* April 22, 1983, p. 9.
19. "Insurers Writing New Healthcare Policy," *Advertising Age,* October 24, 1985, pp. 19–20.
20. Michael S. Joyce, "Grants and Philosophy: The Foundation Perspective" in *The 1978 Longwood Program,* vol. 10 (Newark, Del.: University of Delaware, 1978), p. 5.
21. William Lazer and James D. Culley, *Marketing Management* (Boston: Houghton-Mifflin, 1983), p. 836.
22. "Saving a Nonprofit Program," *Advertising Age,* April 9, 1984, p. M–36.
23. "Make My Day," *Creativity,* January 1988, p. 29.
24. "Advertisers Promote Religion in a Splashy and Secular Style," *The Wall Street Journal,* November 21, 1985, p. 33.
25. Benson P. Shapiro, "Marketing for Nonprofit Organizations," *Harvard Business Review* 51 (September–October 1973):123–132.

BENETTON — THE McDONALD'S OF FASHION

How does a company that was hardly on the map 20 years ago become clothier to the world? Through distribution. The company is Benetton, a name that has achieved worldwide recognition as a manufacturer and distributor of sweaters through a string of 5,000 franchised clothing outlets in 70 countries.[1]

Benetton established its global clout by borrowing a deceptively simple business principle from the Japanese. The principle, called *Kanban* (also known as just-in-time, or JIT) says that a company should produce only what consumers need, when they need it.[2] Until Benetton came along, sweaters were made from pre-dyed yarns. Luciano Benetton, founder of the company, developed a process of coloring sweaters after they are assembled, and determining the right colors based on orders from their retail outlets.

Kanban meant that Benetton could ship products directly to the retail stores that ordered them. The company did not have to keep large product inventories, since the products were pre-sold. Retailers did not have to stock large inventory either. Once the colored sweaters were received, they went right on the shelf and moved briskly off. The result was a highly profitable distribution channel that minimized inventory and warehousing costs and produced profits 30 per cent higher than the U.S. apparel industry average.[3]

With these profit margins, prospective retailers clamored to join Benetton's ranks. Once the *Kanban* system was in place, Benetton rapidly expanded its store outlets in Italy and then in France, adding an average of one new outlet

every working day by the late 1970s. When Benetton moved from Europe to America in 1982, its outlets grew so that by 1988 there were more than 750 stores distributed among all 50 states.[4] The Kelly-green Benetton logo on its storefronts was becoming as familiar as McDonald's golden arches.

To implement *Kanban,* Benetton had to control its distribution outlets. It did so through manufacturers' agents, independent operators who worked exclusively for Benetton to recruit and train retailers and to transmit orders directly to the factories. Retailers had to agree to carry only Benetton merchandise, adhering to suggested markups of about 80 percent over cost, ordering through Benetton's manufacturers' agents, and paying for their orders within 90 days.[5]

Benetton has come a long way from a one-store company in 1969. But growth has created some problems. Rising apparel prices, saturated markets, and shifting tastes in fashion have slowed growth.[6] Some of Benetton's retailers are even losing money, which they attribute to Benetton's opening too many stores too close together.

Still, Benetton remains optimistic as it continues to expand into far-flung markets including Japan, China, and Russia. Although trade restrictions in foreign countries and the vagaries of fashion are question marks for the future, the company's distribution strength is undeniable. Its Kelly-green storefronts are likely to be around as long as McDonald's golden arches. ■

● ● ●

THE IMPORTANCE OF DISTRIBUTION

The Benetton story shows that distribution is a key ingredient in a product's marketing mix, and that it can even be the determining factor in product success. Although Benetton had a $10 million worldwide advertising budget by 1987, advertising did not play a key part in establishing the company. Instead, consumer awareness was created by the presence of Benetton stores in every corner of Italy, and this awareness provided a solid base for global expansion.

If strong distribution was key to Benetton's success, weaknesses in distribution strategy can create handicaps that even a first-rate advertising campaign cannot overcome. When Philip Morris bought Seven-Up Co., it mounted what seemed to be a sure-fire advertising campaign that repositioned 7Up as the caffeine-free alternative to Pepsi and Coke. As we saw in Chapter 4, one reason why the brand failed to take off was because Coke and Pepsi quickly followed suit with their own caffeine-free alternatives. The major reason, however, was poor distribution: Philip Morris never established strong relationships with its bottlers.[7] (In soft drinks, bottlers are the key to distribution since they both bottle and distribute the product.) Philip Morris never gave its bottlers an incentive to push 7Up, and even a good promotional campaign could not rescue a brand that got fourth or fifth place on the supermarket shelf.

Both Benetton and 7Up show the importance of distribution, which is also reflected in its cost (averaging about 25 percent of the product's price).[8] Most manufacturers must use intermediaries, be they retailers, wholesalers, or manufacturers' agents, to ensure that the right product reaches consumers at the right place and at the right time.

This chapter and the next two explore the implementation of distribution systems. Our perspective in this chapter is primarily that of the manufacturer, whose goal is to distribute products to consumers in the most effective manner. Throughout these three chapters, it is important to remember that these distribution strategies must be integrated with other elements of the marketing mix — product, promotion, and price strategies.

FIGURE 13.1
Flows through the
Distribution Channel System

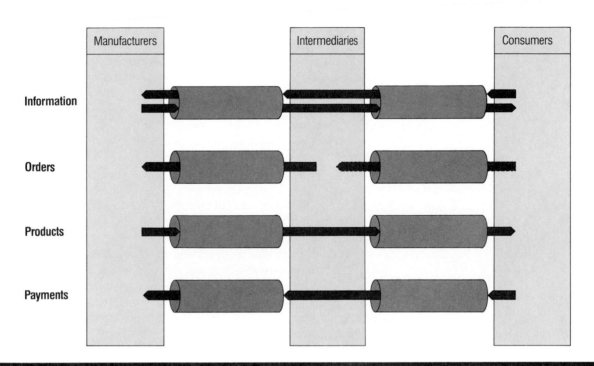

NATURE OF THE CHANNEL SYSTEM

The distribution process has been compared to a pipeline or channel because it represents a series of flows. As Figure 13.1 illustrates, information regarding consumer needs flows to manufacturers, passing through intermediaries on the way. It then flows from manufacturers back to consumers in the form of information on prices, product characteristics, and availability. As we saw, Benetton relies on retail orders to assess consumers' color preferences, and on advertising and store personnel to communicate information to consumers. There is also a flow of orders from intermediaries to manufacturers that reflects consumer needs. The flow of products goes from manufacturers through intermediaries to consumers, and a flow of payment goes from consumers through the channel back to manufacturers.

The distribution of information, orders, products, and payments requires co-operation between manufacturers, wholesalers, and retailers in order to work smoothly. These three parties work as a **channel** (or **distribution**) **system**, that is, a group of independent businesses composed of manufacturers, wholesalers, and retailers designed to deliver the right set of products to consumers at the right place and time. In the following paragraphs, we will look at the role played both by intermediaries and manufacturers within the channel system. First, however, it is important to understand exactly what intermediaries are.

TYPES OF INTERMEDIARIES

There are three general types of intermediaries in the channel system; retailers, wholesalers, and brokers and agents. **Retailers** are distinct from other intermediaries in that they sell to final consumers. As such, they are used by producers of consumer goods, not industrial goods. The importance of retailing is measured by the existence of over 2 million retail establishments in the United States, accounting for over $1 trillion in sales. These establishments range from large department stores such as Dayton Hudson, to supermarket chains such as Kroger, to general merchandisers such as Sears, to small specialty retailers and "mom and pop" food stores.

Wholesalers (also referred to as **distributors**) buy and resell merchandise to other wholesalers or to retailers. (Wholesalers of industrial products are usually called distributors.) Contrary to wholesalers of consumer goods, distributors sometimes sell directly to a buyer. They often specialize in a certain line of industrial goods, and have the sales staff and technical expertise to sell direct.

The third category of intermediaries, agents and brokers, differ from other intermediaries in that they do not take title to products. They provide an important facilitating function by bringing buyers and sellers together, charging a commission for this service.

Agents differ from brokers by serving as an extension of the manufacturer's marketing organization. There are two types: **Manufacturers' agents** sell a company's products in a specific geographic area, usually on an exclusive basis. They specialize in particular product lines and can also carry the products of noncompeting companies. They are used by industrial machinery and equipment producers, auto supply companies, computer firms, and occasionally consumer-goods producers. **Sales agents** go beyond manufacturers' agents in representing the company. They have more authority to set prices and terms of sale, and sometimes even assume the manufacturer's total marketing effort by setting promotional and distribution policy for the line. Sales agents are used by small firms that cannot afford a marketing or sales staff.

In contrast to agents, **brokers** serve solely to bring buyers and sellers together. They have no continuous relation with one seller. They inform sellers of possible buyers and negotiate transactions for a commission. Sellers who are not trying to sell a product or service on a year-around basis, and do not need a permanent sales staff use brokers. Real estate firms, insurance companies, and producers of seasonal items would fit this description. We will discuss these intermediaries further in Chapter 15.

FUNCTIONS OF INTERMEDIARIES

Although some manufacturers, such as Avon, sell directly to consumers, most sell through retailers, wholesalers, agents, or brokers, because these intermediaries provide important services that benefit both manufacturers and consumers through a more efficient exchange of goods.

How Intermediaries Benefit Manufacturers

Intermediaries usually perform three types of functions more efficiently than manufacturers: transactional, logistical, and facilitating functions. **Transactional functions** involve buying products and reselling them to customers, as well as incurring the risks of stocking these products in inventory. **Logistical functions** require assembling a variety of products, storing them, and providing them in smaller units to customers by sorting them out and putting them on the retail shelf. **Facilitating functions** involve obtaining information that manufacturers

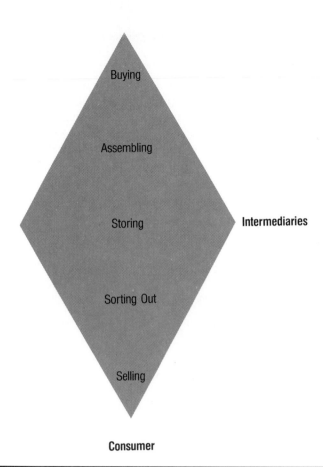

FIGURE 13.2
Transactional and Logistical
Functions of Intermediaries

Buying

Assembling

Storing   **Intermediaries**

Sorting Out

Selling

Consumer

need about market conditions, promoting products through in-store displays or local advertising to facilitate sales, and occasionally extending credit to customers.

The transactional and logistical functions performed by intermediaries are illustrated in Figure 13.2. Assume that J.C. Penney buys athletic shoes and sportswear from four manufacturers: Nike, Reebok, Adidas, and Converse. In so doing, it assembles a variety of different types of products — athletic shoes, jogging outfits, and other sportswear — and stores them in its warehouses. It then distributes them to its retail outlets, which sort out the various shoes by unpacking cartons and showing shoes and clothing samples on the retail floor. As a result of buying, assembling, storing, and sorting out, Penney has made a wide variety of athletic shoes and sportswear available to individual customers so they can buy one pair of shoes or one jogging outfit. In the process, it has also reduced the number of transactions required to buy and sell the manufacturers' products: With four manufacturers and four customers, eight buy-sell transactions are required. (See top of Figure 13.3.)

The bottom of Figure 13.3 shows what would happen without an intermediary. Each manufacturer would have to store its own products, then sort them out. Taking on the storing functions would substantially increase inventory costs, and the sorting functions would substantially increase transportation costs since items would have to be shipped as individual units to customers. Further, with

FIGURE 13.3
How Intermediaries Make
Exchange More Efficient

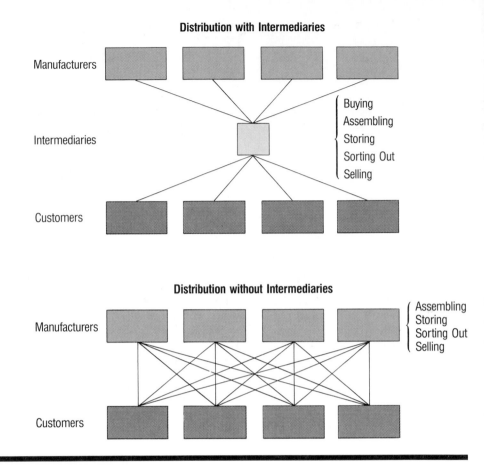

four customers, each manufacturer would have four sales transactions instead of
the one required if a retailer were used. The total number of transactions for the
four manufacturers would be sixteen instead of the eight required with an intermediary. If, as is more likely, there are 1,000 customers instead of four, each
company would have to complete 1,000 transactions to sell to each customer
instead of one shipment to Penney. The total number of transactions for the four
manufacturers would be 4,000 instead of the four required with Penney as an
intermediary.

How Intermediaries Benefit Consumers

Consumers also benefit from intermediaries. Distribution channels create possession, time, and place utility for consumers. **Possession utility** means providing
consumers with the right assortment of products. Benetton's retailers are the
vehicle for determining consumer preferences and allowing the company to make
the right products. **Time utility** means having the product when you want it. A
key ingredient in Benetton's success is the speed with which information on color
preferences reaches the factories, and the speed with which quick-dyed sweaters
are shipped to retail stores. **Place utility** means having the product available in
convenient locations. The number of Benetton outlets in Europe and the United
States gives the company a distinct competitive advantage over other clothing
manufacturers.

If intermediaries play an essential role in the channel system, so does the manufacturer. In some cases, this means selling directly to consumers and taking on the transactional, logistical, and facilitating functions necessary for distributing products and services. Such direct marketing is more prevalent for industrial than consumer goods since industrial markets are likely to have fewer buyers. As a result, there is less need for intermediaries to reduce the number of transactions. Further, the high cost and bulk of many industrial products makes it cheaper to sell them directly than through an intermediary.

Even when manufacturers do not distribute their own goods, they are likely to play an important role in channel coordination and management. Any distribution system needs a **channel leader** to coordinate the flow of information, product shipments, and payment. The largest and most powerful organization in the channel system usually takes on this role, and that is generally the manufacturer (although at times, a large retailer like Sears or wholesaler like McKesson is channel leader). The manufacturer also frequently provides managerial and financial assistance to its intermediaries. For instance, automobile companies often help finance dealers opening new outlets and extend credit to help them maintain an inventory of cars. Manufacturers may also provide dealers with managerial assistance in running their businesses, and may even extend cooperative advertising allowances to pay part of their local advertising costs.

FUNCTIONS OF MANUFACTURERS

SELECTING DISTRIBUTION SYSTEMS AND STRATEGIES

A key marketing decision, generally made by the manufacturer, is that of selecting a channel system to distribute the company's goods. Figure 13.4 presents the steps required in this decision process and serves as a model for the rest of this chapter. The first step requires the market organization to consider alternative forms of distribution and simultaneously evaluate the nature of the distribution environment. The marketer can then identify distribution objectives, determine the channels of distribution to be used, ensure the cooperation of the channel members, and develop distribution strategies to gain adequate coverage. The final step in the process is to evaluate the channel system and consider ways to improve it.

The first step in developing a distribution system is to identify alternative systems, which will vary depending on whether a consumer good, industrial good, or service is being distributed.

IDENTIFY ALTERNATIVE DISTRIBUTION SYSTEMS

Distribution Systems for Consumer Goods
Figure 13.5 shows the five most common types of distribution channels for consumer goods.

Direct Marketing to Consumers Some consumer-goods firms use **direct marketing** to sell products directly to consumers. Three methods are employed: door-to-door sales, company-owned retail stores, and catalogs.

Amway, with 750,000 sales representatives selling soap and related products, and Avon, with over 350,000 reps selling cosmetics, are by far the largest door-to-door sellers. Other companies that rely on door-to-door sales are Mary Kay Cosmetics, Fuller Brush, Electrolux vacuum cleaners, and Shaklee nutritional

FIGURE 13.4
The Process of Selecting Distribution
Systems and Strategies

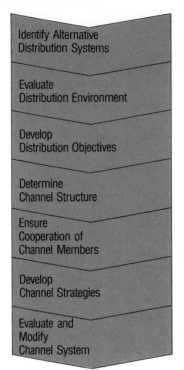

Identify Alternative
Distribution Systems

Evaluate
Distribution Environment

Develop
Distribution Objectives

Determine
Channel Structure

Ensure
Cooperation of
Channel Members

Develop
Channel Strategies

Evaluate and
Modify
Channel System

products. Tupperware sells its housewares directly by having its sales reps arrange Tupperware parties.

Some manufacturers have set up their own retail outlets to sell their goods directly to consumers. This way they bypass the cost of both wholesalers and independent retailers. This strategy is feasible, however, only if manufacturers can perform the wholesaler's and retailer's functions more economically. When IBM began introducing personal computers in 1980, it established two channels, large computer retailers such as Computerland and its own retail stores, called Product Centers. But the Product Centers were soon plagued with inefficient inventory control and high overhead, prompting IBM to conclude that it was more efficient to distribute through intermediaries rather than direct to consumers.[9]

A third means of direct marketing to consumers is through mail-order catalogs. Companies such as L.L. Bean, Fingerhut, Horchow, and the Sharper Image rely primarily on catalogs, whereas others, such as Avon, use them in addition to direct sales. The Sharper Image has been very successful in targeting its catalog to upscale professionals who have little time to shop for gifts or for themselves. More than 3 million people receive the catalog, offering everything from home fitness equipment to furs, every month.

Manufacturer to Retailer Most manufacturers do not market their own products directly to consumers but rely instead on intermediaries. One method, illustrated in the second channel system in Figure 13.5, is to bypass wholesalers and sell directly to retailers. Many larger manufacturers with their own sales staff sell directly to large retailers such as Kroger, K Mart, Sears, and Dayton Hudson. Manufacturers can sell economically to these retailers because they purchase large amounts and, as we noted, can sometimes perform the wholesaler's functions more economically.

Compaq's use of the manufacturer-to-retailer channel system has helped it establish a competitive advantage in the personal computer market by offering retailers a margin of 36 percent of sales, about 10 percent higher than average. It is also responsive to retailers, adding product features and adjusting inventory levels based on their feedback. As a result, Compaq has won the loyalty of computer retailers and is the only company other than IBM and Apple to win substantial shelf space in computer stores.[10]

When a large retailer like Sears is the channel leader, it will sometimes bypass wholesalers and buy directly from manufacturers, thus forming a manufacturer-to-retailer channel. There are several reasons why retailers bypass wholesalers. Like manufacturers, they may be able to perform the facilitating, transactional, and logistical functions more cheaply than wholesalers. In addition, direct contact with manufacturers gives large retailers a better capability to control the assortment of goods they buy. It also may speed delivery, a particularly important factor when goods are perishable.

Manufacturer to Wholesaler to Retailer As shown in the third channel system in Figure 13.5, some manufacturers use wholesalers as intermediaries, either because they are too small to sell directly to retailers, or because the retailers are too small to make direct sales economical. Most large consumer-goods manufacturers such as General Foods or Procter & Gamble use wholesalers to sell to smaller retailers, even though they may sell directly to larger retailers.

FIGURE 13.5
Primary Distribution Channels
for Consumer Goods

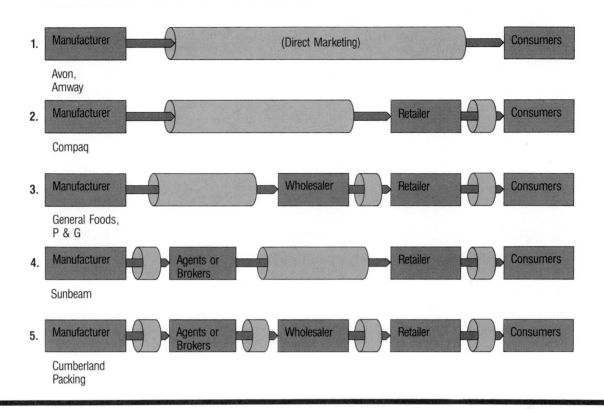

Wholesalers tend to spring up in new business areas when they can assemble a variety of products from many manufacturers more economically than can retailers. For example, wholesalers began to be used by retailers in selling computer software because they could evaluate and screen the many offerings from software manufacturers, both large and small.[11] Few computer retailers had the time or expertise to do so.

Use of Agents and Brokers The last two channel systems in Figure 13.5 use agents or brokers to either sell directly to retailers (system 4) or to sell to wholesalers who then sell to retailers (system 5). Sunbeam's personal care division illustrates the former. The division was too small to develop its own sales staff to sell its line of grooming appliances, so it hired 21 manufacturer's agents to call on retailers, coordinate in-store demonstrations, and present the line in a professional manner. Cumberland Packing Co., producers of Sweet 'n Low artificial sweetener, uses a network of sales agents nationwide to sell to wholesalers. In 1965 Sweet 'n Low was a lackluster sugar substitute with sales of under $3 million. Now its sales have increased tenfold as a result of use of sales agents to convince wholesalers to stock and push the item.[12]

Manufacturers also use brokers to distribute items. When Mr. Coffee, the first electric-drip coffeemaker, was introduced the company used manufacturers'

FIGURE 13.6
Distribution Channels for
Industrial Goods

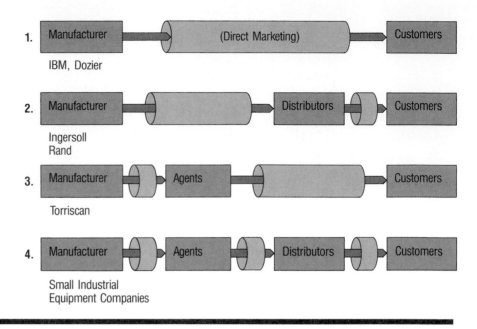

agents to sell both the coffeemaker and filters to appliance and department stores. It soon became apparent, however, that Mr. Coffee users found it inconvenient to go to appliance and department stores to buy the filters; it was much easier to buy the filters in the same food stores where coffee was sold. The company did not have the resources to sell to the 165,000 retail food stores in the United States, so it hired a number of food brokers (brokers who sell a food manufacturer's products on a permanent basis for a commission) to sell the filters to supermarkets and food stores.[13] Today, more of Mr. Coffee's filter sales come from food outlets than from department or appliance stores.

Distribution Systems for Industrial Products

Industrial goods require different types of distribution systems than consumer goods. Figure 13.6 shows the four most common distribution channels for industrial products — direct marketing, and three different systems that involve agents and/or distributors as intermediaries.

Direct Marketing to Industrial Buyers Direct marketing is much more common for industrial than consumer products for a number of reasons. First, many industrial markets have just a few buyers, making direct sales more economical. Second, industrial buyers prefer to deal directly with manufacturers because of the high price and technological complexity of many products. This way they can rely on the technical expertise of the company's sales staff rather than that of an intermediary. One producer of factory automation equipment summarizes the problems of distributing through intermediaries: "You have lots of very fine equipment, lots of industries that can use the equipment, and just about no middlemen who understand how to implement the equipment to the particular needs [of customers]."[14]

Industrial manufacturers use three methods for selling directly to buyers: their own salesforce, telemarketing, and catalog sales. IBM sells most of its mainframe computers and about 20 percent of its PCs to large accounts through its own salesforce. Other large industrial companies such as Hewlett-Packard, GTE, and National Cash Register also sell directly to large accounts.

The high cost of a sales visit makes it impractical for salespeople to contact smaller accounts, so some industrial manufacturers are beginning to use **telemarketing**, which utilizes Wide Area Telephone Services (WATS) lines to reach customers nationwide. Telemarketing is the most cost-effective way to sell to smaller customers directly. AT&T was one of the first to use it for this purpose. A Bell System representative with detailed knowledge of telephone equipment and servicing would call small businesses to determine their communications needs and develop suggestions to meet these needs.

The high costs of personal selling has also prompted firms such as Xerox, Digital Equipment, and IBM to use mail-order catalogs to sell to industrial buyers. Dozier Equipment, a Nashville-based producer of industrial maintenance, materials handling, and safety equipment, sells primarily through a 196-page catalog sent to 200,000 customers nationwide. Catalog sales to industrial firms are sometimes coordinated with a telemarketing program.

Use of Intermediaries in Industrial Distribution The three additional channels for industrial goods, involving selling through agents and/or distributors, pose some risks, since manufacturers lose direct control over sales when intermediaries are involved. It is often more effective for a company sales rep to negotiate product specifications, installation, and maintenance with the buyer. Agents and distributors are usually more effective when a company is trying to reach many smaller buyers and when it is not well-established in the market. Distributors are also more likely to be used for lower-priced items and goods purchased in smaller quantities, in which case they can develop economies by assembling small orders for many different buyers.

Ingersoll-Rand began using distributors (system 2 in Figure 13.6) to sell its pneumatic tools because of expanded use of its lines. Until the mid 1970s, the company had sold directly to large users in the construction industry. But after that, pneumatic tools began to be demanded by smaller buyers, and distributors were able to give better local service to this broader market.

Torriscan Corp., a small regional producer of pressure gauges, is another industrial manufacturer that uses intermediaries. Unlike Ingersoll-Rand, Torriscan uses manufacturer's agents to reach its customers (system 3) because it needs the marketing support that agents provide. Agents allow Torriscan to avoid the fixed expenses of a sales organization, while offering broader territorial coverage and expertise in the product line.[15] The use of agents enabled the company to expand its customer base. With increasing sales, Torriscan might be in a position to sell directly to larger accounts.

Still another industrial channel that involves intermediaries is the use of agents to sell to distributors (system 4 in Figure 13.6). This channel is most effective if a company is selling a new line and is having trouble establishing itself with distributors. Agents have the expertise in industrial products to facilitate product acceptance among distributors. This channel is typically used by small industrial equipment manufacturers who wish to delegate responsibility for marketing their line to sales agents while gaining the broader distribution base afforded by distributors.

FIGURE 13.7
Distribution Channels for Services

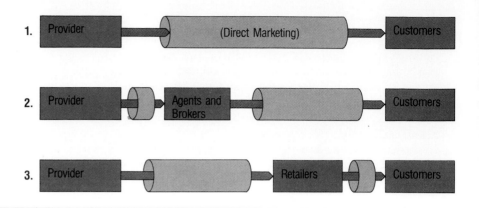

Distribution Systems for Services

As we saw in the last chapter, distribution for services differs from that for products because most services are delivered directly to consumers at the time they are consumed. Figure 13.7 shows three channel systems for services. The first, direct delivery, is the most common. Professional and personal services, health maintenance organizations, airlines, hotels, and cultural organizations generally provide their services directly.

In some cases, these services are sold through agents and brokers. Airline and hotel reservations can be obtained through travel agents and home buyers often use the services of real estate brokers. Consumers are likely to use agents and brokers when they cannot locate the desired service or product on their own. A travel agent might facilitate finding the right vacation package, a real estate broker the right home.

When services are product-related, a retailer is often required to deliver the service. (System 3 in Figure 13.7.) For example, automobile and appliance manufacturers require retailers to provide repair and maintenance services for their products.

Multiple Distribution Systems

Many companies use more than one distribution system. For instance, large consumer-goods firms often sell directly to large retailers but use wholesalers and agents or brokers to sell to smaller retail accounts. Some firms also sell directly to consumers and through intermediaries. GM, Ford, and Chrysler sell most of their cars through independent dealers but also sell directly through company-owned dealerships in some large cities. Company-owned stores are established because it is too expensive for independents to operate them in these markets. The problem is that such dual distribution antagonizes nearby dealers who own their own stores since the company is competing with them.

Many large industrial firms also use a dual-distribution system, selling direct to large accounts and using distributors to reach smaller accounts. In some cases, direct marketing methods such as telemarketing and catalog sales are also used to sell to smaller accounts. As we saw, AT&T sold to smaller accounts directly through WATS lines while selling to larger accounts through its salesforce.

Vertically Integrated Distribution Systems

Regardless what alternative is selected, the distribution system must be coordinated by a single organization (the channel leader) if the channel is to be effective

FIGURE 13.8
Vertically Integrated Distribution Systems

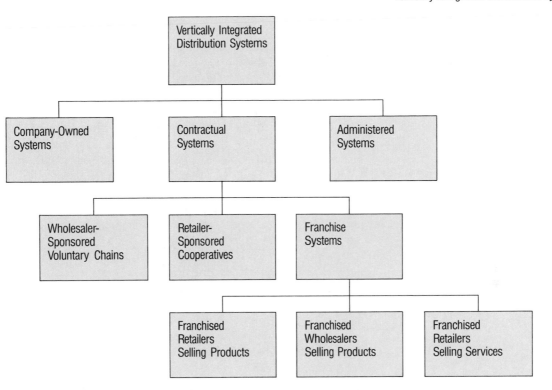

and profitable. This need for coordination requires development of a **vertically integrated channel system**; that is, a system where companies at different levels — manufacturers, wholesalers, retailers — work together to distribute goods. (A **horizontally integrated distribution system** is one in which companies at the same level cooperate to distribute goods; for example, a group of retailers banding together to form a buying cooperative.)

Figure 13.8 illustrates three ways to vertically integrate the distribution system: company ownership, contracting with intermediaries, or a channel leader administering the distribution system. In identifying alternative distribution systems (step 1 in Figure 13.4), the manufacturer must determine which of these three systems is best to achieve vertical integration.

Company-Owned Systems The most direct way to integrate the channel system is to own it outright. When a manufacturer owns the distribution system, it usually owns the retail stores in the system. For example, Goodyear Tire, Sherman Williams paints, and Hart Shaffner and Marx clothing own their own retail outlets. Such ownership allows the manufacturer to control the way its products are sold and to coordinate the activities of its retail outlets for maximum efficiency. Manufacturer ownership of retail outlets is known as **forward integration** because the company is acquiring distribution outlets closer to the consumer.

Intermediaries can also serve as channel leaders for purposes of integrating and controlling their channel activities. When a retailer or wholesaler owns the distribution system, it often owns manufacturing facilities. For example, the wholesaler, McKesson, manufactures some of the food and drug items it distributes. The retailer, Sears Roebuck, obtains 50 percent of its products from manufacturers in which it has part or full ownership. Such ownership gives retailers and wholesalers the means of controlling their sources of supply, and is known as **backward integration** because the intermediaries are acquiring facilities that are further removed from the consumer.

Contractual Systems Another method of integrating distributive functions is through **contractual systems**. Here independent manufacturers enter into a contract with intermediaries to coordinate distributive functions that can be performed more efficiently in tandem than separately. Three types of contractual systems account for about 40 percent of all retail sales: wholesaler-sponsored voluntary chains, retailer-sponsored cooperatives, and franchises.

Wholesaler-sponsored voluntary chains are groups of retailers organized by a wholesaler into a chain operation to help them obtain the same economies in purchasing as larger retail chains. The wholesaler can provide goods and services more economically to the voluntary chain than if it had to sell to each retailer separately. The Independent Grocers Alliance (IGA) is an example — a group of independent grocery stores organized into a buying group by a wholesaler to achieve economies of scale in purchasing.

Retailer-sponsored cooperatives are groups of independent retailers who band together to set up a wholesale buying office. Retailers purchase through this cooperative and collaborate on promoting products and setting prices. An example is Certified Grocers, composed of independent grocers who organized on their own rather than under the sponsorship of a wholesaler, but for the same purpose — to achieve economies of scale in purchasing.

Franchise systems are the most important types of contractual arrangements. A parent company (usually a manufacturer) grants a channel member (usually a retailer, and sometimes called a **dealer**) the right to sell the company's products under its name and according to specific rules laid out in the franchise. The contract usually specifies that the franchisee will be the exclusive representative of the company in a certain area. The franchisor may assist the retailer in establishing the store, promoting it, and training personnel and usually establishes strict guidelines as to how the store is to be laid out and operated. Almost one-fourth of all retail establishments in the United States are franchised, accounting for about one-third of all retail sales.[16]

Table 13.1 shows three types of franchise systems. Manufacturer-sponsored franchise systems generally utilize retailers. Automobile companies and petroleum firms grant franchises to retailers to sell their products under specific conditions. For example, gas stations are required to stay open a certain number of hours and to stock the company's line of products. Auto dealers are required to maintain facilities to service cars. Manufacturer-sponsored systems can also franchise wholesalers. Soft drink companies franchise wholesalers (bottlers) who are required to buy the concentrate from the manufacturer, then bottle, promote, and distribute the product. Pepsi and Coke stipulate that their bottlers cannot enter agreements with other cola lines. As a result, when Seven-Up Co. introduced Like, its caffeine-free cola, the company had difficulty lining up bottlers.

Service firms also franchise retailers. Fast-food outlets such as McDonald's, motel chains such as Howard Johnson, and car rental companies such as Avis franchise their service operations to independent retailers and service establish-

TABLE 13.1
Three Types of Franchise Systems

TYPE OF FRANCHISE	EXAMPLE
Manufacturer-sponsored system franchising retailer	Car dealership
	Gas station
Manufacturer-sponsored system franchising wholesaler	Soft drink bottler
Service firm franchising retailer	Car rental company
	Motel chain

ments. In so doing, they organize a channel system for bringing their services to consumers.

Administered Systems The third type of vertically integrated distribution system is an **administered channel system.** Here, integration of distributive activities is accomplished through the power of a channel member rather than through ownership or contractual arrangements. The most powerful member of the distribution system assumes the role of channel leader and, as such, influences channel members to cooperate in performing distributive functions. Without such cooperation, inefficiencies may occur in delivery, inventory controls, or administration of warranty claims.

Large manufacturers such as Procter & Gamble, General Electric, and IBM have been able to obtain cooperation from retailers regarding displays, preferable shelf space, and pricing policies. In other cases, it is the retailer or wholesaler who assumes the role of channel leader. Thus, the wholesaler, McKesson, is the channel leader for drug retailers; the retailer, Sears, is the channel leader in dealing with its suppliers.

Multiple Vertically Integrated Systems We have presented three vertically integrated channel systems in Figure 13.8 separately. But some firms use these systems in combination. As we saw, IBM uses an administered system when it sells its PCs through independent retailers, and a company-owned system when it sells mainframes direct to large buyers. Companies will establish such multiple systems to satisfy the needs of different markets. IBM's PCs are best sold through independent retailers because these outlets can bring together a variety of hardware and software options for the small buyer in one place. Mainframes are sold through a company-owned system so IBM's sales reps can contact industrial buyers directly to develop customized systems designed for their specific needs.

In 1934 a young Greek immigrant, Thomas Carvelas, borrowed $15 from his wife, filled an old jalopy with ice cream, and started what eventually became an ice cream empire of 865 franchised stores and $300 million in sales.[17] Today Carvel ice cream stores dot the country, and are beginning to dot Europe and Asia as well.

A feisty 83-year-old, Tom Carvel was one of the first to use the franchise system on a national basis, building Carvel's retail network up almost single-

**Tom Carvel —
One Tough Franchisor**

Source: Alan Zale/NYT Pictures.

handedly. He also was perhaps the first CEO to tout his own company's products. His gravelly voice has been heard on radio commercials since 1955.

Carvel sees the company as his own, and this attitude is apparent in his relations with his franchisees. Because of his insistence that all Carvel outlets do business his way, he was once described as an "iron-fisted tyrant." A 1979 anti-trust suit charged Carvel with forcing its dealers to buy everything from cones to napkins at inflated prices. The situation is one of conflict between a franchisor who wants to control and standardize retail operations and independent franchisees who resent this control and want to maintain their independence. Both sides have legitimate points. Carvel does not seem ready to loosen his grip, however. "Sure they call me strict when I try to control them," he says, "but poison one child, and 50 years of business go down the drain."[18] Despite Carvel's tough stance, it is hard to argue with success: the number of outlets and company profits continue to grow.

When asked about retirement, Carvel growls "Why should I retire? . . . When you get up seven days a week and do what you want to do and enjoy doing, that's not work."[19] It may be fun for Tom Carvel, but he makes sure it is work for his franchisees. ◼

EVALUATE THE DISTRIBUTION ENVIRONMENT

As the manufacturer identifies alternative distribution systems, it must also evaluate the distribution environment. These two steps occur simultaneously because environmental factors such as customer needs, competitive practices, legal regulations, and the nature of the company's products largely determine the best channel system for the manufacturer.

Customer and Competitive Factors

Customer characteristics clearly influence channel selection. A company that sells its products to a few large customers in geographically concentrated areas may find that direct marketing is economically feasible. If it sells to many small, geographically dispersed customers, however, that company will need intermediaries.

Competitive factors are also important in selecting a channel system. Compaq chose a retailer-only system that made it a favorite among computer retailers, permitting the company to compete with IBM and Apple. Without strong retailer support, it might have been just another IBM-compatible. Companies may also choose new and innovative channel systems to help them gain competitive advantage. Although L'Eggs stockings had no unique product features, they gained an edge on the market by being the first hosiery product to be distributed through supermarkets.

Legal Regulations

Legal regulations are another important factor in the distribution environment, for they may restrict the choice of intermediaries or otherwise affect distribution strategies. The legality or illegality of several distribution practices often depends on whether they restrict competition. This means that a number of distribution practices may be judged legal in one context but illegal in another.

For example, in **exclusive dealing contracts** the seller requires that its customers handle only the company's line of products. Such contracts violate the Clayton Antitrust Act if they restrain trade by excluding competitors in a market, or if a larger and more powerful seller forces a smaller buyer to accept the exclusive terms. However, such contracts are legal if they are made by smaller manufacturers or those just getting started in a market, since these arrangements do not restrain trade.

A second type of distribution practice that is sometimes judged illegal involves **tying contracts** that require a buyer to take less popular products in a manufacturer's line in order to get the desired merchandise. For example, an automobile manufacturer may insist that a dealer take a quota of less popular models along with the most popular ones. Such arrangements are illegal when the seller is large enough to restrain trade, or when a substantial volume of business is tied to the contract.

Finally, the granting of **exclusive sales territories** by manufacturers to a wholesaler or retailer, giving it the sole right to sell the manufacturer's products in a certain area, is sometimes judged illegal. Such arrangements seek to avoid retailers or wholesalers competing with each other for the same customers when selling the company's products. Their legality is judged on a case-by-case basis. For example, the Supreme Court found territorial restrictions imposed by Schwinn Bicycle on its intermediaries to be illegal because it restrained trade, yet it found soft drink manufacturers to be within their rights in granting bottlers exclusive territories because such contracts do not restrain trade at the retail level.

Product Characteristics

The characteristics of the product are also important in selecting a channel system. One of the most elementary decisions — whether to use intermediaries or to use direct marketing — is in large part dictated by the product. If a product is technologically complex, expensive, or bulky, it is often more effective to market it directly. Mainframe computers fit all three criteria, so most manufacturers sell them directly to industrial buyers. Their complexity makes it necessary to provide the technical expertise of a company's sales staff to explain the product and to service it once it is sold; their high price prompts industrial buyers to insist on dealing directly with the company; and their bulk makes it more economical to avoid the transportation and handling costs of shipping through intermediaries.

Company Characteristics

The characteristics of the company are another consideration in determining what type of distribution system will be most effective for a product. A company that is just starting out may not have the leverage to get its products accepted by wholesalers or retailers; thus, it is more likely to rely upon agents. Once established, it may be able to dispense with the agents' services, and perhaps even with wholesalers. Haagen-Daz began marketing its ice cream in California by using wholesalers to reach the large number of ice cream vendors in the state. As the company became established, it was able to sell directly to supermarket chains.

Size is another important factor in selecting a distribution system. Large companies have more resources to sell directly to customers; they can establish sales staffs and the required warehouse facilities more easily than can small companies. Large companies are also more likely to administer the channel system and to exert control over the operations of their intermediaries.

DEVELOP DISTRIBUTION OBJECTIVES

Once the manufacturer has established the groundwork for selecting a distribution system, it is in a position to develop the objectives that will serve as a guideline for channel selection. When Compaq introduced its line of IBM-compatibles, it knew it did not have the resources to compete head-to-head with IBM's sales staff. This overriding environmental factor determined Compaq's distribution objective: To avoid competing with IBM through direct selling, and to work through intermediaries. This initial objective guided Compaq's selection of a retailer-only system of distribution.

IBM faced a different distribution environment than Compaq; therefore, its distribution objectives differed. Its client base was composed of both large and small accounts, so it developed an objective of selling differently to each group. As a result, it established a dual system of direct sales to large accounts and use of intermediaries to sell to smaller accounts.

DETERMINE THE STRUCTURE OF THE DISTRIBUTION SYSTEM

The key step in selecting a distribution system is to determine its structure. The manufacturer's first decision is whether to use intermediaries or to market directly. If intermediaries are to be used, the next set of decisions involve (1) the length of the channel system and (2) the intensity of distribution. **Length of distribution** refers to the number of different intermediaries that will be used. Direct marketing is, by definition, the shortest channel, since no intermediaries are used. A channel that requires agents, wholesalers and retailers is the longest. **Intensity of distribution** refers to the degree of coverage provided by the distribution system. This can range from the intensive distribution of a product like Hershey bars or Coke, (both of which can be found at virtually any food or candy store) to the exclusive distribution of products such as autos, Rolex watches, or Pucci sportswear.

The final decision in determining the structure of a distribution system is the selection of specific intermediaries to be included in the channel system. Wholesalers and retailers must be selected according to specific criteria, such as their size, location, and expertise in distributing the company's products.

Whether to Use Intermediaries

As we saw, the decision whether to use intermediaries depends on whether the company feels it is more economical to market directly. How can managers estimate these costs? Suppose an industrial manufacturer is faced with the following facts:

- Manufacturers' agents receive a 5 percent commission on sales.
- Company sales representatives receive a 3 percent commission.
- The cost of supporting and administering a company salesforce adds $500,000 a year to the cost of direct selling.

To determine which alternative is more economical, company management must estimate the sales level at which the cost of using either method is equal. This level can be computed by setting the costs of manufacturers' agents and direct selling equal to each other as follows (with x representing the sales level where costs of the two methods are equal):[20]

$$.03x + \$500,000 \text{ (the cost of selling direct)} = .05x \text{ (the cost of selling through manufacturers' agents)}$$

Solving for x, the point of indifference is $25 million. This means that if sales are less than $25 million, it will be cheaper to use manufacturers' agents; but if sales are higher than $25 million, it will be more economical to use company sales representatives. This is logical, because as sales increase, the fixed costs of the company's salesforce will be defrayed. Thus, the decision to use intermediaries depends in large part on the amount of sales a company forecasts.

Even if economies dictate using intermediaries, some companies may still bypass them to control the marketing of their products. IBM continued to sell its PCs through company-owned stores, even when it was uneconomical to do so, in the interest of control.

Length of the Channel

If management determines that intermediaries should be used, the length and intensity of coverage of the channel must be decided upon. Shorter channels offer more control because there are fewer intermediaries. Franchising is popular because manufacturers such as Carvel can deal directly with their franchisees, stipulating conditions for store operations and sales under contract. Large retailers such as Sears or Wal-Mart also prefer shorter channels that permit them to deal directly with their suppliers.

Most smaller consumer packaged-goods companies do not have the luxury of shortening their channels, and require wholesalers to sell to retailers. But even here, some have tried to bypass wholesalers. Goya foods uses 120 salespeople to sell its Hispanic food line to the *Bodegas* (grocery stores) in Spanish-speaking neighborhoods. Goya is able to sell directly to *Bodegas* because they are well-targeted geographically and demographically.

Intensity of Distribution

Distribution coverage can be viewed as a continuum from intensive to exclusive, with selective distribution in between the two extremes. The nature of the product will determine the type of coverage (see Figure 13.9). **Intensive distribution** involves selling in many outlets, and is required for inexpensive, frequently purchased products. A disadvantage of intensive distribution is that it increases the manufacturer's difficulty in controlling the way products are priced and displayed, particularly since retailers can control shelf space.

In **selective distribution,** a limited number of intermediaries who can provide desired sales support and service are used. These intermediaries give the company's products special attention, although they also carry the goods of competitive manufacturers. Selective distribution is common for durable goods such as small appliances, stereo equipment, and furniture, and for industrial goods that are sold on a nonexclusive basis. Buyers often go out of their way to shop for these items, permitting manufacturers to limit distribution to a smaller number of intermediaries and thereby better control how their products are sold.

In **exclusive distribution,** manufacturers grant intermediaries exclusive territorial rights to sell their products in a certain area. Franchises are an example. In addition to industrial goods, exclusive distribution is most common for consumer goods requiring service (autos, appliances) or projecting quality images (jewelry, high styled clothing). This method offers the manufacturer the advantages of distribution of its brands only, no competitive brands on the shelf, and the greatest amount of control over its intermediaries.[21] But exclusive distribution also has disadvantages: There is greater potential for channel conflict as

FIGURE 13.9
Intensity of Distribution Varies
by the Nature of Products

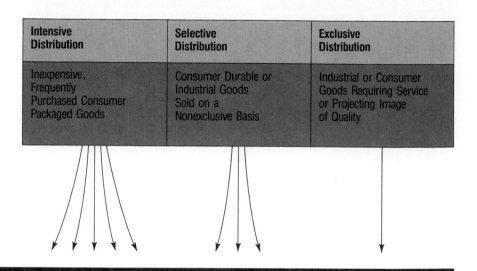

Intensive Distribution	Selective Distribution	Exclusive Distribution
Inexpensive, Frequently Purchased Consumer Packaged Goods	Consumer Durable or Industrial Goods Sold on a Nonexclusive Basis	Industrial or Consumer Goods Requiring Service or Projecting Image of Quality

more powerful manufacturers try to exert control over independent dealers. And the manufacturer may lose some sales in limiting distribution to one intermediary in an area.

Selecting Intermediaries

The most important criterion in selecting intermediaries is their ability to reach the target market and perform the distribution functions at a reasonable cost. Other considerations in selecting wholesalers and retailers are size and financial resources, experience, geographic areas covered, service and delivery record, growth record, product expertise, and reputation in the field.

Thus, industrial firms must seek distributors or agents that have the technical expertise to market their goods, whereas consumer-goods firms must find wholesalers who can distribute economically to smaller retailers. Producers of a variety of products in a particular line must find wholesalers who have the warehousing facilities and inventory control systems to handle many items in small quantities.

ENSURE THE COOPERATION OF CHANNEL MEMBERS

Once the manufacturer has selected a distribution system, it is necessary to ensure the cooperation of channel members (the fifth step in the channel selection process in Figure 13.4). We might assume that such cooperation should be taken for granted since members of a distribution system depend on each other to do business. For example, General Motors needs its network of close to 20,000 dealers to distribute its cars: it would be economically infeasible for even the largest manufacturing entity in the United States to set up 20,000 company-owned dealerships and distribute its cars directly. At the same time, GM dealers cannot do business without the company's cooperation in providing cars and extending financing.

The common desire to make a profit over the long term enforces some degree of cooperation. But as Tom Carvel's case illustrates, conflict sometimes goes hand-in-hand with cooperation, as a natural outgrowth of differing economic objectives among channel members and differing views of the way the business should be run. Let us first review the nature of these distributive conflicts and then discuss how they can be resolved.

Conflict

One source of conflict in distribution systems is differing economic objectives among channel members. The drive to maximize short-run profits sometimes prompts channel leaders to view relations with other channel members as a zero-sum game — that is, my gains are your losses, and vice versa. This was true of many auto manufacturers during the mid 1950s and early 1960s. Having produced too many cars during a period of unstable demand, they typically forced excess inventory on dealers, threatening cutbacks in deliveries and cancellation of franchises if dealers refused to accept additional cars. Dealers had no choice but to cut prices and absorb losses. Similar pressures were put on gas stations by refiners and on TV distributors by manufacturers. Such practices are less common today because manufacturers realized that they were weakening their retail dealer base, ultimately making it more difficult to sell their products.

Another reason for conflict in the distribution system is that a channel leader will sometimes compete with its intermediaries for sales, thus performing the distribution functions of the intermediary. We saw earlier that IBM aggravated computer retailers by selling direct to consumers through its company-owned stores. And, when P&G tried to sell Orange Crush directly to supermarkets, it faced a lawsuit from irate bottlers.[22] Naturally, intermediaries that are bypassed by the channel leader view the action as an economic threat. Their most effective reaction is to prove to the channel leader that they can perform the distributive functions more efficiently. It took four years for IBM to realize that computer retailers could sell PCs to consumers more economically than company-owned stores. On the other hand, IBM continues to bypass distributors when selling to large industrial buyers because it finds direct sales to these accounts more economical than using an intermediary.

A third source of conflict is that manufacturers have a national perspective, whereas most retailers have a local perspective. Having spent millions in product development and advertising, manufacturers want to make sure that intermediaries will sell the product effectively and give it adequate shelf space, so, like Tom Carvel, they often try to exert control over store operations to make sure their product receives the right support. Retailers and wholesalers, on the other hand, often sell many other items besides the manufacturer's line. They are more concerned with local competitive conditions that will affect store sales than the potential of the manufacturer's product for nationwide sales.

In general, channel conflicts are less intense for industrial compared to consumer products, primarily because industrial firms do not use retailers, and many of the conflicts just cited are between manufacturers and retailers. A study of the historic pattern of distribution conflicts in several industries found that the most intense have occurred in the drug, automobile, petroleum, and food industries, all of which use retailers.[23]

Cooperation

Although conflict is virtually inevitable in a distribution system, it impedes the transactional, logistical, and facilitating functions that are necessary for a profitable operation. As the most powerful organization, and the one that has the most at stake, the channel leader usually takes the initiative in providing assistance to other members of the channel.

Manufacturers have tried to ensure the cooperation of intermediaries by helping them make their business operations more profitable. For example, after a period of ignoring the needs of their dealers, auto manufacturers now extend dealers credit and provide them with managerial assistance in areas such as store layout, service operations, and inventory control. They also offer cooperative advertising allowances that share the costs of local dealer advertising and have even established dealer advisory boards to air dealer complaints.

Industrial firms also recognize the importance of gaining the cooperation of their distributors and agents. Parker Hannifin, a producer of power systems for autos, airplanes, and boats, has set up an elaborate system of distributor support. It provides a suggested sales strategy for each of its 2,900 distributors, detailing target markets by product line and geographic segment. Company representatives meet with distributors to make sure the information is understood. In addition, the company offers its distributors a four-day executive development course and a course in telemarketing (reflecting the increasing importance of telephone sales to smaller accounts).[24]

Channel leaders who are intermediaries also offer support to other channel members. McKesson extends finance terms to its 20,000 drug retailers and also provides managerial assistance. Similarly, Sears provides financing and assistance to many of its suppliers.

DEVELOP CHANNEL STRATEGIES

So far in this book, we have emphasized marketing's role in influencing the consumer to buy. But unless intermediaries see the advantage of stocking the company's products, consumers will never have the opportunity to buy. Two types of strategies, *push* and *pull*, are effective in achieving these objectives.

Companies use **push strategies** to influence wholesalers and retailers to stock and promote their products, thus "pushing" the product through the channel to the final consumer. They may offer intermediaries higher margins for carrying a particular product, allowances for retail advertising, quantity discounts, contests and bonuses to reward retailers and wholesalers for higher sales, and in-store promotions and displays to make it easier for the retailer to sell the product.

Pull strategies influence the consumer to go to the store and "pull" a product out of the channel system. Advertising, coupons, and cents-off promotions are used to create brand awareness and encourage consumers to try the product. (We will be discussing push and pull strategies more fully when we consider sales promotional strategies in Chapter 16.)

Manufacturers do not rely solely on either push or pull strategies, since they serve different purposes. The important question is which type of strategy should the company allocate more of its resources to — influencing the trade (push) or influencing consumers (pull). In general, companies that are small or are not yet established in a market must put more emphasis on push than on pull, because getting the product on the shelf is a prerequisite to selling it. As we saw earlier, this strategy proved effective for Compaq.

Industrial companies are also more likely to use push than pull strategies by influencing buyers through their own salesforce or indirectly through intermediaries. Established consumer-goods companies, on the other hand, do not have to rely on push strategies, because wholesalers and retailers will readily stock well-known brands. One wholesaler, commenting on P&G's leverage over its retailers, said "When they [P&G] enter a market with an item, you've got to carry it."[25]

Sometimes, however, established companies may make a mistake in putting too much emphasis on the pull and not enough on the push. We have seen that when Philip Morris bought Seven-Up Co., it ignored the need for a push strategy.

Assuming its distributor relations were rock-solid, the company cut back on promotional support and trade discounts to bottlers and retail stores. When bottlers responded by reducing distribution support, Philip Morris reinstituted a more balanced approach between push and pull.[26]

As Philip Morris's case illustrates, manufacturers must evaluate the performance of the channel system to determine whether changes are needed. This evaluation, the last step in the channel selection process in Figure 13.4, has two purposes: (1) to determine if the channel structure should be changed and (2) to evaluate individual wholesalers and retailers to determine if they should be replaced.

EVALUATE AND MODIFY THE CHANNEL SYSTEM

Such an evaluation led 3M to conclude that it was not economical to distribute its line of office products through its own sales staff. It began instead to use independent dealers and distributors.

Manufacturers must also evaluate how well individual channel members perform by comparing actual sales to projections, as well as evaluating each intermediary's record of inventory levels, on-time deliveries, service fulfillment, and use of in-store displays and promotional programs. Haagen-Daz, the ice cream maker, found that a number of its California wholesalers were not doing an adequate job of selling to large retail accounts. As a result, it terminated these wholesalers and took on the job of selling directly to retail chains.

When a review of channel performance shows a need for change, as in Haagen-Daz's case, management must develop a strategy to modify its channels, either changing their length or their intensity of coverage. For instance, we have seen that both IBM and 3M increased the length of their channels by relying more on retailers and distributors when they saw that direct sales were not economical. Warner Lambert, on the other hand, changed the intensity of distribution for Entenmann's Bakery products after it bought the company. The bakery had previously distributed its products in the northeast and Florida by selling directly to retailers from its own trucks. Within months of acquiring the company, Warner Lambert decided to add trucks, warehouses, and production facilities to make nationwide distribution possible. Entenmann's distribution system did not change; its intensity of coverage did.

SUMMARY

1. Why are intermediaries used to distribute products and services?
Intermediaries such as retailers and wholesalers minimize the number of transactions required to sell products to consumers. They also perform key transactional, logistical, and facilitating functions in getting products to consumers. Manufacturers bypass wholesalers and sell directly to retailers when they determine they can perform these distribution functions more economically.

2. What are channel systems, and what types of channel systems are most effective for distributing consumer goods, industrial goods, and services?
A channel system is a system of interdependent businesses composed of manufacturers and intermediaries designed to deliver the right set of products to consumers at the right place and time. Manufacturers of consumer goods utilize retailers, wholesalers, and agents and brokers to distribute their goods. Industrial firms use distributors (wholesalers distributing industrial goods) and agents. Manufacturers of both consumer and industrial goods also have the option of selling directly to consumers, although this alternative is more likely to be used by industrial

marketers. Most services are distributed directly to customers because they are consumed as they are delivered. Sometimes agents are used to bring buyers and sellers together.

Vertically integrated distribution systems are those that establish the means to coordinate and manage the channel members. These can be company-owned systems, systems using intermediaries that are administered by a channel leader, or contractual systems. The most frequently used contractual systems are franchise systems, in which a parent company grants an intermediary the right to sell its products on an exclusive basis.

3. *What are the key steps in establishing a system of distribution, and in developing distribution strategies?*

When introducing new products, manufacturers must establish a channel system and make key decisions regarding distribution strategies. In so doing, they must first identify the alternative distribution systems available, then evaluate the distribution environment — namely, the nature of customer demand, competitive influences, legal regulations, and product and company characteristics. On this basis, they can identify distribution objectives and determine the channel structure.

Once the channel is selected, manufacturers are in a position to develop distribution strategies to influence intermediaries to stock their goods. The final step in channel development is to evaluate performance of the channel system and to modify the channel if necessary.

4. *Why do conflicts occur within a channel system?*

Conflicts are a natural outgrowth of the differing economic interests of channel members. Actions to maximize profits by one channel member often hurt another. Another reason for conflict is that the channel leader will sometimes bypass its intermediaries and take on their functions, thus competing with them. Conflict also results from the national, product-oriented perspective of the manufacturer versus the local, store-oriented perspective of the retailer.

KEY TERMS

Channel (distribution) system (p. 353)
Retailers (p. 354)
Wholesalers (p. 354)
Distributors (p. 354)
Manufacturers' agents (p. 354)
Sales agents (p. 354)
Brokers (p. 354)
Transactional functions (p. 354)
Logistical functions (p. 354)
Facilitating functions (p. 354)
Possession utility (p. 356)
Time utility (p. 356)
Place utility (p. 356)
Channel leader (p. 357)
Direct marketing (p. 357)
Telemarketing (p. 361)
Vertically integrated distribution systems (p. 363)

Horizontally integrated distribution systems (p. 363)
Forward integration (p. 363)
Backward integration (p. 364)
Contractual systems (p. 364)
Wholesaler-sponsored voluntary chains (p. 364)
Retailer-sponsored cooperatives (p. 364)
Franchise systems (p. 364)
Dealers (p. 364)
Administered systems (p. 365)
Exclusive dealing contracts (p. 367)
Tying contracts (p. 367)
Exclusive sales territories (p. 367)
Intensive distribution (p. 369)
Selective distribution (p. 369)
Exclusive distribution (p. 369)
Push strategies (p. 372)
Pull strategies (p. 372)

QUESTIONS

1. What impact did Benetton's adoption of the *Kanban* process have on its distribution strategy?
2. How did Benetton's distribution strategy create possession, time, and place utility for its consumers?
3. What are the functions of a channel leader in a distribution system?
4. Cite examples of manufacturers that have developed a competitive advantage based on the distribution system they developed. Is their competitive advantage sustainable?
5. What are the differences between industrial and consumer goods firms in (a) the distribution systems they use, and (b) the types of distribution strategies they are most likely to employ?
6. Consider the case of a manufacturer of industrial pipe insulation that sells to many small buyers. Order sizes tend to be small, and sales are fairly routine.

   a. What type of distribution system is this manufacturer likely to develop?
   b. What factors might cause this manufacturer to change the distribution system it is currently employing?

7. Consider the case of a manufacturer of personal computers that is starting to sell to corporate accounts. It is considering two alternative forms of distribution to sell to corporate buyers: through distributors or direct selling. The company has traditionally used distributors because it never developed a strong sales staff. It now feels that the economics of selling direct warrant considering developing its own sales capability.

   a. What specific criteria could management use in evaluating the benefits of direct selling?
   b. Do the pros and cons of selling direct differ for industrial and consumer goods?

8. Why did Tom Carvel establish a franchise system to sell his ice cream? Why is a franchise system a vertically integrated distribution system?

9. What are the bases for the conflicts between Tom Carvel and his dealers? Who do you think has the stronger argument in these conflicts? Why?
10. What environmental factors led Compaq to distribute solely through retailers?
11. Is intensive, selective, or exclusive distribution most likely to be used for the following products? Why?

    a. A new soft drink fortified with calcium.
    b. Low-salt foods.
    c. An electronic mail terminal.
    d. A new low-calorie dog food.

12. An automobile executive cites the changing nature of company-dealer relations as follows:

    > Twenty years ago we would go in and tell the dealer, "Take so many cars or parts and accessories; handle warranty claims in this or that way," and so forth. The company's attitude was that if the dealers didn't like it, let them find someone else to supply them with cars. Today it is totally different. We recognize the dealer as an independent businessperson who might have legitimate grievances, and we try to accommodate our policies to the economic interests of our dealers.

    a. Why do you suppose this automobile manufacturer shifted to a more dealer-oriented view?
    b. What are some recent policies that reflect a greater dealer orientation?

13. Why are companies that first enter the market more likely to use push strategies? What types of push strategies might they use?
14. When Philip Morris first began distributing 7Up, one bottler said, "Philip Morris hasn't recognized that this industry requires as much 'push' at the local level as 'pull' through national ads."[27]

    What are the dangers of too much push and not enough pull? Of too much pull and not enough push?

CASE 13.1

INTEGRATING DISTRIBUTION STRATEGIES IN THE MARKETING MIX: PERRIER MINERAL WATER

Source: Adapted from "Masterminding Distribution and Pricing," *Marketing Communications*, September 1984, pp. 25–34.

How did Perrier mineral water go from $1 million to $16 million in sales in two short years? Because of a shift in distribution strategy. When Great Waters of France (GWF) was formed as the U.S. subsidiary of Perrier in 1976, the product was distributed through specialty food brokers selling primarily to gourmet food outlets in large cities. Retail prices were high and advertising was nonexistent.

GWF saw an opportunity for expanding sales due to the greater health consciousness of the American public and a resulting trend toward lighter beverages and lower-calorie drinks. To get Perrier out of specialty stores into mainstream supermarket distribution, a bold plan was developed. It called first for recruiting wholesalers to reach a broad spectrum of retailers, then lowering the product's price as distribution became more intense and sales increased. National advertising and in-store promotion would follow as distribution expanded.

The program's goal was to increase product exposure through mass market distribution, but the plan could succeed only with a good product. In this respect, Perrier already had a competitive advantage. It had a good-quality image among a small but loyal following, and it was already packaged in a unique, attention-getting bottle.

A network of wholesalers first had to be established to achieve mass distribution. Wholesalers were selected based on coverage in reaching retailers, their effectiveness in executing sales promotional programs for manufacturers, and the margins they required. To ensure the support of retailers and get the product on the shelf, GWF offered retailers margins that averaged 10 percent to 30 percent above those of most other soft drink producers.

Pricing was critical to achieving mass distribution. GWF reduced the retail price from 99 cents to 69 cents a bottle, just 10 cents more than large sizes of club soda. To increase sales to a point permitting such a substantial reduction in price, it inaugurated a national advertising campaign of $800,000, a significant budget considering its previous years' sales were only $1 million. The campaign emphasized Perrier as an alternative to regular sugared soft drinks with the slogan "naturally sparkling."

The marketing program resulted in a sixteenfold increase in sales in two years. Most importantly, this increase was achieved by an integration of distribution, price, and advertising strategies. Expanded distribution permitted a lower price which allowed further expansion of distribution. Advertising fueled this expansion by providing the pull to the initial push given retailers through favorable margins.

1. How did GWF expand distribution for Perrier from specialty stores to supermarkets?
2. In what ways were distribution, pricing, and advertising strategies tied together in the introductory marketing plan for Perrier? Specify how distribution influenced pricing and advertising strategies.
3. What were the pull elements in the strategy? The push elements?

NOTES

1. "Fast Forward," *Business Month,* February 1989, p. 25.
2. "Consumer Draw: From Mass Markets to Variety," *Management Review,* April 1987, p. 22.
3. *Business Month,* February 1989, p. 27; and "McSweater," *Working Women,* May 1986, p. 116.
4. "Why Some Benetton Shopkeepers Are Losing Their Shirts," *Business Week,* March 14, 1988, p. 78.
5. "How Benetton Has Streamlined and Branched Out Worldwide in Casual Clothing Market," *International Management,* May 1986, p. 81.
6. "Benetton Learns to Darn," *Forbes,* October 3, 1988, pp. 122–126.
7. "Weak Bottler Ties Hurt 7-Up in Fight for Share," *The New York Times,* January 20, 1986, p. D1.
8. "Distribution: Industrial Marketing's Neglected Opportunity," *Marketing News,* June 25, 1982, sect. 2, p. 10.
9. "IBM Abandons Product Centers," *High Tech Marketing,* December 1986, pp. 19–21.
10. "Compaq's Grip on IBM's Slippery Tail," *Fortune,* February 18, 1985, p. 76.
11. "New Distribution Channels for Microcomputer Software," *Business,* October–December 1985, p. 20.
12. "Regional Sales Agents Help Cut Rising Staff Costs for Big Firms," *Product Management,* May 1979, p. 6.

13. "Grocers' 'Middlemen' Step to the Forefront," *Advertising Age,* October 11, 1982, pp. M17–M19.

14. "Distribution: More Art Than Science," *High-Tech Marketing,* June 1986, p. 30.

15. "How to Decide Whether the Agency is Practical for You," *Agency Sales Magazine,* November 1983, p. 23.

16. *Franchising in the U.S. Economy* (Washington D.C.: U.S. Department of Commerce, 1984).

17. "A Sweet Job with Sour Notes," *The New York Times,* December 1, 1985, p. F7.

18. Ibid.

19. Ibid.

20. This example is based on a communication from Prof. Roger A. Kerin, professor of marketing, Southern Methodist University.

21. "This Isn't the Legend Acura Dealers Had in Mind," *Business Week,* November 28, 1988, p. 106.

22. "Why Crush Went Flat," Advertising Age, July 10, 1989, p. 1.

23. Henry Assael, "The Political Role of Trade Associations in Distributive Conflict Resolution," *Journal of Marketing* 32(April 1968): 22–23.

24. N. Mohan Reddy and Michael P. Marvin, "Developing a Manufacturer-Distributor Information Partnership," *Industrial Marketing Management* 15(1986): 157–163.

25. "Why P&G Wants a Mellower Image," *Business Week,* June 7, 1982, p. 60.

26. *The New York Times,* January 20, 1986, p. D1.

27. "A Slow Rebound for Seven-Up," *Business Week,* October 12, 1981, p. 107.

TOYS "Я" US'S SECRET OF SUCCESS — PHYSICAL DISTRIBUTION

Toys "Я" Us is in a class by itself — the first retailer to sell toys as a mass merchandiser at discount prices. Its phenomenal success in capturing nearly 25 percent of all toy sales in the United States in 1988 is largely due to its founder, Charles Lazarus.[1] Lazarus opened his first store in 1957. Now, with over $4 billion in sales, 402 stores in the United States and abroad, and an annual growth rate of 27 percent (compared to 2 percent for the rest of the industry), he deserves recognition as being behind one of the great success stories in retailing.[2]

Discount pricing is certainly one factor in the success of Toys "Я" Us — first-quality brand-name toys selling for 20 to 50 percent below standard retail prices. Variety is another factor — 18,000 products, the greatest assortment of toys in the country. But there is also a third, unseen factor — *physical distribution* — that is, the process by which Toys "Я" Us gets products from toy manufacturers to its stores. The heart of the Toys "Я" Us physical distribution process is a computerized information system that hooks up every cash register in every company store to a central computer at company headquarters. By the time a piece of merchandise is in a store, a universal product code has been affixed to its label, so that when a consumer buys it, its code is automatically scanned.

This information is transmitted to the company's central computer. Management can thus determine order quantities for each product and can maintain optimal inventory levels based on consumer purchases. This is an important advantage in a market where tastes can change overnight. Through the cash register, Toys "Я" Us customers themselves ensure that the right mix of products will be delivered to the right store at the right time.

The capability to obtain immediate sales information from its stores permits the company to implement the same *Kanban,* or *just-in-time (JIT),* distribution system as Benetton (discussed in the previous chapter). Merchandise is kept in warehouses for only a short time. Such rapid inventory turnover means higher profits. In addition, rapid delivery is assured by the company's good relations with its suppliers. On-time shipments are made to its 20 warehouses strategically located throughout the country within easy trucking distance of each of the stores serviced. A fleet of Toys "Я" Us trucks ship the merchandise from the warehouses to the retail stores.

A third feature of Toys "Я" Us's physical distribution process is efficient merchandise handling. Many of its warehouses have been transformed into large, modern, automated facilities that process, store, and assemble merchandise for shipment. A good example is the facility designed to service the 112 Kids "Я" Us children's clothing stores. Clothing is moved on hangers from trucks to an overhead monorail. Data on quantity and type of merchandise is fed into a computer at an initial checkpoint. Price tags and labels are printed and attached to the clothing before it reaches its destination in the warehouse. Once the merchandise is designated for a certain Kids "Я" Us store, it is then sorted for shipment in containers holding 1,000 garments. Each store receives the merchandise already hung, sorted by department, and ready to be sold.[3]

Toys "Я" Us's physical distribution system helps target product offerings to customer needs. The efficiency of the system also reduces distribution costs, and these savings are passed on to customers in the form of lower prices. Clearly, physical distribution has enabled this company to gain a competitive advantage and increase profits. ▪

NATURE OF PHYSICAL DISTRIBUTION

Physical distribution is all activities involved in moving goods from where they are produced to where they are purchased or consumed. Toys "Я" Us, for example, orders goods from toy manufacturers, develops its merchandise-handling and storage facilities, and is responsible for transporting goods to its stores for sale to consumers. The combination of order processing, merchandise-handling, inventory, storage, and transportation functions represents its **physical distribution system**.

PHYSICAL DISTRIBUTION AS PART OF THE CHANNEL SYSTEM

Physical distribution is part of the channel system described in the last chapter. It is responsible for the product flows from the manufacturer to the customer and is necessary for manufacturers, as well as retailers like Toys "Я" Us, to ensure that products are delivered on time and in good condition. Toy manufacturers such as Mattel or Hasbro have their own merchandise-handling and storage facilities, and frequently their own trucks to supply merchandise to retailers (such as Toys "Я" Us).

Wholesalers, as well as manufacturers and retailers, require physical distribution systems to deliver goods. W. W. Grainger, one of the largest wholesale distributors of industrial products, services 921,000 customers through 300 branches throughout the United States, using computers to process customer orders and transmit them to automated warehouses where merchandise is retrieved and delivered to loading platforms for shipment. The company stocks 22,000 items in its warehouses, ranging from one-ton industrial generators to featherweight semiconductors.[4]

The channel leader, whether a manufacturer, a wholesaler, or a retailer, has responsibility for integrating these physical distribution systems. As channel leader, Toys "Я" Us will coordinate shipments from manufacturers and wholesalers to fill its orders and will also provide information to help these companies order materials and goods and set their inventory levels.

The Toys "Я" Us example showed a series of steps in physical distribution, illustrated in Figure 14.1. First, a company places an order, based on *customer demand*. At Toys "Я" Us, consumers' purchases indicate which products need re-ordering. For example, if there is a revival of interest in Barbie dolls and a strong increase in sales in the weeks before Christmas, the sales trend would become immediately known to Toys "Я" Us management, and they would order more dolls from Mattel *(order processing)*. Mattel, in turn, would increase its production, if necessary, in order to fill the order.

Once Toys "Я" Us had enough Barbie dolls stocked in its warehouses, it would allocate them to individual stores to fill orders. This would require *merchandise handling* which involves identification of inventory levels by computer and automated processing of orders to locate, assort, and convey the product to the assembly area for shipment. This process assumes a capability for *storing* goods, and a system to determine the optimal level of inventory for storage.

An alternative to maintaining substantial *inventory* levels is the Kanban, or just-in-time (JIT), distribution process that minimizes inventory levels to reduce physical distribution costs. It requires rapid feedback from customers regarding their needs so manufacturers can produce on an as-ordered basis. Toys "Я" Us is able to operate with a JIT system because it can obtain immediate information on customer purchase trends and transmit orders to toy manufacturers on this basis. The result is lower inventory costs, permitting the company to sell its products at lower prices. The company also avoids the risk of holding unsold inventories in the highly volatile toy market, simply by placing more frequent orders with manufacturers.

The final step in the physical distribution process involves the seller shipping merchandise by a particular mode of *transportation* to either an intermediary for resale or to an industrial user. Once the merchandise is received, the buyer will evaluate the on-time reliability and dependability of shipments and the condition of the merchandise. *Customer satisfaction* with physical distribution services is likely to lead to a longer-term relationship between buyer and seller.

THE PHYSICAL DISTRIBUTION PROCESS

The objectives of physical distribution are to provide on-time shipments; dependability of deliveries so that products arrive regularly, safely, and in the correct form and quantity; and accurate information on customer needs. For example, we saw that Toys "Я" Us was able to gain a competitive edge by consistently providing the right mix of products to its stores on time, dependably, and based on accurate customer information.

These purposes are particularly important for industrial marketers, which supply materials that buyers use in the production process, because products that arrive late, in the wrong quantities, or in defective condition can delay production runs and result in substantial losses to buyers.

PURPOSES OF PHYSICAL DISTRIBUTION

The importance of physical distribution is reflected in its cost, estimated by one study at an average of 20 percent of sales.[5] (The average amount spent on advertising or sales promotions is significantly less.) Physical distribution costs for intermediaries are even higher due to their role in assembling and sorting products. Order processing, merchandise handling, storing, inventory management, and transportation all account for a portion of the cost.

Managers view physical distribution as a key component of the marketing mix because of its central role in creating time, place, and possession utility and in

IMPORTANCE OF PHYSICAL DISTRIBUTION

FIGURE 14.1
The Physical Distribution Process

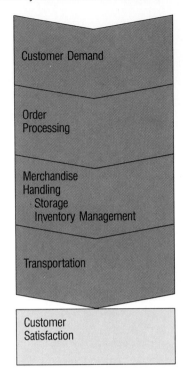

achieving distribution efficiencies. One study of industrial buyers found that they rate physical distribution second to product quality in evaluating alternative suppliers.[6] For many industrial buyers, the starting point in selecting a vendor is not identifying the company offering the lowest price, but the company offering the best delivery and service reliability.

Physical distribution is also rated important by marketers of consumer goods, which cannot afford to risk running out of stock due to poor inventory control or delivery. Consumers are becoming less brand-loyal, and when they find their preferred brand out of stock, are increasingly likely to buy an alternative product.

Physical distribution is also an important means of gaining a competitive advantage. For example, Span-America, a producer of orthopedically designed pads for hospital beds, decided it might have a good product for the consumer market when it found that patients insisted on taking the pads home. The stumbling block to expansion was physical distribution. Moving into the consumer market meant maintaining larger stocks of inventory to fill orders and meeting specific shipping dates set by retail customers. The company met the challenge. Its first problem was that it could not ship rolled-up mattress pads to retailers as it did to hospitals. It designed a new package that reduced shipping size by 75 percent and made the product more stackable in retail showrooms. It also established its own transportation facilities to ensure on-time deliveries and an order completion rate of 98 percent.[7]

Eastman Kodak's experience with instant cameras in the late 1970s serves as an example of poor physical distribution leading to competitive disadvantage. Its promotional campaign aroused consumer interest, but when consumers went to retail stores to look at the camera, retailers were often out of stock.[8] As a result, many consumers lost interest, and sales fizzled. Even the best advertising campaign or the most aggressive pricing strategy is useless if the company does not have an effective physical distribution system to ensure the product is on the right shelves at the right time.

THE PHYSICAL DISTRIBUTION SYSTEM

The functions in Figure 14.1 — order processing, merchandise handling, storage, inventory management, and transportation — combine to form a physical distribution *system* for two reasons. First, they are interrelated; second, they are driven by a common goal, distribution efficiency.

Physical Distribution Tradeoffs

Physical distribution activities are interrelated because they involve cost tradeoffs. Figure 14.2 shows the per-unit costs of physical distribution activities by order quantity (that is, the size of a single order). As order quantity increases per unit transportation costs decrease because of economies of scale in transporting a larger number of items. The cost of processing orders also decreases since larger order quantities result in fewer orders. Storage costs (that is, the costs of building and maintaining warehouses) increase because of the need to maintain more units in stock. Inventory costs (the costs of keeping products in stock) also increase because more inventory capacity is required to handle larger volume.

If a company finds that costs of a certain physical distribution component are too high, it can try to reduce costs of that component; but total costs may not be reduced. For example, if transportation costs are too high, they can be decreased

Per-Unit Costs

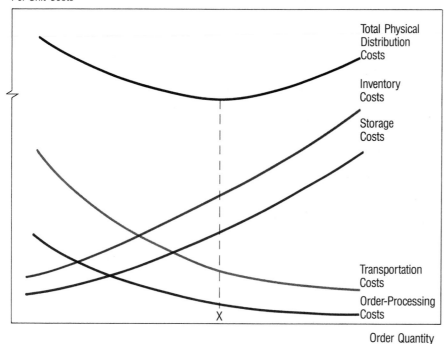

FIGURE 14.2
Physical Distribution Costs

Order Quantity

by using slower means of transport such as rail; but this would increase inventory and storage costs and might also aggravate customers by delaying deliveries.

In summary, Figure 14.2 shows a tradeoff between inventory, transportation, order processing, and storage costs. A just-in-time system increases the frequency of orders and reduces order size. Transportation and order costs are high, but storage and inventory costs are minimal (left-hand side of Figure 14.2). Conversely, accumulating units into one large order minimizes transportation and ordering costs, although it increases storage and inventory costs (right-hand side of Figure 14.2).

Distribution Efficiency

The second reason physical distribution is a system is that the various physical distribution activities are directed to the same goal: distribution efficiency. If we regard the inputs into the physical distribution system as the cost of performing the activities in Figure 14.1 and the outputs as the level of customer satisfaction, then efficiency would be measured by the degree to which the system minimizes distribution costs while maximizing customer satisfaction.

The problem is that there must be a tradeoff between distribution costs and customer satisfaction. Maximizing customer service may require larger inventories to avoid stockouts, speedier transportation to ensure on-time reliability, and more warehouses — all of which increase distribution costs. As a result, distribution managers must decide on the costs deemed necessary for customer satisfaction. One reason why newer automated inventory-control and order-handling systems are a source of competitive advantage is that they are cost-efficient in improving customer service. If physical distribution is to be used as a means of

FIGURE 14.3
Establishing the Physical
Distribution System

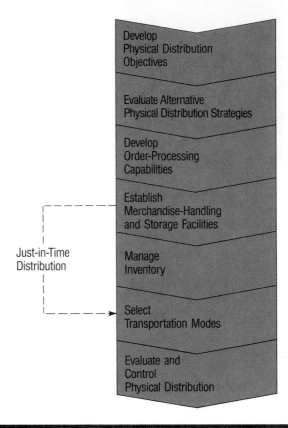

gaining competitive advantage, enough must be spent on it to ensure customer satisfaction and distribution efficiency.

ESTABLISHING THE PHYSICAL DISTRIBUTION SYSTEM

Figure 14.3 shows the steps required to establish the physical distribution system. The first is to establish objectives. Next, managers evaluate alternative physical distribution strategies and develop facilities for order processing, merchandise handling and storage, inventory management, and transportation on this basis. The process also must be evaluated and controlled to produce maximum consumer satisfaction at a reasonable cost. In the remainder of this chapter, we will consider each of these steps.

DEVELOP PHYSICAL DISTRIBUTION OBJECTIVES

Physical distribution objectives can be stated in terms of improving customer satisfaction and/or reducing costs. A customer-oriented objective might be to minimize delivery of damaged goods by use of effective merchandise handling. Another objective might be to minimize out-of-stock conditions through more efficient inventory management procedures. A third might be to ensure on-time delivery of customer orders through an efficient transportation system.

Campbell Soup has established each of these three objectives as general guidelines for physical distribution activities. But Campbell's management recognizes that these objectives are too general to provide operational control over physical distribution activities. Line managers at Campbell are likely to translate the objectives into more specific terms. A reasonable set of physical distribution objectives for, say, Le Menu frozen foods might be

- Merchandise-handling procedures that ensure 98 percent of products arriving damage-free.

- Product turnover so that no product is in inventory more than five days.

- A guaranteed order-to-delivery time of less than three days.

- 100 percent on-time delivery.

Cost objectives could also be specified (for example, physical distribution costs not to exceed 15 percent of sales). The cost of particular physical distribution activities might also be spelled out. If a company uses a just-in-time system, it might want to specify that transportation costs do not exceed 50 percent of total physical distribution costs.

The next step in selecting a physical distribution system is to evaluate alternative strategies in developing the facilities that make up the system. Three alternatives are suggested in Figure 14.2. The first would attempt to minimize total physical distribution costs (the sum of order processing, storage, inventory, and transportation costs). It would require establishing the most cost-efficient order quantity size (x units per order in our example), and developing transportation and storage facilities to handle such order sizes.

EVALUATE ALTERNATIVE PHYSICAL DISTRIBUTION STRATEGIES

But the unknown in this alternative is the cost of maintaining customer service by ensuring on-time delivery and avoiding stockouts. Assume the order quantity that minimizes costs averages 600 units. Would this quantity also be optimal in insuring on time deliveries? Would it produce inventory levels adequate for ensuring against out-of-stock situations? A true cost-minimization approach must account for lost revenue from poor delivery and out-of-stock situations. Yet these costs are not represented in Figure 14.2 and are generally hard to estimate; so a cost-minimization strategy is limited. It cannot account for the costs of potential customer dissatisfaction.

Two other strategies try to optimize customer satisfaction in different ways. The second alternative takes a just-in-time approach to developing the physical distribution system — that is, reduce the order size and increase the number of deliveries to ensure customer satisfaction. Direct shipments in smaller quantities from factory to buyers would reduce the number of warehouses required and would minimize customer stockouts, but would require more expensive modes of transportation to guarantee on-time delivery (left-hand side of Figure 14.2). This strategy would increase the total cost of physical distribution in the short run, but that cost would be offset by greater sales from satisfied customers.

The third alternative takes the opposite approach, accumulating large orders that require fewer deliveries from factory to warehouses (right-hand side of Figure 14.2). To ensure on-time delivery, the strategy calls for more warehouses. This would mean that goods are located closer to customers and can arrive more quickly. As before, overall costs might increase in the short run, but they would be offset by avoiding lost revenues from late deliveries and out-of-stock conditions.

Any of the three alternatives are viable strategies for establishing the physical distribution system as long as managers account for the hidden costs of poor customer service.

FIGURE 14.4
An Automated Order-Processing System

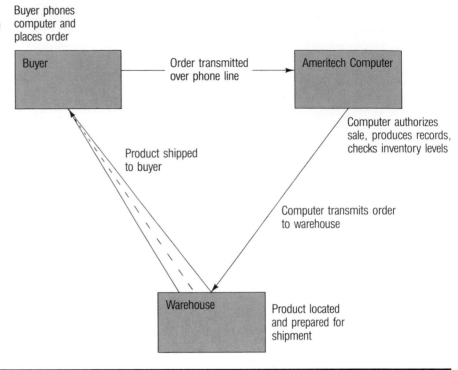

DEVELOP ORDER-
PROCESSING CAPABILITIES

Once the physical distribution strategy is selected, managers must select the components of the system. The first step is to develop **order-processing** capabilities; that is, to receive and process customer orders, transmit them to warehouses, fill the order from inventory, prepare a bill, and issue shipping instructions.

As an example of an order-processing system, Ameritech, a spinoff of AT&T after its divestiture, developed a fairly sophisticated automated system to cut costs and improve customer service (see Figure 14.4). Buyers of Ameritech telecommunications equipment can place orders directly by dialing into an Ameritech computer with a touchtone phone. They enter accounting and authorization data and punch in a seven-digit code for the desired item. The computer checks the authorization and produces the necessary information to develop a record of the order, a bill, and a shipping request. In the process, the computer also checks on inventory levels at Ameritech's warehouse.[9] The order is then transmitted to the warehouse where the product is located, prepared for shipment, and sent to customers.

ESTABLISH MERCHANDISE-
HANDLING AND STORAGE
FACILITIES

The next set of components required for a physical distribution system, merchandise handling and storage facilities, provide the link between order processing and shipment.

Merchandise Handling
The activities of **merchandise handling** are locating an item in inventory, conveying it to an assembly area, where it is sorted and packed for shipping, moving it to a shipping platform, and then loading the item on a transportation vehicle so it can be shipped to the customer. These activities are shown in Figure 14.5.

Ameritech has a merchandise-handling system that operates in conjunction with its order-processing system. Once an order is transmitted to a warehouse, personnel equipped with handheld laser scanners locate the item from inventory by its universal product (or bar) code. Products are arranged in inventory so that the fastest-moving items are located closest to conveyor belts.

Once an item is picked out, it is put into a carrying bag on a conveyor belt and brought to an assembly area, where it is sorted and packed for shipping. The package is then put onto another conveyor and brought to a shipping area, where it gets slotted into one of several shipping lanes. When it arrives at the shipping platform, workers again use a laser scanner to confirm that the item is the correct one for shipment. The product is then loaded on a truck for shipment to the customer.[10]

Storage Facilities

Warehouses permit a firm to consolidate a variety of items in one location close to the buyer. Retailers and wholesalers can buy an assortment of items in larger quantities and take advantage of quantity discounts because of warehouse facilities. Manufacturers can ship larger quantities of items from a warehouse location and save in transportation costs.

Warehouse facilities may be either public or private. **Public warehouses** provide storage facilities to a firm on a rental basis. There are over 10,000 such facilities in the United States. For companies that produce seasonal products or products with cyclical demand, public warehouses are more economical than the fixed costs of building warehouse facilities that would not be needed on a consistent basis. Some public warehouses offer specialized facilities such as refrigeration for frozen foods or climate control for wines and tobacco.

Private warehouses are necessary for firms that need storage facilities on a consistent basis, that is, manufacturers with a large variety of goods requiring storage between production and delivery. Retail chains and distributors shipping to a large number of retail outlets are also likely to own their own facilities.

A recent development is the establishment of large, automated warehouses with computerized order-processing and merchandise-handling facilities, known as **distribution centers.** They are usually one-story facilities, (avoiding the need for elevators) and are located near highways to facilitate transportation (see W. W. Grainger's 1.4 million square-foot distribution center in Exhibit 14.1).

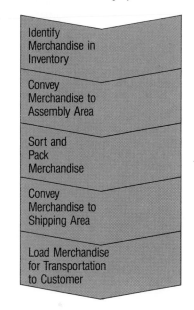

FIGURE 14.5
A Merchandise-Handling System

Identify Merchandise in Inventory

Convey Merchandise to Assembly Area

Sort and Pack Merchandise

Convey Merchandise to Shipping Area

Load Merchandise for Transportation to Customer

EXHIBIT 14.1
A Distribution Center

Toys "Я" Us and Ameritech use distribution centers to handle their products before delivery. Some firms use smaller warehouse facilities to first gather items and then ship them to distribution centers, where they are consolidated for shipment to various points around the country.

Sam Walton — Warehouses Were His Ace in the Hole

Source: Courtesy of Wal-Mart Stores, Inc.

Sam Walton is the richest man in America. As founder and chairman of Wal-Mart stores, his net worth is estimated at $4.5 billion. But you would never know it. He occasionally appears behind a Wal-Mart checkout counter to help the sales clerk approve a personal check. He can be found riding through a Wal-Mart parking lot in his Ford pickup truck counting customers' cars. He has also been known to show up at one of his store's loading docks with a bag of doughnuts for surprised workers.[11]

Wal-Mart's growth is no longer a surprise. It has averaged a steady 35 percent a year, more than triple the growth rate of the retail industry as a whole, making it the third largest retailer in the country. It is projected to be the largest retailer by the early 1990s.[12] When you ask the 70-plus-year-old Walton what is behind Wal-Mart's success, one of the first things he mentions is the company's warehouse facilities. In 1970, when Wal-Mart was only a few years old, the company had difficulty getting supplied by wholesalers. According to Walton, "Our only alternative was to build our own warehouses so we could buy in volume at attractive prices and store the merchandise."[13]

The warehouses helped make Walton a billionaire. Retail stores were clustered within a 200-square-mile area of each warehouse, reducing transportation costs. Today Wal-Mart gets 77 percent of its merchandise from its own warehouses, whereas other chains are forced to buy more of their goods from higher priced intermediaries.

In 1985 Walton began shifting from traditional warehouses to nine large distribution centers, each larger than several football fields, capable of serving between 150 and 200 stores in the 23 southern and southwestern states served by Wal-Mart.[14] The centers are equipped with laser scanning devices to identify products by bar codes and with automated materials-handling equipment. In 1987 the company installed a satellite communications system to enable sales and inventory data to be transmitted from all of Wal-Mart's retail stores (numbering well over a thousand) to company headquarters. The information is then relayed to the company's distribution centers, allowing store inventory to be replenished on an as-needed basis.

If Wal-Mart stores place an order that is not in stock in a distribution center, the order is beamed by satellite direct to the manufacturer, who then arranges for shipment on Wal-Mart trucks to their distribution centers and then to the stores.

Wal-Mart stores receive merchandise an average of 36 hours after placing the order.

This distribution system costs Wal-Mart 3 percent of sales, about half that of most chains. With discounters like Woolco and W.R. Grant failing in recent years because they could not remain cost-competitive, Wal-Mart's physical distribution system gives it an important competitive edge.

Walton started out as an $85-a-month trainee at J. C. Penney in 1940. After a stint in the Army, he bought a Ben Franklin five-and-ten-cent store in 1945. He built up the business to 12 stores, but then decided the future was in discount mass merchandising. Having studied a K mart store in Chicago, he opened the first Wal-Mart store in Rogers, Arkansas in 1962.[15] It has been steady growth ever since, thanks to those original company-owned warehouses. ■

Warehouses and distribution centers require a system to manage inventory. An inventory management system must answer two questions: how much and how often to reorder to maintain optimal inventory levels. The *optimal reorder level* and *optimal reorder frequency* (discussed in more detail later) are easiest to determine for products that have a consistent demand pattern throughout the year. Consumer repurchase rates for items such as toothpaste, cereals, or deodorants are predictable, and inventory levels and reorder frequency can be keyed to known demand. Inventory management is more difficult for seasonal products such as toys, iced tea, or suntan lotion. Companies prefer to manufacture these items year-round to spread out the fixed costs of production facilities and ensure steady work for employees. As a result, inventory builds up in off-season periods. Thus, to operate on a year-round basis, management must trade off lower per-unit production costs against significantly higher inventory carrying costs.

Determining optimal inventory levels and reorder points is most difficult for products with erratic demand such as fashion items or toys. Toys "Я" Us's solution to erratic demand is to maintain minimum inventory levels through a just-in-time system and order by closely tracking consumer demand.

MANAGING INVENTORY

Optimal Reorder Quantity

The optimal amount to reorder to maintain appropriate inventory levels depends on inventory costs. As shown in Figure 14.6, there are three types of inventory costs: carrying costs, out-of-stock costs, and procurement costs. **Carrying costs** are the costs of tying up capital in inventory, and some additional costs such as taxes and insurance on inventory. They can be substantial, often as much as 25 percent of the value of the inventory itself. The longer an item stays in inventory, the higher the carrying costs. **Out-of-stock costs** are the costs of sales lost because the item is not available. The greater the demand for a product, the greater is the out-of-stock cost. **Procurement costs** are the costs of reordering an item. They include the costs of processing and transmitting the order and the cost of the item itself.

The optimal reorder quantity depends on these costs. As inventory levels go up, out-of-stock costs go down, because it is more likely the product will be available. Procurement costs also go down, since orders will be less frequent. But carrying costs will go up. The optimal inventory level is the point where all three of these costs are minimized. This is at point Q in Figure 14.6.

FIGURE 14.6
Inventory Costs

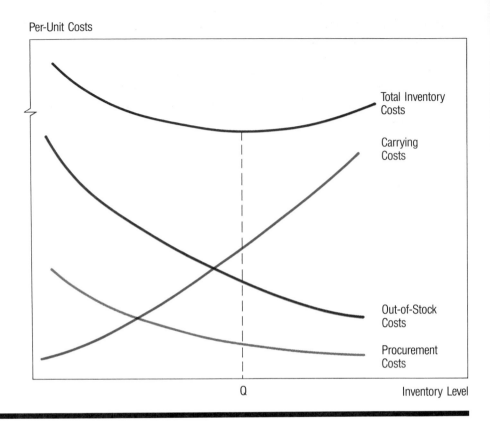

Per-Unit Costs

Total Inventory Costs

Carrying Costs

Out-of-Stock Costs

Procurement Costs

Q

Inventory Level

Frequency of Reorders

The frequency of reorders will depend on the optimal reorder quantity and the level of demand. A firm estimating the number of times it will have to reorder an item might determine that the optimal reorder quantity is at 2,000 units and that estimated annual demand is 50,000 units. The product would then have to be reordered 25 times a year. If demand is consistent, this would mean reordering about every other week. If demand is seasonal or erratic, reorders are likely to cluster at points of peak demand.

Frequent reorders minimize inventory levels and keep inventory carrying costs down. But they increase procurement costs and the chances of being out of stock. Conversely, ordering less frequently requires higher inventory levels, resulting in higher carrying costs but lower procurement costs and less chance of being out of stock.

JUST IN TIME (JIT) DISTRIBUTION

Just-in-time (JIT) distribution means producing exactly what is required by the market just in time to be delivered to customers. Figure 14.3 shows a JIT capability by the dotted line from merchandise handling to transportation. The objective is to minimize inventory and storage costs. JIT systems are most feasible when demand is consistent and predictable.

This system was actually developed by the Japanese as a production control method rather than a distribution system. The idea was to get materials to the production line exactly when they were needed so as to reduce inventory costs involved in production. In its first applications, it was therefore most relevant to industrial marketers trying to ship materials to their buyers (other manufacturers) for use on the production line.

The concept was extended to distribution primarily in the early 1980s when high interest rates substantially increased inventory carrying costs. The best means to reduce carrying costs was by eliminating inventory, and JIT was the way to do it. Not only did it get materials to the production line when needed, but it produced the finished product only when it was needed by customers.

Components of a JIT System

A key component of a JIT system is quick and efficient transportation. The greater frequency of deliveries under this system means that smaller quantities are shipped, thus increasing transportation costs so as to decrease inventory costs. Another essential component is **consolidation centers**. These are ship-through facilities that look like distribution centers — large one-floor buildings — where products are brought for delivery rather than storage.

Computers and universal product (bar) codes are a third component of a JIT system. If products are to pass quickly from manufacturer to customer on an as-ordered basis, then they must be identified on the assembly line to fill customer orders. This must be done by computers, most frequently by laser scanners identifying bar codes with the information fed into the manufacturer's computer at both the plant and the consolidation point.

Example of a JIT System

The Torrington Co., the largest producer and distributor of bearings, introduced a JIT system in the early 1980s because it was experiencing high inventory carrying costs. Figure 14.7 shows Torrington's JIT system, which is representative of most other JIT distribution systems. Products are first identified on the production line for certain customers. Product identification and final destination are entered into a computer, and products are then routed to assembly points. Trucks assemble the products, usually in small quantities, directly at the plant locations for shipment to consolidation centers. Products are collected at these consolidation centers into larger quantities (truckload lots) to reduce transportation costs. They are shipped from the centers twice a week to customers in the same geographic area. Deliveries from the consolidation points are designed to arrive at customers' plants within 15 minutes of the scheduled time. Torrington's JIT system not only reduces inventory costs to almost zero, it also establishes solid customer relations by ensuring close to 100 percent on-time deliveries.

The last physical distribution activity, transportation, accounts for an average of 45 percent of physical distribution costs.[16] This proportion is even higher in JIT systems, since inventory and storage costs are minimized. Because of its cost, selection of transportation facilities is one of the most important decisions in the management of the physical distribution system. The key modes of transport are by truck, rail, air, water, and pipeline. The advantages and disadvantages of each are summarized in Table 14.1.

SELECT TRANSPORTATION FACILITIES

Trucks

More money is spent on truck transportation than on any other mode, even though it comes in second to railroads in terms of total ton-miles of goods delivered. There are over 25,000 independent trucking companies in the United

FIGURE 14.7
Torrington's Just-In-Time System

Source: Torrington's JIT System from *Handling and Shipping Management,* 1985–86, Presidential Issue, pp. 86–89.

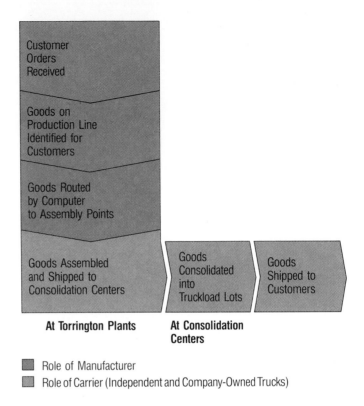

At Torrington Plants

At Consolidation Centers

■ Role of Manufacturer
□ Role of Carrier (Independent and Company-Owned Trucks)

States, shipping a wide variety of products. Most of the products shipped are packaged goods or lighter industrial goods.

The most important advantages of trucks are speed, on-time dependability, and availability of routes. In addition, trucks have the flexibility of picking products up at a plant and delivering them directly to customers, an important advantage in a JIT system. But motor transportation is expensive and cannot carry large loads.

Some of the larger trucking companies provide important services to their customers. John Cheeseman Trucking performed some of Torrington's merchandise-handling and storage functions through its own consolidation centers. Leaseway Trucking has formed a subsidiary, Logistics Resource Inc., as an independent consulting arm to help customers analyze all modes of transportation to come up with the most cost-effective combinations.[17]

Rail

Railroads are the most widely used means of transportation, representing about one-third of all delivered tonnage. In 1950 they represented 57 percent of delivered tonnage. The decrease was due to the increasing use of trucks and the advent of air transportation. With 200,000 miles of lines, railroads provide a wide availability of routes. Companies producing bulky items such as coal, lumber, and paper products usually ship by rail. But railroads are slow, do not ship as frequently as truck and air transport, and have limited flexibility in picking up and delivering products.

TABLE 14.1
Characteristics of Alternative
Modes of Transportation

	ADVANTAGES	DISADVANTAGES
TRUCK	Fast On-time dependability Extensive routes Flexibility in pickup 　and delivery Frequent shipments	High cost Small size of loads Weather-sensitive
RAIL	Extensive routes Handles large loads Handles a variety of 　different products	Slow Limited flexibility 　in pickup and delivery Limited frequency of 　shipments
AIR FREIGHT	Fast Frequent shipments Less risk of damage	High cost Limited variety of 　products can handle Weather-sensitive Limited on-time 　dependability
WATER	Low cost Handles large loads Handles a variety of 　different products	Slow Limited routes Infrequent shipments Limited on-time 　dependability
PIPELINE	Low cost On-time dependability Frequent shipments	Limited variety of 　products can handle Slow Limited routes

Railroad companies are in better shape today than they were 20 years ago. Obsolete tracks and equipment, poor service, and damaged merchandise helped reduce the use of rail transport in the 1950s and 1960s. A series of bankruptcies resulted in the mergers of many railroad lines, leading to modernized equipment and more streamlined companies that offer improved services. One of the most important improvements is **containerization**, that is, putting goods in containers that can be transferred between trucks, ships and railroad cars. **Piggybacking** describes a transfer of containers from truck to rail; **trainship** involves a combination of rail and ship transportation. Such use of combined modes of transport is known as **intermodal transportation**.

Piggybacking is an important means of intermodal transportation because it provides the advantages of door-to-door delivery by truck combined with lower-cost rail transport over long distances. A manufacturer of a bulky item such as an industrial generator might want to ensure prompt delivery to customers. But truck delivery would be too expensive for long distances. The company can use trucks from its plant to railroad yards to ship the product close to the customer by piggybacking on rail transport and then truck the product to the final destination.

CSX, one of the largest railroads, is an intermodal company that offers services in rail, ocean shipping, trucking, and warehousing (see Exhibit 14.2). One service is its Orange Blossom Special for citrus growers, combining rail service through its Seaboard System with CSX-owned trucks that pick up from the growers and deliver directly to customers.[18] CSX provides the advantage of multiple transportation services within one company.

EXHIBIT 14.2
Example of an Intermodal Facility

Another One Of Our Trains Arrives At The Station.

If you think we're just a railroad, take another look.

We're a lot more. We're Sea-Land, one of the largest container ship lines on earth, serving 76 ports in 64 countries.

We're also trucks. Barges. Pipelines. Energy resources. Fiber optics. Resorts and property development. And, of course, the railroad. And we're developing new technology to make it all work together.

We're CSX, the first true global transporter. If you've never heard of one before, it's because there's never been one before. This is a company on the move.

CSX
The Company That Puts Things In Motion.
Transportation/Energy/Properties/Technology

© 1987, CSX Corporation

Air Freight

Air is about three times as expensive as trucks and fifteen times as expensive as rail. As a result, its use is limited to specialized products. But it is very fast and decreases the risk of damaged merchandise. Some combination of truck and air is usually required to get products to airports and then to customers.

Speed is sometimes worth the greater cost of air transport, particularly for perishable goods or high-cost items that must reach customers quickly. Beauty For All Seasons, a cosmetic company, switched from truck to air transport because it cut down on damaged merchandise. The company found that its lipsticks were melting when shipped in the south, and its face creams froze when shipped in the northeast. Quick delivery in temperature controlled planes solved the problem.[19]

Air express companies such as Federal Express and Purolator Courier provide overnight delivery for smaller packages (under seventy pounds) by routing them through central hubs. Emery Air Freight established a niche in the market by concentrating on overnight delivery of heavier packages, making it appealing to companies that need quick delivery as part of a JIT system. Like Federal Express, Emery routes all packages through a hub, Dayton, Ohio, which operates like one giant consolidation center for rerouting to customers nationwide.

Water Transport

Water transport can be by ship on the Great Lakes or the St. Lawrence Seaway, by barges on inland waterways, or trans-oceanic to foreign markets. Water transport is a major means of hauling low-cost, bulky items such as coal and iron. Delivery is slow, the routes are limited to navigable waterways, and shipments are infrequent compared to other modes. But costs are one-fifth that of rail.

Pipelines

Pipelines are used to move liquids such as oil or chemical products and natural gas products over long distances. The over 200,000 miles of pipelines in the United States make them a more flexible means of transportation than many people realize. They are inexpensive and reliable, but slow and limited to certain routes and products.

Once decisions have been made regarding order processing, merchandise handling, storage, inventory management, and transportation, a company must evaluate its performance of these activities (the last step in establishing the physical distribution system). Control requires comparing performance with physical distribution objectives. Looking back to the objectives stated earlier, some key indicators of performance would be

EVALUATION AND CONTROL

- The amount of time it takes to process an order.

- The amount of time it takes to deliver an order.

- The proportion of items that arrive undamaged.

- The amount of time products are in inventory.

- The proportion of times items arrive on time.

- Physical distribution costs as a percentage of sales.

Failure to meet objectives based on these criteria could spell problems with the physical distribution system, warranting examination of each of the activities in the system.

Companies are likely to put more emphasis on controlling particular physical distribution activities, depending on the nature of the system and the strategy they select. For example, a JIT approach requires more emphasis on control of transportation and less on inventory. As a result, managers will keep a closer watch on the proportion of on-time deliveries, and a less careful watch on inventory turnover. Conversely, a company that maintains a large number of warehouses because of seasonal or erratic demand will keep a closer watch on storage and inventory carrying costs.

Regardless of the nature of the physical distribution system, management will track costs as a percentage of sales. If physical distribution costs begin to take up more of the marketing budget, there should be a good reason, such as switching from trucks to air freight for quicker delivery, or changing over from warehouses to distribution centers to improve merchandise handling. When costs rise independent of some planned change in the physical distribution system, it is likely that some activity might be out of control and require corrective action. An example might be excessive inventory carrying costs because of failure to account for swings in customer demand.

As an example of control over physical distribution, the Oldsmobile Division of General Motors has established a special Reduction of Auto Damage (ROAD) team responsible for ensuring damage-free transit and delivery of cars from the assembly line to dealer showrooms. The team analyzes travel conditions along the routes taken by trains transporting Oldsmobile cars, and has authority to alter schedules and routes in response to potential hazards.[20] As a result of ROAD teams, Oldsmobile has cut transit time from an average of 50 hours to 36 hours and substantially reduced delivery of damaged vehicles.

INTEGRATING PHYSICAL DISTRIBUTION INTO THE MARKETING MIX

Physical distribution activities must be integrated with other components of the marketing mix — product, price, promotion, and distribution strategies.

Products can develop a competitive advantage based on the services provided through physical distribution activities. Campbell Soup instituted a JIT system in distributing its Le Menu frozen food line. Products were produced only when needed, improving on-time delivery to supermarkets and reducing damage due to perishability.[21]

Promotional factors also interact with physical distribution. The product must be on the shelf before it is advertised. As we saw, Eastman Kodak failed in this regard with its instant camera line. Its advertising campaign was successful in pulling customers to the store, but the product often was out of stock.

Pricing must also be integrated with physical distribution; its costs must be accounted for in the selling price. For example, one company gave quantity discounts to its customers based on freight costs, ignoring the warehouse handling costs. As a result, some items were underpriced and others overpriced depending on their merchandise-handling requirements.

Since physical distribution is part of the overall *distribution* system, a company must also integrate its physical distribution activities with those of other channel members. Thus, Toys "Я" Us ties its physical distribution system to those of toy manufacturers by sending sales data to them so they can adjust their production to known customer demand.

Physical distribution activities are also sometimes linked to changes in distribution strategies. For instance, Sam Walton has utilized Wal-Mart's advantage in developing its own warehouses and distribution centers by transforming some of these facilities into sales outlets. He has opened 100 Sam's Wholesale Club outlets, which are essentially warehouses that serve as retail outlets for small businesses. He has also transformed four distribution centers into giant retail stores, superstores that offer everything from groceries to hardware in a sprawling one-floor 220,000 square foot emporium.[22]

Walton's strategy has extended traditional physical distribution facilities by opening them up to the customer. Rather than transporting goods from his warehouses and distribution centers to customers, he is asking customers to come to these storage facilities. This allows him to pass on savings in merchandise handling and transportation in the form of prices that are even lower than in the Wal-Mart retail stores.

SUMMARY

1.   What is the nature of the physical distribution process?
Physical distribution is responsible for the flow of products from the manufacturer to the customer. Intermediaries and manufacturers engage in physical dis-

tribution activities to get the right products to customers at the right time and place. These activities are order processing, merchandise handling, development of storage facilities, inventory management, and delivery of products by utilizing various modes of transportation.

2. Why is physical distribution a system?

Physical distribution is a system for two reasons. First, physical distribution activities are interrelated because of cost tradeoffs. For example, decreasing transportation costs may increase storage and order processing costs because of an increase in average order size. Reducing inventory levels by speeding up delivery reduces inventory carrying costs but increases transportation costs. Second, physical distribution activities are designed for a common goal — distribution efficiency in the form of trying to minimize distribution costs and maximize customer satisfaction.

3. What is the nature of physical distribution activities namely, order processing, merchandise handling and storage, inventory control, and transportation?

Order processing requires receiving and processing customer orders, transmitting them to warehouses or distribution centers, filling orders from inventory, and providing billing and shipping instructions.

Merchandise handling requires locating an item in inventory, conveying it to an assembly area where it is sorted and packed for shipping, and then sending it to a shipping platform where it is loaded for shipment. Warehouse facilities permit a firm to consolidate a variety of items in one location, store them, and then select them for shipment. A recent development is the establishment of distribution centers — large, automated warehouses with computerized order processing and merchandise facilities.

Inventory management requires determining how much to reorder to maintain optimal inventory levels, and how often to reorder. The optimal reorder level balances inventory carrying costs, out-of-stock costs, and procurement costs. Finally, transportation modes are selected based on criteria such as cost, speed, on-time reliability, and route availability.

4. What is a just-in-time distribution process?

Just-in-time (JIT) distribution means producing exactly what is required by the market just in time to be delivered to customers. The objective is to minimize inventory levels. A JIT system allows manufacturers to produce on an as-ordered basis. Transportation is a key component, since such a system requires more frequent delivery of smaller quantities. Another essential component of a JIT system is computers and bar codes to allow products to pass quickly from manufacturer to customer.

5. What is the relationship of physical distribution to other components of the marketing mix?

Physical distribution is related to every component of the marketing mix. A product can gain a competitive advantage through on-time, damage-free delivery. Advertising cannot succeed unless physical distribution is effective in putting the product on the shelf in time to meet demand. The price of a product must take account of physical distribution costs. And a company's physical distribution activities must tie in to the distribution activities of other channel members to ensure smooth delivery from manufacturer to consumer.

KEY TERMS

Physical distribution (p. 380)

Physical distribution system (p. 380)

Order processing (p. 386)

Merchandise handling (p. 386)

Public warehouses (p. 387)

Private warehouses (p. 387)

Distribution centers (p. 387)

Carrying costs (p. 389)

Out-of-stock costs (p. 389)

Procurement costs (p. 389)

Just-in-time (JIT) distribution (p. 390)

Consolidation centers (p. 391)

Containerization (p. 393)

Piggybacking (p. 393)

Trainship (p. 393)

Intermodal transportation (p. 393)

QUESTIONS

1. What are the components of Toys "Я" Us's physical distribution system? How does physical distribution give the company a competitive advantage?

2. Why is physical distribution one of the most important marketing activities?

3. One well-known marketing writer commented on management's attitude toward physical distribution thus: "American management's philosophy has been: 'If you're smart enough to make it, aggressive enough to sell it—then any dummy can get it there!' "[23] What is wrong with this philosophy?

4. What are the cost tradeoffs in establishing a physical distribution system? What are the risks involved?

5. A manufacturer of computer chips is considering the three physical distribution strategies cited on p. 385. The manufacturer must ensure on-time delivery of its merchandise to computer manufacturers in damage-free condition.

   a. What are the advantages and disadvantages of each of the three alternatives cited?

   b. Which alternative is the manufacturer most likely to select? Why?

6. A manufacturer of regular and instant coffees is considering coming out with a new line of canned iced coffee. What problems might occur in managing inventory for the new product that the manufacturer did not experience with its regular and instant coffee lines? What can the manufacturer do about these problems?

7. Toy products such as hula hoops and Cabbage Patch dolls experienced a rapid rise in sales, several years of popularity, and then a rapid fall-off. What problems did toy manufacturers have in determining production and inventory levels for these fad items? What solutions might there be for reducing the risk of manufacturing and inventorying such items?

8. Why is transportation the most important physical distribution activity in a just-in-time system? What facilities must transportation companies maintain to insure just-in-time distribution?

9. The manufacturer of the new iced coffee line cited in question 6 maintains a just-in-time system of distribution for its regular and instant coffees. It is considering using the same system for its iced coffees.

   a. What problems might there be in using a JIT system for iced coffees?

   b. What types of companies are most likely to use a JIT system? Why?

10. A producer of over-the-counter pharmaceutical items recently introduced a just-in-time system for most of its products. The distribution manager said:

    > Out JIT system is the greatest thing since sliced bread. It has substantially reduced our inventory costs, improved on-time deliveries, and gotten our products to customers in better condition. If I had my way, I would try to totally eliminate inventory by using even quicker modes of transportation and moving our products more quickly through our distribution centers.

    What are the risks of relying totally on a JIT system?

11. What are the advantages and disadvantages of truck, rail, air, water, and pipeline transportation?

12. What type or types of transportation would be the best for the following products and why:

    a. Fresh lobsters transported to fish markets.

    b. Coal transported to manufacturers.

    c. Natural gas transported to storage facilities.

    d. Soft drinks transported to retail outlets.

13. How do physical distribution requirements affect the following components of the marketing mix:

    a. Promotional strategies.

    b. Packaging.

    c. Pricing strategies.

    How does a product's characteristics affect physical distribution activities?

CASE 14.1

LEVI STRAUSS SUPPORTS ITS RETAILERS THROUGH PHYSICAL DISTRIBUTION

Source: Adapted from David Kiley, "At Levi Strauss, Computers Take Blues Out of Marketing," *Adweek,* November 9, 1987, p. 52. Reprinted with permission of Adweek.

Levi Strauss, the jeans maker, is helping retailers make the transition from outdated inventory and marketing practices to a new era of bar-coding and computerization known as "Quick Response." Quick Response is having the effect of increasing sales for retailers at double-digit rates, while requiring that they stock less inventory.

Ten years ago, Levi practically viewed retailers as a necessary evil, preferring to concentrate its marketing dollars on consumer advertising. Robert Haas, Levi's CEO, admits the company was "arrogant and insensitive" to retail accounts during the magnificent growth in the '70s.

Today, however, manufacturers cannot afford the luxury of arrogance. The relationship between manufacturer and retailer in every business sector has changed substantially. Through scanner data and bar-coding, the retailer is collecting invaluable information at the point of sale that was never before available. Such information will enable the industry to save millions of dollars on improved inventory management.

So the company that stepped on retailers in the '60s and '70s is now courting those same sellers, as well as setting the pace for the rest of the soft-goods industry in one of the most important retail trends of this century — Quick Response inventory management.

Quick Response links the retailer, vendor and textile mill via computers and the bar-coding of all merchandise and inventory documentation. "It's simply the biggest development ever for the retailing industry," says Robert Frazier, executive vice president of the retail consulting firm Kurt Salmon Associates, referring to Quick Response. Frazier points out that 25% of the $100 billion of merchandise that is in the soft-goods pipeline each year is wasted because of out-of-stocks, clearance markdowns and inefficient inventory management.

Through bar-coding and computerization, retailers can automatically record what they are selling right down to the color, size and style. And through Quick Response, stores can use that information for the first time to make small orders from the manufacturer and have them delivered within a week or two. In the past, orders were made two months or more ahead of the selling period. And if the store ran out of a size or a color that was selling fast, that was it. Then, surplus sizes and colors would have to be sold at discount.

According to Paul Benchener, director of retail electronic services at Levi, Quick Response's applications will expand as it becomes more popular. For now, it's mostly used in the form of bar-coded packing slips and advance purchase orders. If that sounds mundane, just those two applications have enabled retailers to cut weeks and months off the ordering and shipping time of goods, as well as enabling companies such as Sears to close major distribution warehouses, where goods previously sat for days and weeks simply waiting to be counted.

According to Benchener, a study done by Levi showed that sales at large chains wired for Quick Response rose at least 13%, and did so on substantially less inventory, reflecting less overstock, not higher prices. And not wanting to discriminate against small retailers who can't afford a sophisticated computer system, Levi has set up a Telerep system, which enables retailers to communicate sales data to Levi over the telephone.

Quick Response enables Levi to set and respond to fashion trends faster than ever before, and faster than foreign competition.

Being the one to introduce retailers to Quick Response, and having been in the forefront of developing its use, Levi has assured its place as a dominant force in leveraging the new data into marketing and product development uses.

1. What is "Quick Response?"
2. Why is Quick Response important to retailers? Why is it important to Levi Strauss?
3. Would you describe Quick Response as a just-in-time system? Why or why not?

NOTES

1. "How Toys 'Я' Us Controls the Game Board," *Business Week,* December 19, 1988, p. 58.

2. Ibid., p. 59; and "Toys 'Я' Us, Big Kid on the Block, Won't Stop Growing," *The Wall Street Journal,* August 11, 1988, p. 6.

3. "Kids 'Я' Us Takes Merchandising Approach," *Chain Store Age Executive,* January 1987, pp. 180, 182; and "Finding Gold in Overalls and Bibs," *The New York Times,* December 25, 1988, p. F1.

4. "Warehousing Success Story in Kansas City," *Material Handling Engineering,* March 1987, p. 70.

5. Roy D. Shapiro, "Get Leverage from Logistics," *Harvard Business Review* 62 (May–June 1984): 124.

6. "Changes in Segmentation, Distribution, Logistics, Demand Analysis Challenge Industrial Marketers," *Marketing News,* June 26, 1981, sect. 2, p. 9.

7. "Casebook: Span-America," *Distribution,* April 1987, pp. 49–50.

8. Thomas C. Kinnear and Kenneth L. Bernhardt, *Principles of Marketing* (Glenview, Ill.: Scott Foresman and Co., 1986), p. 402.

9. "Fast-Track Job Finished on-Time, within Budget," *Modern Materials Handling,* May 1987, p. 65.

10. Ibid., pp. 66–67.

11. "Make That Sale, Mr. Sam," *Time,* May 18, 1987, p. 54.

12. "Wal-Mart: Will It Take Over the World?" *Fortune,* January 30, 1989, p. 52.

13. "Play It Again, Sam," *Forbes* August 10, 1987, p. 48.

14. Ibid.

15. *Fortune,* January 30, 1989, p. 56.

16. "Distribution Can Greatly Boost Productivity," *Distribution Worldwide,* January 1979, pp. 39–40.

17. "Consulting Fever," *Industry Week,* July 8, 1985, p. 24.

18. Roy Dale Voorhees and John I. Coppett, "Marketing Logistics Opportunities for the 1990s," *Journal of Business Strategy,* (Fall 1986): 34.

19. "Casebook: Beauty for All Seasons," *Distribution,* April 1987, p. 51.

20. "A New Facility," *Handling and Shipping Management,* August 1985, pp. 43–44.

21. "Competition Stirs Campbell," *Corporate Strategies,* February 1987, p. 12.

22. "Wal-Mart Stores Penny Wise," *Business Month,* December, 1988, p. 42; and *Time,* May 18, 1987, p. 54.

23. Quote of Bernard J. LaLonde in James C. Johnson and Donald F. Wood, *Contemporary Physical Distribution and Logistics,* (Tulsa: PennWell Books, 1982), p. 3.

K mart is taking aim at Sears for the title of number one retailer. With close to $26 billion in sales in 1988, compared to Sears' $28 billion, it does not have far to go.[1] Its strategy is to upgrade its merchandise and offer name brands in well-defined categories such as home furnishings and kitchen appliances. But why should the company move from its traditional low-priced fare to high-priced name brands? Certainly, it made the right move in the early 1960s when, as S.S. Kresge, it decided to shift from being a five-and-dime chain, with Woolworth as its main competitor, to a discount mass merchandiser. At that time, high-volume discount merchandising was the best way to make a profit. Most consumers were after bargains, and they were not yet attuned to designer names and labels.

By the late 1970s, the company was going full steam ahead, opening an average of 100 stores a year.[2] Customers were streaming to its stores; every other American visited a K mart outlet at least once a month. But as K mart was growing, it began coming up against a demographic juggernaut — the baby-boom generation, more working women, more singles, more dual-earning households. More affluent and aware consumers wanted greater quality and value — which translated into greater style and brand-name consciousness.

By the early 1980s, K mart's earnings had started declining steadily.[3] Management's initial reaction was to repaint the K mart stores, put in new fixtures, and update some of the lines. The focus on bargain-basement items was continued, and K mart's nickname as the ''polyester palace'' (based on its apparel lines) hung on.

It soon became apparent that more than a paint job would be needed. Several managers saw the need to broaden the company's base. In short order, K mart shelled out $1 billion for book, drug, and home-improvement chains.[4] It then started reshuffling the merchandise in its own stores, selecting categories with the greatest profit potential — apparel, electronics, kitchen appliances, home furnishings — and expanded these lines by adding nationally known brand names. Further, it spent $2.2 billion to redesign its stores so each looked like a self-contained retail center, with names like The Kitchen Korner and Home Care Center.[5] In the process, the company provided a more contemporary showcase look for each of these specialty areas.

K mart also upgraded its image by creating its own lines of quality merchandise. It introduced the Jacklyn Smith Signature Collection by using the former star of "Charlie's Angels" as a means of identification. In a further attempt to leave its polyester image behind, the company signed a five-year contract with Martha Stewart, a stylish hostess and author of several cookbooks to become a company-wide spokesperson, featuring her in nationwide TV commercials and in 60 full-page ads in *Family Circle* magazine in 1989.[6]

By 1989 all these pieces were in place to upgrade K mart's image. But will these changes alienate K mart's core economy-minded shopper? The company thinks not. It will continue to offer its traditional bargain-basement fare. The company's $600 million-a-year advertising campaign still features items like $3 frying pans. But now these items will be the lower price points of a broader range of merchandise that includes quality brand names.

If K mart's strategy works, watch out Sears! ☐

CHAPTER

MARKETING BY INTER-MEDIARIES: RETAILING AND WHOLESALING

● ● ●

IMPORTANCE OF RETAILING

We defined retailing in Chapter 13 as the sale of products and services to a final consumer. Many people associate retailing with small stores and independent merchants. This might have been true a hundred years ago, but retailers such as K mart represent large, powerful organizations that serve as the channel leaders in their distribution system.

Compared to manufacturers, retailers are becoming larger and more powerful in the channel system. The growth of private brands has led retailers to rely less on manufacturers for products and has given them more control over what goes on the store shelf. Even when large retailers such as K mart and Sears buy name brands, they are generally in the driver's seat in negotiating price and quantity. Some retail chains even demand payments from manufacturers for putting new products on their shelves. For example, Shoprite Stores asked for $86,000 to stock a new brand—Old Capitol microwave popcorn—then withdrew the brand from its shelves six weeks later.[7]

The importance of retailing can also be measured by its role in the economy. Total retail sales are over $1.5 trillion a year. Retailing is the third largest employer in this country, representing about 14 percent of all jobs. Sales are made by close to 2 million retail establishments.

The importance of retailing goes beyond economic concentration and sales, though. Retailing is essential in providing *time, place,* and *possession utility* to consumers. For example, mass merchandisers such as K mart are giving consumers more possession utility by offering a greater variety of name brands, thus increasing the range of goods available at various prices. They also provide place utility by locating in shopping malls and giving consumers the benefits of one-stop shopping. One-stop shopping also provides time utility by decreasing shopping time.

TRENDS IN RETAILING: PAST AND PRESENT

Retailing is a field of dynamic change, as illustrated by the following description of past and present trends. This dynamism affects the role of retailing in marketing strategies.

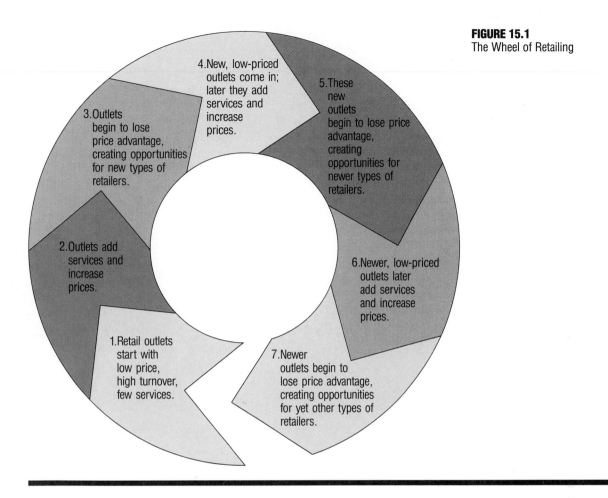

FIGURE 15.1
The Wheel of Retailing

THE WHEEL OF RETAILING

Some writers have seen the emergence of new institutions in retailing as a result of cyclical change that has been described as a **wheel of retailing**.[8] New types of institutions enter into retailing with the same competitive advantage: lower prices as a result of fewer services and lower operating costs. Over time, these outlets begin to add services, increase their prices, and become less efficient, opening up the field for other innovative retailers to come in with the same low-service, low-price advantage. As a result, the wheel of retailing turns again (see Figure 15.1).

This cycle can be seen with the introduction of department stores before the turn of the century. Department stores undercut general stores in price by eliminating personal service and by purchasing in larger quantities. They then became higher priced and added bargain basements for economy-minded shoppers. Higher prices created an opportunity for discount stores to offer lower prices in exchange for reduced services after World War II. The 1970s saw another turn of the wheel with the advent of warehouse clubs. These were the largest outlets yet seen, selling products in a warehouse setting with almost no services and at prices well below discount stores. Warehouse clubs had an opening because discount stores could not hold down operating costs and prices to maintain their competitive advantage.

CURRENT TRENDS

The wheel of retailing continued to turn in the 1980s, with new forms of retailing — specialty retailing, off-price retailing, nonstore retailing, and consolidated retailing.

Specialty Retailing

Specialty retailing emerged in the 1970s as an alternative to mass merchandising. After World War II, retailers such as Sears and Montgomery Ward came to be known as **mass merchandisers** because they offered a wider variety of goods at lower prices. Discount houses such as Korvettes and Goldblatt reinforced the trend to mass merchandising.

The trend to mass merchandising ended in the 1970s, as demographic changes resulted in a fragmentation of the market. Consumers wanted name brands and a greater selection of specialty merchandise. As a result, retailers began offering more limited lines of specialty items, but in deeper assortments. The name of one of the best known specialty clothing stores, The Limited, reflects this strategy. Specialty stores also offered more personalized service in a small shop environment. By 1985 one retail executive noted, "General [mass] merchandisers are getting their heads kicked in by specialty stores."[9]

Mass merchandisers were quick to realize that specialty stores were not the only ones that could engage in specialty retailing. During the 1980s, every leading mass merchandiser climbed on the specialty retailing bandwagon. For example, Sears opened stand-alone hardware and paint stores and launched a chain of children's apparel stores, McKids, with a McDonald's motif.[10] These moves by mass merchandisers show that specialty retailing is not practiced just by specialty stores such as The Limited or The Gap; it is actually a strategy that can be practiced by any retailer that wants to offer more specialized items in deeper assortments.

Off-Price Retailing

A greater emphasis on quality also has led to a trend toward **off-price retailing**, which involves offering brand name merchandise at deep discounts. Many middle-class shoppers, looking for brand names and designer labels as a guarantee of quality, were nevertheless unwilling to pay the high prices charged for such items by department stores. This gave some aware retailers exactly the type of opening predicted by the wheel of retailing — offering the same quality merchandise for lower prices. Stores like Plum's (owned by Dayton-Hudson), Loehmann's (owned by Associated Dry Goods) and T. J. Maxx (owned by Zayre) buy manufacturers' overruns, or orders cancelled by department stores, and sell this merchandise at significant discounts for cash with no exchanges.

Off-price retailing is not restricted to discount retailers such as Plum's or Loehmann's. Like specialty retailing, it is a strategy that can be used by any retailer. In fact, off-price retailing goes hand-in-hand with specialty retailing because both are based on the popularity of high-quality, brand-name merchandise. Thus, when Sears offers name-brand merchandise at reduced prices, it is engaging in both specialty and off-price retailing at the same time. (See Exhibit 15.1 as an example.) In 1989 it reinforced its off-price retailing strategy by further cutting prices on name brands from 10 to 25 percent. Its objective was to stem losses to discount retailers by offering low prices on a consistent basis rather than relying on periodic sales to undercut discounters.[11]

Nonstore Retailing

Another trend in the 1980s has been the increasing importance of **nonstore retailing**, which is any method of selling to a final consumer outside of a store. It includes catalog sales, door-to-door selling, selling by vending machines, and in-home buying by telephone or by newer means such as computer-assisted videotex systems (see Chapter 3). By 1985 nonstore retailing represented about 14 percent of all retail sales, and is projected to account for about one-third of retail sales by 1995.[12]

Although door-to-door selling, catalogs, and vending machines have been around for a long time, two new trends in nonstore retailing emerged in the 1980s. First was the growing importance of catalog sales (in 1986 about half of American adults bought products by mail at least once a year[13]) and their transformation from mass merchandise to specialty vehicles. Second was the increasing importance of in-home shopping, particularly through TV shows.

Consolidated Retailing

In the decade between 1974 and 1984, population grew by 12 percent while space in shopping centers went up by 80 percent.[14] Then retailers began to realize that limited population growth meant fewer shoppers in the long term, so more and bigger stores were obviously not the answer to long-term growth. Rather, smaller and more specialized stores were needed to cater to the needs of more particular and more affluent consumers.

Through **consolidated retailing**, retailers began to consolidate their positions by slowing growth. Many stopped adding new stores. Larger retailers in more mature businesses also felt the best way to grow was by acquiring smaller, faster-growing specialty retailers such as Branden (acquired by Dayton Hudson), and Henri Bendel (acquired by another specialty retailer, The Limited).

TYPES OF RETAILERS

The major types of retailers are divided in Figure 15.2 into merchandisers (sellers of finished, nonfood items) and food stores. These outlets are classified by level of service, price, variety of product lines, depth of assortment in given lines, and size of establishment.

The four types of merchandisers are shown in Figure 15.2 on a continuum, with specialty stores on the full-service, high-price, limited-product-line end of the continuum and discount stores on the limited-service, low-price, and broad-variety end.

Specialty Stores

Stores that are small and carry few product lines in specialty areas but provide a deep assortment of items in these individual lines are **specialty stores**. Examples include clothing stores, furniture outlets, electronics outlets, and stores that sell specialized services such as beauty salons. With the exception of off-price specialty stores such as Loehmann's, they provide full service at higher prices.

Most specialty stores are managed by independent retailers, as opposed to department stores or mass merchandisers that are usually part of a **chain store** (retailers with more than four outlets). As we saw, specialty stores caught the

MERCHANDISERS

FIGURE 15.2
Types of Merchandisers and Food Stores

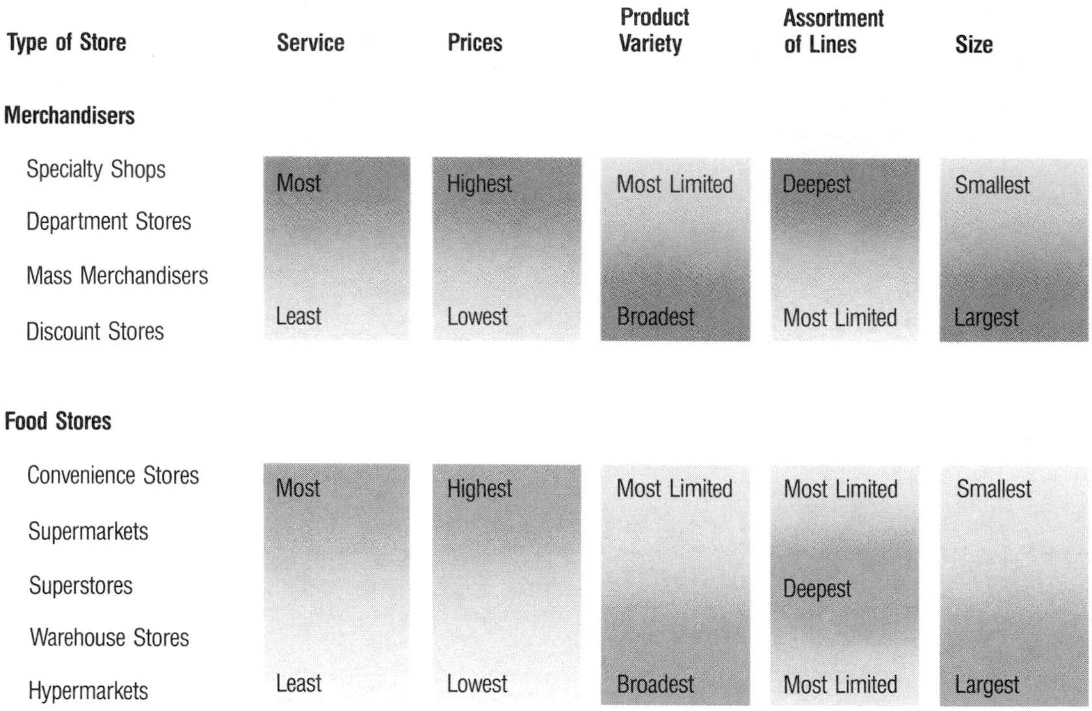

Type of Store	Service	Prices	Product Variety	Assortment of Lines	Size
Merchandisers					
Specialty Shops	Most	Highest	Most Limited	Deepest	Smallest
Department Stores					
Mass Merchandisers					
Discount Stores	Least	Lowest	Broadest	Most Limited	Largest
Food Stores					
Convenience Stores	Most	Highest	Most Limited	Most Limited	Smallest
Supermarkets					
Superstores					Deepest
Warehouse Stores					
Hypermarkets	Least	Lowest	Broadest	Most Limited	Largest

demographic wave in the 1980s and were the fastest growth sector in retailing.[15] The most successful are those that can target their line to a particular niche willing to pay for a wider choice and better service. For example, Georgette Klinger, a New York–based retailer, provides skin-care services to an affluent clientele through a chain of outlets.

Department Stores

In contrast to specialty stores, **department stores** offer a broader choice of merchandise (usually clothing, furniture, and household goods) in some depth. Department stores ran into trouble in the 1980s because they were losing customers on two flanks: (1) specialty stores such as The Limited offered a higher level of service, greater depth of merchandise, and greater responsiveness to fashion trends and (2) mass merchandisers such as K mart and Sears offered lower prices on profitable items such as toys, sporting goods, and appliances.

Many department stores reacted by deciding that "If you can't lick them, join them." For example, Dayton Hudson acquired specialty retailers. Others, such as Macy's and Bloomingdale's, upgraded their lines by establishing departments with higher-quality, specialized merchandise. Some department stores were too late in seeing the need to upgrade their merchandise and establish a new identity. Gimbels took a long sales slide and was finally sold in 1986. Alexander's in New York, Stix Baer & Fuller in St. Louis, and the Wieboldt stores in Chicago all ran into trouble in the 1980s for the same reasons.

Mass Merchandisers

Another type of outlet offering a broad assortment of goods is the **mass merchandiser** such as Sears or K mart. These stores sell at lower prices than department stores or specialty retailers but do not offer the same depth of assortment or service.

Because of their traditional focus on lower-priced, often lower-quality merchandise, mass merchandisers found themselves at a competitive disadvantage to specialty retailers in the 1980s. They tended to concentrate on their own private brands rather than on name brands, and as a result, were bucking the demographic trends that dictated more emphasis on quality and product image.

As we saw, the leading mass merchandisers — Sears, K mart, Montgomery Ward — all finally reacted by moving heavily into specialty retailing without totally giving up their mass-merchandise orientation. Montgomery Ward has taken the most drastic steps to change its merchandise and image. For years it was regarded as the doormat of mass merchandisers because it lacked direction and focus on any particular market segment. A new CEO, Bernard Brennan, moved quickly to transform the company from a mass merchandiser into a collection of value-driven specialty stores. The first prototype specialty store, called Focus Montgomery Ward, was opened in 1986 and carried apparel, home furnishings, appliances, and electronics. Gone were the hardware, gardening and automotive sections typical of mass merchandisers.[16]

Discount Stores

Consumers seeking low prices prefer **discount stores,** which offer goods at the lowest prices on a self-service basis. These stores offer a wide variety of product lines but very limited selections within each line. They first made their appearance in the 1950s when innovative retailers realized they could sell the same merchandise as department stores for substantially less by cutting back on facilities and service. Stores such as Korvette's, Goldblatt's, and Target established themselves as the low-priced alternatives to department stores. As time wore on and the wheel of retailing turned, these stores began to offer more services, their operating costs increased, and they began to lose their price advantage. Many then went out of business. A few, such as Target and T. J. Maxx, survived by discounting brand-name items and becoming off-price retailers.

In the mid 1970s, a new type of discounter emerged, the **warehouse club**. Just as the discount stores of the 1950s undercut the department stores, the warehouse clubs of the 1970s undercut the mass merchandisers. The first was the Price Club, opened in San Diego in 1976. It covered over two acres and stocked a wide variety of products, but with limited assortments in each product line. Customers had to carry heavy items to the cash registers, pay cash, package their own merchandise, and pay a membership fee (hence the term warehouse "club"). The Price Club soon grew to 40 stores, with sales of over $4 billion in 1988.[17]

Although warehouse clubs are not yet widespread, they are a permanent part of the retail landscape. Their no-frills setting and low operating costs will give them a competitive advantage over mass merchandisers into the 1990s.

FOOD STORES

Figure 15.2 shows five types of food outlets, with convenience stores and hypermarkets on the opposite ends of the price, service, and product-variety continuum.

Convenience Stores

Consumers who are willing to pay more in order to buy food quickly often shop at **convenience stores**, neighborhood outlets that stay open longer than supermarkets, carry a limited number of high-turnover convenience items, and charge higher prices because of their higher costs of operation.

Convenience stores have been profitable in recent years because of the greater number of working women requiring off-hour and speedy shopping and the growing number of singles who buy in smaller quantities. The increasing popularity of fast-food establishments has further fueled growth, since consumers are less likely to eat at home and tend to purchase smaller amounts of food, mostly at convenience stores. These stores have grown almost twentyfold in the last 30 years.[18]

Most convenience stores are managed by independent retailers. The largest chain is 7-Eleven, which has over 7,000 stores. It anticipates that demographic trends like the increasing proportion of singles and working women will provide further growth, and is opening up more units as a result.

Supermarkets

Most food purchases are made at **supermarkets** — low-cost, high-volume food outlets that carry an average of 12,000 different products. They offer few services and give most prominent display to high-turnover convenience items. Most supermarkets are chain store operations. The largest are Safeway, Kroger, and American Foods. Many carry their own private brands in competition with national brands.

Demographic trends such as the increasing proportion of singles and working women hurt supermarkets in the 1980s. The greater time crunch led more consumers to use convenience stores, and greater affluence resulted in more consumers eating out, further cutting into supermarket sales.

Supermarkets can ill afford decreased sales. They generally operate on very small profits, averaging 1 percent of sales. Some have tried to increase profits by eliminating low-turnover food items and allocating shelf space to more profitable nonfood items such as toiletries and hardware. The combination of food and nonfood items, known as **scrambled merchandising**, has improved margins.

But most chains have realized that scrambled merchandising is not sufficient to adjust to the environment of the 1980s. They have learned the same lesson as the mass merchandisers — that a highly segmented population means they can no longer take a standardized approach to selling. They have to apply the same concepts of specialty retailing that merchandisers such as Sears and K mart are adopting. Specialty retailing applied to food stores has meant more services such as home delivery and later hours to cater to working women and singles. It has also meant more specialty food items in the stores, such as bakery products, imported goods, and gourmet foods. Some outlets have begun marking store sections more clearly and separating departments to get the busy shopper in and out quickly.

Superstores

As supermarkets introduced a wider variety of food and nonfood lines, they began to expand their size into what became known as **superstores**. Superstores are almost twice as big as the average supermarket — over 40,000 square feet compared to an average of 25,000 square feet for supermarkets — and carry about twice as many items. They offer the deepest assortment of individual food lines. Kroger, Stop & Shop, A&P and Safeway all began building superstores at a fast pace. By 1985 one out of five supermarkets were superstores and they accounted for over 20 percent of total food sales.[19] Kroger's superstores include service departments for meats, cheeses, seafood, deli items, gourmet foods, and baked foods. They also have nonfood sections for drugs, photo finishing, health foods, and flowers. The objective is to compete with convenience stores, stay open just as long, yet also provide the advantage of one-stop shopping through greater variety.

Warehouse Stores

Warehouse stores are deep-discount, no-frills outlets that offer food products in cartons straight from the manufacturer and require customers to bag their purchases. They are the food-outlet equivalent of warehouse clubs. Like the warehouse clubs, they can offer significantly lower prices by buying on a high-volume basis, selling in a warehouse setting, and avoiding service costs. Their operating costs are about one-half those of conventional food stores. Warehouse stores are four times the size of supermarkets and carry more items than superstores. Most carry a wide range of nonfood items. These stores accounted for only 1 percent of food sales in 1976, but by the mid 1980s they accounted for over 10 percent.

The largest chain of warehouse stores is owned by Super Valu, the largest food wholesaler in the country, which runs 16 Cub warehouse stores in the Midwest. Originally, Super Valu viewed the chain as a way to expand its wholesale business, but Cub is now viewed as a profit center in its own right. Supermarket chains began to open warehouse stores in the 1980s. These include Safeway's prototype, Food Barn Warehouse in Kansas City, A&P's Sav-A-Center warehouse stores, and Ralph's Giant stores in Southern California.

Hypermarkets

Continuing the trend to larger food stores offering lower prices has been the establishment of **hypermarkets**, outlets that are combined food stores and mass merchandisers. They offer all the products of a supermarket as well as a larger variety of nonfood items than superstores or warehouse stores. In addition, most hypermarkets have departments typical of mass merchandisers such as automotive supplies, hardware, clothing, and electronics. Some even have beauty salons, fast-food restaurants, and playrooms for children while their parents shop.

To offer the ultimate in one-stop shopping, hypermarkets require huge facilities. Some are over 300,000 square feet, eight times the size of the average superstore, and three times the size of the average warehouse store.[20]

Hypermarkets were first introduced in Europe with the philosophy of providing supermarket facilities, and then drawing shoppers to nonfood items to increase profits. They were introduced into the United States in the early 1970s but failed because American shoppers were not accustomed to buying merchandise and food in the same outlet. As a result, the first hypermarkets could not cover their operating costs. They reappeared on the American scene in earnest in 1987 with the establishment by Carrefour, a large European-based hypermarket operator, of two outlets (see Exhibit 15.2), the opening by Wal-Mart of four hypermarkets, and the planned introduction of additional ones by K mart.[21]

These retailers are reintroducing hypermarkets because the improvements in physical distribution described in the last chapter make it possible to operate these outlets more efficiently than was the case in the early 1970s. It is still too early to tell whether hypermarkets will be accepted by American consumers.

EXHIBIT 15.2
Example of a Hypermarket:
Carrefour USA

Long lines at checkout counters, limited selections, and the trend to specialty retailing rather than one-stop shopping suggest that even the clout of a Wal-Mart or K mart may not be enough to make them successful, despite their advantage of reduced operating costs and low prices.[22]

NONSTORE RETAILERS

Another category of retailers not shown in Figure 15.2 is nonstore retailers, including those selling by catalogs, TV home shopping, door-to-door sales, direct mail, and vending machines. Nonstore retailing is expected to gain an increasing proportion of retail sales in the 1990s due to the increasing numbers of singles and working women, for whom time constraints are most severe and home shopping by catalog and TV home-shopping networks are therefore more desirable.

The importance of catalogs is shown by the number mailed out yearly — close to 9 billion. Sears sends out over 300 million catalogs and generates close to $4 billion in sales from them.[23] Bloomingdale's, Neiman Marcus, and Saks Fifth Avenue use catalogs to sell higher-priced items to an upscale segment. Catalog houses such as L. L. Bean and Spiegel have expanded their business.

Telephone sales through home shopping networks are increasing with the spread of cable TV. By 1987 more than half of all homes with TV sets were able to tune into home shopping networks; 3 million consumers are regular watchers of these shows, and 2 million buy regularly. Many of these people regard home shopping as a social as much as a shopping event, calling in regularly to chat with the host and other viewers. Home shopping has become a cultural phenomenon that is here to stay.

Vending machines are another means of nonstore retailing. They are used to sell to consumers in off-store locations and have the advantage of 24-hour service., The price of vended items is 25 to 30 percent higher than store-bought items because of machine breakdowns, pilferage, and the need to frequently restock widely scattered machines. In addition to convenience items such as candy, soft drinks, and snack foods, recently some retailers have also begun selling clothing and cosmetics through vending machines. In Paris, businesses sell Levi's jeans in vending machines for $47 each.[24]

Other forms of nonstore retailing include door-to-door selling and direct mail. Some manufacturers serve as retailers by selling door-to-door. Companies such as Avon and Mary Kay Cosmetics are essentially nonstore retailers. Consumers can also buy items solicited by direct-mail flyers, letters, and brochures. Certain companies specialize in compiling mailing lists, which are then sold to marketers employing direct mail to sell books, magazines, insurance, and novelty items, to name a few categories.

FIGURE 15.3
Developing Retail Strategies

DEVELOPING RETAIL STRATEGIES

Retailers must develop marketing strategies, just as manufacturers do, but for a different purpose. Retailers' strategies are more focused on getting consumers into their stores and ensuring that they have an assortment of goods to choose from. A marketing planning framework similar to that described in Chapter 8 for manufacturers is also used for developing retailing strategies (see Figure 15.3). Retailers must evaluate their environment, develop objectives, assess alternative strategies, and then evaluate and control them, just as manufacturers do.

Figure 15.3 includes the development of strategies at the level of the entire retail corporation and of the individual store. At the corporate level, retail chains must develop strategic plans that will determine to what extent they will be specialty or general merchandisers, full or off-price merchants, and store or nonstore retailers. Also, corporate planning is necessary to determine whether the company should seek to acquire other retail units, or even other businesses outside of retailing. At the store level, retailers must identify target segments and develop a marketing mix for each store to appeal to these segments.

The first step in developing retail strategies is to evaluate the opportunities and risks in the retail environment. Consumer, competitive, technological, legal, and economic influences are involved.

EVALUATE OPPORTUNITIES IN THE RETAIL ENVIRONMENT

The Consumer

Retailers must assess the environmental trends that affect consumer needs. Two of the most important influences on retail strategies — greater affluence and less time for shopping — have resulted from environmental trends such as the increasing proportion of singles and working women, the greater number of dual-earning households, and the greater affluence of baby boomers as they age. These trends have had a major effect on the strategies of the three key retailing sectors — merchandisers, food stores, and nonstore retailers. It was demographics that led Montgomery Ward to develop its new Focus stores. As Bernard Brennan, president of Montgomery Ward, said:

> We felt that if we wanted to appeal to the . . . Yuppies, we didn't think we could do it with our private labels. So we started adding more brand names. Now we feature almost every major brand in those categories.[25]

Retailers also study the way individual consumers evaluate and select stores. The process of selecting a store to shop in is not that different from the process of brand selection described in Chapter 5. Consumers will process information about a store from various sources — friends, salespeople, advertising, and their own experiences. They will develop an image of the store on this basis. Store image will influence their selection of a store. They will then assess their shopping experience and decide whether they would like to return to the store. If they begin to shop at the same store, they may develop store loyalty, just as they develop brand loyalty for preferred brands.

Retailers attempt to influence consumer images of their stores to foster store loyalty. For example, Macy's tried to establish a new, more trendy image to appeal to the desire for higher fashion and brand-name merchandise among baby boomers. As part of this change, it established a food and kitchenware emporium called Macy's Cellar that was described as "an exciting, sensuous environment [geared to] younger Manhattan lifestyle segments."[26]

Competition

In order to develop a competitive advantage based on price, the quality of merchandise, or service, retailers must evaluate the actions of their competitors. Most retailers were competing on two fronts in the 1980s. First, they were competing with retailers similar to themselves that sold the same types of goods. K mart was competing with Sears, Safeway with Kroger, The Limited with The Gap. Second, they were competing with different types of retailers. When Montgomery Ward started selling electronics in stand-alone stores, it found itself competing with electronics specialty stores such as Newmark and Lewis.

Competition became more intense on both fronts in the last decade. Store expansions in the 1960s and 1970s meant that the same types of stores were competing for consumers. Many of these retailers concluded that the best way to gain a competitive advantage was to go beyond their traditional retail domains and compete in specialty and off-price retailing. As a result, competition between different types of retailers heated up, and the lines between mass merchandisers, department stores, and specialty retailers became more blurred.

Greater competitive intensity during that time decreased retail profits, forcing retailers to reduce their costs in order to maintain profits. More retailers began to use scanners to electronically check out products and automated merchandise-handling systems in their distribution centers as a way to reduce costs. In the last chapter, we saw that Toys "Я" Us and Wal-Mart developed a competitive advantage by selling at lower prices made possible by the lower costs of their more efficient physical distribution systems.

Technology

In addition to electronic checkout systems and automated distribution centers, technology in the 1980s has produced another factor on the retail landscape — electronic retailing, that is, out-of-store kiosks with computer terminals that permit shoppers to obtain product information and to order by using their credit cards (mentioned in Chapter 3). Levi Strauss & Co. has invested in 280 in-store machines with a system, called Jeans Screen™, which serves to communicate, show the product line, and entertain the potential customer. Purchases, however, must still be made through the local retailer (see Exhibit 15.3).[27]

EXHIBIT 15.3
An Example of Electronic Retailing:
Levi's Jeans Screen™

Legal Influences

Retailers are prohibited from engaging in **horizontal price fixing**, which is an agreement among retailers to set a common price in a given area, and **vertical price fixing**, an agreement to fix prices between retailers and manufacturers. In addition, if a larger retailer puts pressure on smaller manufacturers to give it preferential prices, it is guilty of violating the Robinson-Patman Act (see Chapter 3). A&P was involved in a five-year battle with the FTC over charges that it had tried to force its suppliers to grant it lower prices than those charged to other buyers.[28]

Retailers are also prohibited from using deceptive practices such as *bait-and-switch* pricing, in which they systematically advertise products at unusually low prices to get consumers into the store, then claim they are out of the advertised item and attempt to persuade consumers to buy a higher-priced product.

The Economy

Retailers are particularly sensitive to changes in economic conditions because a good proportion of retail sales are tied to disposable income. The only retail segment that is fairly resistant to economic downturns is food stores. Perhaps the sector most sensitive is specialty stores, particularly full-priced retailers. In an economic downturn, consumers are more likely to cut down on purchases of apparel, furniture, jewelry, or gourmet foods than on basics such as food and toiletries. If they do buy specialty items, they are more likely to buy from off-price retailers.

After the stock market crash of October 1987, retailers had a lackluster Christmas season. Most revised their sales estimates downward and put more pressure on store managers to control inventories and cut costs. The stores most adversely affected were specialty apparel retailers such as The Gap and The Limited. Profits for these types of stores in the quarter after the crash were down from 10 to 50 percent.[29]

DEVELOP RETAIL OBJECTIVES

Based on the opportunities identified in its environmental analysis, the retailer sets objectives. These objectives should be broad enough to guide corporate strategies in the form of an overall mission statement, and also specific enough to measure performance at the store level.

Corporate Mission

Retail chains must develop a *mission statement* to guide strategies at the corporate level. For example, Leslie Wexner, founder of The Limited, saw the need for specialty apparel stores across socioeconomic groups. As a result, he developed a mission for The Limited to "blanket every segment of the women's apparel business" with a separate chain of stores.[30] This mission statement determined the company's acquisition strategy in the 1980s.

Performance Goals

Goals must be established to evaluate the performance of the company and of individual stores. Goals at the corporate level involve total company sales, return on investment, and net profits. Goals at the store level involve more specific criteria, such as sales by department and by individual item. A good measure of effective space utilization is *dollar sales per square foot*. Another criterion of performance is the **stock turnover rate**, that is, the rate at which a store's inventory moves over a specific period of time. One study found that retailers with the highest profits also have the highest stock turnover.[31] Supermarkets require stock turns averaging 25 to 30 times a year or about once every other week to be profitable. Mass merchandisers require an average of 15 to 17 stock turns a year.[32]

Another effective measure of performance is **return on assets**, which is the product of the stock turnover and the profit margin. (**Profit margin** is net profits as a percent of sales.) Thus, a supermarket with a stock turnover of 25 and a 1 percent profit margin is achieving a 25 percent return on assets.

DEVELOP CORPORATE RETAIL STRATEGIES

Larger retailers must first develop strategies at the corporate level before considering more specific store strategies. These corporate strategies generally involve decisions regarding whether to promote growth by external acquisitions or by internal development through store expansion.

External Acquisition

Many retail chains have reacted to slow growth in their areas by seeking to acquire higher-growth retailers. For example, Dayton Hudson acquired Branden, a specialty retailer, to better compete on the high-price end of the market, and Mervyn, an off-price retailer, to more effectively compete with mass merchandisers on the low-price end. Dayton Hudson's objective was to broaden its market base in order to appeal to both price-conscious and prestige-oriented consumers.

Some retailers reacted to slow growth by trying to find profit opportunities outside retailing. The leader in this acquisition strategy has been Sears. The company sought growth in financial services by first establishing Allstate Insurance, and more recently, acquiring financial service firms such as Dean Witter, the country's fifth largest stock broker; Coldwell Banker, the largest real estate firm; savings and loan operations in California; and a mortgage life insurance company. Sears introduced many of these financial services in its retail stores. Some

analysts feel that this has sown further confusion in shoppers' minds (see Exhibit 15.4), even though financial services account for close to 40 percent of the company's revenues.[33]

Internal Development

Retailers have promoted growth through internal development, primarily by expanding the number of stores in a chain. Wal-Mart has followed a strategy of store expansion, and with good reason. Its phenomenal success in the South and Southwest can probably be repeated in rural and suburban areas in the rest of the United States.

Retailers can also seek growth through internal development by repositioning themselves, as when the mass merchandiser Montgomery Ward repositioned itself to become a specialty retailer. Such a strategy carries significant risks. First, the Montgomery Ward name will continue to be associated with mass merchandising, not specialty retailing. The company renamed its stores Focus Montgomery Ward and redesigned its logo to try to counteract this. Second, the company may alienate its core customers — middle-to-lower-income, price-conscious consumers — in attempting to attract a more upscale clientele. Third, management is not as familiar with specialty retail operations as it is with mass merchandising.

Because of these risks, a strategy of corporate repositioning should be reviewed carefully and pursued only when sales are stagnating and survival is at stake (which was indeed Montgomery Ward's situation).

IDENTIFY TARGET SEGMENTS AND POSITION STORES

Establishing a corporate mission and growth strategies permits a retailer to identify appropriate target segments for its stores and to position stores to meet the needs of these segments.

We saw that The Limited's corporate mission was to reach as many segments of the women's apparel market as possible. It followed a corporate strategy of both acquisition and store expansion to achieve this aim. Its family of stores is targeted to specific segments with distinct needs. Its flagship chain was designed to appeal primarily to affluent, fashion-conscious baby boomers. But Leslie Wexner, The Limited's founder, realized that in order to catch the next generation of women, he would need a new chain with a trendier image. That is why he started the Limited Express.

He then took aim at the more downscale, price-conscious shopper and bought Lerner Stores to appeal to this group. He spotted yet another segment that he wanted to include in his corporate mix, women that need large-sized apparel. Wexner further split this segment into upscale and budget-conscious women. He acquired Lane Bryant to appeal to the upscale large-apparel market, and Sizes Unlimited to sell budget-priced large sizes.[34]

DEVELOP THE RETAIL STORE'S MARKETING MIX

Once the target segment is identified and a positioning strategy established, retailers can focus on individual stores by developing a marketing mix to give stores a consistent image and to ensure they appeal to the appropriate target segment. A store's marketing mix requires decisions on product mix, service, in-store decor, advertising, price, and location.

Product Mix

Retailers must make decisions about the variety of products they offer and the depth of offerings in individual product lines. J. C. Penney and Sears have followed very different strategies regarding product assortment. Penney has deleted major appliances, paint, hardware, fabric, lawn and garden supplies, and automotive products from its stores, and is increasing the depth of offerings in a more limited line of soft goods. In 1988, clothing accounted for 69 percent of Penney's sales, compared with 49 percent in 1981.[35]

Sears shows no signs of giving up its mass-merchandise orientation, despite its move to include more specialty items in its product mix. The company continues to sell appliances, hardware, automotive supplies, and apparel. The risk is that the combination of general and specialty merchandise may confuse Sears' image.

Service

The level of service offered by a retail store can be the most important component in the marketing mix. One study found that seven of the eleven most important reasons shoppers cited for switching stores were service-related factors such as poor sales help, wrapping, credit, and delivery.[36] Many retail experts identify the quality of sales help as the biggest problem in retailing today. Reduced sales staffs, inadequate employee training, and indifference on the part of sales personnel all contribute to this problem. Retailers such as Bloomingdale's, Dayton Hudson, and Saks Fifth Avenue have instituted sales-training programs to sensitize salespeople to higher service standards.

In-Store Decor

In-store decor (sometimes called **atmospherics**) is an important influence on store image and consumer behavior. The Gap tried to erase its low-price promotional image in the mid 1980s by changing in-store decor to give its stores a more trendy and quality-oriented impression. Out came the 1970s globe lights, cramped stands, and preponderance of blue-denim clothing. In came tiered tables for folded goods, mood-setting pictures on the walls, and more fashionable, color-coordinated clothing.[37]

Advertising

Advertising will also affect a store's image. There are two types of retail advertising: *institutional ads* that attempt to sell the store, and *promotional ads* that attempt to sell the merchandise in the store. Institutional advertising has a longer-

*Highlights from our garment-dyed cotton jersey group. Includes pants, shorts, tops, dresses, and a skirt.
In 7 colors. $14 to $38. Arriving at Gap stores throughout the season.*

EXHIBIT 15.5
Institutionally Oriented Retail Ad

term impact, and many national chains spend millions of dollars on it. (In recent years, K mart's advertising budget has been well over $500 million a year.) Promotional advertising, focusing primarily on price and special sales, has a shorter-term impact and usually appears in newspapers.

Some retailers have moved away from price-oriented promotional advertising in order to attract a more upscale clientele. The Gap switched from promotional newspaper and radio ads to institutionally oriented ads in upscale magazines such as *Vogue* (see Exhibit 15.5).

Price

Consumers could be alienated or confused when a store's advertising (or decor) does not match the price of the merchandise. For example, frequent sales by a store trying to convey a prestige image would be counterproductive. Therefore, retailers must follow a general pricing policy that reflects their store image.

In setting price levels, most retailers use a *markup approach,* adding a certain margin to the cost of the item to cover their expenses and to try to meet profit goals. A typical markup might be 50 percent of the selling price, but the percentage varies greatly among product lines. Lower-priced items can carry lower markups because they are likely to turn over faster.

Other pricing decisions concern the level and timing of markdowns. Discounters and off-price retailers are likely to mark down merchandise early to promote higher stock turnover. Stores that do not mark down on a daily basis run holiday sales or semiannual clearances to sell slow-moving merchandise. Retailers sometimes mark down their merchandise in stages, offering a greater markdown as the item remains in stock longer.

Location

The starting point for a store's locational decisions must be the definition of its target segment. A retailer must first identify the most attractive communities in which to locate by the degree to which they represent the target segment. For example, The Broadway, a department store chain based in Los Angeles, appeals primarily to upscale working women. New store locations should be selected in more affluent areas of the city with a higher proportion of working women. On the other hand, the location of convenience stores such as 7-Eleven cannot be targeted as precisely based on consumer characteristics because these stores must be in diverse neighborhoods to provide easy accessability.

After determining the area, the retailer must choose a specific site, based on pedestrian and vehicular traffic, distance of prospective shoppers from the site, and number of competitive retailers in the area. Additional considerations are local market characteristics such as population size, population density, income level, and household composition.

EVALUATION AND CONTROL

The last step in the process of developing retail strategies is evaluation and control of retail operations. Performance at the company-wide level is compared to projected performance on sales and returns on investment, and at the store level to projected sales by department and product line. Stock turnover and return on assets are also evaluated.

The areas that create the most control problems in retailing are shrinkage, space utilization, inadequate stock turnover, and product proliferation. **Shrinkage** is the theft of merchandise by customers or employees. The cost of shrinkage represents 7 percent of retail sales.[38] Retailers try to control it by store cameras, security guards, and automatic alarms that sound when unchecked merchandise is brought out of the store.

Poor use of space is an even more serious problem, and it is one of the reasons Sears's selling costs are higher than K mart's. Only about 55 percent of Sears's floor space in its large shopping mall stores is devoted to sales compared to nearly 80 percent for K mart stores. Most of the rest of Sears's floor space is used for storage.

Stock turnover is tied to space utilization, since greater turnover means more sales per square foot. When Sears reduced its prices across the board in 1989, it achieved a higher turnover rate on its merchandise, thus reducing its inventories and converting some of its storage space to more profitable sales usage.[39] Reduced inventory as a result of higher turnover could be counterproductive, however, if it leads to out-of-stock situations.

Another control requirement is tracking the profitability of specific products and deleting them if they fail to meet profitability or turnover objectives. Sears had control problems on this score in the 1970s when it failed to delete unprofitable lines. The store now requires that product lines be justified on a profit basis.

Debbi Fields has come a long way since she borrowed $50,000 from her husband in 1977, opened her first Mrs. Fields cookie store, and lured customers in by distributing free cookies outside the store.[40] She was only a 20-year-old novice then, but now owns more than 650 Mrs. Fields bakery cookie stores nationwide and abroad, generating close to $100 million in sales.[41]

**Mrs. Fields —
Is She One Smart Cookie
When It Comes to Control?**

Mrs. Fields Inc. is certainly interesting as a retail success story — a specialty retail chain that started out with an unswerving commitment by one person to product quality and customer service. But there are a lot of interesting retail success stories. The noteworthy factor in Mrs. Fields's story is her day-to-day management of stores from an office in Park City, Utah.

As she became successful, Debbi Fields realized that more was needed than frequent personal visits to her stores. Mrs. Fields Inc. established a computerized management information system that allows two-way contact with the team members in each store. The system tracks past sales performance for each outlet, generates a sales projection for any given day based on past performance, and then computes how many batches of cookie dough have to be mixed to meet demand and to minimize leftovers. As sales are made, they are fed into the computer. The computer then revises projections during the day.

Assisting Debbi Fields are seven store controllers working in Park City from daily store reports and weekly inventory reports. If a store's sales are off, the controller will contact the store and determine why. Are cookies being baked fast enough? Are salespeople doing enough to attract customers into the store? Over and above this level of control, most store owners still rely on yearly visits by Debbi Fields and frequent contacts by electronic mail to keep things moving.

But are there dark clouds on the horizon for Mrs. Fields cookies? Rental and other costs skyrocketed in 1987 and 1988, resulting in sizable losses. Further compounding her problems, Debbi Fields decided to diversify many of her stores to defray costs by selling soup and sandwiches. This diversification has further complicated control issues and may result in company identity problems.[42]

Debbi Field's experience shows that even a sound control system can suffer from rapid growth and unseen environmental factors. For Mrs. Fields cookies, it's a whole new ballgame. ■

IMPORTANCE OF WHOLESALING

As we saw in Chapter 13, wholesaling is the sale of goods to other intermediaries or directly to manufacturers, but not to final consumers. The importance of wholesaling can be measured by its economic magnitude. Wholesale sales are actually greater than retail sales, close to $3 trillion a year. The reason is that the wholesale sector sells both industrial and consumer goods, whereas by definition, retail sales represent only consumer goods.

Wholesaling plays a critical role in providing *time, place* and *possession utility* to industrial customers and final consumers. Without wholesalers, manufacturers would have to deal directly with retailers or with their customers, and retailers would have to buy directly from manufacturers. Most retailers and manufacturers are too small to buy and sell direct; they need wholesalers.

Wholesalers also provide essential services to larger retailers and manufacturers. Many of these firms have found that it is cheaper to use distribution centers and transportation facilities owned by wholesalers rather than to set up their own physical distribution facilities. In fact, the trend in the last decade has been for manufacturers and retailers to increasingly rely on independent wholesalers rather than to sell direct.

Another measure of the importance of wholesaling is its increasing power in the channel system. As wholesalers have provided more services to manufacturers and retailers, they have become a more indispensable part of the distribution link to the customer. Larger wholesalers have served the role of channel leader by managing the flow of goods from manufacturers to retailers and industrial users. For example, McKesson, the largest wholesaler in the country, has helped some of the manufacturers it purchases from to manage inventories, collect and analyze market data, plan sales campaigns, and even develop new products based on market feedback. It is helping its retail customers, particularly independent druggists, by setting up computerized ordering systems, providing in-store promotional programs, and organizing them into voluntary chains so they can achieve economies of scale in buying.

An indication of the increasing power of wholesalers is that some of them have acquired their own retail units. Wetterau, the third largest food wholesaler, established a chain of 93 food stores.[43] Today, close to 20 percent of its sales comes from retailing.

TRENDS IN WHOLESALING: PAST AND PRESENT

Wholesaling was not as important 50 years ago as it is today. The Great Depression in the 1930s caused many manufacturers to become more cost-conscious and reassess the role of the wholesaler. Viewing wholesalers as mere order takers, they decided to "bypass the wholesaler" and perform the wholesale function themselves — usually more cheaply and efficiently.

The trend of bypassing the wholesaler persisted into the 1970s. But then a remarkable shift began taking place in the wholesaler's role from routine order taker to an intermediary providing greater distribution efficiency. Many wholesalers had realized that the only way they could grow was to offer more services, and to do so more efficiently.

This transformation became known as **value-added wholesaling**, which meant improving wholesaling productivity by providing more services and lowering the cost of these services through automation. McKesson was one of the first to implement it — with many of the automated physical distribution facilities described in the last chapter. Its intent was to "make the company so efficient at distribution that manufacturers could not possibly do as well on their own."[44] One result of McKesson's effort was that by 1985 drug companies were selling 65 percent of their products through wholesalers compared with only 45 percent in 1970.[45]

McKesson provided an improved physical distribution system to its retailers as well as to manufacturers. It gave its druggists scanners that allowed them to track inventory and to order based on product bar codes. It started a computerized order-entry and merchandise-handling system that gave each druggist detailed reports showing how its products sold and even suggested the best placement for products on pharmacy shelves. McKesson's shift from an order taker to a value-added wholesaler had an immediate effect on profits, which rose tenfold from 1976 to 1981.[46]

Other wholesalers followed McKesson's lead. The largest food wholesalers — Super Valu, Fleming, Wetterau — have automated distribution centers and computerized systems that equal McKesson's. As a result of their move to value-added wholesaling, the number of retail food chains distributing through wholesalers doubled from 1980 to 1985.[47] Today most wholesalers are following the value-added trend, as indicated by the fact that three out of four have computerized order-processing systems.

TYPES OF WHOLESALERS

The various types of wholesalers in the distribution system are as diverse as the different types of retailers. So far, we have provided examples of independent wholesalers. Figure 15.4 shows that the wholesaling function can also be performed by manufacturers and retailers. In this section, we talk about both company-owned and independent wholesalers.

COMPANY-OWNED WHOLESALE OUTLETS

We saw in Chapter 13 that some manufacturers market directly to their customers, primarily to industrial firms, by integrating forward and assuming the wholesaling function. IBM, 3M, and General Electric have a dual-distribution system in which they market directly and also through independent wholesalers. Manufacturer-owned warehouses designed to handle merchandise and store inventory are known as **sales branches**. Manufacturers use branches to sell to the largest retailers and industrial buyers and distribute to smaller customers through independent wholesalers. Manufacturers' branches represent about 10 percent of all wholesale facilities yet account for over one-third of wholesale volume, reflecting the fact that they sell to the largest accounts.

Large retailers integrate backward by developing their own warehouse and distribution centers. Mass merchandisers such as K mart and Sears, and food chains such as Safeway and Kroger, all have a dual-distribution system in which they buy directly from larger manufacturers and use independent wholesalers to

FIGURE 15.4
Types of Wholesalers

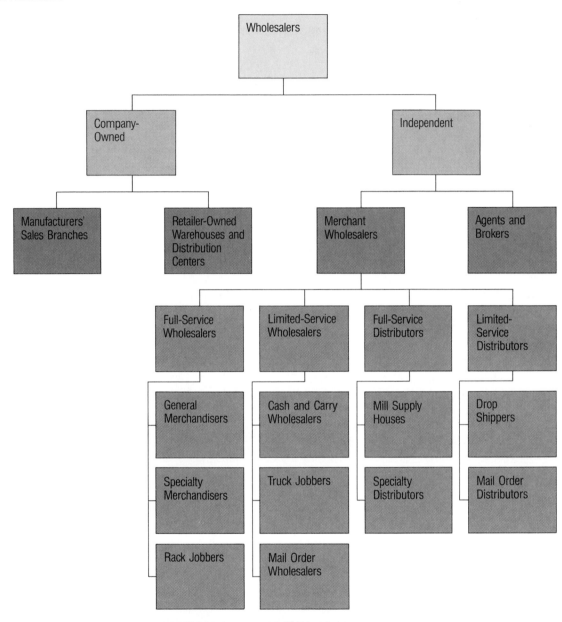

supply them with goods from smaller manufacturers. Retailers use their own distribution centers as ship-through facilities when they buy from larger firms. These facilities provide retailers with less spoilage, better inventory control, and quicker delivery.

INDEPENDENT WHOLESALERS

Independent wholesalers may be merchant wholesalers or agents and brokers. Figure 15.4 shows the various categories of each. **Merchant wholesalers** purchase and take ownership of goods; agents and brokers (discussed in Chapter 13) serve as intermediaries between buyers and sellers without taking ownership of the merchandise. Merchant wholesalers may sell consumer or industrial goods on a full-service or limited-service basis. When they sell industrial goods, they are known as distributors.

Full-Service Wholesalers

Full-service wholesalers perform a wide range of services such as storing goods, controlling inventory, processing orders, and transporting merchandise. Larger full-service wholesalers extend credit to retailers and help them set up order-processing and inventory-control systems. Two examples are McKesson and Super Valu.

Full-service wholesalers are classified by the assortment of merchandise they carry. **General-merchandise wholesalers** carry a broad assortment of merchandise (many different product lines), but in so doing, sacrifice depth in each line. For example, McKesson carries both drug and non-drug items. It stocks almost every product line that can be found in a drugstore, but may not carry every brand of analgesic or stomach remedy. **Specialty merchandise wholesalers** specialize in certain product lines such as health foods, perishable food items, or automotive parts, and carry a deep assortment of alternatives in each line.

A particular type of full-service wholesaler is a **rack jobber**, which displays merchandise in the store by stocking the racks, thus relieving retailers of inventory control and ordering. Rack jobbers sell these items on consignment — that is, they bill the retailer only when the item is sold, in effect extending the retailer credit. They appeared on the scene when food retailers began to stock nonfood items and found the ordering and merchandise-handling costs for these products too high. As a result, independent wholesalers began to take over these functions.

McKesson sometimes acts as a rack jobber for jewelry and cosmetic items in drugstores that lack the time or know-how to properly order and display these items. Close to 1,000 McKesson employees service stores from all 58 of the company's distribution centers. Once McKesson took over as a rack jobber, sales in these categories shot up 80 percent.[48]

Limited-Service Wholesalers

Limited-service wholesalers eliminate certain distributive functions such as transportation, merchandise handling, and credit, and can offer buyers lower prices as a result.

Cash-and-carry wholesalers sell from warehouse facilities. Buyers must pay cash and transport their merchandise. These facilities are the same as retail warehouse clubs, except that cash-and-carry wholesalers will sell only to business firms, whereas retail clubs also sell to consumers. Makro Self-Service Wholesale Corp. is one of the largest cash-and-carry wholesalers in the country. It owns four 200,000-square-foot distribution centers and sells exclusively to business people. Stores carry an average of 35,000 items in a wide variety of categories from food to typewriters. Makro's Washington store has sales of over $200 million a year.[49]

Truck jobbers are small wholesalers that specialize in storing and quickly delivering perishable items such as dairy products, baked goods, fruits and vegetables. They sell directly from their trucks to small retailers for cash.

Mail-order wholesalers sell out of a catalog to small retailers, usually in outlying areas that full-service wholesalers would find too costly to serve. They are used to sell items such as hardware, specialty foods, and jewelry.

Distributors

Distributors can provide full or limited services. Full-service distributors are general or specialty distributors, depending on the assortment of lines carried. A full-service distributor that sells a wide variety of lines is sometimes referred to as a **mill supply house.** In contrast, **specialty distributors** concentrate on specific lines such as generators, power tools, or industrial fasteners.

Two types of limited-service distributors are drop shippers and mail-order distributors. **Drop shippers** (sometimes called desk jobbers) take title to the goods they sell but never possess them. They obtain orders from industrial buyers or other distributors and then forward these orders to producers for shipment. They do not store, handle, or transport the items ordered. They sell primarily bulky items having high transportation costs, such as coal, lumber, chemicals, or industrial machinery. **Mail-order distributors** are the same as mail-order wholesalers except that they sell to industrial buyers. They sell specialized items out of a catalog that can be easily sent by mail.

DEVELOPING WHOLESALE STRATEGIES

Like retailers, wholesalers must establish corporate strategies and a marketing mix. Wholesalers have been less systematic than retailers in developing strategies. With the move to value-added wholesaling, many began to develop strategies based on the steps in Figure 15.3. As with retailers, wholesalers must formulate corporate marketing strategies and a marketing mix that can be implemented by individual wholesale outlets.

CORPORATE WHOLESALE STRATEGIES

Many wholesalers have followed a policy of acquiring other wholesalers as a means of expanding their facilities and offering more and better services. In the early 1980s, McKesson bought four large drug and beauty product wholesalers.[50] It also decided to shore up its drive to automation by buying a 50 percent interest in an inventory-control software firm. The corporate mission guiding these acquisitions was to establish McKesson as a value-added wholesaler and to apply its network of automated services to all of its customers.

Other wholesalers have used acquisitions to get into retailing. Large food wholesalers such as Super Valu and Wetterau have acquired food chains, reasoning that owning their own retail establishments would (1) give them assured outlets for their products and (2) improve efficiency by using one integrated ordering and inventory-control system.

Some wholesalers have sought to grow by internal development rather than by acquisition, building warehouses and distribution centers in new markets. Super Food Services, another food wholesaler, is an example. Its president believes that owning retail stores would mean the company was competing with its own customers. Instead, the company has followed a market-expansion route through a $45-million capital improvement program to build new distribution centers and modernize existing facilities.[51]

THE WHOLESALER'S MARKETING MIX

Like retailers, wholesalers must make product-assortment, price, promotional, and location decisions. Regarding product assortment, wholesalers must decide whether to carry a full line of products or to specialize in a few lines. Just as there is a trend to specialty retailing, there is a strong trend to specialty wholesaling —

concentrating on fewer but more profitable items and providing a higher level of service for those items.

Wholesalers usually set prices on a *markup* basis, often 20 percent, to cover expenses and produce profits that average anywhere from 1 to 3 percent of sales.

Wholesalers generally do little advertising, although some advertise in trade publications. They promote their goods primarily through personal selling. An important aspect of value-added wholesaling is to ensure that the salesperson is more than an order taker, and assists retailers in making the right decisions regarding product assortment and inventory control. In the industrial sector, salespeople must act almost as consultants. One distributor of abrasives and cutting tools goes so far as to say the company does not employ salespeople but rather, "specialists who are qualified to assist our customers with a wide range of questions concerning applications."[52]

Wholesalers must also make decisions about where to locate warehouses and distribution centers. These facilities should be located in areas that will minimize transportation costs to customers. Another factor in the locational decision is the cost of establishing a distribution center that may run several hundred thousand square feet. Low-rent areas and industrial parks are favored.

Overall, wholesalers have become more sophisticated in developing marketing strategies to meet customer needs. They have shown a remarkable resilience in the last decade by increasing their efficiency and demonstrating to manufacturers and retailers that it is generally more economical to use their services rather than bypass them in the distribution channel.

SUMMARY

1. *What are the most significant trends in retailing today?*
The 1980s saw important changes in the retail environment, the most important being the increasing importance of specialty retailing. Greater affluence meant that shoppers wanted name brands and a greater variety of merchandise. Another important trend was off-price retailing, that is, offering high-quality name-brand items at deep discounts. A third trend saw an increase in sales through nonstore retail facilities, particularly catalogs and TV shopping networks. This trend was spurred by the time-saving convenience of buying at home. A fourth trend was the shift from expansion to consolidation in retailing. America became overstored in the 1970s, and many retailers began concentrating on becoming more productive in existing facilities rather than expanding by building new facilities.

2. *What are the most important types of retailers?*
Retailers can be classified as merchandisers, food outlets, and nonstore retailers. The most important merchandisers are specialty stores (small stores carrying a few specialty lines), department stores (full-service outlets that carry a greater number of lines), mass merchandisers (limited-service stores that offer a broad variety of product lines at low prices), and discount stores. Food outlets include convenience stores (neighborhood food stores that offer the convenience of longer operating hours), supermarkets (lost-cost, high-volume outlets that carry many different products), superstores (large stores carrying twice as many items as supermarkets), warehouse stores (deep-discount, no-frills outlets that offer merchandise in warehouse facilities), and hypermarkets (giant-sized outlets that offer both food and a wide variety of non-food items at low prices). Nonstore

retailers include companies that sell by mail order, by telephone, through vending machines, door-to-door, and by direct mail.

3. *How are retail marketing strategies developed at the corporate and store levels?*

Retailers must evaluate their environment, develop objectives, assess alternative strategies, and then evaluate and control them. At the corporate level, they may follow acquisition strategies for growth or grow through internal development by opening new stores or by repositioning themselves to enter new lines.

Retailers must develop a mix of strategies to give their stores a consistent image and to ensure they appeal to the appropriate target group. Store managers must make decisions regarding the product mix, service, in-store decor, advertising, price, and location.

4. *What are the most significant trends in wholesaling today?*

The most significant trend in wholesaling has been a shift from an old-fashioned order-taker mentality to a focus on higher productivity through computerized order-processing systems, automated merchandise-handling methods, and modern distribution centers. This recent focus on efficiency and productivity has come to be known as value-added wholesaling.

5. *What are the most important types of wholesalers?*

Wholesaling can be performed through company-owned or independent wholesalers. Company-owned outlets may be manufacturers using sales branches or retailers using company-owned warehouses. Most wholesalers are independents, divided into those that take title to goods (merchant wholesalers) and those that do not (agents and brokers). Some merchant wholesalers provide full services. These include general-merchandise and specialty wholesalers and rack jobbers. Merchant wholesalers that provide limited services include cash-and-carry wholesalers and truck jobbers. Merchant wholesalers that sell to industrial buyers are called distributors. These may also be full- or limited-service wholesalers.

KEY TERMS

Wheel of retailing (p. 405)
Specialty retailing (p. 406)
Mass merchandisers (p. 406)
Off-Price retailing (p. 406)
Nonstore retailing (p. 407)
Consolidated retailing (p. 407)
Specialty stores (p. 407)
Chain stores (p. 407)
Department stores (p. 408)
Mass merchandisers (p. 409)
Discount stores (p. 409)
Warehouse clubs (p. 409)
Convenience stores (p. 410)
Supermarkets (p. 410)
Scrambled merchandising (p. 410)
Superstores (p. 410)
Warehouse stores (p. 411)
Hypermarkets (p. 411)
Horizontal price fixing (p. 415)
Vertical price fixing (p. 415)

Stock turnover rate (p. 416)
Return on assets (p. 416)
Profit margin (p. 416)
Atmospherics (p. 418)
Shrinkage (p. 420)
Value-added wholesaling (p. 423)
Sales branches (p. 423)
Merchant wholesalers (p. 424)
General-merchandise wholesalers (p. 425)
Specialty merchandise wholesalers (p. 425)
Rack jobbers (p. 425)
Cash-and-carry wholesalers (p. 425)
Truck jobbers (p. 425)
Mail-order wholesalers (p. 425)
Mill supply houses (p. 426)
Specialty distributors (p. 426)
Drop shippers (p. 426)
Mail-order distributors (p. 426)

QUESTIONS

1. Why did K mart move into specialty retailing? What strategies did it use to do so?
2. According to the "wheel of retailing" concept, on what basis do institutions first enter into retailing, and how do they lose their competitive advantage?
3. What have been some of the most significant trends in retailing in the 1980s? Cite examples of each.
4. One department store executive commented on in-home shopping as follows:

   > I just don't think sales through home shopping networks are going to continue to increase. This is a passing fad. Most people want to see merchandise, compare items, and ask a salesperson's advice. Shopping gives a lot of people pleasure. And despite their name, home shopping networks don't let people shop. We were considering buying into a cable home shopping show, but I strongly recommended against it.

   a. Why did in-home shopping increase in the 1980s?
   b. Do you agree with the reasons cited by the executive as to why people are unlikely to buy from home shopping networks?

5. How does Montgomery Ward's strategy to reposition itself as a specialty retailer differ from K mart's? What are the risks of Montgomery Ward's strategy?
6. What was the impact of the following environmental trends on retail strategies in the 1980s?

   a. More singles and working women.
   b. Technological advances in retailing.
   c. The stock market crash of 1987.

7. What corporate strategies have large retailers followed to promote growth? Cite examples.
8. An executive of a large department store chain, reflecting on the company's strategy of acquiring non-retail businesses in the 1970s, said:

   > Buying into businesses that had growth potential looked good on paper. But we quickly discovered we are retailers, not drug manufacturers, electrical distributors, or appliance producers. We had to go back into the retailing business.

   a. Do you agree with the statement? Why or why not?
   b. Why did retailers such as Sears follow a policy of acquiring businesses outside of retailing?

9. How did Leslie Wexner, founder of The Limited, follow an effective market-segmentation strategy in the women's apparel market?
10. What are some key areas of performance that retailers seek to control? Why are these areas of concern to retailers?
11. What is value-added wholesaling? What steps did McKesson take to become a value-added wholesaler?
12. What is the distinction between full-service and limited-service wholesalers? Cite examples of each, specifying why they are full- or limited-service wholesalers.

CASE 15.1

A SUCCESSFUL OFF-PRICE RETAILER: DRESS BARN

Source: Adapted by permission of *Forbes* magazine from "Macy's Buyer Makes Good," by Alyssa A. Lappen, *Forbes,* February 22, 1988, pp. 54–55. © Forbes Inc.

In 1949 Elliot Jaffe graduated from the Wharton School and went to work at Macy's in New York City. For the next six years Jaffe bought baby carriages and girls' sportswear for the big retailer, then became a supervisor. In 1962 he noticed the success that Caldor, then a young Connecticut chain, was enjoying by selling discounted typewriters and television sets. Jaffe, 36 at the time, convinced his wife, Roslyn, that women's fashion apparel could be discounted, too. She volunteered to open a store in Stamford, Conn. with $5,000 of their savings. They called it the Dress Barn.

"It was a concept waiting to happen," Jaffe recalls. He was right. Profits from Roslyn's store began rolling in, enabling Jaffe to quit Macy's and open two more Dress Barn stores in the wealthy suburbs of Wilton, Conn. and Mount Kisco, N.Y.

Did the Jaffes fiddle with their concept? Diversify? They did not. "For 26 years, we have kept the same formula — quality labeled fashions at a 20% to 50% discount from department store prices," says Elliot Jaffe, now 61 and slight, trim and tanned. "We have never carried seconds or irregulars."

Consistency has made Dress Barn a 307-store chain doing business in 26 states, mostly on the East Coast and in the Midwest. Sales have more than doubled since 1984 (to $181 million in the last 12 months), while earnings have quintupled (to nearly $14 million).

As Jaffe tells it, the creation of Dress Barn was easy. It wasn't. At first, few top-line manufacturers saw any benefit in putting first quality clothes on Dress Barn's off-price racks. Sell to the Jaffes at a discount? Forget it. Jaffe was often forced to buy at full wholesale prices through his contacts from Macy's. Some manufacturers insisted that their labels be cut out before Jaffe knocked their goods down. To get around this hurdle, Jaffe's label snippers managed to leave a tantalizing letter or two on the garment — the two E's, say, in an Evan-Picone label — and his salespeople filled in the blanks. Shrewd merchandising, that. What customer doesn't like to think he or she is getting such a deal that the manufacturer is loath to acknowledge it?

By the mid-Seventies, Dress Barn had 18 stores and enough buying clout that manufacturers like Liz Claiborne, Ciao, Jones New York and Calvin Klein Sport were all happy to sell to Jaffe, labels included. Operating from no-frills offices next to a Stamford warehouse, Jaffe was, after all, a steady customer who paid his bills on time — not always a business practice among fashion retailers. Most important, he asked for none of the concessions regularly demanded by department stores — the cooperative advertising allowances, return privileges or subsidies to guarantee a store's gross margins.

By giving Jaffe 20% to 40% discounts, manufacturers found they could fill otherwise unused capacity, or clear out unwanted stock late in the season. Last fall, for example, when millions of sweaters were sitting unsold on the shelves of the Gap and the Limited, Dress Barn was helping importers clear out their slow-moving woolens at steep discounts and selling them for as little as $20.

Can Jaffe continue to produce growth? No guarantees, but he might. Dress Barn is unrepresented in hundreds of markets with high concentrations of the career women who are Dress Barn's best customers — and who will likely remain so if the economy slumps. Dress Barn has yet to open in Delaware, for example, and has only 17 stores on the West Coast.

1. How is Dress Barn able to sell more brands at steep discounts?
2. What recent trends in retailing does Dress Barn's strategy reflect?
3. Is Dress Barn an example of the "wheel of retailing" concept? Why or why not?

CASE 15.2

SEARS MOVES TO SPECIALTY RETAILING

Source: Adapted from Julia Flynn Siler, "New at Sears: Specialty Retailing," *The New York Times,* October 7, 1988, pp. D1, D5.

Struggling to revitalize its lackluster general merchandise business, Sears, Roebuck & Company is taking a lesson from the specialty retailer. It hopes to repeat the success of such specialty stores as the Gap, Circuit City, Toys "Я" Us and the Limited.

Sears has been acquiring specialty store chains like the Western Auto Supply Company, Eye Care Centers of America and Pinstripes Petites, a women's apparel chain. In most cases it plans to operate them separately from Sears stores.

In August Sears opened the first McKids store for children's apparel and toys as part of a licensing agreement with the McDonald's Corporation. And it announced plans to open dozens of these free-standing stores over the next two years.

In addition, for the first time in the company's history, Sears has opened in-store appliance and home electronics outlets known as Brand Central. They will offer many brand-name goods alongside Sears's private-label brands.

And Sears recently created a specialty merchandising unit and restructured its buying operations to more closely resemble those of a specialty retailer.

The changes come at a time when the merchandise group, which provided 52 percent of Sears's net income last year and 58 percent of its revenues, continues to suffer lackluster earnings and falling market share.

"To arrest their loss of retail market share, Sears is becoming more like a specialty store," said N. Richard Nelson Jr., an analyst with Duff & Phelps Inc. in Chicago. "But I don't know if that addresses the fundamental problem within the stores."

At the heart of the retailing problem, analysts say, is that the company has not yet determined what it wants the group to be.

"Consumers either want specialty stores with a depth of merchandise, or warehouse stores with low prices,"

said Louis W. Stern, a marketing professor at Northwestern University's J. L. Kellogg Graduate School of Management. "Sears is neither, and as a result, they're in reasonably serious trouble."

Soon after becoming chairman and chief executive of the group in January 1987, Michael Bozic, who is 47 years old, began addressing that problem, and began modernizing the company's antiquated and costly distribution system.

"We decided not to stand by and watch our market share deteriorate," Mr. Bozic said.

The most significant change is the introduction of the Brand Central in-store home electronic and appliance "superstores."

Although other mass merchandisers, including its cross-town rival, Montgomery Ward, have pursued similar strategies in recent years, the move is significant for the tradition-bound Sears.

Describing Brand Central as "a likely harbinger of our future direction," Mr. Bozic said he planned to apply the concept to auto supplies, lawn and garden products and children's clothing. He is also testing the concept of free-standing appliance and home electronics stores to further compete with chains like Circuit City and Highland.

To Compete With Boutiques

In late August, Sears opened the first McKids store, a licensing venture with McDonald's. Offering name-brand clothing and toys, the chain is designed to enable Sears to compete with the boutiques and department stores.

Sears is optimistic about its children's stores. "I don't think anyone in the industry has positioned quite this mix," said John Whitehead, the chain's national manager.

1. What are the similarities and differences between Sears's move to specialty retailing and K mart's?
2. Does Sears's move to specialty retailing make sense? What are the opportunities and risks?
3. How is Sears implementing its strategy?

NOTES

1. "Attention K Mart Shoppers," *Fortune,* January 2, 1989, p. 41; and "K Mart's Antonini Moves Far Beyond Retail 'Junk' Image," *Advertising Age,* July 25, 1988, p. 1.

2. "New Look at K Mart," *Barron's,* May 11, 1987, pp. 8–9, 30, 35.

3. "Attention K Mart Shoppers: Style Coming to This Aisle," *The Wall Street Journal,* August 9, 1988, p. 6.

4. "K Mart Spruces Up the Bargain Basement," *Business Week,* September 8, 1986, pp. 45, 48.

5. "Mass Appeal," *Forbes,* May 5, 1986, pp. 128, 130.

6. "K Mart's Hyperactive," *Advertising Age,* January 23, 1989, p. 1.

7. "Supermarkets Demand Food Firms' Payments Just to Get on the Shelf," *The Wall Street Journal,* November 1, 1988, p. 1.

8. Malcolm P. McNair, "Significant Trends and Developments in the Postwar Period," in A. B. Smith, ed., *Competitive Distribution in a Free, High-Level Economy and Its Implications for the University* (Pittsburgh: University of Pittsburgh Press, 1958), pp. 1–25.

9. "A Nation of Shopkeepers," *INC,* November 1985, p. 66.

10. "Retailing: Everybody's Getting into the Specialty Act," *Adweek,* September 14, 1987, p. 64.

11. Sears Cutting Prices by as Much as 50% in a Shift of Strategy," *The New York Times,* February 24, 1989, pp. A1, D6, and "The 'Sale' is Fading as a Retailing Tactic," *The Wall Street Journal,* March 1, 1989, p. B1.

12. "The Evolution of Retailing," *American Demographics,* December 1986, p. 30.

13. Ibid., p. 32.

14. "Merchants' Woe: Too Many Stores," *Fortune,* May 13, 1985, p. 62.

15. "Going Shopping in the 1990s," *The Futurist,* December 1983, p. 15.

16. "Brennan: Ward's Man with a Mission," *Chain Store Age Executive,* May 1987, p. 206.

17. "They Get It For You Wholesale," *The New York Times Magazine,* December 4, 1988, p. 25.

18. "Inventory of Formats," *Advertising Age,* April 27, 1981, pp. S-4, S-6.

19. "Bigger, Shrewder, and Cheaper Cub Leads Food Stores into the Future," *The Wall Street Journal,* August 26, 1985, p. 19.

20. "How Much Hype in Hypermarkets?" *Sales & Marketing Management,* April 1988, pp. 51–55.

21. "The Return of the Amazing Colossal Store," *Business Week,* August 22, 1988, p. 59.

22. "Going 'Hyper' in a Hypermarket," *Advertising Age,* May 8, 1989, p. S-21.

23. "A Boutique in Your Living Room," *Forbes,* May 7, 1984, pp. 86–94.

24. "Supermarketing Success," *American Demographics,* August 1985, p. 32.

25. *Chain Store Age Executive,* May 1987, p. 205.

26. Roger T. Blackwell, "Successful Retailers of '80s Will Cater to Specific Lifestyle Segments," *Marketing News,* March 7, 1980, p. 3.

27. "Levi Gets Computer Blues," *Advertising Age,* June 24, 1987, p. 28.

28. Ray O. Werner (ed.), "Legal Developments in Marketing," *Journal of Marketing* 43(Fall 1979):125.

29. "After All the Worry, A Sigh of Relief from Retailers," *Business Week,* January 11, 1988, p. 36.

30. "The Limited Is Aiming Higher," *The New York Times,* November 2, 1985, p. 35.

31. Robert D. Buzzell and Marci K. Dow, "Strategic Management Helps Retailers Plan for the Future," *Marketing News,* March 7, 1980, p. 6.

32. "Safeway: Selling Nongrocery Items to Cure the Supermarket Blahs," *Business Week,* March 7, 1977, p. 54.

33. "Once More with Feeling," *Financial World,* September 8, 1987, pp. 112–114, and "Why Once Rock-Solid Sears Struggles," *Advertising Age,* January 30, 1989, p. 24.

34. *The New York Times,* November 2, 1985, p. 41.

35. "New Shine on a Tarnished Penney," *The New York Times,* April 23, 1989, p. 4.

36. "37 Things You Can Do to Keep Your Customers — Or Lose Them," *Progressive Grocer,* June 1973, pp. 59–64.

37. "A Cinderella Story," *Marketing & Media Decisions,* Winter 1986, pp. 46–50.

38. "More Than One Way to Catch a Thief," *Chain Store Age Executive,* April 1982, p. 39.

39. *The New York Times,* February 24, 1989, pp. A1, D6; and "Minding the Store," *Forbes,* April 7, 1986, pp. 31–32.

40. "How the Cookie Crumbles," *Marketing & Media Decisions,* August 1984, p. 114.

41. "Mrs. Fields' Secret Ingredient," *INC,* October 1987, p. 65.

42. "How the Cookie Crumbled at Mrs. Fields," *The Wall Street Journal,* January 26, 1989, p. B1.

43. "Wholesaling Ignored Despite Modernization," *Marketing News,* February 14, 1986.

44. "Foremost-McKesson: The Computer Moves Distribution to Center Stage," *Business Week,* December 7, 1981, p. 115.

45. "For Drug Distributors, Information is the Rx for Survival," *Business Week,* October 14, 1985, p. 116.

46. James A. Constantin and Robert F. Lusch, "Discover the Resources in Your Marketing Channel," *Business,* July–September 1986, p. 21.

47. *Barron's,* October 14, 1985, pp. 32–37.

48. *Business Week,* December 7, 1981, pp. 115, 118.

49. "Makro's Wholesale Merchandising Machine," *The Discount Merchandiser,* August 1982, pp. 53–54.

50. "Distribution Income," *Forbes,* February 17, 1985, p. 126.

51. "The Education of Jack Twyman," *Forbes,* March 11, 1985, p. 75.

52. "Hotline: Value Added, the Key to Distributor Survival," *IS,* November 1985, p. 58.

When McDonald's talks, its competitors listen. Its promotional budget of close to $1 billion completely eclipses those of its four closest competitors; and although at times McDonald's has moved like a lumbering giant, its recent promotional actions have been swift and effective.[1] For example, in 1986 McDonald's just about smothered Burger King's nationwide "Search for Herb" campaign by an avalanche of advertising and couponing for a new McD.L.T. sandwich. The Burger King campaign, which asked consumers to look for the mythical character "Herb" who never visited a Burger King, never got off the ground. McDonald's barrage of network TV advertising at the rate of $5.5 million a week and its flood of coupons offering free McD.L.T. sandwiches effectively stole poor Herb's thunder. One Burger King franchisee said, "We've never witnessed a bombardment like this from McDonald's before."[2]

McDonald's increasing promotional prowess was also illustrated a few years back by its quick shift from a lackluster "McDonald's and You" advertising campaign to a much more effective and upbeat "It's a good time for the great taste of McDonald's." The theme became a centerpiece for communicating McDonald's traditional image of food, fun, and family values.

Then, in 1987 McDonald's surprised just about everyone with its "Mac Tonight" ads. These takeoffs on the song and character Mac the Knife featured a moonfaced crooner playing a piano atop a giant Big Mac, singing "Dinner/At McDonald's/It's Mac Tonight."[3] The departure from its traditional "family" image (prevailing since its founding in 1955) was successful. McDonald's was learning how to appeal to baby boomers and yuppies, and its dinner business consequently grew.

Advertising is only one of three components of Big Mac's promotional attack. The other two are sales promotions (coupons, contests, price-off promotions)

THE PROMOTIONAL MIX, SALES PROMOTIONS, AND PUBLICITY

and publicity. Since the mid 1980s, McDonald's has been putting more money into sales promotions relative to advertising — and for good reason. By 1988 the company had 10,000 stores worldwide and was serving an average of 17 million Americans a day.[4] Although it was still opening restaurants at the rate of one a day, it saw eventual limits to attracting new customers.

An alternative avenue to growth was to encourage customers to eat at McDonald's more often. To this end, consumers were provided with an immediate incentive to go to a McDonald's restaurant: In 1985 a 39-cent hamburger promotion and a "value pack" of discounted meal coupons were launched. In 1986 a scratch card prize game with a National Football League theme was introduced. In 1987 a Monopoly game promotion gave away $40 million in prizes. McDonald's outlets handed out millions of "deeds" to monopoly board locations, and contestants had to put together the right combination of properties to win. By 1988 the company was offering some special promotion almost every week.[5]

The third leg of McDonald's promotional strategy is publicity. McDonald's has always tried to reinforce a positive corporate image by supporting community programs. Thus far it has opened 107 Ronald McDonald Houses providing free rooms to families visiting children's hospitals.[6] It was also one of the corporate sponsors of the 1988 Olympic games and sponsors other gymnastics and swimming events.

McDonald's huge budget for its mix of advertising, sales promotions, and publicity strategies makes it the largest promoter of any single brand in the United States. With clout like that, it is small wonder that one competitor said, "We don't compete with McDonald's, we try to work around them."[7] ■

● ● ●

MARKETING COMMUNICATIONS

McDonald's advertising, sales promotions, and publicity constitute its **promotional mix** — the combination of strategies that a company uses to communicate its benefits to customers and influence them to buy. Four elements are involved: advertising, sales promotions, personal selling, and publicity. The promotional mix is such an important part of the overall marketing mix that each of its components will be examined in detail — sales promotions and publicity in this chapter, advertising in the next, and personal selling and the management of the sales effort in Chapter 18.

The key process underlying the promotional mix is *communications*. Therefore, to understand how the promotional mix influences customers, we should understand the nature of the communications process, particularly in the field of marketing. Any communication, whether it is an advertisement, a word-of-mouth message such as a friend's opinion about a product, or a news message such as a newspaper report or a TV commentary, has certain elements in common. The top of Figure 16.1 shows the elements in a communications model. The bottom of the figure shows them applied to marketing.

THE SOURCE

The first step in the communications process shows that a communication must have a source. The source of the marketing message is the company offering products or services. In its role as the source, the company develops communications objectives and identifies a target for its communications. As an example, in the early 1980s Polaroid saw sales in its core market of instant cameras almost halved in the face of increasing sales of 35mm cameras. Polaroid's answer, which came in 1986, was the Spectra, an instant camera that produced pictures close to 35mm quality with automatic focusing and a self-timer. The promotional objective was to convince consumers that the Spectra was the equal of 35mm cameras with the added advantage of instant pictures. With its price tag of $225, the camera had to be targeted to a younger and more upscale segment than Polar-

FIGURE 16.1
A Model of the Marketing
Communications Process

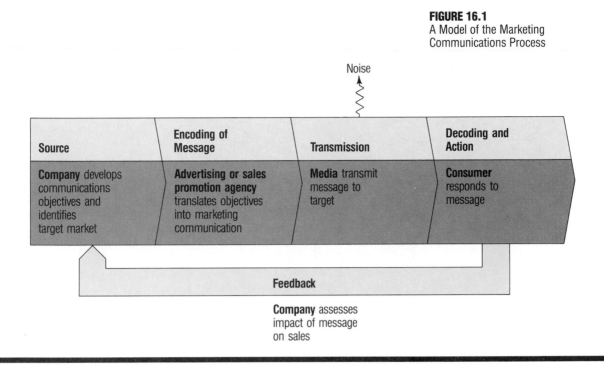

Noise

Source	Encoding of Message	Transmission	Decoding and Action
Company develops communications objectives and identifies target market	**Advertising or sales promotion agency** translates objectives into marketing communication	**Media** transmit message to target	**Consumer** responds to message

Feedback

Company assesses
impact of message
on sales

oid's traditional consumers. As a result, message development and media selection were aimed primarily at baby boomers.[8]

ENCODING

The second step in the marketing communication process is to translate the company's objectives into an advertising or sales promotional strategy that will communicate the appropriate message. This is known as **encoding** the message.

To get across its message of Spectra's parity with 35mm-camera quality, Polaroid's advertising agency decided to use Ben Cross, star of the movie *Chariots of Fire*, as a spokesperson. The agency felt that Cross had an upscale image and that baby boomers would identify with him.

Messages are encoded not only for advertising, but for other forms of marketing communication. For example, Polaroid developed a direct-mail catalogue that emphasized the same message about Spectra as its advertising — the parity of Spectra to 35mm pictures.

TRANSMISSION

The third step in the communications process is transmitting the message to the target audience. Advertising agencies develop a media plan that outlines how to reach the target with a selected mix of vehicles — television, radio, magazines, newspapers, billboards.

Noise in communications is interference that may occur during transmission because of the clutter of messages competing for the consumer's attention. For example, if in the course of a day's viewing, a consumer sees 20 TV commercials, the message communicated in any one commercial may become confused with the others and may be lost in a jumble of competing claims. Such competition for the consumer's attention diminishes a message's effectiveness.

The primary media vehicle to communicate the Spectra message was TV commercials on the major networks. The Ben Cross commercials and other ads comparing Spectra with 35mm pictures appeared on network TV. In addition, print ads were scheduled to appear in all major upscale magazines, and the Spectra was advertised on billboards in 25 markets.[9]

DECODING AND ACTION

The way consumers interpret marketing messages determines how they will react to them. This process of **decoding** involves (1) noticing the message *(awareness)*, (2) interpreting and evaluating it *(comprehension)*, and (3) retaining it in memory *(recall)*.

In our Spectra example, the company hoped that a consumer looking for a simpler alternative to a 35mm camera, who could afford a Spectra, (1) would notice Spectra ads, (2) would interpret and evaluate them as meaning that the Spectra produced comparable pictures to a 35mm camera, and (3) would be likely to remember the message long enough to *act* on it by buying. Judging by the successful introduction of the Spectra camera, the company knew that the basic message had indeed been decoded by the targeted consumers as hoped.

Action — that is, a purchase by the consumer, expressed in sales figures — is the primary criterion for evaluating the effectiveness of a marketing communication. If most consumers had remained unpersuaded that any instant camera could be as good as a 35mm, the sales figures would have shown that the promotional campaign was a failure.

FEEDBACK

Evaluating the impact of communications on sales is termed **feedback**, the final stage of the communications process. As we mentioned, feedback is necessary to judge the success of a communication. Determining this impact is difficult, because the marketer does not know whether a consumer purchases primarily because of the advertising, the recommendations of a friend, a price reduction, poor strategies on the part of competitors, or a host of other environmental factors that might affect consumer actions.

It is almost certain that marketing communications will have some impact on sales. But the key question is how much of an impact. A statement made by John Wanamaker, the famous Philadelphia retailer, over 100 years ago is still largely true today: "I know that half of my advertising expenditures are wasted, but I don't know which half."

One solution to this problem is to look at other criteria in addition to sales — that is, to measure the degree to which consumers are aware of the advertising messages, how they comprehend them, and whether they recall them over time (the three parts of the decoding process). The simple assumption is that a consumer who is aware of the advertising is more likely to buy than one who is not, a consumer who evaluates the ad positively is even more likely to buy, and a consumer who retains the message over time is the most likely to buy. Given the difficulty of linking advertising to sales, advertisers are forced to depend mostly on these measures of effectiveness (awareness, comprehension, and recall).

When the Spectra campaign was evaluated this way, it proved effective on all counts. Awareness of the campaign was high among the target group of affluent baby boomers. They generally evaluated the campaign positively, and a significant proportion recalled the advertising. Sales confirmed these findings, exceeding expectations and reaching close to 800,000 units in the first year.[10] Of equal importance, some experts concluded that the advertising campaign was so successful that it created a more positive image for Polaroid's older instant camera models.

THE PROMOTIONAL MIX

To develop an effective promotional mix, marketers must understand the purposes of each of its elements (advertising, sales promotions, personal selling, and publicity).

Advertising is a paid, ongoing, nonpersonal communication from a commercial source such as a manufacturer or retailer. It communicates messages about a product, service, or company that appear in mass media such as television, magazines, or radio.

ADVERTISING

Advertising has several communications objectives. One is to make consumers aware of a new product. Polaroid introduced the Spectra in 1986 with a $45 million advertising campaign. As a result, the majority of potential purchasers became aware of the availability of the camera. Advertising is also designed to inform. Polaroid's objective was not only to create awareness, but to inform consumers of Spectra's picture quality and features such as the self-timer.

Advertising is also meant to influence consumers to buy. Influencing consumers often requires ads with emotional as well as informational content. "Fly the friendly skies of United" or "It's a good time for the great taste of McDonald's" are themes that are meant to stir up good feelings about the product or service and thus encourage purchase.

Finally, the most important purpose of advertising is to keep the product or service visible to consumers over the long term. The idea is to keep existing customers loyal while ensuring that noncustomers continue to remember the product's existence. In this respect, advertising is insurance against the possibility that the product might fade out of existence. In a sense, it is more of a capital investment, like building a factory to ensure production over the next 20 years, than a short-term expedient to gain sales.

A classic example of the disastrous results of misunderstanding the role of advertising occurred at the turn of the century. The leading bar soap at the time was a brand called Sapolio, with Ivory second. The managers of Sapolio felt their brand was so firmly entrenched that they could cut back on advertising. Soon their market share began slipping, and eventually Sapolio slipped into the history books. Ivory, on the other hand, continued to advertise and thereby has maintained brand awareness to this day.

In contrast to the ongoing role of advertising, **sales promotions** are short-term inducements of value to consumers to encourage them to buy a product or service. Sales promotional tools include *coupons* that can be redeemed for cash; *sweepstakes* and *contests* that involve prizes; and *refunds* on a purchase. Most of these techniques are used to promote consumer packaged goods.

SALES PROMOTIONS

One purpose of sales promotions is to induce nonusers to try a brand in the hope that they will continue to use it. In most cases, consumers who switch into the promoted brand will switch back to their regular brand once the deal is off, but some might switch loyalty to the new brand. And even attracting temporary users over the short term can be profitable. Sales promotions are also designed to motivate existing customers to buy more frequently, like McDonald's sales promotions in the opening vignette. Attracting new customers is secondary in these cases.

Most sales promotions must be combined with advertising to be effective. The price incentive of the sales promotion needs to be complemented by the communication of product or service benefits that advertising provides. When the sales promotion is no longer running and the price incentive is not available, advertising maintains the product's message.

PERSONAL SELLING

Personal selling is face-to-face communication between a company sales representative and a customer designed to influence the customer to buy the company's products or services. It is a powerful element of the promotional mix because the marketer does not have to establish a message beforehand. The salesperson can assess the customer's needs, develop a sales message accordingly, evaluate the customer's reaction, and adjust the approach. Even when it does not result in a sale, personal selling is likely to at least get the attention of the customer and elicit some sort of response that may lead to a later sale.

Advertising and sales promotions tend to support personal selling in that a customer who sees an ad for a product might be more aware of product benefits and therefore more receptive to a salesperson's influence.

Although it is a powerful and effective means of communication, personal selling has two major disadvantages: it is expensive and hard to control. A study by McGraw-Hill estimated that an average call on an industrial buyer costs the selling firm $205, whereas reaching an industrial buyer through a business publication costs an average of only 17 cents.[11] Of course, personal selling is a much more important influence on industrial buyers than magazine advertising, so higher costs are justified. But high costs require managers to maintain tight control over the sales effort. And this brings us to the second disadvantage of personal selling, the difficulty of controlling salespeople's activities. Since a salesperson's message is not prepackaged, it varies tremendously in effectiveness according to the individual salesperson's ability to present it as well as his or her ability to reach the right prospects for a sale.

PUBLICITY

Most companies try to supplement their paid promotional efforts with **publicity**, which is unpaid communication about the company or its product or service in the mass media. Favorable publicity is obtained by providing press releases for radio, newspapers, and magazines; films for television news shows; and public appearances by corporate executives.

Publicity is a subset of a company's broader **public relations** effort, in which it attempts to influence relevant groups such as stockholders, consumers, government and state officials, and other business executives by means of a variety of organized activities. For example, a company might lobby for legislation beneficial to it, or initiate contact with consumer activists such as Ralph Nader in order to convince them that the company is operating in the consumer's interest. Some publicize earnings reports and actions of benefit to the company's stockholders. McDonald's public relations effort involves supporting children's hospitals with its free Ronald McDonald Houses for visitors. Its attempt to communicate these efforts through news releases and reports in the media is the publicity element of its public relations campaign.

Publicity can be both positive and negative. A company tries to encourage positive news and contain or counteract negative news. The oil spill in Alaska in 1989 did tremendous damage to Exxon's image. Some consumers boycotted the company's gas stations. Most of Exxon's top management was preoccupied with damage control of negative publicity for months. Rumors are also a form of negative publicity. The false rumor that Procter & Gamble's man-in-the-moon corporate logo meant that the company's management was tied to a satanic cult was so persistent that the company finally had to drop the logo.

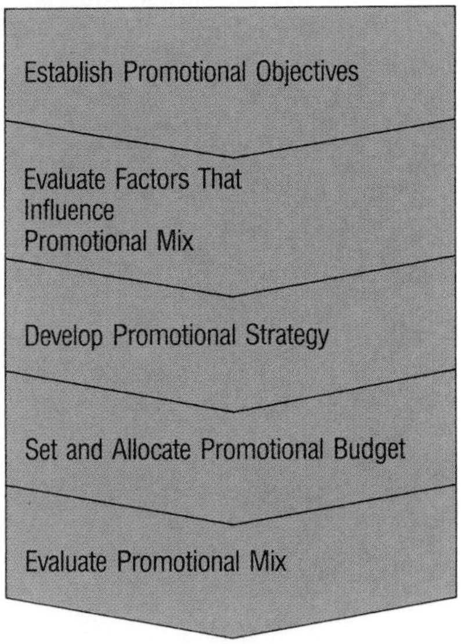

SELECTING THE PROMOTIONAL MIX

FIGURE 16.2
Developing the Promotional Mix

Establish Promotional Objectives

Evaluate Factors That Influence Promotional Mix

Develop Promotional Strategy

Set and Allocate Promotional Budget

Evaluate Promotional Mix

Marketing managers must select a mix of each of the promotional elements of advertising, sales promotion, personal selling, and publicity and allocate resources to each. Firms vary widely in the degree to which they rely on these various elements. Frito Lay relies heavily on TV advertising for its potato chips. Borden Company, its chief competitor, does not have the resources to compete directly with the larger advertising budget of Frito Lay, so it relies almost exclusively on trade discounts and consumer sales promotions in marketing its Cottage Fries potato chips.[12]

Figure 16.2 shows the steps involved in selecting a promotional mix. First come promotional objectives, such as establishing brand awareness, influencing product trial, and encouraging repeat purchasing. Next, managers must evaluate the factors that are likely to influence the promotional mix in order to determine the relative importance of each component. On this basis, a promotional strategy can be developed — that is, the combination of promotional tools required to meet marketing objectives. Now a budget can be formulated in which resources are allocated according to the importance of each element of the promotional mix. The final step is to evaluate the results of the mix and make adjustments where appropriate. Each of these steps will now be examined in detail.

Promotional objectives are formed in terms of what will influence the consumer to buy. If the brand is being introduced, the first objective is to establish brand awareness. The next is to create a positive attitude toward the brand. A third objective is to encourage product trial. And a fourth objective is to influence existing users to buy again. These objectives — awareness, positive brand attitudes, trial, and repeat purchasing — attempt to create a base of loyal consumers over time.

As an example, the promotional objectives for Molson Light, a new Canadian beer import, were to establish brand awareness and influence trial through an advertising campaign linking the beer to the Canadian outdoors. Specific promotional goals might have been to establish brand awareness among 30 percent of beer drinkers in the first six months after introduction into the U.S. market, to achieve trial among 10 percent of all beer drinkers, and to attain a 2 percent share of the beer market within two years after introduction.

ESTABLISH PROMOTIONAL OBJECTIVES

**EVALUATE FACTORS
THAT INFLUENCE THE
PROMOTIONAL MIX**

Once objectives are set, managers must evaluate the factors that determine the relative importance of advertising, sales promotion, personal selling, and publicity. Three factors are particularly important in this regard: the type of customer, type of product, and stage of the product in its life cycle.

Type of Customer

The type of customer the product is targeted to affects the relative emphasis on the various components of the promotional mix. For example, the smaller numbers of industrial buyers, their specialized needs, and their greater geographic concentration make personal selling more important and cost-effective. Advertising would be concentrated in specialized magazines such as *American Machinist, Electrical Construction & Maintenance,* or *Coal Age* because such magazines can reach prospective industrial buyers.

Another set of customers that companies must reach with their promotional mix are retailers and wholesalers. The main vehicles for influencing these intermediaries to stock the company's products are trade promotions and personal selling. Discounts and payments to support a retailer's or wholesaler's promotional efforts are called *push money* because they are designed to push the product through the channel of distribution. Personal selling is part of the push, too.

Companies directing appeals to the final consumer rather than to the trade put more emphasis on advertising and consumer promotions. They rely more on a strategy of *pulling* products through the channels by influencing final consumers to seek them rather than *pushing* products by influencing the trade to offer them. When Polaroid introduced the Spectra, it relied heavily on the pull of advertising to get prospective buyers to camera stores.

In general, more money is spent on trade than on consumer promotions. Without trade support, companies run the risk of spending millions on advertising or consumer promotions only to have consumers unable to find the product.

Type of Product

A product's characteristics will help determine the emphasis placed on each component of the promotional mix. Figure 16.3 shows the relative importance of the four promotional tools for different categories of products — consumer packaged goods, durables, services, and industrial products. Sales promotions are most important for consumer packaged goods because they are frequently purchased, lower-priced items, and consumers are price-sensitive about such items. A consumer intending to buy one roll of Bounty paper towels may buy three rolls during a price promotion. As a result, coupons, premiums, and price deals are effective tools in promoting packaged goods. Sales promotions aimed at the retailer (such as trade discounts) are important in gaining marketers of packaged goods valuable shelf space.

Advertising is most important for consumer durable goods because advertisers must communicate product features and benefits over time. Since consumers pay a higher price for durables such as cars, furniture, or personal computers, advertising must convince prospective purchasers that the product will deliver the expected benefits. Moreover, once a car or a personal computer is purchased, advertising must reassure consumers that they made the right choice.

Personal selling is the dominant element in the promotional mix for service firms because services are often delivered by a salesperson, whether it is a stockholder offering investment advice or a clothing salesperson arranging for alterations and delivery. Also, complex products, products bought on specification,

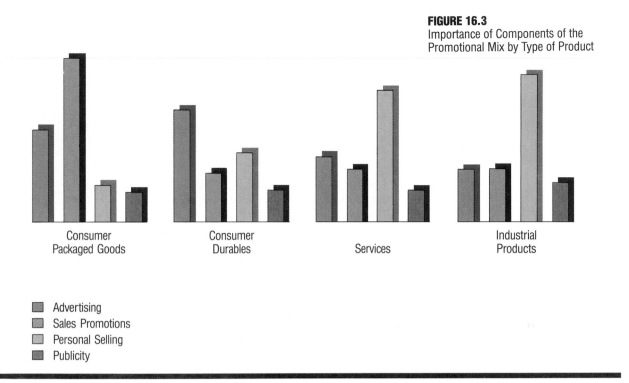

FIGURE 16.3
Importance of Components of the
Promotional Mix by Type of Product

and higher-priced products all warrant an emphasis on personal selling. These characteristics tend to describe industrial goods.

Publicity is likely to be more important for larger firms that must convey a message of corporate good will to stockholders, customers, and other factions of the public than for smaller firms. Such companies cut across all classes of products. But even for larger firms, publicity is rarely a dominant element; rather, it serves an important supporting role.

Stage in the Product's Life Cycle

The composition of the promotional mix will change over a product's life cycle. In Chapter 11, we cited variations in overall marketing strategies across the life cycle. Figure 16.4 shows the impact of these variations on the two most important components of the promotional mix — advertising and sales promotions.

In the *introductory phase* of the life cycle, advertising's role is to create brand awareness. The role of sales promotions is twofold: First, trade promotions provide the *push* to ensure shelf space; second, consumer promotions provide the *pull* to generate product trial. Both advertising and sales promotional expenditures will be high during the introductory period.

When Schering Plough introduced its highly successful Fibre Trim diet product in 1987, it used a combination of advertising, consumer promotions, and trade promotions. Trade promotions to drugstores involved merchandise discounts, premiums, and window decals. Consumer promotions offered first-time purchasers $1 off on the second box. Sales promotions were backed by a $25 million advertising campaign promoting the dietary benefits of fiber. As a result of this strategy, four out of five purchasers said they would rebuy the product, and the introduction was described as the most successful of any diet product.[13]

FIGURE 16.4
The Advertising and Sales Promotional
Mix over the Product Life Cycle

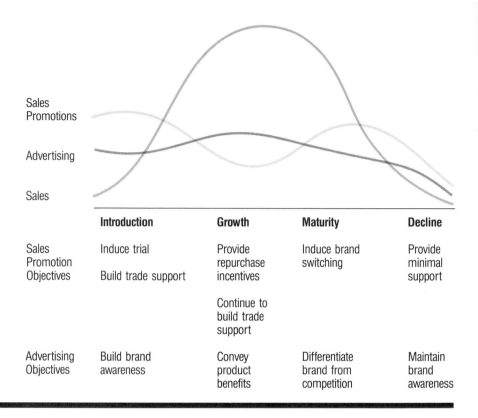

	Introduction	Growth	Maturity	Decline
Sales Promotion Objectives	Induce trial Build trade support	Provide repurchase incentives Continue to build trade support	Induce brand switching	Provide minimal support
Advertising Objectives	Build brand awareness	Convey product benefits	Differentiate brand from competition	Maintain brand awareness

In the *growth phase* of the life cycle, the product is generating increased sales, and advertising expenditures are likely to be maintained or increased. Having established brand awareness, the advertising strategy shifts to communicating product benefits. The purpose is to attract new buyers and convince existing buyers to repurchase. Sales promotional expenditures are likely to take a sharp drop, because many customers have tried the product. Moreover, continued use of consumer promotions might cause buyers to view the brand as a low-priced, low-quality entry.

Sales promotional expenditures are likely to increase in the *maturity phase* of the life cycle, the point where sales growth stabilizes and begins to decline. At this time the company is likely to provide price inducements to coax users of competitive brands to switch to the company's brand. As price competition intensifies, the use of coupons, premiums, and price deals increases. The cigarette industry is in the mature phase of its life cycle, with cigarette sales steady or decreasing slightly. The major cigarette companies have steadily decreased expenditures on magazine advertising and are replacing them with coupons printed on the back of cigarette packs, price deals, and sponsorship of sports events.

Total advertising expenditures in the maturity phase are likely to be maintained, but advertising objectives change. Because products are becoming more standardized, advertisers are unlikely to have a unique set of product benefits to advertise. As a result, advertising shifts from an informational approach to a campaign based more on symbols and imagery. When Pampers were first introduced, Procter & Gamble could rely on advertising the convenience of disposable diapers and their absorbency. As competition intensified, the company focused on attempting to link the concepts of love and security with buying Pampers for the baby. Product characteristics were still important, but symbols and imagery dominated.

The *decline phase* of the life cycle is marked by cutbacks in all promotional expenditures. Sales promotions may support the brand with occasional coupons and price deals, and advertising will attempt to maintain brand awareness among brand loyalists. But it is also possible that the company may choose to *harvest* a brand in the decline phase, meaning it might cut off all promotional support. This was the strategy employed by Standard Brands when it withdrew its support for Chase & Sanborn coffee in the face of a continued sales decline.

The third step in selecting a promotional mix is to develop a strategy that will best meet promotional objectives. If the objective is to gain maximum trial for a new product, then sales promotional components such as coupons and free samples might be employed, combined with merchandise and slotting allowances to influence the trade to stock it. If the primary objective is to gain brand awareness and develop a positive brand image, then advertising will receive the most emphasis. If the main objective is to communicate and demonstrate complex product features, then personal selling will dominate.

DEVELOP A PROMOTIONAL STRATEGY

When Molson Light was introduced into the American market, the primary objective was to induce trial. Accordingly, the brand relied heavily on sales promotional tools such as point-of-purchase displays. The idea was to reinforce the outdoor Canadian imagery of the advertising campaign with colorful display cards and mobiles that provided an eye-catching presentation in the store. Molson also introduced a distributor sales incentive program to encourage stores to stock the brand.[14]

Molson tied sales promotions and advertising together by using the same theme in all its point-of-purchase displays as in its advertising — "Finally Canadian Taste Has Come to Light." The advertising campaign suggested that consumers would enjoy a hearty taste of the Canadian wilderness with each sip of Molson Light. The in-store displays reinforced this image.

The total amount of money that will be spent on the promotional mix will depend on the promotional strategies the firm intends to follow. The amount allotted to each element will depend on its relative importance due to factors like product and consumer characteristics and stage in the life cycle.

SET THE PROMOTIONAL BUDGET

Top-Down versus Bottom-Up Budgeting

Chapter 8 cited two approaches to budgeting, a top-down and a bottom-up approach. Both approaches apply to budgeting for promotion. Figure 16.5 shows that in a top-down approach, managers establish one overall expenditure level for the promotional mix and then allocate these funds to the components of the mix. In contrast, a bottom-up approach first requires developing separate budgets for advertising, sales promotions, personal selling, and publicity. The sum of these four components is the total promotional budget.

A top-down approach has the advantage of treating the promotional mix as an integrated part of marketing strategy and determining how much effort is required overall to inform and influence the consumer. The danger in using a top-down approach is that the manager might lose sight of the specific objectives and roles of the individual components of the promotional mix.

A bottom-up approach has the advantage of focusing on the tasks required to achieve specific advertising, promotional, personal selling, or publicity objec-

FIGURE 16.5
Top-Down versus Bottom-Up
Promotional Budgeting

Top-Down Approach

Set Overall Promotional Budget

Allocate to Components of Promotional Mix

Advertising   Personal Selling   Sales Promotions   Publicity

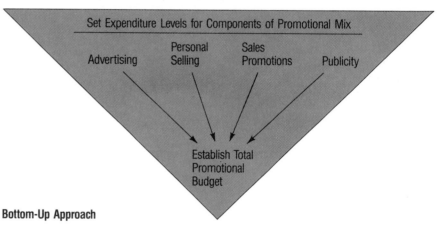

Set Expenditure Levels for Components of Promotional Mix

Advertising   Personal Selling   Sales Promotions   Publicity

Establish Total Promotional Budget

Bottom-Up Approach

tives — but possibly at the expense of exceeding necessary limits on the total promotional budget. In building up a budget, the manager might allocate too much money to the promotional mix, because each promotional component independently establishes a spending level based on its objectives.

McDonald's tends to take a top-down approach to promotional budgeting. It establishes an overall spending level for the year and then allocates expenditures primarily to advertising and sales promotions. Once advertising expenditures are established, the company further allocates resources to network TV, local TV, magazines, radio, and billboard advertising. As we have seen, McDonald's has shifted more resources to sales promotions in recent years, and has allocated the bulk of its advertising budget to network TV.

Techniques for Setting the Promotional Budget

Several budgeting techniques are available and can be used on a top-down or bottom-up basis.

Marginal-Revenue Approach The ideal way to set a promotional budget would be the **marginal-revenue approach,** because it depends on the sales effectiveness of the promotions. It requires determining how much additional *(marginal)* revenue is obtained from each additional dollar spent on the promotional mix *(mar-*

ginal cost). For example, assume that a firm spends $10 million a year on its promotional mix. At this level, it determines it would get $1.10 in revenue if it spent an additional dollar on promotions. Since the firm would receive 10 cents for each additional dollar spent, it can safely increase its promotional budget — and can continue to do so as long as marginal revenues from promotions are above the marginal costs of those promotions.

Suppose the firm in our example increases its promotional budget to $12 million. At this level, it finds it would make an additional one dollar in revenue if it increased its promotional budget by one dollar. Therefore, any increase above $12 million would not contribute to profit. The budget is set at the point where the marginal revenue from promotions equals the marginal cost. It is here that the firm is making the maximum profit possible from promotions.

Most firms view this marginal approach as an ideal rather than an operational basis for setting the promotional budget. The reason is that it is very difficult for a firm to know how much revenue it is getting for each additional dollar spent on promotions.

Objective-Task Approach Given the difficulty of applying a marginal revenue approach, most firms have settled on the next best thing: an **objective-task approach,** which requires defining promotional objectives, determining what strategies (tasks) are required to attain them, and computing how much those strategies will cost. Once the budget is established to fulfill the tasks, the company can determine whether it can afford the expenditures. If not, objectives must be scaled down.

Pillsbury used an objective-task method in setting the advertising budget for its Totino's frozen pizza line. The overall objectives were to increase sales by 30 percent and profits by 100 percent by increasing product quality and distribution. The promotional objectives called for a 70 percent increase in brand awareness, a 20 percent increase in trial, and a 40 percent increase in the repurchase rate.[15] These ambitious goals required Pillsbury to put substantially more money into television advertising while maintaining its level of consumer and trade promotions. Since management felt these goals were attainable, it approved a substantial increase in the advertising budget.

Percent-of-Sales Approach Also frequently used is the **percent-of-sales** approach, in which the promotional budget is set as a certain percentage of sales. For example, in the late 1970s Sears set its advertising budget at 3 percent of forecast retail sales, and advertising expenditures for its catalog were set at 5.75 percent of forecast catalog sales.[16]

This approach has the advantages of being simple and varying promotional expenditures with a brand's performance. But it has serious flaws. First, the level of sales is determining the promotional mix, when actually the opposite should be true — the promotional mix should influence sales results. Second, some products with high sales levels are not particularly profitable. Yet these products would receive more promotional support than more profitable products with lower sales levels. Third, the percent-of-sales approach may inhibit a manager from trying to transform a promising brand into a star. Such an effort would require spending more on promotions than warranted by the brand's sales level.

Competitive-Parity Approach Some firms use a **competitive-parity** approach, in which they set their promotional budgets based on what the competition is doing.

One such approach is to determine advertising expenditures as a percent of sales for a few key competitors or for the industry as a whole and then to use the same percentage to set the budget. Another is to maintain a company's share of advertising over time. For example, if a company represents 15 percent of all promotional expenditures in the industry, maintaining that percent means its promotional spending must go up if industry spending goes up, and down if industry spending goes down.

The problem is that this approach lets competition set the spending pace, and what is right for one company might not be right for another. Moreover, such an approach might just lead a company into following the errors of its competitors.

Arbitrary Approaches Companies that do not have a systematic promotional planning process often use simple and arbitrary methods. Smaller firms that have no formal planning methods are most likely to fall into this category. One such approach is to set budgets for raw materials, production, distribution, and other needs and then allocate what is left over to the promotional mix. Another is to increase the promotional budget by a fixed percent each year. These methods suffer the disadvantage of not being tied to promotional objectives or product performance.

ALLOCATE THE PROMOTIONAL BUDGET

If a company uses a top-down approach in budgeting, the overall promotional budget will be allocated among components of the promotional mix according to the supposed effectiveness of each component. For example, if a company can estimate that it obtains $1.10 in revenues for each additional dollar spent on advertising, and $1.20 for each additional dollar spent on sales promotion, it will allocate more money to sales promotions than to advertising. As more money is spent on sales promotions, the marginal revenues will decrease, because there is a limit to the number of coupons or deals consumers will accept. Once the returns from sales promotions equal those for advertising, managers would stop shifting more money into sales promotions.

The principle is to allocate resources so that each component of the promotional mix is providing the same marginal return. If one component is providing more marginal returns than the others, it should be receiving more money, because the greater marginal return indicates it could be producing more profits if more money were being spent there. The same principle would apply in allocating money to specific sales promotional tools or advertising vehicles. If coupons produce more marginal revenue than deals, more money should be spent on coupons until the marginal revenue equals that of deals. If cable television advertising produces more marginal revenue than network television, more money should be spent on cable until that marginal revenue equals network television's.

EVALUATE THE PROMOTIONAL MIX

The last step in selecting the promotional mix (Figure 16.2) is evaluation. Several key questions are involved here. First, have the promotional objectives been translated into an effective marketing message? Returning to our McDonald's example, the "It's a good time" theme effectively communicated fun and good taste. Its sales promotional strategy was instrumental in conveying value. Second, has the target group been defined? McDonald's primary target group was baby boomers with children. Its secondary target was families in general. Third, is the right promotional mix being used to influence the target group? McDonald's influences baby boomers primarily through network television with a smattering of magazine, billboard, and radio advertising. It also uses sales promotions such as its Monopoly Game promotion and National Football League sweepstakes to appeal to baby boomers. Fourth, to what extent does exposure to each component of the promotional mix result in sales?

As we saw, the ideal approach in evaluating the effectiveness of each component of the promotional mix is to determine how much an additional dollar spent on advertising, sales promotion, personal selling, and publicity produces in sales. But, given the difficulty in determining the sales produced by each component of the promotional mix, managers try to assess the effectiveness of these components by other means — effectiveness in creating brand awareness, conveying product benefits, inducing product trial, or encouraging repurchase of the brand.

Generally, sales promotional strategies are easier to evaluate than advertising because they can often be tied directly to sales. For example, a company can determine the number of products purchased with coupons. Similarly, sales can be related directly to a premium or sweepstakes promotion because these are short-term inducements. Sales increases that occur during the promotional period can generally be attributed to the promotion.

SALES PROMOTIONS

In the remainder of this chapter, we will consider in more detail two components of the promotional mix, sales promotions and publicity. In the next two chapters, we consider the other two components, advertising and personal selling.

The amount of money spent on sales promotions has increased markedly since the mid 1970s. Figure 16.6 shows that in 1976 marketers spent about $30 billion on sales promotions. Ten years later they were spending over $100 billion. Expenditures on advertising also rose during this period, but not as fast. By 1988 more money was being spent on sales promotions ($124 billion) than on advertising ($118 billion).

INCREASING IMPORTANCE OF SALES PROMOTIONS

There are several reasons for this relative shift of promotional dollars from advertising to sales promotions. First, the cost-effectiveness of advertising through the mass media has been decreasing. As markets have become more segmented, it has become increasingly expensive to reach targets through national advertising campaigns. One study estimated that from 1983 to 1987 the amount of revenue produced by the same level of advertising expenditures decreased by almost 20 percent.[17] This decrease in advertising productivity is projected to continue.

Another factor causing a shift from advertising to sales promotions is the increasing popularity of VCRs and cable television, resulting in fewer consumers watching nationally televised commercials. In addition, with more women in the workforce, viewing of daytime television commercials has decreased.

A general decrease in brand loyalty has also led to an increase in the use of sales promotions. Consumers are more willing to buy many products on a price basis, increasing the effectiveness of sales promotional tools such as coupons and price deals. One result of the decrease in brand loyalty is that more consumers are making their purchase decisions in the store rather than deciding on a brand beforehand. A study by the Point-of-Purchase Advertising Institute found that over 80 percent of all supermarket purchases are decided in the store.[18] When consumers make decisions in the store, they are more likely to be influenced by in-store displays, store coupons, and price deals.

FIGURE 16.6
Growth in Sales Promotion and
Advertising Expenditures:
1976–1988

Source: Sales promotion expenditures from "Sales
Promotion: The Year in Review," *Marketing & Media
Decisions,* July 1987, July 1988, and July 1989, pp.
124–126. Advertising expenditures for 1976 and 1981
from *Statistical Abstract,* 1980 and 1987, figures for
1988 from "Ad Spending Outlook Brightens," *Advertising Age,* May 15, 1989.

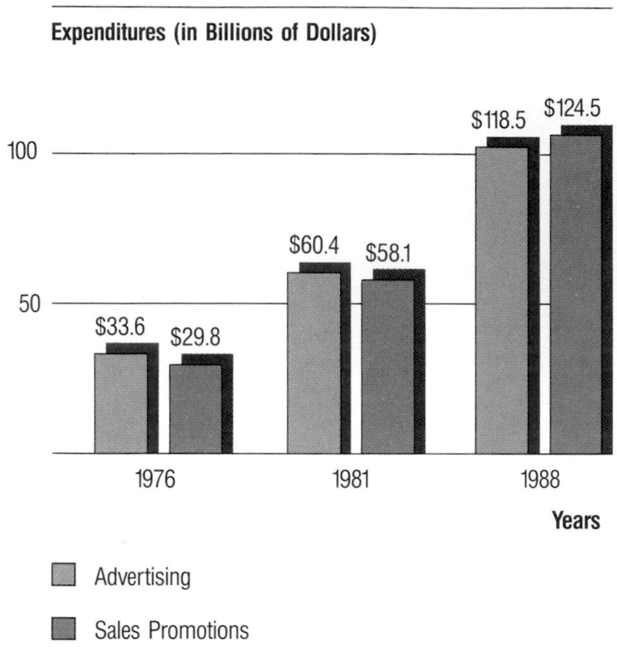

Expenditures (in Billions of Dollars)

Greater similarity among brands in many product categories encourages this
trend. When brands are similar, consumers are more likely to make choices based
on price. As a result, sales promotions are more effective than advertising.

The increasing use of sales promotions is apparent in the marketing of most
consumer packaged goods. Cereal companies such as Quaker have relied on sales
promotions to the point where only 25 cents out of every dollar is now spent on
advertising. And consider the well-known case of Johnson & Johnson, which
used coupons rather than advertising to get Tylenol back on its feet after a series
of cyanide deaths due to tampering. Its mass distribution to American households of 40 million coupons worth $2.50 each (the price of a small bottle of
Tylenol) brought former Tylenol users back to the brand, enabling the company
to recapture lost market share.[19]

RISKS OF INCREASING USE OF SALES PROMOTIONS

Marketers face the risk that their continued emphasis on sales promotions may
condition consumers to expect constant price cuts. Since many consumers see
little difference among brands, when a promotion on a given brand ends, they
will simply switch to another brand being promoted. As a result, many marketers
will be forced to continually use sales promotions to keep their market share from
eroding. Yet the constant use of sales promotions decreases profits.

Increasing expenditures on sales promotions also means less money for advertising — the means of building brand loyalty and communicating consumer benefits. The constant use of sales promotions may, therefore, damage brand loyalties companies have built up over decades.

These risks have caused some companies to reverse the trend shown in Figure
16.6 and to start putting more money into advertising. One such company is
General Foods. In an effort to maintain the value of its brand names, the company is changing its promotional mix to allocate less to sales promotions and

FIGURE 16.7
Distribution of Expenditures by Types of
Sales Promotions

Source: "Sales Promotion: The Year in Review," *Marketing & Media Decisions,* July 1987, July 1988, and July 1989, pp. 124–126.

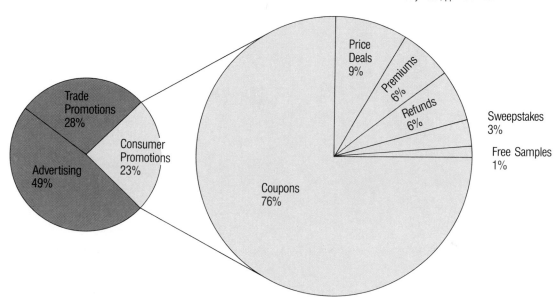

more to advertising.[20] Nevertheless, the relative shift from advertising to sales promotions is likely to continue into the 1990s for most companies.

Sales promotions may be directed to consumers or to the trade. The division of expenditures between advertising, trade promotions, and consumer promotions is shown in Figure 16.7. Somewhat more money is spent on trade than on consumer promotions. Of the $118 billion spent on sales promotions in 1988, about $53 billion was spent on consumer promotions and about $65 billion on trade promotions.

Consumer Promotions

As shown in Figure 16.7, consumer promotions include price deals, premiums, rebates, sweepstakes, and free samples. The vast majority of promotions — 76 percent — are **coupons,** which offer a discount off the regular price of a brand in order to encourage nonusers to try a product or existing users to buy more frequently. Like other sales promotions, coupons are more effective in inducing short-term switches to a brand than in retaining consumers over the long term. Most consumers that have switched to another brand because of coupons will revert to their regular brand when coupons are no longer offered.

In 1986, 202 billion coupons were distributed, and about 7.3 billion of these were redeemed (a redemption rate of 3.6 percent).[21] These redemptions saved consumers a total of $2.75 billion. About 70 percent of coupons are **free-standing inserts,** meaning they are distributed in inserts in newspapers. The remaining 30 percent are distributed by mail, in newspaper or magazine ads, or directly in

TYPES OF SALES PROMOTIONS

EXHIBIT 16.1
Sprite Coupon Promotion
Targeted to Blacks

stores. Health and beauty aids, frozen foods, cereals, prepared foods, and house-hold products use the most coupons. Companies such as Procter & Gamble, Coca Cola, Quaker, and Gillette rely heavily on them (see Exhibit 16.1).

Despite their increasing use, coupons have several disadvantages. First, they are expensive. A single-page, four-color coupon appearing as a free-standing insert in Sunday newspapers across the country costs well over $500,000. In addition, over 95 percent are not redeemed. Finally, the market is becoming saturated with coupons, diminishing their effectiveness. Yet coupons continue to be by far the most widely used sales promotional method because of their effectiveness in inducing consumers to try a brand.

Short-term discounts offered by manufacturers to increase trial or purchase of greater amounts of a brand are called **price deals**. Most price deals are printed directly on the package, indicating so many cents off. These deals are an effective way for a company to meet a competitor's coupon offer or to compete with a price reduction. Some marketers use price deals so frequently that consumers assume they are part of the established price. When the product goes "off deal," consumers may regard it as a price increase and be reluctant to buy it. Constant use of price deals can in this way dilute brand loyalty and discourage repeat purchases.

Products offered free or at a reduced price as an incentive to buy a promoted brand are known as **premiums**. To be most effective, the premium should be related to the product. Family Home Entertainment, a marketer of videocassettes, successfully employed this tool. The company had problems getting video retailers to stock its line of children's tapes, so it attached a related toy worth about $5 to each cassette. One toy, for example, the Transformer, changed from a vehicle to a robot and was attached to a cassette of the same name (see Exhibit 16.2). More than 80,000 cassettes sold out within a few weeks after introducing the premium, and video retailers began clamoring for more stock.[22] Premiums are also directed to existing users to encourage repurchase. Most airlines have frequent-flyer programs that provide passengers with free trips or reduced fares once they travel a certain number of miles with the carrier.

Another form of short-term price inducement, **rebates,** allows the consumer to recover a portion of the original cost of an item. Rebates began to be used widely by auto companies in the mid 1970s as a result of rising gas prices. After almost going into bankruptcy, Chrysler used the technique to help it gain a 12 percent share of the auto market. The use of rebates for autos spurred other industries to try them, sometimes in imaginative ways. Toro realized that consumers were reluctant to buy an expensive snow blower because it did not always snow. As a result, the company started a promotion called "Snow Insurance," involving a rebate of 50 percent to 100 percent off the purchase price if snowfalls were significantly less than average in the buyer's community. Sales exceeded projections by 20 percent during the promotion.[23]

A technique that lends excitement to sales promotions and appeals to the American consumer's sense of gamesmanship is the **sweepstakes,** in which the consumer has a chance to win prizes or sums of money simply by submitting his or her name and address. In a dramatic variation of the sweepstakes idea, Procter & Gamble and General Motors' Chevrolet Division launched a joint promotion, the $9 million Great American Key Hunt, to introduce Chevy's 1988 cars. Hidden inside containers of seven of P&G's top brands were Mylar card keys. Any buyer who found a key was invited to visit a Chevrolet dealer to find out if it was one of the designated keys for 750 cars being given away.[24] Chevrolet was interested in teaming up with P&G because 98 percent of the U.S. households use one or more of the seven P&G products in the promotion. The contest not only sold P&G products, it produced a great deal of traffic in Chevrolet dealerships. It was the biggest promotion run by either P&G or Chevrolet.

An effective way to get consumers to try new products is to offer **free samples.** Free samples are feasible only for low-cost, frequently purchased items; otherwise they become prohibitively expensive. When Gillette introduced its Trac II razor, it distributed over 12 million free samples backed up by a one-dollar refund offer for new purchasers. Thus, a rebate was combined with the free sample. Many free samples are wasted because they are given to nonusers or to people who already use the product. Some companies avoid such waste by offering free samples to consumers who are sufficiently interested to write in for them.

Another sales promotional tool is the **point-of-purchase display,** such as advertising signs, window displays, and end-of-aisle display racks for products. Gillette introduced the Trac II razor at World Series time and provided retailers with streamers and flags tied to the October classic. Such in-store displays combined with price deals provide more impact at the point of purchase.

Companies have often joined forces when using the sales promotional techniques described above. The Great American Key Hunt promotion sponsored by Procter & Gamble and Chevrolet is an example. Joint promotions yield several benefits. They reduce the costs of running expensive efforts such as sweepstakes or premiums, making them affordable even for smaller companies. Given the high cost of sales promotional activities, the use of such joint promotions is likely to increase.

EXHIBIT 16.2
Example of a Premium

A Transformer toy was attached to this video as a premium.

Joint promotions have also been used for products that have complementary associations. A creative example was the joint promotion for Alka Seltzer and H&R Block for a tax-time sweepstakes. Alka Seltzer samples were placed in 7,500 H&R Block tax preparation offices with sweepstakes coupons. A supporting ad campaign plugged Alka Seltzer and H&R Block as the places "where more Americans find fast relief."[25]

Trade Promotions

Trade promotions are directed to retailers and wholesalers to try to get them to stock the company's products. They represent the push in the promotional effort as opposed to the pull provided by consumer promotions and advertising.

Three types of promotions specifically geared to the trade are merchandise allowances, case allowances, and direct payments for stocking goods known as slotting allowances. **Merchandise allowances** are payments by manufacturers to reimburse retailers for in-store support of the product, such as window displays or in-store shelf displays.

Case allowances are discounts on products sold to retailers. Bowater Computer Forms Inc. offers its office supply dealers direct discounts depending on how much paper they agree to buy. The company also absorbs freight costs on shipments of ten cases or more.[26] **Slotting allowances** are direct payments to retailers, generally food chains, for stocking an item. As we saw in the last chapter, some food chains are requiring direct payments of close to $100,000 for each new product introduced. Food companies are increasingly willing to pay these allowances because of the intense competition for shelf space.[27]

Price deals, coupons, and sweepstakes can also be directed to intermediaries as well as to consumers. Bowater offers its dealers premiums such as blank diskettes and computer software in exchange for them stocking its computer forms. It also provides dealers with coupons that are good for discounts on other Bowater products. Another element in Bowater's trade promotional program is direct support for dealers by providing them with in-store product displays, four-color brochures of Bowater's line, and listing dealer names in Bowater's national magazine ads.

Sales Promotions for Industrial Products

Most of the promotions described thus far are for consumer products. Sales promotional tools for industrial products are essentially the same, as those for consumer products. These tools are rarely used for higher-priced industrial products, since buyers are unlikely to select a vendor based on a promotional offer when a substantial purchase is involved. Promotions are used primarily for lower-priced products and services. For example, Airborne Express used a Lotto Sweepstakes to try to influence high-volume corporate customers to use its air freight service. The purpose of the promotion was to build awareness of Airborne and to attract first-time shippers. The total investment was $8 million in network TV advertising and in direct-mail announcements, and a $1 million prize to the winner. Out of 1.3 million mailings, Airborne received only about 20,000 responses.[28] The winner was determined by an airbill number drawn from these responses. Although the promotion did not pay for itself, the company felt it was worth it in building awareness among prospective customers.

One promotional device specific to industrial products is the **trade show,** in which booths are set up by various vendors in one large meeting place to dispense information about their products to prospective customers. Trade shows are instrumental in attracting about one-fourth of all industrial sales.[29] They are particularly important as a means of reaching customers who are not contacted by a company's direct sales force. The trade show provides an efficient means of identifying prospects, introducing new products, and delivering a sales message to many buyers.

Sales Promotions for Services

Sales promotions have become an increasingly important part of the promotional mix for services. Since services cannot be stored, unused service capacity is wasted. Consequently, airlines and hotels use price deals and coupons to encourage customers to use their facilities during off-peak periods. For example, Republic Airlines ran a two-for-one fare offer during the sluggish spring-travel period. Similarly, the Milford Plaza tried to combat sharply reduced hotel occupancies in New York by attracting nonbusiness travelers. Their Broadway Sleeper package offers guests a $10 credit toward a room on presentation of a theater ticket stub.[30]

Financial service firms have also begun to use sales promotions more often. Consumer banking services have become more standardized and competitive, so offering promotions is a way of distinguishing a bank's services. For example, Citibank gave away 500 "Citibikes" in connection with its "Cititour" pro bicycle race. The promotion included a free T-shirt for those who showed a Citibank ATM card, and a free cycling cap for those who had a coupon from the Cititour Sweepstakes brochure.[31] (See Exhibit 16.3.)

PUBLICITY

Publicity has become a more important part of the promotional mix. More companies are recognizing its value — not only as an effective means to get favorable news stories and announcements about a product or company in the mass media but also to counteract negative news.

EXHIBIT 16.3
A Sales Promotion for Financial Services

One advantage of publicity is its credibility. When information appears in a neutral source such as a newspaper or television news broadcasts, it is more likely to be believed than when it comes directly from an advertiser. Most consumers accepted the fact that Johnson & Johnson was not at fault for the cyanide tampering of Tylenol because this view was reported in news stories rather than in company advertising. A second advantage of publicity is that it is inexpensive. There are few costs other than maintaining a public relations department or printing company communications. Third, publicity can support the other components of the promotional mix. The Ronald McDonald Houses providing free rooms to parents with children in hospitals create goodwill for McDonald's and reinforce the image of its prime corporate character in advertising and sales promotions.

Among the drawbacks to the use of publicity, is the fact that it is not within the company's control. When a company sends a press release to the media, it has no influence as to how it will be treated. McDonald's claims of nutritional value for its foods through publicity have sometimes backfired when nutritional groups and state agencies challenged these claims.

A second drawback is that publicity is not always well-coordinated with the other components of the promotional mix. The responsibility for publicity usu-

ADVANTAGES AND DISADVANTAGES OF PUBLICITY

ally lies with a corporate public relations department rather than a marketing group. As a result, strategies to develop favorable publicity for a product or company tend to be divorced from advertising, sales promotion, and personal selling.

Rick Scoville Made Publicity Work for Him

Source: © Keith Glasgow.

Rick Scoville got Artesia Mineral Waters off the ground without a penny of advertising: He did it all with publicity. In 1980 Scoville decided to get into the bottled water business in Texas because he figured San Antonio water, purified by its 176-mile journey over mineral-rich lands, could compete effectively against Perrier. With $25,000 borrowed from a Texas bank, Scoville bought an old bottling plant in San Antonio, dug a well, and began bottling Artesia Waters.

Scoville would pack a few cases of his Artesia mineral water into his van and personally sell it to chic discos, nightclubs, and grocery stores. But he ran into the same problem any small company would face when competing with a giant: How do you knock Perrier off the supermarket shelf and get Artesia Waters on it?

Not one to be discouraged when he started out, Scoville was fond of saying he would "kick Perrier in the derriere."[32] He could not, however, afford advertising in his plan to challenge Perrier in Texas. Instead, he mounted a publicity campaign by writing dozens of letters to media organizations, touting his water as a local product representing the "pure Texas spirit." When a business writer at a Houston newspaper wrote a flattering story about Artesia, Scoville made copies of the article and sent it to other publications. Follow-up calls to newspapers produced a one-paragraph front-page story in *The Wall Street Journal* and a new product feature in *Texas Monthly* magazine about Artesia water's challenge to Perrier. Scoville made sure that every major media organization in Texas got *The Wall Street Journal* article.

Soon after, stories began appearing about Artesia in newspapers in Dallas and San Antonio, and Scoville found himself on radio talk shows and finally on Texas television. The free publicity caused revenue to jump from $100,000 in 1980 to $1.5 million the following year. Scoville could now afford to start a direct mail, outdoor, and print advertising campaign. By 1985 sales were $3 million, and Artesia was the top-selling sparkling water in Texas, bigger even than Perrier.[33]

Then a fellow Texan, Ron Bownds, introduced a competitive product, Utopia Sparkling Water, with a similar "home-grown" theme, sparkling water "deep in the heart of the Texas Hill country."[34] Scoville reacted using the same tool that built Artesia, publicity. He mounted a letter-writing campaign to the Texas Department of Health, to the state's attorney general's office, to media, and to customers that Bownds had misrepresented the product when he claimed Utopia to be natural, pure sparkling water.[35] Bownds sued Scoville for trying to destroy the goodwill Utopia had built up.

Scoville and Bownds finally agreed to call a halt to their feud, recognizing that the major competitive threat was coming from larger companies like Perrier. For Scoville, publicity was certainly the centerpiece of his promotional mix. ■

Most publicity efforts involve press releases, company communications, and, more recently, special events.

Press Releases

Press releases might be used to announce a new product or technology, to communicate news about the company, or to counteract some negative event or rumor. Polaroid came out with a press release to announce its Spectra camera line. Philip Morris sent out a press release to announce its acquisition of General Foods. Johnson & Johnson used a press release to announce that it was reintroducing Tylenol in a tamper-proof package rather than pulling the brand off the market after the cyanide poisonings.

Company Communications

Companies will also try to get stories into newspapers, magazines, or on television news shows in a more comprehensive publicity campaign involving various company communications.

McDonald's mounted an issue-oriented publicity campaign to counter negative publicity generated by nutritional groups' criticisms about the fat and salt content of its foods and the disadvantages of fried foods. The company reduced the sodium level of many of its foods, fried them in vegetable shortening instead of animal fat, and introduced fresh salads on the menu.[36] It publicized these changes through press releases and by offering a booklet in each of its outlets on the nutritional content of its products. The company also introduced a number of ads in medical trade magazines touting the nutritional content of its foods and explaining how they contribute to a balanced diet. (These ads were challenged by several groups, however, as exaggerations.)

Special Events

Increasingly, many companies sponsor special events such as musical or sports events as a means of promoting goodwill among consumers, stockholders, and other relevant portions of the public. These events are then publicized by the company through the mass media.

McDonald's sponsors an All American high school basketball team each year (the "Dream Team" in Exhibit 16.4) comprised of the top senior basketball players in the country. It then holds an annual McDonald's All American game between these players, with the proceeds of the game going to Children's Charities. Millions of viewers watch the game on ABC. As a result, McDonald's gets nationwide publicity and goodwill for its sponsorship of the event.

The effectiveness of a company's publicity efforts can be measured by the amount of space or air time that a company or its product receives, and by the number of people reached by the message. For example, Bacardi Rum mounted an effective publicity campaign to boost public awareness of Puerto Rican rum. Using its test

TYPES OF PUBLICITY

EVALUATING PUBLICITY

EXHIBIT 16.4
An Example of Special Events
Sponsorship

kitchens, Bacardi whipped up a number of recipes using rum and sent them with photographs and articles to newspaper food editors and women's magazines. The articles that were sent received 4,600 column inches in newspapers in the first six months of the campaign and reached an estimated 4.9 million people. Sales of Bacardi rum during this period increased by 20 percent.[37]

Effectiveness can also be measured by the degree to which a campaign changes consumers' opinions. The marketer can measure this by conducting a survey. The Potato Board instituted a publicity campaign to convince consumers that potatoes are not fattening and are actually nutritious. Then it conducted a survey and found that the number of people who believed that potatoes are rich in vitamins and minerals had risen from 36 percent before its publicity campaign to 67 percent after.

A company must also evaluate the effectiveness of the total promotional mix, recognizing publicity as one component of that mix. As we saw, key questions must be addressed, such as whether the company's message is being understood by its intended audience.

SUMMARY

1. What is the nature of the marketing communications process?
Marketing communications require a source (the advertiser) that develops a message (encoding) that is transmitted to an intended receiver who then interprets (decodes) it. The advertiser then evaluates the response to the message

(feedback). Evaluating the effectiveness of the marketing communication process is difficult because a host of other environmental factors influence sales as well.

2. *What are the components of a promotional mix, and the purposes of each component?*

A promotional mix combines advertising, sales promotions, personal selling, and publicity. Advertising is a paid, ongoing, nonpersonal communication from a commercial source such as a manufacturer or a retailer. Advertising is designed to inform consumers about a brand and to influence them to buy. Its primary value is its long-term effect of keeping consumers aware of the brand and maintaining consumer loyalties.

Sales promotions are shorter-term inducements of value to consumers that encourage them to buy a product or service. They are aimed at attracting new users and encouraging existing users to buy more frequently.

Personal selling is face-to-face communication by a company representative to influence the customer to buy a product or service. It is more flexible than other components because the salesperson can assess the customer's needs and design a message accordingly.

Publicity is unpaid communications in the mass media about a company, product or service. Consumers often see it as more believable than advertising, but the message is difficult to control.

3. *How do managers select a promotional mix for a brand or product category?*

Managers first establish promotional objectives. They then evaluate the factors that determine the importance of each component of the promotional mix, such as the type of customer, type of product, and stage in the product's life cycle. On this basis, they develop a strategy that determines the mix of advertising, sales promotion, personal selling, and publicity to effectively promote the product. Next, a promotional budget is determined and allocated to each component of the promotional mix. The final step is to evaluate the promotional mix by assessing its impact on the target audience.

4. *What types of sales promotional tools can be used to promote a brand?*

Sales promotions have become a growing part of the promotional mix, recently exceeding advertising in terms of total expenditures. Consumer promotions are designed to influence consumers to try a brand and to get existing consumers to buy again. Trade promotions are designed to get retailers and wholesalers to stock the brand. Trade promotions push the product through the channels; consumer promotions pull it through.

Coupons are the most frequently used type of consumer promotions. Other types of consumer promotions are price deals, premiums, refunds, sweepstakes, free samples, and point-of-purchase displays. Trade promotions include merchandise allowances, case allowances, and direct payments to get intermediaries to stock a brand.

5. *What types of publicity tools can be used to promote a brand or company?*

Companies use press releases and communications to try to get favorable news disseminated. An increasingly frequent component of publicity efforts is sponsorship of sports or musical events. News of such sponsorship is then publicized to generate goodwill for the sponsor.

KEY TERMS

Promotional mix (p. 436)	Competitive-parity budgeting (p. 447)
Encoding (p. 437)	Coupons (p. 451)
Noise in communications (p. 437)	Free-standing inserts (p. 451)
Decoding (p. 438)	Price deals (p. 452)
Feedback (p. 438)	Premiums (p. 452)
Advertising (p. 439)	Rebates (p. 453)
Sales promotions (p. 439)	Sweepstakes (p. 453)
Personal selling (p. 440)	Free samples (p. 453)
Publicity (p. 440)	Point-of-purchase displays (p. 453)
Public relations (p. 440)	Merchandise allowances (p. 454)
Marginal-revenue budgeting (p. 446)	Case allowances (p. 454)
Objective-task budgeting (p. 447)	Slotting allowances (p. 454)
Percent-of-sales budgeting (p. 447)	Trade shows (p. 454)

QUESTIONS

1. What are the components of McDonald's promotional mix?
2. To evaluate the effectiveness of marketing communications, what basic questions should a promotional manager ask at each stage of the process? Apply these questions to the promotional campaign for Polaroid's Spectra camera.
3. What different roles do advertising, personal selling, sales promotion, and publicity fill in the promotional mix?
4. Why is it easier to evaluate the effectiveness of sales promotions than of advertising? How have advertisers dealt with the difficulty of directly relating advertising to sales?
5. Which component of the promotional mix is likely to be most important for each of the following, and why?

   a. A company marketing pollution control systems to chemical firms.
   b. A leading cereal manufacturer trying to combat competition from lower-priced brands.
   c. A brand of coffee that wants to expand from its western base and is finding it difficult to gain shelf space in supermarkets in the East.
   d. A manufacturer of household products trying to create awareness for a new detergent.
   e. A company trying to create an image for a perfume trageted to the achievement-oriented working woman.
   f. A financial services firm trying to ensure that its customers receive proper attention and advice from its sales representatives.

6. When Pepsi-Cola introduced Slice, it recognized that the roles of sales promotion and advertising would change over the brand's life cycle.

   a. How would sales promotional objectives change from introduction to growth to maturity and to decline for the brand?
   b. How would advertising objectives change over each of these stages of the brand's life cycle?

7. What is the distinction between a top-down and a bottom-up approach to promotional budgeting? What are the advantages and disadvantages of each approach?
8. What are the problems with a percent-of-sales approach and a competitive-parity approach as a basis for establishing the advertising budget? Why are these approaches widely used in setting promotional budgets despite these problems?
9. Why is the marginal-revenue approach the ideal way to establish a promotional budget? What are the problems with using this approach?
10. One product manager for a premium-priced coffee brand made the following comments about sales promotions:

    All I hear these days is the increasing amount spent on sales promotions relative to advertising. I just don't understand it. For my money, advertising will produce higher returns over the long run. It keeps brand awareness high, maintains our loyal customer base, and communicates our product's benefits so as to attract new customers. What do coupons and price deals do? Such promotions may attract some customers based on price incentives. But most of these customers just go right back to their original brand when the promotion is off. So how much have we gained? Even worse, the promotion means our regular customers are buying what they would ordinarily purchase, but at a lower price. Overall, I would put more money into advertising than sales promotions.

a. Do you agree with the product manager's assessment of the value of sales promotions? Why or why not?

b. How is the fact that this executive manages a premium-priced brand likely to color her evaluations of sales promotions?

11. Given the statement of the product manager in the previous question, why has the relative importance of sales promotions increased while that of advertising has declined?

12. What sales promotional tools would you use in each of the following situations, and why?

a. A company introducing a new brand of toothpaste is trying to encourage trial.

b. A company with a coffee brand in the mature phase of the life cycle would like to regenerate interest in the brand.

c. A fast-food chain would like to encourage customers to eat at its outlets more often.

d. A small company introduces flavored sparkling waters and is trying to influence wholesalers and retailers to stock the line.

e. A manufacturer of major kitchen appliances is trying to check a decline in its market share.

13. How can each of the following brands or companies benefit from joint sales promotions?

a. H&R Block and Alka Seltzer.

b. St. Joseph's children's aspirins and Flintstone vitamins.

c. Procter & Gamble brands and Chevrolet cars.

14. A marketing manager for a line of personal computers made the following comments about slotting allowances:

> I think paying retailers to stock our items is outrageous. We spend millions to develop what the consumer wants, so why should we pay retailers to stock our products? I would prefer to use advertising and occasional consumer promotions to pull the products through the store than have to pay retailers to push them through.

a. Do you agree with this executive's position on slotting allowances? What are the risks of his position?

b. Would a manager for a packaged good like cereals take a different position regarding slotting allowances than a manager for a line of personal computers?

15. What are the advantages and disadvantages of using publicity in the promotional mix?

CASE 16.1

USING COUPONS TO SELL BARBIE AND HOT WHEELS

Source: Adapted from Sonia L. Nazario, "Mattel Has New Ploy to Sell Toys: It Will Distribute Discount Coupons," *The Wall Street Journal,* September 12, 1988, p. 24.

Mattel Inc. is preparing to flood the country with 582 million store-redeemable coupons as the centerpiece of a new marketing campaign. The coupons offer discounts of $1 to $5 on toys including Barbie and other dolls, Hot Wheels Speed Shift 500 race sets, TV Play-Along Wheel of Fortune games, and a new line of Disney infant and preschool toys.

While Mattel says the effort will hardly be noticed in the annual total of 540 billion coupons distributed by U.S. retail businesses, the company believes it's the first time a toy maker has emphasized such a campaign in its marketing strategy. Generally, the biggest toy makers depend more heavily on early-morning television ads.

Mattel, based in Hawthorne, Calif., plans to continue that thrust, but it will also employ the coupon strategy to provide an economic incentive for parents to give in and buy.

"We're just adapting a tried and true technique to the toy business," says Robert Sansone, president of the Mattel USA unit, who joined the company last year after a 24-year career at that king of the coupons vendors, General Foods Corp.

The approach could well spread to competitors, according to analysts. "Others will look to see if this works, and if it works, they'll follow," says Gary M. Jacobson, a toy analyst with Kidder Peabody & Co. Mr. Jacobson suggests that the more-traditional rebates currently used in the business (which often involve mailing forms back to the manufacturer and waiting for a check) seem to hassle comsumers, and that coupons could produce at least marginal sales increases for Mattel.

"It's succeeded with the fast food industry. I don't see why it won't succeed here," says Steven Eisenberg of Bear Stearns & Co. The move at Mattel, he believes, is part of a drive to preserve a lead over rivals in some product areas while it tries to capture shelf space lost by troubled Worlds of Wonder Inc. and Coleco Industries Inc., among other competitors.

Other analysts, though, stress that the coupon concept may need fine-tuning. "Barbie is red hot and Hot Wheels has emerged as one of the fastest selling toy lines in the country," says Paul Valentine of Standard & Poor's Corp., noting that parents always seem willing to pay a premium for the hottest toys. "I think they should focus promotions on slower moving products."

The coupons will go out next month and in November by direct mail to 70 million households. The packets offer four or five coupons, and provide rebates of $21 for customers spending a total of $176 on toys. Another part of the campaign is the issuance of coupons in supermarket tie-ins with some soft and fruit drink makers.

The cost of the coupon project — significantly more than $5 million — won't keep Mattel from reducing overall advertising and promotion expenses to $174 million this calender year from $188.2 million last year.

1. How does Mattel's promotional mix differ from that of other toy manufacturers?
2. Why did Mattel begin to use coupons on some of its toys?
3. What are the risks of Mattel's coupon strategy?

CASE 16.2

SWEEPSTAKES FEVER

Source: Adapted by permission of *Forbes* magazine from "Sweepstakes Fever," by Jeffrey A. Trachtenberg. *Forbes*, October 3, 1988, pp. 164–166. © Forbes Inc.

This fall Heinz U.S.A. is using a sweepstakes to increase customer loyalty and generate excitement for its ketchup. It is sponsoring a bright red race car on the Nascar circuit and linking it to a supermarket sweepstakes that has a Buick Regal as the top prize. "Racing means business in the Southeast, because it's something the customers there care about," says Jeff Conner, product manager for Heinz Ketchup. "The prizes are getting larger because people are desensitized to the small things. If you want to get their attention, you have to offer them something exciting."

Product promotion has turned into a giant lottery — or lotteries. "People are developing a pot-of-gold-at-the-end-of-the-rainbow mentality," says Charles Visich, a former marketing consultant, now senior vice president at Southland Corp. Visich attributes much of the trend to the publicity surrounding state lotteries and their growing social acceptance. He says: "When somebody wins $23 million, it makes people who have never won anything think twice. The winners are glamorized on television. Society is telling us it's okay to participate."

And there is a glamour to these product lotteries that cents-off coupons don't have. Visich: "From a marketing point of view, the value of a 50-cent coupon is known in advance. But if I offer a trip to Hawaii, the incentive is much more exciting."

The lotteries have another marketing advantage. Clutter in the mailbox and on television makes it harder for the manufacturer to get its product noticed. But Joe Namath lounging on a beach chair and offering tickets to a football game is instant glamour.

Look at Pine-Sol, the disinfectant manufactured by American Cyanamid Co. The product is marketed as a complete household cleaner. Looking for a clever promotion that would be sure to attract consumer attention, the company hit on the idea of giving away a free house.

"It's the biggest promotion we've ever done," says Paula Shaiman, product manager. "One of our marketing objectives was strong display support in the supermarkets. We're getting it."

Insiders say that the sweepstakes are also less expensive than giving stores straight cash merchandising allowances. That's particularly true if the prize involves a commercial tie-in that promotes a specific airline or hotel. "That trip may be worth $5,000, but it might not cost the sponsor a dime," says one supermarket executive. "Think of the advertising impact in seeing the words

'Disney World' in 23,000 supermarkets nationwide. That has great commercial value."

Everybody, it seems, loves an offer of something for nothing — even manufacturers.

1. Why are companies increasingly using sweepstakes as a promotional tool?

2. Is the prize in the Heinz ketchup sweepstakes related to the product? Is the prize in the Pine-Sol sweepstakes related to the product?

3. Which of the two sweepstakes is likely to influence purchasers the most? Why?

NOTES

1. "Meet Mike Quinlan, Big MAC's Attack CEO," *Business Week*, May 9, 1988, pp. 92–97.

2. "Where's Herb? Lost in McD.L.T. Shuffle," *Advertising Age*, December 23, 1986, pp. 1, 26.

3. "Creativity," *Adweek*, February 1, 1988, p. C.R. 44; and "The Making of 'Mac Tonight,'" *The New York Times*, November 29, 1987, p. F4.

4. "Big Mac Strikes Back," *Time*, April 13, 1987.

5. "McDonald's Corp.," *Advertising Age*, September 24, 1987, p. 129.

6. "Success Formula Pays Off: Kids Rate McDonald's #1," *Sales & Marketing Digest*, March 1988, p. 1; and "Fast-Food Leader: Big Mac Uses Dead Man's Advice and Lively Strategy to Repulse Challenges by Rivals," *The Wall Street Journal*, December 18, 1987, p. 12.

7. "Competitors Face Big Mac Promo Attack," *Advertising Age*, February 9, 1987, pp. 1, 74.

8. "How Polaroid Flashed Back," *Fortune*, February 16, 1987, pp. 72–76; and "Polaroid Snaps the Customer," *American Demographics*, February 1987, pp. 21–22.

9. "Spectra Unites Polaroid's Family," *Advertising Age*, October 6, 1986, pp. 4, 100.

10. "Polaroid Enlarges Ad Budget," *Advertising Age*, February 7, 1987, p. 76.

11. "Cost of Industrial Sales Calls Reaches $205.40," *Labreport* (New York: McGraw-Hill Research, 1983), pp. 1–4.

12. "Marketing without Broadcast Media," *Marketing Communications*, January 1987, pp. 31–32.

13. "Cutting Promotions to Fit the Plan," *Sales & Marketing Management*, January 1987, pp. 79–80.

14. "Building Brand Franchises," *Marketing Communications*, April 1986, p. 54.

15. Malcolm A. McNiven, "Plan for More Productive Advertising," *Harvard Business Review* 58(March–April 1980): 131.

16. "Sears Eyes Lower Ad-to-Sales Ratio," *Advertising Age*, December 4, 1978, pp. 3, 8.

17. "Washday Miracle," *Financial World*, November 3, 1987, p. 26.

18. *Marketing Communications*, January 1987, pp. 31–32.

19. "Special Recovery: Tylenol Regains Most of No. 1 Market Share," *The Wall Street Journal*, December 24, 1982, p. 1.

20. "Big Spenders See Uptick: GF Shifts More to Ads for 1987," *Advertising Age*, November 3, 1986, p. 108.

21. "Targeted Coupons Hit Non-Users," *Advertising Age*, April 27, 1987, p. S-26.

22. "Children's Videos Action-Packed for Promoters," *Advertising Age*, February 6, 1986, p. 16.

23. *Marketing Communications*, April 1986, p. 47.

24. "The Promo Wars," *Business Month*, July 1987, pp. 44–46.

25. "BH&G's Recipes Spice Up Alka-Seltzer Interest," *Advertising Age*, April 27, 1987, pp. S-4, S-6.

26. "Hitting the Market from Both Sides: With Premiums and Incentives," *Business Marketing*, August 1986, pp. 122–126.

27. "Supermarkets Demand Food Firms' Payment Just to Get on the Shelf," *The Wall Street Journal*, November 1, 1988, p. 1; and "Grocer 'Fee' Hampers New-Product Launches," *Advertising Age*, August 3, 1987, pp. 1, 60.

28. "Airborne Sweeps Customers Off Their Feet," *Sales & Marketing Management*, July 1986, pp. 80–82.

29. Joseph A. Bellizzi and Delilah J. Lipps, "Managerial Guidelines for Trade Show Effectiveness," *Industrial Marketing Management*, 13 (1984): 49–52.

30. Christopher H. Lovelock and John A. Quelch, "Consumer Promotions In Service Marketing," *Business Horizons*, May–June 1983, pp. 66–75.

31. "Banks Add Sweepstakes to Financial Rewards," *Advertising Age*, March 23, 1987, p. S-9.

32. "Kicking Perrier in the Derriere," *INC*, September 1981, p. 165.

33. Ibid.

34. "The Great Texas Water War," *INC*, March 1986, p. 70.

35. Ibid, p. 71.

36. *Time*, April 13, 1987.

37. "PR Ripens Role in Marketing," *Advertising Age*, January 5, 1981, pp. S10–S11.

When IBM introduced its personal computer line in 1981, it knew it would have to crack the small-business market to be successful. Yet it faced a double-barreled problem: First, how do you convince millions of managers of small businesses who view computers as beyond their competence that PCs are "user friendly"? Second, how do you overcome an image of IBM as an intimidating monolith that deals only with the Fortune 500?

IBM's answer was an advertising campaign built around the notion of friendliness in the face of high technology. The company's ad agency first considered using the Muppets, or friendly spokespersons such as Bill Cosby or Dick Cavett, to convey a user-friendly image. Someone then hit on the Charlie Chaplin character — a simple, friendly figure who represented Everyman and, even better, could communicate in the least threatening of all manners, in mime.[1]

With one powerful symbol, both of IBM's problems melted away. The Little Tramp's antics allayed the fears about using a personal computer and about dealing with a potentially forbidding IBM. The initial ad, aired in late 1981, opened with a big white block. A voiceover compared the block to early computers that were like closed doors. Then the block sprouted a door that Charlie tried to penetrate, only to have it slam in his face. The block shrank into a package that Charlie opened to find a PC, and within seconds he was sitting at his desk, ready to use it. As the narrator suggested that the PC would make Charlie more productive and creative, the Little Tramp sniffed a red rose, meant to represent creativity.

This ad was so successful that IBM immediately decided to use Charlie as the unifying symbol for its entire PC line. "A tool for Modern Times" (a reminder of Chaplin's most famous movie, *Modern Times*) was the theme. The TV campaign was designed to reach the businessperson at home during prime-time viewing. A print campaign used magazines such as *Business Week, Fortune, Venture,* and *Money* to more specifically target the business segment.

ADVERTISING

By 1983 it was apparent the campaign was a huge success. In that year alone, IBM sold 850,000 PCs.[2] In two short years, the company had about 40 percent of the PC market. But by 1985 IBM's market share started eroding as IBM-compatibles started making a serious dent in sales by offering the same technology and features at lower prices. From 1985 to 1988, IBM's share of the PC market dropped from 40 to 17 percent.[3] IBM knew it had to do something, and it did. In 1987 it introduced a new line of microcomputers, the IBM Personal System/2, that included printers and copiers, as well as PCs, and provided enhanced computing and graphic capabilities.

The introduction of the Personal System/2 line spelled the end of the Little Tramp. The campaign had been running for six years and was wearing thin. IBM had won the battle of making PCs user friendly. Now the company needed a symbol to represent a *team* of products. The agency selected another team, the characters from the popular ''M*A*S*H'' TV show, to represent the Personal System/2 line. The $50 million campaign started in 1987 and featured most of the M*A*S*H characters in business clothes, playing off each other as in the M*A*S*H series.[4]

It was inevitable that the silent spokesperson for the early PCs would eventually have to go: IBM had to tell a different story with the Personal System/2 line. But the M*A*S*H campaign was not the answer.[5] Consumers did not associate the M*A*S*H characters with product benefits. As a result, IBM switched to a new campaign in June 1989 that focused on solutions to customer problems in trendy commercials with the tagline, ''How are you going to do it? PS/2 it!''[6] It remains to be seen whether the new campaign can do for the Personal System/2 what the Little Tramp did for the original IBM PC. ∎

● ● ●

IMPORTANCE OF ADVERTISING

Marketers may be spending more money on sales promotion than advertising, but advertising is still the mainstay of a company's communication strategy, informing the consumer about product benefits and keeping the product visible over time.

ADVERTISING EXPENDITURES

In 1982 total advertising expenditures were about $62 billion. By 1988 they had almost doubled to $118 billion. At the same rate of growth, advertising expenditures would be near $500 billion by the turn of the century.

Table 17.1 lists the ten top advertisers in 1988. Most are firms that sell consumer goods. Philip Morris is the leading advertiser, primarily as a result of its ownership of General Foods, Miller Beer, and more recently, Kraft, subsidiaries that advertise heavily. Procter & Gamble had been the leading advertiser for many years, but slipped into second place in 1988. Producers of consumer packaged goods such as drugs, toiletries, and food typically spend over 5 percent of sales revenues on advertising. Kellogg spends more than 15 percent of sales on advertising. Producers of durable goods spend proportionately less. The leading auto companies spend no more than 2 percent of revenues on advertising.

PURPOSES OF ADVERTISING

Advertising has four basic functions. Exhibit 17.1 provides an example of each. First, advertising makes consumers aware of a product, service, or company. The ad for ICI is meant to increase consumer awareness of the company as the fourth largest chemical producer in the world, and to educate the public about the wide range of products and services ICI offers.

Advertising is also meant to inform customers about product or service benefits. American Express is advertising a new benefit for users of its Gold Card, free insurance if the card is used to rent a car (see Exhibit 17.1). The purpose of this ad is to increase card usage among existing customers and to attract new customers.

Another purpose of advertising is to influence consumers to buy — either by informing them about product benefits or by suggesting these benefits through the use of symbolism and imagery. One of the most effective auto advertising

TABLE 17.1
Leading Advertisers in
the United States for 1988

Source: "100 Leading National Advertisers," *Advertising Age,* September 27, 1989, p. 1.

	ADVERTISING EXPENDITURES (in Millions)	AD EXPENDITURES AS PERCENT OF SALES
1. Philip Morris	$2,058	6.5
2. Procter & Gamble	1,507	7.0
3. General Motors	1,294	1.0
4. Sears, Roebuck	1,045	2.1
5. RJR Nabisco	815	5.3
6. Grand Metropolitan PLC (owns Pillsbury, Burger King, SmithKline Beecham)	774	7.2
7. Eastman Kodak	736	4.3
8. McDonald's	728	4.5
9. Pepsi Co	712	5.5
10. Kellogg	683	15.7

campaigns in the 1980s, the "Heartbeat of America" campaign for Chevrolet, was an example of the latter. The campaign provided little actual information about the car. Rather, it conveyed an image of personal fulfillment and patriotism to the throbbing beat of a score reminiscent of a rock video. Three months after the campaign was introduced in October 1986, Chevy's market share climbed from 12.2 percent to 14.4 percent.[7]

Finally, advertising is designed to maintain product visibility over time. One of the most successful advertising campaigns in history, the Marlboro Man, was launched in the mid 1950s and has been used to maintain product visibility for over 30 years. The image of the strong, quietly confident, masculine cowboy transformed the brand into a market leader.

TYPES OF ADVERTISING

Most advertising campaigns are designed to influence consumers to buy a particular brand. The ads in Exhibit 17.1 for Chevrolet, the Gold Card, and Marlboro all represent brands in a product category. Three other types of advertising can be as important as brand advertising in the promotional mix — product advertising, corporate advertising, and cooperative retail advertising.

BRAND ADVERTISING

Brand advertising is designed to maintain awareness of a brand among consumers and to increase its market share. Marketers try to increase the share of their brands primarily by attracting users of competitive brands. Such brand advertising tries to stimulate **selective demand**; that is, demand for a particular brand. The "Pepsi Challenge" campaign showing Coke users preferring Pepsi was an attempt to stimulate selective demand for Pepsi by attracting Coke drinkers. Brand advertising also attempts to keep current customers "sold" on the brand. Pepsi's campaign was designed to reinforce its current users as well as to attract Coca-Cola drinkers.

PRODUCT ADVERTISING

An alternative to stimulating selective demand is to try to make the industry pie bigger by attracting new users through **product advertising**. Such a strategy is attempting to stimulate **primary demand** — that is, demand for a general

EXHIBIT 17.1
The Purposes of Advertising

Advertising to Create Awareness

Advertising to Inform

Advertising to Influence Purchases

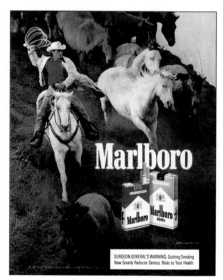

Advertising to Maintain Product Visibility

product — by advertising the product category. The ad for Bayer in Exhibit 17.2 is an example of a company trying to stimulate both primary and selective demand. The company is promoting the product category, aspirin, by advertising its benefits in reducing the chances of a heart attack. It is also promoting its brand by saying that Scott Emerson takes Bayer for this purpose.

Companies also band together at times to advertise a product category on an industrywide basis. Such advertising is usually meant to counter an industry-wide decrease in demand. Rather than spending their money to compete with each other in the face of a shrinking pie, these companies contribute a percentage of their revenues to a cooperative advertising effort to prevent the pie from shrinking further.

Meat producers banded together to advertise beef to combat a decrease in demand. The belief that red meat increases fat and cholesterol resulted in a 20

EXHIBIT 17.2
Advertising Both the Product Category and the Brand

percent decrease in beef consumption from 1976 to 1986 among increasingly health-conscious consumers. Meat producers formed the Beef Industry Council, and contributed $5 million a year to advertise beef as a food that belongs in today's active healthy diet, under the logo "Beef Gives Strength."[8]

CORPORATE ADVERTISING

Companies frequently advertise their corporate name as well as their brands. The ad for ICI in Exhibit 17.1 is an example. There are three types of corporate advertising: patronage, image, and issue advertising.

Many companies employ **corporate-patronage advertising** to encourage customers to patronize the firm. Goodyear advertised "The Blimp's behind you wherever you go" to communicate that the company stood behind its products through its 1,300 service stations coast to coast. The ad in Exhibit 17.3 effectively communicated the message.

Companies often try to establish an identity through **corporate-image advertising.** Bell & Howell conducted research that found that most consumers associated the company with cameras, even though it had sold its camera division in 1979. The company launched a campaign to convey the fact that it was a conglomerate. The ad (see Exhibit 17.4) had little copy and did not detail specific products. Rather, it conveyed an image that the company was in a wide range of product areas.

Corporate-issue advertising states a company's position on an issue of public importance. McDonnell Douglas has advertised the need to maintain the space effort after the Challenger space shuttle disaster by suggesting that Russia could beat out the United States by developing scientific know-how from space stations

EXHIBIT 17.3
Corporate-Patronage Advertising

EXHIBIT 17.4
Corporate-Image Advertising

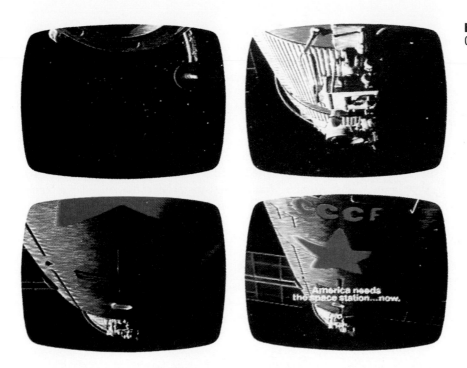

EXHIBIT 17.5
Corporate-Issue Advertising

(see Exhibit 17.5). Since the company is one of the prime contractors for the space shuttle, it has a direct interest in maintaining the space program.

COOPERATIVE ADVERTISING

In **cooperative advertising**, manufacturers offer retailers allowances to advertise their products and permit retailers to insert the store's name in the ad. Cooperative advertising helps manufacturers because it is a means to get retailers to stock and more aggressively sell their products. In this respect, it represents a "push" effort in contrast to the "pull" of brand or product advertising. Cooperative advertising is also important to manufacturers as a source for local advertising to balance their national advertising campaigns.

Cooperative advertising helps retailers as well. Most manufacturers pay from 50 percent to 75 percent of advertising costs. In this way, retailers can afford to advertise in newspapers, on radio, and even on TV. Without such allowances, most retailers could not afford advertising.

Diverse companies such as Levi Strauss, Fram automotive filters, Bristol-Myers, and Apple Computer provide extensive support for cooperative advertising efforts. Apple budgeted $12 million for cooperative advertising in 1986, paying 75 percent of a computer retailer's advertising costs. It links its cooperative ads to national ads that run in such publications as *The Wall Street Journal, USA Today,* and *Fortune* magazine.[9]

DEVELOPING ADVERTISING PLANS AND STRATEGIES

Companies must develop an advertising plan to communicate product benefits to consumers and try to influence them to buy. The process of advertising planning is shown in Figure 17.1. This process parallels the steps in the communications process described in the previous chapter. The advertiser (the source of the mes-

FIGURE 17.1
The Advertising Planning Process

Identify
Target Market

Establish
Advertising
Objectives

Develop
Advertising
Budget

Develop
Advertising
Strategies

Select
Media

Evaluate
Advertising
Effectiveness

sage) identifies the target consumers for the advertising campaign, establishes advertising objectives to influence the target to buy, and develops an advertising budget. The advertising agency then develops an advertising strategy — that is, encoding a set of messages that communicate product benefits — and selects media to transmit the message to target consumers. The advertiser will then evaluate the effectiveness of the campaign based on how consumers interpret (decode) the message and act on it.

A good example of the advertising planning process is a campaign developed by Admiral for its "A La Mode" refrigerator. As the name implies, the refrigerator includes a stir freezer designed to make ice cream and a variety of frozen desserts and yogurt. Admiral was looking for a product that would overcome the natural advantage of the market leaders — GE and Whirlpool — by offering a unique consumer benefit.

Admiral first identified a target for the product — consumers 24 to 54 with income over $40,000.[10] Its advertising objectives were to preempt the market leaders with a unique product, reach at least 80 percent of the target audience nationwide to ensure brand awareness, and at the same time ensure high awareness among appliance retailers. The company set an initial advertising budget of $1.7 million, but initial tests of the concept were so positive that it doubled this to $3.5 million.[11]

Admiral's ad agency developed ads emphasizing different features of the product. One ad showed a little girl eating ice cream, former pro football star Alex Karras claiming he made Paradise Punch, a jogger making blueberry yogurt freeze, and an elegant gourmet making vichyssoise (see Exhibit 17.6).

The media plan involved sinking most of the budget into a short but noticeable two-week TV campaign. Print ads in magazines like *Good Housekeeping, TV Guide,* and *House Beautiful* were used to get year-around coverage. The campaign was a remarkable success. It reached 88 percent of the target group. By the fourth quarter, the total inventory of the product was sold out. The positive evaluation of the campaign led Admiral to invest $35 million in additional production capacity for A La Mode refrigerators.[12]

The remainder of this chapter will consider each of the six steps in the advertising planning process.

IDENTIFYING THE TARGET MARKET

The first step in advertising planning is identifying the target for the advertising campaign. In Chapter 9, we saw that many companies have shifted from a mass market to a segmented approach requiring a more precise definition of the target market. For example, before 1980 most car advertising was targeted to male audiences. With the recognition among marketers that an increasing proportion of women influence and make car buying decisions, the auto companies began targeting ads to specific segments of women buyers such as budget-minded, performance, and luxury-oriented segments.

The definition of the target market will influence the positioning of a product and the advertising themes used. A good example of this link between target market definition and advertising strategy is advertising for wine coolers. California Cooler, the first wine cooler on the market, targeted its initial campaign to people in their twenties with musical video–type ads on network and cable TV. Sun Country paid Ringo Starr a seven-figure salary to appeal to an older group of baby boomers who might fondly remember the former Beatle from the 1960s. Seagram's wine coolers used Bruce Willis, star of Moonlighting, to appeal to young adults somewhere in between the California Cooler and Sun Country age groups. The segment has been described as "a little daffy, irreverent, and clearly more sophisticated," as a reflection of Willis's character.[13] In each case, the selection of a spokesperson and approach was dictated by the definition of the target segment.

ADVERTISING OBJECTIVES

Once marketers identify a target, they must formulate advertising objectives to determine the level of marketing effort needed to influence the target group. These objectives should help advertisers determine the advertising budget and advertising strategies. Objectives also provide the basis for evaluating results of the advertising campaign.

Advertising objectives might be to reach a certain percentage of the target group or to increase the number of times an average consumer in the target group has seen the advertising. As we saw, Admiral's objective was to reach at least 80 percent of the target group of upscale consumers between 24 and 54. Additional objectives might be to achieve awareness of the A La Mode refrigerator within one year among at least two-thirds of the target group, and to create a preference for the product among at least 20 percent of the target.

Ultimately, the key objective must be to influence customer behavior. As a result, advertising objectives are often stated in terms of sales goals; for example, achieving first-year sales of $20 million for the A La Mode refrigerator. Behavioral objectives can also be stated more specifically in terms of goals for increasing new users, increasing usage levels among existing users, or increasing the level of brand loyalty.

DEVELOPING THE ADVERTISING BUDGET

The advertising budget is a component of the overall promotional budget. We described approaches to establishing the promotional budget in the last chapter. Advertisers can use the same approaches to set advertising expenditure levels. They can use a marginal-revenue approach, an objective-task method, a percent-of-sales approach, a competitive-parity approach, or some arbitrary method.

Given the difficulties of applying the marginal-revenue approach, the most effective of these approaches is the objective-task method. Sara Lee used it to establish the advertising budget for its line of Le Sandwiche croissants. The company set a market-share goal for the product line and then determined the proportion of the target group it would have to reach and the frequency of exposures required to attain the market share goal. It then estimated the advertising budget required to meet these "reach" and "frequency" objectives.[14] Sara Lee's approach can be summarized as

EXHIBIT 17.6
Advertising for the
A La Mode Refrigerator

1. OBJECTIVE	2. TASK	3. BUDGET
Market-share goal	→ Reach and frequency required to meet market-share goal	→ Advertising budget to achieve reach and frequency objectives

EXHIBIT 17.7
Ads Based on Information
and Symbolism

Advertising Based on Symbolism   Advertising Based on Information

DEVELOPING ADVERTISING STRATEGIES

The central component of the advertising planning process in Figure 17.1 is developing advertising strategies. Once the target is identified, objectives established, and an advertising budget set, management is ready to consider how to go about influencing the consumer to buy. Advertisers first determine an overall campaign strategy. They then consider what specific messages should be used to inform and influence consumers.

**DETERMINING THE
CAMPAIGN STRATEGY**

Advertising strategies can be designed to maintain a brand's position by continuing an advertising campaign over time, or strategies can be designed to change a brand's image and expand its base of users. A market leader such as Marlboro seeks to maintain its market position and uses advertising as a reminder effect to reinforce current users. But most brands cannot rely on the same campaign for 30 years. They must adapt to changing market conditions by revitalizing their image, which requires a change in advertising strategies over time.

Maintenance or change strategies can be implemented by (1) informing consumers of product benefits and characteristics or (2) using symbols and images to influence consumers to buy. Advertisers often inform consumers about new products or new features and uses for existing products. Informational campaigns are particularly important in industrial advertising, since buyers often make decisions based on product specifications. Informational campaigns are also prevalent for consumer electronics, appliances, and durables because companies can get an edge on their competitors based on product features. The ad for the Sony videocamera in Exhibit 17.7 is meant to inform consumers of product features. The photo is designed to draw consumers into the ad so that they read the copy.

Advertising campaigns can also be based primarily on symbolism and imagery rather than on information. The Halston perfume ad in Exhibit 17.7 is based strictly on imagery. The apple is meant to suggest Eve tempting Adam to eat the forbidden fruit, with the tag line "irresistible."

Types of Campaign Strategies

Figure 17.2 categorizes advertising strategies based on the two factors just cited — maintenance versus change, and information versus imagery. These dimensions do not represent sharp distinctions. Most informational ads have components of imagery. The ad for the Sony videocamera uses images to draw the reader into the ad, but the intent is primarily informational. The ad for Halson shows the product and is therefore partly informational, but the intent is clearly to convey symbolism.

There are four basic types of strategies shown in Figure 17.2. Mercedes has used an **information-oriented maintenance strategy** since the company's advertising has been saying the same thing about its cars for 20 years on an informational basis. Mercedes' advertising agency realized early on that it could not describe Mercedes' quality without using long copy. This approach required print advertising packed with technical facts.

Merrill Lynch has used an **image-oriented maintenance strategy** by consistently relying on the Merrill Lynch bull as a unifying company symbol meant to represent confidence in both the company and the American economy.

Companies use **information-oriented change strategies** to revitalize brands by advertising new product features. For example, Seven-Up Co. shifted from a campaign advertising its flagship brand as "The Uncola" to one touting the caffeine-free benefits of the brand, by using an information approach with the slogan, "Never had it, never will." Information-oriented change strategies are also designed to counter negative information about a brand or company. *USA Today* is countering an image it had since it started in 1982 as fast-food journalism — quick stories short on substance. This image resulted in the unflattering nickname, McPaper.[15] By 1987 the paper felt strong enough to meet the issue head-

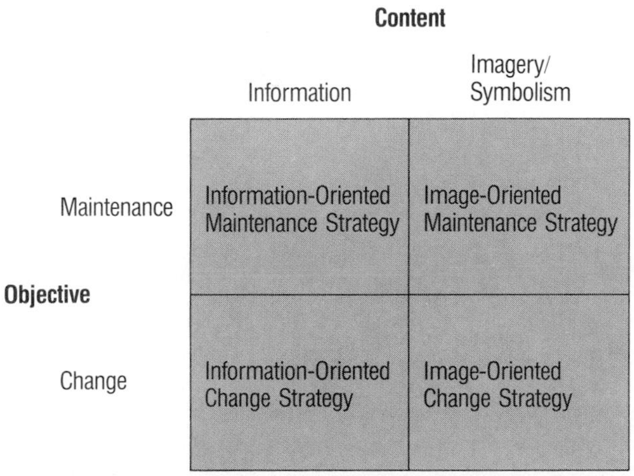

Content

Objective	Information	Imagery/Symbolism
Maintenance	Information-Oriented Maintenance Strategy	Image-Oriented Maintenance Strategy
Change	Information-Oriented Change Strategy	Image-Oriented Change Strategy

FIGURE 17.2
Advertising Campaign Strategies

EXHIBIT 17.8
An Image-Oriented Change Strategy

Surely, she is not telling him about our jeans.

It's also likely she's not saying that Levi's® 501® jeans are made of a special denim that shrinks in the wash to fit only you. Your waist, your hips, *you*.

In fact, she's probably forgotten that while button-fly 501 jeans used to be made just for men, they're now also cut especially for a woman's figure. For a fit so personal, it's like having them custom tailored.

But she *is* wearing 501 jeans. And it *does* look like she's about to have a very special day.

And that's good enough for us.

From

on with the theme, "They used to call us McPaper. Now they call us No. 1." The danger in such a campaign is that it might remind people of the paper's negative image.

An advertiser can also revitalize a brand by an **image-oriented change strategy**. Levi Strauss attempted to increase sales of its jeans by projecting a more youthful and upbeat image to preteens and teenagers. Its ads in Exhibit 17.8 show a change from a focus on young adults to a campaign aimed at a younger segment designed "to sell jeans without mentioning rivets or zippers."[16]

DEVELOPING THE ADVERTISING MESSAGE

Once the direction of the overall campaign is established, advertisers must develop specific messages to communicate product benefits and to influence the consumer to buy. Whether a campaign is based on information or imagery directly affects the development of the advertising message. Advertisers must address certain key issues in developing messages; specifically:

- Should the message be based on emotional or rational appeals?
- Should the advertiser consider using fear appeals to encourage purchase of the brand?
- Should humor be employed?
- Should spokespersons be used to communicate product benefits?
- Should comparative advertising be used to attack competitors?

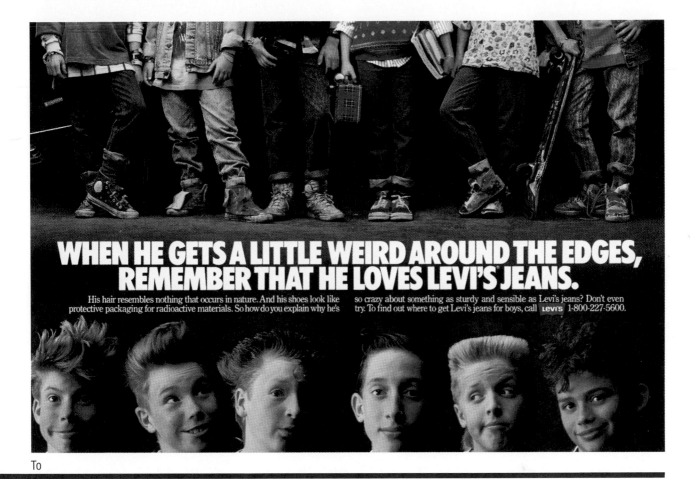

WHEN HE GETS A LITTLE WEIRD AROUND THE EDGES, REMEMBER THAT HE LOVES LEVI'S JEANS.

His hair resembles nothing that occurs in nature. And his shoes look like protective packaging for radioactive materials. So how do you explain why he's so crazy about something as sturdy and sensible as Levi's jeans? Don't even try. To find out where to get Levi's jeans for boys, call LEVI'S 1-800-227-5600.

To

Emotional versus Rational Appeals

An important issue for advertisers is whether the message should "pull at the heartstrings of the consumer" or should be directed to transmitting information. One advertising agency executive voices the consensus among advertisers that the 1980s saw "emotion playing a greater role in advertising [by becoming] less product-feature oriented and much more nonverbal."[17]

Why this recent trend to emotion? There are several reasons. First, many products have become more standardized. When an advertiser for detergents or softeners has no unique product claim, what better approach than to develop an emotionally based positioning? Second, advertisers have begun to recognize that many of the products they advertise are not particularly involving. Emotional advertising is a way to increase that involvement. When Downy fabric softener shows a child at camp complaining that his clothes do not smell as good as home-washed, that is a lot more involving than hearing two adult consumers talking about the merits of the product. Third, the intensity of competition has increased in many categories. More product alternatives makes it harder for any one product to be noticed. What better way to stand out from the crowd than to take an emotional approach?

United attempted to stand out from typical airlines advertising by taking an emotional approach. The ad in Exhibit 17.9 reminisces about a close-knit father-son relationship, the point being that United can fly customers to more hometowns to be reunited with their loved ones.

EXHIBIT 17.9
Using An Emotional Approach

When was your last
home run?
Good of Dad. If he hadn't been there helping
with practice, cheering at the games, it just wouldn't
have been the same.
Isn't it about time to touch base again?
No other airline flies to more hometowns than
United. With convenient flights and great low fares.
Call your Travel Agent. Or call United. It's a home
run you'll never forget.

UNITED
A I R L I N E S

Using Fear Appeals

Most advertising informs consumers of the advantages of using a product. *Fear appeals* focus on the potential problems of not using the product. They are also used for public service advertisements, such as those seeking to discourage smoking. In this case, they are most effective if they do not hit the consumer over the head with their message. Early anti-smoking ads showing terminal cancer patients were ineffective because they produced such a high level of anxiety that many smokers simply chose to ignore them.

Appeals to fear are likely to be effective if they show the consumer what to do to avoid the problem. Kellogg employed a successful appeal to fear when it introduced All-Bran as a high-fiber cereal that could help ward off colon cancer.

Employing Humor

Humor can be a memorable and persuasive way to sell a product. It is a good attention-getting device and also may create a positive mood toward the advertiser, since people like to laugh. Lever started a tongue-in-cheek campaign for Sunlight dishwasher detergent using animated cartoons that make fun of the sexist tone of some household cleaner products. In one ad, a wife furtively clutches a spotty glass and whispers "Clifford's parents will eat me alive." (See Exhibit 17.10.) The ad spoofs traditional fear appeals showing housewives trying to please their husbands through cleaner clothes and spotless dishes.

But humor can be an absolute dud if it is not closely linked to product benefits. Even though the brand in Exhibit 17.10 is poking fun at itself, the message still comes across: Sunlight will get glasses and dishes clean. Burger King, on the other hand, failed in its attempt at humor in a 1985 campaign titled "Where's Herb?"

EXHIBIT 17.10
Use of Humor in Advertising

Designed to find some character called Herb who had never tasted a Whopper, the campaign turned out to be a "$40 million yawn."[18] The focus on Herb as a balding eccentric in glasses, white socks, and gaudy plaids did not get any particular message across regarding the benefits of visiting a Burger King.

Using Spokespersons

Well-known spokespersons can be effective in getting an ad message across if they are likeable. Bill Cosby was a successful spokesperson for General Foods' Jell-o pudding pops because the ads were directed to children who liked Cosby in his TV series. (See Exhibit 17.11.)

Also, if spokespersons are viewed as credible they are more effective in conveying a message. John Houseman was an effective spokesperson for the brokerage house of Smith Barney based on his portrayal of a law professor in the TV series *The Paper Chase*. And when Houseman intoned, "We make money the old fashioned way; we earn it," he seemed to know what he was talking about.

A spokesperson can fall flat if cast in the wrong role. Bill Cosby was used as a spokesperson for the brokerage house, E.F. Hutton, in the hope that his good-guy image would help repair the firm's reputation after it was rocked by a management scandal. But as one wag said, "When Cosby talked, nobody listened." Why? Because his lovable TV character was not perceived as having any special financial know-how. Cosby lacked credibility, which was the main requirement for a spokesperson for a financial services firm. Likewise, John Houseman was not successful as a spokesperson for McDonald's, which tries to communicate warmth and friendliness and therefore requires likeability in its spokesperson. Houseman's TV character was not perceived as being particularly friendly.

EXHIBIT 17.11
Example of a Successful Spokesperson

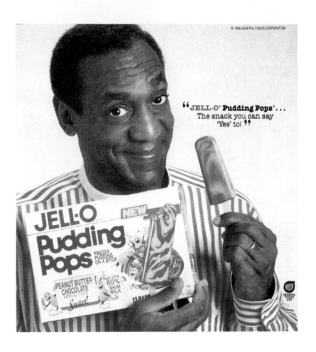

"'JELL-O' **Pudding Pops**'...
The snack you can say
'Yes' to! "

Comparative Advertising

Another issue is whether a message should compare the advertised brand to competition. Such **comparative advertising** names competitors and cites the advantages of the advertised brand. For example, Pan Am inaugurated its new Boston–New York–Washington service by advertising "Your last reason to fly the Eastern Shuttle has just disappeared."

Comparative advertising has been increasing since a 1976 Supreme Court decision that said an advertiser has the right to name a competitor under freedom of speech. The National Broadcasting Company reported that in 1986 half of the commercials it screened were comparative ads, compared to about one-third in 1980.[19] Apparently, companies were finding it increasingly beneficial to meet competitors head-on in advertising.

But there are risks in using comparative advertising. A challenger should steer clear of it unless there is a legitimate claim to superiority. Otherwise, the brand could lose credibility in the consumer's eyes and even risk a court challenge. Another risk is that consumers might confuse the challenger for the competitor, for example, not remembering whether the shuttle ad was sponsored by Pan Am or Eastern.

**Alex Kroll —
From Football Pro to
Master Advertising Strategist**

Source: © Shonna Valeska 1988.

How does an advertising agency make sure its ads stand out in the clutter of TV and print advertising? Ask Alex Kroll, head of Young & Rubicam (Y&R), America's largest ad agency. Kroll is behind ads like the one for Irish Spring soap, where a conservative announcer looks like he is about to launch into a standard pitch only to lose control of the soap as it squirts him in the face and lathers up in his pocket. Kroll is also behind the ad for Colgate's Tartar Control toothpaste that shows construction men inside a "mouth" hacking away at tartar on giant teeth. It took three weeks to build seventeen-feet-high teeth for that commercial.[20]

Kroll and his agency were not always thought of as innovators, ready to take risks with new and unusual approaches to capture consumer attention. In fact, Y&R had a conservative reputation. Kroll originally made his mark by developing ads for run-of-the-mill detergent and household products. One of his biggest coups before heading up Y&R was coming up with the tag line for Spic 'N' Span — "Gets to the dirt liquids leave behind."

Why the change in approach? Because Kroll saw it as necessary to capture new business. When he became CEO in 1985, he began exhorting his troops not to be afraid to come up with the new, the outrageous, the unconventional. Once Y&R employees knew that top management was behind the unconventional, approaches like those for Irish Spring Soap and Colgate Tartar Control were developed. And they were winners. Colgate spent more than $20 million on its "mouth" campaign, helping it attract 8 percent of the $1 billion toothpaste market in nine months.[21] The Irish Spring ads increased formerly flat sales of deodorant soaps.

Although Kroll was puny and uncoordinated as a kid, his one ambition was to be a pro football star. So he started getting up at 2:30 a.m. to lift barbells. By 1961, his senior year at Rutgers, he was captain of an undefeated football team and made All-American. Pro football was next, but after 14 concussions and 9 nose breaks, he decided to accept the offer of a Rutgers alumnus who worked for Y&R, and he joined the agency in 1963.[22] In 1970, on his thirty-third birthday, he was named creative director, the youngest person to reach that position. ("Creative" is the ad industry's jargon for the words, images, and symbols developed for ads.) He then went on to be president in 1975 and CEO in 1985.

Some people say Alex Kroll is not such a nice guy and leads by fear and intimidation. Others say he is fair, straightforward, and inspiring. It is clear that he loves advertising as much as he loved football. In fact, Kroll sees a link between the two. He says, "What I learned from both advertising and football is how really hard it is to win. And how terrific it feels."[23] These days, Alex Kroll is feeling terrific. ■

SELECTING MEDIA

Once advertisers have established a strategy for their brand, they must select the media to transmit the message. Selecting media is a difficult task because of the diversity of options. Advertisers can use TV, radio, magazines, newspapers, billboards, or direct mail, and within each of these categories the number of options is almost limitless.

The media vehicles available to advertisers can be broadly divided into broadcast media (TV and radio) and print media (newspapers, magazines, billboards, direct

TYPES OF MEDIA

FIGURE 17.3
Distribution of Advertising
Expenditures by Type of Media, 1988

Source: "Ad Spending Outlook Brightens," *Advertising Age,* May 15, 1989, p. 24.

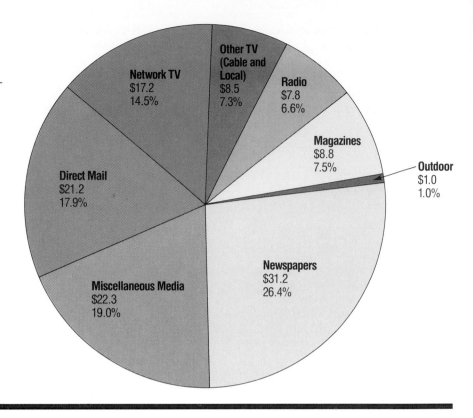

mail). These six types are shown in Figure 17.3. Advertising expenditures in 1988 are shown in dollars and as a percentage of all spending.

Television

The mainstay of most national advertising campaigns is television — a medium in sound, color, and motion that can visually associate symbols with products, demonstrate product usage, and show consumer reactions. Figure 17.3 shows that television (network, local, and cable) accounted for over 20 percent of advertising expenditures in 1988. Over 97 percent of U.S. households have a TV set. These households watch an average of six hours of TV a day, most of the time on one of the three major networks. As a result, network TV is viewed as the most effective medium for mass marketing products.

Network TV's national scope is also a potential weakness, though. The medium is not selective in pinpointing target markets. As a result, advertisers are turning to local TV stations to reach specific geographic markets more effectively, and to cable TV and magazines to reach specific demographic groups. Fewer consumers are watching the networks because of the increasing availability of cable TV and the increasing popularity of VCRs. In addition, with more women in the workforce, daytime TV viewing has dropped, with the networks suffering most of this decrease. The increasing costs of network TV have also led advertisers to allocate less to this medium. Network TV costs rose more than three times from 1967 to 1987, well above the rate of increase for radio, magazines, and direct mail.[24] Despite these weaknesses, network TV remains the single most important part of the media mix for national brands.

Cable TV is in some ways a cross between network TV and magazines. It provides the same visual advantages as network TV, but it also offers the selectivity of magazines. Since most cable channels are oriented to specialized interests such as news, sports, weather, and movies, commercials on these channels can be targeted to better-defined groups than those that watch network TV. As a result, cable TV has come to be referred to as *narrowcasting,* as opposed to network TV's *broadcasting.*

Another advantage of cable is that commercials can be much longer because they cost less. Commercials of more than two minutes are common. Because they can communicate more information, cable TV ads have come to be known as *infomercials* in contrast to network TV's *commercials.* An example is a Crest ad on a cable TV children's show. The ad features detective Philip Molar and his companion, Flossie La Rue. They confront characters such as Madame Decay and the Sugar Fiend while finding decaying food particles and urging kids to floss. Crest is mentioned only briefly at the beginning of the ad.[25]

Radio

Radio is the other major broadcast medium. With an average of over five radios per household and one in 95 percent of cars, it provides constant coverage. The average consumer listens to over three hours of radio a day.[26] Radio is also flexible in reaching a wide range of audiences. This flexibility has led General Motors to increase radio advertising to better target its message to specific audiences. It advertises its Pontiac Bonneville on all-news stations to attract older, upscale listeners. It promotes its less expensive Sprints, Spectrums and Fieros on rock stations. And it advertises its Chevy trucks on an all-night radio network that reaches 650,000 long-haul truckers.[27]

Radio is also more economical. Costs of radio advertising have increased less than those of all the major media. From 1967 to 1987 its rate of increase was half that of network TV.[28] As a result, advertisers have increased radio expenditures from $1.8 billion in 1974 to $7.8 billion in 1988.

Newspapers

Newspapers are the biggest advertising medium, accounting for more than 25 percent of advertising spending. Most of this is for retail advertising. Sales, price specials, coupon offers, and all types of merchandise are advertised on a day-to-day basis. Much of this expenditure might be better categorized as sales promotions rather than advertising, given its short-term nature.

Most national brand advertisers use newspapers on a limited basis, usually in conjunction with retailers by offering allowances for cooperative local advertising. But national advertisers are paying closer attention to newspapers for several reasons. First, they are an excellent medium for targeting specific geographic segments. Second, heavy newspaper readers tend to be upscale and have more discretionary purchasing power. Third, the cost of newspaper advertising has been increasing at a much lower rate than that of television.

These advantages led Peugeot's advertising agency, Ogilvy & Mather, to develop a media mix for the car in which 80 percent of advertising was allocated to newspapers.[29] One of the reasons was that Peugeot's target market was defined as well-educated information seekers, and newspaper advertising was more likely to reach this group with an informative message. Also, newspapers provided the flexibility to vary the amount of expenditures in each local market.

Magazines

Magazines have several major advantages: First, since they are saved, picked up more than once, and often passed along to others, a consumer may be exposed to a magazine ad more than once, and a single ad is likely to be seen by more than one reader. Magazines also provide a means of drawing the consumer's attention to the printed word through illustrations or headlines.

The effectiveness of magazines in communicating information makes them the most important component of the media mix for industrial advertisers. Ads in business publications such as *Iron Age* or *Aviation Week* are likely to reach industrial buyers with purchase influence for the items being advertised. Such ads are essential in providing key information on product attributes and performance, and they pave the way for subsequent sales calls.

Another advantage of magazines is selectivity. Magazines have become the most selective means of reaching target groups based on special interests and demographic characteristics. Since 1970 there has been a flood of specialty magazines geared to special interests such as health, fashion, foods, electronics, sports, and so forth. Magazines are also being targeted to specific demographic groups. The *echo boom* (the increase in the birth rate as baby boomers reached child-bearing age), spawned magazines such as *Motherhood* and *New Mother*. The increase in the proportion of working women resulted in *New Woman* and *Working Woman*. The freer lifestyles and greater self-awareness of older Americans led to the creation of magazines such as *50 Plus* and *Mature Outlook*. These magazines give the advertiser the opportunity to balance mass advertising with targeted advertising in the media mix.

Direct Mail

The mails are another important medium for advertising. Figure 17.3 shows that direct mail (advertising or promotions mailed to specific customers) was the third most prominent medium, representing over 17 percent of all advertising expenditures.

Direct mail has the advantage of being able to target specific segments at relatively low cost compared to the mass media. It is a particularly important vehicle in industrial advertising for delivering catalogs to buyers and providing flyers detailing product specifications and prices. It has the advantage of being able to target advertising directly to the individuals identified as having buying influence without the waste of reaching nonbuyers through mass-media advertising.

Direct mail is also used for consumer goods. Mailing lists have been developed to target specific markets. For example, R. L. Polk, a Detroit-based research group, has data on all households with cars. In 1988 it developed a mailing list for Subaru of 500,000 professional car-owning women with incomes over $35,000. Subaru was interested in this group because more than 60 percent of its cars are bought by women. The mailing included a brochure on Subaru's models and a 13-page kit that provides vehicle purchasing tips, a list of Subaru ownership advantages, and a discussion of leasing versus purchasing.[30]

Outdoor

Outdoor advertising is represented primarily by billboard advertising, but other forms such as advertising on buses and even on parking meters are being used more frequently. It represents only 1 percent of all advertising spending, but it is becoming more important as a means of targeting consumers in specific markets and even in particular neighborhoods.

The cost per advertising exposure is much lower for outdoor than that for TV, radio, or magazine advertising. To be effective, outdoor must convey the message within two or three seconds, so it must capture attention with creative illustrations and few words.

Outdoor advertising is an effective medium for local advertisers, since it can be placed near retail establishments. The billboard in Exhibit 17.12 for Robinson's, a Los Angeles-based 21-store chain, is an example. National advertisers also use outdoor ads. The Gatorade ad in Exhibit 17.12 is for a national campaign.

An advertiser must select media based on their effectiveness in reaching the target group, which is determined by the degree of exposure it produces and its cost.

CRITERIA FOR MEDIA SELECTION

Advertising Exposure

The potential advertising exposure that a particular medium can deliver is determined by its reach and frequency. **Reach** is the number of people exposed to the medium. **Frequency** is the number of times an individual is exposed to the message. Assume Subaru supports its direct-mail campaign to professional women with magazine advertising. It finds that *Working Woman* would reach 30 percent of its target of upscale working women. Subaru plans eight full-page ads a year and estimates readers will be exposed to half of them.

Advertising exposure is based on reach multiplied by frequency, a measure known as **Gross Rating Points (GRPs)**. Subaru's estimated GRPs for *Working Woman* would be 30 (reach) × 4 (frequency), or 120. The company would then investigate other magazines and select those that gave it the highest GRP to the target group at the lowest cost.

There is a tradeoff between reach and frequency. For a given advertising budget, greater emphasis on reach means less on frequency, and vice versa. The balance between the two depends on the advertising objectives. Reach is important for nationally advertised products that cut across many segments — for example, products such as toothpaste, detergents, and soft drinks. Frequency is important when a new product is introduced, to establish brand awareness. Generally, several exposures are necessary for such awareness. Frequency is also more important when trying to influence a particular target group. The objective is to reach fewer people a greater number of times; whereas in advertising on a mass-media basis, the reverse would be true.

In the Subaru example, the advertiser could try to use a greater number of magazines to increase reach to working women. For example, Subaru could advertise in *Time* to reach more working women. But much of this advertising would be wasted on consumers outside the target. A more likely course would be to use fewer magazines and more insertions in each magazine to increase frequency to a more select group of upscale working women.

Advertising Impact

One problem with using advertising exposure to select media is that exposure does not reflect the impact of advertising. Two magazines might deliver the same GRPs, but an advertisement in one might have more of an impact than an ad in the other. An ad for a tennis racket in *Sports Illustrated* is likely to have more of

EXHIBIT 17.12
Local and National Billboard Advertising

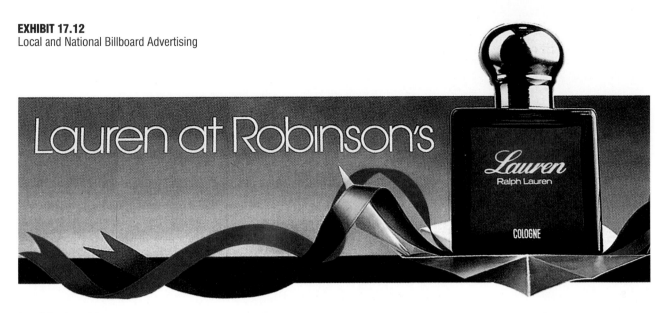

Local Outdoor Ad

National Outdoor Ad

an impact on the reader than the same ad in *Time* because of the differing editorial content of these magazines, even though both might have produced the same GRPs. Media planners must, therefore, account for the nature of the medium and its fit with the product.

Cost

Advertisers select media based on advertising exposure relative to the cost of obtaining such exposure. GRPs alone can not be the basis for media selection. The more appropriate criterion would be the *cost per gross rating point*.

Consider the following example: At one time, McDonald's media plan called for achieving 150 GRPs among children for each weekend of TV, split between

	SAT. MORN. (30 secs.)	SAT. MORN. (15 secs.)	SUN. MORN. (30 secs.)	SUN. MORN. (15 secs.)
1. Frequency (Number of commercials)	2 ads	1 ad	2 ads	1 ad
2. Reach (Percent of children reached)	30%	30%	20%	20%
3. GRPs (1 × 2)	60	30	40	20
4. Total Cost	$300,000	$90,000	$180,000	$55,000
5. Cost per GRP (4 ÷ 3)	$5,000	$3,000	$4,500	$2,750

TABLE 17.2
Selecting Media by Cost per Gross Rating Point

15- and 30-second commercials. The company was willing to allocate up to $650,000 each weekend to achieve this purpose. Suppose the company allocated its advertising as in Table 17.2. On this basis, it would pay the company to put more money into 15-second commercials, since they cost less per GRP. It would also pay to buy more 15-second commercials on Sunday rather than Saturday morning, since the cost per GRP is lower then.

On this basis, the media planner would try to determine the schedule that would achieve the most effective delivery of advertising exposure given the advertising objectives and budgetary constraints.

SELECTING THE MEDIA MIX

Media planners use criteria such as cost per GRP to select a mix of vehicles to advertise their brands. Few rely on only one type of medium. Since there are so many alternatives, computer programs have been developed to help determine the optimal combination of media based on the advertiser's objectives and cost constraints. Such programs might suggest, for example, that Subaru use radio advertising and cable TV as well as magazines to reach upscale working women, and would indicate the most effective combination of these media.

One such program, known as MEDIAC, estimates the GRPs a particular ad might produce in a given medium — for example, the estimated GRPs if Subaru were to run a commercial on a financial news channel on cable TV. It then computes the schedule that will maximize GRPs within budget constraints. These programs cannot take over as a substitute for the advertiser's judgment. In fact, they are based on the objectives and constraints dictated by the advertiser.

Another approach to media selection would be to use marginal analysis. For example, the optimal selection of the media alternatives in Table 17.2 would be at the point where gaining each additional GRP costs the same amount of money. Using marginal analysis, the media planner would shift expenditures from 30- to 15-second commercials and from Saturday to Sunday, until the added cost of achieving an additional GRP is equal across all media vehicles.

ESTABLISHING THE MEDIA SCHEDULE

Once a media mix is selected, a time schedule must be established to specify when the ads will be run. An important consideration in timing is *seasonality* in a product's sales. Many products have some seasonality based either on variations in consumption (iced tea in the summer) or on special events (watches or cameras for graduation and Christmas). Advertisers must decide whether to increase spending during these periods.

Another issue in timing is whether advertisers should spend most of their budgets in a few large bursts at various times (known as **pulsing**), or should spend steadily over time (known as **continuity**). Some advertisers feel that advertising has a greater effect when it is presented in concentrated bursts; others feel it is more effective to advertise consistently over time to constantly keep the brand visible. Research conducted by Anheuser-Busch concluded that advertising for Budweiser could stop for at least a year without any adverse effect on sales. The company could then provide a six-month burst of advertising to maintain previous growth. This finding led Anheuser to adopt a pulsing strategy.

Pulsing is most relevant for new products to provide an initial burst and establish brand awareness. It is also used for seasonal products to advertise more heavily during peak periods. It is sometimes used in conjunction with sales promotions to provide support for price or coupon incentives.

Continuity is used to sustain an ad and establish awareness over time. It is particularly important to maintain a continuous level of advertising expenditures in the face of intense competition. But if the same campaign is run for a long period of time, then there is a danger of consumer **wearout**, that is, a decrease in the effectiveness of advertising because of boredom and familiarity. As a result, advertisers will seek to vary the message when they maintain continuous advertising.

EVALUATING ADVERTISING EFFECTIVENESS

The last step in developing advertising strategies is evaluating the effectiveness of advertising. Overall, advertising has a positive effect on a firm's profits. One study examined advertising expenditures of 700 consumer goods firms from 1970 to 1986 (see Figure 17.4). The study found that firms who advertise much more than their competitors had a significantly higher return on investment (an ROI of 32 percent). Firms that spent much less than average had an ROI of only 17 percent. The study also found that firms that spent much more on advertising had a market share at least twice as great as firms who spent much less. Finally, as more was spent on advertising, consumers' quality perceptions of the product increased.

The study in Figure 17.4 shows that advertising is positively related to profits for some brands and not for others. But what brands and what type of advertising? Advertisers deal with these questions by evaluating their advertising strategies in three ways. First, they evaluate the effects of individual ads on consumers. Does the ad create brand recognition? Does it create a positive attitude toward the brand? Is it likely to influence the consumer to buy? Second, they assess the effectiveness of various media in delivering the message. Third, they evaluate the effect of the overall campaign on sales results.

EVALUATING INDIVIDUAL ADS

Chapter 7 described different techniques to test print and broadcast ads. In each case, ads are tested before they are introduced (pre-testing) and after (post-testing). The most common form of pre-testing print ads is to give respondents a portfolio of dummy ads in a magazine format and ask them to recall copy points. Pre-tests of TV commercials are conducted in theaters and special trailers. In both cases, consumers are asked to record their reactions to the commercials through a hand-held electronic device or by a questionnaire. Testing the ad before it is introduced allows the advertiser to determine the effectiveness of individual ads on criteria such as awareness of the ad, recall, and reaction to the contents.

FIGURE 17.4
Advertising's Effect on Profitability

Source: *The Impact of Advertising Expenditures on Profits for Consumer Businesses* (New York: The Ogilvy Center for Research & Development, 1988), pp. 6, 15.

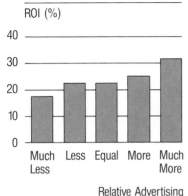

Relative Advertising and Profitability

Relative Advertising and Profitability

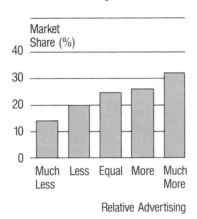

Relative Advertising and Market Share

Advertising Affects Market Share

Relative Advertising and Perceived Quality

Advertising Influences Perceived Quality

The most common method of post-testing print ads is to ask consumers to look through an actual magazine and then report which ads they remember seeing (the *in-magazine recognition test*). The most common method of post-testing TV ads is to interview consumers the day after a TV ad appears to determine what they remember about it (the *day-after recall test*).

EVALUATING MEDIA EFFECTIVENESS

Advertisers must gauge the potential effectiveness of various media in delivering their message. As we saw, the most commonly used measure is cost per gross rating point (GRP). To compute it for magazines or newspapers, the advertiser must know the number of readers a publication reaches and the frequency of exposure to the ad. Some research firms specialize in running syndicated studies to measure readership, the most important being W. R. Simmons for magazines and Scarborough research for newspapers.

To estimate cost per GRP for TV commercials, the advertiser must know how many viewers were exposed to the commercial. Here again, research companies measure exposure through syndicated studies, the most widely used being the A. C. Nielsen service.

EVALUATING ADVERTISING'S EFFECT ON SALES

The most important criterion in measuring advertising effectiveness is its effect on sales. As we saw in the last chapter, relating advertising to sales is difficult because so many other factors might influence a consumer to buy.

The sales effects of certain kinds of advertising are easier to measure than others. Newspaper advertising usually describes store sales and price deals. The retailer can determine whether sales increase during the period of the special promotion. But linking brand advertising to sales is much more difficult, since advertising occurs over time and many other factors influence consumer purchase decisions.

Despite these difficulties, brand advertisers have made important strides in evaluating the sales effectiveness of advertising. The most promising approach uses single-source data to link electronic measurement of TV viewing and electronic scanners to determine consumer purchases. As we saw in Chapter 7, single-source data have given advertisers a means of evaluating the sales effectiveness of their ad campaigns. These new technologies are only now beginning to be widespread.

ENSURING SOCIALLY RESPONSIBLE ADVERTISING

Most advertising is socially responsible. But, unfortunately, some advertising has willfully deceived or misinformed the public, has taken advantage of the naiveté of younger children, or has alienated key consumer groups such as women or minorities with insulting or distasteful representations of their roles.

DECEPTIVE ADVERTISING

Advertising that gives false information or that willfully misleads consumers about the benefits of the brand is **deceptive advertising**. It is unethical, and is controlled both through the self-regulation of responsible advertisers and through government action. The Federal Trade Commission (FTC) monitors advertising and takes action against ads regarded as deceptive by using a cease-and-desist order. For example, several companies were ordered to stop claiming that enzymes in detergents eliminate stains.[31] But such an order cannot correct a false impression created by past advertising, so a second remedy is sometimes applied, **corrective advertising**. Here the company must publicly correct past claims through new advertising. Without corrective advertising, companies might benefit from false claims made in the past, even after they have stopped making them. The FTC required Warner-Lambert to correct the claim that Listerine helps prevent colds. It also required Hawaiian Punch to correct its claim that its drink was composed of natural fruit juices. The impact of corrective advertising was illustrated by a study that found that the proportion of consumers who believed that Hawaiian Punch had little fruit juice went from 20 percent to 70 percent when the company started correcting the claim.[32]

ADVERTISING TO CHILDREN

Advertisers have a responsibility to avoid manipulating younger children, who tend to be more gullible than the rest of the population. One study found that if a child requested a product because it was seen on TV, the parent was more likely to buy it.[33] Yet younger children cannot adequately process information to evaluate advertising claims. The potential for taking advantage of children has led the FTC to propose a ban on advertising sugar-coated foods on children's programs. Others have suggested prohibiting all advertising on programs watched by a significant proportion of children under the age of eight.

PORTRAYAL OF WOMEN AND MINORITIES

Another area in which advertising is sometimes socially irresponsible is in its portrayal of women and minorities. The National Advertising Review Board found that until the late 1970s, women were typically shown as "stupid — too dumb to cope with familiar everyday chores unless instructed by children or a man."[34] In the early 1980s, some advertisers went to the other extreme and portrayed "superwoman" — a working woman who could serve the family breakfast, run off to the office, glide in to make dinner looking perfectly breathtaking, and carry on a stimulating conversation with her husband while taking care of the kids.

Today, offensive role portrayals of women still linger. But advertisers are starting to try to portray women in more realistic roles. Subaru's campaign to women, cited earlier, changed the traditional image of women as being interested only in the styling and interior of a car. Its campaign focused on specific performance characteristics to attract upscale working women.

Advertising's portrayal of blacks has also improved over time. In the past, blacks have been portrayed in subservient roles such as waiters or porters, or as inept and unmotivated. One black advertising executive said "Ten years ago, most portrayals of the black male were of the 'can't-do-anything-but-have-a-good-time' type. Today, much more accurately, the black male is characterized as more ambitious,"[35] and is portrayed in more realistic roles.

SUMMARY

1. What types of advertising do marketers use most widely?
The most common types of advertising are brand, product, corporate, and cooperative advertising. Brand advertising is designed to increase the market share of a brand by getting users of competitive brands to use the company's brand. It is also designed to reinforce the decision of current users to continue to buy the brand.

Product advertising is designed to increase the demand for a product category. Corporate advertising encourages customers to buy the firm's products, tries to establish or change the image of the company, or takes a position on an issue that is important to the company. In cooperative advertising, manufacturers offer retailers an allowance to advertise their stores at the local level. Advertising includes the manufacturer's name and provides a local presence for the manufacturer's products.

2. How do firms develop advertising strategies?
Advertising strategies are developed by an advertising planning process. Advertisers identify a target for their communications, define advertising objectives to influence the target to buy, and establish an advertising budget. The advertising agency is then responsible for developing an advertising strategy. Such strategies may try to maintain a brand's position over time, or may be designed to change a brand's image to expand its base of users. Strategies can be based on transmitting information, developing positive brand associations through images and symbols, or some combination of both. Once strategies are established, the advertising agency selects media to transmit the message to the target. The final step is to evaluate the effectiveness of advertising strategies based on how consumers interpret the message and whether they act on it.

3. What different types of messages do advertisers develop to communicate product benefits?
Advertisers have various alternatives in developing messages. They must decide whether the message should be based on emotional or rational appeals. The trend

in recent years has been to use more emotional appeals, because they are likely to stand out and involve the consumer in the message.

The ad may use fear appeals or humor. A fear appeal can be effective if it provides the consumer a way to remedy the problem that the ad is illustrating. Humor can be effective if it creates a positive mood toward the brand and if it is linked to product benefits.

Another issue in message development is the use of spokespersons. They are effective if they are either seen as experts or are likeable and are matched to an appropriate product. Finally, advertisers must decide whether to attack competitors in their messages. Such comparative advertising is occurring more frequently, but it is risky unless the advertised brand is clearly superior to the named competitor.

4. How do advertisers select media to transmit their messages?

Media are selected primarily based on the degree to which they reach the target group and the frequency of exposure within the group. The combination of reach and frequency is known as gross rating points (GRPs). Cost per gross rating point is the cost of achieving a given level of reach and frequency in the target group when using a particular medium. Another criterion is advertising impact, that is, the effectiveness of the ad in a particular medium based on its editorial content or the nature of its programming. The difficulty in examining the thousands of combinations of media in the process of developing a mix of vehicles has led many ad agencies to use computer programs to help in selecting an effective combination of media vehicles to reach a target group.

5. How do marketers evaluate advertising effectiveness?

Advertisers evaluate individual messages, the media they appear in, and the overall campaign. Print ads are frequently evaluated by in-magazine recognition tests, whereas broadcast commercials are often evaluated based on day-after recall tests. Media are evaluated based on effectiveness in reaching the target group. Evaluating the overall campaign requires relating advertising expenditures to sales. Recently, this has been done by using single-source data, which measure ad exposure and purchases for the same household through electronic means.

6. What is socially responsible advertising?

Advertising is socially responsible if it is truthful and informative. Deceptive advertising willfully misinforms the public. It is combatted by self-regulation through industry standards and by government regulation through the actions of the FTC. Advertisers also have a responsibility to avoid taking advantage of children. Another area in which advertising must demonstrate social responsibility is in portraying women and minority groups realistically.

KEY TERMS

Brand advertising (p. 467)
Selective demand (p. 467)
Product advertising (p. 467)
Primary demand (p. 467)
Corporate-patronage advertising (p. 469)
Corporate-image advertising (p. 469)
Corporate-issue advertising (p. 469)
Cooperative advertising (p. 471)

Information-oriented maintenance strategy (p. 475)
Image-oriented maintenance strategy (p. 475)
Information-oriented change strategy (p. 475)
Image-oriented change strategy (p. 476)
Comparative advertising (p. 480)

Reach (p. 485)
Frequency (p. 485)
Gross rating points (GRPs) (p. 485)
Pulsing (p. 487)

Continuity (p. 488)
Wearout (p. 488)
Deceptive advertising (p. 490)
Corrective advertising (p. 490)

QUESTIONS

1. Why was IBM's use of Charlie Chaplin so successful as a symbol in advertising its personal computers?

2. How do the ads in Exhibit 17.1 illustrate the four basic principles of advertising?

3. What is the distinction between brand and product advertising? What are the purposes of each? Under what circumstances would a manufacturer want to stimulate demand for a product category (like analgesics) as well as demand for the company's brand (such as Bayer)?

4. What are the purposes of the three corporate ads shown in Exhibits 17.3 to 17.5?

5. One manufacturing executive who considered offering retailers advertising allowances stated why he chose not to do so:

   Why should I offer retailers advertising allowances? When I do, half of them don't use it and the other half use it in the wrong way. We spend millions of dollars trying to establish a national message. I want to control my advertising to maintain this image. Retailer cooperative advertising does not permit me that control.

   What are the risks of not having a cooperative advertising program?

6. When would advertisers be most likely to use an informational-oriented advertising campaign? An image-oriented advertising campaign?

7. One advertiser, commenting on the distinction between information- and image-oriented advertising, said:

   That distinction is overdrawn. Sure, there are ads that are primarily informational, and there are ads that are primarily image-oriented. But all advertising really represents a mix between information and image.

   Do you agree? Do the ads in Exhibit 17.7 represent a mix between information and image? In that way?

8. Why are advertisers using emotional themes in their messages more frequently?

9. Do you agree with the following statement?

   United Airlines should not have used an emotional approach in its advertising (see Exhibit 17.9) because airlines are selected based on objective criteria.

   Support your opinion. Can emotional themes be effective in advertising products that are selected based primarily on objective criteria?

10. A number of years ago, the Men's and Boy's Clothing Institute tried to encourage men to be more clothes-conscious by using a fear appeal. Ads showed a daughter concerned with the appearance of her father. She asks her mother, "Couldn't Daddy stay upstairs when Jim comes?" The ad concludes, "Dress Right — you can't afford not to." Based on the requirements for the effective use of fear appeals, do you think this ad was effective in promoting greater clothes-consciousness? Why or why not?

11. Why was Bill Cosby a successful spokesperson for a food product targeted primarily to families but not for a stock brokerage firm?

12. What are the advantages and disadvantages of using network TV as the primary vehicle in a brand's media mix? Why are fewer viewers watching network TV?

13. What might be the primary medium selected by advertisers for each of the following products, and why?

    - An industrial robot used on assembly lines.
    - A new line of Kodak 35mm color film.
    - A special sale of children's clothing at a local department store.
    - A more comprehensive health insurance policy for the elderly.
    - A line of food products targeted to Hispanic families.

14. When should advertising be scheduled based on pulsing? On continuity?

15. What criteria could an advertiser use in evaluating the social responsibility of the firm's advertising?

CASE 17.1

SEVEN-UP IS ADVERTISING TO CHILDREN: IS IT ETHICAL?

Source: Ronald Alsop, "Seven-Up Ads on Children's TV Shows Risk Alienating Health-Conscious Parents," *The Wall Street Journal*, (June 1988), pp. B1, B6.

Seven-Up Co. is breaking the carbonated soft-drink industry's long tradition of not advertising directly to kids on Saturday morning and after-school TV shows. The company is counting on tots to help it reverse a steady decline in market share. The market share for 7 Up and Diet 7 Up in food stores has dropped to about 4.6% from nearly 7% in the early 1980s.

"Establishing brand loyalty during the formative years of a child could give us a big advantage," says Russell Klein, senior vice president of marketing at the Seven-Up division. "We believe kids will tell mom to pick up the 7 Up at the store and that they'll buy it for themselves when they have their own allowances. I've seen reports that kids today have $6 billion in allowances."

But the campaign is also risky. It could alienate parents who don't want more advertisers goading their kids to consume sweet snacks. In fact, some consumer advocates and nutritionists are already riled by the commercials.

For their part, Seven-Up officials defend the children's commercials as responsible and contend that their soft drink is better for kids than some other brands because it doesn't contain caffeine.

Nevertheless, setting the precedent of advertising soda pop directly to kids troubles consumer watchdog groups. Some are concerned that Coke and Pepsi will follow suit.

So far, the $5 million ad campaign looks promising for Seven-Up: Kids under 12 now account for 12% of 7 Up drinkers, compared with 10% in 1987. What's more, only a few months after the campaign began early this year, 93% of children surveyed were aware of the commercials in which the red spots on 7 Up cans spring to life and create mischief.

Seven-Up marketing executives say their campaign is particularly well-timed because so many baby boomers are now having children. Furthermore, kids are an underdeveloped market. Children 12 and under account

Carbonated Soft-Drink Consumption by Age, July 1987–June 1988

Source: MRCA Information Services

AGE	PERCENTAGE
0–5	6.5%
6–12	9.3
13–17	6.4
18–34	25.4
35–54	28.4
55–64	12.7
65+	11.2

for only 15.8% of soft-drink consumption, according to MRCA Information Services, a market-research firm.

Seven-Up's marketers learned in focus groups with kids that the 7 Up brand suffers from an adult, clean-cut, conservative image. What it needed was a "wilder, more fun, footloose image like Coke and Pepsi have," says Mr. Klein.

The company considered concocting a special kids' soft drink — one with a bubble gum flavor — but it figured that probably would be a short-lived fad. Instead, it created the red spot ads.

In the ads, the red spot between "7" and "Up" on the soft-drink can comes alive and wears white sneakers and sunglasses. One of the commercials created by the Leo Burnett ad agency shows a group of dots jumping off the cans and playing a game of baseball in a refrigerator with carrot sticks serving as bats.

The ads aren't just a hit with children. The ads are playing well with teenagers and even adults. Says David Vadehra, editor of Video Storyboard's Commercial Break newsletter: "A lot of teenagers and parents see Saturday morning cartoons, and they're falling for the spot campaign, too."

1. Is Seven-Up's advertising ethical?
2. If you were a commissioner at the FTC, would you restrict the ads or uphold Seven-Up's right to run them? Support your position one way or the other.

CASE 17.2

HEINEKEN LEARNS THE PITFALLS OF CUTTING ADVERTISING EXPENDITURES

Source: Adapted by permission of *Forbes* magazine from "Beer Blunder," by Claire Poole. *Forbes*, February 8, 1988, pp. 128–130. © Forbes Inc.

In early 1933 Leo Van Munching was an ambitious 31-year-old barkeep on a Dutch steamer bound for New York. He heard that a top executive from the Heineken brewery was on board and made it his business to meet him. The executive was so impressed with Van Munching's English and his energy that he hired the young man to help introduce the brew to American beer drinkers. When Prohibition was repealed as expected later that year, Van Munching was back on the steamer — not as a bartender, but as a passenger — along with his country's first 50 cases of Heineken beer and the exclusive rights to import it.

When World War II ended, Van Munching & Co., Inc. saw to it that Heineken was one of the first imported beers to return to the States. Its sharp marketing kept it the top-selling imported beer in the U.S., accounting for almost a quarter of the U.S. import market. It was challenged, but never successfully, by such tough competitors as Beck's from Germany, Kirin from Japan and Molson from Canada.

But now Heineken is slipping. Its sales in 1987 were down 15%, to their 1982 level, and its market share of imported beers went from 38% to 23%. In just three years Corona Extra, brewed by Cervecería Modelo, S.A. in Mexico City, has exploded to become the number two imported beer, with 18.9% of the market, sweeping past Molson and Beck's, the other top contenders. Corona, number one in Mexico, is now within five percentage points of Heineken in the U.S.

Corona's growth is even more extraordinary considering that it is now fully distributed in fewer than 35 states. Market analysts say that later this year — after Corona expands into New England and New York, Heineken's stronghold — nothing will keep the Mexican brew from pushing the Dutch beer off its perch.

What caused Heineken to slide? Van Munching's biggest mistake was slashing its advertising budget. According to Leading National Advertisers, a New York City-based research group, Heineken's media buying fell 78% in the last three years, from $13.2 million in the first three quarters of 1985 to $2.9 million for the same period in 1987. Ads on network radio and television and in newspaper supplements were cut entirely, while magazines and spot television ads were trimmed by more than 70%.

Van Munching's reasoning is simple: The weakening dollar meant sacrificing either ad spending or profit margins. With the dollar weak, it costs Van Munching more to buy the product from Heineken in Amsterdam. So, the importer says, it has less to spend on media buys if it is to maintain profit margins. Because of that weak dollar, Van Munching raised prices by $1.25 a case. A six-pack of Heineken today at Gelson's Market in Los Angeles costs $5.75; a six-pack of number-two seller Corona is $5.19; a six-pack of number three seller Molson Golden is $4.79. Price alone, of course, is not decisive, but by cutting advertising spending Heineken missed the chance to persuade buyers that its brand was worth the extra money.

Leo Van Munching Jr., the son of Van Munching's founder, angrily denies that Heineken is losing its grip. "Complacent? Anybody who says that doesn't know me, doesn't know our organization," he replies. He refers to the challengers as "Johnny-come-latelies that are bringing in Mexican soda pop."

There is a word for what got Heineken into difficulties. Complacency. Mexican beer may be soda pop to Van Munching, but it's trendy brew throughout yuppiedom today.

1. If you were head of Van Munching Importers, would you have cut back on advertising? Why or why not?
2. What actions would you have taken instead of or in addition to advertising cutbacks in order to counter the slide in Heineken's sales caused by Corona's emerging prominence.

NOTES

1. "Using Yesterday to Sell Tomorrow," *Advertising Age,* April 11, 1983, pp. M-4, M-5.

2. "Charlie Chaplin Is Alive and Well," *Marketing & Media Decisions, Business to Business Special,* 1984, p. 88.

3. "Stars Drafted to Revive IBM," *Advertising Age,* April 6, 1987, p. 80; and "IBM in New PS/2 Ad Campaign," *The Wall Street Journal,* June 29, 1989, p. B4.

4. Ibid.

5. "IBM Replays 'New Coke/Old Coke'," *Advertising Age,* September 19, 1988, p. 6.

6. *The Wall Street Journal,* June 29, 1989, p. B4.

7. "Those Heartbeat Ads Are a Hit in the Heartland," *Business Week,* February 23, 1987, p. 107.

8. "Beef Council Leans on Point-of-Purchase," *Advertising Age,* August 15, 1985, p. 33.

9. "Cooperative Advertising," *Sales & Marketing Management,* May 1986, p. 91.

10. "Admiral's One-Shot Television Punch," *Marketing & Media Decisions,* April 1984, pp. 110–114.

11. Ibid., p. 112.

12. Ibid., p. 114.

13. "Cool(ers) and the Gang," *Marketing & Media Decisions,* May 1987, p. 137.

14. "Sara Lee Recipe for Proper Introduction," *Advertising Age,* February 13, 1986, p. 27.

15. "Confronting the Negatives," *Forbes,* April 27, 1987, pp. 83–84.

16. "Hot Raisins and More," *Advertising Age,* July 6, 1987, p. 24.

17. "Nonverbal Messages in Ads Gain New Importance," *Adweek,* January 4, 1988, p. 23.

18. "Burger King Hypes Herb Ads, But Many People Are Fed Up," *The Wall Street Journal,* January 23, 1986, p. 33.

19. "Big Resurgence in Comparative Ads," *Dun's Business Month,* February 1987, pp. 56–58.

20. "An Agency Turns to Madcap Ads," *The New York Times,* June 7, 1987, p. F1.

21. Ibid.

22. "Alex Kroll Got His Training on a Gridiron — and It Shows," *Business Week,* April 4, 1988, p. 78.

23. Ibid.

24. "Radio Days," *Forbes,* November 30, 1987, p. 204.

25. "How Creative Can Cable Advertising Get?" *Madison Avenue,* April 1986, p. 65.

26. *Forbes,* November 30, 1987, p. 204.

27. *Forbes,* November 30, 1987, p. 204; and "More Firms Tune into Radio to Stretch Their Ad Budgets," *The Wall Street Journal,* July 17, 1986, p. 27.

28. "Radio Is Making a Comeback as an Advertising Vehicle," *Sales & Marketing Digest,* September 1986, p. 3.

29. "Peugeot's Newspaper Relaunch," *Marketing & Media Decisions,* July 1982, pp. 48, 49, 222.

30. "Subaru Targets Women," *Advertising Age,* March 28, 1988, p. 38.

31. Boris W. Becker, "Consumerism: A Challenge or a Threat?" *Journal of Retailing* 48 (Summer 1972): 19.

32. William L. Wilkie, Dennis L. McNeil, and Michael B. Mazis, "Marketing's 'Scarlet Letter': The Theory and Practice of Corrective Advertising," *Journal of Marketing* 48 (Spring 1984): 11.

33. Pat L. Burr and Richard M. Burr, "Parental Responses to Child Marketing," *Journal of Advertising Research,* 17 (December 1977): 17–20.

34. "Behind the Wheel of a Quiet Revolution," *Advertising Age,* July 26, 1982, p. M-13.

35. "Blacks' Ambition Enters the Picture," *Advertising Age,* March 14, 1985, p. 26.

FOR HEWLETT-PACKARD, STAYING COMPETITIVE MEANS INCREASING THE EFFECTIVENESS OF ITS SALESFORCE

George Hewitt, a Hewlett-Packard (HP) salesman, looks up from his notes at Ben Schuger, owner of a Stamford, Connecticut, computer store and one of Hewitt's best customers. "Ben," he says, "I've heard that we're coming out with a new version of our Touchscreen" (HP's personal computer that allows the user to touch the screen to develop graphics). Schuger's immediate response is to ask whether he can cancel his existing order for the older Touchscreen model. Hewitt takes out a portable HP computer, punches in a few commands, and gets an immediate reading on the status of Schuger's order. If Schuger wants to cancel, there is still time.[1]

It is surprising that Hewlett-Packard, of all companies, should be the first to supply its salesforce with PCs to allow them instant access to critical information such as the status of a customer's order. Until a few years ago, marketing was not a big part of HP's vocabulary. In the early 1980s the company was a highly regarded producer of test instruments and microcomputers targeted to engineers in high-tech firms. It had been successful for close to 50 years with a philosophy that its products could sell themselves.[2] As a result, HP's salesforce showed little regard for identifying customer needs.

But by 1982, the groundrules were changing. HP, like IBM, realized that companies were no longer buying individual products; they were buying systems solutions. And to sell systems solutions, suppliers had to become aware of customer needs and design a set of interactive products to meet those needs. HP had the technical capability to develop systems but lacked the marketing capability to determine customer needs.

By 1985, the company had only 2 percent of the PC market, its share in microcomputers was slipping, and so were its profits.[3] Management decided that the key to defining customer needs was increasing the effectiveness of its salesforce. It therefore established teams to sell systems solutions to larger accounts. Part of the process was having these teams spend time at customer sites to better understand their needs.[4] In 1986 the company began to systematically train its salespeople in the art of understanding customer needs through a video-training center.[5] In 1987 it went one step further by establishing a telephone information center to identify prospective purchasers and supply its salesforce with this information. Operators at the center handle customer phone inquiries on 800 numbers and determine which customers might be good prospects for a follow-up by the appropriate salesperson.[6]

In 1987 HP implemented its most ambitious step, complete automation of its 2,000-person salesforce with PCs.[7] The PCs quickly became an information lifeline, providing the salesforce with instant information on sales leads, customer orders and shipments, and product and price information. The PC also eliminated hours of paperwork, allowing salespeople to spend 35 percent more time on customer contacts.[8] But the most important competitive advantage was the visible use of HP products at the point of sale.

Hewlett-Packard correctly identified its salesforce as the one component in its marketing mix that might give it a competitive edge over IBM and Apple. The company is still battling its past reputation as a product-oriented engineering firm, but it appears to be winning that battle because of a more customer-oriented salesforce. ■

CHAPTER

PERSONAL SELLING AND SALES MANAGEMENT

● ● ●

THE IMPORTANCE OF PERSONAL SELLING

Many marketers would cite personal selling as the most important component of the promotional mix. Certainly it is the most important component in business-to-business marketing, where face-to-face interaction between buyer and seller is essential because marketers often develop goods to the specification of the buyer. This is true of Hewlett-Packard because it develops systems solutions to meet customer needs. Even when industrial products are not customized, many are complex enough to require personal interaction to explain product features and performance.

By the late 1980s companies were spending over $200 billion annually on personal selling (more than twice as much as on advertising), mostly in the industrial sector. Also, selling expenses in this sector averaged 12 percent of total revenues for office supplies companies, 7 percent for computer companies, and 4 percent for producers of light machinery. In contrast, selling expenses average less than 2 percent of revenues for consumer packaged foods and household items.

The importance of personal selling increased even further in the industrial sector in the 1980s as industrial America became more systems- and productivity-oriented. Marketers responded by developing selling teams to sell a range of integrated products. These salespeople often needed an engineering or design background and frequently acted more as consultants than as traditional salespeople. The character of Willy Loman, the tragic fast-buck salesman in Arthur Miller's play *Death of a Salesman,* was out of touch with the professionalism that characterized much of selling in the 1980s.

Although personal selling dominates the promotional mix for industrial products, it is also important in other areas. As we saw in Chapter 12, it is an essential component of the promotional mix in marketing services. Stockbrokers, real estate agents, and restauranteurs, for example, sell their services at the same time that they perform them, so personal selling becomes their prime means of satisfying customers. Personal selling can also be the primary means of communication and customer satisfaction for some consumer goods, as in Avon's door-to-door selling and General Motor's reliance on its dealer network to sell cars.

TABLE 18.1
Types of Salespeople

	ORDER TAKERS	ORDER GETTERS	PROBLEM SOLVERS
TYPICAL EXAMPLES	Food product salesperson (stocks supermarket shelves)	Door-to-door salesperson	Computer systems salesperson
	Pharmaceutical salesperson (stocks drugstore shelves)	Clothing store salesperson	Pollution control systems salesperson
		Petrochemicals salesperson	Industrial generator salesperson
	Department store salesperson	Steel plate salesperson	Architect (sells home design)
	Office supplies salesperson (takes orders based on inventory levels)	Office supplies salesperson (offers new line of products)	Travel agent (sells vacation package)
SALES APPROACH	Simple inquiry	Structured, one-way	Unstructured, interactive
SALES PRESENTATION	Stimulus–response	Standardized	Need–satisfaction
ORIENTATION	Product	Sales	Customer
CONTROL OVER SALES PROCESS	Buyer in control	Seller in control	Shared control
COMPLEX PRODUCT	No	Sometimes	Usually
LEVEL OF TECHNICAL EXPERTISE	Low	Low to medium	High
TRAINING	Minimal	Moderate	Extensive
PROSPECTING	No	Usually	Usually
TEAM SELLING	No	Rarely	Usually

THE NATURE OF PERSONAL SELLING

The role of the salesperson varies greatly depending on the selling situation. At one end of the spectrum are the sophisticated sales teams developed by companies such as Hewlett-Packard; at the other are simple order takers.

Table 18.1 classifies salespeople on a continuum from simple order-takers to complex problem solvers. In between is a category of salespeople we will refer to as order-getters.

TYPES OF SALESPEOPLE

Order Takers

Table 18.1 shows that an **order taker's** sales approach is a simple inquiry as to stock levels and product needs. It is characterized as a stimulus-response approach. For example, a stimulus such as running low on steel plate in the production line, or running out of paper towels at home, elicits a purchase response. Order takers are product-oriented because they focus on the products required to fill orders. Little technical expertise is required to sell these products, so compa-

EXHIBIT 18.1
An Order Taker

nies do not have to train order takers in the art of determining customer needs. Nor do these salespeople have to seek out potential customers.

Most food and drug companies have what is known as a **route salesforce** composed of order takers responsible for stocking food and drugstore shelves with the company's products. Stocking shelves does not involve selling in the traditional sense. Route salespeople simply enter a store, inspect the shelves, and restock them when required. They have little contact with the buyer (the store manager).

Frito-Lay uses a 10,000-plus route salesforce to stock the shelves of 325,000 food stores. In 1986 the company spent $45 million to equip these salespeople with hand-held computers to track movement of products off the shelf (see Exhibit 18.1) and thus justify a request for more shelf space for its products. The hand-held computers are also used to automate orders and help speed deliveries.[9]

Other types of salespeople are also primarily order takers. A department store salesclerk spends a good deal of time taking merchandise from a customer and ringing up sales. A salesperson for an office supply firm may deal with buyers primarily to take their orders for stationery and other paper products. As we saw in Chapter 6, straight rebuys of industrial products often involve nothing more than informing a salesperson of the need to reorder an item.

Many people regard order takers as low-status positions. But a position as a route salesperson or department store salesclerk is often an entry-level pathway to a higher-paying managerial job. At Frito-Lay, a route sales position is considered one of the most important tasks in the company and is a necessary stepping-stone to a sales management position.

Order Getters

In contrast to an order taker, an **order getter** must search out customers and influence them to buy the company's products. The order-getter's focus is more on closing a sale than it is on solving a customer's problem. Salespeople in clothing stores, door-to-door salespeople, and sellers of standardized industrial prod-

ucts such as petrochemicals or steel plate are examples of order getters. They might also be the same office supply salespeople who were order takers in the last sales visit but are now offering a new line of stationery products and must inform and influence the buyer to switch.

The ad for Willamette Industries in Exhibit 18.2 distinguishes order taking from order getting. The ad says that Willamette's salespeople don't just take orders for the company's line of products, they *fill* them by making sure buyers get exactly what they want.

As the Willamette ad implies, the job of the order getter is to sell a line of standardized rather than custom-made products. The selling process is likely to be a one-way transmittal of information and influence from seller to buyer, often in a standardized presentation (see Table 18.1). The types of products sold are of low to moderate complexity since they are part of a standard line. As a result, the salesperson does not require technical expertise. Some training is required, however, to inform the salesperson of the company's product line and to teach an effective sales approach. Order getters are also expected to prospect for new accounts.

A good example of effective order getting is the sales approach used by Ball Corporation's commercial glass division, which sells a standardized line of glass containers to food packers.[10] Salespeople first inform prospective buyers of Ball's capabilities, including capabilities in its high-tech divisions, such as building guidance systems for space vehicles and launching solar observatories. Then the presentation focuses on Ball's glass container line and specific product benefits. Prospects are invited to visit the company's plant and R&D labs.[11] The primary focus of the sales approach is to inform and influence customers. Communication is essentially one-way, and the sales approach is fairly standardized.

Problem Solvers

The most creative selling is done by **problem solvers** — salespeople who must define customer needs and recommend a set of solutions to meet these needs. A problem-solving salesperson might be an engineer who develops a set of specifications for a custom-designed computer network or air pollution control system, or a travel agent who develops a vacation package to meet a family's needs.

A problem-solving salesperson must develop an intimate knowledge of the customer and the factors underlying customer needs. Rather than making a standardized sales presentation to the buyer, he or she initiates a series of meetings that involve a two-way dialogue to define customer needs. This dialogue could involve a sales team working at the customer's plant or office for several months to fully understand the nature of the operation.

Problem solvers require in-depth technical knowledge and often have an engineering or programming background. Training is extensive. Such salespeople usually have the authority to specify prices, define product specifications, and set delivery dates in negotiations with the buyer. Team selling is the norm, since defining customer needs and developing solutions usually requires a combination of expertise that a single salesperson rarely has.

Hewlett-Packard's strategy to stay competitive in computers was to switch from an order-getting to a problem-solving approach. As we saw, this required selling systems solutions rather than individual products and establishing sales teams rather than relying on individual salespeople. Selling personal computers did not require the same level of expertise as selling computer systems. But even here, HP established a more customer-oriented approach by improving the information capabilities of its salesforce.

TRENDS IN PERSONAL SELLING

The development of selling teams, the increase in information accessible to salespeople, and the greater use of telemarketing to avoid the higher costs of personal selling are the most important selling trends of the 1980s.

National Account Marketing

To more effectively define the needs of their larger customers and develop solutions to meet these needs, many companies have developed **national account marketing (NAM) teams,** groups composed of salespeople and other managers who might be required to define customer needs, such as engineers, information specialists, and production managers. These teams specialize in certain industries and develop an intimate knowledge of their customers' businesses. NAM teams were developed in response to the needs of larger customers to buy complex systems such as those involving computers, factory automation, or medical diagnostics, rather than individual components and equipment. Selling these systems required developing new levels of expertise that went beyond the capabilities of a single salesperson.

Since NAM teams sell to larger customers, they usually represent well over 50 percent of a company's sales. And they are effective. One study found that sales increased in over 90 percent of companies once they established NAM teams.[12]

A NAM team is headed by a **national account manager**, a sort of "super-sales-person" responsible for creating a close working relationship with the customer, coordinating the activities of other members of the NAM team to meet customer needs, providing follow-up service, and maintaining relationships for future sales.

NAM teams usually deal with buying centers (see Chapter 6) in the customer's organization. This facilitates communications in complex sales situations, since an engineer on the NAM team can deal with an engineer in the buying group, an information specialist in the NAM team can deal with the information specialist in the buying group, and so forth.

For Christine Lojacono, negotiating a $2 million contract to sell a system of Xerox workstations is part of a day's work. Lojacono is one of 250 national account managers at Xerox heading teams that sell integrated office equipment and information systems. The purpose of the NAM teams is to "sell a broad range of corporate products within the context of complete management solutions to customer problems."[13]

Christine Lojacono — A Top-Notch National Account Manager

Source: Reprinted by permission of Sales & Marketing Management. Copyright: July 1, 1985.

That is not only the company line, it is also the way Lojacono sees her job. In her words, being a national account manager means "building a rapport with the customer, hanging around customer offices as much as possible, and finding out their particular problems for which Xerox can provide solutions."[14] A critical element in the process is understanding the customer's organization. Lojacono knows, for example, that dealing with a centralized organization means that it is necessary to get to know the headquarters location intimately, since all orders must pass through headquarters. In a decentralized organization, she must get to know the satellite offices.

Lojacono has the authority to pull together the right combination of Xerox people in trying to win a contract — engineers, programmers, service reps, and salespeople with past experience with the client. Meeting a customer's needs means developing a combination of products designed to ensure "plug-to-plug compatibility" in the office. Trying to win a contract also means having the authority to offer customers price and service incentives.

Starting as a regular Xerox sales rep in 1976, Lojacono moved up the sales ladder to become a national account manager. She feels her experience as a regular sales rep was invaluable: "You have to have a thorough understanding of the product line, and that comes only from first-hand selling experience."[15] Lojacono's customer-oriented focus is likely to ensure her continued success as a national account manager. Xerox expressed its confidence by giving her responsibility for five national accounts, whereas most other Xerox national account managers have only one. That could mean that she is five times as effective as the average account manager at Xerox. ■

Information Accessibility

One of the important developments of the 1980s has been the salesforce's greater access to information. The greater emphasis on problem solving means that companies must make information available to their salespeople to allow them to formulate solutions to customer problems. Ryder has supplied its salespeople with computers to enable them to instantly analyze a customer's transportation needs through a program known as Rydernomics. The program includes a computer model that the salesperson uses to help a customer consider the costs of owning versus leasing a fleet of trucks projected over several years. If leasing is determined to be the most economical solution, another model compares the cost of leasing Ryder trucks to that of competitors' trucks. The cards are not always stacked in Ryder's favor, since the model sometimes shows that going with the competitor will be cheaper.[16]

Telemarketing

The escalating costs of a personal sales call have spawned another development in the 1980s, the increasing use of telemarketing. It costs less than one-sixth as much to sell by phone compared to a personal contact.[17] Many industrial firms use telemarketing to sell to smaller accounts, freeing the salesforce to concentrate on more profitable accounts. Dow Chemical, for example, determined that it would be uneconomical for its salesforce to visit accounts representing less than $50,000 in revenue. These accounts are sold by phone.[18]

Firms using telemarketing usually have an outbound and inbound facility. **Inbound telemarketing** takes calls from customers. These inquiries might be generated by ads listing an 800 number for more information. The IBM ad for Computer Assisted Design and Manufacturing Systems in Exhibit 18.3 invites further inquiries about the system. Callers are then likely to be screened to determine whether they are prospects. If the customer is large enough, information on the inquiry will be given to a sales representative for a possible personal sales call. If the prospect is a smaller company, a follow-up might take place through a company's **outbound telemarketing** facility, which involves trained sales representatives making calls and trying to sell the customer by phone.

Sales of complex products such as IBM's Computer Assisted Design and Manufacturing Systems are unlikely to be made by phone. All inquiries from the ad in Exhibit 18.3 will probably be given to an IBM sales representative. But sales of less complex products such as industrial fasteners or steel plate can easily be made by outbound telemarketing facilities.

THE PERSONAL-SELLING PROCESS

A model of the personal-selling process is in Figure 18.1. It reflects a problem-solving approach. An order getter might take only some of the steps, and an order taker even fewer of them. A salesperson first identifies prospects and determines which ones to visit. In making a sales call, the salesperson's first priority is to

determine customer needs. He or she then formulates a sales approach and communicates information to help meet the buyer's needs. In the process of communicating, the salesperson may alter the approach in response to buyer comments. There should be a two-way flow of communication between seller and buyer. In the final step, the salesperson evaluates the effectiveness of the sales approach and modifies it accordingly.

IDENTIFY PROSPECTS

One of the most important roles of a salesperson is to identify new accounts. Such **prospecting** is essential to generate new business and ensure continued profitability. The importance of prospecting has increased as competition, particularly from foreign producers, has intensified. Sellers must generate new accounts to maintain their market share. The rapid rate of technological change means that a company's customer base is also constantly changing, requiring prospecting in new areas. Apple was able to expand its customer base by prospecting large businesses to get them to accept its Macintosh and the related technology for desktop publishing. Furthermore, many companies are going into new business areas, requiring their salespeople to identify prospects in these areas. For exam-

FIGURE 18.1
A Model of the Personal-Selling Process

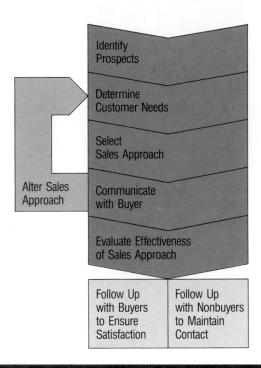

ple, AT&T's expansion into computers and American Can's move into financial services have required identifying new business prospects.

The most frequently used sources for prospecting are leads from other salespeople in the firm and referrals from satisfied customers.[19] But most sales managers agree that their salesforce does not spend enough time on prospecting, since salespeople prefer to visit existing customers rather than new ones. As a result, companies identify prospects for salespeople.

Most companies use two approaches to generate sales leads. One is to identify prospects based on inquiries from 800 numbers. Honeywell generated more than 50,000 sales leads in 1986 from customer inquiries through its inbound telemarketing facility. The company sends these leads to its salesforce by computer within 12 hours of receiving an inquiry.[20]

The second method of prospecting is for a company to generate a customer list from an outside database and then call prospects directly. When IBM decided to target its computerized information systems to scientists and engineers for the first time, it went to an outside database to develop a list of prospective customers in large firms.[21] It obtained the names of subscribers to 15 trade publications read by engineers and scientists and compared them to its existing customer list. This way it identified 22,000 prospects not currently buying IBM equipment. It then sent out a mailing inviting prospects to a free seminar in one of four cities. Close to 1,000 attended, and of these, 30 percent were planning on installing million-dollar information systems. IBM gave its salespeople information on this primary prospect group for follow-up.

DETERMINE CUSTOMER NEEDS

Whether the customer is a prospect or an existing account, the first step in the selling process is to identify needs. There is no formula for identifying customer needs. However, to be prepared to ask the right questions, the salesperson must have information on the customer before the sales call. During the sales call, he or she should encourage two-way communication. The most effective salespeople are problem solvers who consistently probe to determine customer needs, devoting the greater percentage of the sales call to discussing these needs.

Salespeople for Gould Computer (a division of NEC), allow customers to identify their own circuit designs by a computer-aided library of design alternatives. Customers know best what they want in a circuit design, so permitting them to develop their own design allows Gould to meet customer needs effectively while controlling costs.[22]

Once the salesperson has defined customer needs, he or she must select an approach to inform and influence the customer that the company's offerings can meet these needs. Two general strategies are used. The salesperson can emphasize his or her expertise, which requires a demonstration of specialized knowledge, or he or she can emphasize similarity to the customer, which requires building up rapport and showing the customer that the salesperson has had to make similar decisions.

SELECT A SALES APPROACH

Salespeople usually use a combination of both expertise and similarity. But expertise is likely to be more dominant for complex products, particularly in the industrial sector, whereas similarity is more important for consumer services such as life insurance or travel, where personal rapport might be essential.

The sales approach will also vary depending on whether the salesperson is trying to reinforce the customer's preferences or change them. The first task is obviously easier. Inducing the customer to switch to the company's products means that the salesperson must change the customer's beliefs about the relative merits of the company's offerings and requires the presentation of new information on product capabilities, price, delivery, or services.

For example, assume a salesperson for a producer of forklift trucks learns that a new customer needs a fleet of trucks that can carry heavier loads without sacrificing mobility and has reservations about the technical capabilities of the salesperson's company and its ability to deliver trucks on time. The salesperson would seek to communicate technical specifications of the product line to demonstrate its carrying capacity and to assure the buyer that a new just-in-time inventory system has improved delivery. The strategy is to subtly change the buyer's beliefs about the company and its offerings. If the salesperson does not win the buyer over on this sales call, at least a basis has been established for possibly making a sale in future calls.

Having formulated a sales approach, the salesperson must communicate it. Figure 18.2 summarizes three alternatives according to whether communication is from buyer to seller, from seller to buyer, or both. One-way communication from buyer to seller suggests an order taking approach. One-way communication from seller to buyer suggests an order getting approach. Two-way communication between buyer and seller suggests a problem solving approach. In problem solving, the salesperson listens to the customer, evaluates the customer's needs, forms a sales strategy to reinforce or change customer attitudes, communicates information to the customer about the company's products, listens to the customer's reactions, and responds further.

COMMUNICATE WITH THE BUYER

The last box, no communication between buyer and seller, usually depicts an automated order-entry system as a replacement for direct selling. As we saw in

FIGURE 18.2
Alternatives in
Communicating
a Sales Approach

Communication from Buyer to Seller

	Yes	No
Yes	Problem Solver	Order Getter
No	Order Taker	Automated Order Entry Systems

Communication from Seller to Buyer

Chapter 14, such systems are widespread for standardized items that are reordered from a regular supplier.

Our example of the sale of forklift trucks illustrates a two-way flow of communication. The salesperson listened to the customer explaining his needs, and then tried to change the buyer's beliefs about the company's offerings. Assume the customer now expresses interest in several models that can lift heavier loads than his current fleet. He asks specifics on price and potential delivery dates but expresses concern about one product feature, the larger size of the trucks and potential loss of mobility as a result.

The salesperson is pleasantly surprised at the buyer's level of interest and willingness to discuss price and delivery. He decides to alter his sales approach. He will try to close the sale either at this meeting or the next. He assures the customer that the turning radius and speed of the models the buyer is interested in are approximately the same as his current trucks. They buyer still remains unsure about the mobility factor. The salesperson then invites the buyer to try out two models for a week to directly determine both load capacity and mobility based on direct use of the trucks. The buyer agrees. The problem-solving sales approach with two-way communication has paid off.

EVALUATE THE EFFECTIVENESS OF THE SALES APPROACH

After completing the sales call, the salesperson will evaluate the effectiveness of the sales approach to determine what action to take in the future — writing the company off as a prospect, waiting for a while before making the next contact, following up immediately, or possibly even following up with a sales team to provide technical information beyond the salesperson's expertise. The salesperson also evaluates the sales approach to improve his or her effectiveness in future sales contacts.

Evaluating the sales approach provides the information necessary for appropriate follow-up after the sales call. Figure 18.1 shows two types of follow-up. In the absence of a sale, a follow-up maintains contact and builds on the relationship that has been established. If a sale has been made, follow-up is necessary to ensure the customer is satisfied with delivery, service, and product performance.

In our example, the forklift truck salesperson is satisfied that there is an excellent chance the prospect might buy a fleet of trucks from his company. Thus the selling approach is judged to have been appropriate, and follow-up will be made after the buyer has tested the company's products.

MANAGING THE SALES EFFORT

Besides the salesperson, key players in a firm's selling process include divisional sales managers and district sales managers. Both are involved in managing the sales effort. The **divisional sales manager** is responsible for sales of a total division and is often given the title of vice-president of sales. A **district sales manager** usually has responsibility for a particular geographic territory and reports to the divisional sales manager. Nabisco Brands has 20 divisional sales managers who oversee 242 district sales managers. These district sales managers are responsible for Nabisco's 2,500-person salesforce.[23]

A number of steps are involved in managing the sales effort as shown in Figure 18.3. The divisional sales manager is responsible for planning the sales effort, the district sales manager for implementing it. In planning the sales effort, the divisional manager first establishes sales objectives for the division and for individual sales territories. The divisional manager then determines the sales budget and organizes the sales effort.

The district sales manager is responsible for managing the salesforce in his or her territory and implementing the plans laid out by the divisional manager. Implementation requires recruiting salespeople, training them, and motivating them.

The final step in the sales management process is evaluation. The divisional manager evaluates the overall sales performance of the division and the performance of each district sales manager. District managers evaluate the performance of individual salespeople.

Companies establish sales objectives for a total division (such as the personal computer division of a company like Hewlett-Packard), for sales territories within the division, and for individual salespeople within each territory.

Divisional Sales Goals

At most companies, the overall sales goal for a division is based on a *volume target* stated in dollars or units, usually based on a sales forecast for the coming year. Although volume targets are the most common sales objectives, they are not always the most relevant, because a sales manager could achieve volume goals by increasing marketing costs at the expense of profits. Firms are therefore turning more to *profitability objectives*, which consider the expected contribution to profits of a particular product line or sales territory. Profitability objectives have the advantage of accounting for both volume and costs in establishing performance expectations. Alcoa, for example, realized the shortcomings of volume goals in the early 1980s and moved to profitability objectives to measure performance in its sales territories.[24]

Sales Goals by Territory

Volume and profitability objectives are both allocated by territory. A territory's goal is stated as a **sales quota** — that is, the expected sales performance for the area in a given period of time. Territorial quotas can be determined by estimating sales potential of each territory based on potential demand and economic conditions in the territory.

For example, Stark Mill Press, a commercial printing company that sells in the Northeast and in Florida, determined that its sales are closely related to personal income in each of its six sales territories. It therefore uses income to develop its

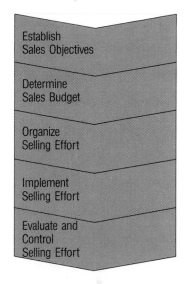

FIGURE 18.3
The Sales Management Process

Establish Sales Objectives

Determine Sales Budget

Organize Selling Effort

Implement Selling Effort

Evaluate and Control Selling Effort

ESTABLISH SALES OBJECTIVES

sales quotas. The Boston area accounted for 26.8 percent of the total personal income of all its sales regions in 1986. Therefore, the Boston area was expected to account for close to 26.8 percent of total sales in 1987.[25] If sales were much below this figure, the divisional manager for Stark Mill Press would take a closer look at performance in the territory to determine why.

Sales goals can also be established based on the characteristics of industries and organizations. A manufacturer of hydraulic lifts might find that sales are greatest among heavy machinery manufacturers with 500 or more employees. A territory that has more companies with these characteristics will have proportionately higher sales goals compared to other territories.

Objectives for Individual Salespeople

Objectives must also be developed for individual salespeople. Many firms allocate a territory's sales quota to individual salespeople based on a combination of past performance, changes in competitive conditions, and changes in demand among the salesperson's customers. If a salesperson accounted for 5 percent of a district's total sales last year, but competition promises to be more intense in the coming year, it would be unfair to hold the salesperson to a goal of 5 percent of total sales. The salesperson's quota should be scaled down.

Total sales volume should be only one among several objectives for salespeople. Objectives might also be stated in terms of *contribution to profit*. Profitability rather than volume objectives might encourage a salesperson to allocate effort to products with the highest profit margins. Other objectives might be to contact a certain number of prospects per week or to make a minimum number of sales calls each week.

DETERMINE THE SALES BUDGET

The sales budget is usually established by determining the number of salespeople required to meet a division's objectives, then calculating the cost to recruit, train, and pay them.

Several methods can be used to determine the optimal size of the salesforce. These methods parallel those described in Chapter 16 to determine the optimal size of the promotional budget — namely, the marginal-revenue, objective-task, percent-of-sales, and competitive-parity approaches.

Marginal-Revenue Approach

The marginal-revenue approach is ideal for determining the sales budget because it identifies the number of salespeople required to optimize contribution to profits. The principle behind this approach is to continue to expand the salesforce as long as the marginal revenue gained from adding a salesperson is greater than the marginal cost of that salesperson. The optimal size of the salesforce is achieved when marginal revenue gained from adding another person equals marginal cost. The problem with this approach is the difficulty of estimating marginal revenues and costs for each additional salesperson.

Objective-Task Approach

The most widely used approach in determining a sales budget is the objective-task method. The size of the salesforce is based on an objective of reaching a certain number of existing and prospective customers and the required sales effort to reach this group. Assume a company wants to reach the following number of large, medium, and small customers each month and estimates the required sales calls to each customer as follows:

	LARGE CUSTOMERS	MEDIUM CUSTOMERS	SMALL CUSTOMERS
Number of customers	200	400	1,000
Estimated sales calls per customer per month	10	5	1
Total number of calls per month	2,000	2,000	1,000

Total calls are estimated at 5,000 per month. If the average salesperson makes 50 calls a month, the size of the sales force should be 100 people. The weakness in this approach is that the number of sales calls may not be related to profitability, so this approach may not identify the salesforce size that maximizes profits.

Percent-of-Sales Approach

A firm can also establish the sales budget as a percentage of sales. The advantage of this approach is that selling costs are controlled because they are a constant percentage of revenues. The problem is that there is no rational basis for setting the sales budget based on a constant percentage. The percentage selected is arbitrary and does not take account of the specific environment the company is facing.

Competitive-Parity Approach

A firm can also base the size of its salesforce on how many salespeople are employed by close competitors. This is the least defensible basis for determining the sales budget, since it assumes that what is right for competitors is also right for the company.

ORGANIZE THE SALES EFFORT

Once a sales budget is established, the divisional sales manager can turn to organizing the salesforce. Developing a sales organization requires several decisions: Should the company maintain one salesforce to service all accounts, or should it develop a **salesforce mix**; that is, a combination of different sales organizations to service large, medium, and small customers? Should it rely on its own employees to sell, or should it use outside facilities? Should it organize its salesforce along product, customer, or geographic lines?

Developing a Salesforce Mix

Many firms have developed a mix of sales organizations to deal with customers. National account marketing teams are designated to deal with the largest clients, individual salespeople with medium-sized clients, and a telemarketing facility to deal with small clients. This organizational mix is shown in Figure 18.4.

Xerox uses such a sales mix. About 250 NAM teams service only 350 customers, but each of these customers represents millions of dollars in sales.[26] Salespeople are in the middle of the salesforce mix in Figure 18.4. Medium-sized customers are served by about 1,000 individual salespeople called "major account

FIGURE 18.4
The Salesforce Mix

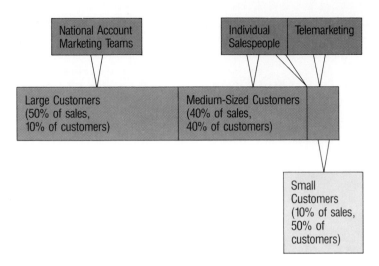

managers." Smaller accounts (under $10,000 in sales) are serviced by about 2,000 salespeople known as "account representatives." Xerox's telemarketing facility also takes up the slack in servicing small orders.

More and more firms are following a sales mix strategy because they find it more cost-effective to let a few salespeople concentrate on several large accounts and to use telemarketing facilities for smaller accounts.

Use of Outside Sales Facilities

Another important organizational decision is whether the firm should use outside facilities such as manufacturers' agents, sales agents, or distributors to supplement, or even to replace, the firm's sales staff. As we saw in Chapter 13, agents and distributors can reduce selling costs by contacting smaller and more geographically dispersed accounts that may be sapping the efforts of the company's own salesforce. If sales revenues are not high enough to support a company's own salesforce, such outside facilities will be used.

For example, Airwick felt its own salesforce was not producing sufficient revenue to justify its cost. So the company replaced its 10 sales offices with 93 independent distributors. The company is helping its distributors hire and train salespeople, control inventory, and install better accounting systems.[27]

Using agents and distributors carries some risks, particularly if they are the primary means of selling. Since they usually work for more than one company, they are less motivated to sell a company's line than the company's sales staff would be. They are also less knowledgeable about the company's products and technical specifications. Apple scrapped its network of manufacturers' representatives in favor of its own salesforce in order to gain better control over its sales effort.[28]

Organizing by Territory, Product, or Customer

Another key decision in organizing the salesforce is whether to structure it by territory, by product, or by customer type. In a *territorial* organization, each salesperson is responsible for selling the complete line of company products to customers in a territory. This organization has the advantage of reducing travel expenses and eliminating duplication of selling effort. But if special expertise is required to sell certain products or to sell to certain customers, a territorial organization will not work.

Companies can also organize the salesforce by *product line*. This type of organization may be logical if the company is selling technical products requiring special sales expertise. However, companies have tended to move away from a product organization because of the trend to systems development. Buyers generally prefer to purchase from one salesperson who can sell an integrated line of products rather than from several salespeople selling individual product lines. If a firm's products are not interconnected, though, a product organization may be feasible.

A salesforce can also be organized by *customer type*. For example, IBM might organize its salesforce for integrated computer systems so that there are sales units for specific industries such as aerospace, automobile, chemical, and metal processing. This type of organization is logical when different buyers have different needs. Salespeople can become more knowledgeable about specific types of buyers and develop a better capability to define their needs. Many companies have moved to a customer-based sales organization because of the greater importance of developing custom-made solutions to customer problems. Hewlett-Packard switched from a product-based to a customer-based organization of its salesforce for this reason. Another factor encouraging a customer-based sales organization is the trend to developing a salesforce mix, since the type of organization shown in Figure 18.4 requires organizing the salesforce by customer size.

IMPLEMENT THE SALES EFFORT

The next set of steps in the sales management process involve implementing the selling effort. At this point, primary responsibility for the sales effort shifts from the divisional manager to the district sales manager, and from planning the sales effort to managing the salesforce. Implementing the selling effort requires recruiting salespeople, training them, and motivating them through compensation plans and other incentives.

Recruitment

One of the most important responsibilities of the sales manager is recruiting salespeople. Effective recruiting means a better performing salesforce and greater profitability from the sales effort. But what makes a good salesperson? Studies have shown that there is no apparent answer to this question. The evidence is contradictory. One study of life insurance salespeople found that industry experience was related to performance; another found it was not.[29] Similarly, one study of oil company salespeople found that their intelligence was related to sales performance; another study found it was not.[30] These contradictory findings probably mean that salespeople need different traits depending on whether they use an order-taking, order-getting, or problem-solving sales approach.

Table 18.2 shows that the main recruitment criteria for an order taker might be that the individual be personable, presentable, reasonably intelligent, able to follow orders, and a high school graduate. An order getter might be required to have a demonstrated ability to absorb information about the product line, be a good communicator, and be persuasive. Some firms might add the need for a college education and industry experience.

In hiring a problem solver, the sales manager would also look for a persuasive individual with good communication skills and a college degree. But in a problem

TABLE 18.2
Recruitment Criteria and Training
Objectives for Different Types of
Salespeople

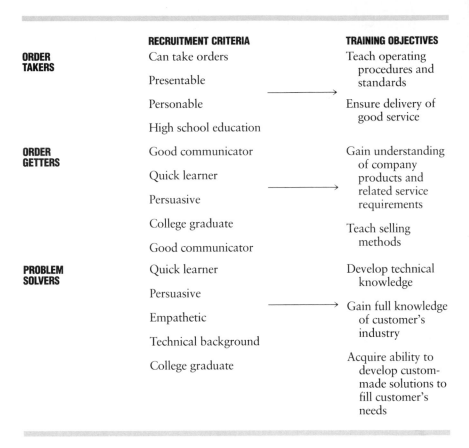

	RECRUITMENT CRITERIA	TRAINING OBJECTIVES
ORDER TAKERS	Can take orders	Teach operating procedures and standards
	Presentable	
	Personable	Ensure delivery of good service
	High school education	
ORDER GETTERS	Good communicator	Gain understanding of company products and related service requirements
	Quick learner	
	Persuasive	
	College graduate	Teach selling methods
	Good communicator	
PROBLEM SOLVERS	Quick learner	Develop technical knowledge
	Persuasive	
	Empathetic	Gain full knowledge of customer's industry
	Technical background	
	College graduate	Acquire ability to develop custom-made solutions to fill customer's needs

solver, the ability to listen and to be empathetic in the communication process is as important as the ability to convey information. In addition, the sales manager would probably look for individuals with technical expertise in the area, through either schooling or industry experience. The overriding concern would be to select an individual the manager feels could effectively define customer needs.

To avoid relying only on subjective criteria, many firms like IBM, Gillette, and Procter & Gamble test their applicants to assist managers in the selection process. These tests are generally developed by the company based on years of experience in observing what factors seem related to sales performance. But these tests are only one element in selection. Ultimately, the sales manager's judgment is the deciding factor.

Training

Sales managers are closely involved in developing training programs for salespeople. Since the cost of training one salesperson averages over $20,000, the sales manager is concerned with developing the most effective program for the money.[31]

The sales manager must decide whether the company should hire experienced salespeople rather than train new ones. Most firms favor training a new staff, because hiring experienced personnel is much more costly. Also, there is always some loss in transferring skills to another company. But in some cases, experienced people are necessary to fill gaps in the salesforce and to establish new capabilities.

Any training program will vary depending on whether a firm is training an order taker, order getter, or problem solver. As Table 18.2 shows, the objectives of a training program for order takers are to communicate proper operating procedures and standards. Burger King established a training program for the employees of its 4,200 fast-food outlets. The objective was to "achieve consistent adherence to strict operating standards" so as to maintain good service.[32]

Training objectives for order getters might be to acquaint them with the company's products and to teach them how to sell. When McKesson Corp., the large drug wholesaler, bought Champion International's office products business in 1984, it inherited a sales staff that McKesson's management decided needed training in selling skills. The company developed a standardized program that was given in each of 17 sales territories.[33] The program is designed to give the office-products salespeople information about McKesson's promotions and programs and to train them in effective presentation skills. It is typical of the focus in order getting on informing customers about a standardized product line and closing the sale.

Problem solvers are likely to go through a more intensive but less structured program. The program will not focus so much on how to sell, but rather on developing technical skills and an understanding of the customer's industry. The purpose of the program is to equip salespeople with the information necessary to develop custom-made solutions to solve customer problems. The training program for Merck's pharmaceutical division is designed for problem solvers.[34] Trainees spend six months to a year on selling the products under supervision to ensure that they understand medical applications and diseases.

Motivation

Salespeople must be motivated to achieve sales objectives; otherwise recruitment and training procedures are meaningless. There are two key issues in motivation: Are sales quotas viewed as attainable? And are the rewards for performance satisfactory?

Quotas must be set in line with the potential in the salesperson's territory. If they are set higher than that, the salesperson might become discouraged. Sales managers must discuss quota objectives with salespeople and try to help them achieve them. Some managers even go on the road with their salespeople to try to help them. Salespeople who see such a commitment on the part of their sales managers are more likely to give their maximum effort.

The second component of motivation — and perhaps the most important — is financial reward. Three types of compensation plans have been used to reward salespeople: straight salary, straight commission, and a combination of the two. A straight salary plan is simple to administer, but it is the least likely compensation plan to stimulate performance, since compensation is not tied to sales levels.

Straight-commission plans provide direct financial incentives tied to sales volume. They encourage salespeople to increase sales and to make more effective use of their time. But a straight-commission plan gives a salesperson no incentive to do anything but sell. Salespeople are also supposed to search for prospects, fill out call reports, supply information to their customers, and help in customer service and product installation. A straight-commission plan does not reward them for these nonsale activities. Moreover, a decrease in industry demand or increase in competition could demoralize a salesforce on straight commission, since sales and compensation would go down for reasons beyond their control.

Problems with straight salary and commission plans have led most companies to adopt a combination plan. One study found that 22 percent of the companies surveyed use straight salary, 21 percent straight commission, and the remaining 57 percent a combination of the two.[35] Combination plans attempt to balance the security of salary and the incentives of commissions.

Nonfinancial incentives such as a sense of accomplishment, respect from one's peers, and recognition are also very important in motivating high performance.[36] These nonfinancial incentives are likely to be influenced by an organization's attitude toward its salesforce. Some organizations treat selling as a low-status position. It is difficult to motivate salespeople in such a climate. Other organizations make it a point to communicate the importance of personal selling.

Some firms use sales contests and recognition programs as nonfinancial incentives to enhance the salesforce's motivation. Companies often have awards for best or most improved performance. Some have special clubs for high performers that enhance their status in the firm. Contests that reward high performers through trips or gifts are also an effective way to increase motivation.

EVALUATE AND CONTROL THE SALES EFFORT

The last step in the sales management process is evaluating and controlling the sales effort. The divisional sales manager evaluates sales performance for the total division; the district sales manager evaluates the performance of individual salespeople in his or her territory. Table 18.3 summarizes the criteria for evaluating the total sales effort and the effort of individual salespeople, along with the problems associated with using each criterion.

Evaluating the Total Sales Effort

The ultimate criterion of the effectiveness of the sales effort is profitability. Ideally, managers would like to establish a relationship between the amount spent on selling and the revenue generated from this effort. But too many other factors affect a customer's decision to buy to be able to isolate the specific impact of a sales contact.

These difficulties have led companies to rely on general measures of sales performance. Divisional managers compare their division's performance to *sales volume* and the *market share* of other companies in the industry. The division's *contribution to profits* is another criterion of evaluation. But it is difficult to isolate the contribution to profits from the sales effort alone as distinct from contributions from advertising, product development, or other components of the marketing mix. In short, there is no one perfect measure of sales performance.

If performance falls short, the divisional manager will want to know whether it was because of environmental factors beyond the firm's control, such as a general decrease in customer demand, or whether it was some shortcoming in the company's sales approach, such as a failure to adequately prospect new accounts.

The divisional manager also evaluates the performance for each sales territory. If a territory is below its quota, the divisional manager will determine if the problem is beyond the district manager's control, or if it is correctible. Low performance could be the result of poor recruitment and training procedures, inadequate prospecting for new accounts, or poor leadership by the district sales man-

TABLE 18.3
Criteria for Evaluating the Sales Effort

	CRITERIA	PROBLEMS AND LIMITATIONS
EVALUATING THE TOTAL SALES EFFORT	Profit return on sales expenditures	Difficult to isolate effects of sales effort on sales results
	Divisional contribution to profits	Difficult to isolate contribution of sales effort as distinct from other components of the marketing mix
	Sales volume	Not necessarily related to profitability
	Contribution to profits by territory	Difficult to determine if performance is result of sales manager's and salesforce's actions or due to uncontrollable market conditions
EVALUATING A SALESPERSON'S PERFORMANCE	Sales quota	Not necessarily related to profitability
	Contribution to profits of salesperson	Difficult to isolate influence of individual salesperson on results
	Sales volume for more profitable product lines	Does not take account of nonsale activities
	Number of new accounts	Does not take account of nonsale activities
	Completion of sales reports	Does not take account of sales performance
	Expenses per sales call	Does not take account of sales performance
	Customer satisfaction	Not empirical, and difficult to assess

ager in motivating the salesforce. Any of these reasons would require corrective action.

Evaluating the Salesperson

In evaluating individual salespeople, the sales manager first looks at their sales volume relative to quota objectives set out at the beginning of the year. But sales volume should not be the only, or even the primary, criterion because it may not reflect profitability. A salesperson might have achieved a high sales volume by pushing less profitable lines that are easier to sell, by failing to prospect for new accounts, or by ignoring the record-keeping required to detail sales calls and results.

Information such as (1) sales volume for more profitable lines, (2) number of new customers sold, and (3) expenses per sales call should be used to evaluate sales performance and determine how much each salesperson contributes to profits. Accordingly, salespeople are required to file *sales reports* that include such information.

Controlling the Salesforce

In controlling the sales effort, the sales manager's primary focus is on expenses. Expenses incurred by salespeople, especially travel and entertainment expenses, must be controlled to maximize profitability.

The sales manager will also try to control the way the salesperson spends his or her time. Since salespeople typically prefer to pursue existing customers, sales managers try to influence them to spend more time on prospecting for new accounts. Salespeople are also notorious in trying to avoid the paperwork associated with sales reports. They feel their time could be better spent in the field trying to close a sale. Sales managers will try to control the allocation of time to ensure that sales reports are submitted. Hewlett-Packard found that an important advantage of supplying its salespeople with personal computers was that less time was spent on paperwork, since salespeople could directly file their sales reports on the computer. This allowed them to spend more time with customers and lessened the need of management to control the completion of paperwork.

The importance placed by marketers on evaluating and controlling the sales effort reflects its role in the promotional mix. In many cases, sales expenditures far outweigh expenditures on advertising and sales promotions, particularly for industrial goods and services. As a result, managers must carefully track the profit results of their sales effort.

ETHICS IN PERSONAL SELLING

The preceding discussion assumes that the salesperson will sell a company's products or services in an ethical manner — making a good-faith effort to determine what the customer wants, conveying truthful and accurate information about the company's products, trying to provide customers with full information, and addressing any subsequent customer complaints.

Unfortunately, such is not always the case. We have all, at one time or another, experienced undesirable high-pressure sales tactics. A play like *Glengarry Glenn Ross,* about real estate agents who would do anything to make a sale, or a movie like *Tin Men,* about sellers of aluminum siding who trick innocent homeowners into signing contracts, highlights the type of unethical sales behavior that can occur. Most salespeople, however, conduct themselves in a responsible manner, especially with today's greater emphasis on a problem-solving approach.

The greatest problem is with order getters, since their canned approach of one-way communication from seller to buyer does not encourage an attempt to understand and satisfy customer needs. In trying to close a sale, order getters have occasionally forgotten their obligation to be truthful and to keep the customer's best interests in mind. Door-to-door encyclopedia salespeople who convince naive and economically deprived consumers to buy expensive encyclopedias, used-car salespeople who are not truthful about defects in their cars, or store salespeople who rely on "bait and switch" advertising to lure consumers into a store with low-priced items and then try to switch them to higher-priced merchandise are all examples of unethical order getters. Of course, there is nothing inherently unethical about order getting. Many order getters are truthful, responsible, and responsive to customer needs.

Government can do little to legislate fair sales practices. If outright fraud has occurred, consumers have recourse in the courts. Otherwise, consumers must rely on the self-regulation imposed by companies. Fortunately, companies have become more sensitive to the need to maintain high standards in selling. The greater complexity of many products, the greater amount of information available to salespeople, and the trend to team selling have encouraged a problem-solving approach that creates higher standards in personal selling.

Many salespeople have begun to view their field as a responsible profession. An example of the professionalization of selling is a certificate program awarded to life insurance salespeople by the American College of Life Underwriters based on a rigorous training course that emphasizes responsible selling.

SUMMARY

1. *How do order-taking, order-getting, and problem-solving approaches to personal selling differ?*

An order taker fills a predefined need, most frequently replenishing a buyer's stocks when inventory is low. Little interaction is required with the buyer. Order getters influence the buyer to select the company's products. The emphasis is on closing the sale. Products are usually part of a standard line and are not highly technical. Problem solvers define the needs of their buyers and develop custom-made solutions to meet these needs. Most often, they sell complex product systems on a team basis. Problem solvers must have a technical background and must develop an intimate knowledge of the customer's operations.

2. *What important trends in personal selling took place in the 1980s?*

One of the most important developments was the establishment of national account marketing (NAM) teams to develop custom-made systems solutions to fill the needs of larger customers. In addition, technology has given salespeople greater access to information. Salespeople with personal computers have almost instant access to information. Finally, telemarketing facilities are increasingly used to handle customer inquiries and to try to sell to smaller customers by phone. Telemarketing is a way to reduce the high costs of personal contacts by limiting these contacts to larger customers.

3. *What is the nature of the selling process?*

The selling process requires a logical series of steps to influence the customer to buy. First, the salesperson must identify a prospective customer. Next, the salesperson determines customer needs by probing for information in a two-way discussion. In so doing, he or she decides on the appropriate approach to inform and influence customers that the company's products and services can fill their needs. Having formulated a sales approach, the salesperson communicates it to try to influence the buyer. Finally, he or she evaluates the effectiveness of that sales approach and decides whether further sales calls are warranted.

4. *What are the key steps in planning the sales effort?*

Planning the sales effort is the responsibility of a divisional sales manager. It requires setting sales objectives and establishing a sales budget for the division, then organizing the salesforce based on (1) what combination of NAM selling teams, individual salespeople, and telemarketing will be used; (2) whether or not outside sales facilities such as manufacturers' agents and distributors will be used; and (3) whether a product, geographic, or customer organization is appropriate.

5. *How is the sales effort implemented and evaluated?*

Implementing the sales effort requires recruiting salespeople, training them, and motivating them to perform. This is the responsibility of the district sales manager. Recruitment criteria and training programs differ for order takers, order getters, and problem solvers. Motivation is frequently based on a combination of straight salary and sales commissions. Implementation requires that the divisional manager evaluate the total performance of the division and that the district sales manager evaluate the performance of individual salespeople based on sales objectives.

KEY TERMS

Order takers (p. 501)
Route salesforce (p. 502)
Order getters (p. 502)
Problem solvers (p. 504)
National account marketing (NAM)
  team (p. 504)
National account manager (p. 505)

Inbound telemarketing (p. 506)
Outbound telemarketing (p. 506)
Prospecting (p. 507)
Divisional sales manager (p. 511)
District sales manager (p. 511)
Sales quota (p. 511)
Salesforce mix (p. 513)

QUESTIONS

1. How did Hewlett-Packard increase the effectiveness of its salesforce in the mid 1980s? What factors prompted the company to make these changes?

2. Why is personal selling the most important component of the promotional mix in business-to-business marketing?

3. What are the differences in the sales approaches of order takers, order getters, and problem solvers? What kinds of products is each type of salesperson most likely to sell?

4. A salesperson of over-the-counter products for a pharmaceutical company says:

   Going in with a canned (standardized) approach usually doesn't work for me. The most difficult part of selling is when you are trying to overcome a customer's resistance to what is new and unfamiliar. For example, it is difficult to try to sell a new high-potency nonprescription pain reliever when the druggist is used to Bayer, Bufferin, and Tylenol. The creative part of selling is adjusting to the customer's frame of reference or trying to change it.

   a. Do you agree with this statement? Why or why not?

   b. What are the implications of the statement for an order-getting versus a problem-solving approach?

5. What reasons are behind the growing use of national account marketing (NAM) teams and telemarketing facilities in the 1980s? What kinds of firms have been most likely to use NAM teams? Why?

6. Consider each of the following situations:

   - A seller of custom-made hydraulic lifts uses the specifications formulated by the customer's engineering department as a basis for submitting a proposal for the sale of the specified product. The salesperson's presentation to the buyer focuses primarily on price, delivery dates, and installation.

   - The sales staff for a leading snack food manufacturer uses its route salespeople to fill orders for supermarket chains. It provides little service or information since chain store buyers know the products they want.

   - The salesforce for a large telecommunications firm communicates the firm's new capabilities in information-processing and office systems.

   - A seller of pollution control systems works jointly with the buyer in developing specifications to the buyer's needs. Both the salesperson and buyer are trained engineers who work together with their design staffs in developing, installing, and servicing the system.

   a. Which sales approach does each of these situations reflect: order taking, order getting, or problem solving? Why?

   b. Do any of these situations reflect the use of a NAM team?

7. A salesman for a small computer company com-

mented on the increasing use of NAM teams to sell as follows:

> I really mistrust selling on a team basis. I realize the team gives you something extra in the expertise of other individuals. But as you bring more people into the selling process, there is more chance of crossed signals between team members and miscommunication with the buyer. I have seen situations where one person on the NAM team says one thing while another says something else. As far as I'm concerned, the best sales approach is one-on-one selling where you can directly influence the buyer and can service the buyer's needs without having to work through a team.

a. Do you agree with the salesperson's criticism of NAM teams? Why or why not?
b. Have you found it difficult to work with teams on school projects? If so, do the salesperson's comments apply to your experiences?
c. What are the advantages and disadvantages of selling on a team basis?

8. When sales of Massey-Ferguson's farm machinery began declining in the early 1980s, the company substantially decreased its salesforce and began using telemarketing facilities to maintain contact with most of its customers.

a. Was this a proper use of telemarketing facilities?
b. How do you think customers reacted to being contacted by phone rather than in person?

9. A sales manager for a producer of hydraulic lifts believes that prospecting has become more important in the last decade. The company is a leader in the field, but the sales manager is concerned that new entrants will have more innovative and technically oriented salespeople who are better able to identify prospects.

a. Is the sales manager's concern well founded?
b. Why has prospecting become more important in the last decade?

10. What are the responsibilities of a divisional sales manager in managing the selling effort? Of a district sales manager?

11. What are the pros and cons of using outside sales facilities like manufacturers' agents and distributors? Why did Apple Computer stop using manufacturers' agents and establish its own salesforce to sell its personal computers?

12. When is a company likely to organize its salesforce by territory, by product, or by customer type? Why have more companies organized their sales effort by customer type in recent years?

13. How will recruitment criteria and training programs differ for order takers, order getters, and problem solvers?

14. Why is a combination of salaries and commissions the most popular method for compensating salespeople?

CASE 18.1

GENERAL ELECTRIC WINS THE GM ACCOUNT WITH TEAM SELLING

Source: "The Sale That Turned GE On," *Sales & Marketing Management,* June 1988, pp. 42–43. Reprinted by permission of Sales & Marketing Management. Copyright June 1988.

Outfitting a new General Motors plant with state-of-the-art electrical gear usually involves more than one supplier, but that's not what happened when marketers at General Electric Co. mustered to land the job at GM's Saturn factory in Spring Hill, TN. "We got the whole thing," says David M. Engelman, vice-president and general manager of GE Electrical Distribution and Control Sales Div. "Everyone was flabbergasted."

Besides beating out rivals for electrifying the plant that'll turn out GM's touted car of the future, the Saturn sale was a landmark in General Electric's sales effort. "For once, we got the whole of GE together," says Engelman, noting that the work is being parceled out to several of GE's 14 businesses. In what is probably one of the most productive opening calls in the history of any industry, vice-chairman Lawrence A. Bossidy led a team of corporate vice presidents that dropped in on General Motors chairman Roger B. Smith nearly two years ago. The message: GE wants to be partners with you on your major projects. Smith liked what he heard and urged the GE team to contact Saturn.

At that point, GE put together a 40-person sales team committed to landing the contract for the Saturn plant. Not only did it include top executives from such diverse operations as plastics and power systems but a deliberate effort was made to match the ages and personalities of GM's Saturn team. GM had some young hotshots, so General Electric included some sales engineers in their early thirties.

By the time they closed the sale last year, the General Electric people had escorted their GM counterparts on tours of GE plants and hammered home the idea that they'd benefit by having a single electrical supplier for the Saturn plant. "They got in on the front end of our product planning," says Engelman, who is convinced that the exchange of specifications and pricing data was a prime reason GE won the contract. "We didn't hold anything back."

Winning the Saturn job brought GE more than just a big chunk of business — specification engineers in other industries tend to look to the automakers for new ideas in manufacturing. Says Engelman, "Now we can go to other industries and say, 'This is the kind of product we used at GM.'"

For Engelman's own division, which this year will sell nearly $1 billion of such things as switchgear, transformers, and motor control centers, the sale was the prize that capped a string of achievements. By redeploying sales engineers and gradually shifting the order-entry process from district offices to his Plainville, CT, headquarters, he was able to reduce personnel by 2 percent and achieve a 13 percent increase in sales productivity. At the same time, he squeezed out a 1.3 percent gain in market share.

Like the other dozen or so sales forces at GE, the Electrical Distribution and Control Sales Division put more emphasis on key account selling last year, partly as a result of the Saturn success. Whether it be with distributors (65% of sales) or original equipment manufacturers, Engelman says, "We're trying to look at the total business and get away from just talking price and products." His organization totals more than 600, including sales engineers, inside salespeople, managers, and support people.

So satisfying was the Saturn effort, in fact, that it fostered renewed interest in pursuing similar sales at key accounts whose product requirements might cut across several of GE's operating businesses. Albert J. Febbo, a corporate vice-president, was put in charge of a strategic account management team in Detroit to concentrate on the automotive market. Sales engineers from the four corners of the company are encouraged to seek sales opportunities for other GE businesses and are rewarded for doing so.

Encouraged by the marketing-oriented philosophy of GE chairman John F. Welch Jr., sales executives and salespeople alike are working closer with major accounts on the complete spectrum of business issues. "The world is different today," says the 55-year-old Engelman. "Before we even start production, our people talk with customers about technical standards and whether we can enhance both our product and theirs to improve our collective profit."

Often these exchanges go beyond mere marketing. GE plant engineers advise customers on upgrading their manufacturing processes. Human resources people provide tips on manpower planning, and financial specialists help with profit analysis. "That way, our customers are more likely to think of us as a total partner," says Engelman, noting that the consulting occasionally extends to the purchasing department. "We're even telling our customers how to *buy* better!"

1. What are the advantages of General Electric's team approach in selling to General Motors?

2. What support was required in team selling to GM?
3. Why did it make sense to sell to GM on a team basis?

NOTES

1. "How Computers Are Reshaping the Sales Process," *Business Marketing,* June 1985, p. 108.

2. "Hewlett-Packard Discovers Marketing," *Fortune,* October 1, 1984, pp. 81–86.

3. "To Market, To Market," *Computerworld,* January 7, 1985, p. 120.

4. "HP Battles Doubts About Systems, Marketing Skills," *Computerworld,* January 5, 1987, p. 32.

5. "Tapping into Corporate Communications," *Marketing Communications,* May 1986, pp. 49–54.

6. "Closing the Loop: Hewlett-Packard's New Lead Management System," *Business Marketing,* October 1987, pp. 74–78.

7. "Hewlett-Packard Gives Sales Reps a Competitive Edge," *Sales & Marketing Management,* February 1987, pp. 36–40.

8. Al Wedell and Dale Hempeck, "Sales Force Automation — Here and Now," *Journal of Personal Selling & Sales Management* 7(August 1987):14.

9. "Getting a Leg Up by Using Handhelds," *Datamation,* January 1, 1987, p. 32.

10. Clifton J. Reichard, "Industrial Selling: Beyond Price and Persistence," *Harvard Business Review* 63(March–April 1985):127–133.

11. Ibid.

12. John Barrett, "Why Major Account Selling Works," *Industrial Marketing Management* 15(1986):63–73.

13. "Reshaping the Sales Structure," *Marketing Communications,* January 1986, p. 19.

14. "Xerox's Sales Force Learns a New Game," *Sales & Marketing Management,* July 1, 1985, p. 51.

15. Ibid.

16. "Ryder Trucks Ahead with Computers," *Marketing Communications,* June 1985, p. 84.

17. "Reps' Fears of Telemarketing Present Management Hurdle," *Marketing News,"* April 25, 1986, p. 8.

18. "Dow Corning Blends Inquiry Handling with Telemarketing," *Business Marketing,* October 1983, p. 116.

19. "High Tech Can't Forget Sales Prospecting," *Industrial Marketing,* November 1981, p. 78.

20. "Sales Lead Management," *Business Marketing,* March 1986, p. 62.

21. "IBM Targets Scientists, Engineers for First Time," *Direct Marketing,* April 1985, pp. 86–90.

22. "Crafting 'Win-Win Situations' in Buyer-Supplier Relationships," *Business Marketing,* June 1986, p. 42.

23. "Nabisco Packages a Meeting for Field Managers," *Sales & Marketing Management,* November 11, 1985, p. 88.

24. "Setting Performance Objectives Requires Lots of Give and Take," *Sales & Marketing Management,* May 19, 1980, p. 86.

25. "The Four Surveys: Putting Them to Work," *Sales & Marketing Management,* July 27, 1987, p. A–10.

26. "Xerox's Makeover," *Sales & Marketing Management,* June 1987, p. 68.

27. "Airwick Drops Sales Offices to Increase Sales," *Marketing News,* February 8, 1980, p. 6.

28. "Apple-Polishing the Dealer," *Sales & Marketing Management,* September 10, 1984, p. 47.

29. Donald Baier and Robert D. Dugan, "Factors in Sales Success," *Journal of Applied Psychology* 41(February 1957):37–40; and Paul J. O'Neill, "Pattern Analysis of Biographical Predictors of Success as an Insurance Salesman," *Journal of Applied Psychology* 53(April 1969):136–139.

30. John B. Miner, "Personality and Ability Factors in Sales Performance," *Journal of Applied Psychology* 46(February 1962): 6–13; and Thomas W. Harrell, "The Relation of Test Scores to Sales Criteria," *Personnel Psychology* 13(Spring 1960):65–69.

31. *Sales & Marketing Management's 1985 Survey of Selling Costs,* February 18, 1985, p. 68.

32. "Burger King Uses A/V 'Their Way'," *Marketing Communications,* April 1986, p. 91.

33. "McKesson Takes to Meeting Monthly," *Sales & Marketing Management,* July 1986, pp. 102, 104.

34. "Merck's Grand Obsession," *Sales & Marketing Management,* June 1987, p. 65.

35. "Motivating Willy Loman," *Forbes,* January 30, 1984, p. 91.

36. Gilbert A. Churchill, Jr., Neil M. Ford, and Orville C. Walker, Jr., "Personal Characteristics of Salespeople and the Attractiveness of Alternative Rewards," *Journal of Business Research* 7(1979):25–50.

Michael Dell founded Dell Computer in 1984 when he was 19. Today, a seasoned veteran in his mid-twenties, he can claim to have started something of a revolution in the computer industry — not a technological revolution, but a pricing revolution. Dell's personal computers sell for 25 percent to 40 percent less than comparable PC models. A PC's Limited Computer (the brand name on all of Dell's models) sells for about $4,500. Comparable IBM and Compaq models sell for about $6,000 to $7,000.[1]

At prices like these, you might ask why everyone does not buy a Dell PC. Well, there is one catch. You can buy Dell computers only directly from the company by phone on one of their 800 lines or by mail. And you had better know the exact options you want, from type of display to disk drives, because the computer is going to be built within three to four days based on the configurations you specify. Dell is the only computer maker that sells directly to its customers, thus eliminating the usual retailer's markup of 22 percent.

At 19, Michael Dell observed that many of his fellow students at the University of Texas knew quite a bit about PCs. They knew the difference between hard and soft disk drives, monochrome and color displays, and fast and slow machine time. Dell started his company to take advantage of the fact that consumers such as these students did not need a retailer's help in selecting PCs and would be happy to avoid paying the retailer's markup.

Eliminating the retailer's markup is not the only reason Dell can sell its computers so cheaply. Michael Dell also knows how to keep manufacturing costs down. When he was 16, he took apart an Apple II to see how it worked and put it back together again.[2] By the time he was in college, he was building a few PCs

for his own use and then began selling them. Next came the realization that he could build a computer much more cheaply by buying many of the components, including the disk drive, from other manufacturers rather than building them himself. Also, Dell Computer assembles computers only after they have been ordered by customers, thereby saving inventory expenses.[3]

Two other components in Dell's low-price strategy give the company a competitive edge — product quality and service. You might assume that lower price means lower quality, but Dell has been able to maintain quality on a par with IBM and Compaq. One computer rating service scored Dell's Model 386 PC higher in performance than the comparable IBM Model 80 and Compaq Deskpro 386.[4]

For service, Dell maintains a staff of 43 people to answer phone inquiries on technical problems. About 90 percent of problems are solved over the phone. If service is required, Dell guarantees its machines for one year. Dell has an agreement with Honeywell Bull Inc. to have its machines serviced in over 200 Honeywell service locations.[5] Without this base of service support, Dell's low-price strategy would not be viable.

This low-price, direct-selling strategy produced $6 million worth of sales in its first year of operation. Just three years later, in 1988, sales were $159 million.[6] Dell is projecting it will become a $1 billion company based on its low-price strategy. While some analysts feel that Dell has come close to saturating the market for computer buffs willing to buy direct, others feel that there are enough price-sensitive consumers to assure Dell of continued growth for years to come.[7] One thing is for sure. Dell has demonstrated the importance of price in the personal computer market.

PRICING INFLUENCES AND STRATEGIES

● ● ●

THE IMPORTANCE OF PRICE

The price level of a product can spell its success or failure. Price must be consistent with the quality consumers perceive they are getting. If it is set too high, consumers will feel they are not getting enough value for their money. If it is set too low, consumers will question the quality of the product because they have learned that in most cases, lower price means lower quality. An important component in Dell's success was convincing consumers that the company was able to deliver a high level of quality at lower prices. The result was that consumers recognized they were getting more value for their money.

PRICE AS A DETERMINANT OF PROFITS

Ultimately, the importance of price must be measured by its impact on a brand's profitability. Profit is total revenue minus total cost, and total revenue is determined by price times quantity. So price is a direct determinant of profits.

These are basic facts known to all marketing managers. Therefore, it is surprising that until recently, price was not regarded as a particularly important decision area in developing marketing strategies. Until the mid 1970s, pricing was primarily a matter of determining costs and adding a target return on investment. This prevailing cost-oriented method of pricing considered consumer demand after the fact. If consumers would not buy at the price that was set, the marketer would reduce the price and see if consumers were then willing to buy.

INCREASING IMPORTANCE OF PRICE IN THE 1970S AND 1980S

In the mid 1970s and early 1980s, marketing executives began to cite price as the most important component of the marketing mix.[8] There were at least four reasons for this increasing emphasis on price. First, the energy crisis in the 1970s resulted in shortages of raw materials in many industries, increasing their costs and therefore prices to consumers. The sharp recession in the early 1980s created a further decrease in consumer purchasing power. As a result, consumers became more price-sensitive. They began to shop around and to buy lower-priced generic brands and private labels. Price thus became a prime weapon to gain competitive advantage.

Foreign competition also increased the strategic importance of price. Lower-priced foreign goods flooded the U.S. market in the 1970s and 1980s, creating downward price pressures in many industries such as autos, electronics, and steel. Some American firms, like Ford Motor Company, have tried to compete directly with foreign producers on a price basis by lowering their costs. Other firms have ceded the low-price end of the market to foreign competitors and are carving a niche on the high end. For example, Zenith, the only remaining company in the United States making TV sets, is focusing on the premium-price niche, offering sets retailing for more than $1,000 with features such as stereo sound and wooden stands.[9]

A third factor increasing the importance of price is the fragmentation of many markets into segments demanding different price levels. Companies that offer one brand to a mass market are losing out to firms that offer premium-priced and lower-priced brands to different segments. Philip Morris, the leading cigarette company, is beginning to segment the market based on price by coming out with lower-priced brands to compete with generics. The company introduced two brands in 1986, Cambridge and Players, priced far below its best-selling Marlboro brand, and its premium-priced Benson & Hedges.[10]

Finally, deregulation has increased the importance of price. Before 1975, pricing was regulated in basic industries such as airlines, trucking, railroads, financial services, and telecommunications. The deregulation of all of these industries resulted in intense price competition. (See Exhibit 19.1 for price-oriented ads as a result of deregulation.) For example, airlines began slashing prices once Congress removed the Civil Aeronautic Board's power to regulate them. In the first five years after deregulation, airline prices decreased 50 percent.[11]

Deregulation has also meant that some industries have had to start pricing their services for the first time. When the Securities and Exchange Commission eliminated fixed commission rates in the sale of stocks in 1975, brokerage houses suddenly had to determine what rates to charge. Managers had to make important pricing decisions that had not been required in a regulated environment.

CHANGES IN PRICE DETERMINATION

The increasing importance of price means that many firms cannot go back to the simple cost-oriented methods of price determination they used in the past. Tacking on a fixed percentage to the cost of a product simply does not take account of consumer demand. If managers are to establish prices in an increasingly competitive market, they have to begin pricing based on what the consumer is willing to pay. As a result, marketers are increasingly using demand-oriented methods that set a price to achieve a particular goal, such as maximization of short-term profits, based on consumer demand at various price levels.

THE PROCESS OF PRICE DETERMINATION

Influences on price, pricing strategies, and pricing methods are all part of the process of price determination. Figure 19.1 presents a model of this process. This chapter examines the steps in the shaded boxes, and the remaining steps will be considered in the next chapter.

EXHIBIT 19.1
Results of Deregulation: Increased Price
Competition in Two Industries

The first step in the model is to establish pricing objectives. For example, Eli Lilly's pricing objective for Treflan, an agricultural herbicide, was to discourage competitive entry into the product category since its patent was about to expire.[12] The company decided to reduce the price of Treflan to deter competition, but the question was by how much?

The next step in Figure 19.1 is to evaluate pricing influences, of which the most important is the customer. Lilly would want to know how much more it could sell to farmers at lower prices. Such an evaluation would require estimating the farmers' demand for Treflan. Costs of producing each unit would also have to be determined, along with environmental factors such as the trade's reaction to decreased margins as a result of Lilly lowering its price.

The third step in setting prices is to develop a pricing strategy that maps out how the company will meet its pricing objectives. Lilly's strategy is to decrease price to discourage competitive entry once its patent expires. Companies set pricing strategies for new as well as for existing products. When Lilly first introduced Treflan, it followed a high-price strategy to try to maximize its profits but had planned to eventually reduce its price. Companies must also set strategies for product lines. Lilly might decide to introduce extensions of Treflan appealing to various price segments — for example, a more expensive stronger version of the product.

Once it has established a pricing strategy, the company should determine the price level at which the product will be sold. Pricing adjustments, such as trade and customer discounts, are likely to follow. For example, Lilly might decide to offer its distributors discounts on merchandise bought after the price decrease as a way to offset their reduced margins.

The last step in Figure 19.1 involves evaluating and controlling prices. To evaluate customer responses to price, the company can measure sales results and determine whether additional customers bought because of a price change. Competitive reactions must also be anticipated. Will a decrease in price discourage companies like Monsanto and American Cyanamid from entering the market once Lilly's patent expires? Prices must be controlled as well as evaluated if sales goals are to be met. Thus, management must make sure that the salesforce is following suggested prices and that discounts are offered uniformly to all customers.

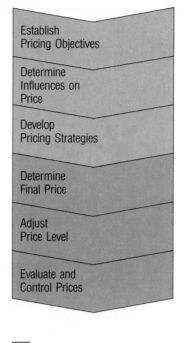

FIGURE 19.1
A Model of Price Determination

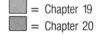
= Chapter 19
= Chapter 20

PRICING OBJECTIVES

A manager's pricing decisions determine price levels based on objectives such as return on investment, market share, and competitive advantage. When Lilly introduced Treflan, its initial objective was to obtain an adequate return to recoup investment in a reasonable period of time. This objective dictated a high-price, or *skimming-the-market,* strategy. When Treflan's patent was about to expire, Lilly changed its objective to one of trying to discourage competitive entry. This led to a reduction in price. Pricing objectives directly influenced pricing strategies and the price level set for Treflan.

Pricing objectives can be based on cost criteria, competitive actions, sales objectives, or customer demand. Cost-oriented methods are still the most common. The most frequently used objective is a *target return on investment.* For example, a firm might cite an objective of a 15 percent return on investment for a product and then set a price that it estimates will meet this goal. In the next chapter, we describe the process of establishing a price based on target return objectives.

Objectives can also be set based on competition such as trying to deter competitive entry. Lilly's low-price strategy for Treflan was based on this objective.

Many firms establish pricing objectives based on sales; that is, they set prices to achieve dollar sales goals. Such goals provide a more direct measure of the firm's success in increasing its revenues through its pricing strategies.

A fourth category of pricing objectives — demand-oriented objectives — are designed to set prices based on customer responses. The most frequently stated demand-oriented objective is short-term profit maximization. But determining customer demand for a brand to set a profit-maximizing price is difficult, because the firm has to estimate how much customers will buy at various price levels.

PRICING INFLUENCES

The two most important environmental influences that affect pricing decisions are demand and cost. Consumer *demand* defines the amount consumers are willing to buy at various prices and determines revenue. *Cost* factors are used to

FIGURE 19.2
Hypothetical Demand Curves
for the Saturn Car

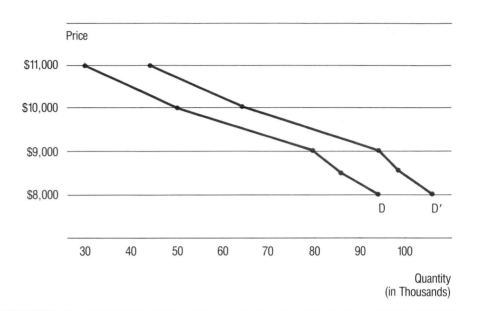

establish prices on a target return or markup basis and define a floor below which prices cannot go. Besides these influences, a number of other environmental characteristics affect price, such as competition and the trade.

As we will be using various demand and revenue concepts in our discussion of pricing, we recommend a review of Appendix 19A, "Basic Demand and Revenue Concepts," at the end of this chapter first before you read further.

DEMAND FACTORS

Marketers should have some idea of the quantity customers are willing to buy at various price levels in order to set prices. This information is estimated in the form of the consumers' *demand curve* and *price elasticity,* or sensitivity to price.

The Consumer Demand Curve

The consumer **demand curve** is a curve that shows the quantity of a product that customers buy at various price levels. Marketers attempt to estimate a demand curve for customers when they introduce new products or want to change prices of existing products.

Suppose General Motors tests five prices ranging from $8,000 to $11,000 for its new subcompact Saturn car line slated for introduction in 1990. Based on these tests, GM estimates demand at 30,000 units at the $11,000 price, 95,000 units at the $8,000 price, and various units in between at the intermediate prices. On this basis, the demand curve for the Saturn is estimated (Curve D shown in Figure 19.2).

Any change in the level of consumer demand at a given price results in a new demand curve. For example, assume that GM introduces the Saturn line at a price of $8,000, then finds that its estimates of demand are fairly accurate. In the first year after introduction, it sells close to the 95,000 cars it projected at a price of $8,000 for total revenue of $760 million (95,000 × $8,000). But now an unanticipated event occurs in GM's favor: Congress imposes a strict import quota on all Japanese cars, resulting in a decrease in competition in the sale of subcompacts. As a result, in the second year after introduction, GM sells 110,000 cars at a price of $8,000. There is now a new demand curve for the Saturn, represented by Curve D′ in Figure 19.2. The demand curve for the Saturn has shifted to the right, meaning that demand has expanded. Now total revenue, at a price of $8,000, is $880 million rather than $760 million. GM has gained a windfall of $120 million more in revenues based on Congress's actions.

On the other side of the coin, suppose Congress took no action, and Japanese manufacturers entered the United States with new lines of cars priced even lower than in previous years. In this case demand for the Saturn would probably decrease, and the demand curve would shift to the left. Thus, an increase in demand means the demand curve shifts to the right; a decrease means it shifts to the left.

Price Elasticity of Demand

Buyers' sensitivity to price is called **price elasticity**. It is measured by the percentage change in quantity that results from a percentage change in price, as shown by the following index:

$$\text{Price Elasticity of Demand} = \frac{\text{Percent Change in Quantity}}{\text{Percent Change in Price}}$$

When the percent change in quantity is more than the percent change in price, consumers are *price-sensitive* (that is, *price elastic*). A decrease in price will produce a more than proportionate increase in quantity, resulting in an increase in revenues. The example in Figure 19.2 shows that demand for the Saturn car is highly elastic. For example, a 10 percent decrease in price from $10,000 to $9,000 results in a 60 percent jump in estimated demand from 50,000 to 80,000 units.

When the percent change in quantity is less than the percent change in price, consumers are *price-insensitive* (that is, *inelastic*). An increase in price will produce a less than proportionate decrease in quantity, resulting in an increase in total revenue. Consider the hypothetical demand curve for a Jaguar auto in Figure 19.3. A 33 percent increase in price from $45,000 to $60,000 results in a decrease in sales from 20,000 to 16,000 units, or only 20 percent. A price increase pays, because at a price of $45,000, total revenue is $900 million ($45,000 × 20,000 cars), whereas at a price of $60,000, total revenue is $960 million ($60,000 × 16,000 cars).

When consumers are price-elastic, they will switch brands based on price. When they are inelastic, they tend to remain loyal to a brand. Price is fairly elastic for items ordinarily purchased in supermarkets or drugstores. It is inelastic for prestige products such as gourmet foods or luxury cars. But demand can be inelastic even for everyday products. The consumer who insists on buying Michelob beer or Pepperidge Farm cookies is loyal to those brands and may continue to buy even if prices increase by 10 or 20 percent.

Upside and Downside Elasticity

Elasticity for a product may differ when prices are increasing (**upside elasticity**) compared to when they are decreasing (**downside elasticity**). For example, consumers may decrease consumption if prices increase, but may not necessarily increase consumption if prices decrease. When coffee prices increased sharply in the mid 1970s, coffee consumption decreased because many consumers switched to tea and other products. When prices began to decrease, some of these consumers continued to drink other products, so consumption did not increase as much

FIGURE 19.3
Example of Inelastic Demand:
Hypothetical Demand Curve
for a Jaguar Car

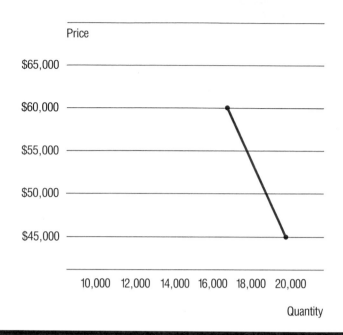

as expected. These consumers demonstrated upside price elasticity (sensitivity to increases in price) and downside inelasticity (insensitivity to decreases in price).

Ideally, a marketer would want things the other way around — upside price inelasticity (no substantial change in consumption as prices go up) and downside elasticity (increased purchases as prices go down). Marketers try to encourage upside price inelasticity by advertising products on a prestige basis. For example, the ad for Red Devil wood stain in Exhibit 19.2 tries to convince the consumer that the product is in a class by itself. Marketers try to encourage downside price elasticity by advertising lower prices and by using price promotions. The ad for the Post Office's Express Mail Service in Exhibit 19.2 is an example of encouraging downside price elasticity by offering a low rate for overnight delivery.

Elasticity by Market Segment
By recognizing that market segments have different price elasticities, marketers can generate more profits by offering products at different prices to different segments — a lower-priced product to the price-elastic segment and a higher-priced product to the price-inelastic segment.

The airlines, for example, have been following a pricing policy based on the fact that business travelers are more price-inelastic than vacationers. They will pay a higher price if they can get to the right place at the right time. Vacation travelers want lower prices more than they want scheduling flexibility, so airlines offer them lower fares at restricted times. The revenues generated by vacation travelers permit the airlines to support more frequent flights and flexible routing for business travelers.[13]

COST-REVENUE RELATIONSHIPS   Estimating the demand curve for a product enables the manager to compute revenues generated at various prices. This information, in turn, is part of the calculation of profits, which are revenues minus costs. Costs are more easily

Creating Upside Price Inelasticity

Creating Downside Price Elasticity

estimated than revenue since the firm already knows its costs for labor, raw materials, marketing, and administration, but must predict revenue. At this point, it would be useful to review the basic cost concepts summarized in Appendix 19B before considering cost-revenue relationships.

Determining Profits

As we noted, the quantity customers are willing to buy at a certain price determines total revenue. If the manager also knows the cost of producing these items, then profits can be determined. Managers will try to set prices at the point where they will maximize profits. The price-quantity relationships in Curve D of Figure 19.2 for the Saturn car are shown in Table 19.1, along with the total costs of production and distribution. The last column shows the profits (total revenue minus total cost).

On this basis, gross profits would be greatest when cars sell for $8,500. Assume GM sets its price for the new cars accordingly. But the company also realizes that if it reduces price to $8,000 because of competitive pressures, or if it

TABLE 19.1
Determining Profits at
Various Price Levels

PRICE *(P)*	QUANTITY *(Q)*	TOTAL REVENUE [P · Q] (in Millions)	TOTAL COST (in Millions)	PROFITS (Total Revenue − Total Cost)
$11,000	30,000	$330	$410	−$ 80
$10,000	50,000	$500	$500	$ 0
$ 9,000	80,000	$720	$600	$120
$ 8,500	87,000	$740	$618	$122
$ 8,000	95,000	$760	$646	$114

decides to raise the price to $9,000, there would be little loss in profits. As a result, GM has price flexibility in the range of $8,000 to $9,000.

Marginal Analysis

The profit-maximizing price is at a point where marginal revenue equals marginal cost. This principle of **marginal analysis** in pricing means that as long as the additional revenue gained from the last unit produced (the marginal revenue) is greater than the cost of producing that last unit (the marginal cost), the company should produce the additional unit. If, for example, the 87,000th Saturn car produces $2,900 in revenue and costs $2,800 to produce, it is profitable to produce the additional car because it is contributing $100 to profits. Once the last unit is no longer contributing to profits, then it does not pay to produce more units.

Putting the principle in the context of setting prices, if demand is elastic, reducing the price increases total revenue. The principle of marginal pricing says that prices should continue to decrease as long as the additional units demanded bring in more revenue than the cost of producing them. This is known as "pricing down the demand curve," since the marketer keeps decreasing prices (moving down the demand curve) as long as these decreases contribute to profit. If demand is inelastic, price increases would accomplish the same purpose, and the marketer would be pricing up the demand curve.

In the Saturn example, demand was elastic. The following marginal revenue and marginal cost figures are in Appendixes 19A and 19B for prices of $9,000, $8,500 and $8,000:

PRICE	QUANTITY	MARGINAL REVENUE (MR)	MARGINAL COST (MC)	MARGINAL CONTRIBUTION TO PROFIT (MR − MC)
$9,000	80,000	$7,330	$3,300	$4,030
$8,500	87,000	$2,860	$2,570	$ 290
$8,000	95,000	$2,500	$3,500	−$1,000

The *marginal contribution to profit* in the preceding table is the contribution made by the last unit produced. As long as the last unit is making a marginal contribution to profit, prices should keep decreasing. At a price of $9,000, each additional unit is making a contribution to profits of $4,030, so it would pay GM

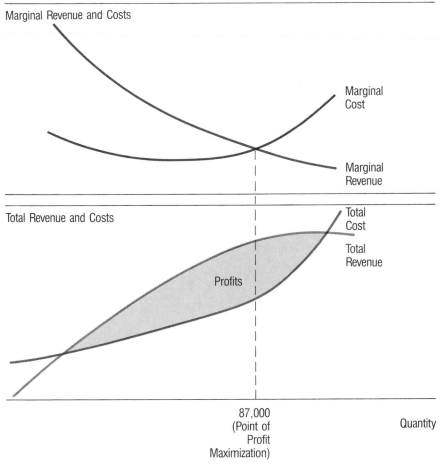

FIGURE 19.4
Defining the Point of
Profit Maximization
for the Saturn Car

Note: Hypothetical example

to reduce the price further so as to sell more cars. At a price of $8,500, marginal revenue is almost the same as marginal cost. By the time we reach a price of $8,000, marginal costs exceed marginal revenue, and there is no contribution to profit by producing any more cars. So the optimal price is close to $8,500, because at that price each additional car produced is making a small ($290) contribution to profit.

At a price much below $8,500, any additional car produced would not be making a contribution to profit. This is exactly the same result we obtained in Table 19.1 when we identified the price that maximizes profits as $8,500. (That is the price at the point of greatest difference between total revenue and total cost.)

This principle of marginal analysis is illustrated in Figure 19.4. The intersection of the marginal revenue and marginal cost curves is at the point that maximizes total profit (that is, the point that produces the greatest spread between total revenue and total cost).

The problem in using marginal analysis to determine the profit-maximizing price is that the method depends on the accuracy of the estimated demand curve. If consumers buy 75,000 units at $8,500 instead of the projected 87,000, then the profit-maximizing price would not be $8,500.

ENVIRONMENTAL PRICE INFLUENCES

In addition to consumer demand and cost factors, a number of environmental factors influence a manager's pricing decisions. These influences include the customer's pricing perceptions, competitive reactions, trade reactions, and economic conditions.

Consumer Price Perceptions

Based on their past experience, customers develop expectations regarding price levels. They judge prices too high or too low based on those expectations. They also frequently regard price as an indicator of product quality. Managers must determine both consumers' pricing expectations and the associations they make between price and quality.

Most consumers develop an idea of an **acceptable price range** for a product category. They will not buy a brand priced above that range because the product is not worth it to them. They will not buy below the range because they fear the product would be of inferior quality. Different segments of the market will have different acceptable price ranges. Luxury-car buyers will have a very different range than economy-car buyers. Therefore, the product manager must determine the acceptable price range for a particular target segment and develop a price within it. For example, assume that the acceptable price range for subcompacts for most consumers is from $6,000 to $11,000. Producers of subcompacts are likely to price somewhere in that range.

Another issue in pricing is the associations consumers make between price and quality. Since many consumers regard price as an indicator of quality, marketers must make sure that price is in line with product quality. Consumers who feel the price was too high for the quality they received will not buy again and may pass the word on to other consumers. And the higher the price, the greater the risk of disappointing the consumer with what is perceived as inferior quality.

Competitive Influences

Marketers must take competitive reactions into account when setting prices. Will a price reduction be quickly followed by competitors? If so, the firm may think twice about lowering price. Companies have also used price to retaliate for competitive actions, sometimes in other product categories. For example, Gillette and Bic have influenced each other's pricing actions for years. When Bic entered the razor market Gillette retaliated by introducing a line of low-priced ballpoint pens to get into Bic's turf.[14] Bic countered by introducing a pen that looked like Gillette's entry, but at an even lower price.

Trade Influences

Manufacturers must anticipate how retailers and wholesalers will react to their pricing strategies. An important consideration for Lilly is the reaction of its distributors to a proposed decrease in prices and dealer margins for Treflan. If many distributors decide to stop carrying the product because of reduced margins, a price decrease could be counterproductive. If manufacturers are small or are new in the business, they may not have the leverage to convince wholesalers and retailers to stock their offerings. Their only option might be to offer the trade higher margins.

Another factor in pricing strategy is the manufacturer's desire to maintain the price of its products at the retail level. When a manufacturer spends millions of dollars in advertising trying to establish a high-quality image for a brand, price discounts at the retail level can undermine the strategy. The manufacturer's ability to police retail prices is limited under prohibitions against price fixing. One legal way to control prices at the retail level is to franchise retailers so that their pricing actions can be controlled by the manufacturer. Another option is for the manufacturer to sell directly to customers through its own outlets. But this is an expensive alternative.

Economic Influences
Periods of inflation, recession, and shortages have a direct affect on pricing actions. In inflation, prices to consumers usually rise to keep pace with the increasing costs of raw materials and labor. Shortages such as the oil crises in the 1970s will also drive up prices because of increased costs. In a recession, marketers face pressures to cut prices to remain competitive because of decreases in demand for many categories.

The combination of recession and inflation in the late 1970s and early 1980s led many marketers to emphasize cost reductions in an attempt to drive down prices, and to shift to more demand-oriented methods of pricing. Another effect of the economic instabilities of the early 1980s was to make consumers more price-sensitive, and more willing to shop for bargains.

PRICING STRATEGIES

Based on its pricing objectives and the influences on price, a company develops an overall pricing strategy for its brand or product line (step 3 in Figure 19.1) that determines a range of prices for a product or service. For example, Helene Curtis decided to buck the trend toward low-priced shampoos and conditioners by introducing a premium-priced brand, Salon Selective. Shampoos had become increasingly undifferentiated, and the company felt it could introduce a brand with a prestige, salon-type image. Helene Curtis's strategy meant pricing significantly above the prevailing $1.40 to $1.60 price range for existing brands. Eventually, it decided on a price of $2.25.[15] The premium price strategy had to be established before the company selected a specific price level.

Pricing strategies can be developed for existing products, for new products, and for product lines.

Pricing strategies for existing products deal with two key areas: the appropriate price level and the changes in price from the current level.

PRICING STRATEGIES FOR EXISTING PRODUCTS

Price Level
Price-level strategies can position a brand from the lowest to the highest price. These extremes are shown in Exhibit 19.3, with the positioning of the Hyundai car at the low end (with a price of $5,724) and BMW at the higher end (with a price of $40,000). Price-level strategies are meant to delineate the pricing position of a brand — as an economy, mid-priced, or premium-priced brand.

The tendency in recent years has been to position products as either economy or premium brands. Low-price strategies are targeted to price-elastic consumer segments. A variety of forces described at the beginning of this chapter have caused marketers to put more emphasis on low-price strategies. And, the increasing popularity of private brands and generics is a reflection of a more price-elastic consumer market. For example, L&M has been able to survive in the cigarette industry by producing generic cigarettes. R. J. Reynolds appealed to more price

EXHIBIT 19.3
Positioning Brands at
Two Extremes of
the Price Range

sensitive smokers by introducing two new cigarette brands, Doral and Century, designed to compete on a price basis with L&M's generic cigarettes.[16]

A high-price strategy is designed to appeal to a price-inelastic segment of the market. There are several reasons why many manufacturers are choosing this course. The increasing proportion of working women and the greater number of single-member households has resulted in more purchasing power for many consumers — and they are more willing to spend on themselves. They are buying products that will give them pleasure and value — gourmet foods, designer clothing, expensive vacations. As a result, a superpremium-price niche has developed in many categories. A superpremium brand like Frusen Gladje ice cream can sell for double the price of a premium brand like Breyers. In the words of one supermarket manager, "It's the quality and the name. People don't care what it costs."[17]

Another reason to target the premium-price segment is to escape competition on the low end. As we saw, Zenith escaped competition from lower-priced Japanese TV sets by going after consumers willing to spend over a thousand dollars for a set.

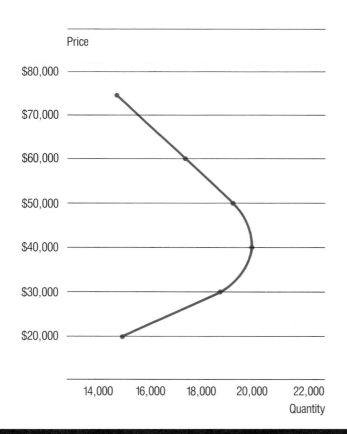

FIGURE 19.5
Demand Curve for a Prestige Product

A third reason companies follow a high-price strategy is as part of an overall marketing strategy to establish a prestige image for a brand. A higher price is consistent with the quality image established in the advertising. Ads for Jaguar make no mention of price (the cars sell for $45,000 to $80,000). They use settings like a 400-year-old manor house in England to reinforce the prestige of the name to a select segment.

One peculiarity of pricing prestige products is that if the price is set too low, demand may actually decrease, because price falls below the consumer's acceptable price range. This is illustrated by the backward-bending demand curve in Figure 19.5. If, for example, the price of a Jaguar was set at $30,000, buyers might feel it had lost its prestige value and might look for another car that had status and prestige at higher prices. Marketers of prestige products want to price above the point at which demand decreases if price goes down. (This would be at a point at or above $40,000 in Figure 19.5.) Backward-bending demand curves are common for prestige products such as designer clothes, yachts, or luxury cars.

Price Stability versus Change

Another major pricing decision for existing products is whether prices should be changed from current levels or should remain stable.

Strategies for Price Stability Some industries try to maintain *price stability* to avoid *price wars*. Price wars are likely to occur in industries with standardized products. Since there is little difference among brands, a decrease in price will attract a large number of customers and force other companies to match the decrease. Some companies may retaliate by decreasing price even further, thus setting off a price war. In such a war, the smaller and weaker companies are forced out of the industry, leaving a few large manufacturers to control prices.

Historically, this type of situation has produced a **price leader**; that is, a company that tacitly sets a price that every other company follows. Having a price leader avoids price wars, since companies in the industry accept the principle that only the leader will change prices. U.S. Steel (now USX), Alcoa, Owens-Illinois, and Dow Chemical assumed price leadership in the steel, aluminum, glass container, and chemical industries to achieve price stability. However, today, many industries can no longer maintain price stability because of foreign competitors coming in with lower prices. As a result, U.S. Steel and Owens-Illinois are no longer price leaders in their industry.

Attempts at price stability are not limited to industries with standardized products. Some candy bar manufacturers have maintained prices by changing the size of their bars. M&M/Mars engineered a disguised price cut by increasing the weight of its bars without changing the price. Its purpose was to gain a competitive advantage, which it held for two years before finally increasing its prices.[18]

Strategies for Price Change Companies may also seek to increase or decrease prices for existing products as a part of their strategy. Companies have increased prices as a result of (1) increases in raw material and labor costs or (2) a change in the quality and features of their product. As we saw, it was an increase in raw material costs that prompted coffee companies to increase their prices in the mid 1970s. In contrast, M&M/Mars increased its prices based on a change in product features. When the company increased the weight of its candy bars, it waited two years before increasing price by five cents a bar. Retailers welcomed the increase, and reacted by increasing the price of all their candy bars by five cents. As a result, other manufacturers had no choice but to follow Mars' price increase.[19]

Price decreases can also be part of a pricing strategy. One reason to reduce prices is to cover overhead when plant capacity is not being fully utilized. The reduced price causes an increase in volume, which covers overhead (fixed costs).

This principle of reducing price so as to use capacity and make a contribution to overhead is well illustrated in airline pricing. If airlines charge regular fares, many of their planes will have empty seats. An empty seat is a lost seat. As long as the airlines can cover the variable cost involved in filling an additional seat (personnel and handling costs for the customer's tickets and baggage), it pays to reduce the price to fill the seat. Any price above its variable costs will contribute to paying off the cost and maintenance of the plane. That is why airlines reduce their fares substantially for standby travelers.

Other firms reduce price because they have been able to reduce costs and hope to gain a competitive advantage by a price reduction. Cummins Engine Company accomplished this in reverse, first reducing prices and then costs. It saw Japanese companies invading the U.S. medium-truck market with lower-priced entries and anticipated the same thing happening in its own heavy-truck market. To avoid being caught at a price disadvantage, the company dropped its prices before the Japanese entered the United States market. Its strategy was to discourage entry by the Japanese so as to maintain its leading position. After reducing prices by one-third, the company began reducing its costs to a point where it could make a profit at the new prices.[20]

A third reason why companies reduce price is as a reactive strategy to a competitive move rather than as a proactive strategy to gain competitive advantage. The major airlines such as American and TWA followed Continental's lead by reducing prices on most of their routes. Similarly, IBM followed the lead of producers of lower-priced clones by slashing its prices on its PCs in 1986.[21] In some cases, companies have gone one better by reducing prices even further than a competitor's initial price decrease. When Arco reduced prices of gasoline by eliminating credit cards and establishing "cash only" pumps, competitors quickly responded by discounting cash sales even further.[22]

Mark Laracy enjoyed the book *Jitterbug Perfume*. It is about a perfume magnate, Luc LeFever, who likes to take chances and is very much like Laracy himself. A former cosmetic company executive, Laracy discovered an untapped price niche in the perfume market, a large group of consumers who want designer perfumes like Calvin Klein's Obsession or Yves Saint Laurent's Opium but cannot afford them.[23] Laracy concluded that these high-priced perfumes did a great job in establishing images that Charles Revson, founder of Revlon, once said "sell hope in a bottle." The problem was that these companies were successful in creating demand for their products among women in Middle America who could not afford prices like $175 an ounce.

Laracy's idea to fill this gap was to come out with lower-priced knockoffs of designer perfumes. He knew that the price structure for the real perfumes looked something like this:[24]

Mark Laracy — From Obsession to Price Concession

Source: © Giorgio Palmisano. New York City.

Raw material and production	10 percent of the price
Packaging and designer royalties	15 percent
Advertising and promotions	50 percent
Profit margins	25 percent

He figured that if he could eliminate most of the advertising and promotions, as well as the cost of royalties to designers, he could make a profit with the knockoffs. And Laracy was in a good position to know. After spending ten years at Chesebrough-Pond's Prince Matchabelli Perfumes division helping to introduce winners such as Aviance and Wind Song perfumes, Laracy moved to Charles of the Ritz to help introduce Yves Saint Laurent's Opium, and got fired in an unsuccessful bid to become CEO. That is when he decided to become the Luc LeFever of designer perfumes.

One of the first things he did was to buy a gas chromatograph that could tell him the exact ingredients in each brand of perfume. His plan was to come out with a near duplicate of the designer brands and use a comparative slogan on the package to advertise it as a designer perfume substitute. He then formed his company, Parfums de Coeur (the name means "perfumes of the heart" in French) and came out with his first product, Ninja, a knockoff of Opium and Cinnabar perfumes. The slogan on the package says "If you like Opium or Cinnabar, you'll love Ninja." After getting assurances from a trademark attorney that his strategy was legal, he moved ahead. The result was $1 million in sales in the first nine months of business in 1981, $5 million in sales by 1983, and $59 million by 1986.[25]

Laracy's success has spawned a number of imitators. Perhaps the most flattering of all has been Avon, which decided to use the same strategy to go after the low-price end of the market. The company has come out with a knockoff of Old Spice called Brisk Spice. Its tag line reads "If you like Old Spice, you'll love Brisk Spice."[26] Sound familiar?

Laracy likes to call the price gap at the low end of the perfume line a chasm rather than a niche. Maybe he is right. ■

STRATEGIES FOR PRICING NEW PRODUCTS

Developing a price for a new product is difficult, since managers have little basis for assessing consumer demand. The more innovative the product, the more difficult it is to assess consumer reactions to price prior to market introduction. As we saw in Chapter 10, two types of strategies used in pricing new products are skimming strategies and penetration strategies.

Skimming Strategies

In a **skimming strategy**, the price is set high with the idea of possibly reducing it as competitors begin to enter the market. A skimming strategy works best if demand for the new product is inelastic and if the company has patent protection. When Polaroid first introduced its instant cameras and film, it could do so at a high price because of the uniqueness of the product. Interested consumers were insensitive to the price, and Polaroid had patent protection. Over time, as the product was adopted on a more widespread basis, Polaroid developed a fuller product line by introducing less expensive cameras positioned to a broader segment of the market while maintaining the positioning of its more expensive cameras to quality-oriented camera buffs.

Polaroid's patent protected it from price competition. Without such patent protection, prices can decrease rapidly as competitors enter the market. When Texas Instruments introduced its 99/4A home computer in the early 1980s, it followed a skimming strategy with a suggested retail selling price of $525. After competitors entered the market, the price fell to $100 in only two years.[27]

Penetration Strategies

In a **penetration strategy**, the company starts out with a low price to deter competitive entry. This makes sense if the company has no patent protection and the demand for the product is elastic.

Bausch & Lomb switched from a skimming to a penetration strategy after it introduced soft contact lenses in the early 1970s. When competitors entered the field with an extended-wear lens, Bausch & Lomb's market share began to shrink. The company then developed an improved version of the extended-wear lens. This time, rather than following a skimming strategy, it priced aggressively with a price 50 percent below the industry norm. When its chief competitor, Cooper-Vision, retaliated by lowering the prices on its lenses, Bausch & Lomb lowered prices even further, to $10 to $15.[28]

A firm can create more profits by offering products to different price segments of the market. Establishing a product line targeted to different segments at specific price points is called **price lining**. In following such a strategy, the company is covering the demand curve by marketing products to appeal to economy-minded customers, customers at the mid-price level, and customers interested in prestige products. Each product is aimed at a segment with a different price elasticity. For example, a clothing manufacturer may establish a line of men's suits priced at $150, $250 and $400, targeted to different segments. The assumption is that consumers tend to buy at these price points. Offering a suit at a price of $200 is unlikely to get the $150 consumers to trade up or the $250 consumers to trade down.

STRATEGIES FOR PRICING PRODUCT LINES

Price lining is an important strategic tool. Scripto used a strategy of price lining for its disposable lighters "to encircle Bic with product offerings aimed at specific segments of the market."[29] On the low end, it introduced its Mighty Match at four for a dollar to undercut Bic's 69-cent lighter. Scripto's Ultra lighter is its mid-price entry at 69 cents, directly competitive with Bic's lowest-priced brand. At the upper end is the Electra, selling for 99 cents. Scripto's purpose in "encircling Bic" is to give consumers more choices at better prices in the hope that many of them will trade up to more expensive lighters. In addition, the assumption is that 25 cents, 69 cents, and 99 cents are logical price points, and that additional offerings at intermediate price ranges will not increase profits.

A company following a strategy of price lining must determine the optimal pricing level for each product in its line. Marginal analysis used for this purpose would state that in a price-elastic market (such as disposable lighters), if one segment is making more of a marginal contribution to profits than another, prices to that segment should decrease so as to increase volume. This is because each additional unit sold to that segment provides more contribution to profits than additional units sold to other segments.

ETHICS AND REGULATIONS IN PRICING

Pricing practices are regulated by the government more forcefully than other areas of the marketing mix (such as personal selling, distribution, or even advertising) in that pricing illegalities are made explicit in acts such as the Sherman Act, the FTC Act, and the Robinson-Patman Act (see Chapter 3). Four areas of pricing are considered unethical and illegal: Deceptive pricing, unfair pricing, discriminatory pricing, and price fixing.

Deceptive prices are those meant to deceive customers and to take unfair advantage of them. They are illegal under the Federal Trade Commission (FTC) Act. **Bait-and-switch pricing** is one type of deceptive price — a low-price offer intended to lure customers into a store, where a salesperson tries to influence them to buy a higher-priced item. Audi was accused of using bait-and-switch tactics in 1988 when it offered rebates on its 5000 line, which was being phased out and was often unavailable, leaving consumers to consider other lines without rebates.[30] Another deceptive practice is to offer a discount off an inflated price. Since the price is inflated, the consumer is not actually getting a discount.

Unfair pricing uses pricing practices to drive competitors out of business. **Predatory pricing** is the most apparent of these practices. A company practices predatory pricing by decreasing its prices, often below cost. When competitors are driven out, the company then raises prices back to their former level. The Sherman Act prohibits such practices. The FTC brought action against General Foods for predatory pricing in 1976. It claimed that GF priced its Maxwell House coffee too low in an attempt to drive competitors like Folgers out of areas where it was the market leader. General Foods claimed that it was competing in good faith against Procter & Gamble's introduction of Folgers into the Eastern market.[31] Since GF did not subsequently raise prices to take unfair advantage of a strong market position, it is questionable whether the company's actions were unethical. In trying to protect General Foods' competitors, the FTC might have been encouraging higher coffee prices.

Price discrimination involves selling the same product to buyers at different prices without any cost justification. Theoretically, price discrimination maximizes profits by enabling sellers to charge price-inelastic customers higher prices than elastic customers are charged. It can be unethical if it leads to charging similar buyers different prices for the same goods based on their ability to pay.

The Robinson-Patman Act of 1936 states that price discrimination is illegal, but it makes a number of important exemptions. First, the restriction applies only to sales to organizational buyers, not to final consumers. General Motors cannot sell the same cars at different prices to its dealers, but the dealers can charge consumers different prices for the same car.

Also, the act says that price differences to similar buyers are legal if such differences have some cost justification. A manufacturer may charge a lower price to a buyer who orders a large quantity or is closer to the factory, since the seller is passing on legitimate savings to the buyer. And a seller may charge different prices for the same item to similar buyers if the seller is meeting lower prices from competitors in certain areas of the country. Finally, if sellers can show that charging different prices for the same product caused no injury to competition, they are unlikely to be prosecuted under the act.

Price fixing is an agreement among firms in an industry to set prices at certain levels. The Sherman Act prohibits it because such actions restrict price competition. Agreements among competitors to fix prices at artificially high levels are known as **horizontal price fixing**. Price-fixing agreements between manufacturers and retailers or between manufacturers and distributors are known as **vertical price fixing**. Generally, vertical price fixing involves an agreement that the product will be sold at the manufacturer's suggested price and will not be discounted by the retailer or wholesaler.

Panasonic was accused of vertical price fixing by forcing its retailers to raise prices of its electronics products by 5 to 10 percent. Retailers who did not comply were threatened with being cut off from Panasonic products. The FTC forced Panasonic to cease the practice, to pay $16 million in rebates to consumers who were charged higher prices, and to advertise the settlement.[32]

As with other areas of the marketing mix, most firms have acted ethically in setting prices. They do not attempt to deceive customers or to use pricing actions to restrain competition. Perhaps the greatest spur to responsible pricing is competitive forces in the market place. Unless it is a monopoly, a firm charging artificially high prices will be undercut by a competitor. A firm willfully deceiving consumers through pricing actions will eventually lose out to more responsible competitors as consumers learn that they are being duped. Although government regulation is important in pricing, competitive forces are the best regulators in insuring ethical pricing.

SUMMARY

1. *Why has price increased in importance as a component of the marketing mix?*

Several factors have led price to become a more important component of marketing strategy. First, economic dislocations in the late 1970s and early 1980s made consumers more price-sensitive. Second, competition from lower-priced foreign imports has led American firms either to try to compete on a price basis, or to escape price competition by going after high-price segments. Third, companies have realized the benefits of segmenting markets by price and are offering high-, medium-, and low-priced brands in a product line. Finally, deregulation in many industries has led to greater price competition, increasing the importance of price.

2. *How does a company go about determining prices for a product?*

A company must first establish price objectives. It must then evaluate pricing influences — in particular, cost and demand for the product. Based on this information, the company establishes pricing strategies that define the general range of prices that the company should consider. The company then determines the price level based on a demand- or cost-oriented method of pricing. It then adjusts the final price to offer consumer and trade discounts. Once the price is set, it evaluates the impact on customers and competitors. In the final step of the price-setting process, the company controls prices by trying to ensure objectives are being met.

3. *How do demand and other environmental factors influence price determination?*

To set prices, marketers should know how customers react to alternative prices. Ideally, a firm will try to establish a demand curve; that is, the amount of a product consumers will purchase at various price levels. This allows marketers to determine total revenue, which information, along with costs, enables marketers to measure profits at various price levels and set the most profitable price. The demand curve also measures price sensitivity. To increase revenues, marketers can set higher prices when customers are less price-sensitive and lower prices when they are more price-sensitive. Marginal analysis identifies a profit-maximizing price as the point where marginal revenues of the last unit sold equal its marginal costs.

A number of environmental factors will influence these pricing decisions, such as customer price expectations, customer price-quality associations, competitive reactions to price, reactions of the trade, and economic conditions.

4. *What types of pricing strategies do companies develop for existing and new products?*

Pricing strategies for existing products focus on establishing the appropriate price level and on deciding whether to change prices from current levels or maintain price stability. Pricing strategies for new products include skimming and penetration pricing. A skimming strategy, which sets a high initial price, is feasible if demand is inelastic or if the company has patent protection. A penetration strategy, which sets a low initial price, makes sense if demand is elastic. Pricing strategies are also developed for product lines. Various offerings in a product line are targeted to different price segments to appeal to economy-minded, mid-price, and prestige-oriented customers.

5. *What types of pricing practices are unethical, and how can they be regulated?*

Several types of pricing practices are unethical, because they either deceive the customer, are discriminatory, or restrain competition. Deceptive pricing attempts to deceive consumers as to product availability at a certain price or as to price level. Discriminatory pricing attempts to sell the same product to similar buyers based on what they are willing to pay, without any cost justification for the price difference. Pricing in restraint of trade involves agreements among competitors to set prices to discourage new entrants, or to set prices below cost to drive existing competitors out.

These actions are illegal under the Sherman, FTC, and Robinson-Patman Acts. Ultimately, competitive forces act as regulators to ensure fair pricing practices, since companies that deceive customers or restrain trade are likely to lose out to companies that price according to customer benefits.

KEY TERMS

Demand curve (p. 532)
Price elasticity (p. 533)
Upside price elasticity (p. 533)
Downside price elasticity (p. 533)
Marginal analysis (p. 536)
Acceptable price range (p. 538)
Price leader (p. 542)
Skimming strategy (p. 544)
Penetration strategy (p. 544)
Price lining (p. 545)
Deceptive pricing (p. 545)
Bait-and-switch pricing (p. 545)

Unfair pricing (p. 546)
Predatory pricing (p. 546)
Price discrimination (p. 546)
Horizontal price fixing (p. 546)
Vertical price fixing (p. 546)
Total revenue (p. 550)
Average revenue (p. 550)
Marginal revenue (p. 551)
Fixed costs (p. 551)
Variable costs (p. 551)
Total costs (p. 551)
Marginal costs (p. 551)

QUESTIONS

1. What is the basis for Dell Computer's low-price strategy? What assumptions did Michael Dell make about his target market in following his pricing strategy?

2. Why did price become a more important element of the marketing mix in the 1980s? How did the increasing importance of price affect the methods used to determine price levels?

3. How can a company estimate the consumers' demand curve for a product? What are the risks of using estimates of consumer responses to various price levels as a basis for setting prices?

4. The demand curve for the Saturn car in Figure 19.2 was cited as probably being elastic. The demand

curve for the Jaguar in Figure 19.3 was cited as probably being inelastic.

a. What does this mean? What are the implications for setting prices?

b. What types of products are likely to have elastic demand? Inelastic demand?

5. What is the distinction between upside and downside price elasticity? Apply these concepts to the experience of coffee producers when coffee prices went way up and then came down again in the mid 1970s.

6. What principle defines the profit-maximizing price for a product? Has this principle been applied to other components of the marketing mix? How?

7. A General Motors dealer, reading the section describing the demand-oriented pricing approach for the company's new Saturn line, said the following:

> I know GM doesn't price like that. They develop a target on their investment and set a price that they think will give them enough revenue to reach the target return. Pricing based on trying to estimate the demand curve for a new car is a pretty chancy proposition. We are not dealing with a brand of cereal or toothpaste that can be test-marketed to determine demand. We are dealing with a car. You might ask people whether they would buy it at a certain price; you might even ask them after they test-drive it. But what they say and do are two different things. I would take your marginal approach to pricing with a grain of salt.

  a. Do you agree with the GM dealer's assessment of using marginal analysis to determine price?
  b. What might be the problem with using a cost-oriented approach like the one the dealer described?

8. What environmental influences should Eli Lilly consider in evaluating a price decrease for its Treflan herbicide?
9. What factors have encouraged companies to follow a low-price strategy for certain products? What factors have encouraged them to follow a high-price strategy?
10. What types of industries are most likely to seek price stability? Why? Why do many of these industries have price leaders?
11. What do we mean by price lining? How can firms better maximize profits through this strategy? What are the risks in following such a strategy?
12. Cite examples of deceptive pricing practices, discriminatory pricing practices, and pricing practices in restraint of trade. How do natural market forces act to discourage these practices?

CASE 19.1

CULINOVA'S TWO-PRICE STRATEGY

Source: Judann Dagnoli, "Culinova Lowers Dinner Prices." Reprinted with permission from *Advertising Age,* February 22, 1988, p. 10, copyright Crain Communications, Inc. All rights reserved.

Culinova is going downscale with its upscale refrigerated dinners.

The price tag for the exotic fare, from $4 to $6.99, has proved to be a stumbling block. So now the company is starting to market slightly less-gourmet Culinova entrees at about half the price.

Culinova is a regional joint venture started by several General Foods Corp. executives with help from GF. The original line of premium-price, restaurant-quality dinners was meant to compete with takeout food.

But the line's high price "put us in a special-occasion niche," said Culinova President Rick Powers. With the new line, "we are priced at a good-value level."

The new entrees start at $2.85 and top off at $3.85. Varieties "are a bit more everyday," Mr. Powers said. Barbecued chicken, lasagne and shrimp fettucine are now on the menu, which originally consisted of such fare as filet mignon madagascar and veal vendee.

Although Mr. Powers called the new entrees "an addition," retail sources called the move "a retrenchment" and said they expect Culinova to phase out the more upscale items.

Price has been the driving force behind the changes at Culinova and a slowdown in premium dinners generally, industry sources said.

Retail sales of premium-price frozen dinners and entrees have gone from virtually nothing to $650 million in the past five years, said Bob Bernstock, general manager-premium dinners at Campbell Soup Co., Camden, N.J. But he added that though tonnage was up 29% in the last fiscal year, it is expected to be flat to down by the end of this year.

Culinova also is facing competition now from grocery store retailers who are marketing upscale dining to go. A&P Co., Montvale, is testing gourmet dinners in several of its stores, said Michael Rourke, VP-communications. "It's similar but not quite as sophisticated as Culinova," he said. The line is marketed under the Food Emporium name in A&P stores and under the A&P label in the company's high-tech Futurestores.

Because the dinners are prepared at the store level,

"they're fresher and have longer shelf life than Culinova," Mr. Rourke said. "We can also make them as demand warrants."

Grand Union Co., Elmwood Park, also is said to be launching a store-prepared line of exotic entrees and reportedly has hired a chef from a well-known Manhattan restaurant to manage the operation. Grand Union executives could not be reached for comment.

Culinova's Mr. Powers stressed that his Hawthorne, N.Y.-based company "is in an expansion mode" and recently signed up Sloan's, a major grocery chain in Manhattan.

Although it is too early to discuss ad plans, "we are putting most of our marketing expenditures behind the new entrees," Mr. Powers said.

1. Do you agree that Culinova should introduce a lower priced line? Why or why not?
2. What risks does Culinova face in offering a lower priced line?

APPENDIX 19A

BASIC DEMAND AND REVENUE CONCEPTS

Total Revenue

Total revenue *(TR)* is the total amount of money received from the sale of a product. It equals the price *(P)* times the quantity sold *(Q)*, or

$$TR = P \times Q$$

Assume General Motors introduces its new Saturn line of low-priced subcompact cars in 1990. GM has planned the introduction of the Saturn line for almost a decade. It has attempted to decrease costs of the car to a level that will enable it to compete with Japanese imports on a price basis. Assume it introduces the car at a price of $8,500 and sells 50,000 cars. Total revenue will be $425 million. Sales of 80,000 cars at this price would produce a total revenue of $680 million.

Average Revenue

Average revenue *(AR)* is the average amount of money received for selling one unit of a product. It is computed as total revenue divided by quantity, so

$$AR = TR/Q$$

In the above example, the average revenue for the Saturn car at 50,000 units is $425 million/50,000 or $8,500. This is also the price of the car, so average revenue is the same as price.

Suppose GM asks consumers whether they would buy a Saturn at $8,000, $8,500, $9,000, $10,000 and $11,000. Consumer responses allow the company to estimate the quantity likely to be purchased at each price. It can then establish a demand curve for the Saturn. Let us assume GM establishes the price-quantity relations in the first two columns of Table 19A.1. The resulting demand curve is shown as Curve D in Figure 19.2 in the chapter.

TABLE 19A.1
Revenue Information from Demand Curve for Saturn Car

PRICE	QUANTITY	TOTAL REVENUE (in Millions) [P × Q]	CHANGE IN QUANTITY	CHANGE IN TOTAL REVENUE (in Millions)	MARGINAL REVENUE [Change in TR/ Change in Q]
$11,000	30,000	$330	—	—	—
$10,000	50,000	$500	20,000	$170	$8,500
$ 9,000	80,000	$720	30,000	$220	$7,330
$ 8,500	87,000	$740	7,000	$ 20	$2,860
$ 8,000	95,000	$760	8,000	$ 20	$2,500

The demand curve is also known as the average revenue curve since it shows the average revenue (i.e., price) that is obtained at various levels of consumer demand (i.e., quantity).

Marginal Revenue

Marginal revenue *(MR)* is the change in total revenue (ΔTR) obtained by selling additional quantities of a product (ΔQ). In the Saturn example, Table 19A.1 shows that a cut in price from $10,000 to $9,000 would result in sales of an additional 30,000 units. The total revenue at $10,000 is $500 million, and at $9,000 it is $720 million. So ΔTR is $220 million, and ΔQ is 30,000. As a result, if 80,000 units are sold, then

$$MR = \$220 \text{ million}/30{,}000 \text{ units} = \$7{,}330$$

The $7,330 in marginal revenue is the revenue derived from selling the 80,001st car.

APPENDIX 19B

BASIC COST CONCEPTS

Fixed Costs

Fixed costs are expenses that are constant regardless of the quantity produced. For example, the cost of constructing a plant is fixed, regardless of the quantity produced in the plant.

Variable Costs

Variable costs vary directly with the amount produced. They include the cost of labor and raw materials used to make the product, plus the cost of distribution and personal selling. *Average variable costs (AVC)* are the variable costs in producing one unit of a product at a certain quantity. *Total variable costs* are average variable costs times the quantity produced; that is,

$$TVC = AVC \times Q$$

Total Costs

Total costs *(TC)* are the total expenses incurred in producing and marketing a product. Total costs are the sum of *total fixed costs (TFC)* and *total variable costs (TVC);* therefore,

$$TC = TFC + TVC$$

Marginal Costs

Marginal costs *(MC)* are the changes in total costs (ΔTC) that result in producing and marketing additional quantities of a product (ΔQ). Therefore,

$$MC = \Delta TC/\Delta Q$$

Cost Interrelationships

The interrelationships between these costs are demonstrated in Table 19B.1. Assume that the fixed costs in

TABLE 19B.1
Cost Factors in Producing the Saturn Car

AVERAGE COST PER UNIT [AVC]		QUANTITY [Q]		TOTAL VARIABLE COSTS [TVC]		TOTAL FIXED COSTS [TFC] (in Millions of Dollars)		TOTAL COSTS [TC]	CHANGE IN Q	CHANGE IN TC (in Millions)	MARGINAL COST [Change in TC/ Change in Q]
$7,000	×	30,000	=	$210	+	$200	=	$410	—	—	—
$6,000	×	50,000	=	$300	+	$200	=	$500	20,000	90	$4,500
$5,000	×	80,000	=	$400	+	$200	=	$600	30,000	100	$3,300
$4,800	×	87,000	=	$418	+	$200	=	$618	7,000	18	$2,570
$4,700	×	95,000	=	$446	+	$200	=	$646	8,000	28	$3,500

establishing the production facilities for the Saturn are $200 million. At 30,000 units of production, average variable costs (*AVC*, that is, the variable costs in producing one unit of a product) are $7,000 per car. Total variable costs would be $210 million ($7,000 × 30,000 units). Total costs would be $410 million (total variable costs plus total fixed costs).

Note that as more cars are produced, average variable costs per unit go down. This is because the company is achieving economies of scale in production. If GM can lower average variable costs sufficiently through better production methods, it can follow a low-price strategy to compete more effectively.

Table 19B.1 also shows marginal costs decreasing until the company produces 87,000 cars. By the time 87,000 units are produced, it costs only an additional $2,570 to produce the 87,001 unit. At this point, marginal costs begin to rise, possibly because the company is coming close to reaching its full production capacity.

NOTES

1. "Computer Technology to Go," *Personal Computing,* November 1987, p. 173.

2. *Personal Computing,* November 1987, p. 170.

3. "Entrepreneur in Short Pants," *Forbes,* March 7, 1988, p. 85.

4. *Personal Computing,* November 1987, p. 174.

5. Dell Computer Corp., *Prospectus,* Goldman, Sachs & Co., June 1988, p. 21.

6. Dell Computer Corp, *Prospectus,* Goldman, Sachs & Co., June 1988, p. 3.

7. "Michael Dell: The Enfant Terrible of Personal Computers," *Business Week,* June 13, 1988, p. 61.

8. "Pricing Competition Is Shaping Up as '84's Top Marketing 'Pressure Point'," *Marketing News,* November 11, 1983, p. 1.

9. "Zenith Is Sticking Its Neck Out in a Cutthroat Market," *Business Week,* August 17, 1987, p. 72.

10. "Cheap Smokes: The Market That's on Fire," *Business Week,* April 14, 1986, p. 41.

11. "Deregulating America," *Business Week,* November 28, 1983, p. 80.

12. "Lilly Cuts Price 12% on Major Herbicide to Lift Market Share," *The Wall Street Journal,* December 15, 1982, p. 10.

13. Thomas Nagle, "Pricing as Creative Marketing," *Business Horizons,* July–August 1983, p. 15.

14. "How Bic Lost the Edge to Gillette," *The New York Times,* April 11, 1982, p. F7.

15. "Helene Curtis' New Line Bucks Price-Brand Trend," *Adweek's Marketing Week,* June 22, 1987, p. 6.

16. *Business Week,* April 14, 1986, p. 41.

17. "Pricey Ice Cream Is Scooping the Market," *Business Week,* June 30, 1986, p. 60.

18. "Chocolate Marketers Fatten Sales with Bigger Bars," *Marketing & Media Decisions,* September 1982, p. 69.

19. *Marketing & Media Decisions,* September 1982, p. 65.

20. "The Price Is Wrong," *Industry Week,* December 8, 1986, p. 28.

21. "IBM Cuts Prices of Personal Computers in Response to Inroads Made by 'Clones'," *The Wall Street Journal,* July 9, 1986, p. 3.

22. "Gas Marketers Are Over a Barrel," *Ad Forum,* November 1982, pp. 12–18.

23. "Mark Laracy's Obsession," *INC.,* May 1988, pp. 70–82.

24. Ibid., p. 70.

25. Ibid., pp. 76–77.

26. Ibid., p. 82.

27. "Computer Firms Push Prices Down, Try to Improve Marketing Tactics," *The Wall Street Journal,* April 29, 1983, p. 35.

28. "Bausch & Lomb: Hardball Pricing Helps It to Regain Its Grip in Contact Lenses," *Business Week,* July 16, 1984, p. 78.

29. "Scripto's New Script," *Madison Avenue,* August 1985, p. 38.

30. "Audi Rebate Plan on 5000 Model Has the Look of Bait and Switch, *The Wall Street Journal,* June 21, 1988, p. 41.

31. Victor E. Grimm, "Some Legal Pitfalls" in *Pricing Practices and Strategies* edited by Earl L. Bailey (New York: The Conference Board, 1978), pp. 19–23.

32. "Panasonic to Pay Rebates to Avoid Antitrust Charges," *The Wall Street Journal,* January 19, 1989, pp. B1, B6.

GENERAL MOTORS — IS ITS COST-ORIENTED PRICING A PROBLEM?

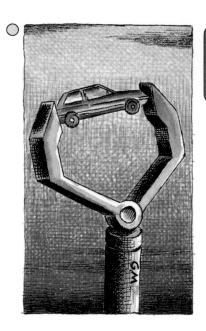

General Motors is in a bind these days, and its cost-oriented approach to pricing may have a lot to do with its problems. Its market share dropped from 45 percent in 1981 to 36 percent in 1988.[1] During these seven years, it went from being the low-cost producer among domestic car makers to being the high-cost producer. And, it saw Ford pull ahead in earnings for the first time.[2]

What happened? For one thing, GM moved quickly to develop smaller cars in response to the energy crisis in the 1970s. A good consumer-oriented response, you might say? Yes, except that redesigning its cars drove costs of production up. The company spent $5.2 billion on new plants and retooling in 1980 alone.[3] As costs went up, prices went up, and GM quickly began losing market share to cheaper Japanese imports. Second, when gas prices came down, many consumers went back to buying larger cars. But GM did not shift gears. It continued along with its small-car strategy while Ford and Chrysler were offering larger cars.

What does all this have to do with cost-oriented pricing? If a company sets its prices based on cost, and it becomes the high-cost producer in the industry, then it is at a competitive disadvantage. It can increase its price above that of competitors, or it can hold the line on price and see its profit margins shrink. Either course is undesirable.

GM prices on a cost-oriented basis. It starts out by designing a car for a particular target segment, checking on competitive prices, and making a rough estimate of the volume that it can sell. The company then estimates its fixed and variable costs per unit at this volume level and adds a certain profit margin to determine the price. It then evaluates the market to determine whether consumers are likely to buy the projected volume at the proposed price. If it appears the

price is too high to achieve the target return, the company can either try to cut costs or withdraw the model.[4]

This pricing method is also used by Ford and Chrysler. Then why is it creating a potential problem for GM? Because GM's costs average $250 per car higher than Ford's or Chrysler's, and at least $1,500 higher than those of Japanese imports.[5] In addition, GM's pricing does not take account of the consumer's response to price. As one auto industry consultant said in commenting on a price rise for GM's 1987 cars:

> *GM in September announced a 5 percent average increase in car prices. They said the reason is our costs went up . . . [But] customers don't care a lot about a company's costs. If prices were set by the relative value of the product offered to the customer, then costs could follow price . . . rather than the other way around.*[6]

In other words, if price is based on consumer demand, then the next step is to determine whether costs permit the company to produce the product profitably at the proposed price. This is what the executive means by costs following price.

GM recognizes it must get its costs down to remain competitive. It has automated many of its plants to reduce labor costs. It has gone overseas to buy cheaper components. It has strengthened its accounting system to keep better track of costs. And it is developing its Saturn cars based on cost-saving statistical control techniques borrowed from the Japanese. Savings of $500 million are expected by replacing obsolete manufacturing operations and plants. Based on some of these steps, it already achieved an overall cost savings of $3.7 billion in 1987 and a significant improvement in profits.[7]

Whether GM will go the one additional step and switch from a cost- to a demand-oriented basis for pricing remains to be seen. ☐

● ● ●

DETERMINING THE FINAL PRICE

In the last chapter, we saw how marketers set the groundwork for determining prices by defining objectives; estimating consumer demand, costs, and profits; and then developing pricing strategies. In this chapter, we continue to focus on the process of determining a particular price for a product. We will now consider the shaded areas shown in Figure 19.1 in the last chapter, namely alternative approaches marketers use to determine the final price, the adjustments they make to this price, and how they evaluate and control pricing actions.

In this section, we will describe three methods of setting prices; cost-oriented, demand-oriented, and competition-oriented pricing methods (see Figure 20.1).

COST-ORIENTED PRICING METHODS

Cost-oriented pricing methods are most widely used because they are simple. Cost-oriented methods tend to lead to stable prices over time since prices are set based on factors internal to the company, such as labor costs and availability of raw materials. The basic limitation of these methods is that they tend to ignore crucial factors outside the company such as customer demand and competition. Cost-based methods work reasonably well only in industries where consumer demand and competition are stable. General Motors' use of cost-based methods could cause problems in the face of a downturn in demand or increased competition from lower-priced imports.

There are two cost-oriented pricing methods: cost-plus pricing and target-return pricing.

Cost-Plus Pricing

In **cost-plus pricing**, the marketer simply determines the unit costs for producing an item (variable and fixed costs per unit) and adds a margin to meet a profit objective. Assume a firm decides to introduce a superpremium brand of ice cream and prices it on a cost-plus basis. It determines its variable costs for producing the superpremium brand (primarily raw materials and labor) at $1.50 per pint. It assumes that variable costs will not change much as a function of quantity because it anticipates few improvements in productivity or other labor efficiencies as volume increases.

The company determines that fixed costs (cost of plant and machinery and administrative costs) are approximately 30 percent of variable costs, or 45 cents

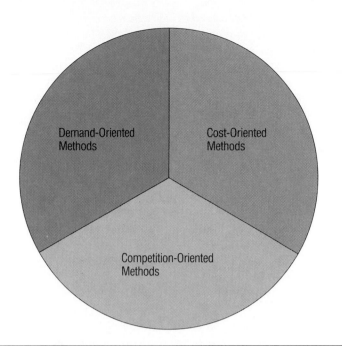

FIGURE 20.1
Methods of Price Determination

per unit. Its profit objective is to achieve a 20 percent return on variable costs, or 30 cents per unit ($1.50 × 20%). On this basis, it computes price as

Variable costs per unit	$1.50
Fixed costs per unit (30% of variable costs)	.45
Profit margin (20% of variable costs)	.30
Price per pint of ice cream	$2.25

The price of $2.25 is what the company charges retailers for its ice cream. Now assume a retailer also uses a cost-plus approach in determining the price it will sell to final consumers. In most cases, retailers will determine a profit margin based on the final selling price rather than the total cost of the item. This profit margin is known as a **markup**. Assume a retailer marks up the ice cream by 25 percent. The final selling price that will give the retailer a profit margin of 25 percent can be computed as follows:

$$\text{Retail Selling Price} = \frac{\text{Average Cost of the Unit}}{1 - \text{Desired Margin}}$$

In our example, this would be:

$$\frac{\$2.25}{1 - .25} = \$3.00$$

The final selling price to the customer would thus be $3.00.

A problem with a cost-plus or markup approach is that there is no guarantee it will produce a final price in line with what consumers are willing to pay. Consumer responses to price never enter into the decision. Further, a company following a cost-plus approach may price itself out of the market if its costs are higher than those of competitors.

Target-Return Pricing

Many firms set a target return on their investment or on costs, and then price to achieve this target. **Target-return pricing** determines the price that will achieve a profit target at a specified volume level. In contrast, cost-plus pricing determines price by tacking a fixed profit margin onto costs regardless of volume.

There are two types of target-return pricing: *target return on investment* and *target return on costs*. The first establishes a *return on investment* (ROI) objective and prices to meet it. Suppose the ice cream producer's initial investment to establish the business and manufacturing plant was $500,000. The company sets an ROI objective of 10 percent, because this is the best return it could expect from putting its $500,000 in some other investment. The company's profit objective in the first year of operation is therefore $50,000.

Assume projected quantity of the superpremium ice cream is 100,000 units. We noted previously that variable costs in producing the ice cream are $1.50 per unit, and fixed costs are 45 cents per unit. So total costs are $195,000 ([$1.50 + .45] × 100,000 units). With a profit goal of $50,000, we can find the price that will achieve that goal as follows:

$$\text{Price} = \frac{\$50,000(\text{Profits}) + \$195,000(\text{Costs})}{100,000 \text{ units}} = \$2.45$$

A price of $2.45 will achieve a profit goal of $50,000 if 100,000 units of ice cream are sold. However, this approach does not tell us whether consumers will actually buy 100,000 units of the ice cream at $2.45.

A firm can also determine price based on a target return on its total costs at a specified volume level. This is the method the American auto companies generally use. An example for pricing a compact is shown in Table 20.1. Variable costs, including raw materials and labor (vehicle assembly), total $3,974. Fixed costs are estimated at 40 percent of variable costs, or $1,590. The profit target is 10 percent of total costs, or $556 (10 percent of $3,974 + $1,590). Additional unallocated costs (research and development, tooling) are $2,472. The sales price to the auto dealer totals $8,592. The dealer's markup of 22 percent would result in a final price of $11,016, but the company might decide to list the car for $10,995 for promotional purposes.

DEMAND-ORIENTED PRICING METHODS

Demand-oriented methods base price on what consumers are willing to buy at various price levels: That is, price is based on the consumers' demand curve. Marketers are paying more attention to demand-oriented pricing because cost-oriented methods are too rigid for the competitive environment of the 1990s. If costs are stable, a company's prices are stable; if costs go up, its prices go up. But price changes are not in response to customer demand or competition.

The need for greater price flexibility became apparent as marketers began to realize that the American consumer was increasingly price-sensitive, and as they

TABLE 20.1
Target Return on Cost Pricing
in the Auto Industry

Source: Adapted from "Why Detroit Can't Cut Prices,"
Business Week, March 1, 1982. Costs adjusted to reflect 1990 prices.

ASSEMBLY PLANT		CORPORATE HEADQUARTERS		DEALER SHOWROOM	
Body	$1,104	Total variable cost (TVC)	$3,974	Cost to dealer	$ 8,592
Trans- mission	$ 180	Fixed costs (TFC): 40% of TVC:	$1,590	Dealer markup	
Engine	$ 622			(22%)	$ 2,424
Chassis	$1,002	Profit target: (10% of TFC + TVC)	$ 556		
Vehicle assembly	$1,066	R&D, special tooling	$2,472		
Total variable costs	$3,974	Total cost to dealer	$8,592	List price	$11,016

became aware that they would have to compete with foreign competitors by providing the same value to consumers, dollar for dollar.

There are three demand-oriented pricing methods to choose from: marginal pricing and flexible break-even pricing, which rely on an estimate of the demand curve, and demand-backward pricing, which does not.

Marginal Pricing

In the last chapter, we saw that if the marginal revenue from the last unit sold is greater than the marginal cost in producing and marketing it, changing the price will increase profits. If demand is inelastic, price would increase; if it is elastic, price would decrease. **Marginal pricing** therefore requires the marketer to change price up to the point where marginal revenue equals marginal cost. At that price, the marginal contribution to profit (marginal revenue less marginal cost) of the last unit produced is zero.

The principle is illustrated using the example of the Saturn in Figure 20.2. In our previous example, GM determined that the point at which marginal revenues equal marginal cost for the last unit produced is at about 87,000 units. This is the point where the marginal revenue and cost curves intersect (point *x* in the figure). But how does GM know what price to charge at that point? By referring to the demand curve. The demand curve in Figure 20.2 (we saw in Appendix 19A in the last chapter that this is the same as the *average revenue curve*) shows that consumers are willing to buy 87,000 units at a price of $8,500. This is determined by identifying the intersection of the marginal revenue and cost curves, and then extending a line up to the average revenue (i.e., *demand*) curve (point *y* in the figure). At that point, the profit-maximizing price is $8,500.

Marginal pricing identifies the profit-maximizing price, but it requires estimating the demand curve. The difficulty in determining how much consumers are willing to buy at various price levels is the main reason that marginal pricing is not used more widely.

FIGURE 20.2
Marginal Pricing

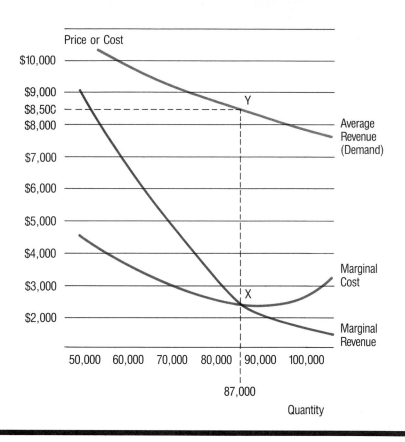

Flexible Break-Even Pricing

Since the method of **flexible break-even pricing** is an offshoot of break-even analysis, it would be helpful to review the principles of *break-even analysis* described in Appendix 20A at the end of this chapter. In this type of pricing, price is determined by maximizing the difference between total revenue and total cost across various levels of demand. A number of alternative prices are considered, producing a different *total revenue curve* for each price. Assume an ice cream manufacturer tests a superpremium ice cream at four prices, $1.75, $2.25, $3.00 and $3.50. Figure 20.3 shows the total revenue (price × quantity) for each price level. The area of profitability is the difference between total revenue and total cost, and this is the shaded area in the figure.

Assume the company tested each price in a test market to estimate demand. At a price of $3.50, demand is estimated at 100,000 units, and at $1.75 it is estimated at 400,000 units. The difference between total revenues and costs at the level demanded at each price is shown by the solid vertical line. The difference between total revenue and total cost is greatest at a price of $3.00. This is shown by the fact that the solid vertical line is longest at a quantity of 300,000 units.

Because flexible break-even pricing requires estimates of consumer responses to prices, it is a demand-oriented method of pricing. It should produce results similar to those of marginal analysis, since both use the criterion of maximizing short-term profit based on consumer demand.

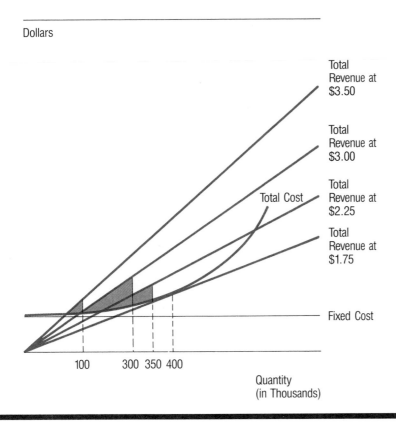

FIGURE 20.3
Flexible Break-Even Pricing

Demand-Backward Pricing

In **demand-backward pricing**, prices are set by determining what consumers are willing to pay for an item, then deducting costs to determine if the profit margin is adequate. This is considered estimating "backwards" because the marketer starts with a final price based on consumer demand and works backward to the profit estimate. It is more common to estimate "forward" by starting with a cost and adding a profit margin.

Demand-backward pricing avoids the complexities of marginal or flexible break-even pricing methods. Instead of determining a series of price-quantity relationships in the form of a demand curve for a product, the marketer only has to learn one price-quantity relationship, the price consumers are willing to pay and the estimated volume for the particular product at that price. The catch is knowing this single price.

Dell Computer used demand-backward pricing when it determined what price for its PCs would be competitive with IBM's Personal System/2 line. It knew it wanted to come in with a price under $1,000 and then determined if it could do so profitably. It did, with a price of $995.

Charles Lazarus, founder of Toys "Я" Us uses demand-backward pricing almost by intuition. Most toy retailers set their price based on what they have to pay wholesalers. According to one of his associates, Lazarus would first say, "I can sell this product in great volumes at a certain price."[8] He would then decide at what price he had to buy it, and would either obtain the item at that price or not sell it. What makes Lazarus the most successful toy retailer in history is the fact that he is right nine times out of ten about that "certain price." One of the few times he was wrong was when he believed that Cabbage Patch Kids would never catch on. His executives prevailed, and Toys "Я" Us carried the item, one of the few items priced on a cost basis rather than on Lazarus's intuitive demand-backward approach.

Jennie Rogers* — Should She Price Based on Costs or Demand?

*The characters cited herein are fictional, but the story is based on actual events.

Jennie Rogers is an eight-year-old entrepreneur who started her own car wash business in the driveway of her home in a suburb of Boston. It all started when she approached her father, the national sales manager for a pharmaceutical company, and asked him if he wanted his car washed for $3.00. He asked her how she arrived at that price. She said she had two friends who would help her, and they wanted $1.00 each, so she thought she should get a dollar also.

Her father thought her pricing method sounded pretty familiar — establish costs and add a profit margin. In fact, that was the pricing method his company had used until the early 1980s. He accepted the $3.00 price, and Jennie made her first sale. She and her friends then set up a big sign in the driveway — "Jennie's Car Wash: $3.00" — and began to solicit neighborhood business on the weekends. The first weekend they got three customers; the next weekend they got four.

Jennie then started thinking, "Should I raise my price to $4.00?" In fairness to her two friends, she would split the $4.00 three ways. (It took a little figuring to determine exactly what that would come to.) She approached her father and asked what he thought about the price increase. "Well," he said, "I'd think twice about having my car washed for $4.00, but I guess I would go ahead and do it maybe once a month. But I have an idea. Why don't you ask a few people around the neighborhood whether they would have their car washed for $4.00 and if not, how they would feel about a $3.00 car wash." Jennie thought that was a great idea.

A few days later, Jennie went back to her father and said, "I talked to eight people. Three said they would have their car washed at $4.00. Another two said no to $4.00 but yes to $3.00. And three said they weren't interested in a car wash." When her father asked her what her pricing decision was, he was surprised by her astute reasoning. "You know," she said, "If I price at $4.00, I'll be making an extra buck per customer, but I'll be losing two customers. If I charge $3.00, I'll keep all five customers. My friends and I figured it out. Three customers at $4.00 is $12.00. But five customers at $3.00 is $15.00, and we decided we would prefer to make the three extra dollars. So we're going to leave the price at $3.00."

Jennie's Dad reflected on her decision process and realized that, in a rather basic way, Jennie had shifted from a cost-oriented to a demand-oriented basis for pricing. She decided between the $3.00 and $4.00 price by talking to prospective customers and determining their intentions. She then selected the price that would maximize her total revenues.

Jennie's father was rather satisfied with her decision because his firm had implemented a demand-oriented pricing approach in the early 1980s, largely on his initiative. As national sales manager, he realized a more flexible approach to pricing was needed than the current cost-plus method, and he convinced his salespeople to try to determine the price sensitivities of their customers. Prices were then based on customers' projected responses to alternative price levels rather than on costs. Profits improved as a result.

A shift from cost to demand-oriented pricing seems to have worked for both Jennie and her father. ◼

Some companies base their prices on what competitors do. In this case, they risk setting prices that do not take account of distinctions between their products and those of competitors. Three types of pricing methods are based on competitive actions: follow-the-leader pricing, pricing pegged to prevailing industry norms, and pricing based on expected competitive responses.

COMPETITION-ORIENTED PRICING METHODS

Follow-the-Leader Pricing

As we saw in the last chapter, industries producing standardized products seek price stability because price competition can lead to destructive price wars. A company emerges that is recognized by others as a price leader, and a tacit understanding develops that companies will use **follow-the-leader pricing**. Such pricing is most likely to occur in an **oligopoly** — that is, an industry dominated by several large companies in which the pricing actions of one company directly affect the others. Since products are standardized, a price reduction by one company would force others to follow, resulting in a price war. As a result, it is in the interest of companies in an oligopoly to create price stability by agreeing to follow a price leader.

Follow-the-leader pricing is less common than it once was, because the government has frowned on such methods as a form of price fixing, even when there is no overt agreement to fix prices. Also, as we saw, greater foreign competition and consumer price sensitivity have led to a need to develop more flexible methods of pricing.

Some industries still have price leaders, however. IBM is regarded as the undisputed price leader in computer software. One software competitor said, "IBM sets the trends we all follow." Another described a clear follow-the-leader policy: "The higher IBM's prices are, the more we can charge."[9] But IBM's prices are not followed as rigorously by competitors as Alcoa's and U.S. Steel's once were in the aluminum and steel industries.

Pegged Pricing

Companies in an industry without a price leader might carry out a strategy for price stability by pegging their prices to industry norms. Candy bar manufacturers have tended to use such **pegged pricing**. They establish a price norm for an individual candy bar, and most companies stick to the norm.

TABLE 20.2
Determining Price Based on Estimated Competitive Responses

[a]Optimal price change to maximize expected ROI

PRICE DECREASE FOR TREFLAN	ESTIMATED RETURN ON INVESTMENT (ROI)	PROBABILITY OF NO COMPETITIVE ENTRY AT STATED PRICE	EXPECTED ROI IF NO ENTRY (ESTIMATED ROI TIMES PROBABILITY OF NO COMPETITIVE ENTRY)
5%	15%	20%	3.0%
10%	12%	40%	4.8%
12%[a]	10%	50%	5.0%
15%	6%	80%	4.8%
20%	4%	90%	3.6%

Some companies use the industry norm as a baseline and price a certain percentage above or below it. This is a common practice for a company trying to establish a niche on the high or low side of the market. The marketer then works back from this premium or economy price to determine if a reasonable profit can be made.

Pricing Based on Projected Reactions by Competitors

Some firms set price levels based on their estimate of competitive responses to their actions. Assume that Eli Lilly is considering the five price reductions for its Treflan herbicide shown in Table 20.2. Return on investment falls with each price decrease: a 15 percent return on investment if the price of Treflan is reduced by 5 percent, a 12 percent ROI if price is reduced by 10 percent, and so forth. Lilly's managers estimate that there is only a 20 percent chance that competition will *not* enter the market if the price of Treflan is reduced by 5 percent, a 40 percent chance if the price is reduced by 10 percent, and so forth (column 3 in Table 20.2).

The last column weights ROI by the chance of *no* competitive entry. As we see, expected ROI is maximized when the price of Treflan is reduced by 12 percent. At that price reduction, *expected* ROI is 5 percent. If the price reduction is any less than 12 percent, the chance of competitive entry is too high. If the price reduction is any more than 12 percent, ROI decreases to unacceptable levels. So management decides to decrease price by 12 percent, largely based on estimated competitive reactions to the company's price changes.

PRICE ADJUSTMENTS

The price that the marketer establishes in the previous step is the quoted price, or **list price**. This is the price that might appear in a catalog or be quoted by a salesperson as the company's "official" price subject to discounts. The list price is sometimes the same as the final selling price. But in the majority of cases, the manufacturer makes some adjustment in the list price. This is the fifth step in the process of price determination.

These adjustments to list price are often made both to the trade and to the final customer. When IBM offers a discount to computer retailers buying a large number of personal computers, when Folgers offers a price promotion on its coffee, or when Ford authorizes its dealer to offer trade-in allowances on used cars, these companies are adjusting their list price downward. The Buick ad in Exhibit 20.1 shows a $19,556 list price for the Electra with options. Two discounts are shown,

EXHIBIT 20.1
An Example of Adjustments
on the List Price

a discount for selecting the option package, and a cash rebate of $1,000. The actual price after adjustments is $18,166.

Five types of adjustments off the list price are frequently used as shown in Figure 20.4: discounts, allowances, price promotions, geographic price adjustments, and odd-even prices.

DISCOUNTS

When a seller offers a buyer a reduction off the list price for taking certain actions that reduce the seller's costs, the reduction is known as a **discount**. The discount could be an incentive to buy in quantity, perform certain marketing functions, buy at a certain time of year, or pay bills quickly.

Quantity Discounts

Quantity discounts are given to buyers for buying in volume. Volume purchases decrease the costs of order taking, processing, and delivery, and may also decrease the unit costs of production because of economies of scale in larger production runs.

Quantity discounts may be noncumulative or cumulative. *Noncumulative discounts* are limited to one order. For example, IBM offers up to 40 percent off list price to retailers buying large numbers of its Personal System/2 computers at one time.[10] *Cumulative discounts* allow a buyer to aggregate all purchases over a year. For example, a manufacturer of industrial generators might offer distributors a 10 percent discount if they buy more than 100 units in a year. Cumulative discounts are an important strategic tool, since they encourage the customer to continue to buy from the same company to qualify for a discount.

FIGURE 20.4
Types of Price Adjustments

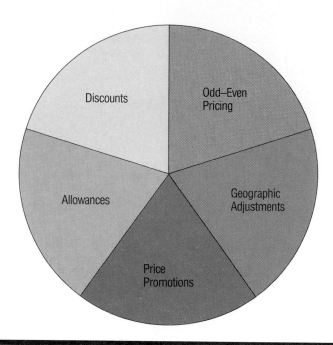

Some companies not only offer cumulative discounts for one of their products, but also allow buyers to accumulate discounts across their product lines. Assume a company like Merrill Lynch buys 20 different computer systems from IBM over the course of a year, and IBM gives Merrill Lynch a 16 percent discount on these purchases. Such a discount encourages customers to buy a range of products from the same manufacturer to qualify for a savings. It is a means of encouraging vendor loyalty.

Trade Discounts

Producers grant **trade discounts** to retailers and wholesalers for performing the marketing functions required to sell to the final consumer. This trade discount is the retailer's and wholesaler's *profit margin*, since it represents the difference between what retailers and wholesalers pay the manufacturer and what they can sell the product for. Trade discounts are also a way producers can get retailers and wholesalers to stock a new item. The traditional retail discount for personal computers is 22 percent. A new computer manufacturer might offer a 30 percent discount to get computer retailers to stock its products.

Table 20.3 shows an example of a trade discount structure for a superpremium ice cream that lists for $3.00 a pint. Assume that the manufacturer distributes the ice cream through food brokers, who then distribute to wholesalers and retailers. The trade discount is stated as $3.00 less 30/10/5. This means the discount is 30 percent to retailers, 10 percent to wholesalers, and 5 percent to food brokers. (The intermediary closest to the consumer is listed first.) The reason that retailers get more of a discount than wholesalers or food brokers is that they usually perform more functions in selling to consumers.

Starting with the list price of $3.00, a 30 percent discount to retailers means they are buying the product at $2.10 per unit. Wholesalers get 10 percent off the suggested retail price of $2.10 and pay $1.89 for the product. Food brokers get 5

TABLE 20.3
Discount Structure from the List Price

List price	$3.00
Trade discount ($3.00 less 30/10/5)	
Retailer discount at 30%	− .90
Wholesaler's selling price to retailer	$2.10
Wholesaler discount at 10%	− .21
Broker's selling price to wholesaler	$1.89
Food broker discount at 5%	− .09
Manufacturer's selling price to broker	$1.80
Quantity discount	
10% off list price	− .30
Manufacturer's selling price to broker with trade and quantity discount	$1.50
Seasonal discount	
4% if purchased from December to March	− .06
Manufacturer's selling price to broker with trade, quantity, and seasonal discount	$1.44
Cash discount (2/10 net 30)	
2% if paid in 10 days; net due in 30 days	− .03
Manufacturer's selling price to broker with all discounts	$1.41

percent off the wholesale price and pay $1.80. The company also offers a quantity discount of 10 percent off the list price of $3.00 for orders of 1,000 or more. Assuming the food broker orders more than 1,000 items, the price would then be $1.50 per item to the broker. An additional seasonal and cash discount could bring the price to the broker down to $1.41 per unit. This is the price that the manufacturer gets for selling the item to the food broker. The spread between the manufacturer's selling price of $1.41 and the final list price of $3.00 is represented by the various discounts in Table 20.3.

Seasonal Discounts

Manufacturers facing seasonal demand for their product offer discounts to encourage customers to buy in the off-season. Buyers obtain the products more cheaply then and stock them for the busy season. **Seasonal discounts** help buyers, since savings are usually more than the additional costs of keeping the products in inventory. They also help sellers to smooth out their production runs. The alternative would be higher unit costs of production in season, and possible layoffs in the off-season.

Products such as boats, skiing equipment, or snow blowers are good candidates for seasonal discounts. Table 20.3 shows a seasonal discount being offered by an ice cream manufacturer in the winter months when demand is lowest. Since ice cream is perishable, the discount is not meant to encourage retailers to stock the item for the summer. Rather, it is meant to get them to spur demand for the product during the winter months through in-store promotions and favorable shelf positions in freezer compartments.

Cash Discounts

Through **cash discounts**, manufacturers encourage buyers to pay their bills quickly. This permits manufacturers to maintain their liquidity and to avoid the costs of collecting bills that are past due. Buyers find it economical to pay quickly, since the savings usually outweigh any revenues they might obtain by holding onto their money longer.

In Table 20.3, the cash discount is stated as 2/10 net 30, which means that the food broker can take a 2 percent discount on the selling price of $1.44 by paying the amount within 10 days of the billing date, but the net amount is due in 30 days. If the food broker buys 2,000 units, this would represent a savings of 3 cents a unit, or $60.

Companies also offer consumers cash discounts. Examples include lower prices at cash-only gas pumps and discounts offered by some stores for cash sales rather than those paid with checks or credit cards.

ALLOWANCES

Allowances are payments to the buyer from the seller in exchange for goods, or for taking certain actions. The most common type is a **trade-in allowance**, which is a price reduction for trading in a used product as part payment for a new one. Car dealers can lower the price of a car without changing the list price by simply offering more for a used car. Some retailers also allow electronics and appliances to be traded in.

Allowances that manufacturers give to retailers to advertise their products are known as **promotional allowances**. As we saw in Chapter 16, such allowances form the basis for cooperative advertising between manufacturers and retailers. Retailers insert their name into the manufacturer's ad, allowing them to advertise on the local level while making the manufacturer's products more visible.

PRICE PROMOTIONS

Price promotions were cited in Chapter 16 as short-term discounts offered by manufacturers to get consumers to try a product. They allow a manufacturer to temporarily reduce price without changing the listed price. Promotions such as cents-off deals are effective in countering competitive price reductions or in getting users of competitive brands to try the product.

Manufacturers use price promotions primarily for lower-priced goods in their line. General Foods frequently runs price promotions for its regular Maxwell House coffee brands but does not run promotions for its top-of-the-line Maxwell House Private Collection coffees. Similarly, our ice cream manufacturer would be wary of running a price promotion on its superpremium brand for fear of hurting its quality image.

If not overused, price promotions are an effective means of adjusting price to short-term changes in competitive conditions.

GEOGRAPHIC PRICE ADJUSTMENTS

Companies also adjust their prices to reflect differences in transportation costs from seller to buyer. These adjustments are most important for bulky products with high transportation costs. The methods for pricing to reflect transportation costs are called *free-on-board* (FOB) *origin pricing* and *delivered pricing*.

FOB Origin Pricing

In **free on board (FOB) origin pricing**, the price is determined at the point of origin and does not include transportation costs. The buyer gets the product delivered on board some vehicle such as a truck or a railroad car at the point of origin (usually the seller's plant) and pays for all transportation costs to the final destination.

Prices quoted FOB are the same to all buyers. Since buyers must absorb transportation costs, the buyer that is most distant from the seller is at a cost disadvantage. As a result, most buyers try to purchase at closer points of origin. Sellers using FOB pricing try to establish plants and warehouse locations across the country so that a point of origin is reasonably close to almost any buyer.

Delivered Pricing

In **delivered pricing**, the price is adjusted to include transportation costs. There are four widely used methods of delivered pricing: Single-zone pricing, multiple-zone pricing, basing-point pricing, and freight-absorption pricing.

Single-zone pricing means that all buyers pay the same price for the product regardless of where they are located. The seller builds in average transportation charges per unit as part of the total cost of the item but does not vary price depending on the buyer's location. This means that buyers close to the seller are subsidizing the transportation costs of buyers further away. General Foods charges the same list price for a can of Maxwell House to retailers across the country. If the point of origin is the New York area, then a supermarket in New York is actually paying a higher price per mile for transportation than a supermarket in California.

A company is most likely to use single-zone pricing when transportation costs are a small part of the final price. In such cases, customers closer to the seller are unlikely to make an issue of the fact they are absorbing freight costs of more distant customers.

In **multiple-zone pricing**, a firm divides its selling territory into geographic zones, and the price depends upon transportation costs from the seller's location to the buyer's zone. A zone system makes sense if transportation costs are high. Customers close to the seller would object to a uniform price. Zones provide a basis for accounting for different transportation costs in different parts of the country. Under such a system, an appliance manufacturer might charge a different price depending on whether a customer is in New England, in the Midwest, in the South, or in the West.

Another delivered-pricing method is **basing-point pricing**, in which the company establishes a location called a *basing point* from which transportation charges are added to the list price. The steel industry used basing-point pricing for years, charging for steel from Pittsburgh, the basing point, because the city was the historic center of the steel industry. Under this system, if a firm is located in Indianapolis and buys steel from nearby Fort Wayne, Indiana, it will still be charged for transportation from Pittsburgh. Such charges for nonexistent freight are known as **phantom freight**.

Multiple-zone and basing-point pricing could both be illegal if there is evidence that firms have conspired to establish the zones and fix prices. If, for example, several firms have exactly the same zones and the same price differences across zones, this would be construed as evidence of collusion in setting up geographic areas and freight charges and would be regarded as illegal.

As the name implies, in **freight-absorption pricing** the seller absorbs the total cost of transportation. The buyer is allowed to deduct the cost of freight from the list price. If freight is an important part of the total cost, absorbing these charges provides the seller with an important advantage over competitors. Companies trying to expand their sales territories absorb freight charges to try to attract buyers in more distant regions. The problem is that such a practice can become very costly.

ODD-EVEN PRICING

A commonly used type of price adjustment is **odd-even pricing**, which adjusts the list price to end in an odd number that is just under a round number. Using odd-even pricing, our ice cream manufacturer might offer regular, premium, and superpremium brands at 99 cents, $1.99, and $2.99 respectively.

Odd-even pricing assumes that consumers see a product as significantly less expensive if it is priced just under the round number — for example, the difference between 99 cents and $1.00 would be perceived as more than one cent. Several studies also have found that odd prices were seen as providing more value than even prices.[11] For this reason, odd-even pricing is sometimes referred to as *psychological pricing.*

The popularity of odd-even pricing is reflected in the fact that 61 percent of supermarket items have prices ending in a 9.[12] Odd-even pricing is also used for a variety of products outside the supermarket. The Chrysler Le Baron is priced at $13,495, not at $13,500. Similarly, Marriott's Courtyard hotels advertise weekend specials at $39 and $49, not $40 and $50 (see Exhibit 20.2).

EVALUATING AND CONTROLLING PRICES

The last step in the process of price determination in Figure 20.1 is to evaluate and control prices after they are introduced into the marketplace. Evaluating prices requires assessing customer and competitive responses to a product's price level. Controlling prices requires determining whether prices should be changed after they have been introduced, and adjusting pricing strategies in response to customers, competitors, and the trade.

EVALUATING CUSTOMER RESPONSES

Evaluating customers' responses to price requires tracking their purchases over time and determining whether estimates of demand are correct. If they are not, the marketer may have to change the price. For consumer packaged goods, the best means of tracking consumer responses to price is *scanner data.* As we noted in Chapter 7, marketers can track the quantity of a product purchased at various price levels in this way, to provide a basis for estimating price-quantity relationships. Marketers can then determine whether an upward or downward change in the price level is warranted based on current demand.

Marketers must also evaluate consumers' responses to price for products not tracked by scanner data — cars and appliances, for example. GM could obtain sales data from its dealers regarding consumer response to a list price of $8,500 for the Saturn. It could also estimate consumer reactions to trade-in allowances, cash rebates, and price deals on options. This should give GM some indication of price elasticity of the Saturn at the $8,500 level and whether a decrease or increase in price is warranted.

EVALUATING COMPETITIVE RESPONSES

Marketers must account for competitive reactions in setting prices. Eli Lilly probably felt a price cut of 12 percent for Treflan was deep enough to deter competitive entry. But Lilly would have to track competitive responses after the price reduction to verify this. If enough competitors entered the market despite the

EXHIBIT 20.2
An Example of Odd-Even Pricing

price cut, Lilly might have to consider an even deeper price cut to deter further competitive entry. On the other hand, if competition was much less than Lilly anticipated, it might consider raising prices close to their former levels, despite the expiration of its patent.

In either case, Lilly would be adjusting prices in response to competitive reactions to its initial price move. Such action and counteraction in response to competition are typical in pricing. Adjusting prices requires carefully assessing competitive responses to the company's pricing strategy to determine if a change from the initial price is warranted.

Managers must be concerned with a number of areas in controlling prices. These are cited in Table 20.4. The most important consideration is to determine whether profit and sales objectives are being met. If not, the firm is likely to take a close look at consumer and competitive responses to its prices to determine if it misestimated customer demand or competitive responses. As we saw, such an evaluation frequently leads the firm to change its initial price.

CONTROLLING PRICE LEVELS AND STRATEGIES

An important question in controlling prices is whether failure to meet profit or sales objectives is due to the firm's pricing actions. Poor performance could be due to advertising strategies, lack of adequate distribution, a weak salesforce, or a host of factors other than price. Unless the impact of price on consumer responses is determined independent of other elements in the marketing mix, the company might wind up changing prices when such a change is not warranted.

TABLE 20.4
Issues in Controlling Prices

KEY QUESTIONS	REQUIRED ACTION
Are profit and sales objectives being met? If not, is it due to price level?	Assess consumer and competitive responses to price. Adjust prices to reflect consumer demand and competitive responses.
Are trade and other discounts adequate?	Improve discounts to trade if required to ensure adequate distribution.
Are prices in product line differentiated to reflect value of each product?	Adjust prices in product line to ensure proper range between premium and economy brands.
Is price in line with quality of product?	Do one of following: Adjust price so it is in line with consumer perceptions of product quality. Adjust product quality so it is in line with price. Advertise to change perception of product value so it is in line with price.
Are price promotions run too frequently?	Control frequency of price deals to ensure that discounted price will not become permanent price.

Here again, scanner data is useful in determining the effects of price on consumer responses. Since scanners immediately record consumer purchases, the marketer can track the amount purchased at various price levels. The marketer also needs to consider other factors, such as changes in the company's advertising expenditures, whether a price deal was running for the product, and whether a competitive promotion was running at the time.

Table 20.4 shows other areas for control. Trade and other types of discounts should be assessed to determine if they are giving the product the distribution clout it needs. Smaller computer companies producing IBM-compatibles have had to provide higher trade discounts to retailers to try to break IBM's hold on the distribution channel.

Another issue is control over prices in a product line. One of GM's problems was that its price-lining strategy was out of control. Models were not sufficiently differentiated across divisions to reflect price differences. In such a case, the company must either realign prices or realign the products to be consistent with current price lines.

A third and related issue is whether the price of a product is in line with consumer perceptions of its quality. Dell Computer's strength is that buyers see value in the product for its price. If consumers do not perceive sufficient value for the price, then the company should consider a price decrease, an upgrade in product quality, or an advertising campaign to educate the consumer about the product's features.

Another area of control in Table 20.4 is price promotions. Marketers must control the frequency of price promotions to avoid a situation where a product is being discounted more often than not. Product managers prefer to promote their products to increase sales and market share. But a longer-range perspective might show that such frequent promotions just encourage consumers to switch in the short term and win very few loyal consumers for the brand.

PRICING SERVICES AND INDUSTRIAL PRODUCTS

Generally, the same methods of determining prices are used for consumer goods, services, and industrial products. But there are enough differences in price determination for services and industrial goods to warrant special attention.

Services are more difficult to price than products for several reasons. First, since services are intangible, it is hard to estimate demand. A company evaluating a new service would have to rely on a description of its features and then ask consumers their intentions to use it. Demand estimates for a product, on the other hand, can rely on actual in-home or market tests to assess customer demand.

PRICING SERVICES

It is also difficult to estimate the cost of a service, particularly a personal service. Costs of producing a product (raw materials and factory labor) are more easily identifiable because products tend to be more standardized. A lawyer's or accountant's fees are often based on hourly rates, but the time required to provide these services is highly variable.

The difficulty in estimating demand for and costs of services means it is harder to apply the most frequently used pricing methods — namely cost-plus pricing, target-return pricing, or demand-oriented approaches. As a result, service marketers have relied on two approaches particular to services: value-based pricing and bundled pricing.

Value-Based Pricing

Value-based pricing attempts to set a price that reflects the highest value a consumer might place on the product. It is pricing by "what the market will bear." In the absence of any systematic demand- or cost-oriented approach, value-based pricing sets the price at a level the marketer thinks the consumer will accept. The price is then gradually raised, almost by trial and error, to test buyers' price elasticities for the service. If a price rise results in a sharp decrease in demand, then the price reverts to its previous level.

Value-based pricing is more complicated than it may sound. It requires establishing prices for different services, often at different rates during different times, depending on the value customers place on the service. Airlines use it in setting fares higher for vacationers during peak holiday periods, and utilities set higher rates during peak usage hours. These differential rates are meant to maintain a constant price-value relationship at different times. That is, if it costs one-half as much for a kilowatt hour of electricity at 4 a.m. compared to noon, the assumption is that electricity is valued twice as much at noon.

Bundled Pricing

The practice of offering two or more products or services as a single package for a special price is **bundling**. For example, some banks offer customers with large certificates of deposit credit cards at no annual fee and free travelers' checks. Airlines sometimes bundle vacation packages combining air travel with car rentals and lodging.

Bundling is more effective for services than for products for two reasons. First, services often are interdependent. Travelers who fly generally need lodging and rental cars. Banking customers who use checking services frequently need loans or want to take out certificates of deposit. It is more economical for a firm to offer such services as a bundle, since demand for one service stimulates demand for the other.

A second reason why bundling is more common for services is that when one agency books airline, hotel, and car rental arrangements, it spreads order-processing and administrative costs across several services. Similarly, when a customer opens a checking account, the marginal costs of servicing the customer on a certificate of deposit or a loan are fairly low. Teller processing, computer time, and sales costs are spread across several services.[13] Costs of bundled services are much lower than if each service were sold separately.

PRICING INDUSTRIAL PRODUCTS

Pricing industrial products is also more difficult than pricing consumer goods because it is harder to estimate customer demand. Demand for industrial goods is derived from demand for consumer goods. Therefore, business-to-business marketers have more than one industry and more than one demand curve to estimate in setting prices. Moreover, this *derived demand* is more volatile than final consumer demand. A change in demand for processed foods will accentuate a change in demand for food machinery.

The volatility of derived demand makes it difficult to use demand-oriented methods of price determination for industrial goods. As a result, the dominant method of setting prices in the industrial sector is based on costs. Although business-to-business marketers use the same type of cost-oriented methods of pricing as consumer marketers — cost-plus and target-return pricing — two pricing procedures are particular to industrial products: bid pricing and delayed-quotation pricing.

Bid Pricing

In **bid pricing**, organizational buyers send out requests for proposals that invite prospective sellers to bid on a set of specifications developed by the buyer. Buyers solicit bids from an approved vendor list and then compare proposals. Generally, the vendor that submits the lowest bid while meeting the buyer's specifications will get the contract.

Sellers must balance the desire to bid low to win the contract with the desire to maintain profit targets in setting the price. In so doing, they must try to estimate the level of competitive bids. Assume that Citicorp sends out specifications for the development of an integrated branch management information system to several vendors on an approved list. One vendor considers four prices for the system and estimates return on investment for each price, as shown in Table 20.5. The vendor then estimates what competitive bids might be and develops a probability of getting the contract at each of the four prices. On this basis, the vendor estimates the highest chance (80 percent) of getting the contract is with a bid of $2 million, but ROI is only 7 percent at that price. The expected ROI weighted by the chance of getting the contract is 5.6 percent (actual ROI of 7 percent times the estimated chance of getting the contract of 80 percent).

Based on the expected ROI, the best price to bid is $3 million, even though there is only a 50 percent chance of getting the contract at that price. The company would prefer to accept a lower probability of getting the contract rather than raising the probability by lowering the price, since lower prices produce unacceptable returns on investment.

Delayed-Quotation Pricing

The production process for industrial goods is usually longer than for consumer goods. For example, the development, sale, and installation of an air pollution control system for a large manufacturer may take years. Costs, specifications,

TABLE 20.5
Example of Bid Pricing

ªOptimal bid price to maximize expected ROI

COMPANY'S BID	ROI ESTIMATE	PROBABILITY OF GETTING CONTRACT WITH THIS BID	EXPECTED ROI (ESTIMATED ROI × PROBABILITY)
$2 Million	7%	80%	5.6%
$2.5 Million	8%	70%	5.6%
$3.0 Millionª	12%	50%	6.0%
$3.5 Million	18%	20%	3.6%

and requirements from regulatory agencies may change significantly during this time. As a result, many business-to-business marketers are reluctant to commit themselves to a fixed price years in advance and will thus delay quoting a price until delivery. Such **delayed-quotation pricing** passes the risk of cost overruns and faulty production schedules to the buyer.

The potential risks of committing to a fixed price are illustrated by Westinghouse's agreement in the mid 1970s to sell 80 million pounds of uranium to nuclear power plants through the 1990s as part of its agreement to sell generating equipment. It committed itself to sell the uranium at $9 a pound. By 1977 uranium was selling at $41 a pound, and Westinghouse sold only one-fifth of the amount contracted.[14] The company wound up losing billions because of these fixed-price contracts.

Some sellers try to balance their risks by quoting a wide price range in advance. This combines a fixed price (since there is a commitment to a price range) and a delayed quote (since the final price is specified within the agreed-to range at the time of delivery).

SUMMARY

1. *How do companies use cost-, demand-, and competition-oriented methods to set price?*

Cost-oriented pricing is usually cost-plus pricing or target-return pricing. In cost-plus pricing, the marketer determines the unit costs of producing an item and adds a margin to meet a profit objective. In target-return pricing, the marketer determines a profit objective based on return on investment or on costs, and then determines the price that will achieve the profit target at a specified volume level.

Demand-oriented pricing methods require estimating consumers' demand curve for a product by asking consumers what they intend to buy, or by using market tests to determine sales at different price levels. Based on this information, companies can set prices with marginal pricing or flexible break-even pricing, both of which seek to maximize short-term profits.

In competition-oriented pricing, marketers base their prices on what competitors do. The company may follow a price leader in the industry, peg prices to a prevailing industry norm, or price based on how competitors might react to the firm's price.

2. *How do companies adjust the final price?*

The price established by a company through cost-, demand-, or competition-oriented methods is the base, or list, price for a product. Adjustments to the base price can be in the form of discounts, allowances, price promotions, geographic adjustments, or odd-even pricing.

Discounts are provided to customers as an incentive to buy in quantity, to perform certain marketing functions that enable customers to buy, to buy at a certain time of year, and to pay bills quickly. Allowances are payments to the buyer in exchange for some benefit to the seller. Price promotions are short-term discounts offered by manufacturers to get consumers to try a product. Geographic adjustments are designed to take account of transportation costs in the final price. In odd-even pricing, the list price is adjusted to end in an odd number that is just under a round number, and gives consumers the impression of being less expensive.

3. *How do companies evaluate and control prices?*

Companies evaluate prices by assessing the responses of customers and competitors to the price levels they set. This requires tracking consumer purchases to determine whether demand estimates on which prices are based are accurate. It also requires evaluating competitive responses to prices to determine whether some countermove is warranted. Both cases might require a change in the list price.

Controlling prices requires a company to determine whether profit and sales objectives have been met and, if not, whether a price change is warranted.

4. *What pricing methods are used for services and for industrial products?*

Service companies tend to price based on their estimate of the value of the service to customers. They are more likely to bundle services into one package at a special price because of the cost efficiencies of bundling.

Sellers of industrial products must face more volatile demand trends for their products. As a result, they are reluctant to commit to fixed prices and are more likely to delay price quotes until the time of delivery. Business-to-business marketers must also respond to requests for bids and must estimate prices in competitive bidding situations.

KEY TERMS

Cost-plus pricing (p. 556)
Markup (p. 557)
Target-return pricing (p. 558)
Marginal pricing (p. 559)
Flexible break-even pricing (p. 560)
Demand-backward pricing (p. 561)
Follow-the-leader pricing (p. 563)
Oligopoly (p. 563)
Pegged pricing (p. 563)
List price (p. 564)
Discount (p. 565)
Quantity discount (p. 565)
Trade discount (p. 566)
Seasonal discount (p. 567)
Cash discount (p. 568)
Trade-in allowances (p. 568)

Promotional allowances (p. 568)
Free-on-board (FOB) origin pricing (p. 568)
Delivered pricing (p. 569)
Single-zone pricing (p. 569)
Multiple-zone pricing (p. 569)
Basing-point pricing (p. 569)
Phantom freight (p. 569)
Freight-absorption pricing (p. 569)
Odd-even pricing (p. 570)
Value-based pricing (p. 573)
Bundled pricing (p. 573)
Bid pricing (p. 574)
Delayed-quotation pricing (p. 575)
Break-even analysis (p. 579)

QUESTIONS

1. A General Motors dealer, after reading the introduction to this chapter, commented as follows:

   > I think you're giving GM a bum rap in implying that they were shortsighted in not getting back into producing larger cars and in using cost-oriented pricing. Their small-car policy was an attempt to meet the needs of the American consumer and to more effectively compete with Japanese imports. Their cost-oriented pricing reflects the realities of the auto industry, namely that we have high fixed costs that must be covered, and that it is very difficult to estimate consumer demand for a new model car. Granted, GM's costs have gone up. But the company is now more conscious of the need to improve productivity and to get its costs down.

   a. Do you agree with this justification of GM's cost-oriented approach to pricing? What are the pros and cons of cost-oriented pricing methods?

   b. What difficulties might GM have if it switched to a demand-oriented basis for pricing?

2. What is the difference between cost-plus pricing and target-return pricing? What are the problems with each method?

3. Demand-oriented pricing methods are based on the assumption that the marketer's objective is to maximize short-term profits. What are the drawbacks with this assumption?

4. Why are demand-oriented pricing methods more flexible than cost- or competition-oriented methods?

5. How can a company estimate a consumer demand curve for new and existing products? What are the problems with using these approaches to estimate demand?

6. What method of pricing does Charles Lazarus, founder of Toys "Я" Us, frequently use? Why is it a demand-oriented pricing approach?

7. Why did companies in the steel and aluminum industries prefer to follow a price leader rather than set prices independently? What was likely to happen if a competitor priced above or below the leader?

8. How does IBM use cumulative discounts to encourage customers to remain loyal to its products?

9. What is the rationale behind odd-even pricing? Should it be used only for low-priced brands? Why or why not?

10. What key areas must be considered in controlling prices? What actions might the marketer take in each of these areas?

11. Why are service firms more likely than other companies to use value-based pricing? Why are they more likely to bundle their services and price them as a single package?

12. Why do marketers of industrial products have more difficulty in estimating customer demand than marketers of consumer goods? What are the implications for determining prices?

CASE 20.1

CATERING TO THE PRICE-SENSITIVE CONSUMER

Source: Adapted by permission of *Forbes* magazine from "When Cheap Gets Chic," by Jeffrey A. Trachtenberg and Christie Brown. *Forbes*, June 13, 1988, pp. 108, 109. © Forbes Inc.

A number of top marketers, including the Marriott Corp., and Miller Brewing have begun catering to the low-budget customers they once purposefully ignored. The reason is that these companies are increasingly anxious about the slowing growth in their traditional, higher-priced markets.

Take the hotel business. Marriott, noted for its full-service hotels ($80 to $120 per night, midweek), is opening a steadily increasing number of Fairfield Inns (under $35 a night). The rooms are smaller, but the towels are just as large. Marriott intends to have 50 to 60 inns in operation by the end of 1989, part of a $500 million commitment.

Marriott has moved into the budget area, in part because that segment is the fastest-growing segment of the hotel industry and in part because it wants to expand into secondary markets like Birmingham, Ala. and Bloomington, Ill. Management believed those secondary markets could not support a full-service Marriott.

Holiday Corp. opened its first low-cost Hampton Inn in August 1984 and is opening a new one every week. Already there are 165 nationwide. A room costs on average $39, compared with $52 at Holiday Inns.

The Hampton Inns were created in part because the 265,000 or so Holiday Inn rooms have saturated the midrange market. When a survey of Holiday Inn guests found one-third wanted to pay less for rooms, management decided to test a smaller facility that didn't offer lounge or food services. Says Ray Schultz, president of Hampton Inn: "We aren't out to cannibalize, but if customers are going to leave the full-service hotels, we want them to stay with us. About half of the Hampton Inn franchisees run Holiday Inns. They know that if they don't have a Hampton Inn somebody else will move into the budget business near them."

Miller Brewing Co., wholly owned by market-smart Philip Morris, went downmarket because it was losing ground in the premium-priced beer business. It brought out Meister Brau (1983) to compete with brands like Anheuser-Busch's Busch, and a year later launched the first nationally distributed budget brand, Milwaukee's Best. With Milwaukee's Best, Miller figured, correctly, that its strong distribution network would quickly gain market share for the new beer. Sales of Milwaukee's Best have grown in three years from an estimated 2.1 million barrels in 1984 to 5.5 million in 1987.

In many businesses, competition from below is so powerful that companies that tried a budget operation and failed are looking again. Hertz, for example, is contemplating opening a low-cost rental business in the next 12 months, spurred by the success of off-airport operators that advertise prices as much as 20% lower. Low-cost rental car chains like Alamo, Thrifty and General have grabbed $1.3 billion of the estimated $7 billion industry.

"We had a division 20 years ago called Valcar, which didn't work, that was ahead of its time," says Hertz Chairman Frank Olson. "Now the time is right. The leisure market, meaning Florida, Colorado, Arizona, Hawaii and California, is especially attractive."

"What you're seeing today is companies extending their lines," says Sidney Levy, chairman of the marketing department at the Kellogg Graduate School of Management at Northwestern University. "If you are upscale, you go downscale. Sometimes it works fine. Sometimes they downgrade but don't know how to manage it. Packard [the once prestigious U.S. motor car] got cheaper and cheaper before it disappeared."

While the cheaper Packards brought new customers, the low-priced cars diluted the exclusive image the once-famed U.S. car company had so painfully built. In the end, Packard lost out on both the low end and the high end of the business. But this is an area where there are no hard and fast rules.

1. What pricing principles explain why many companies have extended their lines to include lower-priced offerings?
2. What are the risks in this strategy?
3. How could Marriott use demand-backward pricing in determining the price per night for its Fairfield Inns?

APPENDIX 20A
BREAK-EVEN ANALYSIS

Break-even analysis identifies the point where total revenue equals total cost and profits are zero. As volume increases beyond the break-even point, the company begins earning profits. To create a break-even chart, first a total revenue curve is determined for a given price level. The chart in Figure 20A.1 is for the Saturn at a price of $11,000. At this price, if the company produces 30,000 units, total revenue will be $330 million. At 40,000 units, total revenue would be $440 million, and so forth. As a result, the total revenue curve at a given price is a straight line representing price times quantity.

The figure shows total fixed costs at $200 million. This remains constant. Total costs rise because total variable costs (primarily raw material and labor) go up as more units are produced. The break-even point for the Saturn at a price of $11,000 would be at 50,000 units. At this price, total revenue and total cost are both $550 million. Beyond 50,000 units, GM would start making a profit.

We know from the appendixes in the last chapter that

$$\text{Total Revenue} = \text{Price } (P) \times \text{Quantity } (Q)$$

and that

$$\text{Total Cost} = \text{Total Fixed Cost } (TFC) + \\ (\text{Average Variable Cost } [AVC] \times \text{Quantity } [Q])$$

Therefore, since the break-even point is where total revenue equals total cost, then

$$P \times Q = TFC + (AVC \times Q)$$

where Q is the amount of production required to break even. Solving for Q gives us

FIGURE 20A.1
Break-Even Chart for the Saturn at a Price of $11,000

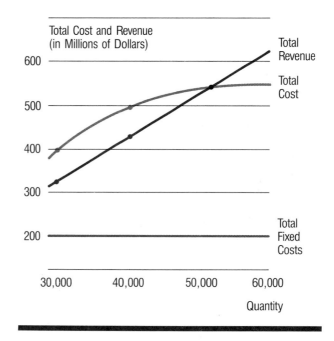

$$Q \text{ (to break even)} = \frac{TFC}{P - AVC}$$

Assuming an average cost per unit of $7,000, the break-even point for the Saturn at $11,000 would be

$$Q = \frac{\$200 \text{ million}}{\$11,000 - \$7,000} = 50,000 \text{ units}$$

NOTES

1. "The U.S. Must Do As GM Has Done," *Fortune,* February 13, 1989, p. 7.

2. *Advertising Age,* January 4, 1988, p. 1.

3. "How GM Is Shifting Gears," *Advertising Age,* January 4, 1988, p. 1; and "General Motors: What Went Wrong," *Business Week,* March 16, 1987, p. 105.

4. "It's Not Easy to Untangle the Web of Auto Pricing," *Iron Age,* January 13, 1982, p. 29.

5. "Why Detroit Can't Cut Prices," *Business Week,* March 1, 1982, p. 111; and *Business Week,* March 16, 1987, p. 106.

6. "The Price Is Wrong," *Industry Week,* December 8, 1986, p. 26.

7. *General Motors, Annual Report,* 1986, p. 4; and *General Motors, Annual Report,* 1987, p. 4.

8. "Founder Lazarus Is a Reason Toy 'Я' Us Dominates Its Industry," *The Wall Street Journal,* November 21, 1985, p. 26.

9. "Software Pricing Strategies," *Computerworld,* January 6, 1986, pp. 53–56.

10. "IBM PS Moves May Cut Prices," *USA Today,* February 10, 1988, p. 7B.

11. Zarrel V. Lambert, "Perceived Prices as Related to Odd and Even Price Endings," *Journal of Retailing* 51(Fall 1975): 13–22; and Robert M. Schindler, "Consumer Recognition of Increases in Odd and Even Prices" in *Advances in Consumer Research,* 11, edited by Thomas C. Kinnear (Provo, Utah: Association for Consumer Research, 1984), pp. 459–462.

12. "Price and Prejudice," *New York Magazine,* June 12, 1989, p. 19.

13. Joseph P. Guiltinan, "The Price Bundling of Services: A Normative Framework," *Journal of Marketing* 51(April 1987): 74–75.

14. "The Opposites: GE Grows While Westinghouse Shrinks," *Business Week,* January 31, 1977, p. 62.

COCA-COLA — THE WORLD BRAND

What is a "world brand"? A brand that sells in 155 countries plus the South Pole, that communicates a single unifying message worldwide, and that so dominates the soft drink market that in many countries it does not compete with other soft drink brands but with generic drinks such as coffee, tea, and even water. You guessed it: The world brand we are citing is Coca-Cola.

There are not many world brands. Colgate toothpaste, McDonald's restaurants, and Marlboro cigarettes all qualify because they market a leading product or service on a worldwide basis with little variation from country to country. And consumers in these countries have similar needs for the product. Coke "is it," whether you live in London, Bangkok, or Rio. McDonald's lets you "have a break today" almost anywhere in the world.

Selling a world brand creates major economic advantages: A company can achieve economies of scale in production because it does not have to develop different products for each country. It achieves economies of scale in marketing by having a worldwide advertising campaign. Its dominant position across many countries is hard to break, giving it a competitive advantage. Coke may be closely competitive with Pepsi in the United States, but on a worldwide basis it outsells Pepsi by three to one,[1] and in some countries, by more than twenty to one. Its overseas operations account for 77 percent of its soft drink income. And the brand's foreign sales are growing at an average of 8 percent a year, twice its domestic growth rate.[2]

But doesn't a world brand contradict the concept that products should be differentiated to meet customer needs? Well, yes, except that Coke is identifying and meeting common consumer needs worldwide. So, except for minor variations, the product is the same from country to country.

The approach to advertising is not as global as the product itself. Coke develops one universal advertising theme, but executions differ from country to country based on differences in cultural norms, interests, and activities. For

example, one campaign centered around a little boy offering a Coke to Mean Joe Greene, the football star, at halftime. Since American football is not played abroad, Coca-Cola adapted the ad using children offering a Coke to soccer stars from different countries. Similarly, when the company launched its General Assembly campaign in 1987, showing children of the world singing the Coke jingle in one big assembly, each country focused on a closeup of a local youngster. The strategy is the same — a unifying theme adapted to different countries.

Coca-Cola also varies other components of its marketing mix to adapt to local markets. For example, in West Germany the use of TV commercials is tightly restricted by the government, so Coke uses a lot of magazine advertising. In Japan, the company found the distribution system so complex that it rejected the use of traditional wholesalers and established its own network of bottlers.[3] In China, Coca-Cola agreed to buy local cashmeres and wine to help the government raise foreign exchange as part of the deal in introducing its flagship brand into the most populous country on earth.[4] Though Coca-Cola may be standardized, its advertising and distribution strategies are not.

Coca-Cola is well positioned to continue to be the world soft drink brand into the next century. It is expanding its base in China with ten bottling facilities. In 1987, it started selling Coke in Russia. It strengthened its dominant position in West Germany by reorganizing the country's bottling system into a stronger and more efficient network.[5] It sees potential growth in the world market as limitless. Consumers abroad drink an average of one soft drink to six for American consumers. In China it is one soft drink to every 150 for American consumers.[6] Coca-Cola figures that if it can get the Chinese to drink half as much as Americans, the additional income would far exceed the company's total revenues. If it gets to that point, Coke might graduate from being a world brand to being *the* universal brand. ■

YOUR FOCUS IN CHAPTER 21

① *What steps are involved in developing an international marketing plan?*

② *What environmental factors are likely to influence a firm's decision to enter foreign markets?*

③ *What are the pros and cons of global versus local international marketing strategies?*

④ *What product-marketing strategies do firms develop for international brands?*

● ● ●

THE NATURE OF INTERNATIONAL MARKETING

International marketing is the marketing of products across national boundaries. From the perspective of the United States, this includes marketing our goods abroad (exports) and marketing foreign goods here (imports). Foreign companies like Sony, Hitachi, Toyota, Mercedes, Nestle, and Unilever have established a major presence in the United States in industries such as autos, electronics, packaged foods, and cosmetics. Likewise, many American companies have established a strong presence abroad. Coca-Cola is sold almost everywhere; a McDonald's hamburger is usually easy to find; Pan Am and TWA have sales offices spanning several continents; and IBM is the world leader in computers. Exhibit 21.1 shows an ad for an American company operating abroad (Hewlett-Packard) and for a foreign firm operating in this country (Iberia).

International marketing in the United States is big business. In 1987 it represented 12 percent of the country's gross national product with exports of $454 billion. Imports of foreign goods were even higher, $585 billion, reflecting our increasing trade gap.[7] Today, more than three-quarters of all manufacturing jobs in the United States are linked to exports, directly or indirectly.[8] International marketing is big business in another sense; it is conducted primarily by large companies. About 80 percent of all exports are sold by 250 of the largest companies in the United States.[9]

Some of these companies, such as Pan Am, Coca-Cola, IBM, Polaroid, Gillette, Johnson & Johnson, and Pfizer earn more of their revenue abroad than here. Moreover, many foreign-owned companies that are often mistaken for American companies — Nestle, Lever, Lipton, Shell Oil — earn a significant percentage of their revenues in the United States. Nestle generates only 5 percent of its earnings in its domestic market (Switzerland), so almost all of its marketing activities are international.

REASONS FOR ENTERING INTERNATIONAL MARKETS

One of the most important reasons for entering a foreign market is enhanced profitability. Anheuser-Busch is looking to foreign markets because it sees little future growth in domestic beer consumption. The industry is in the mature phase of its life cycle, and the overseas market for beer is three times the size of the U.S. market.[10]

American Firm Selling Abroad

Foreign Firm Selling in the United States

Another reason why companies market abroad is that they may be able to benefit from introducing new technologies. General Electric is providing its know-how in building locomotives for China in exchange for a lock on selling the Chinese its engines and parts. It is also seeking to establish a relationship with the Chinese government to sell a variety of other products.[11] Similarly, the Soviet Union let Pepsi-Cola in before Coke because Pepsi was willing to provide the government with bottling technology that could be transferred to other food-processing industries.[12]

Entering foreign markets can also serve as a defensive move against foreign competitors, either going head-to-head against them or escaping from them. When Michelin used its strong European base to enter the U.S. market and attack Goodyear's leading position in the early 1970s, Goodyear struck back by entering Michelin's European markets.[13] In contrast, General Electric reacted to Japanese entry into the television market by ceding TV production to the Japanese and putting its resources behind global expansion in more profitable areas, such as medical imaging and factory automation.

Another important reason to enter foreign markets is to counter adverse environmental trends in a company's domestic markets. Gerber saw that the long-term decrease in the birth rate in this country would mean lower sales of baby foods. At first, it tried to diversify into new businesses. When that did not work, it went back to baby foods by entering markets with increasing birth rates such as Mexico, the Carribean, and Central America.[14]

Other reasons for entering foreign markets include extending a brand's life cycle, as when movie makers export their products abroad once they are seen in this country, and achieving economies of scale in production and marketing, as when Coca-Cola sells one brand with one basic campaign worldwide.

LOCAL VERSUS GLOBAL MARKETING

The major concerns of international marketers are no different from those of domestic marketers: developing a strategic plan for growth; ensuring new product development; positioning products to targeted segments; managing, pricing, advertising, and distributing these products; controlling marketing operations. The major difference is that a new dimension is added — a country. International marketers must adapt their strategies to differences among countries, yet they must also be aware of the opportunity to sell their products worldwide using more standardized approaches. This balance between the necessity of adapting to local needs and customs and the desirability of selling the same product worldwide is the key issue in developing most international marketing strategies.

Local Marketing

International marketers must adjust their marketing strategies to differing customer needs, cultural norms, trade regulations, economic and political conditions, and competitors on a country-by-country basis. For instance, Kellogg knows that most French consumers skip breakfast. Avon knows that most Japanese women are reluctant to sell door-to-door. Coca-Cola knows that TV commercials in Holland are restricted to two 15-minute time periods during the day. Strategies geared to such local differences are **adaptive strategies.**

Such country-specific variations require companies to design advertising, distribution, and product strategies for local markets. Local variations in taste are why a worldwide company like McDonald's offers beer in its German outlets, wine in France, mutton pie in Australia, and McSpaghetti in the Philippines to compete with local noodle houses.[15] Local variations in political conditions are why Coca-Cola does not market in India. In 1977 the Indian government ordered the company to disclose its closely guarded formula or to cease operations.[16] Local variations in advertising regulations are why Kellogg had to develop separate Corn Flakes ads for France, Belgium, and Germany: Children could not be shown in French advertising, so the Corn Flakes kids were out; Belgium did not allow nutritional claims dealing with vitamin content; and Germany did not allow claims comparing Corn Flakes to other cereals.[17]

Some companies follow a local strategy for most of their offerings. Sanyo leaves it up to each of its 73 foreign subsidiaries to develop its own marketing strategies and select its own product offerings based on local conditions. The company churns out variations of its products for individual subsidiaries. The only factor common to Sanyo across national frontiers is its logo.[18]

Global Marketing

Despite the importance of adjusting marketing strategies to local conditions, the trend in international marketing strategies in the last 20 years has been to greater globalization of products and advertising claims. Global strategies cutting across foreign markets are **standardized strategies.**

The advantages of a standardized approach are compelling. Introducing a single standardized brand avoids the significant costs of developing different brands and advertising campaigns for different countries. By reinforcing the same theme in their advertising, companies can build up a world image and a competitive advantage in a product category. Coca-Cola summarizes this advantage as "one look, one sight, one sound," meaning that its advertising message is being constantly reinforced, whether a consumer sees it at home or abroad.

In addition, the world is getting smaller because of greater travel and improved communications. Teenagers the world over are exposed to similar fads, tastes, and peer pressures. A Russian rock band could be mistaken for an American group. Thai, French, and Brazilian teenagers could be wearing the same brand of jeans. And a Sony Walkman is a common sight in the streets of Jakarta, Amsterdam, Tel Aviv, and Shanghai. Improvements in technology are fueling this trend. For example, students the world over are becoming familiar with the common language of personal computers.

As a result, the opportunity for developing world brands is greater. Marketers can now try to introduce brands targeted to global similarities rather than to local differences. That is why Honda created one universal car with minor technical modifications for specific markets.

Making the Key Strategic Decision: Local versus Global

Ultimately, the international marketer's selection of a standardized (global) or an adaptive (local) approach hinges on whether a product category is subject to regional variations in taste and usage. Products like airline travel, cameras, and automobiles reflect universal tastes. Most food and beverage products, clothing, and cosmetics do not. Coca-Cola is the exception as a world beverage. As we will see, the international marketer's decision on where the brand lies on the continuum from local to global will affect every aspect of the marketing mix — product, promotion, distribution, price.

Many international companies consistently pursue either standardized or adaptive strategies as part of their longer-term strategic plan. These companies can be described as primarily global or local. For example, Procter & Gamble follows an adaptive strategy. The smell of Camay, the flavor of Crest, and the formula for Head & Shoulders differ from region to region. The advertising also lacks a universal theme. P&G's local orientation is logical because its toiletries and household products are generally subject to regional variations, and because the company has never linked its products to the P&G name.

A company following a global marketing approach is Black & Decker. In the mid 1970s, Black & Decker was the unchallenged world leader in power tools, with about half of its sales coming from abroad. When lower-priced Japanese imports undermined the company's leading position, it mounted a coordinated worldwide response by looking for similarities among the 50 countries it markets to so as to introduce more standardized products, with relatively minor adjustments to account for different electrical systems and safety and industry regulations. The company is also looking to project a single worldwide image in its corporate advertising.[19]

Most international companies fall somewhere between the extremes of a totally standardized or adaptive approach. Figure 21.1 places several of the companies we have discussed on a continuum from global to local strategies.

FIGURE 21.1
International Marketers Taking a Global
versus a Local Approach

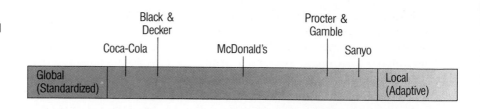

McDonald's is midway because, even though it provides the same services world-wide under the same name, it varies its offerings by region. Coca-Cola and Black & Decker take a more global approach than McDonald's. Procter & Gamble and Sanyo are closer to the local end of the continuum because their brands and subsidiaries operate independently.

OPPORTUNITIES AND THREATS IN INTERNATIONAL MARKETING

The increasing importance of international marketing poses opportunities and threats for American companies into the 1990s. On the positive side, the convergence of tastes and preferences across many countries has provided American firms an opportunity to market globally. IBM's position as world leader in computers is due to the similarity in technological needs across many countries. Coca-Cola achieved world-brand status by ensuring that American GIs could get a Coke during World War II whether they were fighting in the Pacific, Europe, or Africa. As foreign consumers became familiar with the brand and adopted it, Coca-Cola became a permanent fixture abroad.

Another opportunity for American companies is emerging foreign markets. The most interesting is a new "country" called Europe. In 1992 the countries in the European Economic Community (better known as the Common Market) plan to eliminate all trade barriers so that, for trade purposes, Europe will be one country rather than many. A total population of 320 million makes a united European market 25 percent larger than the United States.[20]

In the short run, eliminating trade barriers will make Europe more accessible to U.S. firms. No longer will Kellogg have to worry about different advertising regulations in each country. No longer will American companies have to develop separate distribution channels in each country. An American company will be able to establish one advertising campaign under the same set of regulations and one distribution channel across Europe. But in the longer run, a unified European Community might reintroduce trade barriers and produce larger European companies that might pose more of a competitive threat to American exporters.

Other markets also offer the United States opportunities. The world's two closest trading partners, the United States and Canada, account for $150 billion in trade a year. A free trade agreement was instituted in 1989 to phase out remaining trade barriers between the two nations over a ten-year period.[21] In addition, Japan, long a bulwark of protectionism against American products, began eliminating trade barriers to U.S. goods in the late 1980s. It opened its markets to computers and electronics. China and the Soviet Union offer significant opportunities to firms as these countries loosen trade restrictions. These governments are particularly interested in high-technology products, providing growth opportunities for America's chemical, telecommunications, computer, and space-technology industries. Further, the Soviet government is becoming more interested in supplying its consumers with a wider range of goods, creating opportunities for American companies manufacturing foods, household items, and appliances.

Despite these trends, future threats seem to outweigh opportunities for many American companies in international markets. Lower-priced foreign goods, particularly from the Japanese, have challenged the leadership of American companies in autos, computers, electronics, and even in packaged goods. Their success has led many companies to cede markets to them. As we saw, GE's reaction was to get out of the TV market, while Zenith's was to restrict itself to the high-price end and leave the Japanese unchallenged at the low end. The result of this competition has been to erode America's manufacturing base and limit the ability of many American companies to compete abroad.

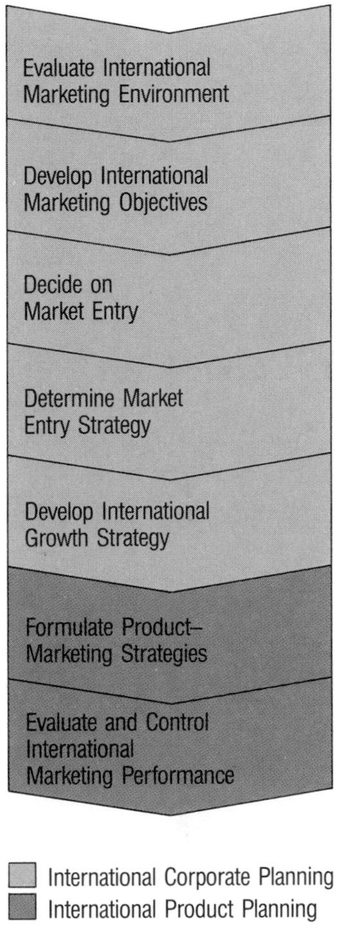

DEVELOPING INTERNATIONAL MARKETING PLANS AND STRATEGIES

Like a brand introduced domestically, a brand introduced into a foreign market requires a marketing plan and a set of strategies. Figure 21.2 shows the process of international marketing planning. It is similar to the marketing planning process described in Chapter 8.

Managers at a company's worldwide headquarters first evaluate the environment the company is facing. For example, Coca-Cola's negotiations with the Chinese government to enter the world's largest market with its flagship brand were at the corporate level. Coca-Cola recognized the limited distribution and advertising capabilities in China and the limited purchasing power of the average Chinese consumer. It also evaluated trade regulations imposed by the Chinese government, political conditions in China, and the likelihood of Pepsi's entry into the market.

Having analyzed the international environment, management then establishes performance objectives such as market share, ROI, and cash flow. Based on the environmental analysis and related objectives, corporate management determines whether to enter the market. Despite environmental limitations, Coca-Cola decided on entry into China primarily because of the size of the market.

The next step in Figure 21.2 is to determine how to enter the market. A market-entry strategy might involve building a plant abroad, entering a joint venture with a domestic company, licensing out the technology, or exporting the product through domestic channels of distribution.

Next, the company incorporates the market-entry strategy into its overall growth strategy that determines whether it will take a global or local approach. Part of the plan is determining the set of product offerings that will be marketed abroad. As we saw, Coca-Cola's strategy for its flagship brand is a global one, with some variation in advertising to reflect local needs and customs. Its product offerings worldwide include not only its flagship brand, but Diet Coke, Cherry Coke, Fanta, and Sprite.

At this point in the process, responsibility for planning shifts from the corporate to the product level, and from corporate managers to an international product manager responsible for a particular brand worldwide or on a regional basis. Procter & Gamble has international product managers responsible for one brand in all countries. In contrast, the worldwide marketing effort for Coca-Cola is too vast to be handled by a single product manager; several market the brand to different regions of the world.

FIGURE 21.2
The International Marketing Planning Process

- Evaluate International Marketing Environment
- Develop International Marketing Objectives
- Decide on Market Entry
- Determine Market Entry Strategy
- Develop International Growth Strategy
- Formulate Product–Marketing Strategies
- Evaluate and Control International Marketing Performance

☐ International Corporate Planning
■ International Product Planning

As Figure 21.2 shows, the international product manager is responsible for developing a brand's marketing strategy. This involves defining the segments to which the product should be targeted and developing a marketing mix for the product on either a global or a local basis. In the final step, the international product manager evaluates the product's performance and controls it by changing the marketing mix or marketing allocations.

In the remainder of this chapter, we will review each of the steps in the international marketing planning process.

EVALUATE THE INTERNATIONAL MARKETING ENVIRONMENT

The main difference between international and domestic marketing is that international marketing strategies must take into account differences among countries. Complete standardization of both product and advertising is almost impossible to attain. Even Coca-Cola, the hallmark of product standardization, introduces some variations in its product, making it less sweet in Thailand, for example, to accommodate local tastes. Thus, before entry, international marketers must thoroughly evaluate a country's environment — its cultural norms, ways of doing business, trade regulations, political and economic environment, and competitive environment.

CULTURAL NORMS

The norms and values of a country (that is, its *culture*) are expressed in customs, language, and symbols that affect how customers react to products and what they buy. There are many examples of American companies failing to take account of cultural norms in foreign markets. In 1981 Campbell was forced to call it quits in Brazil despite a $2 million award-winning advertising campaign because it had failed to recognize that many Brazilian women felt inadequate if they did not make soup from scratch for their families.[22]

Companies have also committed gaffes as a result of a lack of knowledge of local languages and dialects. For example, Gillette had to change the name of its Trac II razor in many foreign markets when research showed that *trac* in some Romance languages means fragile.[23] When Coca-Cola was introduced in China, shopkeepers made their own signs in calligraphy with the words *ke kou ke la,* which meant "bite the wax tadpole," hardly an association that encouraged sales. When the company discovered this, it came out with a different set of characters, *ko kou ko le* which not only sounded more like the real thing, but also meant "may the mouth rejoice."[24]

It is very important that a company study the norms, tastes, preferences, and language of consumers before entering a market. McDonald's undertakes an intensive study of a market, first examining demographic trends, then conducting a political risk analysis, and finally, determining a local population's receptiveness to its products. Further, as we saw, it adapts its product offerings to local tastes.

BUSINESS RELATIONS

One of the frequent failings of international marketers is to assume that business can be conducted abroad in pretty much the same manner as at home. For example, Americans are very time-oriented and believe in getting right to the point in their business dealings. But business people from Asia and many Third World countries spend anywhere from 50 to 80 percent of the time talking about anything but business. Their purpose is to try to establish a personal relationship with the other party — a much less important priority to an American. Warner Lambert failed to realize the importance of personal relationships when it tried to bypass Japanese wholesalers by setting up its own distributors. Making no headway, the company finally sent a new management team in to establish long-lasting relations with local wholesalers.[25]

Another characteristic of American business people that sometimes gets them into trouble in Asian countries is that they are brought up to value individuality and independence of mind. In Japan, the culture dictates that decisions be made mutually. Negotiating sessions among Asians are frequently formalities meant to ratify decisions previously made by consensus. But to Americans, they are seen as a forum for individual give and take that Asians are not prepared for. As a result, misunderstandings develop and business is lost.

American companies are beginning to realize the need to educate their managers in the ways of foreign business relations. Many companies are sending their executives to special courses to prepare them for overseas assignments. Other companies have opted to let local business people represent the company in key dealings.

TRADE REGULATIONS

Countries establish trade regulations to protect their domestic industries from foreign competition. The most common regulation is the **tariff,** a tax on imported goods. Some countries also set import **quotas,** limits on the amount of a product category that can be imported. Until the mid 1980s, the United States set import quotas on Japanese motorcycles to protect domestic manufacturers, primarily Harley-Davidson. Another set of trade barriers are *product standards.* Japan has a variety of such standards to discourage American car manufacturers from exporting their cars. To sell an American car in Japan, one must go through volumes of documents on standards plus local testing, which adds at least $500 to the price of a car.[26]

Since World War II, there have been attempts to ease trade barriers to encourage international trade. In 1947 the United States and 22 other countries signed the General Agreement on Tariffs and Trade (GATT) to reduce tariffs in stages. Since 1947 the GATT agreement has reduced tariffs seven times. The average tariff today is less than one-fifth what it was after World War II. Despite these reductions, some countries make it difficult for foreigners to invest in their economies. So international marketers must determine whether market entry is worth the cost of tariffs, quotas, and rigid product standards.

Governments are motivated by two schools of thought in their attitude toward trade regulations. Some encourage market entry to further development of domestic industries, increase the standard of living, provide sorely needed jobs, and supply foreign currency. For example, the Sudan encourages investments in high-priority industries by exempting foreign investors from corporate taxes for five years. Other governments discourage foreign investment because they want to maintain government control over private enterprise, or they fear foreign domination of their economy. For example, Avon decided against entering the Nigerian market because the government required ownership of 60 percent of Avon's local operations.[27]

POLITICAL ENVIRONMENT

The international marketer must consider the political stability of the host country. The Iran revolution, the crackdown on students in China, and the disintegration of Lebanon show the potential of various countries for instability. American hotel chains such as Holiday Inn saw sizable investments in Lebanon destroyed. Companies may not be able to predict such events, but they can assess the overall political stability of a country. Perhaps spurred by the Bhopal gas leak disaster in India when one of its plants caused almost 2,000 deaths, Union Carbide set up a staff in 1985 that tracks a country's economic conditions and political events and estimates Union Carbide's financial exposure to risk on a country-by-country basis.[28]

ECONOMIC ENVIRONMENT

A country can be classified by its stage of economic development as less developed, developing, or industrialized, depending on its gross national product, per capita income, literacy rates, and the range and quality of products available. As a general rule, opportunities may seem to be greater in industrialized countries because of their greater purchasing power. But competition is also more likely to be intense, and a company may have to look elsewhere for future growth. Companies like McDonald's and Kellogg are already in most of the industrialized nations of the world. Future expansion is more likely to take place in Third World countries.

Another economic factor is the country's industrial facilities — communications, distribution, transportation, and financial. Insufficient facilities may inhibit market entry. China may be encouraging foreign investment, but it lacks facilities to distribute goods outside the major cities. Advertising is restricted to occasional newspaper ads, making it difficult to communicate to potential consumers.

Marketers also must consider exchange rates. As the value of a country's currency increases, its goods become more expensive abroad. Many U.S. companies found themselves at a competitive disadvantage in the early 1980s as the dollar rose against foreign currencies. Japanese goods were finding it easier to make inroads into the American market because they were cheaper based on the currency exchange. When the dollar dropped sharply after 1985, American exporters gained a competitive advantage, since their goods were less expensive abroad.[29]

COMPETITION

International marketers must also consider the degree of competitive intensity in a country when evaluating market entry. If there are many competitors, or if certain companies have a competitive advantage in product quality, price, or distribution, market entry will be more risky. When Procter & Gamble introduced Pampers into Japan in 1977, it failed to evaluate the potential for competitive entry. The company quickly established a 90 percent share of market for disposable diapers, but competition from Japanese companies brought its share down to 7 percent by 1985.[30]

American companies have tended to follow the lead of foreign competitors in the United States. For example, American auto makers followed Japan's lead in producing smaller cars. They are also following Japan's lead in applying techniques to increase productivity and reduce production costs.

DEVELOP INTERNATIONAL MARKETING OBJECTIVES

Once marketers have evaluated the international marketing environment, they must establish objectives for possible entry into foreign markets. A company should be able to establish performance objectives for market share, sales, and return on investment based on its analysis of the potential in a particular country. Coca-Cola might have established objectives for entry into the Chinese market such as a market share of 30 percent, sales of $200 million, and an ROI of 25 percent in the first year.

Additional objectives might be to have its flagship brand available to 50 percent of the Chinese population within three years of entry. It might also set objectives to establish cost limits for raw materials, production, distribution, and advertising.

DECIDE ON MARKET ENTRY

Management's decision on whether to enter a particular market hinges on whether it feels that the environment of the country in question offers opportunities that its company could exploit.

ENVIRONMENTAL ANALYSIS

One approach companies use to decide on market entry is to ask their managers to rate a country on key environmental factors such as barriers to entry, potential stability, and market growth. Assume Coca-Cola's management analyzes the Chinese market by such factors, as shown in Table 21.1. Using a five-point scale, with the most favorable rating being a 5 and the least favorable a 1, it rates China low on cultural norms out of concern that Chinese consumers are not accustomed to drinking soft drinks. (But management feels that soft drinks will become accepted over time.)

Business relations are rated good, since the company has established a solid working relationship with the appropriate government import agencies. However, China has numerous barriers to entry, rigid price controls, and numerous product regulations. Its political stability is rated moderate because of a stable government, but a potential for unrest. (Such unrest was demonstrated by the protests in the spring of 1989 and the government's crackdown. It remains to be seen whether these events will discourage foreign investment in China.) As for additional evaluative factors, inflation is low, and there is little competition in the soft drink market. Of most importance, the size of the potential soft drink market in China is enormous, but management assesses growth to be moderate at first.

Management next computes an overall score representing the desirability of entering the Chinese market. It first rates the importance of each of the ten factors in Table 21.1 based on their impact on profitability. Market growth rate, market size, level of competition, and potential barriers to entry are considered most important. The rating for each factor (the *country value*) is multiplied by the *importance weight* of that factor. The results are added together to yield an overall market-entry score of 89. This score compares favorably with the average of 75 for all the other markets that Coca-Cola is in.

BUSINESS-POSITION ANALYSIS

Having rated a country on environmental factors, a company will then assess its ability to market in that country. Managers can use the same procedure to evaluate its company's business position by using the seven criteria in Table 21.2. There are two types of variables in the table, projected performance (market share, sales, ROI) and company facilities and support (channels of distribution, sales support, plant capacity, capital requirements). On performance, the company estimates it will get a better than 30 percent share of the soft drink market in

TABLE 21.1
Environmental Analysis for Market Entry:
Evaluation of Coca-Cola's Entry into China[a]

[a]The table is hypothetical.
[b]Opportunity rating = Country Value × Importance Weight.
[c]Management's hypothetical rating for Coca-Cola's entry into China.
[d]Total opportunity rating compares favorably with average of 75 for all other Coca-Cola markets.

ENVIRON-MENTAL FACTOR	COUNTRY VALUE	IMPOR-TANCE WEIGHT	OPPOR-TUNITY RATING[b]	ENVIRON-MENTAL FACTOR	COUNTRY VALUE	IMPOR-TANCE WEIGHT	OPPOR-TUNITY RATING[b]
CULTURAL NORMS		3		**POLITICAL STABILITY**		1	
Favorable	5			Stable	5		
Neutral	3			Moderate[c]	3		
Unfavorable[c]	1		3	Unstable	1		3
BUSINESS RELATIONS		3		**INFLATION**		1	
Excellent	5			Very low	5		
Good[c]	4			Low[c]	4		
Fair	3			Medium	3		
Poor	2			High	2		
Very Poor	1		12	Very High	1		4
BARRIERS TO ENTRY		4		**COMPETITIVE LEVEL**		4	
None	5			None	5		
Low	4			Low[c]	4		
Medium	3			Medium	3		
High[c]	2			High	2		
Very high	1		8	Intense	1		16
PRICE CONTROLS		2		**MARKET SIZE**		5	
None	5			Very Large[c]	5		
Low	4			Large	4		
Medium	3			Medium	3		
High	2			Small	2		
Very High[c]	1		2	Very Small	1		25
PRODUCT REGULATIONS		1		**MARKET GROWTH**		5	
Few	5			High	5		
Moderate	3			Medium[c]	3		
Many[c]	1		1	Low	1		15
				Total Market-Entry Score[d] =			89

China because of the lack of competition. Sales are estimated at over $200 million and ROI at more than 25 percent, a relatively high return compared to other countries. But the company has poor support for sales and for establishing channels of distribution because of limited marketing facilities in China. Plant capacity is good, and capital requirements moderate.

TABLE 21.2
Business-Position Analysis: Coca-Cola's Evaluation of Its Position in the Chinese Market[a]

[a]Table is hypothetical.
[b]Business-Position Rating = Country Value × Importance Weight.
[c]Management's hypothetical rating for Coca-Cola's business position in China.
[d]Coca-Cola's average business position in its other markets is 75.

BUSINESS-POSITION VARIABLE	COUNTRY VALUE	IMPORTANCE WEIGHT	BUSINESS-POSITION SCORE[b]	BUSINESS-POSITION VARIABLE	COUNTRY VALUE	IMPORTANCE WEIGHT	BUSINESS-POSITION SCORE[b]
PROJECTED PERFORMANCE				**COMPANY FACILITIES AND SUPPORT**			
Market Share		5	25	Channels of Distribution		3	3
30% or more[c]	5			Strong	5		
25%–29%	4			Average	3		
20%–24%	3			Weak[c]	1		
15%–19%	2						
Under 15%	1						
Sales (in millions)		5	25	Local Sales Support		3	3
Over $200[c]	5			Strong	5		
150–199	4			Average	3		
100–149	3			Weak[c]	1		
50–99	2						
Under 50	1			Plant Capacity		2	8
				Excellent	5		
				Good[c]	4		
Return on Investment		5	25	Fair	3		
				Poor	2		
25% or more[c]	5			None	1		
20–24%	4						
15–19%	3			Capital Requirements		3	9
10–14%	2						
Under 10%	1			Low	5		
				Medium[c]	3		
				High	1		9
				Total Business-Position Score[d] =			98

Management again rates the importance of each variable, multiplies the country value by the importance weight, and sums the seven variables to get an overall business-position score of 98. This compares very favorably with a norm of 75 in the other countries Coca-Cola is in. Overall, management feels it can attain its performance objectives despite lack of marketing facilities, due to the sheer size of the Chinese market and the cooperation of the Chinese government. As a result, Coca-Cola's analysis indicates that it should enter the Chinese market.

DETERMINE A MARKET-ENTRY STRATEGY

Once the international marketer has decided to enter a market, the next question is how. Coca-Cola could enter the Chinese market by establishing a manufacturing plant in that country, or it could enter into a joint venture with the Chinese government, as Avon did with the Nigerian government. It could license its name and manufacturing process to the Chinese government and allow it to manufacture the product. Or it could export Coca-Cola from the United States to China, either directly to local Chinese intermediaries or indirectly through exporters in the United States. As shown on the continuum in Figure 21.3, these five alternatives cover a range from maximum to minimum investment in and control of marketing activities in the foreign country.

DIRECT OWNERSHIP

Investing directly in manufacturing facilities represents the greatest commitment to a foreign market. Such direct investment is most likely when management determines that a country is politically stable, and that therefore the company does not face the risk of expropriation or similarly drastic unforeseen events.

Involvement abroad by American firms has been increasing greatly in recent years for several reasons. American firms generally find it cheaper to produce abroad than at home because of lower labor and materials costs in foreign countries. Also, the firm avoids trade barriers against foreign goods since it is considered a domestic producer. Furthermore, the firm can establish stronger relations with local wholesalers, retailers, and suppliers, making it easier to adapt to local needs. In 1986 Goodyear invested $207 billion, or about 28 percent of its capital spending, in building or upgrading plants abroad. Overall, almost one out of every ten dollars spent by American companies on building is for overseas plants.[31]

JOINT VENTURES

If a firm lacks the expertise and financial resources to enter a foreign market, it might consider entering through a joint venture with a local company. Many Japanese companies use joint ventures to enter the American market. Toshiba, the electronics firm, has a joint venture with Westinghouse to produce color TVs, and a joint venture with AT&T to produce telephone-switching equipment.[32] U.S. companies have also used joint ventures to enter Japan. Apple sells its Macintosh in Japan through Canon, and Ford sells its Taurus in Japan through Mazda.

LICENSING

Licensing involves less investment in and control of foreign markets than does direct ownership or a joint venture. It is a good way to shift the risks of production and marketing to the licensee yet gain the benefits of entry into foreign markets. For example, Weight Watchers International licensed its health products to 13 companies that could guarantee quality in production and could do an effective job of marketing the products abroad.

Licensing creates a risk of lack of control over manufacturing operations, and thus over the quality of the product. PepsiCo licenses production of its flagship brand to government-owned companies in Egypt, and some consumers have complained that the Egyptian version of the drink lacks the flavor of the domestic product.[33]

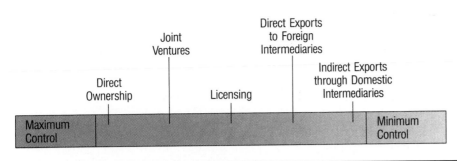

FIGURE 21.3
Market-Entry Strategies

EXPORTING

Exporting involves selling a product abroad from the company's home base. A firm exporting its products does not have to make any substantial investments abroad. As a result, exporting is the most frequently used method for market entry. Hershey exports directly to foreign intermediaries rather than make substantial investments in overseas production or joint ventures. A company can also export indirectly by using home-based organizations such as trading companies to export its goods. This type of entry represents the least involvement in foreign markets, since the company is giving another organization responsibility for marketing its products. It is also the least expensive of the market-entry strategies in Figure 21.3.

A logical strategy for a company first entering international markets is to start off with the least expensive method by exporting through domestic intermediaries. If its products are successful abroad, the company can then consider more direct involvement through licensing, joint ventures, or direct ownership abroad.

ORGANIZING FOR MARKET ENTRY

The international firm must establish an organization to sell its products abroad. The alternative chosen partly depends on the firm's resources and strategies for market entry. A firm that is starting to sell abroad and has not entered into joint ventures or direct ownership will want to use a simple organization. The simplest is an export department, which is an internal company department that handles the paperwork and ships products abroad. If the firm opts to enter foreign markets through direct ownership of manufacturing and marketing facilities, it will need a more complex arrangement, usually the establishment of wholly owned foreign subsidiaries like Gerber's Brazil.

Many firms employ several different entry strategies — licensing in one country, joint ventures in another, direct ownership in a third. In such cases, the firm might establish an international division to handle more complex operations and larger foreign sales on a worldwide basis. This division would have its own budget and planning responsibilities. It could be organized by region or by product groups across regions. If a company follows an adaptive international strategy, it is likely to organize by region, because each region requires different strategies. If it follows a standardized approach, it is likely to organize by product group, since products will be sold in the same way on a worldwide basis.

DEVELOP AN INTERNATIONAL GROWTH STRATEGY

Once the international firm has determined a strategy for market entry, the next step is to establish a **country-product mix**, which defines the company's total product offerings on a global basis. Such decisions should be made in the context

FIGURE 21.4
International Growth Strategies

Breadth of International Effort

		As Many Countries as Possible	A Few Key Countries
Strategic Approach to International Marketing	Standardized (Global)	Worldwide Standardization (World Brands)	Standardization in Key Markets
	Adaptive (Local)	Worldwide Adaptation	Adaptation in Key Markets

of an international growth strategy — that is, an overall game plan for future growth in international markets — evaluating the opportunities in each country and the company's ability to exploit them. For example, General Foods sells chewing gum in France, ice cream in Brazil, and pasta in Italy. If selling chewing gum in France would put General Foods at a competitive disadvantage compared to domestic companies, it would not do so; the company's resources could be better used in another country. In other words, the global game plan requires deciding what products to sell in what countries with an eye on the company's global offerings.

In developing an international growth strategy, a company must make two basic decisions: Should it follow a standardized (global) or an adaptive (local) strategy in introducing its products abroad? And should it try to be in as many countries as possible, or should it focus on a few key countries? The answers to these two questions result in the four strategic alternatives in Figure 21.4.

In **worldwide standardization**, the international firm tries to market in as many countries as possible using a global marketing strategy. This is essentially a world-brand strategy, such as the one Coca-Cola has followed, not only with its flagship brand but with its other soft drink offerings. For example, Diet Coke is marketed in almost as many countries as Coca-Cola. World brands such as Pepsi, Coke, and Black & Decker might advertise one global theme; but they also use local variations in their advertising.

Because standardization provides economies of scale in advertising and production, a standardized strategy usually involves marketing in as many markets as possible (that is, a worldwide strategy). But standardization can also be used effectively on a more limited scale. Companies can use **standardization in key markets** where opportunity is greatest, particularly if customer needs in these markets are similar. For example, Playtex markets its underwire bras in the United States and a few European countries using a standardized approach. The company could try to expand into other countries, but it apparently feels that a product like an underwire bra does not have universal appeal because of different cultural norms outside the United States and Europe. Yet a standardized approach is still desirable, since the size of the United States and European markets makes economies of scale possible.

The most costly strategy is **worldwide adaptation**, which requires selling different variations of a product with consequent differences in advertising, on a worldwide basis. Such adaptation is necessary when differences in needs require product variations by country. Procter & Gamble follows a strategy of worldwide adaptation. Most of its brands are geared to specific countries or regions because of local differences. For example, the American version of Ariel, P&G's top-selling powder detergent, is designed for lower water temperatures, greater sudsing, and faster performance. In Germany, washloads are soaked longer and at higher temperatures, so Ariel matches those conditions. In Japan, the product is formulated for shorter washing cycles and smaller machines.[34]

Adaptive growth strategies are generally directed to a select group of countries rather than to the world at large. Most companies simply do not have the resources of a P&G, allowing a worldwide adaptive strategy. Quaker follows a strategy of **adaptation in key markets**, primarily in Europe. It lets its offices in each European country make their own marketing decisions regarding product offerings and advertising because of variations in needs and tastes for its food products. In contrast to most of the other companies we have cited in this chapter, Quaker is not targeting its international operations for growth. Instead, it is selectively applying its international efforts to a few key markets abroad.[35]

FORMULATE PRODUCT MARKETING STRATEGIES

Having developed an overall game plan for its operations in foreign markets, the international firm is now in a position to take the next step in the planning process in Figure 21.2 — formulating marketing strategies for each of its product lines. The same marketing decisions as those we have described for domestic products are required — defining target segments, positioning products to these segments, and in so doing, developing a marketing mix composed of product, promotion, distribution and pricing strategies. At this point, responsibility for developing international marketing strategies shifts from corporate managers to an international product manager responsible for marketing the product worldwide or for marketing it to specific regions of the world.

MARKET SEGMENTATION AND PRODUCT POSITIONING

The main strategic alternative facing the international marketer is whether to define the segments for a product by geographic region or by consumer types across regions. If there are substantial variations in needs and purchasing behavior across countries or regions, then a geographic definition would make the most sense. On the other hand, if there are universal needs across regions, then defining segments by general consumer needs such as nutrition, convenience, or product quality would be most relevant.

For example, should Kellogg identify the segments for its nutritional cereals abroad as an Asian segment, a Western European segment, a Latin American segment, and so forth? Or should it identify a nutritionally oriented segment, a low-calorie segment, or a taste-oriented segment across these geographic areas? Given the substantial differences in breakfast-eating habits between regions of the world (for example, French consumers regard dry cereals as a crunchy snack), Kellogg defines its markets by region. But as the company's brands become widely known and various regions of the world develop similar breakfast habits, the company might begin to define consumer segments across regional boundaries as nutritional, diet, taste, and fitness-oriented segments.

A product's positioning must be consistent with the segment it is targeted to. Kellogg will vary its advertising depending on the breakfast-eating habits of each

EXHIBIT 21.2
Targeting a Worldwide Consumer
Segment: The Yuppie

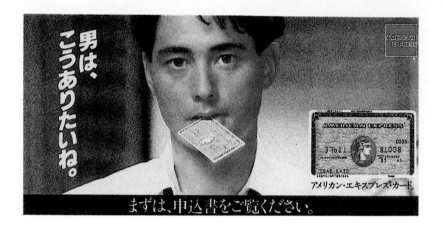

region. American Express uses the more universal theme of status and mobility to target yuppies worldwide. The print ad in Exhibit 21.2 is targeted to the yuppie segment in Japan under a caption implying that young consumers should rely on an American Express card, a variation on the "Don't leave home without it" theme.

THE INTERNATIONAL MARKETING MIX

International marketers must develop product, promotional, distribution, and pricing strategies for each of their products marketed abroad. The major question is the same one we have addressed throughout this chapter: Should these strategies be standardized across markets, or should they be adapted to local conditions?

Most firms do not follow a strictly standardized or adaptive approach. Marketers of world brands usually adjust their advertising to local conditions. And brands designed for local conditions such as P&G's Ariel have a standardized element across regions such as a common product characteristic (powdered detergent) or a common brand name. When firms do follow a strictly standardized or adaptive approach, they tend to run into trouble. For example, Parker Pen tried to standardize every component of its marketing mix in 154 countries and saw its international strategy fail because of inadequate attention to local differences. Its global advertising approach totally overlooked local variations, such as the fact that Scandinavia was a ballpoint-pen market, whereas consumers in France and Italy wanted fancier pens.[36]

Generally, the product component of the international marketing mix is the most standardized, and the advertising component the least standardized. Product and packaging characteristics can be standardized if product needs are similar across regions. But advertising almost always requires variations in language, symbols, and images to conform to local conditions.

Product Strategies

International firms use four types of product strategies (see Figure 21.5), varying from a global to a strictly local approach. Worldwide product standardization is the most global approach. Few brands are completely standardized on a global basis. Coke and Pepsi come close, but there are still minor regional variations in these brands. Black & Decker power tools are also fairly standardized but must vary to conform to local differences in electrical outlets and voltages.

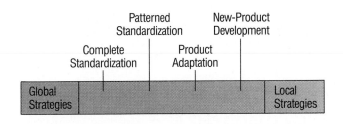

FIGURE 21.5
International Product Strategies

Product standardization could be a risky strategy if a firm decides to export a home-grown success. Kellogg learned this when it assumed it could duplicate its success with Pop Tarts in the United States by selling them in Europe. The product had to be toasted, and few European homes had toasters.[37]

The risks of complete product standardization, coupled with the desirability of economies of scale, have led some companies to develop a common product base that allows for substantial local variations. This approach, called **patterned standardization**, allows companies to take advantage of economies of scale while meeting local needs. U.S. car companies have followed a policy of patterned standardization in selling abroad because they need economies of scale to defray their high fixed costs. General Motors' X-cars were designed with a standardized body and interchangeable parts to allow for adaptation to local conditions. American Motors' Jeep (now owned by Chrysler) has a common design but with variations for 14 different countries.[38]

Another notch toward regional variation is adapting brands so they are totally designed for local needs without a common universal base. Such a strategy denies the firm any advantages of economies of scale, but it is sometimes necessary if there are substantial regional variations in tastes and usages. Local adaptation is most common for food products. For example, Corn Products varies its bouillon cubes to suit local tastes. They are sold in chicken and beef flavors in the United States and Europe, in tomato and shrimp flavors in Mexico, in corn flavors in Argentina, chili in Kenya, mutton in Ireland, and pork in Thailand.[39]

The most locally oriented product strategy is new-product development directed to the needs of foreign markets. Colgate-Palmolive developed a highly profitable new product for Latin American consumers by watching Venezuelan women wash their laundry. Colgate found that instead of detergent, these women were using slivers of bar soap to form a mush. The company decided to manufacture this product, put it in a plastic bowl, and sell it under the name Axion soap. It is now the leading laundry cleaner in many Latin American markets.[40]

Promotional Strategies

Promotional strategies can also vary from a global to a local approach. Completely *standardized* strategies are rare because they risk ignoring differences in local needs. Yet some companies have run exactly the same ad on a worldwide basis with only variations in language. These firms believe that their product has universal appeal and that variations in advertising content are not necessary. For example, Visa has run identical advertisements in various countries for its card with only a change in language (see Exhibit 21.3).

EXHIBIT 21.3
Standardized Advertising in
International Marketing

The more common advertising approach is *patterned standardization*, that is, establishing a universal theme but allowing for variations to account for local differences in needs and customs. The Marlboro cowboy is generally regarded as a universal symbol. But there are significant local differences in implementation, such as showing the cowboy in a white hat on a white horse in Hong Kong because of the positive cultural significance of the color white in the Far East.[41]

Many international firms take an *adaptive* approach to advertising because of pronounced differences in needs or customs between countries. Renault advertised its Renault 5 differently to various European countries because of differences in what consumers consider most important in a car. The company emphasized a "fun" image in France, road performance in Italy (see Exhibit 21.4), quality in Holland, modern engineering in Germany, and construction and reliability in Finland.

The trend in advertising is to greater standardization rather than adaptation. One reason is that consumers are developing similar tastes for many products. A standardized approach can appeal to similar needs for travel, communications, and fashions. In addition, media are cutting across national boundaries, making a standardized approach more feasible. This trend is particularly evident in Europe. Consumers in Belgium, Holland, and France now see the same ads on 14 TV channels via satellite.[42]

EXHIBIT 21.4
Adaptive Advertising in
International Marketing

 Clay Timon learned Japanese when he was the advertising agency executive responsible for Coca-Cola advertising in Japan and Korea in the early 1970s. When his career took him to Brazil several years later, the new arrival found himself unable to communicate with a taxi driver in Portuguese, Spanish, or English. But he and the driver hit on a common language — Japanese.[43]

Timon had a knack for learning the mother tongue wherever he was working on local advertising campaigns — Japan, Brazil, France. And his world travels as an account executive for large ad agencies such as McCann-Erickson make him feel at home almost anywhere in the world. That is one of the reasons he landed a job as director of worldwide advertising for Colgate in 1985.

The post was a new one at Colgate. It was the result of the company's move from an adaptive to a more global, standardized approach in its advertising.

Clay Timon — Colgate's International Advertising Guru

Source: *Advertising Age,* © Crain Communications Inc.

Before 1985 Colgate tended to vary its advertising strategies by region. The one exception was Colgate toothpaste, which maintained a universal advertising theme and tried to emulate Coca-Cola's strategy of "one look, one sight, one sound." Now the company's plan was to do the same for its other brands — establish "a singular look worldwide."[44] And top management felt Clay Timon was the person to accomplish this plan.

Timon is responsible for working with Colgate's management and with its three major advertising agencies to implement a more standardized advertising approach. He operates by consulting with local subsidiaries on advertising approaches rather than by dictating to them. Although pushing for more standardization, he still leaves implementation to local managers in what is clearly a patterned standardization approach.

The fruits of his efforts are apparent. Timon successfully urged a number of Colgate's foreign offices to adopt a campaign successful in England for Colgate Tartar Formula toothpaste. The campaign, known as The Wall, showed little men building a wall of tarter on giant teeth and then being chased away by the toothpaste. Widespread adoption of the campaign resulted in a standardized advertising approach for the brand. In another case, a campaign developed by one of Colgate's ad agencies for Palmolive soap in Costa Rica was so successful that, at Timon's urging, it was adopted in 20 countries around the world.[45]

Given his performance in making Colgate Tartar Formula toothpaste and Palmolive Soap successful worldwide advertising efforts, Colgate might want to officially change Clay Timon's title to International Advertising Guru. ∎

Distribution Strategies

A good distribution system is essential if products are to be marketed abroad. One of the main reasons that Schick has 70 percent of the razor blade market in Japan is its strong distribution system.[46] When the company began doing business in Japan in 1960, it quickly realized the importance of establishing stable personal relationships there. Procter & Gamble was slow to learn this lesson and alienated local wholesalers by discounting Cheer detergent and undercutting their margins. As a result, P&G found itself at a competitive disadvantage to domestic competitors such as Kao with stronger distribution relationships.[47]

Customs and forms of distribution often differ among countries. For example, in Japan 75 percent of all new cars are sold door-to-door by auto salesmen.[48] Apparently dealer showrooms are considered too impersonal.

In selecting distribution channels, international marketers generally choose one of the approaches shown in Figure 21.6. A company can distribute indirectly by selling to domestic intermediaries, which then sell to foreign intermediaries. Or it can sell directly to foreign intermediaries through its headquarters organization. Since smaller companies do not have the resources to sell abroad, they use domestic intermediaries. One is an **export trading company,** which is a company that will buy the firm's products and assume all distribution and marketing abroad. If the firm does not want to give up title to its goods, it can use an **export**

FIGURE 21.6
International Distribution Channels

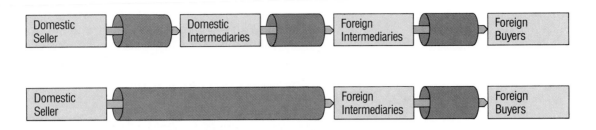

management company, which serves as an export agent by marketing a firm's products overseas on a commission basis.

Larger firms tend to export directly through foreign intermediaries. They may do so through wholesalers, through foreign agents and brokers, or directly to retailers. When Procter & Gamble sells soaps or detergents in Japan, it first sells to general wholesalers, which sell to specialty wholesalers, which sell to regional and local wholesalers, which finally sell to retailers. P&G is not always happy with this mode of distribution, because the longer the channel, the less control it has over the way its products are sold. But the company has little choice since this channel structure is traditional in Japan.

When larger companies can develop more direct control over foreign distribution, they will do so. Deere has set up sales branches in Latin America so it can deal directly with independent dealers that distribute its agricultural equipment. These branches give the company more direct control over the way foreign intermediaries handle sales and service.[49]

One important characteristic of foreign distribution not shown in Figure 21.6 is the high cost of distributing products abroad. Foreign intermediaries are smaller, and the channels of distribution tend to be longer, so prices are higher as a result of the margins required to compensate each channel member. Poor warehousing and storage facilities also increase the costs of distribution. Prices sometimes escalate to three or four times what they would be in the domestic market, largely as a result of these higher distribution costs.

Pricing Strategies

International marketing firms tend to follow two types of pricing strategies. The first is to establish a low price to gain a competitive advantage. Some exporters set prices below cost to stimulate sales in foreign markets, a practice known as **dumping.** Exporters dump products in foreign markets because, even though they are selling below cost, they are still contributing to overhead by getting rid of excess inventories. They also dump to establish a competitive price advantage over producers in foreign markets. Dumping is deeply resented by these producers. Japanese manufacturers have been accused of dumping their products, particularly electronics, in the United States. Their strategy has been to set lower prices to capture market share, often at the expense of profits. In response to charges of dumping, they claim that selling at lower prices permits economies of scale and savings which are passed on to American consumers.

The second pricing strategy is to set prices for foreign goods based on total costs. If the firm exports its products, this approach is likely to lead to prices higher than those in the firm's home markets because of higher costs of distribution. As a result, firms pricing on a total cost basis might find themselves at a disadvantage compared to local competitors. Companies following this pricing strategy do not distinguish between products slated for domestic or foreign markets. Foreign operations are viewed as profit centers that must cover total costs.

EVALUATE AND CONTROL INTERNATIONAL MARKETING PERFORMANCE

The last step in the process of international marketing planning, evaluating and controlling the marketing effort, is more difficult than in domestic marketing for several reasons. One is that international marketers have less control over price because of tariffs and trade regulations. Frequently, the international firm must price its products higher than anticipated. Also, data on international markets are often incomplete, unreliable, and not comparable across countries. Such data are much harder to use for planning purposes. Finally, firms with foreign subsidiaries often find it difficult to control them from the home office because of differences in business customs and environment.

International firms must overcome these difficulties by establishing a system to control their foreign operations. A key requirement is establishing an international marketing information system. Such a system is the same as that described in Chapter 7 with two important exceptions. First, subsystems must be established to provide data on individual countries or regions. In particular, data used to develop estimates of market potential and opportunity must be comparable across countries and regions. A second difference is that international information systems place more emphasis on environmental scanning than domestic systems due to the importance of monitoring variations in political, economic, and cultural factors across countries.

ETHICS IN INTERNATIONAL MARKETING

The nature of international operations has created several ethical issues that have prompted debate in the business community. One is, should an international marketer offer payoffs to buyers abroad if such payoffs are an accepted mode of doing business? Exporters of American products, particularly high-priced industrial goods, often protest that "if we don't, our competitors will, and we will lose the sale." However, such payoffs are little more than bribes for doing business. The fact that competitors offer them does not make the practice ethical. A firm could very well take a position that it sells its products based on quality and that payoffs will not be considered. Such a policy would be most effective if the largest sellers were to publicize it and discourage others from offering payoffs.

A second issue is doing business in countries regarded as having unethical political policies, such as the policy of apartheid in South Africa. Most American companies have withdrawn from South Africa at the urging of the U.S. government. Some, such as Mobil, remain, arguing that it is better to continue to do business in South Africa and try to support blacks economically through higher wages. Mobil finally quit South Africa in April, 1989, on economic rather than ethical grounds, citing restrictive tax laws passed in the United States making it difficult to continue doing business.[50]

A third issue involves charges that some companies from industrialized nations sell products to underdeveloped, Third World countries that have harmful effects on consumers or that take unfair economic advantage of them. The best known case in this regard, arose in the 1970s with evidence of serious health problems among babies in underdeveloped countries being fed Nestle's infant formula products. The company's initial reaction, to fight the allegations and withhold cooperation from investigating agencies, led to a boycott of Nestle products in the United States. Nestle's subsequent cooperation with the World Health Organization and UNICEF and assistance in resolving most of the problems that these organizations identified led to a lifting of the boycott. This case illustrates the special responsibility of international marketers to assure product safety, especially when they sell to less educated and more vulnerable consumers.

SUMMARY

1. What steps are involved in developing an international marketing plan?
The first step in international planning is to evaluate the cultural, political, and economic environment to determine the feasibility of entering the foreign market. If the company decides on entry, it establishes performance objectives and develops a market-entry strategy. Such a strategy might involve building a plant abroad, entering a joint venture with a domestic company, or exporting the product from the company's home base. In the next step, the company develops an overall strategic plan for operations abroad that determines whether it will take a global or local approach and that defines its country-product mix.

The company also develops a marketing plan for each product sold abroad. This requires formulating strategies for product, promotion, distribution, and pricing. In the final step, the company evaluates and controls the international marketing effort.

2. What environmental factors are likely to influence a firm's decision to enter foreign markets?
The international firm must determine cultural norms that might affect consumer needs and their reactions to the company's offerings. It must assess the nature of business relations in each country so that company executives will not blunder in dealing with foreign businesspeople. It must assess trade regulations that might result in taxes, quotas, or restrictions on operations that will directly affect profit potential abroad. Also, it must assess the political and economic environment for signs of instability that might increase the risks of doing business in foreign markets. And, finally, it must evaluate competition to determine the profit potential of operations abroad.

3. What are the pros and cons of global versus local international marketing strategies?
A global (standardized) approach offers one product worldwide and uses a single advertising theme, usually with some local variations. The rationale for such an approach is that the world's consumers are developing similar needs and that a global approach permits companies to achieve economies of scale in production and advertising. But such an approach risks ignoring local differences in needs and customs.

A local (adaptive) approach adjusts marketing strategies to differing customer needs, cultural norms, and other environmental factors on a country-by-country basis. The advantage of this approach is that it directs strategies to the specific needs of individual markets. But it is costly to develop separate products and advertising campaigns for individual countries.

4. *What product-marketing strategies do firms develop for international brands?*

Product strategies can vary from complete standardization worldwide to development of products specifically for local needs. Promotional strategies vary from campaigns with one universal theme to those designed for local markets. Generally, product strategies tend to be more standardized, whereas advertising strategies tend to be more adaptive. Distribution strategies must recognize differences in channels of distribution in foreign countries. The major decision is whether the international firm will sell directly to foreign intermediaries or will use domestic agents to sell abroad. Pricing strategies must establish whether the firm will use a low-price strategy to develop competitive advantage or a high-price strategy that ensures the firm will cover its costs of doing business abroad.

KEY TERMS

International marketing (p. 584)
Adaptive strategies (p. 586)
Standardized strategies (p. 587)
Tariffs (p. 591)
Quotas (p. 591)
Country-product mix (p. 597)
Worldwide standardization (p. 598)

Standardization in key markets (p. 598)
Worldwide adaptation (p. 598)
Adaptation in key markets (p. 599)
Patterned standardization (p. 601)
Export trading companies (p. 604)
Export management companies (p. 604)
Dumping (p. 605)

QUESTIONS

1. On what basis could Coca-Cola be defined as a world brand? Does the brand's strategy account for differences in local needs and customs? If so, in what ways?

2. For what reasons do companies enter foreign markets? Cite examples for each reason.

3. One advertising executive, citing the rationale for a global marketing approach, said

> Different peoples are basically the same . . . An international advertising campaign with a truly universal appeal can be effective . . . The desire to be beautiful is universal. Such appeals as "mother and child," "freedom from pain," "glow of health," know no boundaries.[51]

Another marketing expert, citing the need for local adaptation simply said

> What makes sense in one country may not make sense in another.[52]

a. What are the advantages and disadvantages of a global and a local approach to international marketing?

b. Are the two statements just cited contradictory? Why or why not?

4. Why does McDonald's adapt its offerings to local markets, whereas Coca-Cola generally does not?

5. What are some opportunities and threats for American companies operating abroad in the 1990s?

6. What environmental factors did Coca-Cola have to consider in introducing its flagship brand into China? Make sure to cite cultural, business relations, competitive, political/economic, and regulatory factors.

7. How would a company like Coca-Cola take into account its business position in evaluating entry into a foreign market like China? Cite specific criteria regarding business position the company would have to consider.

8. What market-entry strategies would you suggest for each of the following companies, and why?

   a. An American firm wants to introduce its line of high-quality biscuits in Western Europe, and wants to maintain close control over the manufacture and marketing of the line.

   b. A manufacturer of household cleaners is just starting to sell abroad. It has limited resources for foreign operations but hopes to expand international sales in the future.

   c. A company wants to introduce its line of hydraulic lifts into an Asian country with strict export controls. It would like to establish manufacturing and marketing facilities in that country but does not have the resources to do so. Further, the company is not familiar with local regulations and customs.

9. What alternative strategies for international growth can a company follow? What is the rationale for pursuing each strategy? What are the risks?

10. When Kellogg embarked on a worldwide effort to sell its cereals, it had two options in defining foreign markets. It could have defined these markets on a geographic basis, or it could have defined consumer segments with common needs across geographic regions.

    a. Under what conditions is each approach most relevant?

    b. Which approach do you think Kellogg should choose and why?

11. What is patterned standardization? How would this approach be applied to product and advertising strategies? Cite examples of such applications?

12. The general trend in international advertising strategies is toward greater standardization. Why? Cite examples of this trend?

13. Why was Schick able to establish strong distribution relationships in Japan, whereas Procter & Gamble was not?

14. Why is it more difficult to evaluate and control international marketing operations than domestic operations?

CASE 21.1

MARKETING IN CHINA

Source: "Dispatches from a Chinese Frontier of Capitalism," *The New York Times*, August 15, 1989, p. A4; and "Laying the Foundation for the Great Mall of China," *Business Week*, January 25, 1988, pp. 68–69.

The brutal suppression of the student-led democracy movement in China in June 1989 created only a pause in the government's drive to emphasize private enterprise and consumer goods. In most coastal areas such as Xiamen and Shishi, capitalism seemed to thrive after the crackdown. While tightening the political reins, the government seems to be intent on loosening the economic reins. And no wonder: by attracting foreign goods, the country has started to create foreign currency reserves and more wealth.

Products such as Coca-Cola, Pepsi-Cola, Kodak, and Fuji are common in China. Fast-food outlets such as Kentucky Fried Chicken are becoming widespread. Some American companies are even investing in joint ventures to make their food products in China. Beatrice Foods, for instance, is making ice cream and snack foods in Canton.

But getting into the Chinese market is by no means easy. Foreign marketers rarely reach beyond the 20 percent of the population in the most affluent cities. Regional variations in climate, language, and taste discourage marketers from going nationwide. Further, despite a vast population, China's per capita income is only $300, seriously inhibiting purchases of any foreign goods.

In addition, foreign companies must work through a maze of state-controlled wholesalers and retailers who often sell competitors' products and even refuse to give inventory information to their suppliers. Selling is a foreign concept to these intermediaries, since they have always been able to sell whatever they had.

The lack of any marketing orientation is also apparent in manufacturing. The typical manufacturer leaves its merchandise in the warehouse and waits for customers to pick it up, not even bothering to deliver it to intermediaries.

Changes have begun, however. Coke and Pepsi have

set up direct distribution networks, investing in trucks and refrigeration for retailers. Both companies are also pioneering the development of advertising in China. But socialism and marketing often clash. For example, since commissions are forbidden by law in China, the only incentives a company like Beatrice can offer its salespeople are banquets, ribbons, and T-shirts. It is apparent that

China is still at square one in developing a marketing-oriented economy.

1. What cultural, political, economic, and trade restrictions do foreign companies face in marketing their brands in China?
2. Given these limitations, why do many foreign companies continue to enter the Chinese market?

NOTES

1. "Coke's Intensified Attack Abroad," *The New York Times*, March 14, 1988, p. D1.

2. *The Coca-Cola Company, Annual Report, 1987*, p. 8; and "He Put the Kick Back Into Coke," *Fortune*, October 26, 1987, p. 54.

3. "Opportunities in the Japanese Market," *Management Review*, July 1987, p. 55.

4. "Laying the Foundation for the Great Mall of China," *Business Week*, January 25, 1988, p. 68.

5. *Coca-Cola Annual Report, 1987*, p. 12.

6. *Fortune*, October 26, 1987, pp. 54, 56.

7. *Economic Indicators* (Washington D.C.: U.S. Government Printing Office, January 1988).

8. Teresa Domzal and Lynette Unger, "Emerging Positioning Strategies in Global Marketing," *Journal of Consumer Marketing*, 4(Fall 1987):24.

9. "U.S. Companies Go International," *Advertising Age*, November 24, 1986, p. S-6; and R. Wayne Walvoord, "Foreign Market Entry Strategies," *S.A.M. Advanced Management Journal*, 48(Spring 1983):14.

10. "Bud Is Making a Splash in the Overseas Beer Market," *Business Week*, October 22, 1984, p. 52.

11. "America's International Winners," *Fortune*, April 14, 1986, p. 40.

12. "Eleven Reasons for Firms to 'Go International,' " *Marketing News*, October 17, 1980, p. 1.

13. Gary Hamel and C. K. Prahalad, "Do You Really Have a Global Strategy?" *Harvard Business Review*, 63 (July–August 1985):140.

14. *Marketing News*, October 17, 1980, p. 1.

15. "Ad Fads: Global Sales Pitch by Harvard Guru Appears Much Easier in Theory, Marketers Find," *The Wall Street Journal*, May 12, 1988, p. 4.

16. "Coca-Cola Ordered by India to Disclose Formula for Drink," *The Wall Street Journal*, August 13, 1977, p. 11.

17. "Local Laws Keep International Marketers Hopping," *Advertising Age*, July 11, 1985, p. 20.

18. "Going Global," *Marketing*, December 10, 1987, p. 20.

19. "Global Approach Seeks Similarities in Markets," *Marketing News*, October 11, 1985, p. 12.

20. "The Coming Boom in Europe," *Fortune*, April 10, 1989, pp. 108–114; and "A 'Fortress Europe' in 1992?" *The New York Times*, August 22, 1988, p. A19.

21. "Free Trade or No, Canadians Fear Destruction," *Chicago Tribune*, November 7, 1988, sect. 4, p. 1.

22. "Pitfalls Lie Waiting for Unwary Marketers," *Advertising Age*, May 17, 1982, p. M-9.

23. *Fortune*, April 14, 1986, p. 44.

24. "Foreign Markets: Not for the Amateur," *Business Marketing*, July 1984, p. 112.

25. "When in Japan," *Forbes*, March 10, 1986, p. 153.

26. Philip R. Cateora, *International Marketing* (Homewood, Ill: Richard D. Irwin, 1983), p. 61.

27. *Fortune*, April 14, 1986, p. 36.

28. "How to Analyze Political Risk," *Business Marketing*, January 1987, pp. 52–53.

29. "The Dollar's Tumbling Act," *Adweek*, June 1, 1987, p. G.A. 30.

30. "How P&G Was Brought to a Crawl in Japan's Diaper Market," *Business Week*, October 13, 1986, p. 71.

31. "Trade Barriers and Dollar Swings Raise Appeal of Factories Abroad," *The New York Times*, March 26, 1989, p. 1.

32. "U.S./Japan," *Business Week*, July 18, 1988, p. 50.

33. "Egypt an Oasis for Soft Drinks," *The New York Times*, August 1, 1978, p. D1.

34. "New Foreign Products Pour into U.S. Market in Increasing Numbers," *The Wall Street Journal*, November 11, 1982, p. M-16; and "They Didn't Listen to Anybody," *Forbes*, December 15, 1986, p. 169.

35. "Quaker Tastes Crunch in Overseas Markets," *Advertising Age*, January 28, 1985, pp. 4, 78.

36. "Parker Pen," *Advertising Age*, June 2, 1986, p. 60.

37. "New Foreign Products Pour into U.S. Market in Increasing Numbers," *The Wall Street Journal*, November 11, 1982, p. 22.

38. "Can Ford Stay On Top?" *Business Week*, September 28, 1987, p. 80; and "Detroit Pulls Out Stops to Catch Up with World," *Business Week*, June 22, 1981, pp. S-1, S-44.

39. Eric D. Haueter, "Organizing for 'International Marketing,' " *Vital Speeches of the Day* 49(August 1983):620–624.

40. "Seeing Is Believing," *Marketing & Media Decisions*, February 1988, p. 52.

41. "Marketing Can Be Global, but Ads Must Remain Cultural," *Marketing News*, July 31, 1987, p. 26; and "Goodbye Global Ads," *Advertising Age*, November 16, 1987, p. 22.

42. "Europe's New Mass-Market Appeal," *Adweek*, June 1, 1987, p. 10.

43. "Colgate Ad 'Guru' a Global Marketer," *Advertising Age*, January 31, 1985, p. 39.

44. Ibid.

45. "Colgate," *Advertising Age,* November 17, 1986, p. 106.

46. "Myth and Marketing in Japan," *The Wall Street Journal,* April 6, 1989, p. B1.

47. *Forbes,* December 15, 1986, p. 169.

48. "Marketing, American-Style," *Forbes,* December 29, 1986, p. 91.

49. *Industrial Marketing,* February 1981, p. 68.

50. "Mobil Is Quitting South Africa Blaming 'Foolish' Laws in U.S.," *The New York Times,* April 29, 1989, p. 1.

51. Arthur C. Fatt, "The Danger of 'Local' International Advertising," *Journal of Marketing* (January 1967):60–62.

52. "Multinationals Tackle Global Marketing," *Advertising Age,* June 25, 1984, p. 50.

PART 5

• • •

STRATEGIC PLANNING, EVALUATION, AND CONTROL

In this last section of the book, we consider marketing in a broader perspective. First, we reintroduce the need for a strategic marketing plan to tie together all the components of marketing strategy into an overall corporate game plan. The strategic marketing plan not only coordinates all activities, it also evaluates and controls them to ensure that the company will meet future sales and profit goals. Chapter 22 describes how firms develop strategic plans and focuses on the development of marketing strategies at the corporate and business-unit levels. Chapter 23 focuses on the process of evaluating and controlling the entire marketing effort.

GE is a company that changed rapidly throughout the 1980s. It is not the same company as the one Jack Welch took over as CEO in 1981. Even its name, General Electric, no longer characterizes what it does, for the company has left the electronics field to the Japanese and has concentrated its efforts toward becoming a service and technology powerhouse. Small wonder that management now chooses to identify the company simply with the GE logo, leaving the name General Electric to the history books.[1]

What has made GE a different company? In the 1980s, Welch engineered a remarkable series of sales of existing GE businesses and acquisitions of new businesses that would have made Thomas Alva Edison wonder what happened to the company he had founded. Welch had a basic strategic plan for the 1980s that he vowed would move the company from the tenth largest firm in the United States to first. The plan was to divest the company's low-growth manufacturing businesses and to transform GE into a service and technology support center for the rest of the world. To accomplish this, Welch first divided GE's diverse businesses into three basic sectors that met profitability objectives: advanced technology (including aerospace, medical imaging, and factory automation), services (for instance, financial and communications services), and core manufacturing operations (such as lighting and major appliances).

With these three sectors in mind, Welch made his moves. In 1984 he sold GE's small appliance and housewares business to Black & Decker for $300 million because of low growth, low returns, and increasing foreign competition. He sold the company's mining subsidiary, Utah International, to an Australian mining company for $2.4 billion because it did not fit his strategic plan. In 1987 he made the most radical move. Unwilling to compete with lower-priced Japanese goods in an increasingly standardized, low-margin market, he sold the company's consumer electronics business to Thompson S.A., France's government-owned electronics giant.[2] Welch knew GE's strengths, and competing head-on with the Japanese was not one of them.

STRATEGIC MARKETING PLANNING

GE could not have fulfilled its strategic mission simply by getting rid of low-growth businesses. Its sales had made it cash-rich, and it had to acquire a base of operation in technology and services to carry it into the 1990s. Welch's first move was in financial services, buying Employers Reinsurance Corp. and Kidder Peabody, a stockbrokerage firm. The most important acquisition came next, when RCA was purchased for $6.3 billion in 1986. The biggest non-oil acquisition in U.S. history at the time, this purchase gave GE the National Broadcasting Company (an RCA affiliate) and RCA's aerospace business. But in acquiring what he wanted from RCA, Welch also got rid of what he did not want — RCA's electronics, record, life insurance, and carpet subsidiaries. Finally, when GE sold its electronics business to Thompson S. A., it also acquired Thompson's medical imaging business, making GE the world leader in this field.

Welch's strategic plan relied not only on external acquisitions, but also on internal development. A major move was the investment of $8 billion in R&D, much of it in the technology to develop factory automation systems. Although the business has not yet achieved expected returns, it will be a major component of GE's business mix in the 1990s. By 1987 Welch was well on the road to achieving his strategic goals. GE's corporate realignment was in full swing, with manufacturing representing 30 percent of earnings, down from 50 percent when Welch took over, and projected to be only 20 percent by 1991; services increased from 12 percent of earnings to 29 percent; and advanced technology businesses increased from 38 percent to 41 percent.[3] GE was now the third largest corporate entity in America. Under Welch, earnings had risen an average of 7.6 percent a year, a rate over 50 percent higher than that of his predecessors.[4]

In one respect, Welch's strategic plan mirrors the shift from a manufacturing to a service economy that has taken place in corporate America in the 1980s. In another respect, it represents a bold vision to insure industrial leadership into the 1990s. Without that strategic plan, GE would not be where it is today. ■

● ● ●

THE NATURE OF STRATEGIC MARKETING PLANNING

Until now, we have focused primarily on how to market a product. In this chapter, we take a broader view of marketing and consider the development of an overall corporate "game plan" that will tell the company where it should be going over the next five years. This corporate game plan is known as the **strategic marketing plan**. It differs from the product marketing plan in that it deals with the marketing of all the company's product offerings.

Strategic marketing planning takes place at two levels in the organization, the strategic business unit level (SBU) and the corporate level. (As you may remember from Chapter 2, an SBU is a unit within a company that organizes its marketing effort around customers with similar demand, such as GE's lighting or medical imaging SBUs.) The GE example focused on Jack Welch's corporate strategy in defining what businesses the company should be in, but business units must also develop strategies to determine the mix of products they should offer.

THREE LEVELS OF MARKETING PLANNING

In Chapter 2, we saw that marketing activities take place at three levels in the organization; the corporate level, the strategic business unit (SBU) level, and the product level. Figure 22.1 shows that these three planning levels produce a corporate strategic plan, an SBU strategic plan, and a marketing plan for individual products.

At the corporate level, strategic planning is the responsibility of the company's top management, including an executive VP for marketing. The plan focuses on the firm's **business mix**, that is, the combination of businesses the firm should be in. As we saw, GE changed its business mix by adding factory-automation, financial-services, and medical-imaging SBUs, and by divesting its electronics SBU. These moves were developed in the corporate strategic plan. In the process of determining this mix, top management does two things: First, it formalizes its future plans for the company in the form of a corporate growth strategy that identifies the nature of the business mix. Second, it allocates resources to the SBUs based on the corporate growth strategy. These plans are generally developed with a five-year time horizon.

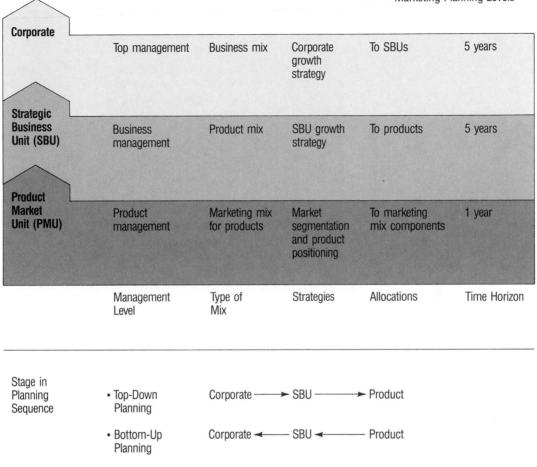

FIGURE 22.1
Characteristics of Three
Marketing Planning Levels

	Management Level	Type of Mix	Strategies	Allocations	Time Horizon
Corporate	Top management	Business mix	Corporate growth strategy	To SBUs	5 years
Strategic Business Unit (SBU)	Business management	Product mix	SBU growth strategy	To products	5 years
Product Market Unit (PMU)	Product management	Marketing mix for products	Market segmentation and product positioning	To marketing mix components	1 year

Stage in Planning Sequence

- Top-Down Planning   Corporate ⟶ SBU ⟶ Product

- Bottom-Up Planning   Corporate ⟵ SBU ⟵ Product

The SBU strategic plan parallels the corporate plan, except it is done at the business-unit level. The plan is the responsibility of the business managers who run the SBU and report to top management, including a marketing manager responsible for the SBU's marketing operations. The SBU strategic plan focuses on the unit's product offerings. For example, the plan for the medical-imaging unit will be concerned with the types of CT-scan imaging machines the unit should produce and whether it should attempt to take the technological lead in developing nuclear imaging devices, among other things. These considerations are incorporated into an SBU growth plan that requires allocations to individual product offerings. Since the SBU plan is submitted to top management to help with the development of corporate plans, the time horizon is also usually five years.

The third level of planning, the product marketing plan, is the responsibility of product managers. As we saw in Chapter 11, their primary concern is developing a mix of product, distribution, promotional, and pricing strategies for their products. In the process, product managers must identify the market segments representing greatest opportunity and position the product to these segments. Product managers make allocations to the individual components of the marketing mix — expenditures for product development, advertising, and distribution. Product marketing plans have a much shorter time horizon, usually one year.

Although strategic plans usually have a five-year time horizon, this does not mean they are developed every five years. In a fast-moving market place, companies can not wait five years to assess their environment. They develop strategic plans yearly, but with a longer-term perspective. As a result, the strategic plan is a moving five-year plan, with objectives and strategies changing yearly to account for changes in the marketing environment.

TOP-DOWN VERSUS BOTTOM-UP STRATEGIC PLANNING

There are two approaches to strategic planning, as shown on the bottom of Figure 22.1: a top-down approach and a bottom-up approach. In the *top-down approach*, allocation decisions are made by a centralized planning group at the corporate level and passed down to the SBUs, which then allocate resources to their individual product lines. Top-down planning is thus a *centralized* planning process in which corporate planners call the shots.

In contrast, the *bottom-up approach* is more *decentralized*, taking place primarily at the SBU level. The central part of the strategic plan is each individual SBU's evaluation of its product mix, but the key factor that drives this evaluation is the product marketing plan. The marketing plan's specification of the sales forecast for a product, the definition of the product's target segment, and its positioning will determine the amount of money the SBU allocates to the product. The company's growth strategy is then a composite of all the SBUs strategies. In the bottom-up approach, the SBU planners call the shots in the strategic planning process: They "drive" the corporate game plan.

The top-down and bottom-up approaches do not merely describe differences in the process of strategic marketing planning, they also describe substantial differences in philosophy and end results. Because it is centered at the corporate level, a top-down approach tends to focus more on corporate resources. Corporate planning managers tend to place more emphasis on the internal evaluation of company strengths and weaknesses than on the external evaluation of environmental opportunities and risks. Concern tends to be more with maximizing shareholder's equity than customer satisfaction, with primary focus on increasing the value of the company's stock.

By definition, a bottom-up approach is more marketing-oriented, focusing on the opportunities in the SBU's markets. SBU managers are more interested in evaluating opportunities and risks, leaving it to the corporate managers to place constraints on the money they can spend. The process is *market-driven* rather than *resource-driven*. In fact, the very term "strategic *marketing* planning" implies a bottom-up approach because of the emphasis on environmental factors in defining opportunity.

GE operated on a top-down basis before Welch took over, with corporate planners determining SBU strategies and direction. This caused some marketing blunders, such as the conclusion among GE's corporate planners that since families were getting smaller, kitchen appliances should get smaller. Line managers at the SBU level realized that the kitchen was one room that was not shrinking, and that working women wanted big refrigerators to reduce shopping trips.[5] The realization that business-unit managers know their markets better than corporate planners caused Welch to cut the corporate planning group from 58 to 33 people, and to follow a bottom-up planning process by giving SBUs responsibility for determining their future course.

Top-down planning is still used in many companies, particularly where a company is in disarray because of rapid environmental changes or a lack of adequate controls on operations. In such cases, a new management team usually steps in and exerts control from the top. If the company is customer-driven, eventually top management will assign strategic planning responsibilities to the SBUs. Since in this text we are following a customer-oriented approach, we will be focusing on a bottom-up planning process.

General Electric was not the only company that shifted from a top-down to a bottom-up strategic planning approach. General Motors did, too, at about the same time. Until around 1980, there was no strategic planning at General Motors' business units. All planning was centralized at the corporate level.

Raymond K. Fears — A Bottom-Up Planner at General Motors

Source: © Peter Yates.

Raymond K. Fears, the strategic planner for GM's Buick division, illustrates the change in strategic planning at General Motors. Fears moved from GM's corporate strategy group to the Buick division in Flint, Michigan, in 1983. His assignment was "To get [operating managers], who are used to thinking in terms of nuts and bolts, to think in strategic terms."[6]

Fears's move was part of General Motors Chairman Roger B. Smith's drive to institute bottom-up planning by involving operating managers from each of GM's five units in the strategic planning process. There was good reason for this move. Top-down planning had created a centralized planning process that led to a series of look-alike cars across its divisions, almost destroying the independent image of its key businesses — Chevrolet, Pontiac, Buick, Oldsmobile, and Cadillac.

Fears's job is to facilitate the changeover to a more decentralized strategic planning focus. Once he completes the task of educating operating managers in developing strategic plans, his job will be phased out. But the goal remains as Roger Smith stated, to ensure that the person in charge of strategic planning is the operating manager at the business unit level.

Does Fears, now in his mid-thirties, have any regrets about moving from headquarters to the "down in the trenches atmosphere of a car plant?" Absolutely not, he says, since he aspires to be an operating manager. "I see the move as getting closer to the action."[7] And the action at General Motors these days is not at corporate headquarters; it is at the business units. ■

THE STRATEGIC MARKETING PLANNING PROCESS

How can strategic marketing plans be developed at the corporate and SBU level to ensure future growth? Figure 22.2 illustrates the required steps, with the corporate planning sequence on the left and the planning sequence at the SBU level

FIGURE 22.2
The Strategic Marketing
Planning Process

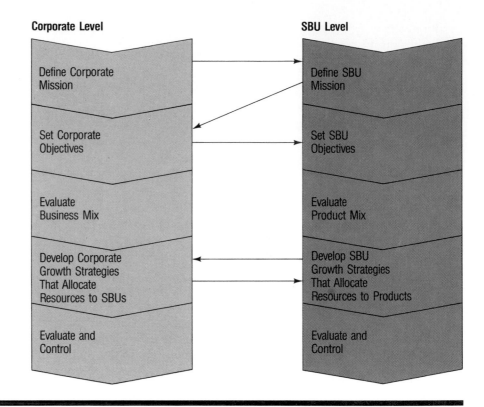

STRATEGIC MARKETING PLANNING AT THE CORPORATE LEVEL

on the right. The figure shows that the planning sequence is essentially the same at both levels.

Developing a strategic marketing plan at the corporate level means that top management must first define the firm's **corporate mission** — that is, what business or businesses the firm should be in. Welch's corporate mission for GE since 1981 has been to make the company a worldwide leader in advanced technology and services.

The company's mission then serves as the basis for defining a set of corporate objectives. These objectives might specify criteria for acquiring new businesses or divesting existing ones, earnings targets, and return on investment goals. As a direct outgrowth of its corporate mission, GE's corporate objectives were:

- To be first or second in key technology and service businesses such as medical imaging and factory automation.
- To change the firm's business mix through acquisitions and divestment, so that 80 percent of earnings would come from technology and services by 1991.
- To maintain a minimum earnings growth rate of 10 percent in each business.
- To achieve a return on investment of 15 percent in each business.

Top management next evaluates the firm's business mix to identify which SBUs should be supported with more investment, which should be maintained at current levels, and which should be divested. Such an analysis evaluates each

SBU's growth and profitability potential, and results in an overall corporate growth strategy designed to allocate funds to each business unit.

The final stage in strategic marketing planning is evaluation and control. Top management must evaluate the plan to determine if corporate objectives have been met, and must also institute controls to make sure the plan remains on course.

The strategic planning process we have just described provides a fairly accurate sketch of how planning takes place in companies like Wrigley that operate within one industry (in Wrigley's case, gum). Wrigley has no SBU structure, for the company is essentially the SBU, so planning occurs only at the corporate level. (The only difference is that instead of a mix of businesses, Wrigley's strategic plan would analyze the mix of gum products it offers.)[8]

STRATEGIC MARKETING PLANNING AT THE SBU LEVEL

Unlike Wrigley, however, firms such as GE have an SBU organization. These firms must ensure that each business unit provides appropriate input into the strategic plan, and that corporate management provides the resources and controls necessary to run the SBUs. The sequence on the right of Figure 22.2 shows that strategic planning at the SBU level requires the same steps as planning at the corporate level. The arrows show how the SBU and corporate plans interact.

There are two important points of interaction between the corporate and SBU levels. The first is when the corporate mission and objectives provide guidelines for the SBUs to establish their mission and objectives. One of the key corporate objectives that emerged from Welch's strategic plan, for instance, was that each of GE's 15 business units in the areas of technology, service, or core manufacturing should be the leader or second in its field.[9] Based on this objective, GE's medical-imaging unit might have established a mission of being the leader in its field through new technologies, with specific objectives to develop nuclear imaging, maintain an earnings growth rate of at least 15 percent (one-third higher than the corporate guideline), and broaden its international marketing base.

Each business unit must evaluate its mix of products in order to meet SBU and corporate objectives. Based on an analysis of the product mix, business-unit managers will then develop an SBU growth strategy spelling out allocations for the unit's product offerings. The second point of interaction between the SBUs and corporate in Figure 22.2 is when the SBUs submit their growth plans to corporate for approval. Top management evaluates each SBUs plans in conjunction with the plans of the other SBUs, and then decides on the funding for each. Once these allocations are made, the SBUs implement their plans, evaluate the results to determine if they are in line with corporate and SBU objectives, and institute controls.

In the remainder of this chapter, we will review the major components of the strategic planning process in Figure 22.2: developing a corporate and SBU mission and objectives, evaluating the firm's business and product mix, developing corporate and SBU strategies, and insuring evaluation and control of the strategic plan.

DEFINE THE CORPORATE MISSION

A corporate mission should give a company's management a sense of purpose and direction. The question "What business are we in?" provides the focus for a corporate mission statement. As we saw in Chapter 2, Kodak changed its mission

EXHIBIT 22.1
Defining Kodak's
Corporate Mission: Imaging

from a "photography company" to an "imaging company." This shift prompted
a change in the company's corporate advertising approach. Before the change in
mission, most of its advertising was for individual products that focused on the
company's photography business. After, the company embarked on an umbrella
campaign that featured electronic publishing, printing, color imaging, and digital
scanning systems. The basic ad theme, "The new vision of Kodak," (see the
bottom of the ad in Exhibit 22.1) reflected the change in corporate mission to
imaging.

Kodak's corporate mission went from a narrow, product-oriented focus to a
broader focus that was centered on customer needs. A strict product focus tends
to be far more limiting than a need-oriented focus, inhibiting the search for new
opportunities. Imagine how history would have changed if railroad companies
such as Penn Central or Baltimore & Ohio had conceived of their business as the
transportation business rather than the railway business. What would have pre-
vented such railroad companies from buying a small airline or bus company in
the 1930s?[10]

On the other hand, there is also a danger that the corporate mission may be
too broad. In the late 1960s and early 1970s many companies stated their mission in terms of maximizing the asset value of the company, then embarked on
acquisitions of high-growth companies that they did not have the know-how to
manage. The problem here was that the corporate mission statement did not give
any guidance as to which companies to acquire and which to avoid: any business
with a good earnings record was a candidate for acquisition.

In the early 1980s, many of these companies redefined their mission as going
back to their core businesses. After Ralston Purina went through an acquisition

binge that included a Colorado resort, a shrimp-breeding company, and the St. Louis Blues hockey team, a new CEO defined the company's business in three key areas — animal feed, restaurants, and domestic grocery products. Similarly, after going into digital watches, calculators, and smoke alarms, Gillette now defines its business as men's and women's grooming and cosmetic products.

In each of the preceding cases, the company's mission statement provides guidelines for acquiring and divesting businesses and for developing new product areas. The development of electronic publishing by Kodak was a natural consequence of its mission statement. Ralston Purina's divestiture of shrimp farms and other businesses was the outcome of its determination to go back to the businesses it knows best.

DETERMINE CORPORATE OBJECTIVES

Although the corporate mission of companies like Ralston Purina and Kodak ultimately leads to strategies such as divesting shrimp farms or developing imaging products, their mission statements are too broad to direct such strategies. Corporate mission statements need to be translated into a set of more specific objectives. That is why GE's mission of growth in its technology and services businesses was translated into the specific objective that these businesses would account for 80 percent of the company's earnings by 1991.

Whirlpool's mission is to compete head-to-head with GE in another area, major appliances. Its ad in Exhibit 22.2 reflects this mission without having to name GE. It also aims to get a bigger chunk of the dishwasher and microwave business. This mission has produced several specific performance objectives: to increase sales by an average of 10 percent a year for the next five years; to increase profits an average of 15 percent per year; and to add $1 billion in sales from new products in the next three years.[11]

EVALUATE THE BUSINESS AND PRODUCT MIX

One of the most important responsibilities of any company's top management is deciding what its business mix should be. In many cases, a company's identity changes when it reorders its business mix. This was true of GE; it is also true of Greyhound. Figure 22.3 shows the changes in Greyhound's business mix. Greyhound went through the same process as Ralston Purina, Gillette, and Kraft, acquiring diverse businesses, including meat and poultry products, computer leasing, and mortgage insurance, that later proved to drag down its earnings. Unlike these other companies, however, Greyhound had no core business. It got rid of its bus line because it was apparent that that business was going nowhere.

If Greyhound is no longer carrying people around in buses, what is it doing? Management saw the need to diversify early on. But when its first batch of acquisitions did not meet earnings objectives, it embarked on a plan to change the company's business mix. As Figure 22.3 shows, from 1982 to 1987 the company divested itself of meat and poultry businesses that represented almost 50 percent of sales, reduced transportation services to almost nothing, and began focusing on three key business areas: consumer products (it acquired Dial soap and Purex Bleach); airport travel services (including airport restaurants and catering services), and financial services. Today, these three areas represent almost 90 percent of sales. Just as the name General Electric no longer applies to that company's business mix, the name Greyhound certainly does not apply to its business mix.

BUSINESS PORTFOLIO ANALYSIS

Before a company can embark on such transformations, management must have some systematic approach to determining its business mix. Such an approach — **business portfolio analysis** — views the corporation as a portfolio or mix of businesses, each with a different mission, market, set of resources, and earnings potential. Each business is evaluated on two familiar sets of criteria: *marketing opportunity* and the company's *business position*, that is, its ability to exploit opportunity (see Figure 22.4). On this basis, management estimates the revenue potential of the business.

The basic concept of portfolio analysis is to develop a mix of businesses that generate and require cash. The revenue-generating businesses will supply cash to fuel future growth opportunities. Thus, GE's manufacturing base in appliances and lighting is meant to generate revenues that can be used to support the basis for future growth in factory automation and medical imaging. In 10 or 20 years, factory automation and medical imaging may be the cash-generating businesses that will support GE's growth opportunities into the twenty-first century.

Based on this framework, there are several approaches to portfolio analysis. They all rely on the common matrix in Figure 22.4 in which opportunity-related criteria are listed on one dimension and company-related factors on the other.

BUSINESS PORTFOLIO STRATEGIES

The four alternatives shown in the matrix in Figure 22.4 are known as business portfolio strategies. If an SBU is in an area of high opportunity and if the firm is in a position to exploit opportunity, then the decision should be for the SBU to *grow*, as shown in the upper-left portion of the matrix. This strategy requires investing in the SBU's future growth potential. If opportunities are low, but the firm is in a strong position, as shown in the lower-left portion of the figure, then the company should invest in the business unit on a limited basis to *maintain* its present position.

If opportunities are good, but the company is in a poor position to exploit them, as in the upper-right quadrant, two strategies are possible: (1) invest in the SBU by acquiring the resources to exploit opportunity, a *build* strategy, or (2) get out of the business, that is *divest*. A company would choose a build strategy only if it felt it could develop the resources to pursue the opportunity. In the late 1970s, GE was at a turning point regarding its medical-imaging business. It could try to build it, or it could get out. GE chose a build strategy because it felt it had sufficient technical expertise and financial resources to develop an emerging opportunity. As a result, medical imaging is now in a grow strategy.

If opportunities are poor, and the company is in a weak position (the lower-right portion of the matrix), its strategy should be to cut back investment in the SBU and *harvest* it by reducing costs faster than decreases in revenues. A profit in the short term can result through these cutbacks. The alternative to harvesting is for the company to divest itself of the business.

Figure 22.5 shows how GE might have applied portfolio analysis in making business-mix decisions concerning a number of its current and past SBUs. Medical imaging, communications, and financial services are seen as strategic windows warranting further investment because of high marketing opportunity and GE's strengths in each area. The portfolio strategy for these businesses is growth through additional investment.

Factory automation, that is, the introduction of robots on the assembly line, is an area of high opportunity. But GE is not in as strong a position here as in the three areas just discussed. It has been slow in adapting the technology to fit the requirements of particular industries and in convincing managers of the need for a changeover from more labor-intensive methods. Despite these problems, the company sees vast potential in this area and is willing to invest resources to follow a build strategy for this unit. Divesting has not been seriously considered as an option.

Lighting and major appliances are mature businesses. Because of their limited growth potential, they are placed in the lower half of the figure. GE's business position is strong because it is the market leader in both areas. As a result, the company will continue to invest in product development, advertising, and distribution to maintain its leadership position.

Consumer electronics, small appliances, and mining were all low-growth areas that were divested. GE's business position in each of these areas was poor — in electronics and small appliances because of lower-cost Japanese competitors, and in mining because of lack of managerial and technical competence. Before divesting the radio and television lines that were part of its electronics business, GE began to cut back investments. This harvesting strategy was a signal that divestment of the electronics business was eventually likely.

The dotted line in Figure 22.5 shows that businesses in low areas of opportunity supply cash for investment in businesses in higher areas of opportunity. Lighting and major appliances supply cash as market leaders; consumer electronics provided cash during the period it was harvested, since marketing costs were cut back substantially; mining and small appliances supplied cash when they were sold to other companies. As a result of these moves, GE is conforming to an

FIGURE 22.3
Changes in Greyhound's Business Mix

Source "Can Greyhound Leave the Dog Days Behind?" Reprinted from June 8, 1987 issue of *Business Week*, p. 72, by special permission, copyright © 1987 by McGraw-Hill, Inc.

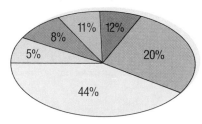

1982
Total Sales: $5 Billion

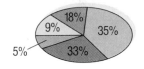

1987
Total Sales: $2.5 Billion

☐ Consumer Products
☐ Airport, Travel, Food Services
☐ Financial Services
☐ Transportation Services
☐ Bus Manufacturing
☐ Meat, Poultry Products

FIGURE 22.4
The Basic Business Portfolio Matrix

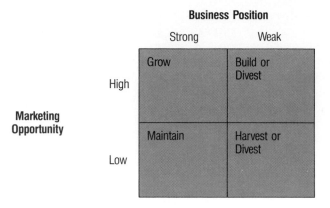

important goal of business portfolio analysis — to ensure a mix of cash-generating and cash-using businesses so that the former can support the latter's growth.

APPROACHES TO BUSINESS PORTFOLIO ANALYSIS

Although the goal of business portfolio analysis is always to provide an optimal mix of businesses, the analysis can be approached in a number of ways. The most widely used approaches are the Boston Consulting Group's (BCG's) growth/ share analysis and GE/McKinsey's market attractiveness/business position analysis. (The latter was developed by General Electric and the large consulting firm, McKinsey & Co., as an alternative to the BCG approach.) We will consider both approaches here because they demonstrate different ways of systematizing the processes of selecting a business mix and allocating funds to businesses.

FIGURE 22.5
GE's Business Portfolio

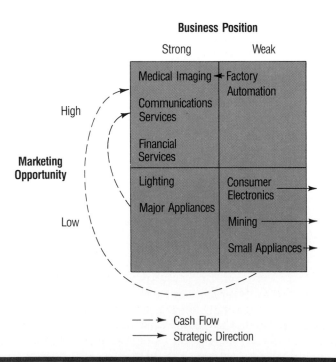

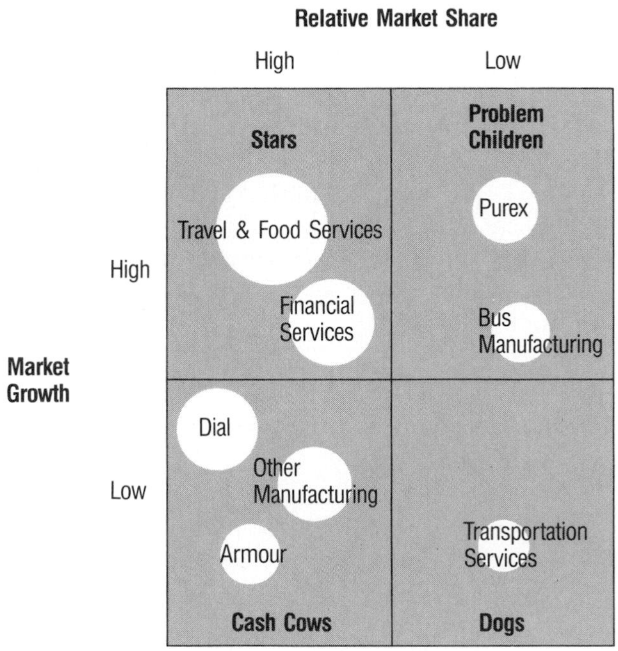

Relative Market Share

High   Low

FIGURE 22.6
Greyhound's Business Mix Utilizing the BCG Growth/Share Matrix

BCG's Growth/Share Analysis

The Boston Consulting group, a leading management consulting company, developed an approach that uses two criteria to evaluate a firm's business units: the market growth rate and the relative market share of its products. **Relative market share** is calculated by dividing the SBU's market share by the market share of its leading competitors. Thus, if Apple's desktop publishing SBU has a 40 percent share of that market and IBM a 20 percent share, Apple's relative share is 2.0 (40/20) and IBM's is .5 (20/40).

The growth rate for an SBU's market is regarded as a summary measure of marketing opportunity, while the firm's relative market share is regarded as a summary measure of its strength or weakness (that is, its business position) in that market. As a result, the BCG matrix parallels the basic portfolio matrix presented in Figure 22.4. The reason BCG uses market growth and relative market share as the two criteria for evaluating SBUs is because studies have shown that these two factors are related to profitability.[12]

BCG's matrix presents four alternative SBU positionings that are shown in Figure 22.6 and parallel those in Figure 22.4:

- *Stars* are products with a high growth rate and market share. These products warrant a growth strategy, and they need significant cash to finance rapid growth.

- *Cash cows* are SBUs in low-growth areas that have high market shares. They generate more cash than is required to maintain them. Excess cash is used to finance high-growth areas.

- *Problem children* are SBUs that have a low relative market share in high-growth situations. Their eventual direction is not clear, and the firm must determine whether to build them into stars or get rid of them. Any course in between is dangerous, since it could just dissipate resources.

- *Dogs* are low-share SBUs in low-growth areas. They should be either harvested for short-term profits or divested.

Figure 22.6 illustrates how Greyhound's business mix fit into the BCG matrix as of 1987. The size of the circles represents the sales of each SBU. The service areas are regarded as stars and are slated for further investment. Most consumer products such as Dial Soap and Armour Meats are cash cows in low-growth areas; they are being maintained for their cash-generating abilities.

The Purex bleach unit is classified as a problem child because Greyhound's strategy to sell its bleach products was to advertise to build brand loyalty, while Purex's strength had actually been its low price appeal. The company has gone back to emphasizing Purex's price, and the unit now seems to be moving out of problem-child status. The bus-manufacturing unit was recently acquired from General Motors. While it has high growth potential, it remains to be seen whether Greyhound can build it into a star. Finally, transportation services is shown as a divestment because of Greyhound's sale of its bus travel business.

Limits of BCG's Portfolio Analysis

The BCG approach provides a useful overview of a company's business mix, and its labels of businesses as stars, cash cows, dogs, and problem children are widely used. But it has serious flaws. The most serious is its assumption that market share is linked to profitability, and that it should be the criterion for a company's strength. Many other factors affect the firm's business position besides market share, including financial resources, marketing know-how, and distribution facilities. And although market share is generally related to profitability, there are many exceptions. As we saw in Chapter 4, low-market-share firms can be very profitable when they operate in protected niches.

A second major flaw in the BCG analysis is that it relies on the single factor of market growth to measure opportunity. As we saw in Part II, a host of factors other than market growth affect marketing opportunity, including competitive intensity, legal and regulatory factors, and technology.

GE's Market Attractiveness/Business Position Matrix

GE began using the BCG analysis in the early 1970s, but it soon recognized the limitations of relying on only one factor to measure opportunity and business position. As a result, GE asked McKinsey & Co., a large management consulting firm, to help it develop a better portfolio approach. The result was a matrix similar to that shown in Figure 22.7, which evaluates market attractiveness and business position according to multiple criteria. This matrix rates an SBU on a number of criteria related to market attractiveness and business position, such as:

MARKET ATTRACTIVENESS	BUSINESS POSITION
Market size	Market share
Growth rate	Product quality
Cyclicality of demand	Price competitiveness
Seasonality of demand	Marketing capability
Competitive intensity	Production strength
Rate of technological change	Financial strength
Barriers to entry	Distribution capability
Economies of scale	Sales effectiveness
Required capitalization	Capacity utilization
Legal regulations	Technological skills

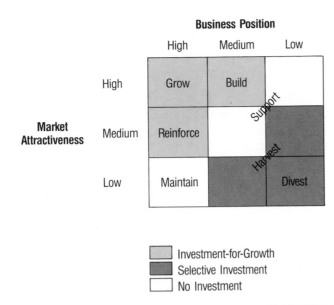

Business Position

	High	Medium	Low
High	Grow	Build	
Medium	Reinforce		Support
Low	Maintain	Harvest	Divest

Market Attractiveness

Investment-for-Growth
Selective Investment
No Investment

FIGURE 22.7
GE's Market Attractiveness/ Business Position Analysis

Once the SBU is rated, it is positioned on the two dimensions in the matrix in Figure 22.7. The matrix shows three general portfolio strategies. SBUs with high market attractiveness that are in a strong business position are candidates for investment for growth. SBUs in the middle range are candidates for selective investment to generate short-term earnings, and SBUs with low attractiveness and business position warrant no further investment.

Figure 22.7 also shows that a company can generate more specific portfolio strategies within each of these three alternatives. In the investment-for-growth area, three strategies are shown: grow, build, and reinforce. As we saw in Figure 22.4, a grow strategy is warranted for a new SBU in a high-opportunity area, and a build strategy if market attractiveness is high but the firm does not have the resources to exploit it. A reinforce strategy is sound for a more mature SBU that is in a strong business position but is facing increasing competition. This strategy requires greater advertising and sales support.

Two different types of portfolio strategies would be appropriate in the selective investment category. A support strategy would apply to an SBU that has a unique competitive advantage in appealing to a particular market segment. The company would allocate resources to the SBU on a selective basis to protect its competitive advantage. For example, American Motors invested selectively in its jeep line to support a protected niche that was not threatened by the big three auto makers. In a maintenance strategy, the company would allocate enough funds to ensure the SBU's leadership position, but would not try to increase market share since the unit is in a stagnant market.

As we saw in Figure 22.4, a firm follows a strategy of harvesting or divesting the SBU when opportunity is low and the business position is poor. A harvesting strategy is best if a firm has a group of loyal customers that will continue to buy its brands despite little advertising and a lack of widespread distribution. In the absence of such a core of loyal users, the business is unlikely to maintain short-term earnings and should be divested.

FIGURE 22.8
Standard Brand's Past Product Mix

Market Attractiveness	Business Position: High	Business Position: Medium	Business Position: Low
High	Pinata Foods	Fleishman's Corn Oil	Souverain Wines
Medium	Planter's Nuts	Fleishman's Yeast Royal Gelatin Desserts	Chase & Sanborne Coffee
Low	Baby Ruth Butterfingers Confectionary Line	Pet Foods	Ufima Coffee

PRODUCT PORTFOLIO ANALYSIS

Just as corporate management evaluates its mix of businesses, SBU managers must evaluate their unit's product mix. In doing so, they use the same principles that top management uses in its portfolio analysis — namely, that a product mix should be balanced so there are enough cash cows to support potential stars, and enough stars to ensure future growth. Business managers thus develop product portfolio strategies, just as top management develops business portfolio strategies: Some brands are built up, others maintained in their cash-generating positions, others harvested, and yet others withdrawn.

Of the two approaches to business portfolio analysis discussed in the preceding section, GE's market attractiveness/business position approach is more suitable for a product portfolio analysis. The reason is because individual products and markets can be analyzed on a range of factors reflecting marketing opportunity. In the late 1970s, for instance, Standard Brands used this approach to analyze its mix of grocery products. The company was concentrating more on brand-name consumer goods and reducing its involvement in commodity food ingredients such as sugar substitutes.[13] Product managers received a data package with projections of inflation, economic growth, demographic shifts, and other environmental changes that they used to evaluate their individual products on market attractiveness and business position.

The result was the product portfolio matrix illustrated in Figure 22.8. Pinata Foods and Planter's Nuts, specialty and snack food categories that the company acquired because of their growth potential, were in an investment-for-growth position. Fleishman Corn Oil was also in the investment-for-growth category. Although an established brand, it had growth potential because corn oil was beginning to be recognized as having nutritional benefits.

Several product lines were in the selective investment category. Souverain Wines was not a major factor in the domestic wine industry because of competition from more established companies such as Gallo. Therefore, Standard Brands had to decide whether to build up the line or to get out of the wine business. Fleishman's Yeast and Royal Gelatin Desserts appealed to well-established consumer segments. Standard Brand's candy bar and confectionary products were in a strong position but in a low-growth market. The company was willing to invest selectively to maintain these brands.

Finally, several products were in the harvest/divest category. Pet foods was a candidate for divestment because of declining sales. Chase & Sanborne, once a leading brand in the coffee market, had only a 4 percent share in 1979. Because the brand had a small but loyal following, management felt it could still generate profits for several years by cutting back marketing expenditures and harvesting it. The same was not true of Ufima Coffee, a French coffee subsidiary. Its low returns prompted Standard Brands to divest it.

This product portfolio strategy produced sound results. Overall, about 50 percent of sales came from brands in the investment-for-growth category, 30 percent from brands in the selective investment category, and 20 percent from brands in the harvest/divest category. This 50/50 split between cash-generating and cash-using brands reflected a balanced product portfolio.

CORPORATE GROWTH STRATEGIES

At the corporate and the SBU level, the key element in the strategic marketing plan is the company's growth strategy — its overall *game plan* for the next five years. A corporate growth strategy can be specified, however, only when the company's mission, objectives, and business portfolio have been developed.

GE's growth strategy is to acquire promising businesses in advanced technology and service areas and to rely on the internal development of new products on a more selective basis. As the company's recent moves illustrate, a major question addressed by corporate growth strategies is what emphasis to place on acquisitions versus internal development for future growth. If a company relies on external acquisitions, this must mean that it is not satisfied with its current business position; it is looking for new businesses to fuel growth. In so doing, it wishes to broaden its resources and capabilities. If it relies on internal development, management must be satisfied with its resource base and is looking for opportunities to better satisfy customer needs by introducing new products.

For instance, Abbott Laboratories, the pharmaceutical company, has rejected a strategy of acquisitions for growth; instead, it is maintaining a competitive advantage in the health-care industry by constantly developing new products in the medical diagnostic market. It developed a desktop blood analyzer that allows physicians to measure glucose and cholesterol levels in just eight minutes in their offices. It was also the first company to come up with a blood test to detect the AIDS virus. Abbott commands more than twice the sales of its nearest competitor in the $5.9 billion medical diagnostic market.[14] Abbott has yet to find an outside business with more profit potential than the businesses it has developed internally. In 1984 its 13.9 percent profit margin was the highest in the pharmaceutical industry, and its 26.8 percent return on equity was one of the best of all U.S. companies.[15]

In contrast to Abbott, Sara Lee is relying on external acquisitions for growth. The company moved from being a packaged foods producer to a consumer products conglomerate by acquiring companies that make shoe polish, insecticides, socks, laundry detergent, and purses. Sara Lee seeks companies that are first or second in their market with a good earnings record. In 1988, it achieved over $10 billion in sales on the strength of its acquisition strategy.[16]

FIGURE 22.9
Corporate Growth Strategies
for Internal Development

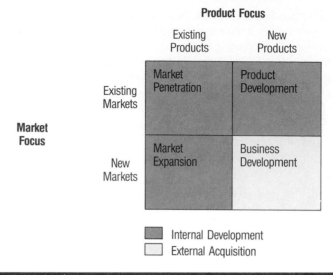

Most companies do not rely on only one strategy for growth. We saw that GE uses internal development as an important vehicle for growing its technology businesses, while it uses acquisitions for expanding its services businesses. One growth strategy does become dominant for many companies, however: external acquisitions for Sara Lee, internal development for Abbott Labs.

INTERNAL DEVELOPMENT STRATEGIES

Figure 22.9 shows three alternative strategies for internal development, and one strategy for external acquisition, each classified by whether the company is concentrating its efforts on new or existing products and on new or existing markets.

Market Penetration

Companies that rely on a **market-penetration strategy** invest in existing brands directed to existing markets. Many of these companies start out by following a strategy of acquisition outside of their core areas, then discover that they do not have the managerial or marketing know-how to run the businesses they have acquired. After a painful process of divestment, they go back to emphasizing existing brands.

General Mills followed this path. In 1985 it got rid of acquisitions in fashion (Izod) and toys (Parker Brothers, Kenner) and went back to emphasizing existing brands in its lower-growth core businesses, cereals and cake mixes. The company is now counting on product reformulations and changes in packaging to sustain older brands such as Cheerios (see Exhibit 22.3), Wheaties, Total, and the Betty Crocker cake mix line.[17]

Market Expansion

A second corporate growth strategy of internal development is to expand existing products into new markets. We saw in Chapter 5 that Kellogg has taken this **market expansion** approach. After seeing sales for many of its cereals stagnate because of decreases in the birth rate, the company is aggressively pursuing new markets for its existing cereal brands by convincing health-conscious adults to eat cereal and by introducing cereals into foreign markets.

Interestingly, Kellogg did not fall into the trap of acquiring diverse businesses when it found itself in a stagnant market. The current CEO remembers going to the chairman of the company in the late 1960s with the idea of diversifying away from cereals as a hedge against the decreasing birth rate. The chairman said no, Kellogg would continue to focus on its core business of cereals. This focus led the company to follow its strategy of market expansion.

Product Development

The third internal strategy for growth is to develop new products or extensions of existing product lines. In most cases, these new products will be directed to existing markets. This strategy is referred to as **product development** in Figure 22.9. Syntex Corp., the first company to make a birth control pill in the 1960s, adopted this strategy when it switched from external acquisitions in the mid 1980s, selling its beauty and eye-care businesses so that it could stick strictly to pharmaceuticals. Committing to pharmaceuticals meant relying on its expertise in biotechnology to introduce new products. The company upped its R&D budget and introduced new drugs to fight ulcers, hypertension, and arthritis. It has doubled its salesforce to help sell these new drugs.[18]

When a company markets new products to totally new markets, it requires new resources such as technology, marketing know-how, distribution networks, a salesforce, and manufacturing facilities. This strategy, shown in the lower right-hand box in Figure 22.9, is referred to as **business development** since it usually involves getting into new businesses and is identified with a strategy of external acquisition. Here, it is important to make a distinction: Until now, our discussion of external acquisitions has focused on companies diversifying into unrelated lines and getting into trouble as a result. There are other less risky routes to external acquisition, however.

Figure 22.10 presents the alternatives for corporate growth through acquisition along two dimensions. First, a company can acquire businesses similar to those it is now in, or it can acquire new businesses in unrelated areas. Second, a strategy of business development can be followed through diversification of its businesses or through integration of its operations.

A strategy of diversifying into new businesses is called **divergent acquisition**, as when GE diversified into financial services. Diversifying into related businesses is called **convergent acquisition**, as when Gillette acquired Braun electric shavers. Companies can also integrate their operations in related or unrelated areas. **Horizontal integration** means acquiring companies in the same industry — for example, GE's acquisition of RCA or Stroh's acquisition of Schlitz beer. In **vertical integration**, a company acquires new facilities in its manufacturing or distribution operations.

Vertical integration can be backward or forward. In **backward integration**, a company acquires facilities that precede its operations in manufacturing and/or distribution. For example, a manufacturing company might acquire a business that produces the raw materials the company uses to make its products, or a retail company might buy a manufacturing plant to insure it will have a source of supply for its own private brands. **Forward integration** is the reverse, when a company acquires facilities that can enable it to carry out tasks that are further along in its manufacturing and/or distribution processes. For instance, a mining company might buy a manufacturing facility, or a manufacturer might acquire retail outlets.

EXHIBIT 22.3
Reinforcing Older Brands through Market Penetration

EXTERNAL ACQUISITION STRATEGIES

FIGURE 22.10
Corporate Growth Strategies for External Acquisition

Type of Business		Type of Strategy: Diversification	Type of Strategy: Integration
	New Businesses	Divergent Acquisitions	Vertical Integration
	Similar Businesses	Convergent Acquisitions	Horizontal Integration

Divergent Acquisitions

We have cited the problems that firms encounter when they acquire businesses outside their core areas. The companies that engaged in divergent acquisitions in the 1960s and 1970s only to find themselves divesting these businesses in the 1980s reads like a roll call of corporate America's best and brightest: Gillette, General Mills, Ralston Purina, Nestle, Union Carbide, Mobile, Westinghouse, Gulf & Western, and so on. In most cases, these acquisitions were made for financial rather than marketing reasons. The guiding rule seemed to be "buy into high-growth businesses with good earnings records to increase the company's worth — and worry about marketing know-how later."

As it turned out, there was plenty to worry about later, as management began to realize they did not know enough about the customers and markets in businesses outside their core areas. The rapid pace of divestment in the 1980s is illustrated by Gulf & Western's sale of many of its divergent acquisitions — Consolidated Cigars, Simmons bedding, and Kayser Roth apparel.

Although this litany of failures may make it appear that the strategy of divergent acquisition should be avoided at all times, such is not the case. Several companies, including GE and Greyhound, have changed their corporate missions to better enter the business environment of the 1990s by defining new businesses as targets outside their traditional areas of competency. The key factor in the success or failure of divergent acquisitions is the attitude of top management. If it is willing to give the acquired company sufficient resources and enough freedom to follow sound marketing strategies, then the business is likely to continue to generate earnings.

Convergent Acquisitions

Companies have also diversified by acquiring businesses within their core areas of competency. Although this strategy of convergent acquisitions appears in the diversification column in Figure 22.10, diversification is a poor description of these actions since they do not take the company far afield from what it is doing. (To coin a word, "conversification" might be more descriptive.)

We saw that some companies such as Quaker arrived at a strategy of convergent acquisition by first following a divergent acquisition strategy that failed. Pet Foods, on the other hand, is a company that did not follow the divergent-acquisition route. It has acquired new businesses within its core area of higher-priced package foods with a quality image. It bought businesses that "hold the high ground" such as Underwood ham spreads, B&M baked beans, Ac'cent, Progresso foods, and Whitman's chocolates.[19] Once it acquires these companies, Pet develops new products within the line. Progresso is best known for its soups. But Pet cashed in on its strong brand name by introducing a line of Progresso frozen Italian dinners. Similarly, Whitman's is best known for boxed chocolates, but Pet leveraged its name by introducing a line of Whitman's frozen chocolate cream pies.

Vertical Integration

Some companies have relied on vertical integration as a central part of their corporate growth strategy, having concluded that integrating their operations, either forward or backward, would improve their competitive position and earnings potential.

Tandy is a company that has relied on both forward and backward integration with mixed results. A manufacturer of electronics goods, the company made an early decision to follow a forward-integration strategy, distributing these products through its own retail Radio Shack stores. Tandy's ownership of its retail stores was motivated by a desire to be closer to the final consumer. But forward integration has not given Tandy a competitive advantage. Radio Shack stores, with poor displays, dim lighting, and inadequate sales help, have hurt the company's image. In an effort to remedy this, Tandy instituted tighter controls over store operations in the mid 1980s.

Tandy has also integrated backwards. It owns companies that make plastic molding, epoxy boards that hold microprocessors, and extruded wire from ingot rods to make electronic cables.[20] These companies provide the materials for the huge variety of electronic parts that Tandy manufactures. Such backward integration gives the company better quality control while holding down costs. But here also, backward integration has not achieved the competitive advantage that the company has sought. New product introductions have not been accompanied by the cost reductions necessary to enable the company to compete in key areas such as laptop computers, VCRs, and cellular telephones.

Horizontal Integration

In horizontal integration, a company acquires a direct competitor and thus expands its market share. This is a quick way for a company to become a market leader. Stroh Brewing Company's acquisition of Schaefer Brewing in 1981, then of Schlitz in 1982, propelled the company from seventh to third in the industry. It also made Stroh a national rather than a regional competitor, placing it in a better position to compete with Anheuser-Busch and Miller, the market leaders.

Horizontal integration may be challenged by the government as restricting trade if the acquisition substantially increases the company's share of industry sales. The Justice Department blocked Mobil's acquisition of Marathon Oil for this reason. It did not block Stroh's acquisitions of Schlitz and Schaefer, however, because of the dominance of Anheuser-Busch and Miller in the beer industry.

EVALUATE AND CONTROL THE STRATEGIC PLAN

Once corporate growth and portfolio strategies have been implemented, management must evaluate the strategic plan to determine if objectives have been met. As Figure 22.2 shows, control over the strategic plan occurs at both the corporate and the SBU level.

At the corporate level, planners must determine whether the necessary resources are being allocated to the business units to achieve objectives. GE's objective of being a leader in factory automation required an investment of billions of dollars in R&D to develop this field. Corporate planners must also ensure that business strategies are consistent with overall objectives. For instance, requests by the lighting or appliance units at GE for increased R&D expenditures that might reduce the funds available for key technology and service areas might be rejected because they are not consistent with GE's overall objective.

The management of strategic business units must also exert controls, tracking allocations to individual products and ensuring that the product mix has the right balance of stars and cash cows, with any dogs being harvested or divested so they do not serve as a cash drain.

One of the most difficult aspects of strategic marketing planning is achieving the delicate balance between too much corporate control, which might stifle the initiative of the business units, and too little control, which might lead units to drift from corporate objectives.

This latter situation occurred at Westinghouse and led to a series of disastrous ventures. Westinghouse formed a business unit to build low-cost housing on government contracts and gave the SBU's management a blank check to achieve growth. The business unit began to acquire contracts without regard for profitability, and substantial losses resulted.

In contrast to Westinghouse, General Mills exerted too much control over some of its business units. When sales started to decrease at Parker Brothers, the company responded by getting involved in a business it did not really know — games. It introduced its own managers into the company, thus undercutting Parker managers who knew the business best. Similarly, when the company's Izod line of clothes began to slip and Izod's managers tried to rush new lines to market, General Mills' corporate staffers held them back, allowing competitors to take business away from Izod.[21] These examples show the importance of effective but not excessive control by corporate management.

SUMMARY

1. *What is the nature of the strategic marketing planning process?*
The purpose of strategic marketing planning is to provide a corporate game plan to chart where the company should be going for the next five years. Developing a corporate game plan requires management to
a. Define the firm's corporate mission and objectives.
b. Evaluate the company's mix of strategic business units.
c. Develop a corporate growth strategy to allocate funds to the SBUs.
d. Evaluate and control the plan.

2. *What is the role of the strategic business unit (SBU)* in the strategic marketing planning process?
Business-unit managers must evaluate the SBU's product mix just as top management evaluates the company's mix of business units. Managers will then develop strategies for each of their products and submit an overall request for funds to corporate management. Once corporate approves funds, business-unit management implements the plan, evaluates results, and institutes controls.

3. *What is the distinction between top-down and bottom-up strategic planning?*

In top-down planning, corporate directions determine strategies for the individual business unit and the unit's product mix. In bottom-up planning, the SBUs provide the basic input into the strategic plan based on their assessment of individual products. This latter process is marketing-oriented because product assessment is based on customer and competitive analysis. Therefore, the foundation for the strategic plan is the analysis by SBU management of the marketing opportunity for individual products.

4. *How can a firm best evaluate its business and product mix?*

A company can best evaluate its business mix through portfolio analysis. This approach views a company's businesses as a portfolio of SBUs that should be balanced between established, cash-generating brands and newer, cash-using brands that have potential for growth. Each business unit is evaluated on two criteria — marketing opportunity and the company's business position in the market. Business units are positioned on these criteria. Portfolio strategies are then developed for each unit depending on its position. For example, a strategy of investment-for-growth would be appropriate for an SBU with high marketing opportunity and in a strong business position. A strategy to maintain a brand would be appropriate for an established SBU in a strong market position but with limited growth potential.

An SBU's product mix can be evaluated on the same basis — analyze marketing opportunity and business position for each product and then develop allocation strategies to achieve a balance between stars (products with high growth potential where the firm is in a strong position to exploit opportunity) and cash cows (established brands that can generate cash to support stars).

5. *What are the alternative routes to corporate growth?*

The strategic marketing plan must specify the degree to which a company will rely on internal product development or external business acquisition for growth. Most companies rely on both, but generally either internal development or external acquisition is more dominant.

One strategy for internal development, market penetration, focuses on increasing the market share for existing products to existing customers through more advertising, more sales promotions, or price cuts. Market expansion looks for growth by identifying new target markets for existing products. In product development, a company introduces new products to existing customers.

Strategies of external acquisition focus on businesses rather than products. These strategies can involve diversification into new businesses or integration of operations. Diversification can be convergent if the company acquires businesses within the company's core market areas, or it can be divergent if businesses in unrelated areas are acquired. Integration is vertical when a company acquires businesses that are earlier or later in the manufacturing and distribution chain — for example, the manufacturer owning its own retail stores, or a retailer owning manufacturing facilities. Integration is horizontal when a company acquires a direct competitor — as when Stroh Brewing acquired Schlitz.

KEY TERMS

Strategic marketing plan (p. 616)
Business mix (p. 616)
Corporate mission (p. 620)
Business portfolio analysis (p. 624)
Relative market share (p. 627)
Market-penetration strategy (p. 632)
Market expansion (p. 632)
Product development (p. 633)

Business development (p. 633)
Divergent acquisitions (p. 633)
Convergent acquisitions (p. 633)
Horizontal integration (p. 633)
Vertical integration (p. 633)
Backward integration (p. 633)
Forward integration (p. 633)

QUESTIONS

1. Consider the following statement:

   Strategic marketing planning is fine for a company organized on a business-unit basis. But a company in one business does not really need strategic planning. What is the point of developing a corporate mission, doing a portfolio analysis, or formulating a corporate growth strategy if you are only in one business?

   Do you agree? Why or why not?

2. What were the changes in GE's corporate mission during the 1980s? What were the implications of these changes for (a) the mix of business units and (b) the company's acquisition and divestment moves in the 1980s?

3. A large Hollywood movie studio establishes a new marketing division with responsibility for researching, advertising, and distributing its movies. The director of the marketing division feels the company's corporate mission should be defined as "developing movies to meet changing customer tastes in a dynamic cultural and social environment."

   a. Do you agree with the definition of corporate mission? Why or why not?
   b. Does the definition of mission exclude certain corporate growth alternatives?

4. What is the distinction between top-down and bottom-up strategic planning? What are the implications of each planning approach for (a) who does strategic planning and (b) what gets emphasized in the strategic plan?

5. What were some of the problems that resulted from a top-down strategic planning approach at General Motors? How did Raymond Fears's strategic planning assignment at GM's Buick Division attempt to overcome some of these problems?

6. Consider the five basic business portfolio strategies — grow, build, maintain, harvest, divest. Which strategy would be most applicable for each of the following businesses and why?

   a. A business with declining sales in a low-growth market, but with a small group of loyal consumers who are likely to continue buying the SBU's products.
   b. A business in a mature industry in which the company has the second largest market share.
   c. A business that has a number of high-technology products developed by the company with good prospects for growth.
   d. A business outside the company's core area that was recently acquired because of a strong R&D capability in a growing industry.

7. What are the limitations of BCG's growth/share approach to portfolio analysis? How does GE's market attractiveness/business position analysis overcome some of these limitations?

8. A marketing executive for a producer of computer software commented on the various alternatives to growth outlined in Figures 22.9 and 22.10 as follows:

   That classification looks logical. But it is a little too simplistic when you look at the way we do things. We don't say we are going to achieve growth in our business through "market penetration" or "market expansion," or "product development." We evaluate each business's potential for increasing sales on a range of factors — competition, customer demand, technology — and then decide how we can apply our expertise to increase growth. We might have ten different growth strategies for ten different businesses. Classifying a business's growth strategy into one of your boxes tends to hide the different and unique conditions each of our businesses face.

Do this executive's comments mean that a business unit should not formulate an integrated corporate growth strategy along the lines suggested in Figures 22.9 and 22.10?

9. What is the distinction between a strategy of market penetration and market expansion? When would a company be likely to use one or the other as the primary vehicle for growth? Give examples.

10. What is the distinction between a strategy of product development and business development? When would a company be likely to use one or the other as the primary vehicle for growth? Give examples.

11. What risks have companies experienced in following (or attempting to follow) strategies of

    a. divergent acquisitions.

    b. vertical integration.

    c. horizontal integration.

Give examples of these risks.

12. What does the term "conversification" attempt to convey? Why is it a more apt term than diversification?

13. When Mobil Oil purchased Montgomery Ward, the large mass merchandiser, Mobil pushed it to take certain actions to improve its earnings record. One action was to expand a Montgomery Ward Florida-based discount chain to national status. On the other hand, when Nestle acquired Beech Nut, it allowed the new SBU's management to develop a plan to challenge Gerber and Heinz. What are the pros and cons of Mobil's more activist position and Nestle's more hands-off attitude?

CASE 22.1

PHILIP MORRIS LOOKS BEYOND CIGARETTES FOR GROWTH

Sources: "Beyond Marlboro Country," *Business Week,* August 8, 1988, pp. 54–58; and "Just Add Billions and Stir," *The Arizona Republic,* May 21, 1989.

For 141 years, tobacco has been the prime source of revenue for Philip Morris, generating the seventh-largest profits of any U.S. corporation. But, in response to the decreasing demand for cigarettes, and despite the continued success of its billion-dollar-plus brand, Marlboro, the company has begun to diversify into other areas. It bought Miller Brewing, then Seven-Up Company in the 1970s, General Foods in 1985, and Kraft in 1988. The last two acquisitions made Philip Morris the second largest food company in the world. (Swiss-based Nestle is the largest.)

With all its marketing savvy, Philip Morris has had a difficult time with its acquisitions. It did well with Miller at first, successfully repositioning High Life to appeal to heavier beer drinkers, and creating the light beer category with Miller Lite. But recently, it has fallen on hard times as market share for High Life took a plunge in the face of Anheuser-Busch's massive advertising spending for Budweiser. Profits have slipped to the point where Philip Morris considered selling Miller.

Its experience with Seven-Up was even worse. Philip Morris tried to impose strategies for soft drinks that worked for cigarettes with disastrous results. The company never understood the importance of bottlers as a source of local distribution and promotions, so it did not give new brands the local sales promotional support they needed. As for the third acquisition, General Foods, when it was acquired in 1985 it was on the skids, with decreasing coffee consumption and little growth in other areas.

The recent acquisition of Kraft might be another story, however. Kraft is renowned as an effective marketer of packaged foods. Further, Philip Morris is combining Kraft and General Foods into one company. The fit between the two is remarkable — General Foods' strength in coffee and desserts, Kraft's in dairy products. Further, their combined operations will give Philip Morris much more clout in advertising and distribution.

Regardless of the Kraft–General Foods' potential, two facts remain: Most of Philip Morris's revenue comes from tobacco products, and it has not faired well in its diversification drive. The future will tell whether it can continue to rely on tobacco, coffee, and beer for growth.

1. What is Philip Morris's growth strategy?
2. What problems has it faced in pursuing this growth strategy?
3. Would you recommend that Philip Morris acquire additional companies? If so, in what industries and why?

CASE 22.2

BORDEN'S REGIONAL ACQUISITION STRATEGY

Source: Adapted from Peter Oberlink, ''Borden's Low-Fat Strategy,'' *Adweek's Marketing Week,* May 16, 1988, pp. 34–42. Reprinted with permission of Adweek's Marketing Week.

In the two years since becoming chairman and chief executive of Borden, Romeo Ventres has led the company in buying out more than 50 businesses here and abroad, putting Borden on or near the top in worldwide production and sales of pasta, snacks, niche grocery items, dairy products, and some non-food areas such as wall coverings.

What sets Borden apart more than the number of buyouts is the kind of acquisitions it has made. Instead of stuffing itself with big-brand companies, which can be tough to digest, Borden snacks on healthy, lean, regional companies whose geographic markets, production capabilities and product lines complement existing Borden brands.

Borden starts out with local winners. Many food companies have written off the kind of small regional brands Borden looks for. Borden's theory is that it's easier to expand from a small base than to shrink a large one.

Borden hit upon its "conquer and divide" strategy the hard way. In 1979, Borden bought The Creamette Co., a Minneapolis pasta company located in the heart of durum wheat country. As a brand, Creamettes resembled scores of other pasta brands across the country: It had a loyal following and good relations with the grocery trade, but a narrow geographic market. "We wanted to become a national pasta company," Ventres recalls, "like a Coca-Cola."

Borden immediately began pushing the Creamette brand east, west and southward, pumping up marketing spending along the way. But the brand didn't move. Instead, sales of local brands rose due to Borden's heavy promotion of its pasta.

Borden regrouped and hit upon a simple alternative. If you can't beat the competition, buy them. Borden targeted 17 strong regional pasta brands that would give it broad geographic coverage, among them Globe A-1 and Anthony's in the Southwest, Luxury and Ronco in the South, R & F and Red Cross in Central and Midwest states; Merlino's in the Northwest; and Gioia, Penn Dutch, Bravo, Vimco and Prince in the Northeast.

The acquisitions gave Borden an extensive distribution network — key to the delivery of brittle pasta products — and allowed Borden to try again with Creamettes. The strategy was a resounding success. Instead of fighting to dislodge these entrenched local brands, Creamettes could now use its entree to the local grocery trade. Borden's U.S. sales of pasta quadrupled to $357 million last year.

Borden has used its experience in pasta as a blueprint for the entire company. "Everything pointed us in the same direction — building by region," says Ventres. "We had been sitting on that strategy all the time, but we're only just recognizing how natural it is for Borden."

So natural that Borden decided to duplicate the formula in its snacks division.

Before 1986 Borden had no interest in emphasizing snacks beyond the East Coast, where its Wise potato chip brand had a local following. In 1986 Ventres and company started moving forward. Borden bought one ripe chip company after another until it had 10 regional companies covering markets in 46 of the 48 contiguous states.

Ventres' unusual game plan does have its critics. Big companies buy big brands for a reason: They have powerful national franchises that can serve as the engine for substantial growth in the future. Borden's cherry-picking approach may look sophisticated, say critics, but when all is said and done, you're left with a collection of minor brands that may solidify your position in the market but won't take you very far. Nonsense, says Ventres. New York Deli chips are now in 26 states, and Borden paid far less to build a national brand that way than to buy it.

Borden has also begun to apply its strategic formula overseas. In the Mediterranean equivalent of carrying coals to Newcastle, Borden is looking to dominate the pasta business in Italy and the rest of Europe. Last year Borden acquired Albadoro SpA., giving it a strong position in the Italian pasta market. With the acquisition of Adria pasta, Brazil's leading brand, Borden has vaulted into the lead as the largest pasta maker in the world.

"The international market will play an increasingly

important role for us," says Ventres, "especially looking ahead to 1992." That's when the European Common Market becomes, in effect, one market. For Elsie, the grass may indeed be greener on the other side of the tariff barrier.

1. What is Borden's growth strategy?
2. What are the risks of this strategy?
3. How does Borden's strategy differ from Philip Morris's as described in the previous case?

NOTES

1. "The Mind of Jack Welch," *Fortune,* March 27, 1989, pp. 39–50; and "The Welch Years: GE Gambles on Growth," *Industry Week,* April 20, 1987, p. 30.

2. "General Electric to Sell Consumer Electronics Lines to Thompson SA," *The Wall Street Journal,* July 23, 1987, p. 3.

3. *Industry Week,* April 20, 1987, p. 32.

4. *Fortune,* March 27, 1989, p. 39.

5. Ibid., p. 40.

6. "The New Breed of Strategic Planner," *Business Week,* September 17, 1984, p. 65.

7. *Business Week,* September 17, 1984, p. 66.

8. "Wrigley Stays True to Gum," *The New York Times,* November 29, 1988, p. D1.

9. *Business Week,* September 17,1984, p. 66.

10. Theodore Levitt, "Marketing Myopia," *Harvard Business Review* 38 (July–August 1960): 45–56.

11. "Whirlpool Puts a New Spin on Its Long-Term Plans," *Marketing & Media Decisions,* Spring 1985, Special Issue.

12. Sidney Schoeffler, Robert D. Buzzell, and Donald F. Heany, "Impact of Strategic Planning on Profit Performance," *Harvard Business Review,* 52 (March–April 1974): 137–145.

13. "Zero Base Helps Rationalize Product Strategy," *International Management,* February 1979, p. 38.

14. "Abbott Labs: Health Care Honcho," *Dun's Business Month,* December 1986, p. 26.

15. Ibid.

16. "Sara Lee's Success with Brands," *The New York Times,* June 19, 1989, p. D4.

17. "General Mills Still Needs Its Wheaties," *Business Week,* December 23, 1985, p. 77.

18. "Syntex Tries to Kick a One-Drug Habit," *Business Week,* December 9, 1985, p. 64.

19. "Take the High Ground," *Forbes,* June 15, 1987, p. 230.

20. "Changing Signals at Radio Shack," *Fortune,* April 29, 1985, p. 180.

21. *Business Week,* July 1, 1985, p. 54.

Alan Canfield's dream seemed to be coming true. Sales of Canfield's Diet Chocolate Fudge soda were taking off beyond his wildest expectations. In the previous 13 years, the soda averaged 60,000 cases a year. In January 1985 sales began booming, and by March the company was selling as much as 20,000 cases in a single day.[1]

What Canfield did not realize was that his dream was about to become a nightmare for one reason: The small Chicago-based beverage company could not sustain such growth. Its production and marketing operations were about to go out of control.

Diet Chocolate Fudge was developed in 1971 when Alan Canfield handed his chief chemist a pound of fudge and asked him to create a diet drink that duplicated the taste. The result was a product that did indeed taste like fudge, but without chocolate. The product nicely complemented Canfield's other beverages such as Hula Punch, Swiss Creme, and Honee Orange.[2] And Canfield Beverages was in the enviable position of being a low-cost producer, so profit margins on Diet Chocolate Fudge were high.

Sales of the brand were modest until an unforseen event occurred. On January 13, 1985, a *Chicago Tribune* reporter was planning to interview someone for his syndicated column when the subject cancelled. As the journalist wondered what to write about, he spied a can of Diet Chocolate Fudge on his desk. (He had been drinking the two-calorie soda because he was on a diet.) He decided to devote his column to the soda, writing that "Taking a sip of the stuff is like biting into a hot fudge sundae."[3] The column appeared in 200 newspapers nationwide, and the next day the phones started ringing at A. J. Canfield.

At first Canfield thought the publicity would increase sales for a few weeks. But by February, he knew something bigger was going on. Sales in a two-day period were higher than for all of 1984. Retailers all over the country were calling to order the soda. Bottlers were jamming the phone lines looking for distribution rights. Among them were the biggest bottlers in the country. The company looked golden.

The first sign that Canfield was losing control of its operations was when the company had to start rationing its product. Plants were running 24 hours a day, seven days a week, without meeting demand. Canfield was starting to run into trouble with some of its loyal retailers. One who had been dealing with the company since 1937 could get only five cases of Diet Chocolate Fudge. The 70-year old owner, reminding Alan Canfield of their long-standing association, said, "If you don't get me a 500-case display by Monday, don't bother coming back when the craze is over."[4] He got the display, but at the cost of other loyal retailers not getting the product.

There were other signs that Canfield was losing control. Factory workers were working 16-hour shifts. One veteran of 20 years, after working for 29 straight days, quit because the grind was ruining his home life. Alan Canfield decided that Diet Chocolate Fudge was getting bigger than the company.

Canfield saw two alternatives. Expand production and distribution, hire hundreds of new people, and pour in the required capital with all the risks involved. Or let someone else take the risks. But how? Canfield came up with the idea of selling the concentrate to bottlers and giving them franchises to produce, bottle, and sell Diet Chocolate Fudge soda. In this way, Canfield did not have to expand facilities and could continue its existing operations on a regional basis. By summer of 1985, eleven bottlers were signed, covering all 50 states and three foreign countries.[5] Canfield's business of selling Diet Chocolate Fudge concentrate became a profitable venture.

Canfield was a regional company that could have gone national with a hot product. But it chose the more conservative course of staying regional for one very good reason. It wanted to *control* its existing operations. ■

EVALUATING AND CONTROLLING THE MARKETING EFFORT

● ● ●

THE NATURE OF EVALUATION AND CONTROL

Control is directing or redirecting a company's actions to ensure that they meet objectives. Evaluation is a necessary adjunct of control because anytime company actions are controlled, they must first be evaluated to determine whether results are on target. This is why we often couple evaluation and control.

The Canfield story illustrates the importance of control, particularly over marketing activities. Canfield was in danger of losing control over distribution of Diet Chocolate Fudge soda. For example, to satisfy some West Coast retailers, Canfield had a truckload of the product driven there. But by the time it arrived, the cans had rubbed against each other for so long that they had started to leak.[6]

In another example, lack of control put Westinghouse at a competitive disadvantage compared to General Electric in the 1970s. The company had no systematic process to identify marketing opportunity, so it haphazardly acquired businesses such as a mail-order house, a watchmaker, and a low-income housing developer. The result was a morass of 135 divisions.[7] As we will see, the story of Westinghouse in the 1980s has been one of building controls over its divisions so that their strategies will meet predefined goals.

When applied to marketing, control has two dimensions: a corporate or SBU dimension and a product dimension. These two dimensions parallel the marketing planning levels cited in the previous chapter. Control at the corporate or SBU level is **strategic control** — that is, an attempt to keep the components of the strategic marketing plan on target and to redirect them if they are not. Control on a product-specific basis is **product-marketing control** — an attempt to keep the components of a product's marketing plan on target.

STRATEGIC CONTROL

Strategic control attempts to evaluate and control the basic components of the strategic marketing plan. This process requires top management to evaluate the company's business mix and SBU management to evaluate the unit's product mix in order to see whether they have effectively judged new business and product opportunities and the company's ability to pursue these opportunities. Unless the strategic plan is absolutely on target (which is unlikely), the process of strategic control will lead managers to make adjustments in resource allocation.

Westinghouse exerted strategic control in the 1980s when it instituted better controls over every aspect of its strategic plan — identification of marketing opportunity, growth strategies, acquisition strategies, and its business mix. A new management team began spinning off dozens of weak divisions — cable television, the major appliance group, the company's lamp business, and its office furniture division. Strict market share and profitability criteria were used to determine these divestments: If a subsidiary was not first or a strong second in its industry, it was a candidate for divestment.

Further, the company increased productivity by cutting costs and improving quality. The workforce was cut by 23,000 employees. Remaining workers were retrained to perform more tasks in smaller work groups and were given more responsibility over their work output. As a result net income per employee more than doubled from 1982 to 1987.[8] Underlying these changes was a reorganization of the planning effort designed to better identify marketing opportunities and to hold SBU managers to tighter profit goals.

PRODUCT MARKETING CONTROLS

Whereas strategic controls deal with the total business and product mix, product marketing controls deal with the marketing mix for an individual product. Product managers must evaluate the effectiveness of product, distribution, promotional, and pricing strategies and reallocate resources as appropriate.

Canfield's immediate focus on control was at the product level: How to control distribution of Diet Chocolate Fudge soda in the face of heavy demand. But the underlying issue was corporate-wide: Should the company remain a regional manufacturer or become a national marketer?

IMPETUS FOR MARKETING CONTROL

The control of marketing operations has received more attention in the 1980s, primarily because of the intensification of foreign competition. As we saw in Chapter 21, foreign competitors, particularly Japanese companies, have been able to capture market share in key industries by offering quality products at lower prices than U.S. companies. The basis for their competitive advantage is no secret — higher productivity because of more efficient production methods and lower labor costs. American companies have reacted by putting more emphasis on productivity. Such improvements in productivity can be achieved only by greater cost and quality controls in production and marketing.

Many American companies have adopted two widespread practices based on the productivity of Japanese competitors: just-in-time distribution systems and quality-circle programs. As we saw in Chapter 14, *just-in-time (JIT) distribution* has cut down on production and distribution costs by producing for existing demand rather than for anticipated demand and by delivering raw materials and finished products on an as-needed basis. **Quality circles** are groups of autonomous workers who are responsible for their output and are motivated to perform quality work based on the recognition that their mistakes will affect the next autonomous work group down the line. Underlying the formation of quality circles is a deceivingly simple notion: It is better to control quality at the point of production to try to avoid mistakes than to identify and correct mistakes through random inspection of products after they are produced.

Another reason why control has received more attention is that poor results from the rash of acquisitions in the late 1960s and early 1970s led many companies to realize that they could not achieve growth simply by gobbling up high-growth businesses that were outside their areas of core competence. That lesson led Westinghouse to specify that acquired companies would have to meet stricter criteria of profitability and debt structure and would have to fit in better with Westinghouse's overall game plan.

A third factor encouraging marketing controls was the traumatic cycle of inflation and recession during the 1970s and early 1980s. Fewer marketing opportunities during this period led managers to try to gain competitive advantage by reducing costs and prices. Higher interest rates also made management more cost-conscious.

A MODEL OF MARKETING EVALUATION AND CONTROL

A firm must have a systematic basis for evaluating and controlling marketing operations at both the corporate and the product level. A model of marketing evaluation and control is in Figure 23.1.

In the first step, the firm must define criteria by which it will evaluate performance. Assume that Westinghouse establishes sales and profitability criteria for its robotics division. It will then project performance of the division on these criteria. It might forecast sales of $65 million in the first year, rising to $120 million by the fourth year, an average of 13 percent return on investment for the first five years, and an expectation that the division will account for 10 percent of Westinghouse's profits at the end of five years. If management finds it unlikely that a business or product will meet its minimal performance goals, it will terminate the business or product and use the funds in some alternative investment opportunity.

The third step in the control process is to establish a marketing organization capable of implementing, evaluating, and controlling marketing plans. Once such an organization is in place, managers can develop and implement a marketing plan to achieve the objectives spelled out in the performance projections. Part of Westinghouse's organizational plan for the robotics division might be to establish quality-circle groups to insure quality control, and establish national account marketing (NAM) teams to sell to large users of factory automation systems such as General Motors.

Once the plan is implemented at both the strategic and product marketing level, performance is evaluated. Evaluation requires a control system that will allow a company to track costs and revenues and determine whether profit and ROI goals have been met. If performance is on target, implementation of the plan can continue. If it is not, corrective action should be considered.

Westinghouse's robotics division did not meet expectations when it was first acquired in 1983. Sales were expected to rise above $60 million the year after the business was purchased but reached only $40 million. Part of the reason was that General Motors, the unit's largest customer, went into a joint venture to produce automated systems for itself. Also, many companies preferred electric robots to Westinghouse's hydraulic robots.[9]

In the final step, the company determines whether corrective action is necessary and what steps to take. If such action successfully redirects efforts to meet objectives, it will serve as input into the next planning cycle. If corrective action is

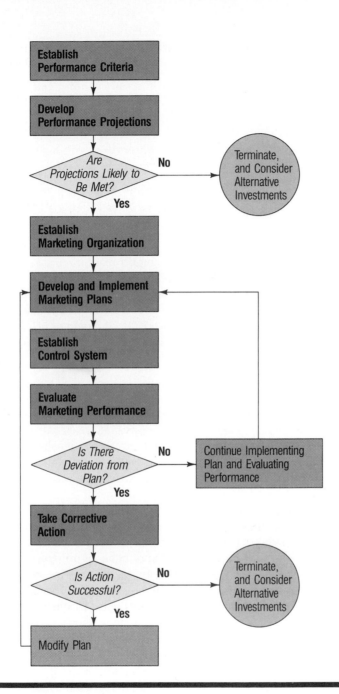

FIGURE 23.1
A Model of Evaluation and Control

not successful, the business will be divested or the product eliminated. In Westinghouse's case, corrective action might include switching product design from hydraulic to electric robots, seeking clients outside the auto industry, and putting even more emphasis on productivity to become more cost-competitive. Westinghouse did in fact try to improve the productivity of its division by establishing a productivity center to develop new techniques for cost reductions and quality control.[10]

The remainder of this chapter considers each of the steps in evaluation and control in Figure 23.1.

ESTABLISH PERFORMANCE CRITERIA

The three primary criteria used to evaluate performance at both the product and the corporate/business-unit level are profits, sales volume, and market share. In some cases, these criteria do not always move in tandem, and a firm may consciously emphasize one at the expense of another. For example, a firm entering a market might try to "buy" market share at the expense of profits by advertising heavily and by providing retailers and wholesalers with higher margins. Since costs increase to achieve market share, profits go down. The firm might incur these additional expenses to establish itself in a market, but the goal remains maximization of long-term profits.

Computer companies such as Compaq have followed this strategy to get their products on retailer shelves in an effort to compete with IBM. Compaq *pulls* its products through the distribution channel by advertising to consumers and *pushes* them through by giving retailers higher margins.

This chapter is particularly concerned with profit criteria, since they ultimately dominate evaluation of a product's or business unit's performance. The profit criteria most commonly used in evaluating performance are *contribution to margin* and *return on investment* (ROI). It would be helpful at this point to review the cost and profit concepts involved by turning to the appendix to this chapter.

CONTRIBUTION TO MARGIN

Contribution to margin is a logical criterion for evaluating product performance because it takes into account only those costs that are directly assignable to the product. As a result, it is also known as *direct* (i.e., assignable) *costing*. In contrast, an approach based on net profit and return on investment is known as *full costing*, since it takes account of all costs, both assignable (direct) and nonassignable (indirect).

Product managers tend to object to the use of full-costing measures to evaluate performance because such criteria require allocating nonassignable costs like production facilities, corporate advertising, or executive salaries to a product, and the fairness of such allocations is questionable. A product may account for, say, 20 percent of a company's sales yet use significantly less than 20 percent of production facilities, or be a smooth-running cash cow that management does not have to spend much time on. The product manager might object to burdening such a product with 20 percent of the company's nonassignable costs. A contribution-to-margin approach is simply more clear-cut in evaluating product performance.

This approach also makes it easier to evaluate marketing expenditures. Procter & Gamble evaluates its products using an approach it calls Direct Product Profitability (DPP), which relies solely on direct costs to evaluate product performance. The DPP approach has shown that some products with high sales volume have a low contribution to margin because they have high handling costs. P&G began focusing on reducing handling costs so as to increase margins. For example, it found that if it redesigned its Ivory shampoo bottle from a teardrop shape to a cylindrical container, it would save 29 cents a case in handling and storage costs.[11] (See Exhibit 23.1.) If P&G had evaluated Ivory shampoo based on net profits or return on investment, it would have had to allocate indirect (nonassignable) costs to the product, and the importance of reducing handling costs might have been overlooked.

From

To

**NET PROFIT/RETURN ON
INVESTMENT (ROI)**

Return on investment (ROI) is based on net profits and therefore requires allocating all costs to a product or business unit. As is shown in Figure 1 of the appendix, projected allocation of nonassignable costs to the Westinghouse Robotics Division five years after its acquisition is $15.5 million. With a contribution to margin of $29.5 million, net profit is projected at $14 million ($29.5 million minus $15.5 million). Since it cost Westinghouse $107 million to acquire the division,[12] return on investment is estimated at 13.1 percent ($14 million divided by $107 million).

Given the problems cited with allocating nonassignable costs, why would a firm use net profits or return on investment as a performance criterion? One reason is that return on investment gives a firm some indication as to how effective it is in using its capital. Was Westinghouse's expenditure of $107 million to acquire the robotics business worthwhile? The best way to answer that is to consider alternative uses of the capital. Five years after Westinghouse acquired the division (1988), had it put the money in the bank, it might have received a 10 percent return at best. So a projected 13.1 percent in 1988 would be a good return on investment.

A second reason for using a return-on-investment measure is that it is more valid when evaluating a business unit rather than a product. This is because most of the costs incurred by a business unit are assignable. For example, most of the costs of manufacturing automated equipment can be directly assigned to the robotics division. But if the division produces 20 different robotics systems, it would be difficult to allocate manufacturing costs to each of these products. So, in general, it is much easier to allocate costs to a business unit than to a product. This is demonstrated in Figure 1 of the appendix. Of total manufacturing costs, $28 million are directly assignable to the division, whereas only $11 million are not directly assignable. The nonassignable manufacturing costs are those that are shared with other Westinghouse units — for example, the costs of manufacturing transistors that might also be used by other divisions.

USE OF PERFORMANCE CRITERIA

What criteria are used most frequently in evaluating marketing performance? A study of 233 American firms found that sales volume was by far the most frequently used criterion of performance, with 88 percent of the companies in the study using it. The next most frequently used criterion was contribution to margin, used by 44 percent of the companies, followed by net profit/ROI used by 30 percent.[13] The finding that sales is a more popular performance measure than profitability should be of concern if it reflects current procedures in corporate America. As we know, sales are not always related to profitability. A firm that does not use some profitability criterion can quickly lose sight of rising costs.

Among firms that use a profitability criterion, contribution to margin was the more popular yardstick. This shows that many firms recognize the importance of measuring product performance by direct costing. But the study also shows that many firms use both a direct and a full-cost approach in evaluating marketing performance.

DEVELOP PERFORMANCE PROJECTIONS

Once the firm has established the criteria it will use to evaluate marketing performance, it develops performance projections for products and business units in the form of a profit and loss (P&L) statement.

THE PROJECTED PROFIT AND LOSS (P&L) STATEMENT

Performance projections are in the form of expected performance, usually for a minimum of one and a maximum of five years. The best way to set out these projections is in a *profit and loss (P&L) statement* for a product or business unit.

Assume that Westinghouse's management developed a five-year P&L projection for the robotics division when it was purchased in 1983. The projected P&L is in Table 23.1. Sales are forecast at $65 million in the first year after acquisition, and are expected to increase to $80 million in Year 2, $110 million in Year 3, and then level off thereafter. Variable costs rise more sharply at the start of business and then level off as learning effects begin to reduce the average cost of production and marketing per unit. Assignable fixed costs are more constant since they do not vary as much with sales volume. Contribution to margin is projected to rise steadily from $7 million in the first year to $29.5 million in Year 5. When nonassignable fixed costs are allocated, there is a net loss in the first year, but a more substantial net profit by Year 3 that then levels out, producing an ROI of 12 to 13 percent.

Since the five-year P&L is a projection, it serves as a performance yardstick. The comparison of actual to projected performance gives management a basis for determining whether corrective action is necessary to try to get performance on target. As we know, sales of the robotics division did not meet expectations after the unit was purchased, and it probably took longer than three years to make the division profitable.

TABLE 23.1
Hypothetical Five-Year Profit and Loss (P&L) Projections for Westinghouse's Robotics Division (In Millions)

| | **YEAR** | | | | |
	1	**2**	**3**	**4**	**5**
1. Sales	$65.0	$80.0	$110.0	$120.0	$114.0
2. Variable Costs	30.0	40.0	48.0	55.0	50.0
3. Assignable Fixed Costs	28.0	30.5	34.0	35.0	34.5
4. Contribution to Margin $(1 - [2 + 3])$	7.0	9.5	28.0	30.0	29.5
5. Nonassignable Fixed Costs	9.0	10.5	15.0	16.0	15.5
6. Net Profits $(1 - [2 + 3 + 5])$	−2.0	1.0	13.0	14.0	14.0
Contribution to Margin as a Percent of Sales (4/1)	10.8%	11.9%	25.5%	25.0%	25.9%
Return on Investment (row 6/initial investment of $107 million)	0	.9%	12.1%	13.1%	13.1%

To develop a profit and loss statement, management must establish a budget for a product or SBU that will provide cost and revenue estimates, which yield an estimate of profits. In past chapters we have seen that managers can develop budgets based on marginal revenues, past sales, competitors' activities, or the marketing strategies needed to fulfill specific objectives (an objective-task approach). Today, many companies are using a variation of an objective-task approach known as **zero-based budgeting** in which the budget is determined at the beginning of each year on a clean slate. Managers do not look at past sales or competitive expenditures. Instead, they formulate certain profitability goals, ask themselves what actions are required to meet these goals, and then estimate the necessary expenditures. Zero-based budgeting is popular because it provides a cleaner basis for evaluating marketing performance.

Zero-based budgeting simplifies evaluating product or divisional performance because expenditures are evaluated from a zero starting point. Many firms assess marketing expenditures by comparing them to expenditures in previous years. A firm might say that a $5 million advertising budget for this year is 10 percent higher than last year's and evaluate advertising results on this basis. But the fallacy is that last year's budget might have been too high or too low to begin with. Zero-based budgeting overcomes this problem by assessing costs from a base of zero, so that if $5 million is spent on advertising this year, the basis for assessing the value of this expenditure is the profit it produces without reference to past expenditures.

Heinz's president describes its zero-based budgeting approach as a process of asking managers to assume that they are starting a new business, even for an old product like Heinz ketchup, then determining what is required and what the costs would be.[14] The process forces managers to justify costs based on specific profitability objectives rather than to take the easy way out and say, for example, that advertising expenditures should increase because of increases by competitors.

ZERO-BASED BUDGETING

FIGURE 23.2
Two Types of Marketing Organizations

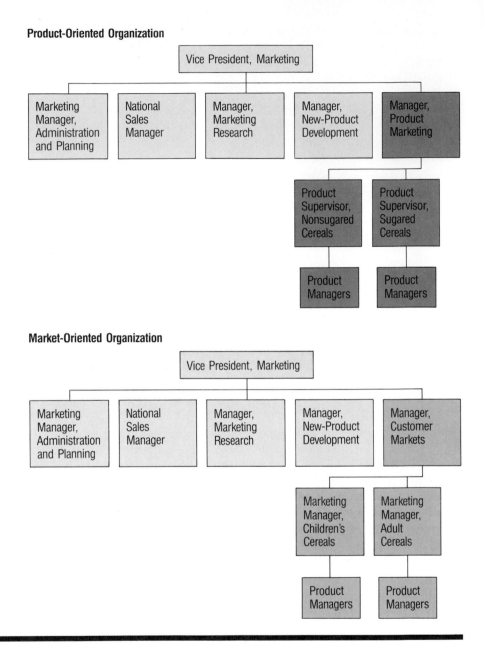

Product-Oriented Organization

Market-Oriented Organization

DEVELOP A MARKETING ORGANIZATION

The next step in the process of evaluation and control requires establishing a marketing organization capable of implementing and evaluating marketing strategies. The two most widely used approaches to organizing the marketing effort are a product-based organization and a market-based organization. These approaches are shown in Figure 23.2.

In each case, the marketing organization is headed by a vice-president of marketing. Under the vice-president are several marketing managers responsible for various functional tasks. There is a marketing manager for administration and planning who is responsible for developing marketing plans for each product and for supplying input into the business unit's strategic plan. A national sales manager is responsible for overseeing the efforts of regional and district managers to ensure that existing and prospective customers are contacted and sold. A marketing research manager is responsible for providing line managers with enough information on customer needs and the marketing environment to make marketing decisions. And a marketing manager for new-product devleopment initiates new-product ideas and oversees the process of development, product testing, and test marketing.

The two organizational charts differ in the way marketing strategies are implemented. At the top of Figure 23.2 is a product-oriented form of organization. Take Kellogg as an example: The basic product division might be between sweetened and unsweetened cereals. A manager of product marketing might be responsible for both units. Under this manager might be a supervisor of all sweetened cereals and a supervisor of all unsweetened cereals. Under each of these supervisors would be product managers for individual cereal brands.

The alternative to a product-oriented organization is organizing marketing activities by broad customer segments (see the bottom of Figure 23.2). The basic organization is the same except that under the vice-president of marketing is a manager of consumer markets. Kellogg is actually organized on this basis, across two broad markets, children and adult cereals. A consumer market manager is responsible for each of these groups across all product categories. For example, the market manager for children's cereals is responsible for marketing all brands to this market. Product managers responsible for individual brands then report to their respective market managers.

A product-based organization is most appropriate when customer needs are differentiated by product characteristics. For example, a basic distinction in soft drinks is between cola and noncola products. Cola drinks tend to appeal more to teens because they are sweeter and more carbonated. Noncola drinks appeal more to adults because they are less sweet and more flavor-oriented. In contrast, in cereals, the basic distinction is not between product characteristics but between markets. The appeal to children is based on taste and nutrition; the appeal to adults is based on diet, health, and fitness. Although sweetened cereals are primarily positioned to children, many nonsweetened products are also. Kellogg's corn flakes directs appeals to both groups. Given that this basic distinction between the needs of children and adults frequently cuts across individual products, a market-based organization makes sense.

DEVELOP AND IMPLEMENT THE MARKETING PLAN

Much of this book has been devoted to the process of developing and implementing marketing plans. What we have not discussed is the human dimension of implementation — that is, the problems managers encounter in trying to implement marketing plans and the importance of adequately motivating subordinates to try to meet objectives. Evaluation and control involve not only costs and revenues, but also people.

One large consulting firm, McKinsey and Company, believes that one of the recent problems with implementation in American industry is that management has focused too much on analytical techniques and not enough on the human element. Japanese companies may have attained higher productivity precisely because they have done the exact opposite. The development of quality circles is an example of a focus on the human element in implementation.

PROBLEMS IN IMPLEMENTATION

One source of problems in implementing marketing plans is resistance to change. The more far-reaching the changes in the marketing plan, the greater the potential for such resistance. A common scenario is a company in trouble and a new management team coming in with a strategic plan calling for changes such as severe cost cutting, more emphasis on new-product development, divestment of certain business units, or entry into new lines of business. These changes contradict "the way we do things around here" and are resisted.

AT&T ran into serious problems in implementing a new set of strategies after divestiting its subsidiaries in 1984. In that year, James Olsen, the company's chief financial officer, tried to implement a plan to strengthen the company's core business of long-distance services and phone equipment and to strengthen its fledgling computer business. But the strategy involved cooperation and trade-offs between divisions — for example, combining the salesforce for telephone and computer equipment and eliminating duplication in accounting and data-processing services across various divisions. Managers refused to buy in because they ran their divisions like fiefdoms in the old Bell System and were not used to compromise.[15] Only when Olsen was promoted to chairman two years later would they agree to the plan. But AT&T's top management is still likely to find it difficult to implement Olsen's plan.

Managers also face problems in implementing plans because of conflicts between corporate staffers and line (operational) managers. Line managers see staffers as being divorced from day-to-day operations and concerned primarily with analytical planning techniques that often produce unrealistic goals. Conversely, staffers feel that line managers do not see the "big corporate picture" and are too focused on their individual tasks.

As a result of this conflict, alienated line managers often ignore staffers, even when they are right. For example, GE's corporate staffers correctly predicted that Japanese manufacturers would make a dent in the U.S. small-appliance market as early as 1970, but the warning was ignored by the Appliance Group's line managers.[16] On the other hand, GE staffers recommended building smaller appliances because of smaller families. Line managers could have told them that kitchens were not getting smaller, despite smaller families.

REQUIREMENTS FOR EFFECTIVE IMPLEMENTATION

There are no clear-cut solutions to implementation problems, but there are a few prescriptions to take account of the human element. One is to ensure that performance goals are understood and that managers accept them. Olsen saw this requirement as his major task when he took over as head of AT&T in 1986.

Another prescription is to reward management for good performance. When Tony O'Reilly became president of Heinz in 1973, he pursued a single-minded strategy of making Heinz the low-cost producer in packaged foods. Managers who were not rigorous enough in cutting costs were weeded out. Those who remained were given more autonomy, and a lucrative compensation plan tied to their performance.[17]

A third prescription is to foster open communications and participative management. A study of 43 successful U.S. companies found that most had a high level of informality and a decentralized structure that fostered open communications. Quality circles are highly motivated because of their autonomy and informality. Productivity of these groups tends to be much higher than that of traditional ones supervised by foremen.

A fourth prescription for effective implementation is to make sure that people know their responsibilities. One of the problems at Canfield Beverage was that tasks and responsibilities were not being defined as sales for Diet Chocolate Fudge soared. As a result, shipments were going astray, and delivery dates were being missed.

ESTABLISH A CONTROL SYSTEM

Once marketing plans are implemented, one step remains before these plans can be evaluated — establishing a control system to track performance and let managers know when corrections are necessary. Companies use three types of systems to control marketing performance: after-the-fact, steering, and adaptive control.

After-the-Fact Control System

An **after-the-fact control system** controls marketing performance at the end of the planning period. If performance does not meet objectives, managers take corrective action to bring performance back into line for the next planning cycle. Consider the hypothetical projections of performance for Westinghouse's robotics division in Table 23A.1 of the appendix. The projections were made when the division was purchased (1983) and are for the fifth year after purchase (1988). Assume Westinghouse finds its sales revenues in 1988 were close to projections but distribution costs were higher than the projected $10.5 million. Management breaks out distribution costs further to compare projected to actual performance and finds the following:

DISTRIBUTION COSTS	PROJECTED	ACTUAL	PERCENT DIFFERENCE
Transportation costs	$6.2 million	$8.2 million	+32%
Inventory costs	$2.7 million	$3.7 million	+37%
Order-handling and processing costs	$1.6 million	$1.7 million	+6%

Management further determines that (1) transportation costs are out of line because of increases in trucking costs and (2) inventory costs are above projections because products are staying in inventory longer than expected. Management decides to institute a just-in-time (JIT) system so that production will be more closely tied to existing orders, thus reducing product inventory levels. It must continue to ship by truck because of the need for rapid delivery with a JIT system, but it institutes a more rigorous review of alternative shippers in an attempt to control transportation costs.

FIGURE 23.3
Control Charts for a Steering
Control System*

*Hypothetical Distribution Costs for Westinghouse's
Robotics Division, 1988

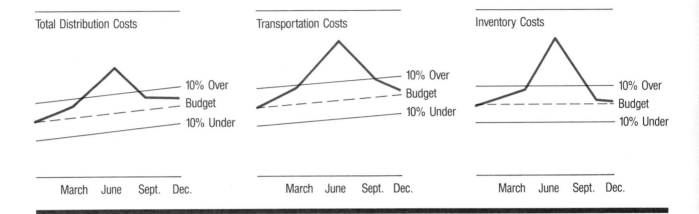

Steering Control System

The problem with an after-the-fact control system is that since management waits until the end of the planning period to make adjustments, delays could cost a company millions of dollars. A **steering control system** avoids this problem. Deviations in performance are detected during rather than at the end of the planning period, allowing for prompt corrective action.

A way to implement such a system is through the use of control charts, such as the ones in Figure 23.3 that track hypothetical distribution costs for Westinghouse's Robotics Division. The control charts show the projected (dotted line) and actual (heavy solid line) distribution costs by quarter in 1988. The parallel lines above and below projected costs are an allowed 10 percent deviation above or below budget. If costs stray more than 10 percent beyond projections, the deviation is immediately brought to management's attention so it can attempt to "steer" costs back into line. The control charts show that by the second quarter of 1988, transportation and inventory costs were out of line and needed to be brought into control.

Since taking corrective action more quickly makes the most sense, why would any company use an after-the-fact control system? Because after-the-fact control is simpler to implement. Many companies do not have the resources and managerial know-how to implement a steering control system. In some cases, however, after-the-fact control may be justified in its own right because expenditures cannot be changed until the end of the planning period. For example, media schedules are fixed well in advance, and it might not be feasible to change advertising expenditures during the year.

Adaptive Control System

Both after-the-fact and steering control systems are designed to bring performance into line with prior objectives. But what happens when the environment changes to such a degree that the objectives are no longer relevant? Such a situation calls for an **adaptive control system** that allows for changes in objectives as well as in performance to meet objectives. This system requires tracking environmental factors such as competitive intensity, level of customer demand, and technology to determine if objectives are still relevant. If not, objectives are changed to meet the new environmental contingencies, resulting in a new set of guidelines for performance.

For example, Westinghouse may have been overly optimistic in its expectations that factory automation might be the answer to increasing productivity. Rather than relying solely on automation to increase productivity, many companies have begun to rely more on quality circles to reduce labor costs. As a result, sales of factory robots have begun to lag behind forecasts. If Westinghouse had established an adaptive control system, it might have scaled back its sales and cost forecasts rather than waiting until the end of the planning period to make adjustments.

Both adaptive and steering control allow for changes during the planning period. The difference is that with adaptive control, objectives can change, whereas with steering control, they remain fixed. In this way, adaptive control is a *proactive* system: management anticipates changes in the environment and acts to develop a new set of ground rules for evaluating and controlling performance. After-the-fact and steering control are *reactive* systems: management reacts to a situation that is out of control, and tries to repair it.

Adaptive control systems are essential in strategic control because they account for environmental changes over the long term. Without the ability to adjust the plan to a changing environment, a firm might be locked into unrealistic goals that were made five years ago. RCA grossly overestimated the sales of its videodisc players in the early 1980s. If an adaptive control system had been in place, the company might have been more proactive in anticipating a basic change in the environment — the rising popularity of VCRs and the importance of their recording capability. RCA might then have withdrawn its videodiscs and moved more quickly to produce VCRs.

EVALUATE MARKETING PERFORMANCE

Once plans are implemented and a control system is established, managers are able to evaluate performance. There are two dimensions in marketing evaluation: the strategic dimension, which evaluates corporate and business unit performance, and the product-marketing dimension, which evaluates product performance.

STRATEGIC MARKETING EVALUATION

The elements of marketing performance we will consider in strategic evaluation involve costs, product quality, corporate growth, and acquisitions. Costs and product quality determine a company's level of productivity. As we have seen, one of the major concerns of American firms is their level of productivity compared to that of foreign competitors. America's future economic well-being is likely to be determined by the degree to which American companies increase their productivity.

Marketing Productivity
The productivity of a company's marketing operations is defined by its *efficiency*, which is the ratio of output to input: Increased efficiency means more output for less input. In this context, **marketing productivity** could be defined as the ratio of marketing performance to the costs involved.

FIGURE 23.4
The Productivity Triangle

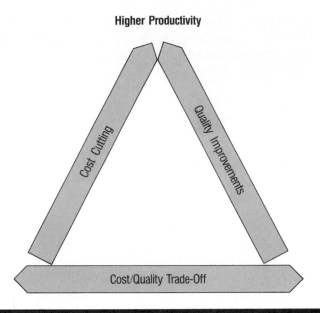

What is the best measure of overall marketing performance at the corporate level? Given the importance of satisfying customer needs, marketing productivity should be tied to the quality level of a company's product offerings, but with the proviso that quality be attained at reasonable cost. Therefore, marketing productivity can best be measured by the ratio of product quality to the cost of producing and marketing the item. This is illustrated in Figure 23.4 as the marketing productivity triangle. One leg of the triangle is lower costs, the other is higher quality. The higher the quality and the lower the cost, the higher the company's marketing productivity and profitability. The cost/quality trade-off at the bottom of the triangle means that an emphasis on higher quality could result in higher costs, and lower costs could result in lower quality.

Cost Cutting Chrysler is a good example of a company that has emphasized cost-cutting as the primary means to improve productivity. When Lee Iacocca took over as president in 1978, it was on the brink of bankruptcy and had to rely on an unprecedented government loan to keep it afloat. Iacocca knew what he had to do: cut costs unmercifully while maintaining quality. In the space of four years, he cut the workforce in half, eliminated one-third of Chrysler's plants, reduced fixed costs of production by $2 billion a year, and shook out an additional $1 billion in inventory costs by cutting in half the parts used in manufacturing Chrysler cars.[18] Iacocca also borrowed a page from the Japanese by instituting just-in-time inventory and production methods.

Iacocca did not ignore quality in his drive to reduce costs. In his words, "Chrysler launched an all-out . . . program to improve the quality of both its finished products and components [through] the latest methods of preventive surveillance and statistical controls."[19] But the primary focus of his efforts was on cost-cutting. The result of these efforts was a total turnaround at Chrysler. The company repaid its multi-billion-dollar government loan by 1983 and began showing a profit. Its market share started going up, primarily at the expense of General Motors. Most marketers agree that the turnaround was due to Iaccoca's success in getting managers to evaluate every aspect of Chrysler's performance.

**Anthony O'Reilly —
Heinz's Cost-Cutter Supreme**

When Tony O'Reilly became president of Heinz in 1973, he defined his first mission as getting managers of the different product lines to begin cutting costs. One of the division heads said, "The [corporate] culture has been chip, chip, chip."[20]

In 1982, after he became chairman, O'Reilly initiated further cost cuts in earnest with his *low-cost operator (LCO)* program. LCO meant specific cost-cutting goals for each of Heinz's subsidiaries. Managers were given little choice — either achieve the cost-cutting goals or start looking for another job — but they were given a great deal of latitude in how they could achieve these goals. In one case, the ketchup group discovered that they could save $4 million a year by getting rid of the back label on ketchup bottles.[21] Based on his LCO initiative, O'Reilly wound up closing 16 plants, eliminating one-third of the managerial jobs at Heinz, and generating an average of about $55 million a year in profits from cost cuts.

Why the emphasis on cost-cutting? Because O'Reilly realized that with Heinz charging premium prices for its products, any additional profits would have to come from lower costs, not increased prices. Further, most of Heinz's products are in the mature stages of their life cycle, with growth inching ahead at an average of 2 percent a year. In O'Reilly's words, "If you can't get growth out of [increasing] volume, you've got to get it out of cost."[22]

O'Reilly's strategy has been to take the money saved in cost cuts and plow it into marketing. He has doubled expenditures on marketing, most of the increase going into advertising. Has the strategy worked? In the four-year period from 1983 to 1987, sales increased by $1 billion and profits by $500 million. In an industry where contribution to margins averages 35 percent of sales, Heinz's is 42 percent.[23] Overall, O'Reilly's consistent focus on evaluating every aspect of Heinz's operations with an eye to reducing costs has worked. Heinz has established a distinct advantage as the low-cost producer in packaged foods.

Tony O'Reilly did not start on the road to fame as a manager. Like John Akers of IBM and Alex Kroll of Young & Rubicam, O'Reilly started off as a sports star — a world-class Irish rugby player whose scoring records set in the late 1950s still remain unbroken.[24] Today, O'Reilly takes most pride in his success in turning Heinz from a mediocre company to what one analyst described as "the best run, best structured of the major food companies."[25] Despite his sports laurels, Tony O'Reilly would probably prefer the label of "Heinz's cost-cutter supreme." ■

Quality Control The second leg of the productivity triangle is quality. Many American companies have subscribed to the traditional notion that quality control is best attained by inspections after the fact. As a result, they have been at a

EXHIBIT 23.2
Ford's Emphasis on Quality Control

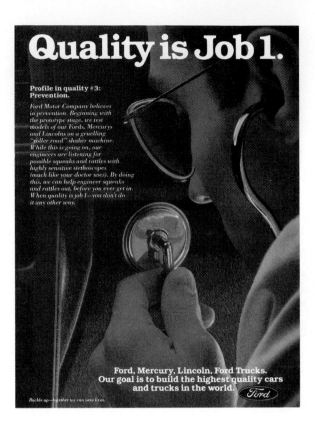

competitive disadvantage to foreign competitors, particularly the Japanese. One estimate is that one-fourth of American workers are employed to fix the mistakes of the other three-fourths, and that quality control costs the average American firm 10 to 20 percent of sales.[26]

In contrast, the Japanese have adopted the concept of **statistical process control,** which seeks to control defects at the time they occur rather than after the fact. This is done by giving workers responsibility for identifying defects in their own work and encouraging them to be as conscious of quality as possible. It requires that workers have the greatest amount of autonomy possible.

Effective quality control decreases the incompatability between high quality and lower costs, since quality can be improved while costs are reduced. This has been Ford's approach to improving productivity: let improvements in quality drive cost cuts, the idea being that product quality, not costs, is the key to marketing success. (Chrysler's approach has been the opposite: Let cost cuts drive any subsequent improvements in quality.)

Ford's approach to quality control has been to establish quality circles, each trained to regard itself as a customer of the preceding group on the assembly line and as a supplier to the next group. If one group assembles circuit boards, it is a customer of whoever makes the chips for the board, and it is a supplier to the next group down the line who gets the board and puts it into the car. Being accountable to one's co-workers for quality makes each member of the quality circle more responsible for his or her work output.[27] The ad in Exhibit 23.2 illustrates Ford's approach: quality control through prevention rather than through correction.

The focus on product quality has produced results. Ford averages 10 percent fewer defects in producing its cars compared to General Motors and Chrysler,

FIGURE 23.5
Results of Ford's Drive
for Product Quality

Source: "Can Ford Stay on Top?" Reprinted from
September 28, 1987 issue of *Business Week,* p. 82,
by special permission, copyright © 1987 by McGraw-
Hill, Inc.

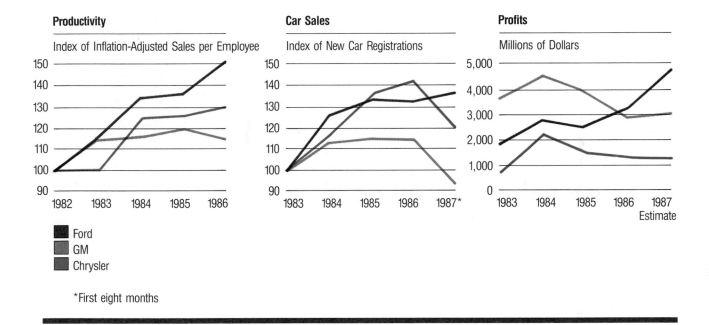

and from 1982 to 1987, its sales have grown faster than those of GM and Chrysler. Further, in 1986 Ford's net income outstripped GM's for the first time (see Figure 23.5). It is apparent that the evaluation of performance in the context of product quality is paying off.

Corporate Growth

Corporate growth strategies are another component of the strategic marketing plan that must be evaluated and controlled. Canfield Beverages recognized the limitations of unbridled growth and pulled back before operations went out of control. As we saw in Chapter 12, one company that did not realize the limits of unbridled growth was People Express. When it started flying from Newark in 1981 as a low-cost, no-frills airline, it avoided competition by choosing lesser routes such as Newark to Buffalo. But its immediate success prompted Donald Burr, the company's founder, to expand into bigger cities such as Chicago and Dallas, and to begin acquiring small commuter airlines such as Britt, Frontier, and Provincetown-Boston Airlines.

The problem was that all this activity was not controlled. According to one company consultant, the airline was "flinging aircraft at cities with only a vague idea as to whether the routes were profitable."[28] When the larger carriers began reducing their fares, People's main advantage, lower prices, was gone. And it did not have the resources to compete with the larger airlines based on service. The beginning of the end was when management decided to raise fares. At that point,

People found itself filling only 50 percent of its seats compared to an industry average of 62 percent.[29]

Had management exerted better controls over People's growth, the company might have survived. This required a mentality more like Alan Canfield's than Donald Burr's — namely, a recognition of the limits of growth. When it was evaluating routes, it should have analyzed the associated costs and projected the profitability of each route. And when it bought Britt, Provincetown, and Frontier, it should have calculated the risks of such large capital expenditures and its ability to manage these airlines.

Acquisitions

An important component in evaluating corporate growth strategies is company acquisitions. As we noted in the last chapter, the late 1960s and the 1970s saw many of the largest companies in America acquiring firms far from their core areas of expertise. These companies wrongly assumed they could run these businesses. When they found that they did not have the managerial or marketing know-how to do so, most of the acquisitions were divested.

The key requirement in evaluation and control is for a company to establish marketing, managerial, and financial criteria for acquisitions. For example, Lipton specifies that any company it considers for acquisition should have a leading position in its market (a marketing criterion). Further, the company must have an uncomplicated management and employment situation (a managerial criterion). Lipton also requires high profits and a low ratio of capital to sales (financial criteria).[30]

PRODUCT MARKETING EVALUATION

The second area that must be evaluated for purposes of control is the product marketing plan. Management will want to evaluate three product-specific areas: the adequacy of the new-product development process in adding profitable products to the company's offerings; the adequacy of the company's process of deleting unprofitable products; and the effectiveness of the product's marketing mix — that is, advertising, sales, distribution, and pricing strategies.

Product Additions

As we saw in Chapter 10, firms emphasize new-product development to sustain profitability over time. A typical objective for firms such as DuPont, Westinghouse, and 3M is that one-fourth of their earnings come from products developed in the last five years. The effectiveness of the new-product development process can be measured by the number and profitability of the products introduced.

When Gordon McGovern became president of Campbell in 1980, his primary goal was to energize the company into becoming a more diversified packaged food firm through new-product development. Over 300 new products were introduced in the first five years of McGovern's reign. New-product introductions were so fast-paced that inadequate cost control and research preceded many of the launches. There were some big winners such as the Le Menu line of premium frozen dinners, but there were too many losers. By 1985 McGovern recognized the need to exert tighter control over the new-product development process to improve profitability. He admitted that "brand managers became so involved in looking at new products that they ignored the base businesses."[31] Tighter control meant moderating the rate of new-product introductions and putting more emphasis on improving the productivity of existing products.

A possible consequence of a lack of control over new product introductions is **unplanned cannibalization,** which occurs when a new brand unexpectedly draws sales from an existing brand and reduces profits below the firm's expectations. General Motors has had a serious cannibalization problem in recent years because of the similarity of the design of its new car models. The company had tried to integrate the design process across its divisions to reduce costs, but the result was a number of look-alike models. When Chevrolet introduced models such as the Corsica and Beretta, sales came largely from other Chevrolet models such as the Cavalier and Celebrity rather than from competitors.[32] Better control over new-product development might have led Chevrolet's management to more sharply differentiate its cars, or to stagger their introduction in different model years.

Product cannibalization can also be planned. **Planned cannibalization** results when new technologies create new products that might compete with other products in the company's line. General Foods introduced Maxim freeze-dried coffee knowing it would cannibalize sales of Instant Maxwell House. But if it did not introduce the product, it would have lost customers to Nestle's Tasters' Choice (also a freeze-dried brand). It was better to have customers switch from one of the company's brands to another than lose them to another company.

An irony of GM being subjected to the unplanned cannibalization just described is that it was one of the originators of the notion of planned cannibalization. The original idea in having various GM divisions competing with each other was to have a customer stay with GM cars for life by trading up from one division to another. Planned cannibalization was a means of retaining customer loyalty as long as there were sufficient differences between divisions. When these differences started to blur, planned cannibalization turned into unplanned cannibalization.

Product Deletions

Given the emphasis on new-product development, many firms tend to ignore the other side of the coin, product deletions. New products are more glamorous, more fun to work on, and more closely linked to profitability than existing ones. Product deletions tend to be associated with failure. Few managers want to make a career of wielding the axe on existing products. Also, companies rarely reward managers for sound decisions to eliminate existing products; they reward them for introducing successful new products.

Figure 23.6 presents a systematic approach to product deletions. Take the example of Chase & Sanborne, at one time a leading coffee brand marketed by Standard Brands (now Nabisco Brands). In evaluating the brand, the first step is to determine if it is meeting sales, profitability, and market-share objectives. If so, the product is retained. Since Chase & Sanborne's sales and market share were sliding, the next question was the brand's future growth potential. If a brand has growth potential, the company will change the marketing strategy to try to revitalize it. Chase & Sanborne had little growth potential because most former buyers preferred newer freeze-dried and premium coffees and were unlikely to switch back to the brand.

Given a lack of growth potential, the next question is whether deleting a brand would have a negative impact on other coffee brands in the line. If so, deletion

FIGURE 23.6
A Product Deletion Model

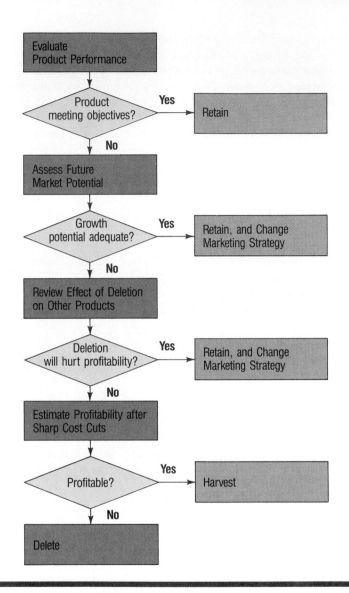

might actually decrease profits, despite the brand's poor performance. For example, a buyer of steel plate might not deal with a company unless it offers various qualities of plate. High-quality steel plate may be a loss item because of the expense of processing, yet the seller must maintain it in the line to satisfy customers. Although it may not be profitable, the product has a positive impact on the line. In such a case, the company would retain the product and change its marketing strategy to try to increase its sales. In Chase & Sanborne's case, however, customers did not link purchase of one coffee brand to availability of another, so deleting the product would not harm the company.

The final decision in Figure 23.6 is whether to harvest or delete the product. If a product still has a small but loyal following, then eliminating advertising and sales promotional expenses and minimizing other costs could make the product profitable. If such a harvesting strategy is unlikely to produce profits, then the product should be deleted. Chase & Sanborne did have a small group of loyal

TABLE 23.2
Criteria for Evaluating
Components of the
Marketing Mix

MARKETING MIX COMPONENT	CRITERIA
Product	Sales
	Market share
	Contribution to profit
	Net profit
Distribution	Cost of on-time delivery
	Amount of time to process an order
	Amount of time to deliver an order
Sales Promotion	Cost of coupon redemption
	Cost of attracting customer to store with in-store promotions
Advertising	Cost of reaching a target customer
	Cost of creating brand awareness for a target customer
	Cost of creating favorable brand attitudes for a target customer
Personal Selling	Cost of acquiring a new account
	Number of sales calls per completed sale
	Contribution to margin of a salesperson or a sales branch
Price	Evaluation of price relative to product quality
	Evaluation of price relative to customer's perceived product value
	Evaluation of adequacy of trade discounts to win trade support

consumers, so Standard Brands decided to harvest it, with the possibility of deleting it should market share shrink further.

The Marketing Mix

In previous chapters, we discussed the evaluation of various components of the marketing mix — the product, distribution, sales promotions, advertising, personal selling, and price. Some of the criteria we discussed for evaluating these strategies are summarized in Table 23.2.

Many of these criteria reflect measures of marketing productivity based on cost inputs and performance outputs. For example, distribution performance could be measured by the cost (input) of on-time delivery (output), or by the amount of time it takes (input) to deliver an order (output). Similarly, sales promotional effectiveness could be measured by the cost to the company of an average coupon redemption, or by the cost of attracting customers through in-store promotions. These measures give the manager some insight into the effectiveness of the marketing strategy.

Evaluating marketing performance requires a comprehensive, periodic, and independent review of a company's or SBU's marketing operations known as a **marketing audit**. It is a comprehensive review because it should evaluate every aspect

THE MARKETING AUDIT

TABLE 23.3
Key Questions in a Marketing Audit

THE STRATEGIC MARKETING AUDIT

1. Are the firm's business mission and corporate objectives clearly stated?
2. Has the company established a reasonable organizational and planning framework based on customer needs?
3. Is there an environmental scanning system in place capable of identifying marketing opportunity?
4. How has the company adjusted to key changes in demographics, technology, the economy, and legal and regulatory requirements?
5. Has the company effectively anticipated competition?
6. Is product quality satisfying customer needs?
7. Is the firm sufficiently conscious of cost-cutting opportunities?
8. Are there adequate criteria for reviewing potential acquisitions?
9. Has the firm been effective in applying its research and development resources to pursue opportunities?
10. Has the firm adequately exploited opportunities through new-product development?

THE PRODUCT MARKETING AUDIT

1. Have the needs of current and potential customers been adequately identified?
2. Have the major market segments been defined?
3. Have products been effectively positioned to these segments?
4. What is the profitability of each product?
5. What is the profitability of each product line?
6. Does the company have an effective system for new-product introductions?
7. Does it have an effective system for product deletions?
8. Are product, distribution, promotional, and pricing objectives clear for each product and product line?
9. Are expenditures allocated to each component of the marketing mix based on a set of defined criteria?
10. Are the marketing mix components effective in contributing to profits? (See specific marketing mix criteria in Table 23.2.)

of marketing performance. It is a periodic review because frequent changes in the environment mean that an audit should be an ongoing process. It is an independent review because it should be conducted by a team outside of marketing (a team of marketing auditors) with no vested interest in the results.

Table 23.3 shows that there are two components to a marketing audit, a strategic and a product component. In the strategic component, the auditors assess the firm's or SBU's strategic planning capabilities and the effectiveness of the firm in responding to environmental change. Key questions asked in a strategic marketing audit are listed in the top of the table — for example, whether the firm has adequately anticipated environmental changes and competitive actions in its planning. Usually, these questions are framed in a longer checklist than that in Table 23.3, but the questions in the table indicate the environmental focus of the strategic marketing audit.

In Westinghouse's case, a marketing audit might review the future prospects for factory automation, competitive threats from large producers of automated equipment such as General Electric, satisfaction with existing systems among large customers such as General Motors, and the potential threat of foreign competition on the company's business. The auditors will also consider Westinghouse's efficiency in producing and marketing their machines, and the company's adaptability to produce custom-made systems.

In the product marketing component of the audit, the focus is on the company's or SBU's ability to exploit specific opportunities through development of an effective marketing mix. The key factors that auditors will evaluate in their review are listed in the bottom of Table 23.3 — for example, whether the firm is effective in identifying customer needs and in targeting a product to specific market segments. Auditors will also review management's effectiveness in developing the marketing mix for individual products based on the criteria listed in Table 23.2.

TAKE CORRECTIVE ACTION

The last step in the evaluation and control process is taking corrective action if needed. We have referred to corrective actions at various points in our discussion — Canfield Beverages' shift from producing and marketing Diet Chocolate Fudge soda to franchising it to bottlers; Campbell's cutback in its emphasis on new product development; People Express's cutback in routes and increase in fares; Chrysler's sharp cost-cutting and institution of a just-in-time system.

Sometimes corrective actions fail, as in the case of People Express. In such cases, the firm must terminate the product or business and look for alternative investment opportunities. If corrective action looks as if it will be profitable, then a new planning cycle begins.

Two types of conditions require corrective action. The first is when objectives are not being met. The difference between objectives and performance is known as **performance variance**. For example, if Campbell's return on investment goal for new products is 15 percent, and it is actually attaining a 10 percent ROI, the performance variance is 5 percent. In such a case, a company will usually reallocate resources to try to attain the original goals. Campbell might increase advertising for new products, invest more money in concept and product testing, or allocate more funds to coupons and in-store promotions in the first few months after introduction. All three control systems — after-the-fact, steering, and adaptive control — allow for corrective action due to performance variance.

The second condition for corrective action is particular to an adaptive control system. It allows for adjustments in objectives because of changes in environmental conditions. The difference between the original objective and the new objective is known as **forecasting variance**. If Campbell decided that its ROI objectives were too optimistic in an increasingly competitive environment and scaled them back from 15 percent to 12 percent, the forecasting variance would be 3 percent. It would then determine performance variance based on the new ROI objective. Forecasting variance therefore requires corrective action in the form of a change in objectives, whereas performance variance requires corrective action in the form of a change in resource allocations.

If an adaptive control system is in place, a firm will usually require corrective actions as a result of both forecasting and performance variance. In the process of strategic marketing planning, it is rare that a firm has gauged the marketing environment so precisely as to require no change in projections.

For example, General Foods' evaluation of its pet food business resulted in both types of corrective action. Growth in pet foods slowed in the early 1980s because of a slowing of new household formations, growth of generic pet foods, and a severe recession. Competition was more intense for a shrinking market because many competitors had built plants in the expectation of increasing demand. As a result of forecasting variance, the division cut back its sales objectives for the Gaines Division in the expectation of slower growth. Performance variance also led General Foods to cut costs by reducing advertising spending, consolidating manufacturing to two plants from three, and cutting back on marketing personnel.[33]

Managers should not regard the necessity for corrective action as a failure of the marketing planning process. Corrective action reflects the need to keep a pulse on a constantly changing marketing environment and adapt plans accordingly. Such a process of adaptation suggests that managers are sensitive to customer needs. And, ultimately, that is what marketing is all about!

SUMMARY

1. What is the distinction between strategic control and product marketing control?

Strategic control attempts to ensure that the components of the strategic marketing plan are on target. Product marketing control attempts to ensure that the components of a product's marketing plan will meet objectives. The strategic dimension of control focuses on evaluating and controlling corporate and business-unit strategies, whereas the product marketing dimension focuses on controlling the components of the marketing mix.

2. How do companies control marketing operations?

Firms must have a systematic basis for evaluating and controlling marketing operations. The first step is to define criteria for evaluation. The two most widely used profit criteria are contribution to margin and return on investment (ROI). Next, the firm projects cost estimates and revenues in a profit and loss (P&L) statement for a product or a business unit. The third step is to establish a marketing organization that is capable of implementing and controlling marketing activities. Next, the firm must develop and implement a plan to achieve the objectives spelled out in the projections. Once the plan is implemented, a control system is established to enable the company to evaluate marketing performance. In the final step, the company determines whether corrective action is necessary.

3. What is the primary focus of strategic control?

The primary focus for control at the corporate and business-unit levels is the product quality of the firm's offerings and the costs of producing and marketing the product. The relationship between product quality and costs measures marketing productivity. Another area of strategic control is corporate growth. A corporate growth plan requires control over new-product development, market entry, and marketing expenditures if costs are to be kept in line. A third area is to control acquisition strategies by establishing appropriate criteria to evaluate prospective acquisitions.

4. What is the primary focus of product-marketing control?

Firms must control marketing performance at the individual product level on several dimensions. First, they must control product additions to ensure that overzealous product managers do not come out with unprofitable new products. Second, firms must have a systematic process for deleting unprofitable products from the line. The third area for evaluation and control is the product's marketing mix. The product's distribution, advertising, personal selling, sales promotion, and pricing strategies must be evaluated. Productivity measures should be established that measure the performance of these strategies relative to their cost.

5. What types of systems do companies use to implement control processes?
Firms use after-the-fact, steering, and adaptive systems to implement marketing controls. In an after-the-fact control system, managers wait until the end of the planning period to take corrective action. In a steering control system, corrective action is taken during the planning period by tracking performance and steering it back to the desired objectives if it goes out of control. An adaptive system recognizes that environmental changes over time might require a change in forecasts and objectives as well as a change in strategies. Such a system is more proactive in that it anticipates environmental change, whereas after-the-fact and steering control systems are more reactive in that they deal with changes after they occur.

KEY TERMS

Control (p. 644)
Strategic control (p. 644)
Product-marketing control (p. 644)
Quality circles (p. 645)
Zero-based budgeting (p. 651)
After-the-fact control system (p. 655)
Steering control system (p. 656)
Adaptive control system (p. 656)
Marketing productivity (p. 657)
Statistical process control (p. 660)
Unplanned cannibalization (p. 663)

Planned cannibalization (p. 663)
Marketing audit (p. 665)
Performance variance (p. 667)
Forecasting variance (p. 667)
Assignable fixed costs (p. 672)
Nonassignable fixed costs (p. 672)
Contribution to margin (p. 672)
Profit and loss (P&L) statement
  (p. 673)
Return on investment (ROI) (p. 673)
Net profit (p. 673)

QUESTIONS

1. What signals indicated that Alan Canfield was losing control over the production and marketing of Diet Chocolate Fudge?
2. In what way was Westinghouse's attempt to bring its operations under control in the 1980s an example of strategic control?
3. What factors led firms to give more attention to control of marketing operations in the 1980s?
4. Why do product managers prefer using contribution to margin as a criterion of performance rather than return on investment? What are the advantages of using return on investment?
5. What is meant by zero-based budgeting? What are its advantages?
6. One of the top executives of an electronics company that has found itself losing market share to Japanese competitors made the following statement:

    Contrary to popular belief, one of the reasons our Japanese competitors have a productivity advan-

tage is that they are people-oriented, whereas we [American companies] tend to be machine-oriented. They reduce costs by motivating their people to work efficiently on a team basis and provide better quality control. We try to reduce costs by replacing people with robots. Overall, human quality control seems to be working better than factory automation as the best road to increasing productivity.

  a. Do you agree or disagree with the executive? Why?
  b. What evidence in this chapter supports your position?

7. What is the distinction between a product-based marketing organization and a market-based organization? How might the development of marketing plans and strategies at Kellogg differ depending on whether the company is organized on a product or market basis?

8. What are some principles for ensuring effective implementation of the marketing plan? Cite examples demonstrating each of these principles?

9. The two components of marketing productivity defined in Figure 23.4 are lower costs and higher product quality.

   a. Cite examples of companies focusing primarily on cost-cutting and companies focusing primarily on product quality to increase productivity.
   b. Are these two approaches mutually exclusive? Explain.

10. Looking back over the last ten years, a former CEO of a firm producing plastics is concerned with America's economic outlook. He says:

    We are slowly losing our manufacturing base as foreign competitors. In particular the Japanese are undermining domestic companies in the auto, computer, electronics, and small-appliance industries. As a result, we are becoming a service economy as more of our gross national product shifts from manufacturing to services. And I do not see this trend being arrested in the near future. That spells serious trouble for us and our children.

    a. Is the former CEO being overly pessimistic? Why or why not?
    b. Is there any evidence in this chapter that American companies can recapture sales lost to foreign competitors? Explain.

11. How did lack of adequate controls lead to People Express's demise?

12. Consider the following statement:

    New products insure future profitability. Therefore, a company should ensure that it comes out with a steady stream of new products every year.

    a. What risks are involved in trying to ensure a steady stream of new products every year?
    b. What was Campbell's experience in emphasizing new-product development? What questions of control are raised by Campbell's experience?

13. Why do most companies pay much more attention to the process of product additions than product deletions? Do you agree with the greater emphasis on additions compared to deletions? Why or why not?

14. In the past, General Motors followed a policy of planned product cannibalization. Now it is plagued with unplanned cannibalization.

    a. What is meant by product cannibalization?
    b. What is the distinction between planned and unplanned cannibalization?
    c. What was General Motors' policy of planned cannibalization? Why is the company now plagued with unplanned cannibalization?

15. What are the differences between after-the-fact, steering, and adaptive control systems? In what sense is an adaptive control system proactive, whereas after-the-fact and steering control systems are reactive? Under what conditions is an adaptive control system most appropriate?

CASE 23.1

CONTROL PROBLEMS AT WORLDS OF WONDER INC.

Source: Adapted from Carrie Dolan, "Yesterday's Marvel, Worlds of Wonder Inc., Is in Worlds of Trouble," *The Wall Street Journal*, October 28, 1987, pp. 1, 18.

When it comes to his company's products, Donald Kingsborough behaves like a proud father showing off his adorable children. In an office here, the 40-year-old chairman of Worlds of Wonder Inc. opens a book with built-in microchips and touches a picture of a frog. The frog croaks. The chairman beams.

Next, Mr. Kingsborough sets a radio beside two stuffed dolls. The dolls start to shake and bump into each other. Mr. Kingsborough exclaims: "Aren't they great!"

Richard Brady, executive vice president of Play Co., a Southern California toystore chain, is less enthusiastic about Mr. Kingsborough's prides and joys. Mr. Brady hasn't received a shipment of those dancing dolls, promised him in June. And he is fed up with Worlds of Wonder, which in the industry is more familiarly, if not always approvingly, referred to as WOW. He says sales of older WOW toys are slowing and adds that every product that Play Co. has ordered from WOW has been delivered late. "The company has a tremendous credibility problem," he says.

Times have changed — rapidly. Founded in early 1985, WOW chalked up the fastest two-year sales growth of any new manufacturing concern by producing two huge hits: Teddy Ruxpin, a $70 stuffed bear that moves its mouth and eyes in sync with a tape-recorded spiel, and Lazer Tag, a gun game in which players "shoot" one another with beams of infrared light.

But now Worlds of Wonder is plagued by declining sales and by delivery problems. Some new products show promise, but not on the scale of WOW's two big sellers. It is thus becoming less able to afford the huge advertising budgets needed to persuade parents to buy its expensive, high-tech toys for their children.

In August, WOW laid off 55 workers. Two weeks ago, Mr. Kingsborough dismissed an additional 60 employees. Mr. Kingsborough says "We've been hurt by our inability to deliver, not by our lack of ideas." Furthermore, he attributes many of WOW's woes to the company's explosive growth.

WOW's experience is the classic management story of a supersalesman who launches an extraordinarily suc-

cessful product but has difficulty mastering the complex manufacturing operations and runaway growth that result.

Mr. Kingsborough believed he could make a market niche for WOW by adapting new technology, particularly inexpensive microchip advances, to toys such as talking and animated stuffed animals and dolls. He thought such products could have life cycles far longer than most toys because his company would continually develop new tapes or chips to give the toys new acts. He would produce toys cheaply by contracting most manufacturing to plants in the Far East. He also planned to beat imitators by obtaining licenses to produce dolls of such well-known characters as Mickey Mouse, Snoopy, and the Muppets.

But almost from the beginning, WOW was plagued by delays in toy development and by overseas production gaffes. Last Christmas, when Lazer Tag was the hottest toy around, the company couldn't get enough of the product to stores until it was too late. By the time the season was over, retailers had a pile of Lazer Tag guns, many of which are still sitting on store shelves.

In 1987, WOW allowed its costs to balloon in an attempt to develop as many as 150 different products, but its production problems also ballooned. Five stuffed Muppets, radio-controlled to talk to one another, were originally set to go on sale at Christmas but were delayed until next year. Wondervision, a videocassette recorder aimed at teens, met a similar fate. A talking Snoopy is available now, but not his pal, Charlie Brown, reportedly because Charlie's mouth doesn't work right. Little Boppers were shipped late because of early manufacturing problems. The books with croaking frogs and other talking characters have also been delayed. Mr. Kingsborough still expects diversification to bear fruit, and some retailers report that a line of school accessories, called Class Act, did well late this summer.

But at the annual meeting last week, Mr. Kingsborough was pelted with angry questions from stockholders, who asked why corporate officers sold their WOW shares.

After several questions, Mr. Kingsborough said, "We have to be going now" and left. Other officers stayed behind, and one, Thomas Liddy, demonstrated the $100 Julie doll. He asked her, "Julie, are you hungry?" and she responded, "Can we talk about your friends?" He repeated the question. This time, Julie replied: "Ooh, it's nice to have friends."

Said Mr. Liddy, chuckling: "Sometimes I want to smack her."

1. What are the areas that Worlds of Wonder (WOW) must control? What corrective action is required?

2. What are the similarities in control problems between WOW and Canfield Beverages?
3. What kind of control system should WOW institute? Why?

APPENDIX 23A
COST AND PROFIT CONCEPTS FOR EVALUATING AND CONTROLLING MARKETING PERFORMANCE

COST CONCEPTS

Costs may be variable or fixed. *Variable costs* vary directly with the amount produced and include cost of labor, raw materials, transportation charges, order processing costs, and sales commissions. *Fixed costs* are not determined by the amount produced.

There are two types of fixed costs, assignable and nonassignable. **Assignable fixed costs** are those that can be associated with the production or distribution of a product and can therefore be assigned to the product. For example, product advertising is an assignable fixed cost because advertising expenses do not vary directly with quantity produced yet can be assigned to a particular product. Other assignable fixed costs are the salary of a product manager, sales promotions, retooling costs for a product on the assembly line, and inventory carrying charges.

Nonassignable fixed costs are those that cannot be directly linked to the production or distribution of a product. If an auto plant produces many models, the plant and its facilities would be nonassignable since they are not product-specific. For the same reason, corporate advertising expenditures, a research and development facility, and salaries of general managers are nonassignable fixed costs.

PROFIT CONCEPTS

The distinction between assignable and nonassignable costs defines the distinction between contribution to margin and return on investment. **Contribution to margin** is the amount left over after all costs directly related to

TABLE 23A.1
Profit and Loss Projection for Westinghouse's Robotics Division in Fifth Year after Acquisition (in Millions)

Sales revenue			$114.0
Variable costs		$50.0	
Labor	$22.0		
Raw materials	15.5		
Distribution	10.5		
Sales commissions	2.0		
Assignable fixed costs		34.5	
Assignable Manufacturing costs	28.0		
Product advertising	5.0		
Sales promotions	0.5		
Assignable salaries	1.0		
Contribution to margin[a]			29.5
Nonassignable fixed costs		15.5	
Nonassignable Manufacturing costs	11.0		
Nonassignable salaries	2.0		
Research and development	2.5		
Net profit[b]			14.0

[a]Contribution as a percent of sales is 25.9 percent.
[b]Total investment to buy the robotics division was $107 million. Therefore, projected return on investment in the fifth year is $14 million divided by $107 million, or 13.1 percent.

the product are deducted. As a result, contribution to margin equals

Total Sales − Variable Costs − Assignable Fixed Costs

The *margin* is defined as nonassignable costs plus profits. Thus, the amount left over after deductions for direct product costs is a *contribution* to nonassignable fixed costs and to profits; that is, a contribution to margin.

A **profit and loss statement** is a statement of the actual or projected revenue costs and profits for a product, an SBU, or a company. An example of a projected profit and loss statement for Westinghouse's robotics division in the fifth year after its acquisition is shown in Table 23A.1. Projected sales in the fifth year after acquisition are $114 million. Variable costs and assignable fixed costs are estimated at $50.0 million and $34.5 million, respectively, leaving $29.5 million as the contribution to margin. Another frequently cited profitability measure, the contribution as a percentage of sales, is 25.9 percent ($29.5 million divided by $114 million).

The second most frequently used measure of profitability is **return on investment,** which is net profit divided by total investment, where **net profit** equals

Total Sales − Variable costs −
Assignable Fixed Costs − Nonassignable Fixed Costs

To compute net profits for a product or business unit requires the allocation of nonassignable fixed costs to a product or business unit. For example, a portion of the salaries of Westinghouse executives would have to be allocated to the robotics division. Similarly, a portion of the costs of maintaining Westinghouse's research and development facility and productivity center would have to be allocated to the division. One way to do that might be based on sales. For example, if the robotics division accounts for 7 percent of Westinghouse's total sales, then 7 percent of nonassignable fixed costs would be allocated to the division.

In this example, management projects that $15.5 million of nonassignable costs will be allocated to the robotics division, producing a net profit of $14 million. Since the initial investment in buying the division was $107 million, the return on investment is 13.1 percent ($14 million divided by $107 million).

NOTES

1. "Too Hot to Handle," *Inc.,* March 1987, p. 54.

2. Ibid.

3. Ibid., p. 53.

4. Ibid., p. 56.

5. Ibid., p. 57.

6. Ibid., p. 56.

7. "How Westinghouse Is Revving Up After the Rebound," *Business Week,* March 28, 1988, p. 47.

8. Ibid., pp. 47, 50.

9. "Operation Turnaround," *Business Week,* December 5, 1983, p. 133; and *Business Week,* March 28, 1988, pp. 50, 52.

10. "You Can Be Sure . . . If It's Danforth," *Nation's Business,* March 1985, p. 85.

11. "Procter & Gamble's Comeback Plan," *Fortune,* February 4, 1985, pp. 30, 32.

12. *Business Week,* March 28, 1988, p. 50.

13. Donald W. Jackson, Jr., Lonnie L. Ostrom, and Kenneth R. Evans, *Cost & Management,* July–August 1985, p. 20.

14. "Heinz Pushes to Be the Low-Cost Producer," *Fortune,* June 24, 1985, p. 44.

15. "AT&T: The Making of a Comeback," *Business Week,* January 18, 1988, pp. 56–62.

16. "The New Breed of Strategic Planner," *Business Week,* September 17, 1984, pp. 62–68.

17. "At Heinz, a Bottom-Line Leader," *The New York Times,* May 8, 1988, p. F1.

18. Ibid., and "Can Chrysler Keep Its Comeback Rolling?" *Business Week,* February 14, 1983, p. 132.

19. Lee Iacocca, "The Rescue and Resuscitation of Chrysler," *Journal of Business Strategy* (Summer 1983):67.

20. "The King of Ketchup," *Forbes,* March 21, 1988, p. 59; and *Fortune,* June 24, 1985, p. 44.

21. Ibid., p. 50.

22. *The New York Times,* May 8, 1988, p. F6.

23. *Forbes,* March 21, 1988, p. 59.

24. "Tony O'Reilly of Heinz: His Day Has 57 Varieties," *Business Week,* December 17, 1984, pp. 72–73; and *The New York Times,* May 8, 1988, pp. F1, F6.

25. *Business Week,* December 17, 1984, p. 73.

26. Joel E. Ross, "Making Quality a Fundamental Part of Strategy," *Long-Range Planning* 18(1985):55; and "America's Quest Can't Be Half-Hearted," *Business Week,* June 8, 1987, p. 136.

27. "Can Ford Stay on Top?" *Business Week,* September 28, 1987, p. 84.

28. *The Wall Street Journal,* July 31, 1986, pp. 1, 17.

29. Ibid., p. 17.

30. H. M. Tibbetts, "The Product-Line Audit: An Approach to Profit-Oriented Marketing," *Management Review* 66(March 1977):14–17.

31. "Burned By Mistakes, Campbell Soup Co. Is in Throes of Change," *The Wall Street Journal,* August 14, 1985, p. 16.

32. "'Cannibal' Peril for GM Sales," *The New York Times,* October 9, 1987, p. D5.

33. "GF Execs: Committed to Lean Pet Foods Unit," *Advertising Age,* November 8, 1982, p. 4.

APPENDIX 1

MARKETING MATHEMATICS

The goals of marketing activities are often expressed and discussed in financial terms — net profit, contribution margin, return on investment. Certainly, many marketing decisions, such as adding a new product, changing channels of distribution, adjusting prices of products, or choosing among alternative promotional programs, have a significant financial impact on an organization. Consequently, marketing decision makers must understand certain basic financial concepts. Four areas of financial analysis are examined in this section: financial operating statements (including operating ratios), selected performance ratios, markups, and markdowns. Bear in mind, however, that financial considerations are only one aspect of marketing decision making.

OPERATING STATEMENTS

One of the primary financial statements used by any company is the *operating statement* (which may also be referred to as the *income statement* or the *profit and loss statement*). This document summarizes company sales, cost of goods sold, and expenses incurred during a given time period, usually a monthly, quarterly, or yearly period, although it can be any length. The length is chosen for a particular reason, such as monitoring monthly sales in a region or reporting annual income of the company. The statements may be for the company as a whole or for some operating division, profit center, or even a single product. A typical operating statement is shown in Table 1. The amount of detail in the statement may vary depending on how it is used. Typical uses include determining net income, finding the relationship between sales and the cost of goods sold, analyzing changes in inventory, identifying total expenses and the amounts of expenses by category, and comparing current operating results with past results. Table 1 shows the major sections and some typical subsections and categories included in most statements. Each one of the major sections is examined next.

Sales

The first element of any income statement is *sales,* the total dollar amount the company received for the goods or services it sold during the period. For most companies, this gross sales amount must be adjusted for goods returned by customers. Returns occur for many reasons, including products damaged in transit, errors made in filling customer orders, or perhaps a change in the customer's mind. For goods actually returned for credit, the term *return* is used. If the customer keeps the merchandise but an adjustment is made in its price, the term *allowance* is used. The two amounts are often lumped together, but they may be reported separately if desired. Subtracting total sales returns and allowances from gross sales yields *net sales,* the revenue actually received from sales.

Cost of Goods Sold (CGS)

Often the most complicated part of the operating statement, the *cost of goods sold* (CGS) reflects the amount the company actually spent for the merchandise sold during the period. This section is complicated by the presence of inventory. If a company has no inventory at the beginning of the period *(beginning inventory)* and no inventory at the end of the period *(ending inventory),* then the cost of goods sold is simply *net purchases.*

Gross sales			$20,420
Less: sales returns and allowances			157
Net sales			$20,263
Cost of goods sold:			
Beginning inventory 1/1/89 (at cost)		$ 3,770	
Net purchases:			
Gross purchases	$10,367		
Plus: freight in	628		
Less: purchase discounts	925		
Net purchases		$10,070	
Ending inventory 12/31/89 (at cost)		2,827	
Cost of goods sold (beginning inventory + net purchases − ending inventory)			11,013
Gross margin (net sales − cost of goods sold)			$ 9,250
Expenses:			
Selling expenses:			
Sales salaries and commissions	$ 2,510		
Advertising and promotion	350		
Travel	276		
Total selling expenses		$ 3,136	
Administrative expenses:			
Office salaries	$ 1,256		
Supplies	175		
Miscellaneous	280		
Total administrative expenses		$ 1,711	
General expenses:			
Rent	$ 620		
Utilities	200		
Miscellaneous	150		
Total general expenses		$ 970	
Total expenses			$ 5,817
Net income before taxes (gross margin − total expenses)			$ 3,433

Net purchases is *gross purchases,* which includes both the actual cost of the merchandise and any additional costs involved with the actual purchase, such as freight costs, less *purchase discounts.*

When a company has *inventory* (material purchased or manufactured for resale, but not yet sold), the cost of goods sold is still net purchases, but now this amount must be adjusted by the net change in inventory during the period. If ending inventory is larger than beginning inventory, this means that some purchases were not sold and are being held in inventory. If ending inventory is smaller than beginning inventory, this means that not only was the total amount of purchases sold, but also some of the beginning inventory was sold as well.

So the cost of goods that were actually sold during a given period is the amount we started with (beginning inventory), plus net purchases for the period, less the amount we had left over at the end of the period (ending inventory).

Gross Margin

Gross margin is the difference between net sales and the cost of goods sold. Gross margin represents the amount available to the company to pay for its other expenses (and profit or loss).

Expenses

Expenses not directly related to purchases are usually categorized as selling expenses, administrative expenses, and general expenses. *Selling expenses* relate directly to the activities involved in selling, such as sales salaries and commissions, advertising, sales promotion, and other miscellaneous selling expenses. *Administrative expenses* usually relate to the operation of offices and the salaries of those people not directly involved in selling. *General expenses* are all those other expenses (sometimes called *overhead expenses*) that are not directly related to selling or administration. Examples include rent, utilities, insurance, depreciation, property taxes, uncollectable accounts, and miscellaneous other expenses.

Net Income before Taxes

Total expenses are subtracted from gross margin to determine net income before taxes. If total expenses exceed gross margin, there is a *net operating loss*. Otherwise, there is a *net profit* from operations from which, in the case of a corporation, both state and federal income taxes must be subtracted to arrive at *net income.*

OPERATING RATIOS

The income statement may be used directly by marketing managers to improve their decision-making abilities. Actual amounts in various categories may be compared with previously forecasted or budgeted amounts. Differences between actual and budgeted amounts may identify activities that warrant further investigation by the manager.

For example, if actual sales are less than budgeted (or forecasted) sales, the problem might be poor forecasting, sales performance below expectations in one or more areas, or unexpected changes in customer demand. Higher than expected customer returns might indicate problems with the product design or package, damage in transit, or poor order-filling procedures. Similarly, higher than expected expense categories might point to inefficient operations. In all cases, the marketing manager must be a good detective to track down the underlying marketing problem.

The manager can be aided in this investigation in several ways. Income statement amounts may be recalculated as percentages of sales and then compared to budgeted percentages, similar percentages from previous periods, and/or percentages reported for similar businesses in trade publications. Table 2 shows the income statement data from Table 1 expressed as percentages of sales. Because many expenses are directly linked to sales and because sales vary each period, converting all amounts to percentages of sales will allow multiple-period data to be compared directly. These percentages are actually simplified *operating ratios*.

Operating statement amounts reflect only cost and revenue amounts. They provide no information concerning the efficiency or the effectiveness of spending. Nor do these amounts identify the type or composition of inventory or purchases.

Notice that changes in income statement amounts may or may not indicate a desirable development. For example, is an increase in selling expense desirable or not? It may reflect rising competition and thus suggest the need to advertise more. Or it may reflect ineffective advertising. The manager must make the determination. Changes in income statement amounts also do not indicate the efficiency or the effectiveness by which expenses are incurred. Improving office efficiency

Net sales			100.00%
Cost of goods sold:			
Beginning inventory 1/1/89 (at cost)		18.60%	
Net purchases:			
Gross purchases	51.16%		
Plus: freight in	3.10%		
Less: purchase discounts	4.56%		
Net purchases		49.70%	
Ending inventory 12/31/89 (at cost)		13.95%	
Cost of goods sold (beginning inventory + net purchases − ending inventory)			54.35%
Gross margin (net sales − cost of goods sold)			45.65%
Expenses:			
Selling expenses:			
Sales salaries and commissions	12.39%		
Advertising and promotion	1.73%		
Travel	1.36%		
Total selling expenses		15.48%	
Administrative expenses:			
Office salaries	6.20%		
Supplies	0.86%		
Miscellaneous	1.38%		
Total administrative expenses		8.44%	
General expenses:			
Rent	3.06%		
Utilities	0.99%		
Miscellaneous	0.74%		
Total general expenses		4.79%	
Total expenses			28.71%
Net income before taxes (gross margin − total expenses)			16.94%

TABLE 2
Operating Statement in Percentages: Ace Analytical Instruments, Inc. Operating Statement For the Year Ended 12/31/89

might reduce administrative expense, but improving the efficiency or effectiveness of the salesforce might increase sales commissions (due to increased sales).

Operating ratios express amounts on the income statement as a percentage of sales. The three most important operating ratios are

$$\text{Gross Margin Ratio} = \frac{\text{Gross Margin}}{\text{Net Sales}} = \frac{\$9,250}{\$20,263} = 45.65\%$$

$$\text{Net Income Ratio} = \frac{\text{Net Income}}{\text{Net Sales}} = \frac{\$3,433}{\$20,263} = 16.94\%$$

$$\text{Operating Expense Ratio} = \frac{\text{Total Expense}}{\text{Net Sales}} = \frac{\$5,817}{\$20,263} = 28.71\%$$

In addition to investigating changes in income statement amounts, marketing managers might also use *performance ratios* in their financial analysis of company operations.

A discussion of some useful performance ratios follows.

PERFORMANCE RATIOS

Inventory Turnover. Sometimes called the *stockturn rate*, the *inventory turnover* identifies the number of times an inventory is sold during one year.

$$\text{Inventory Turnover} = \frac{\text{Cost of Goods Sold}}{\text{Average Inventory}} = \frac{\$11{,}013}{(\$3{,}770 + \$2{,}827)/2}$$

$$= 3.3 \text{ times}$$

Whether an inventory turnover rate is too high or too low depends upon the type of industry and management customer service policy. Generally, the higher the turnover number, the better the performance. Higher turnover rates not only mean that sales are being made with a relatively small investment in inventory, but also that the composition of the inventory is more current (and so less likely to become obsolete). However, turnover rates that are too high could foretell shortages and thus reduced customer satisfaction.

Return on Investment (ROI). A measure of the efficiency with which company management can generate sales based upon the amount invested in the company is the *return on investment* (ROI).

$$\text{Return on Investment} = \frac{\text{Net Income}}{\text{Total Investment}}$$

The "Total Investment" amount comes from the balance sheet of the company. (A balance sheet shows the amounts of assets, debt, and net worth of a company at a given point in time.) Total investment may be interpreted as either total assets or net worth (net assets) of the company.

MARKUPS

A *markup* is a dollar amount added to the cost of an item to determine its selling price. As a result:

$$\text{Selling price} = \text{Cost} + \text{Markup}.$$

The amount of the markup must cover all the selling, administrative, and general expenses related to the item, and some additional amount to contribute to profit. Markups are widely used in wholesaling and retailing businesses, although other types of businesses may use them as well.

For ease of use, markups are often expressed as a percentage of either the selling price of the item or its cost. Most consumer goods middlemen use selling price as the basis for the markup.

$$\text{Percentage Markup on Selling Price} = \frac{\text{Dollar Markup}}{\text{Dollar Selling Price}}$$

Cost could also be used as the base for the markup:

$$\text{Percentage Markup on Cost} = \frac{\text{Dollar Markup}}{\text{Dollar Cost}}$$

To better understand markups, consider the following example: The Suitery is a retail clothing store specializing in men's suits. What should be the selling price of its TruFit brand if the suit costs The Suitery $99.90 each and the markup on selling price is 55 percent?

$$\text{Selling Price} = \text{Cost} + \text{Markup}$$
$$\text{Selling Price} = \$99.90 + (55\% \times \text{Selling Price})$$
$$\text{Selling Price} - (55\% \times \text{Selling Price}) = \$99.90$$
$$\text{Selling Price} = \$99.90/.45 = \$222.00$$

What is the dollar amount of the markup?

$$\text{Selling Price} = \text{Cost} + \$ \text{ Markup}$$
$$\$ \text{ Markup} = \text{Selling Price} - \text{Cost}$$
$$\$ \text{ Markup} = \$222.00 - \$99.90 = \$122.10$$

or you could determine the dollar amount of the markup as

$$\$ \text{ Markup} = \% \text{ Markup} \times \text{Price}$$
$$\$ \text{ Markup} = .55 \times \$222.00 = \$122.10$$

Sometimes a retailer might want to set a retail price first, and then determine the markup percentage. Let's consider The Suitery again. The Suitery would like to sell its BestFit brand of suit for a higher price than its TruFit brand ($222.00). The company thinks that customers would be willing to pay $335. If BestFit suits cost The Suitery $134.00 each, what percentage markup on selling price is being received?

$$\text{Percentage Markup on Selling Price} = \frac{\$ \text{ Markup}}{\text{Selling Price}} = \frac{\$335 - \$134}{\$335.} = 60\%$$

Chains of Markups. Each middleman in the channel of distribution generally adds a markup to the selling price of a product, thus creating a chain of markups. Although somewhat more complicated, the basic principle for calculating markups is still the same. Consider this example: The TruFit suits being sold by The Suitery were purchased from Suit City Wholesalers for $99.90 who, in turn, bought them from the manufacturer, Suits-R-US. If Suit City uses a 20 percent markup on its selling price, what was the cost of the suit to Suit City (or the Suits-R-US selling price)?

$$\text{Selling Price} = \text{Cost} + \$ \text{ Markup}$$
$$\$99.90 = \text{Cost} + (.20 \times \$99.90)$$
$$\text{Cost} = \$99.90 - \$19.98 = \$79.92$$

In other words,

Wholesaler's Cost	= $ 79.92	(Manufacturer's Price)
Wholesaler's 20%	= 19.98	(.20 × $99.90)
Retail Cost	= $ 99.90	(Wholesaler's Price)
Retailer's 55%	= 122.10	(.55 × $222.00)
Consumer's Cost	= $222.00	(Retailer's Price)

MARKDOWN RATIOS

A *markdown* is a reduction in the retail selling price of an item. Markdowns are used by retailers as a way of encouraging customers to buy. They are necessitated by such things as style changes, inventory overstock reductions, damage, original markups being too high, or some type of miscalculation. The computation of markdown ratios is not related to the operating statement because the markdown is given to the customer prior to the sale. Operating statement gross revenue is recorded as the actual amount received from the sale after the markdown.

Markdown ratios are an important tool for retailers trying to measure the efficiency of individual departments within the retail company. They are computed for each department and not for each product line. Different department ratios may then be compared to each other and/or over time. The markdown ratio may be calculated as follows:

$$\text{Markdown Ratio} = \frac{\text{Total Markdowns in Dollars}}{\text{Total Net Sales in Dollars}}$$

Assume total markdowns for the Suitery were $50,000 on net sales of $500,000. The markdown ratio would then be 10 percent.

QUESTIONS AND PROBLEMS

1. Define the following based on the income statement:

   a. Net sales
   b. Net purchases
   c. Gross margin
   d. Cost of goods sold.

2. Using the following data, calculate the net income from operations for the Big Zap Electric Supply Co.:

Administrative expense	$ 14,137
Beginning inventory (cost)	25,132
Ending inventory (cost)	21,991
General expense	4,712
Gross sales	169,646
Purchases (net cost)	84,823
Sales returns and allowances	12,566
Selling expense	31,415

3. The shoe department of the Stupendous Sportswear Co. has the following operating data:

Cost of goods sold	$376,842
Gross sales	942,478
Markdowns	62,816
Returns and allowances	57,106
Ending inventory	93,711

   Calculate the markdown ratio for the department.

4. Consider the following income statement:

   ABC Company
   Income Statement
   Year Ended 12/32/89

Sales		$113,097
Sales returns and allowances		10,178
Net sales		$102,919
Cost of goods sold		43,811
Gross margin		$ 59,108
Selling and administrative expense	$ 23,909	
Miscellaneous expense	14,622	
Total expenses		$ 38,531
Net income		$ 20,577

   Calculate the following:

   a. Gross margin ratio
   b. Net income ratio
   c. Operating expense ratio

5. The Better Bicycle Co. had net sales of $1,000,000 last year and a gross margin percentage of 24 percent. What must its average inventory be in order to achieve a stockturn rate of 12?

ANSWERS

1. a. Net sales is equal to gross sales minus sales returns and allowances.
   b. Net purchases is equal to gross purchases minus purchases returns and allowances.
   c. Gross income is a synonym for net sales. Gross margin is net sales minus cost of goods sold.
   d. Cost of goods available for sale is beginning inventory plus net purchases. Cost of goods sold is cost of goods available for sale minus ending inventory.

2.

Big Zap Electric Supply Co.
Income Statement
For the Period Ended — —

Gross sales		$169,646
Less sales returns and allowances		12,566
Net sales		$157,080
Cost of goods sold:		
Beginning inventory (cost)	$ 25,132	
Purchases (net cost)	84,823	
Cost of goods available for sale	$109,955	
Ending inventory (cost)	21,991	
Cost of goods sold		$ 87,964
Gross margin		$ 69,116
Expenses:		
Selling expense	$ 31,415	
Administrative expense	14,137	
General expense	4,712	
Total expenses		$ 50,264
Net income (before tax)		$ 18,852

3. Markdown Ratio $= \dfrac{\text{Markdowns}}{\text{Net Sales}} =$

$$\dfrac{\$62,831}{\$942,478 - \$57,106} = 8.0\%$$

4. a. Gross Margin Ratio $= \dfrac{\text{Gross Margin}}{\text{Net Sales}} =$

$$\dfrac{\$59,108}{\$102,919} = 57.4\%$$

b. Net Income Ratio $= \dfrac{\text{Net Income}}{\text{Net Sales}} =$

$$\dfrac{\$20,577}{\$102,919} = 20.0\%$$

c. Operating Expense Ratio $= \dfrac{\text{Total Expenses}}{\text{Net Sales}} =$

$$\dfrac{\$38,531}{\$102,919} = 37.4\%$$

5. Cost of Goods Sold (CGS) $= .76 \times \$1,000,000 = \$760,000$

Stockturn Rate $= \dfrac{\text{CGS}}{\text{Average Inventory}}$

Average Inventory $= \$760,000/12 = \$63,333$.

APPENDIX 2
CAREERS IN MARKETING

Students often find themselves attracted to marketing as a career because of the creative challenge it poses. The field is so diverse, however, that selecting a specific career goal presents a dilemma. Marketing is now being used not only for products, but also for services, and not only by for-profit companies, but also by nonprofit and government organizations. It has been estimated that there were 9,498,000 workers employed in marketing in 1987.[1]

This appendix has been designed to help in the selection of a specialty in marketing. Since career goals represent long-term planning, we will focus on those positions that can lead to the executive suite. The percentage of CEOs from marketing is higher than that of any other group.[2] As competition heats up, companies tend to turn to marketers for leadership.

The positions that will be described as well as the typical career paths are

PRODUCT	Product Manager
PROMOTION	Advertising
	Account Executive
	Media Director
	Creative Director
	Sales Promotion
	Sales Promotion Manager
	Public Relations
	Public Relations Manager
	Personal Selling
	Sales Manager
DISTRIBUTION	Physical Distribution Manager
RETAILING	Merchandise Manager
	Store Manager
	Retail Buyer
MARKETING RESEARCH	Project Manager

Of course, the precise titles may differ from company to company, and the levels to reach them may vary by company structure and size.

The one association that covers the entire spectrum of marketing is

American Marketing Association
250 S. Wacker Drive
Chicago, IL 60606

PRODUCT MANAGER

While the position of *product manager* may be found in both the consumer and industrial sectors, producers of consumer products who follow a multi-brand strategy seem to be most in need of product managers. Product managers are the "champions" for the product or brand they are responsible for. They must compete with all of the other product managers for the resources of the company. This generalist position carries with it a high level of responsibility, and many graduates choose product management as a career goal because it may be a fast track into general management.

Sample Job Description

Your marketing career begins with a thorough period of training for about six months including field sales experience, assignments in an advertising agency, and in the marketing services and budget departments. When you begin with a product group, your responsibilities include the full spectrum of product marketing; you help develop the budget and play a significant part in planning and evaluating advertising programs. Your work also involves product development with research and development (R&D) people. You will also be gathering information to effect workable marketing programs for new and existing products, as well as suggesting product ideas and consumer/trade promotion programs. Market research also comes into play as new products, advertising, and promotions are consumer tested. Finally, you must implement marketing decisions and assess their impact on sales, consumer franchises, and profitability. If you perform well, you can expect to be managing your own product about two years after joining a product group. Specific responsibilities are to:

- Gather, analyze, and interpret sales, marketing, and market research data. Write reports on important trends for specific brand/product category and maintain familiarity with general market conditions.

- Assist in the development, organization, coordination, and follow-up on multifaceted marketing assignments. This requires interface with finance, purchasing, graphics, promotion, market research, and sales departments.

- Participate and assist in the development of short- and long-term product marketing programs that identify level of profitability and potential opportunities for the brand.

- Prepare brand reports and update required brand information including forecasts, P&L, and general brand performance.

- Participate in the development of consumer/trade promotions.

- Prepare special reports or participate in special projects as requested by management.

Career Path for Product Manager

Future product managers are hired as *marketing assistants*. The prerequisite may be either an M.B.A. or a bachelor's degree, depending upon the company. They are given detailed tasks covering a variety of functional areas. For example, one assignment may take them into a test market, another into monitoring a promotional program. After a year, or less, they may be promoted to *assistant product manager* and begin to work closely with the product manager in planning and development. In another year or two, they may move up to product manager, usually for a different product or brand than they were involved in as assistant product manager.

Information Sources for Product Manager Careers

Consumer product companies in the Fortune 500, or the top 100 advertisers listed by *Advertising Age* annually are the companies that would be most likely to use the product manager form of organization.

Business publications such as *Business Week, Forbes,* and *Fortune* frequently have articles about product management.

ADVERTISING ACCOUNT EXECUTIVE

Advertising account executives are the interface between the agency and the client. They have to interpret the client's objectives to the agency's creative group and then sell the creative group's strategy for meeting those objectives to the client. Once a campaign has been agreed upon, the account executive must coordinate the actions of the media and the production people to implement it.

In large agencies, the account executive may be assigned to a single brand. The account responsibility in smaller agencies may be more diverse and may include new-account solicitation.

This position is very stressful because if the agency loses an account, the account executive's job is often at stake.

Sample Job Description of Assistant Account Executive

A starting position is as an assistant account executive. The major functions of the position include:

- Attaining an understanding of client's business, brand's position in the market, and marketing goals.
- Assisting in brand strategy planning.
- Communicating client needs to all appropriate agency departments.
- Coordinating the creation and implementation of the agency's advertising product with creative, media, and other departments.
- Communicating agency policies, recommendations, or relevant problems to client.
- Production — the production of finished commercials and advertisements.
- Preparing and presenting periodic reports.
- Developing media plans.

Careers in account management can develop from account representative to account supervisor, to management supervisor, ultimately to group account director and on to top management within the agency.

Career Path for Account Executive

Advertising is a difficult field to get into. Because of the glamour associated with the industry, the competition for jobs is intense, allowing compensation for entry-level positions to be on the low side.

The largest agencies are located in New York. They have formal training programs wherein trainees are rotated through all of the departments to give them exposure to everything the agency does. In six months or less the trainee becomes an *assistant account executive* and continues learning the business on the job until such time as an account executive's position opens up.

Smaller agencies may not offer such training. They also do not usually have many openings.

MEDIA DIRECTOR

Advertisers want to make sure that their message is reaching their customers as efficiently as possible. The media department of an advertising agency plans and analyzes purchases of broadcast time and space in print media so as to achieve the client's goal.

The *media director* is responsible for the media department and in that capacity oversees the work of media buyer analysts. He or she may also be involved in corporate level planning.

Career Path for Media Director

Media directors usually start out as *assistant buyers*, receiving on-the-job training in that position. Many menial tasks are involved, including the processing of large quantities of data. A specific type of degree is not as important for this position as relevant quantitative skills. After experience at this level, the next step is to be promoted to *media buyer*.

The media specialist must not only be an expert on costs, but must also be able to match the medium with the demographic characteristics that best represent the target market(s). After all of the variables are considered and alternatives weighed, the media buyer must exercise personal judgment based upon experience to produce a proposal that the account executive can present to the client with confidence.

Larger agencies have *associate media directors* who manage smaller groups of media analysts and become involved in more costly media buys that may involve longer time spans.

Information Sources for Media Director

Publications of interest to the media specialist are *Marketing and Media Decisions*, *Media Decisions*, and *Broadcasting*.

CREATIVE DIRECTOR

The *creative director* manages the creative department of the advertising agency, which includes copywriting and art. Since ideas and strategies are the creative director's forte, there may be a considerable amount of client contact involved, and this may include participation in getting new accounts. The creative director usually starts either as a copywriter or as an artist.

Career Path for Creative Director: Copywriter

The job of the *copywriter* is to take the client's objectives and creatively transform them into words that can be used in the advertisement. These words must be concise, yet effective in creating images in the mind of the reader. Getting an entry-level job as a copywriter means convincing the agency that you possess this talent.

The copywriter is not allowed the luxury of having "writer's block." Deadlines have to be met, that may require putting in long hours at times.

Copy writers eventually are given supervisory responsibilities over other copywriters and then follow the path to *associate creative director*.

Career Path for Creative Director: Art Director.

Both agencies and company art departments require *art directors*. Just as the copywriter is responsible for the words in an ad, the art director is responsible for everything that is visual. The two have to work closely together to rightly interpret what the client wants. They usually work with free-lance photographers and illustrators rather than producing art and photography in-house. They also coordinate the activities of production people, printers, typesetters, and so forth.

The art director administers a portion of the budget for each assignment. If the client requires it, he or she may also get involved in package and display design.

The entry level may be as an *assistant art director* who may be doing the layouts, or *mechanicals* (putting the ad components together). An art degree of some sort helps, but you don't have to be able to produce finished art. Visualization is an essential skill, and the ability to communicate this visualization to others is important.

Information Sources for Creative Director Career
The "bible" of the advertising industry is *Advertising Age. AdWeek* is another magazine that has wide readership. The following associations are relevant to people pursuing advertising careers.

> *American Advertising Federation*
> *1400 K Street NW, Suite 1000*
> *Washington, DC 20005*

> *American Association of Advertising Agencies*
> *666 Third Avenue*
> *New York, NY 10017*

> *Business/Professional Advertising Association*
> *205 E. 42nd Street*
> *New York, NY 10017*

> *International Advertising Association*
> *475 Fifth Avenue*
> *New York, NY 10017*

> *Women in Advertising and Marketing*
> *4200 Wisconsin Avenue, N.W., Suite 106–238*
> *Washington, DC 20016*

SALES PROMOTION MANAGER

When a company is looking for an immediate response, it will spend a larger portion of its promotional budget on sales promotion. It may have a staff group in-house, use an advertising agency, or hire the services of a sales promotion agency. The *sales promotion manager* is someone whose experience lends itself to developing and executing short-term incentives such as sweepstakes, coupons, and premiums to augment the other promotional efforts of the firm. He or she will interface with clients so as to communicate the promotion to the purchaser.

This position is usually found in the area of consumer products. Industrial firms may also get involved in sales promotion, but usually not to the degree of requiring a specialist.

Career Path for Sales Promotion Manager
There are no distinct career paths for a sales promotion manager. Product knowledge is essential, so it is not unusual for them to have some sales experience. This is also a position that *assistant product managers* may go into instead of into product management. A less likely route would be that of *promotion assistant*, since this position does not exist in too many companies. Companies look for someone who has experience not only in promotion, but also in selling and marketing.

PUBLIC RELATIONS MANAGER

The position of *public relations manager* can be an in-house or an agency one. There are agencies that specialize in public relations as well as advertising agencies that offer public relation services for their clients. The public relations manager deals with the company's image rather than with its products. Because the ability to get favorable "press" may depend to a large extent on contacts in the media, journalistic experience is often looked upon favorably for this position.

Public relations managers must communicate with every one in the organization so that they can stay abreast of all activities. If something newsworthy is planned, they have to know about it so that they can obtain media coverage. They may also create newsworthy events to generate publicity. And they often help key executives in preparing for public appearances. Perhaps their most important role, though, is to overcome any negative publicity that may accrue to the company.

Career Path for Public Relations Manager: Company
The entry-level position may be as a researcher or writer for the public relations staff. This is the point at which networks can be developed and contacts made that will provide the ingredients necessary for promotion to *public relations officer* and, ultimately, *director of public relations*.

Career Path for Public Relations Manager: Agency
The starting position in an agency may be as an *assistant account executive* or *staff writer*. These positions are regarded as on-the-job training for public relations.

Information Sources for Public Relations Career
Publications dedicated to the public relations field are the *Public Relations Quarterly* and the *Public Relations Journal*. Other publications of interest are *Communication World*, *Communication Illustrated*, and *PR News*. Relevant associations are

Public Relations Society of America
845 Third Avenue
New York, NY, 10021

International Association of Business Communicators
870 Market Street, Suite 940
San Francisco, CA 94102

Marketing Communications Executives International
412 Ocean Avenue
Seabright, New Jersey

SALES MANAGER

Any organization of any size that employs salespeople will have a *sales manager*. There is a greater demand for sales managers than for any other key position in marketing. Their responsibilities are significant. They not only have to develop short- and long-range sales goals, but they have to plan strategies for achieving them and control mechanisms for monitoring progress.

In addition, they may have to plan the sales territories so that the coverage required by the company is attained while providing equitable opportunities for the representatives. This may be done geographically, or by product line, or both.

The sales manager must also staff the territories by recruiting and selecting new sales personnel. Training of these new representatives as well as ongoing training of the entire sales force might be delegated to a training specialist in larger firms, but the responsibility is still that of the sales manager.

Other possible areas of involvement for the sales manager are sales compensation and budgeting. They also must evaluate the performance of salespeople. And they frequently represent the company at trade association meetings and trade shows where products are displayed.

In cases where the sales task is delegated to manufacturer's representatives, dealers, or distributors, the sales manager may have to work with these independent sales staffs.

The modern sales manager must be conversant with computers, as a great deal of software has been developed to assist in territory development and management, budget control, and so on.

Since revenues are generated by sales, the sales manager's position is an extremely visible and important one. Moreover the results of his or her efforts are easily quantified.

Career Path for Sales Manager

It is critical that sales managers have experience in sales and marketing, so the entry-level position is usually that of a *sales representative*. What may be frustrating to the college graduate is that sales positions do not always require a degree. Yet as products become more complex and the market more sophisticated, a degree is becoming a threshhold requirement. High-technology firms may require a technical degree in addition to a business degree. Even in the case where completing college is not an entry-level requirement, the graduate will often have a decided edge when it comes to promotion.

There are over 240 separate job descriptions listed under sales in the *Dictionary of Occupational Titles* (4th Ed. 1977, U.S. Department of Labor). A generic description follows:

> *SALES REPRESENTATIVE*
>
> *Sells products to business and industrial establishments or individual for manufacturer or distributor at sales office, store, showroom, or customer's place of business, utilizing knowledge of product sold; Compiles lists of prospective customers for use as sales leads, based on information from newspapers, business directories, and other sources. Travels throughout assigned territory to call on regular and prospective customers to solicit orders or talks with customer on sales floor or by phone. Displays or demonstrates product using samples or catalog, and emphasizes saleable features. Quotes prices and credit terms and prepares sales contracts for orders obtained. Estimates dates of delivery to customer based on knowledge of own firm's production and delivery schedules. Prepares reports of business transactions and keeps expense accounts.*

Many college students have a negative bias toward sales because they think the objective is to sell a product or service to the consumer, usually as the result of a single call. Encyclopedias and vacuum cleaners are examples of products that have been successfully sold door to door. There is no attempt to develop long-term relationships. These types of salespeople are usually paid a straight commission and are often considered independent contractors rather than employees of the firm.

Other sales positions, however, emphasize call-backs and building long-term relationships. The responsibilities differ markedly by industry and company. Some represent different levels in the channel of distribution: manufacturers selling to wholesalers, wholesalers to retailers, and so on. They emphasize the benefits that the next channel level will receive in terms of profit margins, inventory turnover, and so forth, by including their products in their mix. Assistance may be given in merchandising, display, inventory management, and other areas to reduce the cost of the channel member. A sales representative for a food broker, for example, will check the inventory levels in each store, make sure that the product(s) are displayed properly and adequately on the shelves, put up special displays, and credit merchandise that is being returned.

Sales personnel in the industrial field may be involved in either basic, semi-technical products or very complex technical products. While providing a high level of service is important in both instances, as products become more complex, product knowledge becomes a critical factor. At the extreme, a technical degree may be considered essential.

What is satisfying about a sales position is the ability to work without close supervision and to be measured by the results you produce. It can be a time-intensive occupation, however, and field representatives may find themselves traveling a good portion of the time.

Information Sources for Sales Manager Career

The best generic information source for sales positions is *Sales and Marketing Management* magazine. *Business Marketing* addresses sales management in the industrial area. In addition, every industry has at least one trade journal. These are listed in Standard Rate and Data's *Business Periodical Index,* which most advertising agencies subscribe to. Marketing faculty can obtain old copies from Standard Rate and Data for use in the classroom.

The following associations are relevant to sales managers.

Bureau of Salesmens National Association
1718 Peachtree Street NW, Suite 600
Atlanta, GA 30309

Direct Marketing Association
6 E. 43rd Street
New York, NY 10017

Direct Selling Association
1730 M Street N.W. Suite 610
Washington, DC 20036

National Association for Professional Saleswomen
Box 255708
Sacramento, CA 95865

National Association of Wholesaler-Distributors
1725 K St. N.W.
Washington, DC 20006

Sales and Marketing Executives International
6151 Wilson Mills Rd., Suite 200
Cleveland, OH 44143

PHYSICAL DISTRIBUTION MANAGER

Every company is involved in physical distribution, so the position will vary in scope by industry and company size. The *physical distribution manager* manages both people and resources. Because the cost of physical distribution is often a large part of the final cost of the product, the management of this function is becoming increasingly more sophisticated. The larger the firm, the more likely it is to have a professional in charge of physical distribution.

The responsibilities include determining the number, location, and type of warehouses necessary, the method of inventory management, and the appropriate transportation and order-processing methods, as well as interacting with all of the other functions to make sure that they are coordinated with physical distribution.

Career Path for Physical Distribution Manager

Because of the diverse number of career opportunities in this field, a generic career path is impossible to devise. What companies are looking for is someone who may have had some experience in physical distribution. A knowledge of marketing as well as the ability to use computers is increasingly important. Problem-solving abilities as well as financial knowledge are also important.

Information Sources for Physical Distribution Manager Career

Publications that address this area are *Handling and Shipping Management, Distribution World Wide, Industrial Distribution*, and *Transportation Journal.* Relevant associations are

> *American Society of Transportation and Logistics*
> *P.O. Box 33095*
> *Louisville, KY 40232*
>
> *National Council of Physical Distribution Management*
> *2803 Butterfield Road*
> *Oak Brook, IL 60521*

MERCHANDISE MANAGER (RETAILING)

The *merchandise manager* is responsible for the activities of all of the buyers within a product area. This includes overseeing the planning of assortments, merchandising, planning promotions, and budgeting. Depending upon the size of the chain, the merchandise manager may report to a *general merchandise manager* who may have the title of *vice-president of marketing.*

Career Path for Merchandise Manager

Employees on this career track begin as *executive trainees*. They are exposed to company policies and procedures as well as how the firm approaches retailing in general. After a relatively short orientation of 16 weeks or less, they are promoted to the position of *assistant buyer*. Working with a buyer, they check deliveries, make sure that merchandise is displayed, communicate price information to the department managers, and distribute promotional material. The buyer may bring them along on buying trips, where they learn about planning merchandise assortments. They will then be promoted to the position of *buyer,* where they will be responsible for administering a rather rigid budget in their merchandise area. They must know what has sold in the past as well as being able to anticipate what will sell in the future. They must be prepared to negotiate with suppliers on quantities, price, and delivery.

Merchandise managers must work with the advertising people and the various departments of the company to make sure that the merchandise moves in a timely manner. Having to mark down prices to move products will result in smaller budgets in the future.

STORE MANAGER (RETAILING)

The other route to the top in retailing is the position of *store manager.* One of the prime responsibilities of this position is in the personnel area, making sure the company has adequate numbers of people, properly trained, and that labor costs are in line. The performance of the store manager is measured by the profit contribution that the store makes, and labor is the cost that the manager has the most control over. He or she must also be sure that the store has the proper amount of inventory and that it is displayed properly.

Providing customer service is an extremely important part of this job, because dissatisfied customers will ultimately reflect on the patronage and profitability of the store. To ensure adequate customer service requires constant interaction with the department managers and sales support groups as well as the corporate officers of the company.

Career Path for Store Manager

After orientation as an executive trainee, the employee aiming for store manager will proceed through sales management positions, where training will be given in supervising sales personnel. He or she may pass through several levels of sales management where wider experience is attained in such areas as display, promotion, and price administration.

Information Sources for Store Manager Career

Many trade journals are product-specific (e.g., publications on furniture or jewelry retailing). In addition, useful publications include *Chain Store Age, Stores,* and the *Journal of Retailing.* The association that pertains to store managers is

National Retail Merchants Association
100 31st Street
New York, NY 10017

RETAIL BUYER

Whenever retailing students are asked about their future aspirations, invariably a great number respond that they would like to be buyers. The buying function seems to be the most glamorous aspect of the retail operation. Perhaps to the inexperienced it is a chance to spend a great deal of money in sums that one could never spend for his or her own needs. While the buying job does often present glamorous and exciting moments, few jobs in retailing require more ability and disciplined training. Duties and responsibilities are as follows:

- Most important is the actual purchasing of merchandise. The buyer is faced with the perennial problems of what merchandise to choose and from which vendors, how much of each item to purchase, and the correct timing of delivery to meet with customers' demands.

- After buying arrangements have been worked out, the buyer must price the merchandise to conform with the policies of the store and his or her particular department.

- After goods are received and marked and come to the selling floor, the placement of the goods is often determined by the buyer.

- Depending on the store, the buyer may be involved in the final selection of employees for the department, the supervision of selling, and the arrangement of sales meetings.

- The buyer selects merchandise for promotions, for special displays, and for advertisements. She or he plans fashion shows, then relevant, and any special events that might promote goods.

MARKETING RESEARCH PROJECT MANAGER

The marketing research project manager works with the clients to determine what their information needs are and develops methodology that will efficiently and effectively meet those needs. The project manager has total responsibility for the success of the research project. Based upon information received from the client, a budget is drawn up and a proposal is made. When the research is completed, the account executive presents the results to the client.

The position also entails keeping present clients happy and looking for new customers. At this level the account executive does not engage in any of the research activities personally, but rather acts as a consultant.

Career Path for Marketing Research Project Director

There are a number of entry-level positions that involve gathering data and "number crunching" — jobs such as *field supervision* and *coding and tabulating*. The next level is that of *assistant project director* and *project director*, which are supervisory positions. Communication skills are important because project directors not only have to write reports, but they must also communicate with other research functions and with the client. Competence in statistical analysis as well as knowledge of computer applications is essential.

Qualifications for such a position, besides having proficiency in various research techniques, include excellent analytical and written skills, and an ability to work with people and organize projects. Responsibilities of an assistant or associate usually include most of the following:

- Write proposals for minor research projects.
- Submit budget proposals.
- Prepare research designs, write questionnaires, and create processing plans.
- Supervise data collection.
- Analyze and interpret research results and review these with the supervisor.
- Write final research reports.
- Present findings.

Most of these activities are performed with other members of the research staff. A research associate, however, should be able to head up a research project or be able to execute all elements of the project individually.

Promotion to a research director position usually requires well-developed project management skills. This includes the ability to construct an entire research project, manage personnel well, and lead them in the project. A research director should be knowledgeable in a variety of research designs and analytical techniques.

Depending on the firm, a research director may interact with clients or the managers of the various marketing divisions to suggest and assist in formulating research that will be useful in making marketing decisions. The directors' duties usually include:

- Developing junior staff members.
- Overseeing all major research projects.
- Analyzing research designs.
- Writing and editing reports.
- Ensuring that projects are completed on time and within budget.
- Making certain that research projects satisfy the needs of the requesting division or client.

Opportunities for employment in market research can be found in a variety of different firms: advertising agencies, manufacturers, data supply firms, and consulting organizations. Depending on the particular firm, movement from a position in market research to one in marketing management can be readily accomplished.

Information Sources for Marketing Research Career
Publications of interest in this career area are the *Journal of Marketing Research* and *Research Management*. Relevant associations are

Marketing Research Association
111 E. Wacker Drive
Chicago, IL 60601

Marketing Science Institute
1000 Massachusetts Ave.
Cambridge, MA 02138

Compensation for the various marketing positions varies geographically and by industry. Below are salary data that are typical of what you will find in the library.

OVERVIEW OF COMPENSATION

MARKETING, ADVERTISING, AND PUBLIC RELATIONS MANAGERS

Median	$35,400 (1986)
Lowest 10%	17,700 or less
Top 10%	52,000 or more

MANUFACTURER'S SALES WORKERS

Median	$25,600 (1986)
Middle 50%	18,300–36,200
Bottom 10%	13,200 or less
Top 10%	50,900 or more

WHOLESALE AND RETAIL BUYERS

Median	$20,700 (1986)
Lowest 10%	11,400 or less
Top 10%	41,300 or more

MARKET RESEARCH ANALYSTS

Starting salary	$19,300 (1986)

Note: The median salaries are the closest estimate of starting salaries.
Source: *Occupational Outlook Handbook, 1988–1989*. U.S. Department of Labor.

(THE DARTNELL CORPORATION, *SALES FORCE COMPENSATION*)

INDUSTRY	SALES TRAINEES (STARTING SALARIES)	EXPERIENCED
Aerospace	22,000–33,000	35,000–50,000
Airlines	N/A	30,000
Appliances, household	18,000–19,000	21,000–29,000
Automotive parts	15,000–20,400	25,800–30,500
Auto and truck	18,000–25,000	24,000–30,500
Banks	12,000–20,000	18,000–24,667
Building materials	18,000–22,000	25,717–32,000

(continued)

(THE DARTNELL CORPORATION, *SALES FORCE COMPENSATION*) *(continued)*

INDUSTRY	SALES TRAINEES (STARTING SALARIES)	EXPERIENCED
Chemicals	20,000–22,300	30,000–35,000
Computer products	20,000–35,000	25,500–45,000
Cosmetics	22,000–24,500	23,000–32,000
Electrical equipment	36,000	27,000–34,000
Electronics	30,000–43,500	35,000–47,500
Fabricated metal prod.	18,000–25,000	22,200–40,000
Food Products	13,340–18,000	20,400–23,000
General machinery	18,000–27,000	28,000–36,000
Glass	22,300	24,000
Healthcare products	16,500–35,000	21,000–42,500
Housewares	21,000	34,000
Instruments	26,900–25,000	34,000–38,000
Iron and steel	22,200–22,500	28,800–29,500
Insurance, casualty	19,000–20,000	24,500–30,000
Paper	15,000–25,500	20,000–45,500
Printing	24,700–35,000	25,600–38,250
Publishing	20,600–21,000	18,000–26,500
Radio and television	15,000–24,000	28,800–40,456
Service industries	15,800–23,000	20,100–33,000
Transportation	20,000–25,283	31,500–36,119
Utilities	9,000	16,250–21,000

Source: *The American Almanac of Jobs and Salaries,* 1987–88 ed. John W. Wright. New York: Avon (1987).
(The Dartnell Corporation, *Sales Force Compensation*)

ALL FIRMS — TOTAL COMPENSATION

POSITION	MEAN	QUARTILE RANGE
Gen. Mktg. & Sales Mgr.	71,575	50,932–86,477
Marketing Manager	61,416	50,575–75,560
General Sales Manager	64,062	62,005–71,463
Regional Sales Manager	53,568	46,775–59,526
Field Sales Rep.	34,407	28,814–41,360
Commission Sales Rep.	34,779	27,825–41,421
Sales Engineer	39,636	37,200–42,180
Mkt. Research Analyst	32,447	27,095–37,478
Ad/Sales Promo. Mgr.	45,320	35,980–52,716
Ad/Sales Promo. Spec.	29,031	25,636–31,759
Dist. Center/Whse. Mgr.	42,148	33,360–49,200
Senior Buyer	32,427	26,722–36,568
Public Relations Mgr.	45,364	35,110–52,601

Note: These numbers represent middle management salary levels.

WHAT YOU CAN DO WHILE STILL IN SCHOOL

Once you have selected your marketing career, you can tailor your studies and extracurricular activities to position yourself for an entry-level position.

Curriculum

Two skills necessary in all career tracks are oral and written communications. Take elective courses in communications and writing to hone those skills as finely as possible. Also important is the ability to use computers and work with spreadsheets and databases. In addition, those heading toward the quantitative areas such as marketing research should take as many math, computer science, and statistics courses as they can squeeze into their programs.

Employment

Many students work part-time during the school year and summer. Some of the entry-level positions do not require a degree, so they afford a good opportunity for work experience. Marketing research companies often hire students as interviewers, and working with the public is a good background for any marketing career.

Working as a temporary may also be beneficial, as it offers flexible hours plus the chance to observe an organization from the inside.

Organizations

Become part of and active in any student organization that is career-related. The American Marketing Association has student chapters on many campuses. Professional chapters located in every major market welcome students to their meetings. Not only will you benefit from networking with professionals, but you will have a chance to exhibit your leadership abilities, which many employers look for in those they hire for management career tracks.

Campus organizations need help in fund-raising, recruiting new members, and publicity. Campus newspapers and radio stations need help in selling advertising. These all offer opportunities for marketing experience.

Internships and Cooperative Field Experiences

Some schools have cooperative field experience programs where you actually work for a firm in your career field for one or more terms. Others have internship programs that permit you to work for a company part-time. You will have a chance to apply what you've learned in the classroom. In both cases you will be supervised by the faculty and receive academic credit plus job experience. Interns are frequently hired after graduation by the firms that they worked for.

Placement Service

Become acquainted with the people in your placement service as early as possible. Find out what services they offer. For example, they can help you with your resume writing and your interviewing skills, and they have access to a wide range of career-related materials, including brochures and videotapes supplied by organizations who are interested in recruiting at your school. They can also tell you what employers will be conducting campus interviews and when. Some have computer programs to help you in developing career goals.

Testing Services

If you're still at sea as to your career choice, avail yourself of the testing services that many schools provide to reveal your vocational interests, aptitudes, and personality strengths.

Class Projects

Many of your marketing classes will include experiential projects or simulations. Do these as professionally as you can. Make sure that they are typed or reproduced on a word processor or computer. Keep a copy for yourself. These can become an important part of your portfolio to show to prospective employers.

Company Information

It is a good idea to research companies you are interested in. Good sources of information on specific companies are their annual reports and 10K reports required by the Securities and Exchange Commission. Both are probably available in your library. You might also consider doing a computer search on specific companies using your library's on-line search programs.

Outside Reading

Read business publications regularly to be informed about what is happening to companies and industries. *The Wall Street Journal, Business Week, Advertising Age, Fortune, Forbes,* and *Marketing News* are recommended.

THE RESUME AND COVER LETTER

Resumes serve two purposes: to get an interview, and to remind the employer of you after the interview. A good resume will not get you the job but a poor resume can eliminate you from consideration. The very best resumes are those that are targeted toward a specific employer and reflect that organization's needs.

Prior to writing the resume, therefore, you should do two things. One is to develop a database of your traits, abilities, and accomplishments. They do not necessarily have to be business related. For example, holding an office in a student organization can show leadership, the ability to set and achieve goals, and the ability to motivate others. The other is to find out as much about the employer as possible. Library research can reveal a lot of information about publicly-held companies. An informational interview with someone who works for the employer can be invaluable.

The two basic types of resumes are the chronological resume and the functional resume. The chronological resume is more traditional and is often preferred by personnel professionals. The functional resume may be a better one, however, for recent graduates who do not have work experience, or whose experience may not be related to the career field they are pursuing.

The chronological resume lists employers and positions held starting with the most recent job. The functional resume shows experience under general headings such as "Leadership," "Sales Experience," "Communication Skills," and so forth.

In either case, recent graduates would do well to show their educational achievements first. Both resumes can be fleshed out by adding subheadings such as "Honors and Awards," "Other Interests and Activities," and so forth. Do not include personal data such as age, sex, or marital status unless you believe including this information will be to your advantage.

Resumes should be kept to one page or two pages at the most. Use a terse writing style and avoid personal pronouns. Don't just create "laundry lists"; try to describe as briefly as possible what you've done and what the results were.

Unless you are applying for a creative position (such as an artist), it is best to have your resume look as conservative and professional as possible. Use headings, subheadings, and indentations so that it does not look crowded. Use a good quality white paper.

Every resume that is sent by mail should include a cover letter. You should introduce yourself and explain why you are writing in the first paragraph. The second and third paragraphs should address your qualifications and how they match what the employer is looking for. You should ask for an interview in the final paragraph.

Even if you use a stock resume, you should customize the cover letter for every job you are applying for.

CHRONOLOGICAL RESUME

FIRST I. LASTNAME
1234 Anyplace Drive
Anywhere, WA 98202

(206) 000–0000

OBJECTIVE:

This is optional. It should relate to the position you are seeking. State the entry level and where you want the job to lead.

EMPLOYMENT

From (date) to present	*Exact Job Title* Company/Organization A Address: Company/Organization A
	Tell what you were responsible for and what you accomplished in this job.
From (date) to (date)	*Exact Job Title* Company/Organization B Address: Company/Organization B
	Tell what you did in this job that prepared you for your present position.
From (date) to (date)	*Exact Job Title* Company/Organization C
	Tell what your accomplishments were when you first started working.

EDUCATION

From (date) to (date)	Your School Address: Your School Degree earned Major area of concentration, additional coursework, G.P.A.
Activities	Athletic activities, volunteer activities, professional associations, etc. Active hobbies are better than sedentary ones.
HONORS AND AWARDS	Scholarships, honor societies, leadership positions, etc.
REFERENCES	The finest of references are available upon request.

**FUNCTIONAL
RESUME**

FIRST I. LASTNAME
1234 Anyplace Drive
Anywhere, WA 98202

(206) 000–0000

OBJECTIVE:
Optional. I am looking for a position in which I can grow and achieve my personal goals by helping a dynamic company achieve its goals.

EDUCATION	Degree and major
	Your school
	Address: Your school
	Discuss all courses taken that are pertinent to the position being applied for:
	Advertising (describe)
	Other (describe)
EXPERIENCE	*Leadership*
	Use functional titles and describe the pertinent work experience.
	Organizing
	If you want to mention an organization, start out by saying, "While a (job title) at (company name), I . . . (follow with what you did."
	Controlling
	You can also provide dates, but de-emphasize them by placing them at the end of your descriptions: Company A (date) to (date).
OTHER EXPERIENCE	Under this category you can list all of your other experience that may be work related, but is not a result of employment.
MAJOR INTERESTS	Athletic activities, professional associations, etc., can be listed here.
REFERENCES	The finest of references are available upon request.

Final Note

It is important that you answer the question, "What do I do with a degree in marketing?" While still in school, research the occupations and the industries of interest to you. With good preparation your question at graduation will not be, "Where can I find a job?" but rather, "Which offer should I accept?"

NOTES

1. Martha C. White, *Occupational Outlook Quarterly,* Washington D.C.: Department of Labor (Spring 1989), p. 3.
2. "What Is the Fastest Track to the Executive Suite? Sales/Marketing," *Marketing News,* July 6, 1984, p. 7.

GLOSSARY

Acceptable price range A price range the customer views as realistic. If the product is priced below this range, quality is suspect. If the product is priced above, the consumer refuses to buy.

Accessories *See* Installations and accessories.

Adaptation in key markets International growth strategy where a firm channels resources into certain key markets. Within these markets, local employees make decisions on the product marketing strategy, fitting it to each country's particular culture and economy. This type of strategy works for companies with limited resources, but which want to sell in certain overseas markets.

Adaptive control system Control that allows for changes in objectives as well as in performance to meet those objectives; requires tracking environmental factors such as competitive intensity, level of customer demand, and technology to determine if objectives are still relevant or need to be changed.

Adaptive strategies International marketing strategies which reflect the local differences in customer needs, cultural norms, trade regulations, economic and political conditions, and competitors. Adaptive strategies allow companies to make changes in their marketing plans when the needs of a particular country dictate, rather than trying to make one strategy work everywhere.

Administered systems Systems in which integration of distributive activities is accomplished through the power of a channel member rather than through ownership or contractual arrangements.

Advertising Paid, ongoing, nonpersonal communication from a commercial source such as a manufacturer or retailer. It communicates messages about a product, service, or company that appears in mass media such as television, radio, and magazines.

After-the-fact control Compares actual product performance at the end of a planning period with expected performance and determines the causes for any deviations in sales results. On this basis, management can institute changes in both marketing objectives and strategies to increase profitability in the next planning period. One shortcoming of this approach is that it corrects for deviations after they occur rather than before.

Assignable fixed costs Fixed costs that can be associated with the production or distribution of a product and can therefore be assigned to the product.

Atmospherics In-store decor.

Attitudes The consumer's tendency to evaluate an object in a favorable or unfavorable way. Attitudes are determined by our needs and perceptions.

Audimeter Machine attached to a TV set to record the station it is tuned to; used to calculate TV ratings.

Augmented product Product that includes elements other than the *tangible product*, including delivery, installation, warranties, and service.

Average revenue Average amount of money received from selling one unit of a product; computed as total revenue divided by quantity. Also equals price.

Backward integration A type of vertical integration in which the company acquires facilities earlier in the distribution and manufacturing process.

Bait-and-switch pricing Offering one product at a low price in order to lure customers into the store, where a salesperson tries to influence them to buy a higher-priced item instead.

Basing-point pricing Delivered pricing method in which the price is set by adding transportation costs to a base price. These costs are developed by using a particular location, such as a historical industry center, as the starting point, regardless of whether or not the goods actually leave from that city.

Battle of the brands The fight for retail shelf space and consumer dollars between controlled and national brands. Controlled brands have a price advantage and national brands have an advertising advantage.

Behavioral segmentation Identification of consumer groups by differences in behavior (e.g., users versus nonusers or heavy versus light users). Market segments are identified by what consumers do.

Benefit segmentation Identification of a group of consumers based on similarity in needs. Often marketing opportunities are discovered by analysis of consumers' benefit preferences. Frequently, one or more segments are identified that are not being adequately served by existing brand alternatives.

Bid pricing Pricing in which organizational buyers send out requests for proposals that invite prospective sellers to bid on a set of specifications developed by the buyer.

Brand A name or symbol that represents a product.

Brand advertising Type of advertising which is designed to increase market share of a brand by attracting customers who currently use a competitor's brand, and by maintaining awareness among existing customers.

Brand equity Refers to the value of a brand name.

Brand establishment strategy Creating market position of a new brand by building a distribution network and by establishing awareness and initiating trial among consumers.

Brand image Represents overall perception of the brand, formed from information about the brand and past experience. The set of beliefs that forms a complete picture of the brand.

Brand leveraging Taking advantage of a strong brand image by introducing related items under the well-known brand name.

Brand loyalty Commitment to a certain brand because of prior reinforcement (satisfaction as a result of product usage). Brand loyalty is a result of two components: (1) a favorable attitude toward the brand, (2) repurchase of the brand over time. Causes repeat purchases made with little thought or deliberation, but with high involvement due to continued satisfaction with a product.

Brand manager *See* product manager.

Brand revitalization Strategy used when a brand reaches the mature phase of the product life cycle and faces decreasing profits. One or all of the following approaches may be used: market expansion, product modification, or brand repositioning.

Branded The existence of a name or symbol to identify a product, as opposed to no defined name or symbol. Generics, private labels, and commodity products are generally considered to be unbranded.

Breadth of the line Refers to the diversity of a product line. A line is broadened by adding products beyond its current range (as compared with *deepening* a line by adding products within its current range).

Break-even analysis Identifies the point where total revenue equals total cost and profits are zero.

Brokers People who bring buyers and sellers together. Brokers do not have a formal relationship with either party; they simply serve as an intermediary between the two. Brokers are used primarily by firms which do not need to maintain a permanent sales force.

Bundling pricing Offering two or more products or services as a single package for a special price.

Business-to-business marketing The sale of products to firms for use in manufacturing and processing other products or supporting such activities.

Business development Growth strategy of marketing new products to totally new markets.

Business manager Manager of a business unit usually responsible for formulating the marketing strategy for that unit.

Business mix Combination of businesses the firm is in.

Business portfolio analysis Systematic approach to evaluating the corporation as a mix, or portfolio of businesses, each with a different mission, market, and resources. Each business is examined according to its opportunity for growth and profit, and its fit with the company's corporate strategy and objectives.

Business position A company's ability to exploit opportunity.

Buying center A group of executives providing the different skills necessary to make important decisions in organizational buying. The decision-making unit to select products and vendors in an organization.

Cannibalization Occurs when a new brand draws consumers away from the same company's existing brands. **Unplanned cannibalization** is unexpected and reduces the company's profits. This is most likely to happen if the products are not sufficiently different from one another in the consumer's mind. **Planned cannibalization** occurs when new technologies create new products that might compete with other products in the company's line, so the company prefers to have its customers switch to another of the company's brands rather than to a competitor's brand.

Carrying costs Costs of tying up capital in inventory, plus some additional costs such as taxes and insurance on inventory.

Case allowance Type of trade promotion where discounts are given to products sold to retailers depending on how much they buy.

Cash-and-carry wholesalers Wholesalers that sell from warehouse facilities. Buyers must pay cash and transport their merchandise. These facilities are the same as retail warehouse clubs except that they will sell only to business firms, whereas retail clubs also sell to consumers.

Cash discount Discount to buyers who pay bills within a specified time.

Category manager *See* Product-line manager.

Chain stores Retailers with more than four outlets.

Channel (distribution) system A group of independent businesses composed of manufacturers, wholesalers, and retailers designed to deliver the right set of products to consumers at the right place and time.

Channel leader Coordinates the flow of information, product shipments, and payment in a distribution system. Generally, the most powerful member of the system.

Communications system System that informs customers of products available and influences them to buy.

Comparative advertising The naming of a competitive product in the marketer's advertisement. Advertisers use comparative advertising to point out weaknesses in and to create a less favorable attitude toward the competitive brand, thus increasing the likelihood of buying the marketer's brand. It has become an important means of competitive positioning.

Comparative influence Influence a membership group exerts in the process of comparing oneself to other members of the group. Provides a basis for comparing one's attitudes and behavior to those of the group.

Competitive advantage Gained when a company capitalizes on a marketing opportunity by producing a better product, selling it at a lower price, distributing it more widely, providing better services, or offering a wider variety of product options than competing companies.

Competitive analysis Assessing a competitors' strengths and weaknesses.

Competitive-parity budgeting Requires setting the promotional budget according to what the competition is doing. One example would be to determine advertising expenditures as a percent of sales for a few key competitors and then use the same percentage to set the budget.

Complex decision making Associated with a high-involvement purchase that is important to the consumer and entails a significant financial outlay. The buyer is motivated to undertake a process of active search for information and based on this information, alternative brands are evaluated on specific criteria. The cognitive process of evaluation involves consumer perceptions of brand characteristics and development of favorable or unfavorable attitudes toward a brand. The assumption is that consumer perceptions and attitudes will precede and influence behavior.

Concentrated segmentation Also referred to as a *market niche strategy*, this approach targets a single product to a single market segment. Best suited to a firm with limited resources because it avoids conflicts with major competitors in larger market segments.

Concept test A method of product testing where consumers evaluate the product idea prior to actual production.

Consistency Refers to product lines that are related to each other.

Consolidated retailing A strategy of growth through the acquisition of retailers, rather than through store expansion. Many retailers began using this approach as a way of combating "overstoring."

Consolidation centers A part of the physical distribution system used in the implementation of a just-in-time distribution system. These centers resemble distribution centers, and serve as assembly facilities for different items which are to be delivered to each customer.

Consumer The final user of a product or service.

Consumer socialization Process by which people learn to be consumers as they are taught from childhood by their families.

Containerization A form of intermodal transportation used by shippers in the physical distribution system. Containerization involves putting the product into a container which is in turn loaded onto another form of transport, such as rail.

Continuity A means of advertising, where the message is dispersed steadily over time.

Contractual systems Systems where independent manufacturers and intermediaries enter into a contract to coordinate distributive functions that can be performed more efficiently in tandem than separately.

Contribution to margin Product revenues less costs directly assigned to the product. A measure of product profitability.

Control Directing or redirecting a company's actions to ensure that they meet objectives.

Convenience goods Products that consumers purchase frequently with little deliberation or effort.

Convenience stores Neighborhood food outlets that stay open longer than supermarkets, carry a limited number of high-turnover convenience items, and charge higher prices because of their higher costs of operation.

Convergent acquisition Strategy of acquiring related businesses.

Cooperative advertising A type of product-related advertising in which manufacturers and retailers pool resources to promote both the product and the store. Manufacturers offer retailers allowances to advertise the manufacturer's products, permitting retailers to insert the name of the store and, in some cases, details about the retail establishment.

Core product Characteristics of the product seen as meeting customer needs.

Corporate-brand-names strategy *See* corporate brand name.

Corporate-image advertising Advertising which is designed to create and promote a corporate identity. In this way, consumers will know more about the company and its products.

Corporate-issue advertising Advertising which relays a company's position on a particular issue that is important to consumers.

Corporate brand name Using the company name as part of the brand, thereby linking the brand name to the company name. An advantage of this strategy is that consumer loyalty can be better cultivated if the consumer can identify which brands belong to the company.

Corporate family name A brand identification strategy where all of the company's products are included under a corporate umbrella as a family of brands. This strategy works well when the company's product mix is not too diverse, the company has a strong corporate identity, and individual brand identification is difficult.

Corporate growth strategy Decisions regarding the future of the businesses in which a company currently competes. This is the game plan it will use to exploit marketing opportunities. Corporate strategies usually cover a five-year time span.

Corporate marketing manager Manager at the headquarters level.

Corporate mission Statement of what business or businesses the firm should be in.

Corporate-patronage advertising Type of advertising used to promote the company's offerings. The purpose is to influence consumers, so that they purchase the company's line of products.

Corrective advertising Advertising in which a company corrects false claims it has made in the past. It is often a result of a FTC order stemming from an ad campaign deemed to be deceptive or misleading.

Cost advantage A type of competitive advantage a firm may have which is gained by reducing production or marketing costs below those of competitors and thereby being able to reduce prices or channel the savings into other areas.

Cost-plus pricing A simple pricing method whereby the firm determines its costs and then adds the desired profit margin. This approach tends to encourage price stability since most competitors will arrive at similar acceptable margins.

Country-product mix The decision made by international marketers as to what products will be sold in each country. The ultimate mix is dependent on the overall international strategy chosen by the company.

Coupons Printed material that offers a discount off the regular price of a brand if presented at the time of purchase.

Cultural values An especially important class of beliefs shared by the members of a society about what is desirable or undesirable. Beliefs that some general state of existence is personally and socially worth striving for. Cultural values in the United States include achievement, independence, and youthfulness.

Culture The implicit beliefs, norms, values, and customs that underlie and govern conduct in a society. The norms, beliefs, and customs learned from society. Culture leads to common patterns of behavior.

Customer orientation When a firm develops products and strategies directed to meeting customer needs.

Customized marketing Strategy of offering tailor-made products to meet the needs of individual buyers.

Dealers Channel members who are granted the right to exclusively sell a company's products in a franchise contract.

Dealing contract A contract that requires that the customer handle only the seller's line of products. These contracts are illegal if they exclude competitors in a market, or are forced on the buyer.

Deceptive advertising Advertising which makes false claims, or is misleading to consumers. The Federal Trade Commission monitors advertising, to ensure that manufacturers and retailers do not indulge in this practice.

Deceptive pricing Any type of pricing used to deceive customers and take unfair advantage of them. Examples are bait-and-switch pricing, unfair pricing, predatory pricing, price discrimination, and price fixing.

Decision maker Family member who is responsible for the final selection of a product or service.

Decoding Process in which the target audience (1) notices the message (awareness), (2) interprets and evaluates it (comprehension), and (3) retains it in memory (recall).

Delayed-quotation pricing Industrial pricing method where the risk of cost overruns and imprecise production schedules is passed on to the buyer, because the seller delays quoting a price until delivery.

Delivered pricing Pricing method where the final price is adjusted to include transportation costs. The seller includes delivery costs in the quoted price, and is responsible for getting the product to the buyer.

Delphi method Requires experts to make individual forecasts without meeting and to state their reasoning in writing. Forecasts are pooled and sent to participants who are then asked to make a second forecast. A consensus is usually achieved after three or four rounds. This method overcomes some of the problems of panel forecasts, namely strong participant personalities and senior management influence.

Demand-backward pricing Pricing set by determining what consumers are willing to pay for an item, then deducting costs to see if the profit margin is adequate.

Demand curve Curve showing the quantity of a product that customers buy at various price levels.

Demographics Objective characteristics of consumers, such as age, income, occupation, marital status, location, or education. This information is characteristically used for media planning.

Demographic segmentation Strategy in which market segments are identified by variables such as income, education, occupation, age, sex, or race.

Department stores Full service stores that offer a broad choice of merchandise.

Depth interviews Unstructured, personal interviews in which the interviewer attempts to get subjects to talk freely and to express their true feelings. Can be conducted individually or in groups (focus group interviews). The latter have the advantage of eliciting more information because of group interaction.

Depth of the line Refers to the number of different types of brands, sizes, and models within the current range of a particular product line.

Derived demand Demand for one product may be determined by the demand for the good the product is used to manufacture, i.e., the demand for industrial goods is derived from the demand for consumer goods.

Desk jobber *See* Drop shipper.

Deterministic models Predict a particular course of action based on such input variables as consumer characteristics, brand attitudes, consumer needs, etc. Deterministic models attempt to predict behavior in exact or nonprobabilistic terms (e.g., purchase versus no purchase).

Differential advantage *See* Competitive advantage.

Differentiated segmentation Strategy in which product offerings are differentiated to meet the needs of particular market segments. A firm using this approach introduces many products within a product category to appeal to a variety of market segments. Separate marketing strategies are needed for each segment. By offering a full line of products, the firm establishes a strong identification with that product category.

Direct marketing Selling directly to consumers by door-to-door sales, company-owned retail stores, catalogs, and other means.

Discount Type of price adjustment, where the seller makes a reduction off of the list price. Discounts serve as an incentive to buy in quantity or during a particular time of the year, to pay in cash, or to handle certain marketing functions.

Discount stores Stores that offer goods at low prices on a self-service basis. These stores offer a wide variety of product lines but very limited selections within each line.

Discretionary income Amount of income left after paying for necessities and taxes.

Dissonance A state of tension because information about a brand is not consistent with the consumer's expectations (e.g., negative information about a favored brand). Doubts about whether the right purchase decision has been made.

Distribution centers Centralized distribution facilities that serve broader markets than warehouses. They maintain full product lines, consolidate large shipments from different production points, and usually have computerized order-handling systems.

Distribution system (Channel system) A group of independent businesses composed of manufacturers, wholesalers, and retailers designed to deliver what the customer wants, when and where the customer wants it. *See also* Channel system.

Distributors Generally, wholesalers of industrial products. *See also* Wholesalers.

District sales manager Manager responsible for a particular geographic territory; reports to the divisional sales manager.

Divergent acquisitions Retail strategy in which the company seeks growth by moving into areas outside of retailing. In this way, retailers can continue to grow even when the retail industry is experiencing a slowdown.

Divisional sales manager Manager responsible for sales of a total division; often given the title of vice-president of sales.

Downside price elasticity Price-elasticity changes in response to decreased prices.

Drop shippers Limited-service wholesalers, also called *desk jobbers,* who take title to the merchandise they sell but do not take physical possession. They obtain orders from wholesalers and retailers and forward these orders to the manufacturer, who then sends the goods directly to the wholesaler or retailer. Used mostly in the distribution of bulky goods that have high transportation costs (e.g., lumber).

Dumping The practice of selling merchandise in foreign markets at prices lower than those charged in domestic markets to absorb excess production or inventory.

Durable goods Products that are used over time (the most tangible type of product).

Economies of scale Reductions in the per-unit cost of manufacturing or marketing a product as the amount produced increases.

Electronic retailing Process by which customers call up product information through computer terminals in shopping kiosks in various locations and place orders by credit card.

Encirclement strategies Strategy in which the market leader is challenged on several fronts at the same time or in quick succession.

Encoding Translating the company's objectives into an advertising or sales promotional strategy that will communicate the appropriate message. The good advertising campaign is one in which the encoding process uses information, symbols, or imagery that successfully communicate the product benefits to the consumer.

Environmental scanning Collecting and assessing environmental information from diverse sources to judge where future opportunities and threats might lie. Changes that may affect the scope of opportunity include competitive activity, technology, the economy, and social and cultural trends.

Equipment based services When products play a supportive role in delivering a service, such as ATMs providing banking services.

Exclusive dealing contract Formal arrangement in which the seller requires that its buyers carry the company's line of products on an exclusive basis. Such an agreement is illegal if it restrains trade or if smaller buyers are coerced into making the arrangement.

Exclusive distribution Distribution strategy where manufacturers give intermediaries exclusive territorial rights to sell the product in a specified area. This is most often used when the product requires service, or projects a quality image that could be diluted by a wide distribution channel.

Exclusive sales territories Exclusive rights to a geographic area offered by manufacturers to wholesalers and retailers to prevent intermediaries from competing with one another. (Franchises are an example.) These contracts are judged on a case-by-case basis to determine whether they restrict competition and violate antitrust rulings.

Expected value method Tool for determining the best strategy given certain expected trends. Managers are asked to estimate the probability of various scenarios occurring and to predict the sales results as a consequence.

Experimentation Attempting to control extraneous factors to establish a cause and effect relationship between a marketing stimulus (e.g., advertising) and consumer responses (e.g., intention to buy or sales).

Export management companies (EMCs) Organizations that are similar to export trading companies except that they do not take title to goods and are paid on a commission basis. They serve as the export department for many domestic manufacturers by marketing and distributing their products overseas.

Export trading companies (ETCs) A domestic merchant, the export trading company buys the firm's merchandise and assumes all responsibility for distribution and marketing abroad. Smaller companies are likely to use ETCs because they reduce their costs and avoid the risk of marketing abroad.

Eye pupil dilation test A physiological method of evaluating ads, which uses pupil dilation as an indicator of consumer interest. This is a useful, objective test because pupil dilation is an involuntary response, and not an active choice by the viewer.

Facilitating functions Activities performed by intermediaries in the distribution channel which help manufacturers obtain information about market conditions, and the effect of marketing mix variables.

Facilitating marketing systems Systems that provide the means for an exchange process in which there is a transfer of goods from manufacturers to customers, and a reverse transfer of payments from customers to manufacturers.

Factory shipments Goods a firm sells to retailers and wholesalers.

Family life cycle The progression of a family from formation, to child-rearing, to middle age, and finally to retirement.

Feedback Information received by a company on the impact of its communications on sales; the final stage of the communication process.

Fighting brands *See* Price brands.

Fixed costs Costs that are constant regardless of the quantity produced.

Flanking strategies Strategy of challenging the market leader in an area not currently contested; that is, offering customer benefits the leader has overlooked.

Flexible break-even pricing An offshoot of break-even analysis; price is determined by maximizing the difference between total revenue and total cost across various levels of demand.

Focus-group interviews Informal marketing research interviews with eight to twelve respondents who are asked to focus on a particular topic in an open-ended discussion guided by a trained moderator.

Follow-the-leader pricing Pricing strategy whereby the leader in an industry sets prices, and the other competitors use basically the same price structure. This often occurs in industries which are standardized, or where one company is the undisputed leader. Also, this pricing method tends to create stability and deter price wars.

Follow-the-leader strategies Strategy that copies the leader but also adds some sort of customer benefit. Minimizes the risks of retaliation due to a direct or indirect challenge to the market leader.

Forecasting variance The difference between the original objective and the new objective that was set due to changes in environmental conditions.

Forward integration A type of vertical integration in which the company acquires facilities closer to the consumer in the manufacturing and distribution chain. (For example, manufacturer ownership of retail or wholesale outlets.)

Four Ps of marketing Product, promotion, place, and pricing strategies.

Franchise systems Distribution systems in which a parent company (usually the manufacturer) grants a wholesaler or retailer the right to sell the company's products exclusively in a certain area. One of the fastest-growing forms of distribution, franchised establishments account for about one-third of all retail sales.

Free-on-board (FOB) origin pricing Geographic price adjustment based on having the buyer take ownership at the point of origin, and not delivery. The buyer is responsible for providing and paying for transportation. The quoted price is lower than it would otherwise be, because the seller does not incur delivery costs.

Free samples New products offered free as a way to get consumers to try them.

Free-standing inserts Coupons distributed as inserts in newspapers.

Freight-absorption pricing Pricing method in which the seller absorbs the total cost of transportation. This type of pricing is used if the freight charges are small, or if they are large enough to provide the seller with a competitive advantage if this pricing method is employed.

Frequency The average number of times, within a specified time period, that an individual is exposed to the message as a result of the media plan.

Gatekeeper Person in the purchasing process who controls the flow of information to the buying center.

General-merchandise wholesalers Full service wholesalers that carry a broad assortment of merchandise but in doing so, sacrifice depth in each product line. They also perform a number of services, like storing and controlling inventory, processing orders and transporting goods.

Generic brands Goods sold without brand names and identified only by their contents; "no-frills" goods. They are not advertised or promoted.

Government agencies From the marketing perspective, buyers of products and services to implement government services.

Gross rating points (GRPs) The *total number of exposures* produced by the media schedule, this measurement is determined by the reach times the frequency.

Grow strategy One of the business portfolio strategies in which the business being considered is in a high opportunity area, and one that the firm wants to take advantage. Investing in this opportunity usually requires significant resources, but the firm is willing to do so because of the future potential of the market.

Growth phase Phase of the product life cycle in which a product is generating increased sales.

Habit A connection between stimuli and/or responses that has become virtually automatic through experience, usually resulting in the purchase of the same brand. A limitation or absence of (1) information seeking and (2) evaluation of alternative brand choices.

Harvesting strategy A method used by marketers to reap short-term profits by withdrawing most marketing expenditures and reducing manufacturing costs before pulling the product out of the market.

Head-to-head competition Strategy in which a competitor in the industry challenges the leader.

Hierarchy of effects Process in the marketing communications process in which consumers pass through stages from attention to comprehension of the message, to retaining it. How far the consumer progresses up this ladder of attention-comprehension-retention is an indicator of the likelihood of purchase.

High-involvement purchases Purchases that are more important to the consumer, are related to the consumer's self-identity, and involve some risk. It is worth the consumer's time and energies to consider product alternatives more carefully in the high-involvement case. Therefore, a process of complex decision making is more likely to occur when the consumer is involved in the purchase.

Historical analogy Method used to forecast sales based on past sales results of a similar product.

Horizontal integration Growth strategy in which a company acquires businesses in the industry within which it is currently operating.

Horizontally integrated distribution systems Systems where companies at the same level cooperate to distribute goods.

Horizontal price fixing Competitors within an industry agree to maintain a certain price, thus eliminating price competition and limiting consumer choice. This action is prohibited by the Sherman Antitrust Act.

Hypermarkets Outlets that are combined food stores and mass merchandisers. They offer all the products of a supermarket as well as a larger variety of nonfood items than superstores or warehouse stores.

Image oriented change strategy Strategy to revitalize a brand by using image-oriented advertising.

Image oriented maintenance strategy Strategy to use imagery to reinforce current advertising campaign.

Impulse purchasing When a purchase decision is made on the spur of the moment. Motivation for an impulse purchase might be the desire to switch from an existing brand or to buy something new.

Inbound telemarketing Telemarketing facility that enables the company to receive product inquiries from customers. Toll free telephone lines are generally used to ask for further information.

Individual-brand-names strategy Strategy in which new brands are identified with the company name.

Industrial buyers Buyers of products and services to be used to further process other products, such as products used in manufacturing, mining, and construction.

Industrial products Products used to further produce other products, or those used to support the production of these products.

Inertia A passive process of information processing, brand evaluation, and brand choice. The same brand is frequently purchased by inertia to save time and energy.

Influencer Family member who establishes the criteria by which brands are compared and is instrumental in influencing others in the family.

Informational influence The influence of experts or experienced friends or relatives on consumer brands evaluations.

Information gatherer Family member who collects information and is likely to be the most knowledgeable about what sources of information to consult.

Information oriented change strategy Strategy to change consumer perception of a product or service by advertising new features or by providing additional information.

Information oriented maintenance strategy Strategy to maintain and reinforce existing perceptions of a product or service by using advertising that primarily provides information about a product.

Innovations Products that are new to both consumers and to a company. Often results in a change in consumption patterns.

Installations and accessories Industrial goods used in support of the manufacturing process.

Institutional buyers Buyers of products to be used to provide services (rather than to process products).

Intensity of distribution The degree of coverage provided by a distribution system.

Intensive distribution Distributing a product through most retail outlets in an area. Most often used for inexpensive, frequently purchased items. These are low-involvement products. If a store does not have a particular brand, the consumer will buy an alternative. Thus intensive distribution is necessary for these goods to avoid losing sales.

Intermodal transportation A means of moving physical goods from the manufacturer to the consumer by utilizing multiple delivery methods, such as air, truck, and rail, and thus allowing a single shipper to more efficiently move a customer's products door-to-door.

International marketing The development of marketing strategies to sell goods abroad and to integrate these strategies across various countries. Factors that must be taken into account include cultural and linguistic differences and political and foreign exchange risks as well as differences in regulatory structures.

Introductory phase Phase of the product life cycle in which a new product is presented to the public.

Just-in-time (JIT) distribution Producing exactly what is required by the market just in time to be delivered to customers. In so doing, maintaining inventory levels at a minimum.

Learning In marketing, refers to purchase behavior based on a consumer's past experiences. Purchases based on habit are usually the result of learning.

Length of distribution The number of different intermediaries that will be used by a distribution system.

Lifestyles An individual's mode of living as identified by his or her activities, interests, and opinions. Lifestyle variables have been measured by identifying a consumer's day-to-day activities and interests.

Lifestyle segmentation Strategy in which market segments are identified by consumers' attitudes, interests, and opinions.

Limited decision making Decision making that is not automatic but requires little information search.

Line extensions Additions to a product line that serve to *deepen* the line.

Line pruning Reducing the depth of a product line by cutting back on the number of offerings in a particular product category.

Line retrenchment Reducing the breadth of a product line by cutting back on the diversity of items offered across product categories.

List price The quoted price that might appear in a catalog or be quoted by a salesperson as the company's official price before discounts. Also referred to as the final selling price.

Logistical functions Assembling a variety of products, storing them, and providing them in smaller units to customers by sorting them and putting them on the retail shelf.

Low-involvement decision making A decision-making process whereby the consumer is not heavily involved with the product and, therefore, does not put much time into information processing and brand evaluation. An implication of low-involvement decision making is that consumers are less likely to pay attention to advertising so the focus should be on a simple message.

Low-involvement purchases Purchases that are less important to the consumer. Identity with the product is low. It may not be worth the consumer's time and effort to search for information about brands and to consider a wide range of alternatives. Therefore, low-involvement purchases are associated with a more limited process of decision making.

Mail-order distributors Distributors that are the same as mail-order wholesalers except that they sell to industrial buyers. They sell specialized items out of a catalog that can be easily shipped by mail or truck.

Mail-order wholesalers Limited service wholesalers that sell out of a catalog to small retailers, usually in outlying areas that full-service wholesalers would find too costly to serve.

Manufacturers' agents Agents that sell a company's product offering in a specific geographic area, often on an exclusive basis. They carry product lines of several noncompeting manufacturers and restrict their activities to selling to wholesalers, retailers, and industrial buyers. They do not take title to the goods they sell and are paid on a commission basis.

Manufacturer's brand A brand that is both produced and marketed by the manufacturer; also known as *national* or *regional brand.*

Marginal analysis Principle that as long as the additional revenue gained from the last unit produced (the marginal revenue) is greater than the cost of producing that last unit (the marginal cost), the company should produce it.

Marginal costs The changes in total costs that result from producing and marketing additional quantities of a product.

Marginal pricing Demand oriented pricing method which is based on pricing at the point where marginal revenue equals marginal cost.

Marginal revenue The change in total revenue obtained by selling additional quantities of a product.

Marginal-revenue budgeting Method of setting the promotion budget, which requires determining the additional revenue that would be earned from each additional dollar spent. Based on this approach, more money can be spent on promotion as long as marginal revenue exceeds marginal cost.

Market A group of customers who seek similar product benefits.

Market expansion strategy A marketing strategy which targets existing products to new markets in order to expand the entire product category.

Marketing All individual and organizational activities directed to identifying and satisfying customer needs and wants.

Marketing advantage A type of competitive advantage in which a superior marketing strategy is developed that outperforms competing strategies in meeting consumers' needs.

Marketing audit A periodic and comprehensive review of marketing operations. The marketing audit is designed to (1) identify changes in the environment requiring reassessment of marketing opportunities, (2) evaluate marketing planning and control procedures, and (3) appraise marketing strategy to determine if any changes would increase profitability.

Marketing concept The philosophy that all marketing strategies must be based on known consumer needs. Marketers must first define the benefits consumers seek from particular products and gear marketing strategies accordingly. Based on a *customer orientation.*

Marketing Information System (MIS) The system of people, technology, and procedures designed to acquire and generate information from both the marketing environment and the firm. Such information is integrated, analyzed, and communicated to improve marketing planning, execution, and control.

Marketing mix The marketing variables within the control of the marketing manager that are selected to elicit the desired response from the target market. Combination of strategies involving "the four Ps": product, promotion, place, and price.

Marketing opportunities Changes in environmental factors which create new opportunities to meet customers' needs.

Marketing plan The vehicle for developing marketing strategies.

Marketing planning A function of the product or brand manager that involves developing the product, defining its target market, and formulating marketing strategies.

Marketing productivity The ratio of marketing performance to the costs involved.

Marketing threats Changes in the environment which are a threat to the success of a company's marketing efforts.

Market niche Segments of a market that appear to be targets of opportunity.

Market penetration strategy *See* Penetration strategy.

Market potential The total demand for a product category in the market.

Market segmentation The process of subdividing a large undefined market into smaller groups of consumers with similar needs, characteristics, or behavior. This enables the marketer to effectively allocate marketing resources to satisfy the needs of a well-defined group of consumers.

Market-segment expansion Strategy that involves targeting one product to several market segments.

Market share The amount of sales a brand receives expressed as a percent of total sales generated in the brand's product category.

Market share protection strategy Competitive strategy used by a market leader wherein the goal is to protect its current share. While the market leader has more to protect, it should find this task easier because it usually has higher margins and, therefore, more resources at its disposal.

Market strategy The basic approach a company will take in trying to influence customers to buy a product.

Markup The profit margin realized when a cost plus pricing method is used; it is the percent added to the price after taking into consideration the seller's costs.

Mass marketing Strategy of offering one basic product without distinguishing among different customer needs and characteristics.

Mass merchandisers Stores that sell at lower prices than department stores or specialty stores but do not offer the same depth of assortment or service. Their merchandise is often of lower quality also.

Maturity phase Phase of the product life cycle in which a product's sales growth stabilizes and begins to decline.

Merchandise allowances Payments by manufacturers to reimburse retailers for in-store support of the product, such as window displays or in-store shelf displays.

Merchandise handling The component of the physical distribution system which links order processing and shipment. Merchandise handling activities include locating an item in inventory, moving it through the warehouse, and readying it for shipment.

Merchant wholesalers Independent wholesalers that purchase and take ownership of goods.

Mill supply house Full-service distributor that sells a wide variety of lines to industrial buyers.

Modified rebuy Recurring purchase of an industrial product that is less routine than a straight rebuy, requiring some information search and perhaps reevaluation of a straight rebuy because of a new product introduction or a change in technology.

Multiple exchanges The different types of exchanges of resources that nonprofit services must deal with.

Multiple publics The different groups that nonprofit services market to, including donors as well as clients.

Multiple sourcing Buying from several vendors so that the risk is spread among them.

Multiple zone pricing Type of delivered pricing method in which the price within a geographic zone is the same for all buyers, but the price between zones differs.

National account manager The leader of a national account marketing team, who is responsible for creating a working relationship with the customer, coordinating the activities of other members of a NAM team, and maintaining the relationship.

National account marketing (NAM) team Selling team composed of a national account manager and other salespeople, who work together to service large clients. NAM teams are usually used in complex industries, when customers need more than just facts about the product.

National/regional brands Brands that are marketed nationally by the manufacturer. Regional and local brands are sometimes lumped together with national brands to distinguish them from private brands and generics. *See also* Manufacturer's brands.

Need-gap analysis The identification of important consumer needs that are not being met by existing products. Defining such a gap represents an opportunity to the firm to meet these needs by introducing a new product or repositioning an existing one.

Needs Forces directed towards achieving a particular goal. The motive behind purchasing behavior.

Net profit Sales less variable costs, assignable fixed costs, and nonassignable fixed costs. Net profit is used to determine the return on investment for a particular product or business.

New buy Purchase of an industrial product (or service) that has not been made before; usually involves extensive information search.

New-product development strategy A strategy for new products where the new item is targeted to new or existing customers. These strategies apply to completely new-product offerings for the company.

New-product duplications Products that are known to the market but are new to the company.

Noise in communications Interference that occurs during the transmission of a message to the consumer. Noise can be competitive communications or misperception of the company's communication.

Nonassignable fixed costs Fixed costs that cannot be directly linked to the manufacturing or distribution of a product, and are therefore allocated across all products.

Nondurable goods Products that are consumed in one or a few uses.

Nonprobability sampling A sample selected primarily according to the researcher's judgment rather than according to the scientific rules of probability sampling; used when representativeness is less important.

Nonprofit services Services similar to those in the profit sector except that they usually offer a public service and are not geared to producing a profit.

Nonstore retailing Any method of selling to the final customer, which does not involve a store. Examples include catalogs, door-to-door sales, and the home shopping networks on television.

Normative influence Exerted by a reference group by persuading consumers to conform to its norms.

Objective-task budgeting This approach develops a promotional budget by specifically defining promotional objectives, determining the tasks required to meet those objectives, and estimating the costs associated with the performance of these tasks.

Odd-even pricing Sometimes referred to as psychological pricing, odd even pricing is used by manufacturers and retailers in the belief that consumers are more likely to purchase a product if its price ends with an odd number just under a round number (e.g., a price of $2.99 instead of $3.00).

Off-price retailing Offering brand-name merchandise at deep discounts.

Oligopoly An industry in which two or three firms dominate and the actions of one firm directly affect those of another.

Opinion leaders Individuals regarded by a reference group as having expertise and knowledge on a particular subject.

Order getters Salespeople who search out customers and persuade them to buy the company's products. The focus is on closing the sale, rather than taking an order.

Order processing Refers to the paperwork required to receive and process customer orders, transmit them to warehouses, fill the order from inventory, prepare a bill, and issue shipping instructions.

Order takers Salespeople who make an inquiry as to stock levels and product needs, and then take the order. Order takers are product oriented, and have a minimal amount of customer contact.

Outbound telemarketing Involves trained sales representatives making calls and trying to sell the customer by phone or providing prospective customers with information.

Out-of-stock costs One type of physical inventory costs, out-of-stock costs indicate the amount of sales lost due to the unavailability of an item at the retail or wholesale level.

Patent Grants exclusive rights to manufacture a product utilizing a new process or technology. The patent is in effect for 17 years.

Patterned standardization A compromise between standardized and localized international marketing strategies. This approach requires that the company establish global marketing strategies but leave the implementation of marketing plans to executives in local markets who are aware of national traits and customs. Strategy is developed at the corporate level, while tactics are developed at the local level.

Payback period The number of years it takes to recoup investment.

Pegged pricing Pricing strategy used by companies in an industry without a price leader, to establish price stability by setting prices at, above, or below the industry norm.

Penetration pricing strategy Pricing strategy of introducing a brand at a low price to induce as many consumers as possible to try it; usually coupled with price deals and coupons. This strategy works best when consumer demand for the product is price elastic.

People-based services Services which rely only on people in order to be delivered, as distinct from equipment-based services.

People meters Hand-held devices used to measure which TV shows are being watched by viewers in a household. People meters replaced diaries as the way households recorded when they started and stopped watching TV.

Percent-of-sales budgeting Technique of setting the promotional budget, which involves determining how much to spend based on a percentage of sales.

Perceptions The way consumers organize and interpret information about objects like brands and companies.

Perceptual map A method that seeks to position various brands on a "map" based on the way they are perceived by the consumer. The closer one brand is to another on the map, the more similar it is to the other brand. The basic assumption is that if consumers see two brands as being similar, they behave similarly toward the two brands.

Performance variance The difference between objectives and performance.

Personality Consistent and enduring patterns of behavior. Represents a set of consumer characteristics that have been used to describe target segments.

Personal selling Aspect of the promotional mix which involves face-to-face communication between a sales rep of the company and the consumer. The goal is to sell the product or service to the consumer.

Phantom freight Type of charge which results from the use of basing point pricing. It is the freight fees charged from the basing point to the delivery city, even if the goods are not actually moved.

Physical distribution Part of the distribution channel system involving the movement of goods from where they are produced to where they are consumed.

Physical distribution system A company's combination of order processing, merchandise handling, inventory, storage, and transportation functions. The physical distribution system is the means by which manufacturers get the product to the consumers.

Piggybacking Intermodal transportation, whereby a loaded truck is put onto a railroad car. Because of the use of two means of distribution, a shipper can provide door-to-door service at a lower cost than with trucking alone.

Place utility Benefit received by consumers because of the existence of the distribution system, wherein products are available at convenient locations.

Planned cannibalization *See* cannibalization.

Point-of-purchase displays Displays for products in the store, such as advertising sign, window display, or end-of-aisle display rack.

Population The total market under study.

Possession utility Consumer benefit provided by the distribution system whereby a channel member makes available an assortment of goods for consumer purchase.

Postpurchase process Maintenance or service provided by the vendor after the sale. Particularly important in organizational buying.

Predatory pricing An attempt to reduce competition by pricing below cost, thus forcing the failure of existing competitors and deterring new entrants into the market. Once competition has decreased, the company can again raise its prices. This action is prohibited by the Sherman Antitrust Act.

Preemptive action Strategy in which the market leader enters a market to anticipate or discourage competitive entry.

Premiums Products offered free or at a reduced price as an incentive to buy a promoted brand.

Price brands Low-priced brands under the manufacturer's control that are sold with minimal advertising and promotional expenditures; also called *fighting brands*.

Price deals Short-term discounts offered by manufacturers to induce customers to try products they have not bought before or to buy greater amounts of products they are already in the habit of buying.

Price discrimination Price differences given by sellers to intermediaries or organizational buyers that are not offered equally to the same types of buyers. This action is prohibited by the Clayton Act and the Robinson-Patman Act.

Price elasticity Measured by the percentage change in quantity purchased resulting from a percentage change in price.

When the percentage change in quantity is less than the percentage change in price, consumers are relatively price insensitive and demand is inelastic (price elasticity index less than 1). When the percentage change in quantity is greater than the percentage change in price, consumers are relatively sensitive to price changes (price elasticity index greater than 1). The equation to determine the price elasticity index (PEI) is % change in quantity/% change in price = PEI.

Price fixing Occurs when competitors agree to maintain fixed price levels to avoid competition based on price. *See also* Horizontal price fixing; Vertical price fixing.

Price leader Company that tacitly sets a price which every other company in the industry follows. A price leader tends to prevent price wars, because the other companies will not change prices unless the leader does.

Price lining Introducing various brands in a product line at different prices, thus appealing to consumers with different price elasticities (e.g., the quality-conscious consumer, the average consumer, and the economy-minded consumer).

Pricing strategy The price of a product set by the brand manager as a part of the marketing mix strategy.

Primary data Data originally collected by the marketing organization for its own immediate well-defined purposes. Methods of collecting primary data include survey research and depth interviews.

Primary demand Demand for a general product category rather than a particular brand.

Private brands Brands sold under a wholesaler's or retailer's label, usually at a lower price than national brands.

Private warehouse Warehouse facilities owned by a firm which needs storage facilities on a consistent basis. Because of the fixed maintenance costs, only companies with continual storage needs usese private warehouses.

Proactive strategy Marketing strategy that attempts to anticipate future competitive actions and environmental trends to exploit the resulting market opportunities; an offensive rather than defensive strategy.

Probabilistic models Sales forecasting models that treat the response of consumers in the marketplace as the outcome of a probabilistic process over time. They attempt to explain brand loyalty and switching behavior based on past purchases.

Probability sampling Techniques in which every possible sampling unit drawn from a specified population has a known chance of being selected. As a result, the reliability of data from the sample can be estimated (i.e., the sampling error).

Problem solvers Salespeople who define customer needs, and then recommend a set of solutions to meet these needs. This type of selling involves the most customer contact and in-depth understanding of the clients' needs and the market.

Procurement costs A cost of maintaining physical inventories. These costs are basically the expenses involved in placing reorders, such as processing, order transmitting, and the cost of the product itself.

Product The features of the item offered and the benefits, both tangible and intangible, that the consumer receives from it. Includes goods, services, and ideas.

Product advertising Designed to maintain awareness of a product category among consumers rather than a particular brand. Sometimes sponsored by competitors within an industry, and designed to maintain awareness of a total product category among consumers, as opposed to a particular brand. In such cases, the purpose is to counter an industry-wide drop in demand for the product, rather than a loss in market share for one competitor.

Product category The generic class to which a brand belongs.

Product development Growth strategy of developing new products or extensions of existing product lines, usually directed to existing markets.

Product extensions Products that are not new to the company but have some new dimension for consumers. There are three types: revisions, additions, and repositionings.

Product Life Cycle (PLC) The phases a product goes through — introduction, growth, maturity, and decline. Changes are required in marketing strategies to meet changing consumer demand and competitive conditions at each phase. A brand's position on the life cycle directly influences positioning, advertising, pricing, and distribution strategies.

Product line A line of offerings within a certain product category, frequently having the same name to facilitate identification. *See also entries under* Line.

Product-line brand name Brand name applied to several products within a product line.

Product-line breadth The diversity of products in a line, or the range of its items. Broad lines can provide a choice to various segments of the market, but too much breadth can lead to cannibalization because of product overlap.

Product-line depth The number of different types of brands, sizes, or models within a particular line of products. Deep product lines offer the consumer more choices, but too much depth can lead to cannibalization.

Product-line extensions New variations of an existing product.

Product-line manager Manager who coordinates marketing strategies of various brands in a product line; also called *category managers*.

Product-line segmentation Strategy that involves targeting several products to one market segment.

Product management system The system within which brand or product managers work.

Product manager (also **Brand manager**) Person responsible for formulating, implementing, and controlling a given product's marketing mix.

Product-marketing control Activities which are designed to keep the components of a product's marketing plan on track, in order to meet the product objectives.

Product marketing plan Defines the marketing strategy (4 Ps) for a given product or service, generally over a one-year period.

Product-market matrix A method of delineating product categories by market type. A matrix is constructed with product categories listed down the side and markets listed across the top. This process is vital to new product development because it identifies market segments whose needs are not being served by the firm and who therefore represent marketing opportunities.

Product market unit (PMU) Set of products aimed at defined markets.

Product mix All of the products that a business unit or company markets.

Product-mix consistency The relationship of a company's product lines to each other. Companies can have consistent product lines, which means they are in similar businesses, or diverse product lines, which encompass multiple industries.

Product positioning The use of advertising and other marketing mix variables to communicate the benefits of the product.

Product-related services Services that play a supporting role to tangible products. Examples include warranties, food delivery, and repair service.

Product specifications Performance requirements set by prospective users of the product (such as lifting capacity for forklift trucks). Usually applies to industrial buyers.

Production goods Products that are used to manufacture a final product.

Production orientation Firms focus primarily on production efficiency and product availability with little regard for the needs of consumers.

Profit and loss (P&L) statement A method used to set out a business unit's or product's performance projections, usually for the next one to five years. The P&L statement usually details revenues and expenses to determine net profits.

Profit margin Net profits as a percent of sales.

Projective techniques Techniques used for detecting and measuring wants and attitudes not readily discernable through more direct methods. Consists of the presentation of ambiguous materials (e.g., ink blots, untitled pictures, etc.). In interpreting this material, the viewer "projects" tendencies of which he or she may be unaware or may wish to conceal. Diagnostic devices in which interpretation of ambiguous stimuli are taken to reveal something about the observer, based on previous experience and motives, needs, and interests in play at the time.

Promotion The tactics a company uses to communicate the product's positioning.

Promotional allowances Price reductions given by the manufacturers to retailers in exchange for advertising the manufacturer's products. Promotional allowances are the foundation for cooperative advertising.

Promotional mix The combination of strategies that a company uses to communicate its benefits; includes advertising, sales promotions, publicity, and personal selling; a part of the marketing mix.

Prospecting An important sales function which enables a salesperson to identify new accounts. Sources used include referrals, telemarketing, and mail-in information cards.

Psychological set Consumer's predisposition to react positively or negatively toward a brand, product, or company.

Publicity A marketing communication which appears in the mass media, and is about a company or product. It is distinguished from advertising in that publicity is not paid for by the company.

Public relations A form of marketing communications which attempts to influence stockholders, consumers, government officials, and other business people. Public relations is an organized effort to present a positive image of the company and its products.

Public warehouse Warehouse that provides storage facilities to a firm on a rental basis.

Pull strategies Promotional strategies directed at end users as a means of stimulating demand. The strategy "pulls" the product through the distribution channel. Examples of pull strategies are couponing and consumer advertising.

Pulsing A way to advertise in which ads are distributed in a few large burst, as opposed to a steady stream of commercials. Pulsing is commonly used with new products, to gain initial customer awareness.

Purchase intentions The likelihood that a consumer will buy the product based on the extent to which it meets his or her need.

Purchasing agent Family member who buys the product. May also be the decision maker or may be just an "order taker."

Push strategies Promotional strategy (e.g., trade discounts, advertising allowances) directed to channel members. This approach is said to "push" the merchandise from the manufacturer through the channels of distribution.

Qualitative research Research that asks consumers to respond to questions in an unstructured manner and is not generally quantifiable.

Quality circles Groups of autonomous workers who are responsible for their output and are motivated to perform high-quality work based on the recognition that their mistakes will affect the next autonomous work group down the line.

Quantity discounts Discounts given for volume purchases.

Quota International trade regulation set by the individual country, which limits the amount of product within a particular category that can be imported.

Rack jobber Limited-service wholesaler who supplies supermarkets and other retail stores with nonfood items such as housewares and health and beauty aids. The rack jobber owns the goods and the displays (racks) that are supplied and splits the profits with the retailer.

Reach The number of people or households exposed to one or more of the vehicles in the media plan during a specified time period.

Reactive strategy Marketing strategies in which the company lets the competition make the major moves before the company responds. This is a defensive strategy.

Rebates Promotion that allows consumer to recover a portion of the purchase price.

Reference groups Groups with which an individual identifies such that he or she tends to use the group as a standard for self-evaluation and as a source of personal values and goals. Groups that serve as a reference point for the individual in the formation of beliefs, attitudes, and behavior. Such groups provide consumers with a means of comparing and evaluating their own brand attitudes and purchasing behavior.

Regional brands Manufacturer's brands sold on a regional basis.

Relative market share The strategic business unit's market share divided by the market share of its leading competitors.

Reliability Measurement of marketing information that insures unbiased data and thus allows accurate conclusions to be drawn about its implications.

Representativeness The degree to which a sample of consumers represents the characteristics of a population.

Resellers Wholesalers and retailers that buy products to resell. They do not process goods but, rather, act as intermediaries for other organizational buyers or for the final consumer.

Retailers Members of the distribution system who sell directly to the consumer. The retailer is the final link in the distribution channel, and ensures that products are made available to consumers.

Retailer-sponsored cooperatives A type of contractual system that integrates the distributive function among smaller retailers. In an effort to protect themselves against the larger chains with greater purchasing power, groups of smaller retailers acquire and operate their own wholesale facilities. This permits them to obtain the quantity discounts available to the chains.

Return on assets Measure of performance used by retailers, which is equal to stock turnover multiplied by profit margin.

Return on investment (ROI) Net profits divided by total investment.

Route salesforce Type of salesperson who routinely checks store shelves, and restocks as necessary. These people are primarily order takers, and most commonly work for drug and food companies.

Sales agents Sales agents serve as an extension of the manufacturer's salesforce, particularly in industrial marketing. Sales agents have fuller authority to set prices and terms of sales than manufacturer's agents and at times even assume the manufacturer's total marketing effort by specifying promotional and distribution activities for the product line. They specialize in certain lines of trade and are paid on a commission basis.

Sales branches A type of wholesale outlet where manufacturer-owned warehouses are designed to handle merchandise and store inventory. Companies use these types of warehouses to sell to large retailers and industrial buyers.

Salesforce mix Combination of different sales methods to service large, medium, and small customers.

Sales orientation Firms that focus primarily on selling what the company makes as opposed to what the consumer needs.

Sales promotions Short-term inducement of value to encourage consumers to buy a product or service; includes coupons, sweepstakes and contests, refunds on a purchase.

Sales quota The expected sales level per territory, per measurement period. Sales quotas are the expression of a territory's volume and profitability objectives.

Sales wave experiment Preliminary market tests in which the new product is placed in the consumer's home for his or her use. Consumers are given the opportunity to repurchase the new product or competitive products up to six times at reduced prices (six sales waves). Researchers can then better estimate the repurchase rate of the new product.

Scanner systems In-store technology that uses laser beams to read the Universal Product Code (UPC) from packaged goods. The information contained in the UPC is then fed into a computer that tracks sales for inventory purposes and for marketing research.

Scrambled merchandising Combining food and nonfood items in order to increase profits by allocating shelf space to more profitable nonfood items.

Seasonal discounts Discounts for buying a product with seasonal demand in the off-season.

Secondary data Data collected previous to the current study and not designed specifically to meet the firm's immediate research needs. Sources of secondary data include syndicated research services and the government.

Segmenting by consumer characteristics Strategy in which market segments are identified by consumer characteristics.

Selective demand Consumer demand for a particular brand within a product category. Companies stimulate selective demand when they try to maintain their current customer base and persuade others to switch brands.

Selective distribution Most often used for durable goods like small appliances, stereo equipment, and furniture, selective distribution is a compromise between intense and exclusive distribution. The marketer selects a limited number of intermediaries who can provide the desired sales support and service. Because durable goods have higher prices, consumers are more likely to shop around, enabling manufacturers to limit distribution. Selective distribution allows manufacturers more control over the way their products are sold and also decreases the likelihood of price competition between intermediaries.

Service management system The equivalent of a product management system for service firms.

Service manager Manager who develops marketing strategies for a service and has profit responsibility for service performance.

Services Intangible benefits purchased by consumers that do not involve ownership.

Shopping goods Those products that consumers are likely to spend more time shopping for. The consumer is involved with the product.

Shrinkage Theft of merchandise by customers or employees.

Simulated store test Test in which customers shop in experimental supermarket facilities in which new products are introduced and their purchases are tracked.

Single-source data Data on an individual consumer's purchases and media exposure from the same source.

Single-zone pricing Form of delivered pricing method where all buyers pay the same price regardless of where they are located.

Situation analysis Preliminary evaluation of the market for a product, including identifying the key characteristics of the market, the size of the market, and other products that are likely to compete with the company's brand.

Skimming pricing strategy A strategic option establishing a high price for a new product entry and "skimming the cream of the market" by aiming at the most price inelastic consumer. Advertising and sales promotion would be limited to specific targets, and distribution would be selective.

Slotting allowances Direct payments to retailers, generally food chains, for stocking an item.

Social class A division of society made up of persons possessing certain common social and economic characteristics resulting in equal-status relations with one another and restricting interaction with members of other social classes.

Source attractiveness Refers to the likability of the salesperson or spokesperson. Factor which is included in the encoding process, and is used to judge its effectiveness.

Source credibility Describes the believability of the salesperson or spokesperson. A factor which helps determine the effectiveness of the encoding process.

Specialty distributors Distributors that concentrate on specific lines.

Specialty goods Products with unique characteristics that consumers make a special effort to search for and buy.

Specialty merchandise wholesalers Wholesalers that specialize in certain product lines (such as health foods or automotive parts) and carry a deep assortment of alternatives in each line.

Specialty retailing Retailers that offer limited, specialized lines of merchandise, with a wide assortment within these lines.

Specialty stores Stores that are small and carry a few product lines in specialty areas. Although these stores do not have a variety of products, they do have a wide assortment within the lines that they carry.

Standardization in key markets Standardization strategies applied (in international markets) only to markets where opportunity is greatest, particularly if customer needs in these markets is similar.

Standardized strategies This approach to international marketing assumes that some products have universal appeal. It is thus unnecessary to develop individual marketing strategies on a market-by-market basis. Companies such as Pepsi-Cola, Ford, and Goodyear utilize this strategy. Its advantages over localized strategies are lower unit marketing costs and greater control over local marketing operations.

Statistical process control Concept of quality control where defects are controlled when they happen instead of after the product is completed. Workers are given responsibility for identifying the defects in their own work, which serves as a motivator to produce quality output.

Status quo strategy A strategy to avoid competition where the company seeks to keep things in the industry the way they are. This strategy of not rocking the boat can be appealing because it is less expensive than taking on the competition directly.

Steering control system A method of evaluating marketing performance during the planning period rather than at the end of the period. Performance projected during the period is compared to the performance projected at the beginning of the period. If performance deviates from objectives, corrective action is taken to bring the plan back into control.

Stock turnover rate Rate at which a store's inventory moves out over a specified time period. Retailers use the stock turnover rate as a measurement of performance.

Store audits A source of retail sales information for the manufacturer that measures retail sales by subtracting end of period inventory for a product from inventory at the beginning of the period plus shipments. A. C. Nielsen is one organization that conducts audits and supplies information to manufacturers on a syndicated basis.

Straight rebuy Recurring purchase of industrial products that can be handled on a routine basis; usually involves standardized products and requires little information search.

Strategic Business Units (SBUs) Division level units within the organization that act as autonomous profit centers. SBU management is responsible for establishing strategic marketing plans. The boundaries of SBUs are generally defined by markets based on homogeneous consumer demand.

Strategic control Attempt made at the corporate level to keep the components of the strategic marketing plan on target, and modify them if they are not.

Strategic marketing concept Concept emphasizing the identification of marketing opportunity as a basis for marketing planning; emphasizes marketing's role in developing products and services, as well as its broader and longer-term role in charting a course for corporate growth. Compared to the *marketing concept*, which is based on a customer orientation, the *strategic marketing concept* focuses on both customers and competitors.

Strategic marketing plan A corporate and SBU-level function that (1) defines the corporate mission, (2) establishes guidelines for long-term corporate growth, (3) guides the development of the firm's overall product mix, and (4) allocates available resources to each of the firm's business units.

Strategic window of opportunity A term used to describe a situation in which the firm's competencies are at an optimum to exploit marketing opportunities. *See also* Window of competitive opportunity.

Subcultures Broad groups of consumers that have similar values that distinguish them from society as a whole.

Supermarkets Low cost, high volume food retailer. Supermarkets carry a wide range of products and offer few services. Most supermarkets are part of a national or regional chain.

Superstores Very large supermarkets that engage in extensive scrambled merchandising. They are at least twice as large as the average supermarket. The goal of a superstore is to provide service and one-stop shopping.

Supplies and services Products that support the manufacturing process but are not part of it.

Sustainable competitive advantage Meeting the customer's needs while maintaining an advantage over competitors in terms of product uniqueness or lower costs.

Sweepstakes Allow consumers a chance to win prizes or sums of money simply by submitting their name and address.

Syndicated research firms Sources external to the firm that collect consumer and product information and sell it to subscribing clients. It is not collected for a singular purpose but rather for the multiple needs of various clients and is thus considered secondary data.

Tangible product Product attributes representing desired benefits.

Target market (segment) A group of consumers with similar needs that can be identified and appealed to by a specific product or product line.

Target-return pricing Pricing method in which the return on investment that a company wants to achieve is stated, and the price is then set based on this target. With this method, demand is not estimated, but instead, price is set relative to expected volume.

Tariff International trade regulation in the form of a tax on imported goods. Tariffs are used to protect domestic industries.

Telemarketing A sales method whereby the telephone is used to contact existing customers and prospects directly. A telemarketing sales call is significantly less expensive than a face to face contact, and just as effective. Telemarketing is commonly used to sell to smaller clients.

Test marketing Placing products in company selected markets for a period of time in order to gather pertinent sales information; conducted as part of a complete marketing plan to simulate a national introduction.

Time utility Benefit provided by distribution intermediaries, wherein the products are made available to consumers, when they want them.

Total costs Total costs incurred in producing and marketing a product; the sum of total fixed costs and total variable costs.

Total revenue Total amount of money received from the sale of a product.

Trade discounts Discounts given to retailers and wholesalers for performing the marketing functions required to distribute a product.

Trade-in allowance An adjustment to price which results from trading in a used product. The trade-in allowance is used as a partial payment in the purchase of a new item. Trade-ins are usually durable goods, such as cars.

Trademarks The way a company registers its brand names and symbols to protect them from being duplicated.

Trade shows Booths set up by various vendors in one large meeting place to dispense information about their products to prospective customers.

Trainship Combination of rail and ship transportation.

Transactional functions Function performed by intermediaries in the distribution system, which involves the buying of products and reselling them to customers. The members of the distribution channel who undertake this function also incur the risks of stocking inventory.

Truck jobbers Small wholesalers selling directly from their trucks, and specializing in storing and quickly delivering perishable goods.

Tying contracts The requirement by a manufacturer that a buyer purchase unwanted or less desirable products, in order to obtain the products which are desired. These contracts are illegal when they are in restraint of trade, or cover a significant volume.

Unfair pricing Pricing practices designed to drive competitors out of business. *See* Predatory pricing; Price discrimination; Price fixing.

Uniform Product Code The set of numbered vertical lines that appear on most packaged foods. The code can be read by scanner systems and contain such information as product type, brand, weight, and expiration date. UPCs can also be used to help track goods through the physical distribution system.

Unplanned cannibalization *See* Cannibalization.

Upside elasticity Price-elasticity changes in response to increased prices

Validity Marketing information that satisfactorily meets the purposes for which it was gathered is said to have validity.

Value-added wholesaling Improving wholesaling productivity by providing more services and lowering the cost of these services through automation.

Value-based pricing Method of pricing services based on what the consumer is willing to pay. In other words, it is setting the price at the level the market will bear.

Variable costs Costs that vary directly with the quantity produced.

Variety seeking Occurs when the consumer tries a variety of brands to create some interest and avoid boredom with low-involvement purchases.

Vertical integration Corporate growth strategy of adding new facilities to existing manufacturing or distribution operations.

Vertically integrated distribution system Distribution system in which institutions at different levels (e.g., manufacturer, wholesaler, and retailer) combine to distribute goods. Integration requires the management of the system so that common objectives (e.g., adequate inventory, quick delivery) are attained and conflicting ones (e.g., level of discounts, use of company's promotional aids) resolved.

Vertical price fixing This type of price fixing involves an agreement between manufacturers and retailers that the manufacturers' suggested retail price will actually be charged by the retailer. Once thought of as a means of ensuring manufacturers' profits and legalized by fair trade laws, it is now considered in restraint of trade.

Videotex systems Two-way (interactive) cable television systems in which the consumer can select information by requesting it through a home computer terminal and can also order merchandise through the terminal.

Warehouse clubs Type of discounter that offers extremely low prices on a self-service basis, stocking a wide variety of product lines but limited selections within each line. The main differences between warehouse clubs and traditional discount stores are lower prices and a warehouse-like facility.

Warehouse stores Deep-discount, no-frills outlets that offer food products in cartons straight from the manufacturer and require customers to bag their purchases. These are the food-outlet equivalent of warehouse clubs.

Warranty Written statement of the manufacturer's commitment to replace or repair a product that is defective or performs poorly.

Wheel of retailing The cyclical emergence of new retailers as the existing ones become less price competitive. Innovative retailers come in offering lower prices based on low overhead.

Wholesalers Organizations that buy and resell merchandise to other businesses. They sell to other wholesalers, retailers, and industrial buyers, but not to the final consumer.

Wholesaler-sponsored voluntary chains Groups of retailers organized by a wholesaler into an integrated chain operation. Both wholesaler and retailers benefit; costs are reduced because of increased purchasing power and more efficient wholesale operations.

Window of competitive opportunity The combination of competitive weakness, market attractiveness, and corporate capabilities that allows a firm to establish competitive advantage.

Word-of-mouth communication Face-to-face, personal communication.

Worldwide adaptation Global marketing strategy in which different variations of a product are sold in each country. The marketing mix variables, such as advertising, and distribution are adapted to meet the individual needs of each country. This is the most expensive international marketing strategy, but it affords the company the most flexibility.

Worldwide standardization Global marketing strategy employed by firms which is fairly standardized across countries. This is also known as a world brand strategy, because the underlying assumption is that the band has universal appeal, and is not country specific.

Zero-based budgeting Method for evaluating performance in which the budget is determined at the beginning of each year on a clean slate, without carrying over any charges from prior years. The budget is based on what is expected, and what activities are necessary to meet these objectives.

Name Index

Company Index

Subject Index

Accessories, installations and, 270
Accounting, 14
Account representatives, 514
Acquisition (of companies), 18–19, 416–417, 426
  by Borden, 640–641
  by General Electric, 605
  by Philip Morris, 639
  by Sara Lee, 631
  marketing control and, 646
  strategic marketing evaluation and, 662
  types of strategies for, 633–635
Activities (consumer), 129
Adaptive control system, 655–656, 667
Adaptive strategies, 586–587, 588, 590
  international growth strategies and, 598, 599
  marketing mix and, 600, 602
  organizing by region and, 597, 599, 601, 604
Added product, 271, 662–663
Administered channel system, 365
Advertising, 465–496
  accessibility of market segment and, 248–249
  budget for, 473
  business portfolio strategies and, 629
  combined with sales promotions, 440, 445
  comparative, 217–218, 480
  of convenience goods, 268
  cooperative, 357
  dependence of on distribution, 382
  developing message in, 476–480
  for durable goods, 267, 442
  ethics concerning, 78
  evaluation of, 488–490
  example of Alex Kroll's success in, 480–481
  example of cutting back on, 495
  example of IBM's campaign, 464–465
  example of McDonald's, 434–435
  fear appeals in, 478
  government regulations concerning, 75, 76
  Gross Rating Points (GRPs) in, 485, 486, 487, 489
  for habit purchases, 123
  home entertainment technology and, 74
  humor in, 478–479
  importance of, 466–467
  informational. *See* Informational ads/ approach
  in international marketing, 582–583, 588

  of innovations, 272
  in introductory phase, 443
  by lawyers, 328
  market segmentation and, 232
  for nonprofit services, 341
  objectives of, 439, 473
  in organizational buying, 151, 161
  personality segmentation and, 245
  personal selling supported by, 440
  physical distribution and, 396
  product, 467–479
  product life cycle stages and, 443–445
  as part of promotional mix, 436, 439
  promotions vs., 450, 451, 466
  push strategies and, 372
  reformulating after test marketing, 283
  retailing strategies and, 418–419
  sales volume and, 438, 489–490
  for services, 335–336
  socially responsible, 490–491
  target market for, 472–473
  top ten companies in expenditures for, 466, 467
  types of, 467–471
  wholesaling strategies and, 427
Advertising agency, 13, 188
Advertising campaign, 13, 474–476
Advertising costs, 284, 466, 486–487
  example of pitfalls of cutting, 495
  statistics on, 449
Advertising exposure, 190–191, 485
Advertising impact, 485–486
Advertising plan, 471–472
Advertising strategies
  adaptive. *See* Adaptive strategies
  for business-to-business marketers, 164–165
  consumer personality and, 132
  developing, 471–472, 474–481
  for high- vs. low-involvement purchases, 124
  marketing mix and, 218
  product life cycle and, 312
  for reference groups, 135–136
  for social classes, 134–135
  spokespersons and, 136
  standardized. *See* Standardized strategies
Advertising tests, 118, 178, 188, 189, 488–489
After-the-fact control system, 655, 656, 657, 667
Age composition, 66–68

Age segmentation, 243
  See also Senior citizens
Agents, 354, 359, 424–425
  for industrial products, 361
  in international marketing, 605
  as primary means of selling, 514
  for services, 362
Air freight, 395
Alaskan oil spill, 441
Allowances, 568
Alternative marketing strategies, 43–45, 219–220
  marketing research and, 178, 189, 194
  product marketing plan and, 43–45
AMA Code of Ethics, 78–79
American Marketing Association (AMA), 78
Antitrust laws, 108
Apartheid, 606
Asia, 590, 591
Atmospherics, 418
Attitudes (consumer), 116, 118, 126–128
  toward brand, 441
  market segmentation and, 244
  MIS and, 174
  term defined, 125
Audimeter, 191, 192
Augmented product, 265
Average revenue, 550, 559
Awareness (of communications), 438, 439
  See also Brand awareness

Baby boomers, 66–70, 131
  age segmentation and, 243
  aging of, 59, 413
  Campbell Soup Co.'s focus on, 230
  conservative lifestyle of, 68, 69, 70
  discount mass merchandising and, 402
  echo boom due to, 484
  as "emerging investors," 325, 334
  health consciousness of, 115, 117
  new products aimed at, 289
  trend to sedentary, at-home lifestyle among, 175
Backward integration, 364, 423, 633
Bait-and-switch, 415, 520, 545–546
Bargain basements, 405
Basing-point pricing, 569
BCG's growth/share analysis, 626, 627–628
Behavioral segmentation, 238, 241–242
  industrial, 253, 254
BehaviorScan, 197–198
Belongers, 61

Boldface entries indicate key concepts.

Credits